The Expositor's Bible
The Gospel of St. John Volumes I & II
By Marcus Dods, D.D.
Edited by Anthony Uyl

Woodstock, Ontario, 2017

The Expositor's Bible: The Gospel of St. John Volumes I & II
By Marcus Dods, D.D.
Professor of exegetical theology, New College, Edinburgh
Edited by Anthony Uyl
Originally edited by the Rev. W. Robertson Nicoll, M.A., LL.D.

Originally Published by:
New York: A. C. Armstrong and Son, 51 East Tenth Street (near Broadway). 1891.

The text of The Expositor's Bible: The Gospel of St. John Volumes I & II is all in the Public Domain. This edition is published by Devoted Publishing a division of 2165467 Ontario Inc.

What kind of philosophies do you have?
Let us know!

Contact us at: devotedpub@hotmail.com
Visit us on Facebook: Devoted Publishing
Get more products via our website: www.devotedpublishing.com
Published in Woodstock, Ontario, Canada 2017.

For bulk educational rates, please contact us at the above email address.

ISBN: 978-1-988297-97-2

Table of Contents

VOLUME I 6
INTRODUCTORY NOTE 6
THE DIVISIONS OF ST. JOHN'S GOSPEL 8
I. THE INCARNATION 9
    Footnotes: 13
II. RECEPTION CHRIST MET WITH 14
    Footnotes: 17
III. THE BAPTIST'S TESTIMONY 18
IV. THE FIRST DISCIPLES 24
    Footnotes: 27
V. THE FIRST SIGN--THE MARRIAGE IN CANA 28
    Footnotes: 32
VI. THE CLEANSING OF THE TEMPLE 33
VII. NICODEMUS 37
VIII. THE BRAZEN SERPENT 42
    Footnotes: 45
IX. THE WOMAN OF SAMARIA 46
    Footnotes: 50
X. JESUS DECLARES HIMSELF 51
XI. THE SECOND SIGN IN GALILEE 55
    Footnotes: 59
XII. SABBATH CURE AT BETHESDA 60
    Footnotes: 63
XIII. JESUS LIFE-GIVER AND JUDGE 64
    Footnotes: 68
XIV. JESUS THE BREAD OF LIFE 69
    Footnotes: 73
XV. THE CRISIS IN GALILEE 74
    Footnotes: 78
XVI. JESUS DISCUSSED IN JERUSALEM 79
    Footnotes: 83
XVII. THE WOMAN TAKEN IN ADULTERY 84
XVIII. CHRIST THE LIGHT OF THE WORLD 88
    Footnotes: 91
XIX. JESUS REJECTED IN JERUSALEM 92
XX. SIGHT GIVEN TO THE BLIND 96
    Footnotes: 100
XXI. JESUS THE GOOD SHEPHERD 101
    Footnotes: 105

XXII. JESUS, SON OF GOD ... 106
    Footnotes: ... 110
XXIII. JESUS THE RESURRECTION AND LIFE ... 111
XXIV. JESUS THE SCAPEGOAT ... 116
NOTE ON CHAP. VI., Vers. 37, 44, 45 ... 121
VOLUME II ... 122
I. THE ANOINTING OF JESUS ... 122
    Footnotes: ... 126
II. THE ENTRY INTO JERUSALEM ... 127
    Footnotes: ... 129
III. THE CORN OF WHEAT ... 130
IV. THE ATTRACTIVE FORCE OF THE CROSS ... 134
V. RESULTS OF CHRIST'S MANIFESTATION ... 139
    Footnotes: ... 141
VI. THE FOOT-WASHING ... 142
    Footnotes: ... 146
VII. JUDAS ... 147
    Footnotes: ... 151
VIII. JESUS ANNOUNCES HIS DEPARTURE ... 152
    Footnotes: ... 155
IX. THE WAY, THE TRUTH, AND THE LIFE ... 156
    Footnotes: ... 159
X. THE FATHER SEEN IN CHRIST ... 160
XI. THE BEQUEST OF PEACE ... 166
    Footnotes: ... 170
XII. THE VINE AND THE BRANCHES ... 171
    Footnotes: ... 175
XIII. NOT SERVANTS, BUT FRIENDS ... 176
XIV. THE SPIRIT CHRIST'S WITNESS ... 179
    Footnotes: ... 185
XV. LAST WORDS ... 186
XVI. CHRIST'S INTERCESSORY PRAYER ... 191
XVII. THE ARREST ... 196
    Footnotes: ... 200
XVIII. PETER'S DENIAL AND REPENTANCE ... 201
    Footnotes: ... 204
XIX. JESUS BEFORE PILATE ... 205
    Footnotes: ... 210
XX. MARY AT THE CROSS ... 212
    Footnotes: ... 215
XXI. THE CRUCIFIXION ... 216

XXII. THE RESURRECTION	220
Footnotes:	223
XXIII. THOMAS' TEST	224
Footnotes:	228
XXIV. APPEARANCE AT SEA OF GALILEE	229
XXV. RESTORATION OF PETER	234
XXVI. CONCLUSION	238

VOLUME I

INTRODUCTORY NOTE

In order to read the Gospel of St. John with some intelligence, it is necessary to understand its purpose and its plan. For in the whole range of literature there is no composition which is a more perfect work of art, or which more rigidly excludes whatever does not subserve its main end. From the first word to the last there is no paragraph, sentence, or expression which is out of its place, or with which we could dispense. Part hangs together with part in perfect balance. The sequence may at times be obscure, but sequence there always is. The relevancy of this or that remark may not at first sight be apparent, but irrelevancy is impossible to this writer.

The object which the Evangelist had in view in writing this Gospel we are not left to find out for ourselves. He explicitly says that his purpose in writing was to promote the belief that "Jesus is the Christ, the Son of God" (chap. xx. 31). This purpose, he judges, he will best accomplish, not by writing an essay, nor by framing an abstract argument in advocacy of the claims of Jesus, but by reproducing in his Gospel those manifestations of His glory which elicited faith in the first disciples and in others. That which had produced faith in his own case and in that of his fellow-disciples, will, he thinks, if fairly set before men, produce faith in them also. He relates, therefore, with the utmost simplicity of language, the scenes in which Jesus seemed to him most significantly to have revealed His power and His goodness, and most forcibly to have demonstrated that the Father was in Him. At the same time he keeps steadily in view the circumstance that these manifestations had not always produced faith, but that alongside of a growing faith there ran an increasing unbelief which at length assumed the form of hostility and outrage. This unbelief he feels called upon to account for. He feels called upon to demonstrate that its true reason lay, not in the inadequacy of Christ's manifestations, but in the unreasonable and unspiritual requirements of the unbelieving, and in their alienation from God. The Gospel thus forms the primary apologetic, which by its very simplicity and closeness to reality touches at every point the underlying causes and principles of faith and unbelief.

The object of the Gospel being kept in view, the plan is at once perceived. Apart from the Prologue (chap. i. 1--18) and the Appendix (chap. xxi.), the body of the work falls into two nearly equal parts, chaps. i. 19--xii. and xiii.--xx. In the former part the Evangelist relates, with a singular felicity of selection, the scenes in which Jesus made those self-revelations which it was most important that men should understand, and the discussions in which their full significance was brought out. Thus he shows how the glory of Christ was manifested at the marriage in Cana, in the cleansing of the Temple, in the conversation with the Samaritans, in the healing of the impotent man, in the feeding of the five thousand, in the cure of the man born blind; and how, through these various signs or object-lessons, Jesus makes Himself known as the Life, the Light, the Judge of men, or, in one word, as the Son doing the Father's works, manifesting the Father's presence, disclosing in His various words and deeds "the glory as of the only begotten of the Father, full of grace and truth."

These manifestations culminate in the raising of Lazarus, recorded in the eleventh chapter. This final sign, while in "many of the Jews" (xi. 45) it produced faith, aggravated at the same time the unbelief of the authorities, who "from that day forth took counsel together for to put Him to death" (xi. 53). The twelfth chapter, therefore, holds a place by itself. In it we have three incidents related, and all related for the same purpose, namely, to demonstrate that there was now no further need of such manifestations of the glory of Jesus as had already been given, and that all things were now ripe for the catastrophe. The incidents in which this became apparent were Mary's anointing of Jesus, His triumphal entry into Jerusalem, and the enquiry of the Greeks. By introducing these three incidents together at this point, John wishes to show (1) that Jesus was now embalmed in the love of His intimate friends, (2) that He had found in the untutored instincts of the people a response to His claim, and (3) that even in the still wider circle of the outlying nations His name was known. He may, therefore, now safely finish His self-revelation. It has done its work. And the completeness of its result is seen, not only in this widely-extended impression and firmly-rooted attachment, but also in the maturity of unbelief which now took active steps to take Jesus and put Him to death.

This part of the Gospel therefore appropriately closes with the words: "These things spake Jesus and departed, and did hide Himself from them" (xii. 36). The public manifestation of Jesus is closed.

Between the first and the second part of the Gospel there is interposed a paragraph (xii. 37--50), in which John briefly points out that the rejection of Jesus by the Jews was no more than had been predicted by the prophet Isaiah, and that it reflects no suspicion on the manifestations of His relation to the Father which Jesus had made. He then sums up in one or two sentences the significance and consequences of receiving and of rejecting Jesus.

In the second part of the Gospel the writer is still guided by the same purpose of showing how Jesus manifested His glory. This is obvious not merely from the contents of this second part, but also from the fact that in the language of John the death of Jesus is constantly referred to as His glorification, being the "lifting up" which was an essential step to, or part of, His glorification. Before entering upon the last scenes, which are described in chaps. xiii.--xix., Jesus is assured that in His death the Father is to glorify His Name (xii. 28); and in the prayer recorded in the seventeenth chapter, which closes the explanations which our Lord Himself made of His work, it is still the manifestation of His glory that is in His thoughts. The characteristic which distinguishes this second part of the Gospel is, that Jesus no longer manifests His glory to the people in signs of manifest power, but now, in chapters xiii.--xvii., further discloses His glory privately to the Twelve; and in chapters xviii. and xix. passes triumphantly through the ultimate trial which still lay between Him and the final consummation of His glory. That this final glory has been achieved is witnessed by the Resurrection, the record of which, and of its results in faith, occupies the twentieth chapter. De Wette has the credit of being the first to discern that the entire Gospel is held together by this idea of the manifestation of Christ's glory, and that "the glory of our Lord appears in all its brightness in the second part of the narrative (xiii.--xx.), and that (a) inwardly and morally in His sufferings and death (xiii.--xix.), and (b) outwardly and sensibly, in the triumphant event of the Resurrection."

The best tabulated division of the Gospel with which I am acquainted is that which the Rev. A. Halliday Douglas, M.A., of Huntly, has printed for private circulation. By the kindness of the author I am allowed to publish it here.

THE DIVISIONS OF ST. JOHN'S GOSPEL

The Prologue or Introduction. Chap. i. 1--18.
    Part I. The Manifestation of Christ's Glory in Life and Power. Chap. i. 19--xii. 36.
        1. Christ's Announcement of Himself, and the Beginnings of Faith and Unbelief. Chap. i. 19--iv.
        2. The Period of Conflict. Chap. v.--xii. 36.

The Evangelist's Pause for Reflection, and Review of Christ's Teaching. Chaps. xii. 36--50.
    Part II. The Manifestation of Christ's Glory in Suffering and Death. Chaps. xiii.--xx.
        1. Moral Victory in Suffering:--
            a. In Anticipation. Chaps. xiii.--xvii. [Faith finally settled in the disciples, and unbelief cast out from among them.]
            b. In the Actual Struggle. Chaps. xviii., xix. [Unbelief apparently victorious, faith scarcely saved.]
        2. Actual Victory over Death. Chap. xx. [Faith proved right, and unbelief condemned.]

The Epilogue or Appendix. Chap. xxi.

Marcus Dods, D.D.

I. THE INCARNATION

"In the beginning was the Word, and the Word was with God, and the Word was God. The same was in the beginning with God. All things were made by Him; and without Him was not any thing made that hath been made. In Him was life; and the life was the light of men. And the light shineth in the darkness; and the darkness apprehended it not. There came a man, sent from God, whose name was John. The same came for witness, that he might bear witness of the light, that all might believe through him. He was not the light, but came that he might bear witness of the light. There was the true light, even the light which lighteth every man, coming into the world. He was in the world, and the world was made by Him, and the world knew Him not. He came unto His own, and they that were His own received Him not. But as many as received Him, to them gave He the right to become children of God, even to them that believe on His name: which were born, not of blood, nor of the will of the flesh, nor of the will of man, but of God. And the Word became flesh, and dwelt among us (and we beheld His glory, glory as of the only begotten from the Father), full of grace and truth. John beareth witness of Him, and crieth, saying, This was He of whom I said, He that cometh after me is preferred before me: for He was before me. For of His fulness we all received, and grace for grace. For the law was given by Moses; grace and truth came by Jesus Christ. No man hath seen God at any time; the only begotten Son, which is in the bosom of the Father, He hath declared Him."--John i. 1--18.

    In this brief introduction to his Gospel John summarises its contents, and presents an abstract of the history he is about to relate in detail. That the Eternal Word, in whom was the life of all things, became flesh and was manifested among men; that some ignored while others recognised Him, that some received while others rejected Him,--this is what John desires to exhibit at large in his Gospel, and this is what he summarily states in this compact and pregnant introductory passage. He briefly describes a Being whom he names "The Word;" he explains the connection of this Being with God and with created things; he tells how He came to the world and dwelt among men, and he remarks upon the reception He met with. What is summed up in these propositions is unfolded in the Gospel. It narrates in detail the history of the manifestation of the Incarnate Word, and of the faith and unbelief which this manifestation evoked.

    John at once introduces us to a Being whom he speaks of as "The Word." He uses the term without apology, as if already it were familiar to his readers; and yet he adds a brief description of it, as if possibly they might attach to it ideas incompatible with his own. He uses it without apology, because in point of fact it already had circulation both among Greek and Jewish thinkers. In the Old Testament we meet with a Being called "The Angel of the Lord," who is at once closely related, if not equivalent, to Jehovah, and at the same time manifested to men. Thus when the Angel of the Lord had appeared to Jacob and wrestled with him, Jacob called the name of the place Peniel, for, said he, "I have seen God face to face." [1] In the apocryphal books of the Old Testament the Wisdom and the Word of God are poetically personified, and occupy the same relation to God on the one hand, and to man on the other, which was filled by the Angel of the Lord. And in the time of Christ "the Word of the Lord" had become the current designation by which Jewish teachers denoted the manifested Jehovah. In explaining the Scriptures, to make them more intelligible to the people, it was customary to substitute for the name of the infinitely exalted Jehovah the name of Jehovah's manifestation, "the Word of the Lord."

    Beyond Jewish circles of thought the expression would also be readily understood. For not among the Jews only, but everywhere, men have keenly felt the difficulty of arriving at any certain and definite knowledge of the Eternal One. The most rudimentary definition of God, by declaring Him to be a Spirit, at once and for ever dissipates the hope that we can ever see Him, as we see one another, with the bodily eye. This depresses and disturbs the soul. Other objects which invite our thought and feeling we easily apprehend, and our intercourse with them is level to our faculties. It is, indeed, the unseen and intangible spirit of our friends which we value, not the outward appearance. But we scarcely separate the two; and as we reach and know and enjoy our friends through the bodily features with which we are familiar, and the words that strike upon our ear, we instinctively long for intercourse with God and knowledge of Him as familiar and convincing. We put out our hand, but we cannot touch Him. Nowhere in this world can we see Him more than we see Him here and now. If we pass to other worlds, there, too, He is concealed from our sight, inhabiting no body, occupying no place. Job is not alone in his painful and baffling search after God. Thousands continually cry with him, "Behold, I go forward, but He is not there; and backward, but I cannot perceive Him: on the left hand, where He doth work, but I cannot behold Him: He hideth Himself on the right hand, that I cannot see Him."

In various ways, accordingly, men have striven to alleviate the difficulty of mentally apprehending an invisible, infinite, incomprehensible God. One theory, struck out by the pressure of the difficulty, and frequently advanced, was not altogether incompatible with the ideas suggested by John in this prologue. This theory was accustomed, although with no great definiteness or security, to bridge the chasm between the Eternal God and His works in time by interposing some middle being or beings which might mediate between the known and the unknown. This link between God and His creatures, which deemed to make God and His relation to material things more intelligible, was sometimes spoken of as "The Word of God." This seemed an appropriate name by which to designate that through which God made Himself known, and by which He came into relations with things and persons not Himself. Vague indeed was the conception formed even of this intermediary Being. But of this term "the Word," and of the ideas that centred in it, John took advantage to proclaim Him who is the manifestation of the Eternal, the Image of the Invisible. [2]

The title itself is full of significance. The word of a man is that by which he utters himself, by which he puts himself in communication with other persons and deals with them. By his word he makes his thought and feeling known, and by his word he issues commands and gives effect to his will. His word is distinct from his thought, and yet cannot exist separate from it. Proceeding from the thought and will, from that which is inmost in us and most ourselves, it carries upon itself the imprint of the character and purpose of him who utters it. It is the organ of intelligence and will. It is not mere noise, it is sound instinct with mind, and articulated by intelligent purpose. By a man's word you could perfectly know him, even though you were blind and could never see him. Sight or touch could give you but little fuller information regarding his character if you had listened to his word. His word is his character in expression.

Similarly, the Word of God is God's power, intelligence, and will in expression; not dormant and potential only, but in active exercise. God's Word is His will going forth with creative energy, and communicating life from God, the Source of life and being. "Without Him was not any thing made that was made." He was prior to all created things and Himself with God, and God. He is God coming into relation with other things, revealing Himself, manifesting Himself, communicating Himself. The world is not itself God; things created are not God, but the intelligence and will that brought them into being, and which now sustain and regulate them, these are God. And between the works we see and the God who is past finding out, there is the Word, One who from eternity has been with God, the medium of the first utterance of God's mind and the first forthputting of His power; as close to the inmost nature of God, and as truly uttering that nature, as our word is close to and utters our thought, capable of being used by no one besides, but by ourselves only.

It is apparent, then, why John chooses this title to designate Christ in His pre-existent life. No other title brings out so clearly the identification of Christ with God, and the function of Christ to reveal God. It was a term which made the transition easy from Jewish Monotheism to Christian Trinitarianism. Being already used by the strictest Monotheists to denote a spiritual intermediary between God and the world, it is chosen by John as the appropriate title of Him through whom all revelation of God in the past has been mediated, and who has at length finished revelation in the person of Jesus Christ. The term itself does not explicitly affirm personality; but what it helps us to understand is, that this same Being, the Word, who manifested and uttered God in creation, reveals Him now in humanity. John wishes to bring the incarnation and the new spiritual world it produced into line with the creation and God's original purpose therein. He wishes to show us that this greatest manifestation of God is not an abrupt departure from previous methods, but is the culminating expression of methods and principles which have ever governed the activity of God. Jesus Christ, who reveals the Father now in human nature, is the same Agent as has ever been expressing and giving effect to the Father's will in the creation and government of all things. The same Word who now utters God in and through human nature, has ever been uttering Him in all His works.

All that God has done is to be found in the universe, partly visible and partly known to us. There God may be found, because there He has uttered Himself. But science tells us that in this universe there has been a gradual development from lower to higher, from imperfect towards perfect worlds; and it tells us that man is the last result of this process. In man the creature at last becomes intelligent, self-conscious, endowed with will, capable to some extent of meeting and understanding its Creator. Man is the last and fullest expression of God's thought, for in man and man's history God finds room for the utterance not merely of His wisdom and power, but of what is most profoundly spiritual and moral in His nature. In man God finds a creature who can sympathise with His purposes, who can respond to His love, who can give exercise to the whole fulness of God.

But in saying that "the Word become flesh" John says much more than that God through the Word created man, and found thus a more perfect means of revealing Himself. The Word created the visible world, but He did not become the visible world. The Word created all men, but He did not become the human race, but one Man, Christ Jesus. No doubt it is true that all men in their measure reveal God, and it is conceivable that some individual should fully illustrate all that God meant to reveal by human nature. It is conceivable that God should so sway a man's will and purify his character that the human will should be from first to last in perfect harmony with the Divine, and that the human character should exhibit the character of God. An ideal man might have been created, God's ideal of man might have been realized, and still we should have had no incarnation. For a perfect man is not all we have in Christ. A perfect man is one thing, the Word Incarnate is another. In the one the personality, the "I" that uses the human nature, is human; in the other, the personality, the "I," is Divine.

By becoming flesh the Word submitted to certain limitations, perhaps impossible for us to define. While in the flesh He could reveal only what human nature was competent to reveal. But as the human nature had been created in the likeness of the Divine, and as, therefore, "good" and "evil" meant the same to man as to God, the limitation would not be felt in the region of character.

The process of the Incarnation John describes very simply: "The Word became flesh, and dwelt among us." The Word did not become flesh in the sense that He was turned into flesh, ceasing to be what He had previously been, as a boy who becomes a man ceases to be a boy. In addition to what He already was He assumed human nature, at once enlarging His experience and limiting His present manifestations of Divinity to what was congruous to human nature and earthly circumstance. The Jews were familiar with the idea of God "dwelling" with His people. At the birth of their nation, while they were still dwelling in tents outside the land of promise, God had His tent among the shifting tents of the people, sharing all the vicissitudes of their wandering life, abiding with them even in their thirty-eight years' exclusion from their land, and thus sharing even their punishment. By the word John here uses he links the body of Christ to the ancient dwelling of God round which the tents of Israel had clustered. God now dwelt among men in the humanity of Jesus Christ. The tabernacle was human, the indwelling Person was Divine. In Christ is realized the actual presence of God among His people, the actual entrance into and personal participation in human history, which was hinted at in the tabernacle and the temple.

In the Incarnation, then, we have God's response to man's craving to find, to see, to know Him. Men, indeed, commonly look past Christ and away from Him, as if in Him God could not be satisfactorily seen; they discontentedly long for some other revelation of the unseen Spirit. But surely this is to mistake. To suppose that God might make Himself more obvious, more distinctly apparent to us, than He has done, is to mistake what God is and how we can know Him. What are the highest attributes of Divinity, the most Divine characteristics of God? Are they great power, vast size, dazzling physical glory that overpowers the sense; or are they infinite goodness, holiness that cannot be tempted, love that accommodates itself to all the needs of all creatures? Surely the latter, the spiritual and moral qualities, are the more Divine. The resistless might of natural forces shows us little of God till we have elsewhere learned to know Him; the power that upholds the planets in their orbits speaks but of physical force, and tells us nothing of any holy, loving Being. There is no moral quality, no character, impressed upon these works of God, mighty though they be. Nothing but an impersonal power meets us in them; a power which may awe and crush us, but which we cannot adore, worship, and love. In a word, God cannot reveal Himself to us by any overwhelming display of His nearness or His power. Though the whole universe fell in ruins around us, or though we saw a new world spring into being before our eyes, we might still suppose that the power by which this was effected was impersonal, and could hold no fellowship with us.

Only, then, through what is personal, only through what is like ourselves, only through what is moral, can God reveal Himself to us. Not by marvellous displays of power that suddenly awe us, but by goodness that the human conscience can apprehend and gradually admire, does God reveal Himself to us. If we doubt God's existence, if we doubt whether there is a Spirit of goodness upholding all things, wielding all things, and triumphant in all things, let us look to Christ. It is in Him we distinctly see upon our own earth, and in circumstances we can examine and understand, goodness; goodness tried by every test conceivable, goodness carried to its highest pitch, goodness triumphant. This goodness, though in human forms and circumstances, is yet the goodness of One who comes among men from a higher sphere, teaching, forgiving, commanding, assuring, saving, as One sent to deal with men rather than springing from them. If this is not God, what is God? What higher conception of God has any one ever had? What worthy conception of God is there that is not satisfied here? What do we need in God, or suppose to be in God, which we have not in Christ?

If, then, we still feel as if we had not sufficient assurance of God, it is because we look for the wrong thing, or seek where we can never find. Let us understand that God can best be known as God through His moral qualities, through His love, His tenderness, His regard for right; and we shall perceive that the most suitable revelation is one in which these qualities are manifested. But to apprehend these qualities as they appear in actual history we must have some sense for and love of them. They that are pure in heart, they shall see God; they who love righteousness, who seek with lowliness for purity and goodness, they will find in Christ a God they can see and trust.

The lessons of the Incarnation are obvious. First, from it we are to take our idea of God. Sometimes we feel as if in attributing to God all good we were dealing merely with fancies of our own which could not be justified by fact. In the Incarnation we see what God has actually done. Here we have, not a fancy, not a hope, not a vague expectation, not a promise, but accomplished fact, as solid and unchangeable as our own past life. This God whom we have often shunned, and felt to be in our way and an obstacle, whom we have suspected of tyranny and thought little of injuring and disobeying, has through compassion and sympathy with us broken through all impossibilities, and contrived to take the sinner's place. He, the ever blessed God, accountable for no evil and sole cause of all good, accepted the whole of our condition, lived as a creature, Himself bare our sicknesses, all that is hardest in life, all that is bitterest and loneliest in death, in His own experience combining all the agonies of sinning and suffering men, and all the ineffable sorrows wherewith God looks upon sin and suffering. All this He did, not for the sake of showing us how much better a thing the Divine nature is than the human, but because His nature impelled Him to do it; because He could not bear to be solitary in His blessedness, to know in Himself the joy of holiness and love while His creatures were missing this joy and making themselves incapable of all good.

Our first thought of God, then, must ever be that which the Incarnation suggests: that the God with whom alone and in all things we have to do is not One who is alienated from us, or who has no sympathy with us, or who is absorbed in interests very different from ours, and to which we must be sacrificed; but that He is One who sacrifices Himself for us, who makes all things but justice and right bend to serve us, who forgives our misapprehensions, our coldness, our unspeakable folly, and makes common cause with us in all that concerns our welfare. As while on earth He endured the contradiction of sinners, and waited till they came to a better mind, so does He still, with Divine patience, wait till we recognise Him as our Friend, and humbly own Him as our God. He waits till we learn that to be God is not to be a mighty King enthroned above all the assaults of His creatures, but that to be God is to have more love than all besides; to be able to make greater sacrifices for the good of all; to have an infinite capacity to humble Himself, to put Himself out of sight, and to consider our good. This is the God we have in Christ; our Judge becoming our atoning Victim, our God becoming our Father, the Infinite One coming with all His helpfulness into the most intimate relations with us; is this not a God to whom we can trust ourselves, and whom we can love and serve? If this is the real nature of God, if we may always expect such faithfulness and help from God, if to be God be to be all this, as full of love in the future as He has shown Himself in the past, then may not existence yet be that perfect joy our instincts crave, and towards which we are slowly and doubtfully finding our way through all the darkness, and strains, and shocks that are needed to sift what is spiritual in us from what is unworthy?

The second lesson the Incarnation teaches regards our own duty. Everywhere among the first disciples was this lesson learned and inculcated. "Let this mind," says Paul, "be in you which was also in Christ Jesus." "Christ suffered for us," says Peter, "leaving us an example." "If God so loved us, we ought also to love one another" is the very spirit of John. Look steadily at the Incarnation, at the love which made Christ take our place and identify Himself with us; consider the new breath of life that this one act has breathed into human life, ennobling the world and showing us how deep and lovely are the possibilities that lie in human nature; and new thoughts of your own conduct will lay hold of your mind. Come to this great central fire, and your cold, hard nature will be melted; try in some sort to weigh this Divine love and accept it as your own, as that which embraces and cares for and carries you on to all good, and you will insensibly be imbued with its spirit. You will feel that no loss could be so great as to lose the possession and exercise of this love in your own heart. Great as are the gifts it bestows, you begin to see that the greatest of them all is that it transforms you into its own likeness, and teaches you yourself to love in the same sort. Understanding our security and our joyful prospect as saved by the care of God, and as provided for by a love of perfect intelligence and absolute resource; humbled and softened and melted by the free spending upon us of so Divine and complete a grace, our heart overflows with sympathy. We cannot receive Christ's love without communicating it. It imparts a glow to the heart, which must be felt by all that comes in contact with the heart.

And as Christ's love became incarnate, not spending itself in any one great display, apart from the needs of men, but manifesting itself in all the routine and incident of a human life; never wearying through the monotonous toil of His artisan-life, never provoked into forgetfulness in His boyhood; so must our love derived from Him be incarnated; not spent in one display, but animating our whole life in the flesh, and finding expression for itself in all that our earthly condition brings us into contact with. The thoughts we think and the actions we do are mainly concerned with other people. We are living in families, or we are related as employer and employed, or we are thrown together by the hundred necessities of life; in all these connections we are to be guided by the spirit which prompted Christ to become incarnate. Our chance of doing good in the world depends upon this. Our review of life at the close will be satisfactory or the reverse in proportion as we have or have not been in fact animated by the spirit of the Incarnation. We must learn to bear one another's burdens, and the Incarnation shows us that we can do so only in so far as we identify ourselves with others and live for them. Christ helped us by coming down to our condition and living our life. This is the guide to all help we can give. If anything can reclaim the lowest class in our population, it is by men of godly life living among them; not living among them in comforts unattainable by them, but living in all points as they live, save that they live without sin. Christ had no money to give, no knowledge of science to impart; He lived a sympathetic and godly life, regardless of Himself. Few can follow Him, but let us never lose sight of His method. The poor are not the only class that need help. It is our dependence on money as the medium of charity that has begotten that feeling. It is easy to give money; and so we discharge our obligation, and feel as if we had done all. It is not money that even the poorest have most need of; and it is not money at all, but sympathy, which all classes need--that true sympathy which gives us insight into their condition, and prompts us to bear their burdens, whatever these are. There are many men on earth who are mere hindrances to better men; who cannot manage their own affairs or play their own part, but are continually entangled and in difficulties. They are a drag on society, requiring the help of more serviceable men, and preventing such men from enjoying the fruit of their own labour. There are, again, men who are not of our kind, men whose tastes are not ours. There are men who seem pursued by misfortune, and men who by their own sin keep themselves continually in the mire. There are, in short, various classes of persons with whom we are day by day tempted to have no more to do whatever; we are exasperated by the discomfort they occasion us; the anxiety and vexation and expenditure of time, feeling, and labour constantly renewed so long as we are in connection with them. Why should we be held down by unworthy people? Why should we have the ease and joy taken out of our life by the ceaseless demands made upon us by wicked, careless, incapable, ungrateful people? Why must we still be patient, still postponing our own interests to theirs? Simply because this is the method by which the salvation of the world is actually accomplished; simply because we ourselves thus tax the patience of Christ, and because we feel that the love we depend upon and believe in as the salvation of the world we must ourselves endeavour to show. Recognising how Christ has humbled Himself to bear the burden of shame and misery we have laid upon Him, we cannot refuse to bear one another's burdens, and so fulfil the law of Christ.

Footnotes:

1. See also Gen. xvi. 13, xviii. 22; Exod. iii. 6, xxiii. 20; Judges xiii. 22.
2. For the need of intermediaries, see Plato, Symposium, pp. 202--3: "God mingles not with men; but there are spiritual powers which interpret and convey to God the prayers and sacrifices of men, and to men the commands and rewards of God. These powers span the chasm which divides them, and these spirits or intermediate powers are many and divine." See also Philo (Quod Deus Immut., xiii.): "God is not comprehensible by the intellect. We know, indeed, that He is, but beyond the fact of His existence we know nothing." The Word reveals God; see Philo (De post. Caini, vi.) "The wise man, longing to apprehend God, and travelling along the path of wisdom and knowledge, first of all meets with the Divine words, and with them abides as a guest."

II. RECEPTION CHRIST MET WITH

John i. 1--18.

In describing the Word of God, John mentions two attributes of His by which His relation to men becomes apparent: "All things were made by Him," and "the life was the light of men." By whom were all things made? what is the originating force which has produced the world? how are we to account for the existence, the harmony, and the progress of the universe?--these are questions which must always be put. Everywhere in nature force and intelligence appear; the supply of life and power is unfailing, and the unconscious planets are as regular and harmonious in their action as the creatures that are endowed with conscious intelligence and the power of self-guidance. That the whole universe is one does not admit of a doubt. Far as the astronomer can search into infinite space, he finds the same laws and one plan, and no evidence of another hand or another mind. To what is this unity to be referred? John here affirms that the intelligence and power which underlie all things belong to the Word of God: "without Him was not anything made which was made."

"In Him was life." In this Divine Being, who was "in the beginning" before all things, there was that which gives existence to all else. "And the life was the light of men." That life which appears in the harmony and progress of inanimate nature, and in the wonderfully manifold and yet related forms of animal existence, appears in man as "light"--intellectual and moral light, reason and conscience. All the endowment possessed by man as a moral being, capable of self-determination and of choosing what is morally good, springs from the one fountain of life which exists in the Word of God.

It is in the light of this close relationship of the Word to the world and to men that John views the reception He met with when He became flesh and dwelt among us. This reception forms the great tragedy of human history. "In Agamemnon returning to his palace after ten years' absence, and falling by the hand of his unfaithful spouse, we have the event which is tragical par excellence in pagan history. But what is that outrage when compared with the theocratic tragedy? The God invoked by the nation appears in His temple, and is crucified by His own worshippers." To John it seemed as if the relationship borne by the Word to those who rejected Him was the tragical element in the rejection.

Three different aspects of this relationship are mentioned, that the blindness of the rejecters may more distinctly be seen. First, he says, although the very light that was in man was derived from the Word, and it was by His endowment they had any power to recognise what was illuminating and helpful to their spiritual nature, they yet shut their eyes to the source of light when presented in the Word Himself. "The life was the light of men.... And the light shineth in darkness, and the darkness apprehended it not." This is the general statement of the universal experience of the Eternal Word, and it is illustrated in His incarnate experience summarily related in verses 10 and 11. Again: "He was in the world, and the world was made by Him, and the world knew Him not." So little had men understood the source of their own being, and so little had they learned to know the significance and purpose of their existence, that when their Creator came they did not recognise Him. And thirdly, even the narrow and carefully-trained circle of the Jews failed to recognise Him; "He came unto His own"--to everything which had pointedly and of set purpose spoken of Him, and could not have existed but to teach His character--"and His own received Him not."

1. "The light shineth in the darkness; and the darkness apprehended it not." As yet John has said nothing of the Incarnation, and is speaking of the Word in His eternal or pre-incarnate state. And one thing he desires to proclaim regarding the Word is, that although it is from Him every man has such light as he has, yet this light is commonly rendered useless, and is not cherished. As it is from the Word, from God's uttered will, that all men have life, so it is from the same source that all the light which is in reason and in conscience is derived. Before the Word appeared in the world, and shone out as the true light (ver. 9), He was in all rational creatures as their life and light, imparting to men a sense of right and wrong, and shining in their heart with some of the brightness of a Divine presence. This sense of a connection with God and eternity, and this moral faculty, although cherished by some, were commonly not "comprehended." Evil deeds have been suffered to darken conscience, and it fails to admit the true light.

2. "He was in the world, and the world was made by Him, and the world knew Him not." When our Lord came to earth the heathen world was mainly represented by the Roman Empire, and one of the earliest events of His life on earth was His enrolment as a subject of that empire. If we had been invited

Marcus Dods, D.D.

before His coming to imagine what would be the result upon this empire of His appearance, we should probably have expected something very different from that which actually happened. The real Sovereign is to appear; the Being who made all that is, is to come and visit His possessions. Will not a thrill of glad expectancy run through the world? Will not men eagerly cover up whatever may offend Him, and eagerly attempt, with such scant materials as existed, to make preparations for His worthy reception? The one Being who can make no mistakes, and who can rectify the mistakes of a worn-out, entangled world, is to come for the express purpose of delivering it from all ill: will not men gladly yield the reins to Him, and gladly second Him in all His enterprise? Will it not be a time of universal concord and brotherhood, all men joining to pay homage to their common God? "He was in the world, and the world was made by Him"--that is the true, bare, unvarnished statement of the fact. There He was, the Creator Himself, that mysterious Being who had hitherto kept Himself so hidden and remote while yet so influential and supreme; the wonderful and unsearchable Source and Fountain out of which had proceeded all that men saw, themselves included,--there at last He was "in the world" Himself had made, apparent to the eyes of men, and intelligible to their understandings; a real person whom they could know as an individual, whom they could love, who could receive and return their expressions of affection and trust. He was in the world, and the world knew Him not.

Indeed, it would not have been easy for the world to show a more entire ignorance of God than while He was upon earth in human form. There was at that time abundance of activity and intelligent apprehension of the external wants of men and nations. There was a ceaseless running to and fro of the couriers of the empire, a fine system of communications spread over the whole known world like a network, so that what transpired in the most remote corner was at once known at the centre. Rome was intelligent to the utmost circumference through all its dominions; as if a nervous system radiated through the whole of it, touch but the extremity in one of the remotest colonies and the touch is felt at the brain and heart of the whole. [3] The rising of a British tribe, the discovery of some unheard-of bird or beast, the birth of a calf with two heads--every scrap of gossip found its way to Rome. [4] But the entrance of the Creator into the world was an event of such insignificance that not even this finely sympathetic system took any note of it. The great Roman world remained in absolute unconsciousness of the vicinity of God: they registered His birth, took account of Him as one to be taxed, but were as little aware as the oxen with whom He shared His first sleeping-place, that this was God; they saw Him with the same stupid, unconscious, bovine stare. [5]

3. But in this great world of men there was an inner and specially trained circle, which John here designates "His own." For although the world might be called "His own," as made and upheld by him, yet it seems more likely that this verse is not a mere repetition of the preceding, but is intended to mark a deeper degree of insensibility on the part of Christ's rejecters. Not only had all men been made in God's image, so that they might have been expected to recognise Christ as the image of the Father; but one nation had been specially instructed in the knowledge of God, and was proud of having His dwelling-place in its midst. If other men were blind to God's glory, the Jews at least might have been expected to welcome Christ when He came. Their temple and all that was done in it, their law, their prophets, their institutions, their history and their daily life, all spoke to them of God, and reminded them that God dwelt among them and would come to His own. Though all the world should shut its doors against Christ, surely the gates of the Temple, His own house, would be thrown open to Him. For what else did it exist?

Our Lord Himself, in the parable of the Wicked Husbandmen, makes even a heavier accusation against the Jews, intimating, as He there does, that they rejected Him not because they did not recognise Him, but because they did. "This is the Heir. Come, let us kill Him, that the inheritance may be ours." In any case their guilt is great. They had been definitely and repeatedly admonished to expect some great manifestation of God; they looked for the Christ to come, and immediately before His appearance they had been strikingly awakened to prepare for His coming. But what was their actual state when Christ came? Again and again it has been pointed out that their whole thoughts were given to the schemes which usually distract conquered nations. They were "tossing in unhelpful and inefficacious sedition," resenting or paying hollow homage to the rule of the foreigner, looking uneasily for deliverance, and becoming the dupes of every fanatic or schemer that cried, "Lo here!" or "Lo there!" Their power of discerning a present God and a spiritual Deliverer was almost as completely gone as that of the heathen, and they tested the Divine Saviour by external methods which any clever charlatan could have satisfied. The God they believed in and sought was not the God revealed by Christ. They existed for Christ's sake, that among them He might find a home on earth, and through them be made known to all; they believed in a Christ that was to come, but when He came the throne they raised Him to was the cross. And the suspicion that perhaps they were wrong has preyed on the Jewish mind ever since, and has often pricked them on to a fierce hatred of the Christian name, while sometimes it has taken almost the form of penitence, as in the prayer of Rabbi Ben Ezra,--

"Thou! if Thou wast He, who at mid-watch came,
By the starlight, naming a dubious name!
And if, too heavy with sleep--too rash
With fear--O Thou, if that martyr-gash
Fell on Thee coming to take Thine own,
And we gave the Cross, when we owed the Throne,--
Thou art the Judge."

It is the detailed history of this rejection which John presents in his Gospel. He tells the story of Christ's miracles, and the jealousy they excited; of His authoritative teaching and the opposition it aroused; of His unveiling His Divine nature, His mercy, His power to give life, His prerogative of judgment, His humble self-sacrifice, and of the misunderstanding which ran parallel to this manifestation. He tells how the leaders strove to entangle Him and find Him at fault; how they took up stones to stone Him; how they schemed and plotted, and at length compassed His crucifixion. The patience with which He met this "contradiction of sinners" was a sufficient revelation of His Divine nature. Though rudely received, though met on all hands with suspicion, coldness, and hostility, He did not abandon the world in indignation. He never forgot that He came, not to judge the world, not to deal with us on our merits, but to save the world from its sin and its blindness. For the sake of the few who received Him He bore with the many who rejected Him.

For some did receive Him. John could say for many, along with himself, "We beheld His glory," and recognised that it was Divine glory, such as none but an Only-begotten in the image of His Father could manifest. This glory dawned upon believing men, and gradually encompassed them in the brightness and beauty of a Divine revelation, by the appearance among them of the Incarnate Word, "full of grace and truth" (ver. 14). Not the works of wonder which He did, not the authority with which He laid the angry waves and commanded the powers of evil, but the grace and truth which underlay all His works, shone into their hearts as Divine glory. They had previously known God through the law given by Moses (ver. 17); but coming as it did through law, this knowledge was coloured by its medium, and through it God's countenance seemed stern. In the face of Jesus Christ they saw the Father, they saw "grace," an eye of tender compassion and lips of love and helpfulness. In the law they felt that they were seeing through a dimmed glass darkly; they became weary of symbols and of forms in which often they saw but flitting shadows. What must it have been for such men to live with the manifested God; to have Him dwelling among them, and in Him to handle and see (1 John i. 1) the "truth," the reality to which all symbol had pointed? "The law was given by Moses; grace and truth came by Jesus Christ." [6]

And to those who acknowledge in their hearts that this is Divine glory which is seen in Christ, the glory of the Only-begotten of the Father, He gives Himself with all His fulness. "As many as received Him, to them gave He the right to become children of God." This is the immediate result of the acceptance of Christ as the Revealer of the Father. In Him we see what true glory is and what true sonship is; and as we behold the glory of the Only-begotten, sent to declare the Father to us, we acknowledge the unseen Father, and His Spirit brings us into the relationship of children. That which is in God passes into us, and we share in the life of God; and this through Christ. He is "full" of grace and truth. In all He is and does, grace and truth overflowingly manifest themselves. And "of His fulness have all we received, and grace upon grace." [7] John read this off his own experience and that of those for whom he could confidently speak. What they had seen and valued in Christ became their own character. The inexhaustible fulness of grace in Christ renewed in them grace according to their need. They lived upon Him. It was His life which maintained life in them. By communion with Him they were formed in His likeness.

The presentation of Christ to men now divides them into two classes, as at the first. There are always those who accept and those who reject Him. His contemporaries showed, for the most part, a complete ignorance of what might be expected of God, a native inability to understand spiritual greatness, and to relish it when presented to them. And yet Christ's claims were made with such an air of authority and truth, and His whole character and bearing were so consistent, that they were half persuaded He was all He said. It is chiefly because we have not a perfect sympathy with goodness, and do not know its value, that we do not at once and universally acknowledge Christ. There is in men an instinct that tells them what blessings Christ will secure to them, and they decline connection with Him because they are conscious that their ways are not His ways, nor their hopes His hopes. The very presentation to men of the possibility of becoming perfectly pure reveals what at heart they are. By the judgment each man passes on Christ he passes judgment on himself.

Let us stir ourselves to a clearer decision by remembering that He is presented to us as to His contemporaries. Time was when any one going into the synagogue of Nazareth would have seen Him, and might have spoken with Him. But the particular thirty years during which this manifestation of God on earth lasted makes no material difference to the thing itself. The Incarnation was to be some time, and it is as real having occurred then as if it were occurring now. It occurred in its fit time; but its bearing on us is not dependent on the time of its occurrence. If it had been accomplished in our day, what should we have thought of it? Would it have been nothing to us to see God, to hear Him, perhaps to have had His eye turned upon us with personal observation, with pity, with remonstrance? Would it have been nothing to us to see Him taking the sinners place, scourged, mocked, crucified? Is it conceivable that in presence of such a manifestation of God we should have been indifferent? Would not our whole nature have burned with shame that we and our fellow-men should have brought our God to this? And are we to suffer the mere fact of Christ's being incarnate in a past age and not in our own, to alter our attitude towards Him, and blind us to the reality? Of more importance than anything that is now happening in our own life is this Incarnation of the Only-begotten of the Father.

Footnotes:

3. See Isaac Taylor's Restoration of Belief.
4. See Pliny's Letters to Trajan, 23, 98.
5. Cp. Faber's Bethlehem.
6. The first introduction in the Gospel of the name of Jesus Christ.
7. This expression means a succession of graces, higher grace ever taking the place of lower.

III. THE BAPTIST'S TESTIMONY

"There came a man, sent from God, whose name was John. The same came for witness, that he might bear witness of the light, that all might believe through him. He was not the light, but came that he might bear witness of the light.... John beareth witness of Him, and crieth, saying, This was He of whom I said, He that cometh after me is preferred before me: for He was before me. For of His fulness we all received, and grace for grace. For the law was given by Moses; grace and truth came by Jesus Christ. No man hath seen God at any time; the only begotten Son, which is in the bosom of the Father, He hath declared Him. And this is the witness of John, when the Jews sent unto him from Jerusalem priests and Levites to ask him, Who art thou? And he confessed, and denied not; and he confessed, I am not the Christ. And they asked him, What then? Art thou Elijah? And he saith, I am not. Art thou the prophet? And he answered, No. They said therefore unto him, Who art thou? that we may give an answer to them that sent us. What sayest thou of thyself? He said, I am the voice of one crying in the wilderness, Make straight the way of the Lord, as said Isaiah the prophet. And they had been sent from the Pharisees. And they asked him, and said unto him, Why then baptizest thou, if thou art not the Christ, neither Elijah, neither the prophet? John answered them, saying, I baptize with water: in the midst of you standeth One whom ye know not, even He that cometh after me, the latchet of whose shoe I am not worthy to unloose. These things were done in Bethany beyond Jordan, where John was baptizing. On the morrow he seeth Jesus coming unto him, and saith, Behold, the Lamb of God, which taketh away the sin of the world! This is He of whom I said, After me cometh a Man which is preferred before me: for He was before me. And I knew Him not; but that He should be made manifest to Israel, for this cause came I baptizing with water. And John bare witness, saying, I have beheld the Spirit descending as a dove out of heaven; and it abode upon Him. And I knew Him not: but He that sent me to baptize with water, He said unto me, Upon whomsoever thou shalt see the Spirit descending, and abiding upon Him, the same is He that baptizeth with the Holy Spirit. And I have seen, and have borne witness that this is the Son of God."--John i. 6--8, 15--34.

In proceeding to show how the Incarnate Word manifested Himself among men, and how this manifestation was received, John naturally speaks first of all of the Baptist. "There came a man, sent from God, whose name was John. The same came for witness ... that all might believe through him." The Evangelist himself had been one of the Baptist's disciples, and had been led to Christ by his testimony. And to many besides, the Baptist was the true forerunner of the Messiah. He was the first to recognise and proclaim the present King. John had come under the Baptist's influence at the most impressible time of his life, while his character was being formed and his ideas of religion taking shape; and his teacher's testimony to the dignity of Jesus had left an indelible print upon his spirit. While his memory retained anything it could not let slip what his first teacher had said of Him who became his Teacher and his Lord. While, therefore, the other Evangelists give us striking pictures of the Baptist's appearance, habits, and style of preaching, and show us the connection of his work with that of Jesus, John glances very slightly at these matters, but dwells with emphasis and iteration on the testimony which the Baptist bore to the Messiahship of Jesus.

To us, at this time of day, it may seem of little importance what the Baptist thought or said of Jesus. We may sympathise rather with the words of the Lord Himself, who, in allusion to this witness, said, "I receive not testimony from man." But it is plain that, at any rate from a Jewish point of view, the witness of John was most important. The people universally accepted John as a prophet, and they could scarcely think him mistaken in the chief article of his mission. In point of fact, many of the most faithful adherents of Jesus became such through the influence of John; and those who declined to accept Jesus were always staggered by John's explicit indication of Him as the Christ. The Jews had not only the predictions of prophets long since dead, and descriptions of the Christ which they could perversely misconstrue; they had not merely pictures of their Messiah by which they might identify Jesus as the Christ, but of which it was also quite possible for them to deny the likeness; but they had a living contemporary, whom they themselves acknowledged to be a prophet, pointing out to them another living contemporary as the Christ. That even such a testimony was to a large extent disregarded shows how much more the inclination to believe has to do with our faith than any external proofs.

But even to us the testimony of a man like John is not without importance. He was, as our Lord bore witness, "a burning and a shining light." He was one of those men who give new thoughts to their generation, and help men to see clearly what otherwise they might only dimly have seen. He was in a position to know Jesus well. He was His cousin; he had known Him from His childhood. He was also in a position to know what was involved in being the Messiah. By the very circumstance that he himself had been mistaken for the Messiah, he was driven to define to his own mind the distinctive and characteristic marks of the Messiah. Nothing could so have led him to apprehend the difference between himself and Jesus. More and more clearly must he have seen that he was not that light, but was sent to bear witness of that light. Thus he was prepared to receive with understanding the sign (ver. 33) which gave him something more than his own personal surmises to go upon in declaring Jesus to the world as the Messiah. If there is any man's testimony we may accept about our Lord it is that of the Baptist, who, from his close contact with the most profligate and with the most spiritual of the people, saw what they needed, and saw in Jesus power to give it; the business of whose life it was to make Him out, and to arrive at certain information regarding Him; a man whose own elevation and force of character made many fancy he was the Messiah, but who hastened to disabuse their minds of such an idea, because his very elevation gave him capacity to see how infinitely above him the true Christ was. Seen from the low ground the star may seem close to the top of the mountain; seen from the mountain-top it is recognised as infinitely above it. John was on the mountain-top.

Of John's person and work nothing need here be said save what serves to throw light on his witness to Christ. Going from the comfortable home and well-provided life and fair prospects of a priest's family, he went to the houseless wilderness, and adopted the meagre, comfortless life of an ascetic; not from any necessity, but because he felt that to entangle himself with the affairs of the world would be to blind him to its vices, and to silence his remonstrance, if not to implicate him in its guilt. Like thousands besides in all ages of the world's history, he felt compelled to seek solitude, to subdue the flesh, to meditate undisturbed on things Divine, and discover for himself and for others some better way than religious routine and the "good wine of Mosaic morality turned to the vinegar of Pharisaism." Like the Nazarites of the earlier times of his country, like the old prophets, with whose indignation and deep regret at the national vices he was in perfect sympathy, he left the world, gave up all the usual prospects and ways of life, and betook himself to a life of prayer, and thought, and self-discipline in the wilderness. When first he went there, he could only dimly know what lay before him; but he gathered a few friends of like disposition around him, and, as we learn, "taught them to pray." He formed in the wilderness a new Israel, a little company of praying souls, who spent their time in considering the needs of their fellow-countrymen, and in interceding with God for them, and who were content to let the pleasures and excitements of the world pass by while they longed for and prepared themselves to meet the great Deliverer.

This adoption of the rÃ´le of the ancient prophets, this resuscitation of their long-forgotten function of mourning before God for the people's sin, and addressing the nation authoritatively as God's voice, was outwardly shown by his assumption of the prophet's dress. The rough skin for a cloak; the long, uncared-for hair; the wiry, weather-beaten frame; the lofty, calm, penetrating eye, were all eloquent as his lips. His whole appearance and habits certified his claim to be the "voice" of one crying in the wilderness, and gave him authority with the people. Slightly altering what has been said of a great modern, we may much more truly say of the Baptist,--

"He took the suffering human race,
He read each wound, each weakness clear:
He struck his finger on the place,
And said, Thou ailest here, and here.'
He looked on (Isr'el's) dying hour
Of fitful dreams and feverish power,
And said, The end is everywhere,
(Christ) still has truth, take refuge there.'"

He was listened to. It is so always, in our own day as in others; the men who are unworldly and have the good of their country or of any class of men at heart, the men who are saintly and of few desires, these are listened to as the commissioned messengers of heaven. It is to these men we look as the salt of the earth, who preserve us still from the corrupting, disintegrating influence of doubt. To these men, no matter how different they be from us in creed, we are forced to listen, because the Holy Spirit, wherever He is, is the Spirit of God; and all men instinctively acknowledge that those who are themselves in the kingdom of God have authority to summon others into it, and that those who are themselves unworldly have alone a right to dictate to worldly men. There is no power on earth like the power of a holy, consecrated life, because he who is leading such a life is already above the world, and belongs to a higher kingdom. There is hope for our country, or for any country, when its young men have something of John's spirit; when they school the body until it becomes the ready instrument of a high and spiritual intention, fearless of hardship; when by sympathy with God's purposes they apprehend what is most needed by men, and are able to detect the weaknesses and vices of society, and to bear the burden of their time.

But the Baptist's equipment for the most responsible office of proclaiming the Messiahship of Jesus was not completed by his own saintliness of character and keen perception of the people's needs, and knowledge of Jesus, and incorruptible truthfulness. There was given to him a sign from heaven, that he might be strengthened to bear this responsibility, and that the Messiah might never seem to be only of the Baptist's appointing and not of God's. Some degree of disappointment may be felt that external signs should have intruded on so profoundly spiritual and real an occasion as the baptism of Christ. Some may be ready to ask, with Keim, "Is it, or was it ever, the way of God, in the course of His spiritual world, above all upon the threshold of spiritual decisions affecting the fate of the world, and in contradiction to the wise economy of revelation pursued by His supreme ambassador Himself, to take away from seeking and finding souls the labour of deciding their own destiny?" But this is to suppose that the signs at the baptism of Jesus were mainly for His encouragement, whereas John describes them as being given for the certification of the Baptist. "I knew Him not"--that is, I did not know He was the Messiah--"but He that sent me to baptize with water, He said unto me, Upon whomsoever thou shalt see the Spirit descending, and abiding upon Him, the same is He that baptizeth with the Holy Spirit. And I have seen, and have borne witness that this is the Son of God."

The baptism of Jesus was, in fact, His anointing as the Messiah; and this anointing by which He became the Christ was an anointing, not with a symbolic oil, but with the Divine Spirit (Acts x. 38). This Spirit descended upon Him "in a bodily shape" (Luke iii. 22), because it was not one member or faculty or power which was communicated to Jesus, but a whole body or complete equipment of all needful Divine energies for His work. "God giveth not the Spirit by measure unto Him;" there is no gauge, no metre checking the supply. Now for the first time can the whole Spirit be given, because now for the first time in Jesus is there room to receive it. And that the Baptist may confidently proclaim Him as King the sign is given,--not the outward sign alone, but the outward sign accompanying and tallying with the inward sign; for it was not said to the Baptist, "Upon whomsoever thou shalt see a dove descend," but, "upon whomsoever thou shalt see the Spirit descend."

This anointing of Jesus to the Messiahship occurred at the moment of His truest identification of Himself with the people. John shrank from baptizing One whom he knew to be already pure, and to have no sins to confess. But Jesus insisted, identifying Himself with a polluted people, numbered with transgressors. It was thus He became true King and Head of mankind, by identifying Himself with us, and taking upon Him, through His universal sympathy, all our burdens, feeling more shame than the sinner's self for his sin, pained with the suffering in all their pain. It was the Divine Spirit of universal love, attracting Him to all sorrow and suffering, which identified Him in the mind of His first confessor as the Christ, the Son of God. This to the Baptist was the glory of the Only-begotten, this sympathy which felt with all, and shrank from no sorrow or burden.

Thus equipped, the Baptist gives his testimony with confidence. This testimony is manifold, and uttered on several occasions,--to the Sanhedrim's deputation, to the people, and to his own disciples. It is negative as well as positive. He repudiates the suggestions of the deputation from Jerusalem that he himself is the Christ, or that he is in their sense Elijah. But the most remarkable repudiation of honours which could be rendered to Christ alone is found recorded in chap. iii. 22--30, when the growing popularity of Jesus excited the jealousy of those who still adhered to the Baptist. Their complaint was the occasion of calling up clearly in the Baptist's own consciousness the relation in which he stood to Jesus, and of prompting the most emphatic enouncement of the unrivalled dignity of our Lord. He says to his jealous disciples, "If I do not gather a crowd of followers while Jesus does, this is because God has appointed to me one place, to Him another. Beyond God's design no man's destiny and success can extend. What is designed for me I shall receive; beyond that I desire to receive and I can receive nothing. Least of all would I covet to be called the Christ. You know not what you say in even remotely hinting that such a man as I could be the Christ. It is no mere unworldliness or purity which can raise a man to this dignity. He is from above; not to be named with prophets, but the Son of God, who belongs to the heavenly world of which He speaks."

To make the difference between himself and Christ clear, the Baptist hits upon the happy figure of the Bridegroom and the Bridegroom's friend. "He that has and keeps the Bride is the Bridegroom. He to whom the world is drawn, and on whom all needy souls lean, is the Bridegroom, and to Him alone belongs this special joy of satisfying all human needs. I am not the Bridegroom, because men cannot find in me satisfaction and rest. I cannot be to them the source of spiritual life. Moreover, by instigating me to assume the Bridegroom's place you would rob me of my peculiar joy, the joy of the Bridegroom's friend." The function of the bridegroom's friend, or paranymph, was to ask the hand of the bride for the bridegroom, and to arrange the marriage. This function the Baptist claims as his. "My joy," he says, "is to have negotiated this matter, to have encouraged the Bride to trust her Lord. It is my joy to hear the glad and loving words that pass between Bridegroom and Bride. Do not suppose I look with sadness on the defection of my followers, and on their preference for Christ. These crowds you complain of are evidence that I have not discharged the function of paranymph in vain. To see my work successful, to see Bride and Bridegroom at length resting in one another with undisturbed, self-forgetting confidence, this is my joy. While the Bridegroom cheers the Bride with His voice, and opens to her prospects which only His love can realize, shall I obtrude myself and claim consideration? Is it not enough for one life to have had the joy of identifying the actually present Christ, and of introducing the Bride to her Lord? Has not that life its ample reward which has been instrumental in achieving the actual union of God and man?"

Probably, then, the Baptist himself would think we waste too much emotion over his self-sacrifice and magnanimity. After all, it not being possible to him to be the Messiah, it was no small glory and joy to be the friend, the next, to the Messiah. The tragic character of the Baptist's death, the despondent doubt which for a time shook his spirit during his imprisonment, the severe life he had previously led, all tend to make us oblivious of the fact that his life was crowned with a deep and solid joy. Even the poet who has most worthily depicted him still speaks of

"John, than which man a sadder or a greater
Not till this day has been of woman born."

But the Baptist was a big enough man to enjoy an unselfish happiness. He loved men so well that he rejoiced when he saw them forsake him to follow Christ. He loved Christ so well that to see Him honoured was the crown of his life.

Besides this negative repudiation of honours that belonged to Jesus, the Baptist emits a positive and fivefold testimony in His favour, (1) to His dignity (vv. 15, 27, 30), "He that cometh after me is preferred before me;" (2) to His pre-existence (vv. 15, 30), which is adduced as the reason of the foregoing, "for He was before me;" (3) to His spiritual fulness and power (ver. 33), "He baptizeth with the Holy Ghost;" (4) to the efficacy of His mediation (ver. 29), "Behold, the Lamb of God, which taketh away the sin of the world;" (5) to His unique personality (ver. 34), "this is the Son of God."

1. Three times over the Baptist declared the superiority of Jesus; a superiority so immense that language failed him in trying to represent it. The Rabbis said, "Every office which a servant will do for his master a scholar should perform for his teacher, except loosing his sandal-thong." But this exceptionally menial office the Baptist declares he was not worthy to perform for Jesus. None so well as the Baptist himself knew his limitations. He had evoked in the people cravings he could not satisfy. There had gathered to him a conscience-stricken people, longing for renewal and righteousness, and demanding what he had no power to give. Therefore, not merely his explicit enouncements from time to time, but his entire ministry, pointing to a new order of things which he himself could not inaugurate, declared the incomparable greatness of Him that was to come after him.

2. This superiority of Christ was based on His pre-existence. "He was before me." It may appear unaccountable that the Baptist, standing on Old Testament ground, should have reached the conclusion that Jesus was Divine. But it is at any rate evident that the Evangelist believed the Baptist had done so, for he adduces the Baptist's testimony in support of his own affirmation of the Divine glory of the Incarnate Word (ver. 15). After the wonderful scene at the Baptism, John must have talked closely with Jesus regarding both His work and His consciousness; and even if the passage at the close of the third chapter is coloured by the Evangelist's style, and even by his thought, we must suppose that the Baptist had somehow arrived at the belief that Jesus was "from above," and made known upon earth the things which He, in a pre-existent state, had "heard and seen."

3. The Baptist pointed to Jesus as the source of spiritual life. "He baptizeth with the Holy Ghost." Here the Baptist steps on to ground on which his assertions can be tested. He declares that Jesus can communicate the Holy Ghost--the fundamental article of the Christian Creed, which carries with it all else. No one knew better than the Baptist where human help failed; no one knew better than he what could be effected by rites and rules, by strength of will and asceticism and human endeavour; and no one knew better at what point all these become useless. More and more they seemed to him but a cleansing with water, a washing of the outside. More and more did he understand that, not from without, but from within, true cleansing must proceed, and that all else, save a new creation by the Spirit of God, was inefficacious. Only Spirit can act upon spirit; and for true renewal we need the action upon us of the Divine Spirit. Without this no new and eternal kingdom of God can be founded.

4. The Baptist pointed to Jesus as "the Lamb of God, that taketh away the sin of the world." That by this title he meant only to designate Jesus as a person full of gentleness and innocence is out of the question. The second clause forbids this. He is the Lamb that takes away sin. And there is only one way in which a lamb can take away sin, and that is, by sacrifice. The expression no doubt suggests the picture in the fifty-third of Isaiah of the servant of Jehovah meekly enduring wrong. But unless the Baptist had been previously speaking of this chapter, the thoughts of his disciples would not at once turn to it, because in that passage it is not a lamb of sacrifice that is spoken of, but a lamb meekly enduring. In the Baptist's words sacrifice is the primary idea, and it is needless to discuss whether he was thinking

of the paschal lamb or the lamb of morning and evening sacrifice, because he merely used the lamb as the representative of sacrifice generally. Here, he says, is the reality to which all sacrifice has pointed, the Lamb of God.

5. The Baptist proclaims Jesus as "the Son of God." That he should do so need not greatly surprise us, as we read in the other Gospels that Jesus had been thus designated by a voice from heaven at His baptism. Very early in His ministry, not only His disciples, but also the demoniacs ascribe to Him the same dignity. In one sense or other He was designated "Son of God." No doubt we must bear in mind that this was in a rigidly monotheistic community, and in a community in which the same title had been freely applied to Israel and to Israel's king to designate a certain alliance and close relation subsisting between the human and the Divine, but of course not suggesting metaphysical unity. But considering the high functions which clustered round the Messianic dignity, it is not unlikely that the Messiah's forerunner may have supposed that a fuller meaning than had yet been recognised might be latent in this title. Certainly we are safe in affirming that by applying this title to our Lord, the Baptist intended to indicate His unique personality, and to declare that He was the Messiah, God's Viceroy on earth.

Whether we can add to this testimony the thoughts contained in the closing paragraph of the third chapter may be doubted. The thought of the passage moves within the circle of ideas familiar to the Baptist; and that the style is the style of the Evangelist does not prevent us from receiving the ideas as the Baptist's. But there are expressions which it is difficult to suppose that the Baptist could have used. The preceding conversation was occasioned by the growing popularity of Jesus; was this, then, an occasion on which it could be said, "No one receives His testimony"? Is this not more appropriate to the Evangelist than to the Baptist? It would seem, then, that in this paragraph the Evangelist is expanding the Baptist's testimony, in order to indicate its application to the eternal relations subsisting between Jesus and men generally.

The contents of the paragraph are a most emphatic testimony to the pre-existence and heavenly origin of Christ. In contrast to persons of earthly origin, He is "from heaven." He "cometh" from above, as if His entrance into this world were a conscious transition, a voluntary coming from another world. His origin determines also His moral relationships and His teaching. He is "above all," in dignity, in authority, in spirit; and He speaks what He has seen and heard. But in the thirty-fourth verse a new idea is presented. There it is said that He speaks the words of God, not directly, because He is from above, and speaks what He has seen and heard, but "because God giveth not the Spirit by measure unto Him." What are we to understand by this double Divine inhabitation of the humanity of Jesus? And what are we to understand by the Spirit being given without measure to the Incarnate Word?

In the Old Testament two ideas present themselves regarding the Spirit which illustrate this statement. The one is that which conveys the impression that only a limited amount of spiritual influence was communicated to prophetic men, and that from them it could be conveyed to others. In Numb. xi. 17 the Lord is represented as saying to Moses, "I will take of the Spirit which is upon thee, and will put it upon them;" and in 2 Kings ii. 9 Elisha is represented as praying that the eldest born's portion, the two-thirds of Elijah's spirit, might be bequeathed to him. The idea is a true and instructive one. The Spirit does, in point of fact, pass from man to man. It is as if in one receptive person the Divine Spirit found entrance through which He might pass to others. But another idea is also frequent in the Old Testament. The Spirit is spoken of rather as conferring a gift here and a power there than as dwelling wholly and permanently in men. One prophet had a dream, another a vision, a third legislated, a fourth wrote a psalm, a fifth founded an institution, a sixth in the power of the Spirit smote the Philistines, or, like Samson, tore a lion in pieces.

In Christ all powers are combined--power over nature, power to teach, power to reveal, power to legislate. And as in the Old Testament the Spirit passed from man to man, so in the New Testament Christ first Himself receives and then communicates to all the whole Spirit. Hence the law noticed at a subsequent stage of this Gospel that "the Spirit was not yet given; because Jesus was not yet glorified" (vii. 39). We cannot see to the bottom of the law, but the fact is apparent, that until Christ received into every part of His own humanity the fulness of the Divine Spirit, that Spirit could not fill with His fulness any man.

But why was the Spirit needed in a personality of which the Word, who had been with God and known God, was the basis? Because the humanity of Christ was a true humanity. Being human, He must be indebted to the Spirit for all impartation to His human nature of what is Divine. The knowledge of God which the Word possesses by experience must be humanly apprehended before it can be communicated to men; and this human apprehension can only be arrived at in the case of Christ by the enlightenment of the Spirit. It was useless for Christ to declare what could not be apprehended by human faculty, and His own human faculty was the measure and test of intelligibility. By the Spirit He was enlightened to speak of things Divine; and this Spirit, interposed, as it were, between the Word and the human nature of Jesus, was as little cumbrous in its operation or perceptible in consciousness as our breath interposed between the thinking mind and the words we speak to declare our mind.

To return to the direct testimony of the Baptist, we must (1) acknowledge its value. It is the testimony of a contemporary, of whom we know from other sources that he was generally reckoned a prophet--a man of unblemished and inviolable integrity, of rugged independence, of the keenest spiritual discernment. There was no man of larger size or more heroic mould in his day. In any generation he would have been conspicuous by his spiritual stature, his fearless unworldliness, his superiority to the common weaknesses of men; and yet this man himself looks up to Jesus as standing on quite a different platform from his own, as a Being of another order. He can find no expressions strong enough to mark the difference: "I am not worthy to loose His shoe latchet;" "He that is of the earth" (that is, himself) "is earthly, and speaketh of the earth: He that cometh from heaven is above all." He would not have used such expressions of Isaiah, of Elijah, of Moses. He knew his own dignity, and would not have set so marked a difference between himself and any other prophet. But his own very greatness was precisely what revealed to him the absolute superiority of Christ. These crowds that gathered round him--what could he do for them more than refer them to Christ? Could he propose to himself to found among them a kingdom of God? Could he ask them to acknowledge him and trust in him for spiritual life? Could he promise them His Spirit? Could he even link to himself all kinds of men, of all nationalities? Could he be the light of men, giving to all a satisfying knowledge of God and of their relation to Him? No; he was not that light, he could but bear witness of that light. And this he did, by pointing men to Jesus, not as a brother prophet, not as another great man, but as the Son of God, as One who had come down from heaven.

It is, I say, impossible that we can make nothing of such a testimony. Here was one who knew, if any man ever did, spotless holiness when he saw it; who knew what human strength and courage could accomplish; who was himself certainly among the six greatest men the world has seen; and this man, standing thus on the highest altitudes human nature can reach, looks up to Christ, and does not only admit His superiority, but shrinks, as from something blasphemous, from all comparison with Him. What is the flaw in his testimony, or why are we not accepting Christ as our light, as able to take away our sins, as willing to baptize us with the Holy Ghost?

But (2) even such testimony as John's is not sufficient of itself to carry conviction to the reluctant. None knew better than John's contemporaries that he was a true man, not liable to make mistakes in a matter of this kind. And his testimony to Christ did stagger them, and often held them in check, and no doubt threw a kind of undefined awe over the person of Christ; but, after all, not many believed on account of John's testimony, and those who did were not influenced solely by his testimony, but by his work as well. They had become concerned about sin, sensitive to defilement and failure, and were thus prepared to appreciate the offers of Christ. The two voices chimed, John's voice saying, "Behold, the Lamb of God!" the voice of their own conscience crying for the taking away of sin. It is so still. The sense of sin, the feeling of spiritual weakness and need, the craving for God, direct the eye, and enable us to see in Christ what we do not otherwise see. We are not likely to know Christ until we know ourselves. What is the man's judgment regarding Christ worth who is not conscious of his own littleness and humbled by his own guilt? Let a man first go to school with the Baptist, let him catch something of his unworldliness and earnestness, let him become alive to his own shortcomings by at last beginning to strive after the highest things in life, and by seeking to live, not for pleasure, but for God, and his views of Christ and his relation to Him will become satisfactory and true.

IV. THE FIRST DISCIPLES

"Again on the morrow John was standing, and two of his disciples; and he looked upon Jesus as He walked, and saith, Behold, the Lamb of God! And the two disciples heard him speak, and they followed Jesus. And Jesus turned, and beheld them following, and saith unto them, What seek ye? And they said unto Him, Rabbi (which is to say, being interpreted, Master), where abidest Thou? He saith unto them, Come, and ye shall see. They came therefore and saw where He abode; and they abode with Him that day: it was about the tenth hour. One of the two that heard John speak, and followed Him, was Andrew, Simon Peter's brother. He findeth first his own brother Simon, and saith unto him, We have found the Messiah (which is, being interpreted, Christ). He brought him unto Jesus. Jesus looked upon him, and said, Thou art Simon the son of John: thou shalt be called Cephas (which is by interpretation, Peter). On the morrow he was minded to go forth into Galilee, and he findeth Philip: and Jesus saith unto him, Follow Me. Now Philip was from Bethsaida, of the city of Andrew and Peter. Philip findeth Nathanael, and saith unto him, We have found Him, of whom Moses in the law, and the prophets, did write, Jesus of Nazareth, the son of Joseph. And Nathanael said unto him, Can any good thing come out of Nazareth? Philip saith unto him, Come and see. Jesus saw Nathanael coming to Him, and saith of him, Behold, an Israelite indeed, in whom is no guile! Nathanael saith unto Him, Whence knowest thou me? Jesus answered and said unto him, Before Philip called thee, when thou wast under the fig tree, I saw thee. Nathanael answered him, Rabbi, Thou art the Son of God; Thou art King of Israel. Jesus answered and said unto him, Because I said unto thee, I saw thee underneath the fig tree, believest thou? thou shalt see greater things than these. And He saith unto him, Verily, verily, I say unto you, Ye shall see the heaven opened, and the angels of God ascending and descending upon the Son of man."--John i. 35--51.

In the prosecution of his purpose to tell how the Incarnate Word manifested His glory to men, John proceeds to give one or two instances of the eagerness with which prepared souls welcomed Him, and of the instinctive perception with which true and open minds confessed Him Son of God and King of Israel. This paragraph is the continuation of that which begins at ver. 19 with the general title, "This is the witness of John." We are now introduced to some of the results of John's witness, and are shown that Christ is King, not only by official proclamation, but by the free choice of men. These instances here cited are but the first among countless numbers who in every generation have felt and owned the majesty of Christ, and who have felt irresistibly drawn to Him by a unique affinity. In the spell which His personality laid upon these first disciples, in the uninvited yet cordial and assured acknowledgments of His dignity which they felt drawn to make, we see much that is significant and illustrative of the allegiance He evokes from age to age in humble and open-minded men.

In proceeding to gather to Himself subjects who might enter into His purposes and loyally serve Him, Jesus shows a singularly many-sided adaptability and inexhaustible originality in dealing with men. Each of the five disciples here introduced is individually dealt with. "The finding of the one was not the finding of the other. For John and Andrew there was the talk with Jesus through the hours of that never-to-be-forgotten evening; for Simon, the heart-searching word, convincing him he was known and his future read off; for Philip, a peremptory command; and for Nathanael, a gracious courtesy disarming him of prejudice, assuring him of a perfect sympathy in the breast of the Lord. Thus there are those who seek Christ, those who are brought by others to Christ, those whom Christ seeks for Himself, those who come without doubts, and those who come with doubts." [8]

The two men who enjoyed the signal distinction of leading the way in owning the majesty and attaching themselves to the person of Christ were Andrew and probably John who wrote this Gospel. The writer, indeed, does not name himself, but this is in accordance with his habit. The suppression of the name is an indication that he himself was the disciple spoken of, since had it been another he could have had no scruple in mentioning his name. We know also that the families of Zebedee and Jonah were partners in trade, and it was likely that the young men of the families would go in company to visit the Baptist when the fishing was slack. These two young men had already attached themselves to the Baptist; had not merely passed through the fashionable ceremony of baptism, and returned home to talk about it, but were laid hold of by John's teaching and character, and had resolved to wait with him till the predicted Deliverer should appear.

And at length the day came when the master whom they trusted as God's prophet suddenly checked them in their walk, laid his hand breathlessly upon them, and gazing at a passing figure, said, "Behold, the Lamb of God!" There in actual bodily presence was He for whom all ages of their people had longed; there within sound of their voice was He who could take away their sin, lift off the burden and the trouble of life, and let them know the blessedness of living. We are ever ready to think it was easy for those who saw Christ to follow Him. Could we read His sympathy and truthfulness in His face, could we hear His words addressed directly to ourselves, could we ask our own questions and have from Him personal guidance, we fancy faith would be easy. And no doubt there is a greater benediction pronounced on those who "have not seen, and yet have believed." Still, the advantage is not wholly theirs who saw the Lord growing up among other boys, learning His trade with ordinary lads, clothed in the dress of a working man. The brothers of Jesus found it hard to believe. Besides, in giving the allegiance of the Spirit, and forming eternal alliance, it is well that the true affinities of our spirit be not disturbed by material and sensible appearances.

These two men, however, felt the spell, and "followed Jesus"--representatives of all those who, scarcely knowing what they do or what they intend, are yet drawn by a mysterious attraction to keep within sight of Him of whom they have ever been hearing, and whom all ages have sought, but who now for the first time stands clear before their sight. Without a word to their teacher or to one another, silent with wonder and excitement, they eagerly follow the passing figure. So does enquiry begin with many a soul. He who is much spoken of by all, but of whom few have personal knowledge, suddenly assumes a reality they scarcely were looking for. It is no longer the hearing of the ear, but now, whispers the soul, mine eye seeth Him. The soul for the first time feels as if some action were demanded of it; it can no longer just sit and listen to descriptions of Christ, it must arise on its own account, and for itself seek further knowledge of this unique Person.

"Then Jesus turned and saw them following,"--turned probably because He heard them following, for He suffers none to follow in vain. Sometimes it may seem as if He did; sometimes it may seem as if the best years of life were spent in following, and all to no purpose. It is not so. If some have spent years in following, and cannot yet say that Christ has turned and made them conscious that He is responding to their search, this is because in their path lie many obstacles, all of which must be thoroughly cleared away. And no man should grudge the time and the toil that is spent on honestly clearing away whatever prevents a perfect cohesion to this eternal Friend.

The question put by Jesus to the following disciples, "What seek ye?" was the first breath of the winnowing fan which the Baptist had warned them the Messiah would use. It was not the gruff interrogation of one who would not have his retirement invaded, nor his own thoughts interrupted, but a kindly invitation to open their minds to Him. It was meant to help them to understand their own purposes, and to ascertain what they expected in following Jesus. "What seek ye?" Have you any object deeper than mere curiosity? For Christ desires to be followed intelligently, or not at all. At all times He used the winnowing fan to blow away the chaff of the great crowds that followed Him, and leave the few immovably resolute souls. So many follow because a crowd streams after Him and carries them with it; so many follow because it is a fashion, and they have no opinion of their own; so many follow experimentally, and drop off at the first difficulty; so many follow under misapprehension, and with mistaken expectations. Some who came to Him with great expectations left in shame and sorrow; some who thought to make use of Him for party ends left Him in anger when they found themselves unmasked; and one who thought skilfully to use Him for the gratification of His own selfish worldliness, discovered that there was no surer path to eternal ruin. Christ turns away none for mere slowness in apprehending what He is and what He does for sinful men. But by this question He reminds us that the vague and mysterious attraction which, like a hidden magnet, draws men to Him, must be exchanged for a clear understanding at least of what we ourselves need and expect to receive from Him. He will turn from none who, in response to His question, can truly say, We seek God, we seek holiness, we seek service with Thee, we seek Thyself.

The answer which these men returned to the question of Jesus was the answer of men who scarce knew their own minds, and were suddenly confused by being thus addressed. They therefore reply, as men thus confused commonly reply, by asking another question, "Rabbi, where dwellest Thou?" Their concern was about Him, and so far the answer was good; but it implied that they were willing to leave Him with only such information as might enable them to visit Him at some future time, and so far the answer was not the best. Still their shyness was natural, and not without reason. They had felt how the Baptist searched their soul, and of this new Teacher the Baptist himself had said he was not worthy to loose his sandal-thong. To find themselves face to face with this greatest person, the Messiah, was a trying experience indeed. The danger at this point is hesitation. Many persons fail at this point from a native reluctance to commit themselves, to feel pledged, to accept permanent responsibilities and bind themselves with indissoluble ties. They are past the stage of merely keeping Christ in view, but very little past it. The closer dealings they have had with Him have as yet led to nothing. Their fate hangs in the balance.

Out of this condition our Lord delivers these two men by His irresistible invitation, "Come and see." And well for them it was that He did so, for next day He left that part of the country, and the mere knowledge of His lodging by the Jordan would have availed them nothing; a warning to all who put themselves off with learning more about salvation before they accept it. An eagerness in acquiring knowledge about Christ may as effectually as any other pursuit retard us in making acquaintance with Him. It is mere trifling to be always enquiring about One who is Himself with us; the way to secure that we shall have Him when we need Him is to go with Him now. How can we expect our difficulties to be removed while we do not adopt the one method God recognises as effectual for this purpose, fellowship with Christ? Why enquire longer about the way of salvation, and where we may find it at a future time? Christ offers His friendship now, "Come with Me, now," He says, "and for yourself enter My dwelling as a welcome friend." Can the friendship of Christ do us harm, or retard us in any good thing? May we not most reasonably fear that hesitation now may put Christ beyond our reach? We cannot tell what new influences may enter our life and set an impassable gulf between us and religion.

Sixty years after, when one of these men wrote this Gospel, he remembered as if it had been yesterday the very hour of the day when he followed Jesus into His house. His whole life seemed to date from that hour; as well it might, for what could mark a human life more deeply and lift it more surely to permanent altitude than an evening with Jesus? They felt that at last they had found a Friend with human sympathies and Divine intelligence. How eagerly must these men who had of late been thinking much of new problems, have laid all their difficulties before this master-mind, that seemed at once to comprehend all truth, and to appreciate the little obstacles that staggered them. What boundless regions of thought would His questions open up, and how entirely new an aspect would life assume under the light He shed upon it.

The astonished satisfaction they found in their first intercourse with Christ is shown in the bursting enthusiasm with which Andrew sought out his brother Simon, and summarily announced, "We have found the Christ." That is how the Gospel is propagated. The closer the tie, the more emphatic the testimony. It is what brother says to brother, husband to wife, parent to child, friend to friend, far more than what preacher says to hearer, that carries in it irresistible persuasive power. When the truth of the utterance is vouched for by the obvious gladness and purity of the life; when the finding of the Christ is obviously as real as the finding of a better situation and as satisfying as promotion in life, then conviction will be carried with the announcement. And he who, like Andrew, can do little himself, may, by his simple testimony and honest life, bring to Christ a Simon who may become a conspicuous power for good. The mother whose influence is confined to the four walls of her own house may lodge Christian principle in the heart of a son, who may give it currency in one form or other to the remotest corner of the earth.

The language in which Andrew announced to Simon his great fortune was simple, but, in Jewish lips, most pregnant. "We have found the Christ!" What his people had lived and longed for through all past ages, "I have found" and known. The perfect deliverance and joy which God was to bring by dwelling with His people, this at last had come. Taught to believe that all evil and disappointment and thwarting were but temporary, the Jew had waited for the true life of man--a life in the presence and favour and fellowship of the Highest. This was to come in the Messiah, and Andrew had found this. He had entered into life--all darkness and shadow were gone; the light shone round him, making all things bright, and piercing into eternity with clear radiance.

The words with which Jesus welcomes Simon are remarkable: "Thou art Simon, son of John: thou shalt be called Cephas." This greeting yields its meaning when we recall the character of the person addressed. Simon was hot-headed, impulsive, rash, unstable. When his name was mentioned on the Lake of Galilee there rose before the mind a man of generous nature, frank and good-hearted, but a man whose uncertainty and hastiness had brought him and his into many troubles, and with whom, perhaps, it was well to have no very binding connection in trade or in the family. What must the thoughts of such a man have been when he was told that the Messiah was present, and that the Messianic kingdom was standing with open gates? Must he not have felt that this might concern others,--decent steady men like Andrew,--but not himself? Must he not have felt that instead of being a strength to the new kingdom he would prove a weakness? Would not that happen now which so often before had happened--that any society he joined he was sure to injure with his hasty tongue or rash hand? Other men might enter the kingdom and serve it well, but he must remain without.

Coming in this mood, he is greeted with words which seem to say to him, I know the character identified with the name "Simon, son of John;" I know all you fear, all the remorseful thoughts that possess you; I know how you wish now you were a man like Andrew, and could offer yourself as a serviceable subject of this new kingdom. But no! thou art Simon; nothing can change that, and such as you are you are welcome; but "thou shalt be called Rock," Peter. The men standing round, and knowing Simon well, might turn away to hide a smile; but Simon knew the Lord had found him, and uttered the very word which could bind him for ever to Him. And the event showed how true this appellation was. Simon became Peter,--bold to stand for the rest, and beard the Sanhedrim. By believing that this new King had a place for him in His kingdom, and could give him a new character which should fit him for service, he became a new man, strong where he had been weak, helpful and no longer dangerous to the cause he loved.

Such are the encouragements with which the King of men welcomes the diffident. He gives men the consciousness that they are known; He begets the consciousness that it is not with sin in the abstract He takes to do, but with sinners He can name, and whose weaknesses are known to Him. But He begets this consciousness that we may trust Him when He gives us assurance that a new character awaits us and a serviceable place in His kingdom. He assures the most despondent that for them also a useful life is possible.

As Andrew, in the exuberant joy of his discovery of the Messiah, had first imparted the news to his own brother Simon, so Philip, when invited by Jesus to accompany him to Galilee, sought to bring with him his friend Nathanael Bartholomew (son of Tolmai). This was one of the devout Jews who had long been wondering who that mysterious Personage should be of whom all the prophets had spoken, and for whom the world waited that He might complete it. The news that He was found seemed only too good to be true. He had come too easily and unostentatiously, and from so unlooked-for a quarter, "Can any good come out of Nazareth?" Good men, as well as others, have their narrow views and illiberal prejudices, and mark off in their own minds as hopeless and barren whole religions, sects, or countries out of which God determines to bring that which is for the healing of the nations. To rise above such prejudices we must refuse to accept current rumours, traditional opinions, proverbial or neat dicta which seem to settle a matter; we must conscientiously examine for ourselves,--as Philip says, "Come and see." He instinctively knew how useless it was to reason with men about Christ's claims so long as they were not in His presence. One look, one word from Himself will go further to persuade a man of His majesty and love than all that any one else can say. To make Christ known is the best way to prove the truth of Christianity.

The shade of the fig-tree is the natural summer-house or arbour under which Eastern families delight to take their meals or their mid-day rest. Nathanael had used the dense foliage of its large and thick leaves as a screen behind which he found retirement for devotional purposes. It is in such absolute seclusion, retirement, and solitude that a man shows his true self. It was here Nathanael had uttered himself to his Father who seeth in secret; here he had found liberty to pour out his true and deepest cravings. His guilelessness had been proved by his carrying into his retirement the same simple and unreserved godliness he professed abroad. And he is astonished to find that the eye of Jesus had penetrated this leafy veil, and had been a witness to his prayers and vows. He feels that he is known best at the very point in which he had most carefully contrived concealment, and he recognises that no one is more likely to be the fulfiller of his prayers than that same Person who has manifestly been somehow present at them and heard them.

To the man of prayer a suitable promise is given, as to the man of uncertain character a promise fitting his need had come. Under his fig-tree Nathanael had often been in sympathy with his forefather Jacob in his great experience of God's attentiveness to prayer. When Jacob fled from home and country, a criminal and outcast, he no doubt felt how completely he had himself fallen into the pit he had digged. Instead of the comforts of a well-provided household, he had to lie down like a wild beast with nothing between him and the earth, with nothing between him and the sky, with nothing but an evil conscience to speak to him, and no face near save the haunting faces of those he had wronged. A more miserable, remorseful, abandoned-looking creature rarely lay down to sleep; but before he rose he had learned that God knew where he was, and was with him; that on that spot which he had chosen as a hiding, because no one could find him, and scarcely his own dog track him to it, he was waited for and met with a loving welcome by Him whom he had chiefly wronged. He saw heaven opened, and that from the lowest, most forlorn spot of earth to the highest and brightest point of heaven there is a close connection and an easy, friendly communication. If Jesus, thought Nathanael, could reopen heaven in that style, He would be worthy of the name of King of Israel. But he is now to learn that He will do far more; that henceforth it was to be no visionary ladder, swept away by the dawn, which was to lead up to heaven, but that in Jesus God Himself is permanently made over to us; that He, in His one, visible person, unites heaven and earth, God and man; that there is an ever-living union between the highest height of heaven and the lowest depth of earth. Profound and wide as the humanity of Christ, to the most forgotten and remote outcast, to the most sunken and despairing of men, do God's love and care and helpfulness now come; high and glorious as the divinity of Christ may the hopes of all men now rise. He who understands the Incarnation of the Son of God has a surer ground of faith, and a richer hope and a straighter access to heaven, than if the ladder of Jacob stood at his bed-head and God's angels were ministering to him.

Footnotes:

8. See Mr. Reith's rich Handbook on The Gospel of John (Clark).

V. THE FIRST SIGN—THE MARRIAGE IN CANA

"And the third day there was a marriage in Cana of Galilee; and the mother of Jesus was there: and Jesus also was bidden, and His disciples, to the marriage. And when the wine failed, the mother of Jesus saith unto Him, They have no wine. And Jesus saith unto her, Woman, what have I to do with thee? Mine hour is not yet come. His mother saith unto the servants, Whatsoever He saith unto you, do it. Now there were six waterpots of stone set there after the Jews' manner of purifying, containing two or three firkins apiece. Jesus saith unto them, Fill the waterpots with water. And they filled them up to the brim. And He saith unto them, Draw out now, and bear unto the ruler of the feast. And they bare it. And when the ruler of the feast tasted the water now become wine, and knew not whence it was (but the servants which had drawn the water knew), the ruler of the feast calleth the bridegroom, and saith unto him, Every man setteth on first the good wine; and when men have drunk freely, then that which is worse: thou hast kept the good wine until now. This beginning of His signs did Jesus in Cana of Galilee, and manifested His glory; and His disciples believed on Him."--John ii. 1--11.

Having recorded the testimony borne to Jesus by the Baptist, and having cited instances in which the overmastering personality of Jesus elicited from simple-hearted and godly men the acknowledgment of His majesty, John now proceeds to relate the homely incident which gave occasion to the first public act in which His greatness was exhibited. Testimony comes first; inward and intuitive recognition of the greatness declared by that testimony second; perception that His works are beyond the reach of human power comes last. But in the case of these first disciples, while this order was indeed maintained, there was no great interval between each step in it. It was but the "third day" after they had in their hearts felt His impressiveness that He "manifested forth His glory" to them in this first sign.

From the place where they first met Him to Cana of Galilee was a distance of twenty-one or twenty-two miles. [9] Thither Jesus repaired to be present at a marriage. His mother was already there, and when Jesus arrived, accompanied by His new-found friends, all were invited to remain and share in the festivities. Owing probably to this unexpected increase to the number of the guests, the wine begins to fail. Among the minor trials of life there are few which produce more awkwardness than the failure to provide suitable entertainment for a specially festive occasion. Mary, with the practised eye of a woman whose business it was to observe such matters, and perhaps with a near relative's charge and liberty in the house, perceives the predicament and whispers to her Son, "They have no wine." This she said, not to hint that Jesus would do well to retire with His too many friends, nor that He would cover the lack of wine by brilliant conversation, but because she had ever been accustomed to turn to this Son in all her difficulties, and now that she sees Him acknowledged by others her own faith in Him is stimulated.

Considering the simple manner in which He had walked in, and taken His place among the other guests, and partaken of the refreshment, and joined in the conversation and mirth of the day, it would seem more likely that she should have had no definite expectation as to the way in which He would extricate the host from his difficulty, but only turned to Him on whom she was accustomed to lean. But His answer shows that he felt Himself urged to action of some kind by her appeal; and her instructions to the servants to do whatever He ordered indicates that she definitely expected Him to relieve the embarrassment. How He would do so she could not know, and had she definitely expected a miracle she would probably have thought the help of the servants unnecessary.

But though Mary did not anticipate a miracle, it had already occurred to our Lord that this was a fit occasion for manifesting His kingly power. His words grate somewhat on the ear, but this is partly due to the difficulty of translating fine shades of meaning, and to the impossibility of conveying in any words that modification of meaning which is given in the tone of voice and expression of face, and which arises also from the familiarity and affection of speaker and hearer. In His use of the word "Woman" there is really no harshness, this being the ordinary Greek term of address to females of all classes and relationships, and being commonly used with the utmost reverence and affection. The phrase "What have I to do with thee?" is a needlessly strong translation, although it might be difficult to find a better. It "implies a certain resistance to a demand in itself, or to something in the way of urging it;" but might be quite sufficiently rendered by such an expression as "I have other thoughts than thine." There is nothing approaching angry resentment at Mary's inviting His aid, nothing like repudiation of any claim she might have upon Him, but only a calm and gentle intimation that in the present instance she must allow Him to act in His own way. The whole phrase might be rendered, "Mother, you must let

Me act here in My own way: and My time for action is not yet come." She herself was perfectly satisfied with the answer. Knowing her Son well, every gleam of His expression, every tone of His voice, she recognised that He meant to do something, and accordingly left the matter in His hands, giving orders to the servants to do whatever He required.

But there was more in the words of Jesus than even Mary understood. There were thoughts in His mind which not even she could fathom, and which had He explained them to her then she could not have sympathized with. For these words, "Mine hour is not yet come," which she took to be the mere intimation of a few minutes' delay before granting her request, became the most solemn watchword of His life, marking the stages by which He drew near to His death. "They sought to take Him, but no man laid hands on Him, because His hour was not yet come." So again and again. From the first He knew what would come of His manifesting His glory among men. From the first He knew that His glory could not be fully manifested till He hung upon the cross.

Can we wonder, then, that when He recognised in His mother's request the invitation from God, though not from her, that He should work His first miracle and so begin to manifest His glory, He should have said, "My thoughts are not yours; Mine hour is not yet come"? With compassion He looked upon her through whose soul a sword was to pass; with filial tenderness He could only look with deep pity on her who was now the unconscious instrument of summoning Him to that career which He knew must end in death. He saw in this simple act of furnishing the wedding guests with wine a very different significance from that which she saw. It was here at this wedding feast table that He felt Himself impelled to take the step which altered the whole character of His life.

For from a private person He became by His first miracle a public and marked character with a definite career. "To live henceforth in the vortex of a whirlwind; to have no leisure so much as to eat, no time to pray save when others slept, to be the gazing-stock of every eye, the common talk of every tongue; to be followed about, to be thronged and jostled, to be gaped upon, to be hunted up and down by curious vulgar crowds; to be hated, and detested, and defamed, and blasphemed; to be regarded as a public enemy; to be watched and spied upon and trapped and taken as a notorious criminal"--is it possible to suppose that Christ was indifferent to all this, and that without shrinking He stepped across the line which marked the threshold of His public career?

And this was the least of it, that in this act He became a public and marked character. The glory that here shed a single ray into the rustic home of Cana must grow to that dazzling and perfect noon which shone from the cross to the remotest corner of earth. The same capacity and willingness to bless mankind which here in a small and domestic affair brought relief to His embarrassed friends, must be adapted to all the needs of men, and must undauntedly go forward to the utmost of sacrifice. He who is true King of men must flinch from no responsibility, from no pain, from no utter self-abandonment to which the needs of men may call Him. And Jesus knew this: in those quiet hours and long, untroubled days at Nazareth He had taken the measure of this world's actual state, and of what would be required to lift men out of selfishness and give them reliance upon God. "I, if I be lifted up, will draw all men unto Me"--this was even now present to His mind. His glory was the glory of absolute self-sacrifice, and He knew what that involved. His kingship was the rendering of service no other could render.

The manner in which the miracle was performed deserves attention. Christ does all while the servants seem to do all. The servants fill in the water and the servants draw off the wine, and there is no apparent exercise of Divine power, no mysterious words of incantation uttered over the waterpots, not so much as a command given that the water should become wine. What is seen by the spectators is men at work, not God creating out of nothing. The means seem to be human, the result is found to be Divine. Jesus says, "Fill the water pots with water," and they filled them; and filled them not as if their doing so were a mere form, and as if they would leave room for Christ to add to their work; no, they filled them up to the brim. Again He says, "Draw out now, and bear to the governor of the feast," and they bore. They knew very well they had only put in water, and they knew that to offer water to the governor of a marriage feast would be to insure their own punishment; but they did not hesitate. There seemed every reason why they should refuse to do this, or why they should at least ask some explanation or security that Jesus would bear the evil consequences; but there was one reason on the other side which outweighed all these--they had the command of Him whom they had been ordered to obey. And so, where reasoning would have led them to folly, obedient faith makes them fellow-workers in a miracle. They took their place and served, and they who serve Christ and do His will must do great things; for Christ wills nothing that is useless, futile, not worth doing. But this is how we are tried: we are commanded to do things which seem unreasonable, and which we have no natural ability to do. We are commanded to repent, and are yet told that repentance is the gift of Christ; we are commanded to come to Christ, and are at the same time assured that we cannot come except the Father draw us; we are commanded to be perfectly holy, and yet we know that as the leopard cannot change his spots, nor one of us add a cubit to his stature, so neither can we put away the sins that stain our souls and walk uprightly before God. And yet these commands are plainly given us, not only to make us feel our helplessness, but to be performed. We feel our inability, we may say it is unreasonable to demand from us what we cannot perform, to require that out of the thin and watery substance of our human souls we should produce wine that may be poured out as an offering on the holy altar of God; but this is not unreasonable. It is our part in simplicity to obey God; what is commanded we are to do, and while we work He Himself will also work. He may do so in no visible way, as Christ here did nothing visibly, but He will be with us, effectually working. As the will of Christ pervaded the water so that it was endowed with new qualities, so can His will pervade our souls, with every other part of His creation, and make them conformable to His purpose. "Whatsoever He saith unto you, do it;" this is the secret of miracle-working. Do it, though you seem to be but wasting your strength and laying yourself open to the scorn of onlookers; do it, though in yourself there is no ability to effect what you are aiming at; do it wholly, up to the brim, as if you were the only worker, as if there were no God to come after you and supply your deficiencies, but as if any shortcoming on your part would be fatal; do not stand waiting for God to work, for it is only in you and by you that He performs His work among men.

The significance of this incident is manifold. First, it gives us the key to the miracles of our Lord. It has become the fashion to depreciate miracles, and it is often thought that they hamper the gospel and obscure the true claim of Christ. It is often felt that so far from the miracles verifying Christ's claim to be the Son of God, they are the greatest obstacle to His acceptance. This is, however, to misunderstand their significance. The miracles unquestionably formed a most important element in Christ's life; and, if so, they must have served an important purpose; and to wish them away just because they are so important and make so large a demand upon faith seems to me preposterous. To wish them away precisely because they alter the very essence of the religion of Christ, and give it that very power which through all past ages it has exerted, seems unreasonable.

When the Jews discussed His claims among themselves or with Him, the power to work miracles was always taken into account as weighing heavily in His favour. He Himself distinctly stated that the crowning condemnation of those who rejected His claims arose from the circumstance that He had done among them the works which none other man had done. He challenges them to deny that it was by the finger of God that He wrought these works. After His withdrawal from earth the miracle of the Resurrection was still appealed to as the convincing proof that He was all He had given Himself out for. There can be no doubt, therefore, that the power of working miracles was one great evidence of the Divine mission of Christ.

But though this is so, we are not on that account warranted in saying that the only purpose for which He wrought miracles was to win men's belief in His mission. On the contrary, we are told that it was one of His temptations, a temptation constantly resisted by Him, to use His power for this object without any other motive. It was the reproach He cast upon the people that except they saw signs and wonders they would not believe. He would never work a miracle merely for the sake of manifesting His glory. Whenever the unsympathetic, ignorant crowd clamoured for a sign; whenever with ill-concealed dislike they cried, "How long dost Thou make us to doubt? Show us a sign from heaven, that we may believe," He was silent. To create a mere compulsory consent in minds which had no sympathy with Him was never a sufficient motive. Was there a sick child tossing in fever, was there a blind beggar by the roadside, was there a hungry crowd, was there even the joy of a feast interrupted: in these He could find a worthy occasion for a miracle; but never did He work a miracle merely for the sake of removing the doubts of reluctant men. Where there was not even the beginning of faith miracles were useless. He could not work miracles in some places because of their unbelief.

What then was the motive of Christ's miracles? He was, as these first disciples owned Him, the King of God's kingdom among men: He was the ideal Man, the new Adam, the true Source of human goodness, health, and power. He came to do us good, and the Spirit of God filled His human nature to its utmost capacity, that it might do all that man can do. Having these powers, He could not but use them for men. Having power to heal, He could not but heal, irrespective of the result which the miracle might have on the faith of those who saw it; nay, He could not but heal, though He straitly charged the healed person to let no man know what had been done. His miracles were His kingly acts, by which He suggested what man's true life in God's kingdom should be and will be. They were the utterance of what was in Him, the manifestation of His glory, the glory of One who came to utter the Father's heart to His strayed children. They expressed good-will to men; and to the spiritual eye of a John they became "signs" of spiritual wonders, symbols and pledges of those greater works and eternal blessings which Jesus came to bestow. The miracles revealed the Divine compassion, the grace and helpfulness that were in Christ, and led men to trust Him for all their needs.

We must, therefore, beware of falling into the error that lies at either extreme. We must neither, on the one hand, suppose that Christ's miracles were wrought solely for the purpose of establishing His claim to be God's Viceroy on earth; nor, on the other hand, are we to suppose that the marvels of beneficence by which He was known did nothing to prove His claim or promote His kingdom. The poet writes because he is a poet, and not to convince the world that he is a poet; yet by writing he does convince the world. The benevolent man acts just as Christ did when He seemed to lay His finger on His lips and warned the healed person to make no mention of this kind act to anyone; and therefore all who do discover his actions know that he is really charitable. The act that a man does in order that he may be recognised as a good and benevolent person exhibits his love of recognition much more strikingly than his benevolence; and it is because the miracles of Christ were wrought from the purest and most self-denying compassion that ever explored and bound up the wounds of men, that we acknowledge Him as incontestably our King.

2. In what respects, then, did this first miracle manifest the glory of Christ? What was there in it to stir the thought and attract the adoration and trust of the disciples? Was it worthy to be the medium of conveying to their minds the first ideas of His glory they were to cherish? And what ideas must these have been? The first impression they must have received from the miracle was, no doubt, simple amazement at the power which so easily and unostentatiously turned the water into wine. This Person, they must have felt, stood in a peculiar relation to Nature. In fact, what John laid as the foundation of his Gospel,--that the Christ who came to redeem was He by whom all things were at first made,--Jesus also advanced as the first step in His revelation of Himself. He appears as the Source of life, whose will pervades all things. He comes, not as a stranger or interloper who has no sympathy with existing things, but as the faithful Creator, who loves all that He has made, and can use all things for the good of men. He is at home in the world, and enters physical nature as its King, who can use it for His high ends. Never before has He wrought a miracle, but in this first command to Nature there is no hesitation, no experimenting, no anxiety, but the easy confidence of a Master. He is either Himself the Creator of the world He comes to restore to worth and peace, or He is the Delegate of the Creator. We see in this first miracle that Christ is not an alien or an usurper, but one who has already the closest connection with us and with all things. We receive assurance that in Him God is present.

3. But it was not only the Creator's power which was shown in this miracle, but some hint was given of the ends for which that power would be used by Christ. Perhaps the disciples who had known and admired the austere life of the Baptist would expect that He whom the Baptist proclaimed as greater than himself would be greater in the same line, and would reveal His glory by a sublime abstemiousness. They had confessed Him to be the Son of God, and might naturally expect to find in Him an independence of earthly joys. They had followed Him as the king of Israel; was His kingly glory to find a suitable sphere in the little family difficulties that poverty begets? It is almost a shock to our own ideas of our Lord to think of Him as one of a marriage party; to hear Him uttering the ordinary salutations, civilities, and enquiries of a friendly and festive gathering; to see Him standing by while others are the principal figures in the room. And we know that many who had opportunity to observe His habits could never understand or reconcile themselves to His easy familiarity with all kinds of people, and to His freedom in partaking in mirthful scenes and hilarious entertainments.

And just because of this difficulty we find in reconciling religion with joy, God with nature, does Christ reveal His glory first at a marriage-feast, not in the temple, not in the synagogue, not by taking His disciples apart to teach them to pray, but at a festive gathering, that thus they may recognise in Him the Lord of all human life, and see that His work of redemption is co-extensive with human experience. He comes among us, not to crush or pour contempt on human feelings, but to exalt them by sharing in them; not to show that it is possible to live separate from all human sympathies, but to deepen and intensify them; not to do away with the ordinary business and social relations of life, but to sanctify them. He comes sharing in all pure feelings and joys, sanctioning all natural relationships; Himself human, with interest in all human interests; not a mere spectator or censor of human affairs, but Himself a man implicated in things human. He shows us the folly of fancying that God looks with an austere and morose eye upon outbursts of human affection and joy, and teaches us that to be holy as He is holy we are not required to abandon the ordinary affairs of life, and that however we make them the apology for worldliness, it is not the necessary duties or relations of life that prevent our being Christlike, but these are the very material in which His glory may be most clearly seen, the soil in which must grow and ripen all Christian graces and fruits of righteousness.

This, then, was the glory Christ wished His disciples first of all to see. He was to be their King, not by drilling men to fight for Him, nor by interrupting the natural order and upsetting the established ways of men, but by entering into these with a gladdening, purifying, elevating spirit. His glory was not to be confined to a palace or to a small circle of courtiers, or to one particular department of activity, but was to be found irradiating all human life in its most ordinary forms. He came, indeed, to make all things new, but the new creation was the fulfilment of the original idea: it was not to be achieved by thwarting nature, nor by a one-sided development of some elements of nature, but by guiding the whole to its original destination, by lifting the whole into harmony with God. We see the glory of Christ, and accept Him as our Ruler and Redeemer, because we see in Him perfect sympathy with all that is human.

4. While enjoying the bounty of Christ at the marriage feast, John cannot have yet understood all that was involved in His Master's purpose to bring new life and happiness to this world of men. Afterwards, no doubt, he saw how appropriately this miracle took the first place, and through it read his Lord's own thoughts about His whole work on earth. For it is impossible that Christ Himself should not have had His own thoughts about the significance of this miracle. He had, during the previous six

weeks, passed through a time of violent mental disturbance and of supreme spiritual exaltation. The measureless task laid upon Him had become visible to Him. Already He was aware that only through His death could the utmost of blessing be imparted to men. Is it possible that while He first put forth His power to restore the joy of these wedding guests, He should not have seen in the wine a symbol of the blood He was to shed for the refreshment and revival of men? The Baptist, whose mind was nourished with Old Testament ideas, called Christ the Bridegroom, and His people the Bride. Must not Jesus also have thought of those who believed in Him as His bride, and must not the very sight of a marriage have set His thoughts working regarding His whole relation to men? So that in His first miracle He no doubt saw a summary of His whole work. In this first manifestation of His glory there is, to Himself at least, a reminder that only by His death will that glory be perfected. Without Him, as He saw, the joy of this wedding feast had been brought to an untimely close; and without His free outpouring of His life for men there could be no presenting of men to God unblemished and blameless, no fulfilment of those high hopes of mankind that nourish pure characters and noble deeds, but a swift and dreary extinction of even natural joys. It is to the marriage supper of the Lamb, of Him who was slain, and has redeemed us by His blood, that we are invited. It is the "Lamb's wife" that John saw adorned as a bride for her Husband. And whosoever would sit down at that feast which consummates the experience of this life, terminating all its vacillation of trust and love, and which opens eternal and unlimited joy to the people of Christ, must wash and make white his garments in this blood. He must not shrink from the closest fellowship with the purifying love of Christ.

5. His disciples, when they saw His power and His goodness in this miracle, felt more than ever that He was the rightful King. They "believed on Him." To us this first of signs is merged in the last, in His death. The joy, the self-sacrifice, the holiness, the strength and beauty of human character which that death has produced in the world, is the great evidence which enables many now to believe in Him. The fact is indubitable. The intelligent secular historian, who surveys the rise and growth of European nations, counts the death of Christ among the most vital and influential of powers for good. It has touched all things with change, and been the source of endless benefit to men. Are we then to repudiate Him or to acknowledge Him? Are we to act like the master of the feast, who enjoyed the good wine without asking where it came from; or are we to own ourselves debtors to the actual Creator of our happiness? If the disciples believed on Him when they saw Him furnish these wedding guests with wine, shall we not believe, who know that through all these ages He has furnished the pained and the poor with hope and consolation, the desolate and broken-hearted with restoring sympathy, the outcast with the knowledge of God's love, the sinner with pardon, with heaven, and with God? Is not the glory He showed at this marriage in Cana precisely what still attracts us to Him with confidence and affection? Can we not wholly trust this Lord who has a perfect sympathy guiding His Divine power, who brings the presence of God into all the details of human life, who enters into all our joys and all our sorrows, and is ever watchful to anticipate our every need, and supply it out of His inexhaustible and all-sufficient fulness? Happy they who know His heart as His mother knew it, and are satisfied to name their want and leave it with Him.

Footnotes:

9. Modern topography inclines to identify this Cana, not, as formerly, with Kafr-Kenna, but with KÃ¢net-el-Jelil, some six miles N.E. of Nazareth. It is called Cana of Galilee to distinguish it from Cana in Asher, S.E. from Tyre (Joshua xix. 28).

Marcus Dods, D.D.

VI. THE CLEANSING OF THE TEMPLE

"After this He went down to Capernaum, He, and His mother, and His brethren, and His disciples: and there they abode not many days. And the Passover of the Jews was at hand, and Jesus went up to Jerusalem. And He found in the temple those that sold oxen and sheep and doves, and the changers of money sitting: and He made a scourge of cords, and cast all out of the temple, both the sheep and the oxen; and He poured out the changers' money, and overthrew their tables; and to them that sold the doves He said, Take these things hence; make not My Father's house a house of merchandise. His disciples remembered that it was written, The zeal of Thine house shall eat me up. The Jews therefore answered and said unto Him, What sign showest Thou unto us, seeing that Thou doest these things? Jesus answered and said unto them, Destroy this temple, and in three days I will raise it up. The Jews therefore said, Forty and six years was this temple in building, and wilt Thou raise it up in three days? But He spake of the temple of His body. When therefore He was raised from the dead, His disciples remembered that He spake this; and they believed the Scripture, and the word which Jesus had said."--John ii. 12--22.

Whether the Nazareth family returned from Cana to their own town before going down to Capernaum, John does not inform us. Neither are we told why they went to Capernaum at all at this time. It may have been in order to join one of the larger caravans going up to Jerusalem for the approaching Feast. Not only the disciples, some of whom had their homes on the lake-side, accompanied Jesus, but also His mother and His brothers. The manner in which the brothers are spoken of in connection with His mother suggests that He and they bore to her the same relation. They remained in Capernaum "not many days," because the Passover was at hand. Having come to Jerusalem, and appearing there for the first time since His baptism, He performed several miracles. These John omits, and selects as more significant and worthy of record one authoritative act.

The circumstances which occasioned this act were familiar to the Jerusalem Jew. The exigencies of Temple worship had bred a flagrant abuse. Worshippers coming from remote parts of the Holy Land, and from countries beyond, found it a convenience to be able to purchase on the spot the animals used in sacrifice, and the material for various offerings--salt, meal, oil, frankincense. Traders were not slow to supply this demand, and vying with one another they crept nearer and nearer to the sacred precincts, until some, under pretence perhaps of driving in an animal for sacrifice, made a sale within the outer court. This court had an area of about fourteen acres, and was separated from the inner court by a wall breast high, and bearing intimations which forbade the encroachment of Gentiles on pain of death. Round this outer court ran marble colonnades, richly ornamented and supported by four rows of pillars, and roofed with cedar, affording ample shade to the traders.

There were not only cattle-dealers and sellers of pigeons, but also money-changers; for every Jew had to pay to the Temple treasury an annual tax of half a shekel, and this tax could be paid only in the sacred currency. No foreign coin, with its emblem of submission to an alien king, was allowed to pollute the Temple. Thus there came to be need of money-changers, not only for the Jew who had come up to the feast from a remote part of the empire, but even for the inhabitant of Palestine, as the Roman coinage had displaced the shekel in ordinary use.

There might seem, therefore, to be room to say much in favour of this convenient custom. At any rate, it was one of those abuses which, while they may shock a fresh and unsophisticated mind, are allowed both because they contribute to public convenience and because they have a large pecuniary interest at their back. In point of fact, however, the practice gave rise to lamentable consequences. Cattle-dealers and money-changers have always been notorious for making more than their own out of their bargains, and facts enough are on record to justify our Lord calling this particular market "a den of thieves." The poor were shamefully cheated, and the worship of God was hindered and impoverished instead of being facilitated and enriched. And even although this traffic had been carried on under careful supervision, and on unimpeachable principles, still it was unseemly that the worshipper who came to the Temple seeking quiet and fellowship with God should have to push his way through the touts of the dealers, and have his devotional temper dissipated by the wrangling and shouting of a cattle market. Yet although many must have lamented this, no one had been bold enough to rebuke and abolish the glaring profanation.

Jesus on entering the Temple finds Himself in the midst of this incongruous scene--the sounds and movements of a market, the loud and eager exclamations of competing traders, the bustle of selecting one animal out of a flock, the loud talk and laughter of the idle groups of onlookers. Jesus cannot stand it. Zeal for the honour of His Father's house possesses Him. The Temple claims Him as its vindicator from abuse. Nowhere can He more appropriately assert His authority as Messiah. Out of the cords lying about He quickly knots together a formidable scourge, and silently, leaving the public conscience to justify His action, He proceeds single-handed to drive out cattle and traders together. A scene of violence ensued,--the cattle rushing hither and thither, the owners trying to preserve their property, the money-changers holding their tables as Jesus went from one to another upsetting them, the scattered coin scrambled for; and over all the threatening scourge and the commanding eye of the Stranger. Never on any other occasion did our Lord use violence.

The audacity of the act has few parallels. To interfere in the very Temple with any of its recognized customs was in itself a claim to be King in Israel. Were a stranger suddenly to appear in the lobby of the House of Commons, and by sheer dignity of demeanour, and the force of integrity, to rectify an abuse of old standing involving the interests of a wealthy and privileged class, it could not create a greater sensation. The Baptist might be with Him, cowing the truculent with his commanding eye; but there was no need of the Baptist: the action of Christ awakening conscience in the men themselves was enough to quell resistance.

No doubt Jesus began His work at the house of God because He knew that the Temple was the real heart of the nation; that it was belief in God which was their strength and hope, and that the loss of that belief, and the consequent irreverence and worldliness, were the most dangerous features of Jewish society. The state of matters He found in the Temple could not have been tolerated had the people really believed God was present in the Temple.

Such an act could not pass without being criticised. It would be keenly discussed that evening in Jerusalem. At every table it would be the topic of conversation, and a most serious one wherever men in authority were meeting. Many would condemn it as a piece of pharisaic ostentation. If He is a reformer, why does He not turn His attention to the licentiousness of the people? Why show such extravagant and unseemly zeal about so innocent a custom when flagrant immoralities abound? Why not spend His zeal in clearing out from the land the polluting foreigner? Such charges are easy. No man can do everything, least of all can he do everything at once. And yet the advocate of temperance is twitted with his negligence of other causes which are perhaps as necessary; and he who pleads for foreign missions is reminded that we have heathen at home. These are the carping criticisms of habitual fault-finders, and of men who have no hearty desire for the advancement of what is good.

Others, again, who approved the act could not reconcile themselves to the manner of it. Might it not have been enough to have pointed out the abuse, and to have made a strong representation to the authorities? Was it fair to step in and usurp the authority of the Sanhedrim or Temple officials? Was it consistent with prophetic dignity to drive out the offenders with His own hand? Even those most friendly to Him may have felt a little jarred as they saw Him with uplifted scourge and flaming eyes violently driving before Him men and beasts. But they remembered that it was written, "The zeal of Thine house will consume Me." They remembered perhaps how the most popular king of Israel had danced before the ark, to the scandal indeed of dull-souled conventionalists, but with the approval of all clear-seeing and spiritually-judging men. They might also have remembered how the last of their prophecies had said, "Behold, the Lord whom ye seek shall suddenly come to His temple. But who may abide the day of His coming, and who shall stand when He appeareth?"

This zeal at once explained and justified His action. Some abuses may be reformed by appeal to the constituted authorities; others can be abolished only by the blazing indignation of a righteous soul who cannot longer endure the sight. This zeal, conquering all consideration of consequences and regard to appearances, acts as a cleansing fire, sweeping before it what is offensive. It has always its own risks to run: the authorities at Jerusalem never forgave Jesus this first interference. By reforming an abuse they should never have allowed, He damaged them in the eyes of the people, and they could never forget it. Zeal also runs the risk of acting indiscreetly and taking too much upon it. In itself zeal is a good thing, but it does not exist "in itself." It exists in a certain character, and where the character is imperfect or dangerous the zeal is imperfect or dangerous. The zeal of the proud or selfish man is mischievous, the zeal of the ignorant fraught with disaster. Still, with all risks, give us by all means rather the man who is eaten up, possessed and carried away, by a passionate sympathy with the oppressed and neglected, or with unquenchable zeal for rectitude and honourable dealing or for the glory of God, than the man who can stand and be a spectator of wrong because it is no business of his to see that injustice be withstood, who can connive at unrighteous practices because their correction is troublesome, invidious, hazardous. He who lays a sudden hand on wrong-doing may have no legal authority to plead in his defence when challenged, but to all good men such an act justifies itself. It was a similar zeal which at all times governed Christ. He could not stand by and wash His hands of other men's sins. It was this which brought Him to the cross, this which in the first place brought Him to this world at all. He had to interfere. Zeal for His father's glory, zeal for God and man, possessed Him.

Marcus Dods, D.D.

It was therefore no concern of Jesus to make Himself very intelligible to those who could not understand the action itself and demanded a sign. They did not understand His answer; and it was not intended they should. Frequently our Lord's answers are enigmatical. Men have opportunity to stumble over them, if they will. For frequently they asked foolish questions, which admitted only of such answers. The present question, "What sign showest Thou unto us, seeing that Thou doest these things?" was absurd. It was to ask for a light to see light with, a sign of a sign. His zeal for God that carried the crowd before it, and swept God's house clean of the profane, was the best proof of His authority and Messiahship. But there was one sign which He could promise them without violating His principle to do no miracle merely for the sake of convincing reluctant minds. There was one sign which formed an integral part of His work; a sign which He must work, irrespective of its effect on their opinion of Him-- the sign of His own Resurrection. And therefore, when they ask Him for a sign of His authority to reform the abuses of the Temple, He promises them this sign, that He will raise the Temple again when they destroy it. If He can give them a Temple He has authority in it. "Destroy this Temple, and in three days I will raise it up."

What did He mean by this enigmatical saying, which not even His disciples understood till long afterwards? We cannot doubt that in their resistance to His first public act, righteous and necessary, and welcome to all right-hearted men, as it was, He plainly saw the symptom of a deep-seated hatred of all reform, which would lead them on to reject His whole work. He had meditated much on the tone of the authorities, on the religious state of His country--what young man of thirty with anything in him has not done so? He had made up His mind that He would meet with opposition at every point, and that while a faithful few would stand by Him, the leaders of the people would certainly resist and destroy Him. Here in His very first act He is met by the spirit of hatred, and jealousy, and godlessness which was at last to compass His death. But His rejection He also knew was to be the signal for the downfall of the nation. In destroying Him He knew they were destroying themselves, their city, their Temple. As Daniel had long ago said, "The Messiah shall be cut off ... and the people of a prince who shall come shall destroy the city and the sanctuary."

To Himself therefore His words had a very definite meaning: Destroy this Temple, as you certainly will by disowning My authority and resisting My acts of reform, and at length crucifying Me, and in three days I will raise it. As by denying My authority and crucifying My Person you destroy this house of My Father, so by My resurrection will I put men in possession of God's true dwelling-place, and introduce a new and spiritual worship. "It is in Christ's person this great drama is enacted. The Messiah perishes: the Temple falls. The Messiah lives again: the true Temple rises on the ruins of the symbolical temple. For in the kingdom of God there is no simple restoration. Every revival is at the same time an advance" (Godet). A living Temple is better than a Temple of stone. Human nature itself, possessed and inspired by the Divine, that is the true Temple of God.

This sign was in two years given to them. As Jesus drew His last breath on the cross the veil of the Temple was rent. There was no longer anything to veil; the unapproachable glory was for ever gone. The Temple in which God had so long dwelt was now but a shell, mocking and pathetic in the extreme, as the clothes of a departed friend, or as the familiar dwelling that remains itself the same but changed to us for ever. The Jews in crucifying the Messiah had effectually destroyed their Temple. A few years more and it was in ruins, and has been so ever since. That building which had once the singular, wonderful dignity of being the spot where God was specially to be found and to be worshipped, and where He dwelt upon earth in a way apprehensible by men, was from the hour of Christ's death doomed to vacuity and destruction.

But in three days a new and better Temple was raised in Christ's body, glorified by the presence of the indwelling God. Forty and six years had the Jews spent in rearing the magnificent pile that astonished and awed their conquerors. They had thus themselves rebuilt more splendidly the Temple of Solomon. But to rebuild the Temple they destroyed in crucifying the Lord was beyond them. The sign of rebuilding their Temple of marble, which they scouted as a ridiculous extravagance, was really a far less stupendous and infinitely less significant sign than that which He actually gave them in rising from the dead. If it was impossible to rear that magnificent fabric in three days, yet something might be done towards it: but towards the raising of the dead body of Christ nothing could be done by human skill, diligence, or power.

But it is not the stupendous difficulty of this sign which should chiefly engage our attention. It is rather its significance. Christ rose from the dead, not to startle godless and truth-hating men into faith, but to furnish all mankind with a new and better Temple, with the means of spiritual worship and constant fellowship with God. There was a necessity for the resurrection. Those who became intimately acquainted with Christ slowly but surely became aware that they found more of God in Him than ever they had found in the Temple. Gradually they acquired new thoughts about God; and instead of thinking of Him as a Sovereign veiled from the popular gaze in the hidden Holy of holies, and receiving through consecrated hands the gifts and offering of the people, they learned to think of Him as a Father, to whom no condescension was too deep, no familiarity with men too close. Unconsciously to themselves, apparently, they began to think of Christ as the true Revealer of God, as the living Temple who at all hours gave them access to the living God. But not till the Resurrection was this transference complete--nay, so fixed had their hearts been, in common with all Jewish hearts, upon the Temple, that not until the Temple was destroyed did they wholly grasp what was given them in the Resurrection of Jesus. It was the Resurrection which confirmed their wavering belief in Him as the Son of God. As Paul says, it was the resurrection which "declared Him to be the Son of God with power." Being the Son of God, it was impossible He should be held by death. He had come to the Temple calling it by an unheard-of name, "My Father's house." Not Moses, not Solomon, not Ezra, not the holiest of high priests, would have dreamt of so identifying himself with God as to speak of the Temple, not even as "our Father's house" or "your Father's house," but "my Father's house." And it was the Resurrection which finally justified His doing so, declaring Him to be, in a sense no other was, the Son of God.

But it was not in the body of Christ that God found His permanent dwelling among men. This sacred presence was withdrawn in order to facilitate the end God has from the first had in view, the full indwelling and possession of each and all men by His Spirit. This intimate fellowship with all men, this free communication of Himself to all, this inhabitation of all souls by the ever-living God, was the end aimed at by all that God has done among men. His dwelling among men in the Temple at Jerusalem, His dwelling among men in the living Person of Christ, were preliminary and preparatory to His dwelling in men individually. "Ye," says Paul, "are built up a spiritual house." "Ye are builded together for a habitation of God." "Ye are the temple of the living God." This is the great reality towards which men have been led by symbol--the complete pervasion of all intelligence and of all moral beings by the Spirit of God.

For us this cleansing of the Temple is a sign. It is a sign that Christ really means to do thoroughly the great work He has taken in hand. Long ago had it been said, "Behold the Lord, whom ye seek, shall suddenly come to His Temple; and He shall sit as a refiner and purifier of silver." He was to come where holiness was professed, and to sift the true from the false, the worldly and greedy religious from the devoted and spiritual. He was not to make pretence of doing so, but actually to accomplish the separation. To reform abuses such as this marketing in the Temple was no pleasant task. He had to meet the gaze and defy the vindictiveness of an exasperated mob; He had to make enemies of a powerful class in the community. But He does what is called for by the circumstances: and this is but a part and a sample of the work He does always. Always He makes thorough, real work. He does not blink the requirements of the case. We shrug our shoulders and pass by where matters are difficult to mend; we let the flood take its course rather than risk being carried away in attempting to stem it. Not so Christ. The Temple was shortly to be destroyed, and it might seem to matter little what practices were allowed in it; but the sounds of bargaining and the greedy eye of trade could not be suffered by Him in His Father's house: how much more shall He burn as a consuming fire when He cleanses that Church for which He gave Himself that it might be without spot or blemish. He will cleanse it. We may yield ourselves with gladness to His sanctifying power, or we may rebelliously question His authority; but cleansed the house of God must be.

VII. NICODEMUS

"Now when He was in Jerusalem at the passover, during the feast, many believed on His name, beholding His signs which He did. But Jesus did not trust Himself unto them, for that He knew all men, and because He needed not that any one should bear witness concerning man; for He Himself knew what was in man. Now there was a man of the Pharisees, named Nicodemus, a ruler of the Jews: the same came unto Him by night, and said to Him, Rabbi, we know that Thou art a teacher come from God: for no man can do these signs that Thou doest, except God be with Him. Jesus answered and said unto him, Verily, verily, I say unto thee, Except a man be born anew, he cannot see the kingdom of God. Nicodemus saith unto Him, How can a man be born when he is old? can he enter a second time into his mother's womb, and be born? Jesus answered, Verily, verily, I say unto thee, Except a man be born of water and the Spirit, he cannot enter into the kingdom of God. That which is born of the flesh is flesh; and that which is born of the Spirit is spirit. Marvel not that I said unto thee, Ye must be born anew. The wind bloweth where it listeth, and thou hearest the voice thereof, but knowest not whence it cometh, and whither it goeth: so is every one that is born of the Spirit."--John ii. 23--iii. 8.

The first visit of Jesus to Jerusalem was not without considerable effect on the popular mind. Many who saw the miracles He did believed that He was a messenger from God. They saw that His miracles were not the clever tricks of an impostor, and they were prepared to listen to His teaching and enrol themselves as members of the kingdom He came to found. Yet our Lord did not encourage them. He saw that they misunderstood Him. He recognised their worldliness of heart and of aim, and did not admit them to the intimacy He had established with the five simple-minded Galileans. The Jerusalem Jews were glad to fall in with one who seemed likely to do honour to their nation, and their belief in Him was the belief men give to a statesman whose policy they approve. The difference between them and those who rejected Christ was not a difference of disposition such as exists between godly and ungodly men, but consisted merely in the circumstance that they were convinced that His miracles were genuine. Had our Lord encouraged these men they would ultimately have been disappointed in Him. It was better that from the first they should be stimulated to reflect on the whole matter by being coldly received by the Lord.

It is always a point that calls for reflection: we have to consider not only whether we have faith in Christ, but whether He has faith in us--not only whether we have committed ourselves to Him, but whether that committal is so genuine that He can build upon and trust it. Can He count upon us for all service, for fidelity in times when much is needed? Thoroughgoing confidence must always be reciprocal. The person you believe in so utterly that you are entirely his, believes in you and trusts himself to you--his reputation, his interests are safe in your keeping. So is it with Christ. Faith cannot be one-sided here any more than elsewhere. He gives Himself to those who give themselves to Him. They who so trust Him that He is sure they will follow Him even when they cannot see where He is going; they who trust Him, not in one or two matters which they see He can manage, but absolutely and in all things,--to these He will give Himself freely, sharing with them His work, His Spirit, His reward.

To illustrate the state of mind of the Jerusalem Jews and Christ's mode of treating them, John selects the case of Nicodemus. He was one of those who were much impressed by the miracles of Jesus, and were prepared to attach themselves to any movement in His favour. He belonged to the Pharisees; to that party which, with all its narrowness, pedantry, dogmatism, and bigotry, still preserved a salt of genuine patriotism and genuine godliness, and reared high-toned and cultivated men like Gamaliel and Saul. Nicodemus, whether a member of the Sanhedrim's deputation to the Baptist or not, certainly knew the result of that deputation, and was aware that a crisis in the national history had arrived. He could not wait for the community to move, but felt that whatever conclusion regarding Christ the Pharisees as a body might arrive at, he must on his own responsibility be at the bottom of those extraordinary events and signs that clustered round the person of Jesus. He was a modest, reserved, cautious man, and did not wish openly to commit himself till he was sure of his ground. He has been blamed for timidity. I would only say that, if he felt it dangerous to be seen in the company of Jesus, it was a bold thing to visit Him at all. He went by night; but he went. And would that there were more like him, who, whether cautious to excess or not, do still feel constrained to judge for themselves about Christ; who feel that, no matter what other men think of Him, there is an interest in Him which they cannot wait for others to settle, but must for themselves settle before they sleep.

Probably Nicodemus made his visit by night because he did not wish to precipitate matters by calling undue attention to the position and intentions of Jesus. He probably went with the purpose of urging some special plan of action. This inexperienced Galilean could not be supposed to understand the populace of Jerusalem as well as the old member of the Sanhedrim, who was familiar with all the outs and ins of party politics in the metropolis. Nicodemus would therefore go and advise Him how to proceed in proclaiming the kingdom of God; or at least sound Him, and, if he found Him amenable to reason, encourage Him to proceed, and warn Him against the pitfalls that lay in His path. Modestly, and as if speaking for others as much as for himself, he says: "Rabbi, we know that Thou art a Teacher come from God, for no man can do these miracles that Thou doest except God be with Him!" There is here neither patronizing acknowledgment nor flattery, but merely the natural first utterance of a man who must say something to show the state of his mind. It served to reveal the point at which Nicodemus had arrived, and the ground on which the conversation might proceed. But "Jesus knew what was in man." In this acknowledgment of His miracles on the part of Nicodemus, Jesus saw the whole mental attitude of the man. He saw that if Nicodemus had uttered all that was in his mind he would have said: "I believe you are sent to restore the kingdom to Israel, and I am come to advise with you on your plan of operation, and to urge upon you certain lines of action." And therefore Jesus promptly cuts him short by saying: "The kingdom of God is quite another thing than you are thinking of; and the way to establish it, to enlist citizens in it, is very different from the way you have been meditating."

In fact, Jesus was becoming embarrassed by His own miracles. They were attracting the wrong kind of people--the superficial worldly people; the people who thought a daring and strong hand with a dash of magic would serve all their turn. His mind was full of this, and as soon as He has an opportunity of uttering Himself on this point He does so, and assures Nicodemus, as a representative of a large number of Jews who needed this teaching, that all their thoughts about the kingdom must be ruled by this principle, and must start from this great truth, that it was a kingdom into which the Spirit of God alone could give entrance, and could give entrance only by making men spiritual. That is to say, that it was a spiritual kingdom, an inward rule over the hearts of men, not an outward empire--a kingdom to be established, not by political craft and midnight meetings, but by internal change and submission in heart to God--a kingdom, therefore, into which admission could be given only on some more spiritual ground than the mere circumstance of a man's natural birth as a Jew.

In our Lord's language there was nothing that need have puzzled Nicodemus. In religious circles in Jerusalem there was nothing being talked of but the kingdom of God which John the Baptist had declared to be at hand. And when Jesus told Nicodemus that in order to enter this kingdom he must be born again, He told him just what John had been telling the whole people. John had assured them that, though the King was in their midst, they must not suppose they were already within His kingdom by being the children of Abraham. He excommunicated the whole nation, and taught them that it was something different from natural birth that gave admission to God's kingdom. And just as they had compelled Gentiles to be baptized, and to submit to other arrangements when they wished to partake of Jewish privileges, so John compelled them to be baptized. The Gentile who wished to become a Jew had to be symbolically born again. He had to be baptized, going down under the cleansing waters, washing away his old and defiled life, being buried by baptism, disappearing, from men's sight as a Gentile, and rising from the water as a new man. He was thus born of water, and this time born, not a Gentile, but a Jew.

The language of our Lord then could scarcely puzzle Nicodemus, but the idea did stagger him that not only Gentiles but Jews must be born again. John had indeed required the same preparation for entrance to the kingdom; but the Pharisees had not listened to John, and were offended precisely on the ground of his baptism. But now Jesus presses upon Nicodemus the very same truth, that as the Gentile had to be naturalized and born again that he might rank as a child of Abraham, and enjoy the external privileges of the Jew, so must the Jew himself be born again if he is to rank as a child of God and to belong to the kingdom of God. He must submit to the double baptism of water and of the Spirit--of water for the pardon and cleansing of past sin and defilement, of the Spirit for the inspiration of a new and holy life.

Our Lord here speaks of the second birth as completed by two agencies, water and the Spirit. To make the one of these merely the symbol of the other is to miss His meaning. The Baptist baptized with water for the remission of sins, but he was always careful to disclaim power to baptize with the Holy Ghost. His baptism with water was of course symbolical; that is to say, the water itself exercised no spiritual influence, but merely represented to the eye what was invisibly done in the heart. But that which it symbolised was not the life-giving influence of the Holy Spirit, but the washing away of sin from the soul. Assurance of pardon John was empowered to give. Those who humbly submitted to his baptism with confession of their sins went from it forgiven and cleansed. But more than that was needed to make them new men--and yet more he could not give. For that which would fill them with new life they must go to a Greater than he, who alone could bestow the Holy Ghost.

These then are the two great incidents of the second birth--the pardon of sin, which is preparatory, and which cuts our connection with the past; the communication of life by the Spirit of God, which fits us for the future. Both of these are represented by Christian baptism because in Christ we have both; but those who were baptized by John's baptism were only prepared for receiving Christ's Spirit by receiving the forgiveness of their sins.

Having thus declared to Nicodemus the necessity of the second birth, He goes on to give the reason of this necessity. Birth by the Spirit is necessary, because that which is born of the flesh is flesh, and the kingdom of God is spiritual. Of course our Lord does not mean by flesh the mere tangible substance of the body; He does not mean that our first and natural birth puts us in possession of nothing but a material frame. By the word "flesh" He signifies the appetites, desires, faculties, which animate and govern the body, as well as the body itself--the whole equipment with which nature furnishes a man for life in this world. This natural birth gives a man entrance into much, and for ever determines much, that has important bearings on his person, character, and destiny. It determines all differences of nationality, of temperament, of sex; apart altogether from any choice of his it is determined whether he shall be a South Sea Islander or a European; an antediluvian living in a cave or an Englishman of the nineteenth century. But the kingdom of God is a spiritual kingdom, into which entrance can be had only by a man's own will and spiritual condition, only by an attachment to God which is no part of a man's natural equipment.

As soon as we clearly see what the kingdom of God is, we see also that by nature we do not belong to it. The kingdom of God so far as man is concerned is a state of willing subjection to Him--a state in which we are in our right relation to Him. All irrational creatures obey God and do His will: the sun runs his course with an exactness and punctuality we cannot rival; the grace and strength of many of the lower animals, their marvellous instincts and aptitudes, are so superior to anything in ourselves that we cannot even comprehend them. But what we have as our speciality is to render to God a willing service; to understand His purposes and enter sympathetically into them. The lower creatures obey a law impressed upon their nature; they cannot sin; their performance of God's will is a tribute to the power which made them so skilfully, but it lacks all conscious recognition of His worthiness to be served and all knowledge of His object in creation. It is God serving Himself: He made them so, and therefore they do His will. So it is with men who merely obey their nature: they may do kindly, noble, heroic actions, but they lack all reference to God; and however excellent these actions are, they give no guarantee that the men who do them would sympathize with God in all things, and do His will gladly.

Indeed, to establish the proposition that flesh or nature does not give us entrance into God's kingdom, we need go no further than our own consciousness. Remove the restraints which grace puts upon our nature, and we are aware that we are not in sympathy with God, fond of His will, disposed for His service. Let nature have its swing, and every man knows it is not the kingdom of God it takes him to. To all men it is natural to eat, drink, sleep, think; we are born to these things, and need to put no constraint on our nature to do them; but can any man say it has come naturally to him to be what he ought to be to God? Do we not to this hour feel drawn away from God as if we were not in our element in His presence? Flesh, nature, in God's presence is as much out of its element as a stone in the air or a fish out of water. Men who have had the deepest religious experience have seen it most clearly, and have felt, like Paul, that the flesh lusts against the spirit, and draws us ever back from entire submission to God and delight in Him.

Perhaps the necessity of the second birth may be more clearly apprehended if we consider it from another point of view. In this world we find a number of creatures which have what is known as animal life. They can work, and feel, and, in a fashion, think. They have wills, and certain dispositions, and distinctive characteristics. Every creature that has animal life has a certain nature according to its kind, and determined by its parentage; and this nature which the animal receives from its parents determines from the first the capabilities and sphere of the animal's life. The mole cannot soar in the face of the sun like the eagle; neither can the bird that comes out of the eagle's egg burrow like the mole. No training can possibly make the tortoise as swift as the antelope, or the antelope as strong as the lion. If a mole began to fly and enjoy the sunlight it must be counted a new kind of creature, and no longer a mole. The very fact of its passing certain limitations shows that another nature has somehow been infused into it. Beyond its own nature no animal can act. You might as well attempt to give the eagle the appearance of the serpent as try to teach it to crawl. Each kind of animal is by its birth endowed with its own nature, fitting it to do certain things, and making other things impossible. So is it with us: we are born with certain faculties and endowments, with a certain nature; and just as all animals, without receiving any new, individual, supernatural help from God, can act according to their nature, so can we. We, being human, have a high and richly-endowed animal nature, a nature that leads us not only to eat, drink, sleep, and fight like the lower animals, but a nature which leads us to think and to love, and which, by culture and education, can enjoy a much richer and wider life than the lower creatures. Men need not be in the kingdom of God in order to do much that is admirable, noble, lovely, because their nature as animals fits them for that. If we were to exist at all as a race of animals superior to all others, then all this is just what must be found in us. Irrespective of any kingdom of God at all, irrespective of any knowledge of God or reference to Him, we have a life in this world, and a nature fitting us for it. And it is this we have by our natural birth, a place among our kind, an animal life. The first man, from whom we all descend, was, as St. Paul profoundly says, "a living soul," that is to say, an animal, a living human being; but he had not "a quickening spirit," could not give to his children spiritual life and make them children of God.

Now if we ask ourselves a little more closely, What is human nature? what are the characteristics by which men are distinguished from all other creatures? what is it which marks off our kind from every other kind, and which is always produced by human parents? we may find it hard to give a definition, but one or two things are obvious and indisputable. In the first place, we could not deny human nature to men who do not love God, or who even know nothing of Him. There are many whom we should naturally speak of as remarkably fine specimens of human nature, who yet never think of God, nor in any way acknowledge Him. It is plain, therefore, that the acknowledgment and love of God, which give us entrance into His kingdom, are not a part of our nature, are not the gifts of our birth.

And yet is there anything that so distinctly separates us from the lower animals as our capacity for God and for eternity? Is it not our capacity to respond to God's love, to enter into His purposes, to measure things by eternity, that is our real dignity? The capacity is there, even when unused; and it is this capacity which invests man and all his works with an interest and a value which attach to no other creature. Man's nature is capable of being born again, and that is its peculiarity; there is in man a dormant or dead capacity which nothing but contact with God, the touch of the Holy Ghost, can vivify and bring into actual exercise.

That there should be such a capacity, born as if dead, and needing to be quickened by a higher power before it can live and be of use, need not surprise us. Nature is full of examples of such capacities. All seeds are of this nature, dead until favouring circumstances and soil quicken them into life. In our own body there are similar capacities, capacities which may or may not be quickened into life. In the lower animal-creation many analogous capacities are found, which depend for their vivification on some external agency over which they have no control. The egg of a bird has in it the capacity to become a bird like the parent, but it remains a dead thing and will corrupt if the parent forsakes it. There are many of the summer insects which are twice-born, first of their insect parents, and then of the sun: if the frost comes in place of the sun, they die. The caterpillar has already a life of its own, with which, no doubt, it is well content, but enclosed in its nature as a creeping thing it has a capacity for becoming something different and higher. It may become a moth, or a butterfly; but in most the capacity is never developed, they die before they reach this end--their circumstances do not favour their development. These analogies show how common it is for capacities of life to lie dormant: how common a thing it is for a creature in one stage of its existence to have a capacity for passing into a higher stage, a capacity which can be developed only by some agency peculiarly adapted to it.

It is in this condition man is born of his human parents. He is born with a capacity for a higher life than that which he lives as an animal in this world. There is in him a capacity for becoming something different, better and higher than that which he actually is by his natural birth. He has a capacity which lies dormant or dead until the Holy Ghost comes and quickens it. There are many things, and great things, man can do without any further Divine assistance than that which is lodged for the whole race in the natural laws which make no distinction between godly and ungodly; there are many and great things man may do by virtue of his natural birth; but one thing he cannot do--he cannot quicken within himself the capacity to love God and to live for Him. For this there is needed an influence from without, the efficient touch of the Holy Spirit, the impartation of His life. The capacity to be a child of God is man's, but the development of this lies with God. Without the capacity a man is not a man, has not that which is most distinctive of human nature. Every man is born with that in him which the Spirit of God may quicken into Divine life. This is human nature; but when this capacity is so quickened, when the man has begun to live as a child of God, he has not lost his human nature, but has over and above become a partaker of the Divine nature. When the image of God, as well as of his earthly parents, becomes manifest in a man, then his human nature has received its utmost development,--he is born again.

Of the Agent who accomplishes this great transformation there is need only to say that He is free in His operation and also inscrutable. He is like the wind, our Lord tells us, that blows where it lists. We cannot bring the Spirit at will; we cannot use Him as if He were some unintelligent passive instrument; neither can we subject all His operations to our control. The grub must wait for those natural influences which are to transform it; it cannot command them. We cannot command the Spirit; but we, being free agents also, can do more than wait,--we can pray, and we can strive to put ourselves in line with the Spirit's operation. Seamen cannot raise the wind nor direct its course, but they can put themselves in the way of the great regular winds. We can do the same: we can slowly, by mechanical helps, creep into the way of the Spirit; we can set our sails, doing all we think likely to catch and utilize His influences--believing always that the Spirit is more desirous than we are to bring us all to good. Why He breathes in one place while all around lies in a dead calm we do not know; but as for the wind's variations so for His, there are doubtless sufficient reasons. We need not expect to see the Spirit's working separate from the working of our own minds; we cannot see the Spirit in Himself--we cannot see the wind that moves the ships, but we can see the ships moving, and we know that without the wind they could not move.

If this, then, be the line on which our human nature can alone be developed, if a profound harmony with God be that which can alone give permanence and completeness to our nature, if in accordance with all that we see in the world around us some men fail of attaining the end of their creation, and lie for ever blighted and useless, while others are carried forward to fuller and more satisfying life, we cannot but ask with some anxiety to which class we belong. Good and evil are in the world, happiness and misery, victory and defeat; do not let us deceive ourselves by acting as if there were no difference between these opposites, or as if it mattered little in our case whether we belong to the one side or the other. It matters everything: it is just the difference between eternal life and eternal death. Christ did not come to play with us, and startle us with idle tales. He is the centre and fountain of all truth, and what He says fits in with all we see in the world around us.

But in endeavouring to ascertain whether the great change our Lord speaks of has passed upon us, our object must be not so much to ascertain the time and manner of our new birth as its reality. A man may know that he has been born though he is not able to recall, as no man can recall, the circumstances of his birth. Life is the great evidence of birth, natural or spiritual. We may desire to know the time and place of birth for some other reason, but certainly not for this, to make sure we have been born. Of that there is sufficient evidence in the fact of our being alive. And spiritual life quite as certainly implies spiritual birth.

Again, we must keep in view that a man may be born though not yet full grown. The child of a day old has as truly and certainly a human nature as the man in his prime. He has a human heart and mind, every organ of body and soul, though as yet he cannot use them. So the second birth impresses the image of God on every regenerate soul. It may not as yet be developed in every part, but all its parts are there in germ. It is not a partial but a complete result which regeneration effects. It is not one member, a hand or a foot that is born, but a body, a complete equipment of the soul in all graces. The whole character is regenerated, so that the man is fitted for all the duties of the Divine life whensoever these duties shall come before him. A human child does not need additions made to it to fit it for new functions: it requires growth, it requires nurture, it requires education and the practice of human ways, but it requires no new organ to be inserted into its frame; once born it has but to grow in order to adapt itself with ease and success to all human ways and conditions. And if regenerate we have that in us which with care and culture will grow till it brings us to perfect likeness to Christ. If we are not growing, if we remain small, puny, childish while we should be adult and full grown, then there is something seriously wrong, which calls for anxious enquiry.

But above all let us bear in mind that it is a new birth that is required; that no care spent on our conduct, no improvement and refinement of the natural man, suffices. For flying it is not an improved caterpillar that is needed, it is a butterfly; it is not a caterpillar of finer colour or more rapid movement or larger proportions, it is a new creature. We recognise that in this and that man we meet there is something more than men naturally have; we perceive in them a taming, chastening, inspiring principle. We rejoice all the more when we see it, because we know that no man can give it, but only God. And we mourn its absence because even when a man is dutiful, affectionate, temperate, honourable, yet if he have not grace, if he have not that peculiar tone and colour which overspread the whole character, and show that the man is living in the light of Christ, and is moved by love to God, we instinctively feel that the defect is radical, that as yet he has not come into connection with the Eternal, that there is that awanting for which no natural qualities, however excellent, can compensate--nay, the more lovely and complete the natural character is, the more painful and lamentable is the absence of grace, of Spirit.

VIII. THE BRAZEN SERPENT

"Nicodemus answered and said unto Him, How can these things be? Jesus answered and said unto him, Art thou the teacher of Israel, and understandest not these things? Verily, verily, I say unto thee, We speak that we do know, and bear witness of that we have seen; and ye receive not our witness. If I told you earthly things, and ye believe not, how shall ye believe, if I tell you heavenly things? And no man hath ascended into heaven, but He that descended out of heaven, even the Son of man, which is in heaven. And as Moses lifted up the serpent in the wilderness, even so must the Son of man be lifted up: that whosoever believeth may in Him have eternal life. For God so loved the world that He gave His only begotten Son, that whosoever believeth on Him should not perish, but have eternal life. For God sent not the Son into the world to judge the world; but that the world should be saved through Him. He that believeth on Him is not judged: he that believeth not hath been judged already, because he hath not believed on the name of the only begotten Son of God. And this is the judgment, that the light is come into the world, and men loved the darkness rather than the light; for their works were evil. For every one that doeth ill hateth the light, and cometh not to the light, lest his works should be reproved. But he that doeth the truth cometh to the light, that his works may be made manifest, that they have been wrought in God."--John iii. 9--21.

There are two great obstacles to human progress, two errors which retard the individual and the race, two inborn prejudices which prevent men from choosing and entering into true and lasting prosperity. The first is that men will always persist in seeking their happiness in something outside themselves; the second is that even when they come to see where true happiness lies they cannot find the way to it. In our Lord's time even wise and godly people thought the permanent glory and happiness of men were to be found in a free state, in self-government, lightened taxes, impregnable fortresses, and a purified social order. And they were not altogether wrong; but the way to this condition, they thought, lay through the enthronement of a strong-handed monarch, who could gather round his throne wise counsellors and devoted followers. This was the form of worldliness which our Lord had to contend with. This was the tendency of the unspiritual mind in His day. But in every generation and in all men the same radical misconceptions exist, although they may not appear in the same forms.

In dealing with Nicodemus, a sincere and thoroughly decent but unspiritual man, our Lord had difficulty in lifting his thoughts off what was external and worldly and fixing them on what was inward and heavenly. [10] And in order to effect this, He told him, among other things, that the Son of man was indeed to be lifted up--yes, but not on a throne set up in Herod's palace. He was to be conspicuous, but it was as the Brazen Serpent was conspicuous, hanging on a pole for the healing of the people. His lifting up, His exaltation, was secure; He was to be raised above every name that is named; He was destined to have the pre-eminence in all things, to be exalted above all principalities and powers; He was to have all power in heaven and in earth; He was to be the true and supreme Lord of all,--yes; but this dignity and power were to be attained by no mere official appointment, by no accidental choice of the people, by no mere hereditary title, but by the sheer force of merit, by His performing services for men which made the race His own, by His leaving no depth of human degradation unexplored, by a sympathy with the race and with individuals which produced in Him a total self-abandonment, and suffered Him to leave no grievance unconsidered, no wrong unthought of, no sorrow untouched. There is no royal road to human excellence; and Jesus could reach the height He reached by no swift ascension of a throne amidst the blare of trumpets, the flaunting of banners, and the acclamations of the crowd, but only by being exposed to the keenest tests with which this world can confront and search human character, by being put through the ordeal of human life, and being found the best man among us; the humblest, the truest; the most faithful, loving, and enduring; the most willing servant of God and man.

It was this which Christ sought to suggest to Nicodemus, and which we all find it hard to learn, that true glory is excellence of character, and that this excellence can be reached only through the difficulties, trials, and sorrows of a human life. Christ showed men a new glory and a new path to it--not by arms, not by statesmanship, not by inventions, not by literature, not by working miracles, but by living with the poor and becoming the friend of forsaken and wicked men, and by dying, the Just for the unjust. He has been lifted up as the Brazen Serpent was, He has become conspicuous by His very lowliness; by a self-sacrifice so complete that He gave His all, His life, He has won to Himself all men and made His will supreme, so that it and no other shall one day everywhere rule. He gave Himself for the healing of the nations, and the very death which seemed to extinguish His usefulness has made Him the object of worship and trust to all.

This is certainly the point of analogy between Himself and the Brazen Serpent which our Lord chiefly intended to suggest--that as the serpent was lifted up so as to be seen from every part of the camp, even so the death of the Son of man was to make Him conspicuous and easily discernible. It is by their death that many men have become immortalized in the memory of the race. Deaths of gallantry, of heroism, of self-devotion have often wiped out and seemed to atone for preceding lives of dissipation and uselessness. The life of Christ would have been inefficient without His death. Had He only lived and taught, we should have known more than was otherwise possible, but it is doubtful whether His teaching would have been much listened to. It is His death in which all men are interested. It appeals to all. A love that gave its life for them, all men can understand. A love that atoned for sin appeals to all, for all are sinners.

But though this is the chief point of analogy there are others. We do not know precisely what the Israelites would think of the Brazen Serpent. We need not repeat from the sacred narrative the circumstances in which it was formed and lifted up in the wilderness. The singularity of the remedy provided for the plague of serpents under which the Israelites were suffering, consisted in this, that it resembled the disease. Serpents were destroying them, and from this destruction they were saved by a serpent. This special mode of cure was obviously not chosen without a reason. To those among them who were instructed in the symbolic learning of Egypt there might be in this image a significance which is lost to us. From the earliest times the serpent had been regarded as man's most dangerous enemy-- more subtle than any beast of the field, more sudden and stealthy in its attack, and more certainly fatal. The natural revulsion which men feel in its presence, and their inability to cope with it, seemed to fit it to be the natural representative of the powers of spiritual evil. And yet, strangely enough, in the very countries in which it was recognised as the symbol of all that is deadly, it was also recognised as the symbol of life. Having none of the ordinary members or weapons of the wilder lower creatures, it was yet more agile and formidable than any of them; and, casting its skin annually, it seemed to renew itself with eternal youth. And as it was early discovered that the most valuable medicines are poisons, the serpent, as the very "personification of poison," was looked upon as not only the symbol of all that is deadly, but also of all that is health-giving. And so it has continued to be, even to our own days, the recognised symbol of the healing art, and, wreathed round a staff, as Moses had it, it may still be seen sculptured on our own hospitals and schools of medicine.

But whatever else the agonised people saw in the brazen image, they must at any rate have seen in its limp and harmless form a symbol of the power of their God to make all the serpents round about them as harmless as this one. The sight of it hanging with drooping head and motionless fangs was hailed with exultation as the trophy of deliverance from all the venomous creatures it represented. They saw in it their danger at an end, their enemy triumphed over, their death slain. They knew that the manufactured serpent was only a sign, and had in itself no healing virtue, but in looking at it they saw, as in a picture, God's power to overcome the most noxious of evils.

That which Moses lifted up for the healing of the Israelites was a likeness, not of those who were suffering, but of that from which they were suffering. It was an image, not of the swollen limbs and discoloured face of the serpent-bitten, but of the serpents that poisoned them. It was this image, representing as slain and harmless the creature which was destroying them, which became the remedy for the pains it inflicted. Similarly, our Lord instructs us to see in the cross not so much our own nature suffering the extreme agony and then hanging lifeless, as sin suspended harmless and dead there. All the virus seemed to be extracted from the fiery, burning fangs of the snakes, and hung up innocuous in that brazen serpent; so all the virulence and venom of sin, all that is dangerous and deadly in it, our Lord bids us believe is absorbed in His person and rendered harmless on the cross.

With this representation the language of Paul perfectly agrees. God, he tells us, "made Christ to be sin for us." It is strong language; yet no language that fell short of this would satisfy the symbol. Christ was not merely made man, He was made sin for us. Had He merely become man, and thus become involved in our sufferings, the symbol of the serpent would scarcely have been a fair one. A better image of Him would in that case have been a poisoned Israelite. His choice of the symbol of the brazen serpent to represent Himself upon the cross justifies Paul's language, and shows us that He habitually thought of His own death as the death of sin.

Christ being lifted up, then, meant this, whatever else, that in His death sin was slain, its power to hurt ended. He being made sin for us, we are to argue that what we see done to Him is done to sin. Is He smitten, does He become accursed, does God deliver Him to death, is He at last slain and proved to be dead, so certainly dead that not a bone of Him need be broken? Then in this we are to read that sin is thus doomed by God, has been judged by Him, and was in the cross of Christ slain and put an end to--so utterly slain that there is left in it not any so faint a flicker or pulsation of life that a second blow need be given to prove it really dead.

When we strive to get a little closer to the reality and understand in what sense, and how, Christ represented sin on the cross, we recognise first of all that it was not by His being in any way personally tainted by sin. Indeed, had He Himself been in the faintest degree tainted by sin this would have prevented Him from representing sin on the cross. It was not an actual serpent Moses suspended, but a serpent of brass. It would have been easy to kill one of the snakes that were biting the people, and hang up its body. But it would have been useless. To exhibit one slain snake would only have suggested to the people how many were yet alive. Being itself a real snake, it could have no virtue as a symbol. Whereas the brazen serpent represented all snakes. In it each snake seemed to be represented. Similarly, it was not one out of a number of real sinners that was suspended on the cross, but it was one made "in the likeness of sinful flesh." So that it was not the sins of one person which were condemned and put an end to there, but sin generally.

This was easily intelligible to those who saw the crucifixion. John the Baptist had pointed to Jesus as the Lamb of God that taketh away the sin of the world. How does a Lamb take away sin? Not by instruction, not by example, but by being sacrificed; by standing in the room of the sinner and suffering instead of him. And when Jesus, Himself without sin, hung upon the cross, those who knew His innocence perceived that it was as the Lamb of God He suffered, and that by His death they were delivered.

Another point of analogy between the lifting-up of the serpent and the lifting-up of the Son of Man on the cross is to be found in the circumstance that in each case the healing result is effected through a moral act on the part of the healed person. A look at the brazen serpent was all that was required. Less could not have been asked: more, in some cases, could not have been given. If deliverance from the pain and danger of the snake-bite had been all that God desired, He might have accomplished this without any concurrence on the part of the Israelites. But their present agony was the consequence of their unbelief, and distrust, and rebellion; and in order that the cure may be complete they must pass from distrust to faith, from alienation to confidence and attachment. This cannot be accomplished without their own concurrence. But this concurrence may be exercised and may be exhibited in connection with a small matter quite as decisively as in connection with what is difficult. To get a disobedient and stubborn child to say, "I am sorry," or to do the smallest and easiest action, is quite as difficult, if it be a test of submission, as to get him to run a mile, or perform an hour's task. So the mere uplifting of the eye to the brazen serpent was enough to show that the Israelite believed God's word, and expected healing. It was in this look that the will of man met and accepted the will of God in the matter. It was by this look the pride which had led them to resist God and rely upon themselves was broken down; and in the momentary gaze at the remedy appointed by God the tormented Israelite showed his reliance upon God, his willingness to accept His help, his return to God.

It is by a similar act we receive healing from the cross of Christ. It is by an act which springs from a similar state of mind. "Every one that believeth,"--that is all that is required of any who would be healed of sin and its attendant miseries. It is a little and an easy thing in itself, but it indicates a great and difficult change of mind. It is so slight and easy an action that the dying can do it. The feeblest and most ignorant can turn in thought to Him who died upon the cross, and can, with the dying thief, say, "Lord, remember me." All that is required is a sincere prayer to Christ for deliverance. But before anyone can so pray, he must hate the sin he has loved, and must be willing to submit to the God he has abandoned. And this is a great change; too difficult for many. Not all these Israelites were healed, though the cure was so accessible. There were those who were already insensible, torpid with the heavy poison that ran through their blood. There were those whose pride could not be broken, who would rather die than yield to God. There were those who could not endure the thought of a life in God's service. And there are those now who, though they feel the sting of sin, and are convulsed and tormented by it, cannot bring themselves to seek help from Christ. There are those who do not believe Christ can deliver them; and there are those to whom deliverance weighted with obligation to God, and giving health to serve Him, seems equally repugnant with death itself. But where, there is a sincere desire for reconcilement with God, and for the holiness which maintains us in harmony with God, all that is needed is trust in Christ, the belief that God has appointed Him to be our Saviour, and the daily use of Him as our Saviour.

In proceeding to make a practical use of what our Lord here teaches, our first duty, plainly, is to look to Him for life. He is exhibited crucified--it is our part to trust in Him, to appropriate for our own use His saving power. We need it. We know something of the deadly nature of sin, and that with the first touch of its fang death enters our frame. We have found our lives poisoned by it. Nothing can well be a fitter picture of the havoc sin makes than this plague of serpents--the slender weapon sin uses, the slight external mark it leaves, but, within, the fevered blood, the fast dimming sight, the throbbing heart, the convulsed frame, the rigid muscles no longer answering to our will. Do we not find ourselves exposed to sin wherever we go? In the morning our eyes open on its vibrating fangs ready to dart upon us; as we go about our ordinary employments we have trodden on it and been bitten ere we are aware; in the evening, as we rest, our eye is attracted, and fascinated, and held by its charm. Sin is that from which we cannot escape, from which we are at no time, nor in any place, secure; from which, in point of fact, no one of us has escaped, and which in every case in which it has touched a man has brought death along with it. Death may not at once appear; it may appear at first only in the form of a gayer and intenser life; as, they tell us, there is one poison which causes men to leap and dance, and another which distorts the face of the dying with a hideous imitation of laughter. Is that not a diseased soul which has no vigour for righteous and self-sacrificing work; whose vision is so dim it sees no beauty in holiness?

Of this condition, faith in God through Christ is the true remedy. Return to God is the beginning of all healthy spiritual life. Faith means that all distrust, all resentment at what has happened in our life, all proud and all despondent thoughts, are laid aside. To believe that God is loving us tenderly and wisely, and to put ourselves unreservedly into His hand, is eternal life begun in the soul.

Footnotes:

10. In saying, "Art thou the teacher of Israel, and knowest not these things?" our Lord hints that it is bad enough for an ordinary Israelite to be so ignorant, but for a teacher how much worse. If the teacher is thus obtuse, what are the taught likely to be? Is this the state of matters I must confront? And in saying that the subjects of conversation were "earthly" (ver. 12) He meant that the necessity of regeneration or entrance into the kingdom of God was a matter open to observation and its occurrence a fact which might be tested here upon earth.

IX. THE WOMAN OF SAMARIA

"When therefore the Lord knew how that the Pharisees had heard that Jesus was making and baptizing more disciples than John (although Jesus Himself baptized not, but His disciples), He left Judæa, and departed again into Galilee. And He must needs pass through Samaria. So He cometh to a city of Samaria, called Sychar, near to the parcel of ground that Jacob gave to his son Joseph: and Jacob's well was there. Jesus therefore, being wearied with His journey, sat thus by the well. It was about the sixth hour. There cometh a woman of Samaria to draw water: Jesus saith unto her, Give Me to drink. For His disciples were gone away into the city to buy food. The Samaritan woman therefore saith unto Him, How is it that Thou, being a Jew, askest drink of me, which am a Samaritan woman? (For Jews have no dealings with Samaritans.) Jesus answered and said unto her, If thou knewest the gift of God, and who it is that saith to thee, Give Me to drink; thou wouldest have asked of Him, and He would have given thee living water. The woman saith unto Him, Sir, Thou hast nothing to draw with, and the well is deep: from whence then hast Thou that living water? Art thou greater than our father Jacob, which gave us the well, and drank thereof himself, and his sons, and his cattle? Jesus answered and said unto her, Every one that drinketh of this water shall thirst again: but whosoever drinketh of the water that I shall give him shall never thirst; but the water that I shall give him shall become in him a well of water springing up unto eternal life. The woman saith unto Him, Sir, give me this water, that I thirst not, neither come all the way hither to draw. Jesus saith unto her, Go, call thy husband, and come hither."--John iv. 1--16.

Jesus left Jerusalem because His miracles were attracting the wrong kind of people, and creating a misconception of the nature of His kingdom. He went into the rural districts, where He had simpler, less sophisticated persons to deal with. Here He gained many disciples, who accepted baptism in His name. But here again His very success endangered His attainment of His great end. The Pharisees, hearing of the numbers who flocked to His baptism, fomented a quarrel between His disciples and those of John; and would, moreover, have probably called Him to account for presuming to baptize at all. But why should He have feared a collision with the Pharisees? Why should He not have proclaimed Himself the Messiah? The reason is obvious. The people had not had sufficient opportunity to ascertain the character of His work; and only by going about among them could He impress upon susceptible spirits a true sense of the nature of the blessings He was willing to bestow. To the woman of Samaria He did not hesitate to proclaim Himself, because she was a simple-minded woman, who was in need of sympathy and spiritual strength. But from controversial Pharisees, who were prepared to settle His claims by one or two trifling theological tests, He withdrew. The time would come when, after conferring on many humble souls the blessings of the kingdom, He must publicly proclaim Himself King; but as yet that time had not arrived, and therefore He left Judæa for Galilee.

A line drawn from Jerusalem to Nazareth would pass through the entire breadth of Samaria, and quite close to the town of Sychar. Between Judæa, where Jesus was, and Galilee, where He wished to be, the province of Samaria intervened. It stretched right across from the sea to the Jordan, so that the Jews, who were too scrupulous to pass through Samaritan territory, were compelled to cross the Jordan twice, and make a considerable détour if they wished to go to Galilee. Our Lord had no such scruples; besides, the springs near Salim, where John was baptizing, were not far from Sychar, and He might wish to see John on His way north. He took, therefore, the great north road, and one day at noon [11] found Himself at Jacob's well, where the road divides, and where, at any rate, it was natural that a tired traveller should rest during the mid-day hours. Jacob's well is still extant, and is one of the few undisputed localities associated with our Lord's life. Travellers of all shades of theological opinion and of no theological opinion are agreed that the deep well, now much choked with débris, lying twenty minutes east of Nablûs, is the veritable well on the stone rim of which our Lord sat. Ten minutes' walk north of this well lies a village now called El-Askar, which represents in name and partly in locality the Sychar of the text. Partly in locality I say, for "Palestine was ten times as populous in the days of our Lord as it is at present;" and there is therefore good ground for the supposition that although now but a little village or hamlet, Sychar was then considerably larger, and extended nearer to the well. Coming, then, to this well, and being tired with the forenoon's walk, our Lord sat down, while the disciples went forward to the town to buy bread.

And thus arose that conversation with the woman of Sychar, which has brought hope and comfort to many a thirsting and weary soul besides. That which struck the woman herself and the disciples is not that which is likely to impress us most distinctly. We all feel the unsurpassed delicacy and grace of the whole scene. No poet ever imagined a situation in which the free movements of human nature, the picturesqueness of outward circumstance, and the profoundest spiritual interests were so happily, easily, and effectively combined. Yet the chief thing which struck the woman herself and the disciples was the ease with which Jesus broke down the wall of partition which the hatred of centuries had erected between Jew and Samaritan.

To estimate aright the magnanimity and originality of our Lord's action in making Himself and His salvation accessible to this woman, the marked separation that had hitherto existed must be borne in mind. The Samaritans were of heathen origin. In the Second Book of Kings, chap. xvii., we read that Shalmaneser, King of Assyria, pursuing the usual policy of his empire, carried the Israelites to Babylonia, and sent colonists from Babylonia to occupy their cities and land. These colonists found the country overrun by wild beasts, which had multiplied during the years of depopulation; and accepting this as proof that the God of the land was not pleased, they begged their monarch to send them an Israelitish priest, who would teach them the manner of the God of the land. Their application was granted, and an adulterated Judaism was grafted on their native religion. They accepted the five Books of Moses, and looked for a Messiah--as indeed they still do. The origin of their hatred of the Jews is told in Ezra. When the Jews returned from exile and began to rebuild the temple, the Samaritans begged to be allowed to share in the work. "Let us build with you," they said, "for we seek your God as ye do; and we sacrifice unto Him since the days of Esarbaddon." But their request was bluntly refused; they were treated as heathens, who had no part in the religion of Israel. Hence the implacable religious enmity which for centuries manifested itself in all sorts of petty annoyances, and, when occasion offered, more serious injuries.

This Samaritan woman, then, was taken quite aback when the quiet figure on the well, which by dress and accent she had recognised as that of a Jew, uttered the simple request, "Give me to drink." As any Samaritan would have done, she twitted the Jew with showing a frankness and friendliness which she supposed were wholly due to His own keen thirst and helplessness to quench it. But, to her still greater surprise, He does not wince before her thrust, nor awkwardly apologise, or seek to explain, but gravely and earnestly, and with dignity, utters the perplexing but thought-provoking words: "If thou knewest the gift of God, and who it is that saith to thee, Give me to drink, thou wouldest have asked of Him, and He would have given thee living water." He perceived the interest of the situation, saw with compassion her entire ignorance of the presence in which she stood, and of the possibilities within her reach. So do the most important issues often hinge on slight, trivial, every-day incidents. The turning-points in our career have often nothing to show that they are turning-points. We unconsciously determine our future, and bind ourselves with chains we can never break, by the way in which we deal with apparent trifles. We do not know the forces that lie hidden all around us; and for want of knowledge we miss a thousand opportunities. The sick man drags out a miserable existence, incapacitated and useless, while within his reach, but unrecognised, is a remedy which would give him health. It is often by a very little that the scientific or philosophical student fails to make the discovery he seeks; one more fact known, one idea fitted into its proper place, and the thing is done. The gold-digger throws aside his pick in despair at the very point where another stroke would have turned up the ore. So with some among ourselves; they pass through life alongside of that which would make all eternity different to them, and yet for lack of knowledge, for lack of consideration, the thin veil continues to hide from them their true blessedness. Like the crew that were perishing from thirst, though surrounded by the fresh waters of the River Amazon that penetrated far into the salt ocean, so we, surrounded on all hands by God and upheld by Him, and living in Him, yet do not know it, and refrain from dipping our buckets and drawing out of His life-giving fulness. How often, looking on those who, like this Samaritan woman, have gone wrong and know no recovery, who go through their daily duties sad and heavy at heart and weary of sin--how often do these words rise to our lips, "If only thou knewest." How often does one long to be able to shed a sudden and universal light into the minds of men that would reveal to them the goodness, the power, the all-conquering love of God. Yes, and even in those who can speak intelligently of things Divine and eternal, how much blindness remains. For the knowledge of words is one thing, the knowledge of things, of realities, is another. And many who can speak of God's love have never yet seen what that means for themselves. Certainly it is true of us all, that if we are not deriving from Christ what we recognise as living water, it is because there is a defect in our knowledge, because we do not know the gift of God.

In two particulars this woman's knowledge was defective: she did not know the gift of God, nor who it was that spoke to her.

She did not know the gift of God. She was not expecting anything from that quarter. Her expectations were limited by her earthly condition and her physical wants. With affections worn out, with character gone, with no purifying joy, she came out listlessly day by day, filled her pitcher, and went her weary way. She had no thought of God's gift, no belief that the Eternal was with her, and desired to communicate to her a spring of deep and ever-flowing joy. Doubtless she would have acknowledged God as the Giver of all good; but she had no idea of the completeness of His giving, of the freeness of His love, of His perception and understanding of our actual wants, of the joy with which He provides for them all. Through all ages and for all men there remains this gift of God, sought and found by those who know it; different from and superior to the best human gifts, inheritances, and acquisitions; not to be drawn out of the deepest, most cherished well of human sinking; steadily arrogating to itself an infinite superiority to all that men have regarded and busily sunk their pitchers in; a gift which each man must ask for himself, and having for himself knows to be the gift of God to him, the recognition by God of his personal wants, and the assurance to him of God's everlasting regard. This gift of God, that carries to each soul the sense of His love, is His deliverance from evil. It is His answer to the misery and vanity of the world which He has resolved to redeem to worth and blessedness. It is all that is given in Christ, the hope, the holy impulses, the new views of life--but above all it is the means of conveyance that brings God to us, His love to our hearts.

What, then, can teach a man to know this gift? What can make a man for a while forget the lesser gifts that perish in the using? What can reasonably induce him to turn from the accredited sources round which men in all ages have crowded, what can induce him to forego fame, wealth, bodily comfort, domestic happiness, and seek first of all God's righteousness? May we not all well pray with Paul, "that we may have not the spirit of the world but the Spirit of God, that we may know the things that are freely given us of God;" that we may see the small value of wealth or power or any of those things which can be won by mere worldly prudence or greed; and may learn fixedly to believe that the things of true value are the internal, spiritual possessions, which the unsuccessful may have as well as the successful, and which are not so much won by us as given by God?

Jesus further describes this gift as "living water," a description suggested by the circumstances, and only figurative. Yet it is a figure of the same kind as pervades all human language. Water is an essential of animal and vegetable life. With a constantly recurring appetite we seek it. To have no thirst is a symptom of disease or death. But the soul also, not having life in itself, needs to be sustained from without; and when in a healthy state it seeks by a natural appetite that which will sustain it. And as most of our mental acts are spoken of in terms of the body, as we speak of seeing truth and grasping it, as if the mind had hands and eyes, so David naturally exclaims, "My soul thirsts for the living God." In the living soul there is a craving for that which maintains and revives its life, which is analogous to the thirst of the body for water. The dead alone feel no thirst for God. The soul that is alive sees for a moment the glory and liberty and joy of the life to which God calls us; it feels the attraction of a life of love, purity, and righteousness, but it seems continually to sink from this and to tend to become dull and feeble, and to have no joy in goodness. Just as the healthy body delights in work, but wearies and cannot go on exerting itself for many hours together, but must repair its strength, so the soul soon wearies and sinks back from what is difficult, and needs to be revived by its appropriate refreshment.

And this woman, if for a moment she felt as if Christ were playing with her or making her enigmatical offers that could never bring her any substantial good, was immediately made aware that He who made these offers had fully in view the harshest facts of her domestic life. Mystified, she is also attracted and expectant. She cannot mistake the sincerity of Jesus; and, scarcely knowing what she asks, and with her mind still running on relief from her daily drudgery, she says, "Sir, give me this water, that I thirst not, neither come hither to draw." In prompt response to her faith Jesus says, "Go, call thy husband, and come hither." The water which He means to give cannot be given before thirst for it is awakened. And in order to awaken her thirst He turns her back upon the shameful wretchedness of her life, that she may forget the water of Jacob's well in thirst for relief from shame and misery. In requiring her thus to face the facts of her guilty life, in encouraging her to bring clear before Him all her sinful entanglement, He responds to her request, and gives her the first draught of living water. For there is no abiding spiritual satisfaction which does not begin with a fair and frank consideration of our past, and which does not proceed upon the actual facts of our own life. If this woman is to enter into a hopeful and cleansed life, she must enter through confession of her need of cleansing. No one can slink out of his past life, forgetting or huddling up what is shameful. It is only through truth and straightforwardness we can enter into that life which is all truth and integrity. Before we drink the living water we must truly thirst for it.

If the inquiry be more closely pressed, and if it be asked what this Samaritan woman would find to be living water to her, what it was which, after Christ had gone, would daily renew in her the purpose to live a better life and to bear her burden cheerfully and hopefully, it will be seen that it must have been simply the remembrance of Christ; the knowledge that in Christ God had sought her, had claimed her in the midst of her evil life for some better and holier thing, had, in a word, loved her through all her sin, and sent deliverance to her. It is still, and always, this knowledge which comes with fresh exhilarating power to every disconsolate, despairing, fainting soul. The knowledge that there is One, the Holiest of all, who loves us, and who will be satisfied with nothing short of the purest blessedness for us; the knowledge that our God follows us, forgives us, elevates and purifies us by His love, this is living water to our souls; this revives us to the love of goodness, and braces us for all effort. It is not a little cistern that soon runs dry. To the end of a Christian's life this fact of God's love in Christ comes as fresh and as reviving to the soul as at first; to us this day it has the same power of supplying motive to our life as it had when Christ spoke to the woman.

He further defines the gift as "a well of water in the soul itself springing up to everlasting life." This peculiarity of the water He would give was remarked upon here for the sake of contrasting it with the well outside the city to which the woman in all weathers had to repair; often wishing, no doubt, as she went out in the heat or in the rain, that she had a well at her door. The source of spiritual life is within; it cannot be inaccessible; it does not depend on anything from which we may be separated. And this is man's victory and end when within himself he has the source of life and joy, so that he is independent of circumstances, of position, of things present and things to come. It was a commonplace even of heathen philosophy, that no man is happy until he is superior to fortune; that his happiness must have an inward source, must depend on his own spiritual state, and not on outward circumstances. Similarly Solomon thought it a saying worthy of preservation that "the good man is satisfied from himself;" that is, he shall not look to success in life, or to comfortable circumstances, or even to domestic happiness or the society of old friends, as a sure and unfailing source of joy; but shall be at bottom independent of everything save what he carries always and everywhere in himself. Nothing is more pitiable than the restlessness one sees in some people; how they can find nothing in themselves, but are ever going from place to place, from entertainment to entertainment, from friend to friend, seeking something to give them rest, and finding nothing, because they seek it without and not within. It is Christ dwelling in the heart by faith that is alone the fountain of living water. It is His inward presence, apprehended by faith, by imagination, by knowledge, that revives the soul continually. It is thus that God makes us partakers of the life that is only in Him, linking us to Himself by our will, by all that is deepest in us, and so producing true and lasting spiritual life.

The woman was blinded by her ignorance on a second point; she did not know who it was that said to her, "Give Me to drink." Until we know Christ we cannot know God: it is to Christ we owe all our best thoughts about God. This woman, when she had met the absolute goodness and kindness of Christ, had for ever different thoughts of God. So as we look at Christ our thought of God expands, and we learn to expect substantial good from Him. Yet often, like this woman, we are in Christ's presence without knowing it, and listen, like her, to His appeals without understanding the majesty of His person and the greatness of our opportunity. He does offer largely; He speaks as if He were perfect master of the human heart, knew its every experience, and could satisfy it. He speaks of the gift He has to bestow in terms which convict Him of silly and heartless extravagance if that gift be not perfect; He has, in plain words, misled and deceived a large part of mankind, and especially those who were well inclined and thirsting for righteousness, if He cannot perfectly satisfy the soul. He challenges men in the most grievous and undone conditions to come to Him; He calls them off from every other source and stay, and bids them trust to Him for everything. If a man expects to find in Him all that the human heart can contain of joy, and all that the human nature is susceptible of, he does not expect more than the explicit offers of Christ Himself warrant. Manifestly such offers are at least worth considering. May it not be true that if we were to awake to the knowledge of Christ, we might now find His pretensions to be well founded? He professes to bestow what is worth our immediate acceptance, His friendship, His Spirit. What if it should be now that He seeks to come to our heart with these words, "If thou knewest who it is that speaketh." Yes, if but for one hour we saw God's gift, and Him through whom He offers it, we should become the suppliants. Christ would no longer need to knock at our door; we should wait and knock at His.

For in truth it is always the same request He urges to all. In His words to the woman, "Give Me to drink," there was more than the mere request that He would lift her pitcher to His lips. Driven from Judæa, wearied as much with the blindness of men as with His journey, He sat on the well. Everything He saw had that day some spiritual meaning for Him. The bread His disciples brought reminded Him of His true support, the consciousness that He was doing His Father's will; the fields whitening for harvest suggested to Him the nations unconsciously ripening for the great Christian ingathering. And when He said to the woman, "Give Me to drink," He thought of the intenser satisfaction she could give Him by confiding in Him and accepting His help. In her person there stands before Him a new, untried race. Oh that she may prove more accessible than the Jews, and may allay His thirst for the salvation of men! His parched tongue seems forgotten in the interest of His talk with her. And to which of us has He not in this sense said, "Give Me to drink"? Is it cruelty to refuse a cup of cold water to a thirsting child, and none to refuse to quench the thirst of Him who hung upon the cross for us? Ought we to feel no shame that the Lord is still in want of what we can give? This woman knew it was a real thirst which could induce a Jew to ask drink from her. Has He not sufficiently shown the reality of His thirst for our friendship and trust? Could it be a feigned desire that led Him to do all He has done? Are we never to have the joy of appropriating His love as spent upon us; are we never with humble ecstasy to exclaim:--

"Weary satst Thou seeking me,
Diedst redeeming on the tree.
Can in vain such labour be"?

Footnotes:

11. Some good authorities hold that John reckoned the hours of the day from midnight, not from sunrise. It is, however, probable that John adopted the Roman reckoning, and counted noon the sixth hour.

Marcus Dods, D.D.

X. JESUS DECLARES HIMSELF

"The woman answered and said unto Him, I have no husband. Jesus saith unto her, Thou saidst well, I have no husband: for thou hast had five husbands; and he whom thou now hast is not thy husband: this hast thou said truly. The woman saith unto Him, Sir, I perceive that Thou art a prophet. Our fathers worshipped in this mountain; and ye say, that in Jerusalem is the place where men ought to worship. Jesus saith unto her, Woman, believe Me, the hour cometh, when neither in this mountain, nor in Jerusalem, shall ye worship the Father. Ye worship that which ye know not: we worship that which we know: for salvation is from the Jews. But the hour cometh, and now is, when the true worshippers shall worship the Father in spirit and in truth: for such doth the Father seek to be His worshippers. God is a Spirit: and they that worship Him must worship in spirit and truth. The woman saith unto Him, I know that Messiah cometh (which is called Christ): when He is come, He will declare unto us all things. Jesus saith unto her, I that speak unto thee am He."--John iv, 17--26.

In this conversation at Jacob's well the woman for some time, quite naturally, misses the point of what Jesus says. It does not occur to her that by "water" He means anything else than what she could carry in her pitcher. Even when He speaks of causing a well to spring up "within herself," she still thinks merely of the domestic convenience of some such arrangement, and begs Him to give what would save Her the endless trouble of coming to draw water out of Jacob's well. This simplicity has its good side, as also has her obvious confidence in His words. Jesus sees in this child-like simplicity and directness a much more hopeful soil for His message than He had found even in a thoughtful man of education like Nicodemus. He seeks, therefore, to prepare the soil further by quickening within her a sense of spiritual want. This may best be effected by backing her into her actual life. Therefore He says, "Go, call thy husband, and come hither." And in this simple way He leads the woman at once to recognise His prophetic insight into her condition, and to bring His offers into connection with her character and her life. And there was that in her manner of owning Him as a prophet, a frankness and a simplicity in uttering her mind and listening to His explanations, that prompted Him explicitly to say, "I that speak unto thee am the Messiah."

To this unfortunate and ill-living alien woman, then, Jesus declared Himself as He had not declared Himself to the well-to-do, respectable Jewish rabbis. The reason of this difference in our Lord's treatment of individuals arises from the different dispositions they manifest. Acknowledgment of His power to work miracles may seem at first sight as good a certificate for Christian discipleship as acknowledgment of His prophetic power. But it is not so; because such an acknowledgment of His prophetic insight as this woman made is an acknowledgment of His power over the human heart and life. He who is thus felt to penetrate to the hidden acts, and to lay His hand upon the deepest secrets of the heart, is recognised as in a personal connection with the individual; and this is the foundation on which Christ can build, this is the beginning of that vital connection with Him which gives newness of life. Those who are merely solving a problem when they are considering the claims of Christ, are not likely to have any personal revelation made to them. But to every one, who, like this woman, shows some desire to receive His gifts, and who is not above owning that life is a very poor affair without some such thing as He offers; to every one who is conscious of sin, and who looks to Him as able to deliver from all its foul entanglement, He does make Himself known. To such persons He will disclose Himself when He sees that they are ripe for the disclosure. To such the moment of moments will come, when to them He will say: "I that speak unto thee am He."

This distinction between the chemist who analyses the living water, and the thirsting soul that uses it, runs very deep, and may be commended to the consideration of any who are apt to be carried away by the current of unbelief that characterizes much of our literature. I think it may be said that in writers distinguished by a lack of Christian belief there will commonly be found an absence of what is popularly and fitly called "an awakened conscience." It will be found that they do not know what it is to look at Christ from the point of view of this woman, from the point of view of a shattered and wretched life, and a conscience that day by day is saying, It is I myself who have broken my life, and doing so I have become a transgressor, and need pardon, guidance, strength. Acute thought, an admirable faculty of explaining and enforcing what is thought, we find in abundance; but we certainly do not find a spirit humbled by a sense of sin and a conscience alive to the deepest obligations. So far as can be gathered from the writings of the most conspicuous unbelievers, they do not possess the first requisite for discerning a Saviour--namely, a sense of need. They lack the prime preparation for speaking on such a subject; they have never dealt fairly with their own sin. We do not consult a deaf man if we wish to ascertain whether the noise we have heard is thunder or the rumbling of a cart; neither can we expect that those will be the best teachers regarding God in whom the faculty by which we chiefly discern God--viz., the conscience--has been less exercised than any other. It is through the conscience God makes Himself most distinctly felt; it is in connection with the moral law we come most clearly in contact with Him; and convictions of God's Being and connection with us root themselves in the soul that a sense of sin has ploughed.

I am far from saying that in deciding upon the claims of Christ the understanding is to have no voice. The understanding must have a voice here as elsewhere. But it is a strong presumption in Christ's favour that He offers precisely what sinners need; and it is decisive in His favour when we find that He actually gives what sinners need. If it is practically found that He is the force that lifts thousands and thousands of human beings out of sin; if He has, in point of fact, brought light to those in deep darkness, comfort and courage to the desolate and heavily burdened, consecration and purity to the outcast and the corrupt, then, plainly, He is what He claims to be, and we owe Him our faith.

If God is to reveal Himself at all, the revelation must be made not solely or chiefly to the understanding, but to that part of us which determines character, and is capable of appreciating character. The revelation must be moral not intellectual. As our Lord's ministry proceeded He recognised that it was always the simple who most readily accepted and trusted Him; and He recognised that this was a thing to be thankful for: "I thank Thee, O Father, Lord of heaven and earth, that Thou hast hid these things from the wise and prudent, and hast revealed them unto babes." And every one who thinks of it sees that it must be so--that a man's destiny must be decided not by his understanding, but by his character and leanings; not by his ability or disability to believe this or that, or to prove that his belief is well grounded, but by his aspirations, by the real bent of his heart. We should feel that there was something very far wrong if our faith depended upon proofs that not every one could master, and if thus the clever man had an advantage over the humble and contrite. "The evidence must be such that spiritual character shall be an element in the acceptance of it." And such we find it to be. The reality and the significance of the revelation of God in Christ are more readily apprehended by the spiritually than by the intellectually gifted. Persons who are either by nature humble and docile, or whom life has taught to be so, persons who feel their need of God, and deeply long for an eternal state of peace and purity, these are the persons to whom God finds it possible to make Himself known. And if it be thought that this circumstance, that simple and docile spirits are convinced while hard-headed men are unconvinced, throws some suspicion on the reality of the revelation, if it be thought that the God and the eternity they believe in are but fancies of their own, it may fairly be replied, that there is no more reason for such a thought than for supposing that the rapture of a trained musician is fanciful and self-created, and not excited by any corresponding reality, because it is not shared by those whose taste for music is unawakened.

Convinced that Jesus was a prophet, the woman proposes to Him the standing subject of debate between Jews and Samaritans. Her statement of it is abrupt, and offers some appearance of being intended to turn the conversation away from herself; but this does not harmonise with her simple and direct character, and it is quite possible that in the midst of her confused and disappointed life she had sometimes wondered whether all her misery did not arise from her being a Samaritan. She knew what the Jews said of the Samaritan worship. She knew that they mocked at the Temple which stood on the hill over against Jacob's well; and when she found how very little her worship had helped her, she may have begun to suspect that there was truth in the Jewish allegations. Evidently the aspect of the Messiah, which had chiefly struck her, was His power to lead men into all truth, to teach them all things. Persons in her station, and quite as much overborne by sin as she, often retain their hold upon religious teaching; and in the midst of much that is superstitious they have a spark of true hope and longing for redemption. Jesus shows by the gravity and importance of His answer that He considered the woman sincere in the statement of her difficulty, and anxious to know where God might really be found. Perplexed and bewildered by her earthly experience, as so many of us are, she suddenly awakes to the consciousness that here, before her, and conversing with her, is a prophet; and at once she utters to Him what had been burning in her heart, "Where, where is God to be found?"

And so in reply to the inquiry of one sincere woman Jesus makes that great announcement which has ever since stood as the manifesto of spiritual worship. Not in any particular and isolated place, He tells the woman, is God to be found, not in the temple at Jerusalem, nor in the rival structure on Gerizim, but in spirit. "God is a Spirit, and they that worship Him must worship in spirit and in truth." As our Lord intimates, this was a new kind of worship, essentially different from that to which Jews and Samaritans, and indeed all men, had hitherto been accustomed.

The magnitude of the contents of such sayings can as little be comprehended as their significance can be exhausted. We have first of all the central affirmation: "God is a Spirit." To fill out this definition with intelligible ideas is difficult. It implies that He is a Personal Being, that He is self-conscious, possessed of intelligence and will; but although Personal His Personality transcends our conception. So far as regards the immediate application of the definition by our Lord at this time, it suffices to note its primary meaning that God has not a body, and consequently is subject to none of the limitations and conditions to which the possession of a body subjects human persons. He needs no local dwelling-place, no temple, no material offerings. In local worship there was an advantage while the world was young, and men could best be taught by symbols. A house in their midst, of which they might say, "God is there," was undoubtedly an aid to faith. But it had its disadvantages. For the more a worshipper fixed his mind on the one local habitation, the less could he carry with him the consciousness of God's presence in all places.

Very slowly do we learn that God is a Spirit. We think nothing is more surely believed among us. Alas! make almost any application of this radical truth, and we find how little it is believed. Take, for example, the appearances and voices by which intimations were made to godly men in Old Testament times. Why are many people reluctant to allow that these manifestations were inward and to conscience, that they came as convictions wrought by an unseen power, rather than as outward appearances or audible voices? Is it not because the truth that God is a Spirit is not adequately apprehended? Or why again do we so crave for signs, for clearer demonstrations of God's being and of His presence? Ought we not to be satisfied if He responds to spiritual aspirations, and if we find that our craving for holiness is met and gratified?

The inference drawn by our Lord from the truth that God is a Spirit is one which needs still to be pressed. God seeks to be worshipped not by outward forms or elaborate ritual but in spirit. Ordinary teachers would have put in a saving clause to preserve some forms of worship; Christ puts in none. Let men worship God in spirit, and let forms take their chance. To worship God in spirit is to yield the unseen but motive powers within us to the unseen but Almighty influences which we recognise as Divine. It is to prostrate our spirit before the Divine Spirit. It is in our deepest being, in will and intention, to offer ourselves up to Him in whom goodness is personified. When a man is doing that, what does it matter what he says to God, or with what forms of worship he comes before Him? That alone is acceptable worship which consists in the devout approach of the human spirit to the Divine; and that is accomplished often as effectually in our business intercourse with men when tempted to injustice, or in our homes when tempted to anger or to laxity, as when we are in the house of God. Worship in the spirit needs no words, no appointed place, but only a human soul that bows inwardly before the goodness of God, and submits itself cordially to His sovereign and loving will.

This certainly is a strong argument for simplicity of worship. Why, it may indeed be said, why have any outward worship at all? Why have churches and why have Divine service? Well, it would have been better for the Church if there had been far less outward worship than there commonly has been. For by its elaborate services the Church has far too much identified religion with that worship which can only be rendered in church. No one can be surprised that in utter disgust at the disproportion between outward and spiritual worship, between the gorgeous and fussy services that profess so much, and the slender and rare devotion of the soul to God, discerning men should have turned their back on the whole business, and declined to be partakers in so huge and profane a farce. Milton in his later years attended no Church and belonged to no communion. This certainly is to run to the opposite extreme. No doubt that worship may be real and acceptable which is offered in the silence and solitude of a man's spirit; but we naturally utter what we feel, and by the utterance strengthen the feelings that are good, and rid ourselves of the bitterness and strain of those that are painful and full of sorrow. Besides, the Church is, before all else, a society. Our religion is meant to bring us together; and though it does so more effectually by inspiring us with kindliness and helpfulness in life than by a formal meeting together for no purposes of active charity, yet the one fellowship aids the other, as many of us well know.

While, then, we accept Christ's statement in its fullest significance, and maintain that our "reasonable service" is the offering of ourselves as living sacrifices, that spiritual worship is offered not in church only or mainly, but in doing God's will with a hearty good-will, we all the rather see how needful it is to utter ourselves to God as we do in our social worship; for as the wife would need some patience who was cared for indeed by her husband in the supply of her common wants, but had never a word of affection spoken to her, so our relations to God are not satisfactory unless we utter to Him our devotion as well as show it in our life. He was one of the wisest of English writers who said, "I always thought fit to keep up some mechanical forms of good breeding (in my family), without which freedom ever destroys friendship." Precisely so, he who omits the outward and verbal expression of regard to God, will soon lose that regard itself.

But if the words of Christ were not intended to put an end to outward worship altogether, they do, as I have said, form a strong argument for simplicity of worship. No forms whatever are needed that our spirit may come into communion with God. Let us begin with this. As true and perfect worship may be rendered by the dying man, who cannot lift an eyelid or open his lips, as by the most ornate service that combines perfect liturgical forms with the richest music man has ever written. Rich music, striking combinations of colour and of architectural forms, are nothing to God so far as worship goes, except in

The Expositor's Bible: The Gospel of St. John Volumes I & II

so far as they bring the human spirit into fellowship with Him. Persons are differently constituted, and what is natural to one will be formal and artificial to another. Some worshippers will always feel that they get closer to God in private, in their own silent room, and with nothing but their own circumstances and wants to stimulate them; they feel that a service carefully arranged and abounding in musical effects does indeed move them, but does not make it easier for them to address themselves to God. Others, again, feel differently; they feel that they can best worship God in spirit when the forms of worship are expressive and significant. But in two points all will agree: first, that in external worship, while we strive to keep it simple we should also strive to make it good--the best possible of its kind. If we are to sing God's praise at all, then let the singing be the best possible, the best music a congregation can join in, and executed with the utmost skill that care can develop. Music which cannot be sung save by persons of exceptional musical talent is unsuitable for congregational worship; but music which requires no consideration, and admits of no excellence, is hardly suitable for the worship of God. I do not know what idea of God's worship is held by persons who never put themselves to the least trouble to improve it so far as they are concerned.

The other point in which all will agree, is that where the spirit is not engaged there is no worship at all. This goes without saying. And yet, subtract from our worship all that is merely formal, and how much do you leave? Worse still, there are those who do not even strive after the fit and decorous form, who do not bow their heads in prayer, who are not ashamed to be seen looking about them during the most solemn acts of worship, who show that they are indevout, thoughtless, profane.

The true worshippers shall worship the Father not only "in spirit," but also "in truth." The word "truth" here probably covers two ideas--the ideas of reality and of accuracy. It is opposed to symbolic worship and to ignorant worship. It does not mean that worship was now to be sincere, for that it had already been both among Samaritans and Jews. But among the Jews the worship of God had been symbolical, and among the Samaritans it had been ignorant.

The Jewish worship had been symbolical, every person and thing, every colour, gesture, movement, having a meaning for the initiated. The time for this, says our Lord, is past. We are to worship really. They need no longer take an animal to the temple to symbolise that they gave themselves to God; they were to spend their whole care on the real thing, on giving themselves to God; they were not to set candles about their altars to show that light was come into the world, they were themselves to shine as lights lit by Christ; they were not to swing censers to symbolise the sweet-smelling prayers of the saints, they were to offer prayers from humble hearts. In effect Christ said, You are grown up now, and can understand the realities; put away then these childish things. And those who continue to worship with various robes, and prescribed gesticulations and movements, and pictures, and altars, and everything to impress the senses, write themselves down children among grown-up people.

Truth is opposed also to error or misconception about the object of worship. Christ, by His presence, enables men to worship the Father in truth. He gives them the true idea of God. He makes God real, giving an actuality to our thought of God which we could not otherwise arrive at; and He shows us God as He truly is, connected with ourselves by love; holy, merciful, just.

Marcus Dods, D.D.

XI. THE SECOND SIGN IN GALILEE

"In the mean while the disciples prayed Him, saying, Rabbi, eat. But He said unto them, I have meat to eat that ye know not. The disciples therefore said one to another, Hath any man brought Him aught to eat? Jesus saith unto them, My meat is to do the will of Him that sent Me, and to accomplish His work. Say not ye, There are yet four months, and then cometh the harvest? behold, I say unto you, Lift up your eyes, and look on the fields, that they are white already unto harvest. He that reapeth receiveth wages, and gathereth fruit unto life eternal; that he that soweth and he that reapeth may rejoice together. For herein is the saying true, One soweth and another reapeth. I sent you to reap that whereon ye have not laboured: others have laboured, and ye are entered into their labour. And from that city many of the Samaritans believed on Him because of the word of the woman, who testified, He told me all things that ever I did. So when the Samaritans came unto Him, they besought Him to abide with them: and He abode there two days. And many more believed because of His word; and they said to the woman, Now we believe, not because of thy speaking: for we have heard for ourselves, and know that this is indeed the Saviour of the world. And after the two days He went forth from thence into Galilee. For Jesus Himself testified, that a prophet hath no honour in his own country. So when He came into Galilee, the Galilæans received Him, having seen all the things that He did in Jerusalem at the feast: for they also went unto the feast. He came therefore again unto Cana of Galilee, where He made the water wine. And there was a certain nobleman, whose son was sick at Capernaum. When he heard that Jesus was come out of Judæa into Galilee, he went unto Him, and besought Him that He would come down, and heal his son; for he was at the point of death. Jesus therefore said unto him, Except ye see signs and wonders, ye will in no wise believe. The nobleman saith unto Him, Sir, come down ere my child die. Jesus saith unto him, Go thy way; thy son liveth. The man believed the word that Jesus spake unto him, and he went his way. And as he was now going down, his servants met him, saying, that his son lived. So he inquired of them the hour when he began to amend. They said therefore unto him, Yesterday at the seventh hour the fever left him. So the father knew that it was at that hour in which Jesus said unto him, Thy son liveth: and himself believed, and his whole house. This is again the second sign that Jesus did, having come out of Judæa into Galilee"--John iv. 31--54.

The disciples, when they went forward to buy provisions in Sychar, left Jesus sitting on the well wearied and faint. On their return they find Him, to their surprise, elate and full of renewed energy. Such transformations one has often had the pleasure of seeing. Success is a better stimulant than wine. Our Lord had found one who believed Him and valued His message; and this brought fresh life to His frame. The disciples go on eating, and are too busy with their meal to lift their eyes; but as they eat they talk over the prospects of the harvest in the rich fields through which they have just walked. Meanwhile our Lord sees the men of Sychar coming out of the town in obedience to the woman's request, and calls His disciples' attention to a harvest more worthy of their attention than the one they were discussing: "Were you not saying that we must wait four months till harvest comes again [12] and cheapens the bread for which you have paid so dear in Sychar? But lift up your eyes and mark the eager crowd of Samaritans, and say if you may not expect to reap much this very day. Are not the fields white already to harvest? Here in Samaria, which you only wished quickly to pass through, where you were looking for no additions to the Kingdom, and where you might suppose sowing and long waiting were needed, you see the ripened grain. Others have laboured, the Baptist and this woman and I, and ye have entered into their labours."

All labourers in the Kingdom of God need a similar reminder. We can never certainly say in what state of preparedness the human heart is; we do not know what providences of God have ploughed it, nor what thoughts are sown in it, nor what strivings are being even now made by the springing life that seeks the light. We generally give men credit, not perhaps for less thought than they have, for that is scarcely possible, but for less capacity of thought. The disciples were good men, but they went into Sychar judging the Samaritans good enough to trade with, but never dreaming of telling them the Messiah was outside their town. They must have been ashamed to find how much more capable an apostle the woman was than they. I think they would not wonder another time that their Lord should condescend to talk with a woman. The simple, unthinking, untroubled directness of a woman will often have a matter finished while a man is meditating some ponderous and ingenious contrivance for bringing it to pass. Let us not fall into the mistake of the disciples, and judge men good enough to buy and sell with, but quite alien to the matters of the Kingdom.

> "There is a day in spring
> When under all the earth the secret germs
> Begin to stir and glow before they bud.
> The wealth and festal pomps of midsummer
> Lie in the heart of that inglorious hour
> Which no man names with blessing, though its work
> Is bless'd by all the world. Such days there are
> In the slow story of the growth of souls."

Such days may be passing in those around us, though all unknown to us. We can never tell how many months there are till harvest. We never know who or what has been labouring before we appear on the scene.

The woman's testimony was enough to excite curiosity. The men on her word came out to judge for themselves. What they saw and heard completed their conviction; "And they said to the woman, Now we believe, not because of thy speaking: for we have heard for ourselves, and know that this is indeed the Saviour of the world." This growth of faith is one of the subjects John delights to exhibit. He is fond of showing how a weak and ill-founded faith may grow into a faith that is well rooted and strong.

This Samaritan episode is significant as an integral part of the Gospel, not only because it shows how readily unsophisticated minds perceive the inalienable majesty of Christ, but also because it forms so striking a foil to the reception our Lord had met with in Jerusalem, and was shortly to meet with in Galilee. In Jerusalem He did many miracles; but the people were too political and too prejudiced to own Him as a spiritual Lord. In Galilee He was known, and might have expected to be understood; but there the people longed only for physical blessings and the excitement of miracles. Here in Samaria, on the contrary, He did no miracles, and had no forerunner to herald His approach. He was found a weary wayfarer, sitting by the roadside, begging for refreshment. Yet, through this appearance of weakness, and dependence, and lowliness, there shone His native kindness, and truth, and kingliness, to such a degree, that the Samaritans, although naturally suspicious of Him as a Jew, believed in Him, delighted in Him, and proclaimed Him "Saviour of the world."

After two days of happy intercourse with the Samaritans Jesus continues His journey to Galilee. The proverbial expression which our Lord used regarding His relation to Galilee--that a prophet has no honour in his own country--is one we have frequent opportunity of verifying. The man that has grown up among us, whom we have seen struggling up through the ignorance, and weakness, and folly of boyhood, whom we have had to help and to protect, can scarcely receive the same respect as one who presents himself a mature man, with already developed faculties, no longer a learner, but prepared to teach. Montaigne complained that in his own country he had to purchase publishers, whereas elsewhere publishers were anxious to purchase him. "The farther off I am read from my own home," he says, "the better I am esteemed." The men of Anathoth sought Jeremiah's life when he began to prophesy among them.

It is not the truth of the proverb that presents any difficulty, but its application to the present case. For the fact that a prophet has no honour in his own country would seem to be a reason for His declining to go to Galilee, whereas it is here introduced as His reason for going there. The explanation is found in the beginning of the chapter, where we are told that it was in search of retirement He was now leaving the popularity and publicity of Judæa, and repairing to His own country.

But, as frequently on other occasions, He now found that He could not be hid. His countrymen, who had thought so little of Him previously, had heard of His Judæan fame, and echoed the recognition and applause of the south. They had not discovered the greatness of this Galilean, although He had lived among them for thirty years; but no sooner do they hear that He has created a sensation in Jerusalem than they begin to be proud of Him. Every one has seen the same thing a hundred times. A lad who has been despised as almost half-witted in his native place goes up to London and makes a name for himself as poet, artist, or inventor, and when he returns to his village everybody claims him as cousin. Such a change of sentiment was not likely to escape the observation of Jesus nor to deceive Him. It is with an accent of disappointment, not unmingled with reproach, that He utters His first recorded words in Galilee: "Except ye see signs and wonders, ye will in no wise believe."

This sets us in the point of view from which we can clearly see the significance of the one incident which John selects from all that happened during our Lord's stay in Galilee at this time. John wishes to illustrate the difference between the Galilean and the Samaritan faith, and the possibility of the one growing into the other; and he does so by introducing the brief narrative of the courtier from Capernaum. Accounts, more or less accurate, of the miracles of Jesus in Jerusalem had found their way even into the household of Herod Antipas. For no sooner was He known to have arrived in Galilee than one of the royal household sought Him out to obtain a boon which no royal favour could grant. The supposition is not without plausibility that this nobleman was Chuza, Herod's chamberlain, and that this miracle, which had so powerful an effect on the family in which it was wrought, was the origin of that devotion to our Lord which was afterwards shown by Chuza's wife.

The nobleman, whoever he was, came to Jesus with an urgent request. He had come twenty miles to appeal to Jesus, and he had been unable to trust his petition to a messenger. But instead of meeting this distracted father with words of sympathy and encouragement, Jesus merely utters a general and chilling observation. Why is this? Why does He seem to lament that this father should so urgently plead for his son? Why does He seem only to submit to the inevitable, if He grants the request at all? Might it not even seem as if He wrought the miracle of healing rather for His own sake than for the boy's or for the father's sake, since He says, "Except ye see signs and wonders, ye will in no wise believe"--that is, will not believe in Me?

But these words did not express any reluctance on the part of Jesus to heal the nobleman's son. Possibly they were intended, in the first instance, to rebuke the desire of the father that Jesus should go with him to Capernaum and pronounce over the boy words of healing. The father thought the presence of Christ was necessary. He had not attained to the faith of the centurion, who believed that an expression of will was enough. Jesus, therefore, demands a stronger faith; and in His presence that stronger faith which can trust His word is developed.

The words, however, were especially a warning that His physical gifts were not the greatest He had to bestow, and that a faith which required to be buttressed by the sight of miracles was not the best kind of faith. Our Lord was always in danger of being looked upon as a mere thaumaturge, who could dispense cures merely as a physician could within his own limits order a certain treatment. He was in danger of being considered a dispenser of blessings to persons who had no faith in Him as the Saviour of the world. It is therefore with the accent of one who submits to the inevitable that He says, "Except ye see signs and wonders, ye will in no wise believe."

But especially did our Lord wish to point out that the faith He approves and delights in is a faith which does not require miracles as its foundation. This higher faith He had found among the Samaritans. Many of them believed, as John is careful to note, because of His conversation. There was that in Himself and in His talk which was its own best evidence. Some men who introduce themselves to us, to win our countenance to some enterprise, carry integrity in their whole bearing; and we should feel it to be an impertinence to ask them for credentials. If they offer to prove their identity and trustworthiness we waive such proof aside, and assure them that they need no certificate. This had been our Lord's experience in Samaria. There no news of His miracles had come from Jerusalem. He came among the Samaritans from nobody knew where. He came without introduction and without certificate, yet they had discernment to see that they had never met His like before. Every word He spoke seemed to identify Him as the Saviour of the world. They forgot to ask for miracles. They felt in themselves His supernatural power, lifting them into God's presence, and filling them with light.

The Galilâ¡an faith was of another kind. It was based on His miracles; a kind of faith He deplored, although He did not quite repudiate it. To be accepted not on His own account, not because of the truth He spoke, not because His greatness was perceived and His friendship valued, but because of the wonders He performed--this could not be a pleasant experience. We do not greatly value the visits of a person who cannot get on without our advice or assistance; we value the friendship of him who seeks our company for the pleasure he finds in it. And although we must all be ceaselessly and infinitely dependent on the good offices of Christ, our faith should be something more than a counting upon His ability and willingness to discharge these good offices. A faith which is merely selfish, which recognises that Christ can save from disaster in this life or in the life to come, and which cleaves to Him solely on that account, is scarcely the faith that Christ approves. There is a faith which responds to the glory of Christ's personality, which rests on what He is, which builds itself on the truth He utters, and recognises that all spiritual life centres in Him; it is this faith He approves. They who find in Him the link they have sought with the spiritual world, the pledge they have needed to certify them of an eternal righteousness, they to whom the supernatural is revealed more patently in Himself than in His miracles, are those whom the Lord delights in.

But the lower kind of faith may be a step to the higher. The agony of the father can make nothing of general principles, but can only reiterate the one petition, "Come down ere my child die." And Jesus, with His perfect knowledge of human nature, sees that it is vain trying to teach a man in this absorbed condition of mind, and that probably the very best way to clarify his faith and lead him to higher and worthier thoughts is to grant his request--a hint not to be overlooked or despised by those who seek to do good, and who are, possibly, sometimes a little prone to obtrude their teaching at most inopportune seasons--at seasons when it is impossible for the mind to admit anything but the one absorbing topic. Circumstances are, in general, much better educators of men than any verbal teaching; and that verbal teaching can only do harm which interposes between the moving events that are occurring and the person who is passing through them. The success of our Lord's method was proved by the result; which was, that the slender faith of this nobleman became a genuine faith in Christ as the Lord, a faith which his whole household shared.

From the very greatness of Christ, and our consequent inability to bring Him into comparison with other men, we are apt to miss some of the significant features of His conduct. In the circumstances before us, for example, most teachers at an early stage in their career would have been in some excitement, and would probably have shown no reluctance to accede to the nobleman's request, and go down to his house, and so make a favourable impression on Herod's court. It was an opportunity of getting a footing in high places which a man of the world could not have overlooked. But Jesus was well aware that if the foundations of His kingdom were to be solidly laid, there must be excluded all influence of a worldly kind, all the overpowering constraint which fashion and great names exercise over the mind. His work, He saw, would be most enduringly, if most slowly, done in a more private manner. His own personal influence on individuals must first of all be the chief agency. He speaks, therefore, to this nobleman without any regard to his rank and influence; indeed, rather curtly dismisses him with the words, "Go, thy son lives." The total absence of display is remarkable. He did not go to Capernaum, to stand by the sickbed, and be acknowledged as the healer. He made no bargain with the nobleman that if his son recovered he would let the cause be known. He simply did the thing, and said nothing at all about it.

Though it was only one in the afternoon when the nobleman was dismissed he did not go back to Capernaum that night--why, we do not know. A thousand things may have detained him. He may have had business for Herod in Cana or on the road as well as for himself; the beast he rode may have gone lame where he could not procure another; at any rate, it is quite uncalled for to ascribe his delay to the confidence he had in Christ's word, an instance of the truth, "He that believeth shall not make haste." The more certainly he believed Christ's word the more anxious would he be to see his son. His servants knew how anxious he would be to hear, for they went to meet him; and were no doubt astonished to find that the sudden recovery of the boy was due to Him whom their master had visited. The cure had travelled much faster than he who had received the assurance of it.

The process by which they verified the miracle and connected the cure with the word of Jesus was simple, but perfectly satisfactory. They compared notes regarding the time, and found that the utterance of Jesus was simultaneous with the recovery of the boy. The servants who saw the boy recover did not ascribe his recovery to any miraculous agency; they would no doubt suppose that it was one of those unaccountable cases which occasionally occur, and which most of us have witnessed. Nature has secrets which the most skilful of her interpreters cannot disclose; and even so marvellous a thing as an instantaneous cure of a hopeless case may be due to some hidden law of nature. But no sooner did their master assure them that the hour in which the boy began to amend was the very hour in which Jesus said he would get better, than they all saw to what agency the cure was due.

Here lies the special significance of this miracle; it brings into prominence this distinctive peculiarity of a miracle, that it consists of a marvel which is coincident with an express announcement of it, and is therefore referrible to a personal agent. [13] It is the two things taken together that prove that there is a superhuman agency. The marvel alone, a sudden return of sight to the blind, or of vigour to the paralysed, does not prove that there is anything supernatural in the case; but if this marvel follows upon the word of one who commands it, and does so in all cases in which such a command is given, it becomes obvious that this is not the working of a hidden law of nature, nor a mere coincidence, but the intervention of a supernatural agency. That which convinced the nobleman's household that a miracle had been wrought was not the recovery of the boy, but his recovery in connection with the word of Jesus. What they felt they had to account for was not merely the marvellous recovery, but his recovery at that particular time. Even though it could be shown, then,--as it can never be,--that every cure reported in the Gospels might possibly be the result of some natural law, even though it could be shown that men born blind might receive their sight without a miracle, and that persons who had consulted the best physician suddenly recovered strength--this, we are to remember, is by no means the whole of what we have to account for. We have to account not only for sudden, and certainly most extraordinary cures, but also for these cures following uniformly, and in every case the word of One who said the cure would follow. It is this coincidence which puts it beyond a doubt that the cures can be referred only to the will of Christ.

Another striking feature of this miracle is that the Agent was at a distance from the subject of it. This is, of course, quite beyond our comprehension. We cannot understand how the will of Jesus, without employing any known physical means of communication between Himself and the boy, without even appearing before him so as to seem to inspire him by look or word, should instantaneously effect his cure. The only possible link of such a kind between the boy and Jesus was that he may have been aware that his father had gone to seek help for him, from a renowned physician, and may have had his hopes greatly excited. This supposition is, however, gratuitous. The boy may quite as likely have been delirious, or too young to know anything; and even though this slender link did exist, no sensible person will build much on that. And certainly it is encouraging to find that even while on earth our Lord did not require to be in contact with the person healed. "His word was as effective as His presence." And if it is credible that while on earth He could heal at the distance of twenty miles, it is difficult to disbelieve that He can from heaven exercise the same omnipotent will.

Note.--It is not apparent why John appends the remark, "This is again the second sign that Jesus did, having come out of Judæa into Galilee." He may, perhaps, have only intended to call attention more distinctly to the place where the miracle was wrought. This idea is supported by the fact that John shows, on parallel lines, the manifestation of Christ in Judæa and in Galilee. It is just possible that he may have wished to warn readers of the Synoptical Gospels, that Jesus had not yet begun the Galilæan ministry with which these Gospels open.

Footnotes:

12. The words (ver. 35) have quite the ring of a proverb--a proverb peculiar to seed-time and for the encouragement of the sower. If uttered on this occasion in seed-time, this gives December as the date.

13. This is lucidly taught in Mozley's Bampton Lectures.

XII. SABBATH CURE AT BETHESDA

"After these things there was a feast of the Jews; and Jesus went up to Jerusalem. Now there is in Jerusalem by the sheep gate a pool, which is called in Hebrew Bethesda, having five porches. In these lay a multitude of them that were sick, blind, halt, withered. And a certain man was there, which had been thirty and eight years in his infirmity. When Jesus saw him lying, and knew that he had been now a long time in that case, He saith unto him, Wouldest thou be made whole? The sick man answered Him, Sir, I have no man, when the water is troubled, to put me into the pool: but while I am coming, another steppeth down before me. Jesus saith unto him, Arise, take up thy bed, and walk. And straightway the man was made whole, and took up his bed and walked. Now it was the Sabbath on that day. So the Jews said unto him that was cured, It is the Sabbath, and it is not lawful for thee to take up thy bed. But he answered them, He that made me whole, the same said unto me, Take up thy bed, and walk. They asked him, Who is the man that said unto thee, Take up thy bed, and walk? But he that was healed wist not who it was: for Jesus had conveyed Himself away, a multitude being in the place. Afterward Jesus findeth him in the temple, and said unto him, Behold, thou art made whole: sin no more, lest a worse thing befall thee."--John v. 1--14.

The miracle here recorded is selected by John because in it Jesus plainly signified that He had power to quicken whom He would (v. 21), and because it became the occasion for the unbelief of the Jews to begin the hardening process and appear as opposition.

The miracle was wrought when Jerusalem was full; although whether at the Feast of Tabernacles, or Purim, may be doubted. The pool at the sheep-gate or sheep-market is commonly identified with the Fountain of the Virgin, which still supplies a bath known as Hammam esh Shefa, the Bath of Healing. It seems to have been an intermittent spring, which possessed some healing virtue for a certain class of ailments. Its repute was well established, for a great multitude of hopeful patients waited for the moving of the waters. [14]

To this natural hospital Jesus wended His way on the Sabbath of the feast. And as the trained eye of the surgeon quickly selects the worst case in the waiting-room, so is the eye of Jesus speedily fixed on "a man which had an infirmity thirty and eight years," a man paralysed apparently in mind as well as in body. Few employments could be more utterly paralysing than lying there, gazing dreamily into the water, and listening to the monotonous drone of the cripples detailing symptoms every one was sick of hearing about. The little periodic excitement caused by the strife to be first down the steps to the bubbling up of the spring was enough for him. Hopeless imbecility was written on his face. Jesus sees that for him there will never be healing by waiting here.

Going up to this man, our Lord confronts him with the arousing question, "Are you desiring to be made whole?" The question was needful. Not always are the miserable willing to be relieved. Medical men have sometimes offered to heal the mendicant's sores, and their aid has been rejected. Even the invalid who does not trade pecuniarily on his disease is very apt to trade upon the sympathy and indulgence of friends, and sometimes becomes so debilitated in character as to shrink from a life of activity and toil. Those who have sunk out of all honest ways of living into poverty and wretchedness are not always eager to put themselves into the harness of honest labour and respectability. And this reluctance is exhibited in its extreme form in those who are content to be spiritual imbeciles, because they shrink from all arduous work and responsible position. Life, true life such as Christ calls us to, with all its obligations to others, its honest and spontaneous devotion to spiritual ends, its risks, its reality, and purity, does not seem attractive to the spiritual valetudinarian. In fact, nothing so thoroughly reveals a man to himself, nothing so clearly discloses to him his real aims and likings, as the answer he finds he can give to the simple question, "Are you willing to be made whole? Are you willing to be fitted for the highest and purest life?"

The man is sufficiently alive to feel the implied rebuke, and apologetically answers, "Sir, I have no one to put me into the pool. It is not that I am resigned to this life of uselessness, but I have no option." The very answer, however, showed that he was hopeless. It had become the established order of things with him that some one anticipated him. He speaks of it as regularly happening--"another steps down before me." He had no friend--not one that would spare time to wait beside him and watch for the welling up of the water. And he had no thought of help coming from any other quarter. But there is that in the appearance and manner of Jesus that quickens the man's attention, and makes him wonder whether He will not perhaps stand by him and help him at the next moving of the waters. While these thoughts are passing through his mind the words of Jesus ring with power in his ears, "Rise, take up thy bed, and walk." And he who had so long waited in vain to be healed at the spring, is instantaneously made whole by the word of Jesus.

John habitually considered the miracles of Jesus as "signs" or object lessons, in which the spiritual mind might read unseen truth. They were intended to present to the eye a picture of the similar but greater works which Jesus wrought in the region of the spirit. He heals the blind, and therein sets Himself before men as the Light of the world. He gives the hungry bread, but is disappointed that they do not from this conclude that He is Himself the Bread sent by the Father to nourish to life everlasting. He heals this impotent man, and marvels that in this healing the people do not see a sign that He is the Son who does the Father's works, and who can give life to whom He will. It is legitimate, therefore, to see in this cure the embodiment of spiritual truth.

This man represents those who for many years have known their infirmity, and who have continued, if not very definitely to hope for spiritual vigour, at least to put themselves in the way of being healed--to give themselves, as invalids do, all the chances. This crowding of the pool of Bethesda--the house of mercy or grace--strongly resembles our frequenting of ordinances, a practice which many continue in very much the state of mind of this paralytic. They are still as infirm as when they first began to look for cure; it seems as if their turn were never to come, though they have seen many remarkable cures. Theoretically they have no doubt of the efficacy of Christian grace; practically they have no expectation that they shall ever be strong, vigorous useful men in His Kingdom. If you asked them why they are so punctual in attendance on all religious services, they would say, "Why, is it not a right thing to do?" Press them further with our Lord's question, "Are you expecting to be made whole? Is this your purpose in coming here?" They will refer you to their past, and tell you how it has always seemed to be some other person's case that was thought of, how the Spirit of God seemed always to have other work than that which concerned them. But here they are still--and commendably and wisely so; for if this man had begun to disbelieve in the virtue of the water because he himself had never experienced its power, and had shut himself up in some wretched solitude of his own, then the eye of the Lord had never rested upon him--here they are still; for the best part of a lifetime they have been on the brink of health, and yet have never got it; for eight-and-thirty years this man had seen that water, knew that it healed people, put his hand in it, gazed on it,--yes, there it was, and could heal him, and yet his turn never came. So do these persons frequent the ordinances, hear the word that can save them, touch the bread of communion, and know that by the blessing of God the bread of life is thereby conveyed, and yet year by year goes past, and for them all remains unblessed. They begin despairingly to say--

"Thy saints are comforted, I know,
And love Thy house of prayer;
I therefore go where others go,
But find no comfort there."

This miracle shows such persons that there is a shorter way to health than a languid attendance on ordinances--an attendance that is satisfied if there seems to be still in operation what may be useful to others. It is the voice of Christ they need to hear. It is that voice summoning to thought and hope that we all need to hear, "Wilt thou be made whole?" Are you weary and ashamed of your infirmity; would you fain be a whole man in Christ, able at last to walk through life as a living man, seeing the beauty of God and of His work, and meeting with gladness the whole requirements of a life in God? Does the very beauty of Christ's manhood, as He stands before you, make you at once ashamed of your weakness and covetous of His strength? Do you see in Him what it is to be strong, to enter into life, to begin to live as a man ought always to live, and are you earnestly looking to receive power from on high? To such come the life-giving voice of the Word who utters God, and the life that is in God.

It is important to notice that in Christ's word to the sick, "Rise, take up thy bed, and walk," three things are implied--

1. There must be a prompt response to Christ's word. He does not heal any one who lies sluggishly waiting to see what that word will effect. There must be a hearty and immediate recognition of the speaker's truth and power. We cannot say to what extent the impotent man would feel a current of nervous energy invigorating him. Probably this consciousness of new strength would only succeed his cordial reliance on the word of Christ. Obey Christ, and you will find strength enough. Believe in His power to give you new life, and you will have it. But do not hesitate, do not question, do not delay.

2. There must be no thought of failure, no making provision for a relapse; the bed must be rolled up as no longer needed. How do those diseased men of the Gospels rebuke us! We seem always half in doubt whether we should make bold to live as whole men. We take a few feeble steps, and return to the bed we have left. From life by faith in Christ we sink back to life as we knew it without Christ--a life

attempting little, and counting it a thing too high for us to put ourselves and our all at God's disposal. If we set out to swim the Channel we take care to have a boat within hail to pick us up if we become exhausted. To make provision for failure is in the Christian life to secure failure. It betrays a half-heartedness in our faith, a lurking unbelief which must bring disaster. Have we rolled up our bed and tossed it aside? If Christ fails us, have we nothing to fall back upon? Is it faith in Him that really keeps us going? Is it His view of the world and of all that is in it that we have accepted; or do we merely take a few steps on His principles, but in the main make our bed in the ordinary unenlightened worldly life?

3. There must be a continuous use made of the strength Christ gives. The man who had lain for thirty-eight years was told to walk. We must confront many duties without any past experience to assure us of success. We must proceed to do them in faith--in the faith that He who bids us do them will give us strength for them. Take your place at once among healthy men; recognise the responsibilities of life. Find an outlet for the new strength in you. Be no longer a burden, a charge to others, but begin yourself to bear the burdens of others, and be a source of strength to others.

Before the man could get home with his bed he was challenged for carrying it on the Sabbath. They must surely have known that he himself, and many more, had that very morning been carried to Bethesda. But we can scarcely conclude from the Jews thus challenging the healed man that they sought occasion against Jesus. They would have stopped any one going through the streets of Jerusalem with a bundle on the Sabbath. They had Scripture on their side, and founded on the words of Jeremiah (xvii. 21), "Take heed to yourselves, and bear no burden on the Sabbath day." Even in our own streets a man carrying a large package on Sunday would attract the suspicion of the religious, if not of the police. We must not, then, find a malicious intention towards Jesus, but merely the accustomed thoughtless bigotry and literalism, in the challenge of the Jews.

But to their "It is not lawful," the man promptly answers, perhaps only meaning to screen himself by throwing the blame on another, "He that made me whole, the same said unto me, Take up thy bed." The man quite naturally, and without till now reflecting on his own conduct, had listened to Christ's word as authoritative. He that gave me strength told me how to use it. Intuitively the man lays down the great principle of Christian obedience. If Christ is the source of life to me, He must also be the source of law. If without Him I am helpless and useless, it stands to reason that I must consider His will in the use of the life He communicates. This must always be the Christian's defence when the world is scandalised by anything he does in obedience to Christ; when he goes in the face of its traditions and customs; when he is challenged for singularity, overpreciseness, or innovation. This is the law which the Christian must still bear in mind when he fears to thwart any prejudice of the world, when he is tempted to bide his time among the impotent folk, and not fly in the face of established usage; when, though he has distinctly understood what he ought to do, so many difficulties threaten, that he is tempted to withdraw into obscurity and indolence. It is the same Voice which gives life and directs it. Shall I then refuse it in both cases, or choose it in both? Shall I shrink from its directions, and lie down again in sin; or shall I accept life, and with it the still greater boon of spending it as Christ wills?

But though the man had thus instinctively obeyed Jesus, he actually had not had the curiosity to ask who He was. It is almost incredible that he should have so immediately lost sight of the person to whom he was so indebted. But so taken up is he with his new sensations, so occupied with gathering up his mats, so beset by the congratulations and inquiries of his comrades at the porch, that before he bethinks himself Jesus is gone. Among those who do undoubtedly profit by Christ's work there is a lamentable and culpable lack of interest in His person. It does not seem to matter from whom they have received these benefits so long as they have them; they do not seem drawn to His person, ever following to know more of Him and to enjoy His society, as the poor demoniac would have done, who would gladly have left home and country, and who cared not what line of life he might be thrown into or what thrown out of, if only he might be with Christ. If one were to put the case, that my prospects were eternally and in each particular changed by the intervention of one whose love is itself infinite blessing, and if it were asked what would be my feeling towards such a person, doubtless I would say, He would have an unrivalled interest for me, and I should be irresistibly drawn into the most intimate personal knowledge and relations; but no--the melancholy truth is otherwise; the gift is delighted in, the giver is suffered to be lost in the crowd. The spectacle is presented of a vast number of persons made blessed through the intervention of Christ, who are yet more concerned to exhibit their own new life and acquirements, than to identify and keep hold of Him to whom they owe all.

Although the healed man seems to have had little interest in Christ, Christ kept His eye upon him. Finding him in the Temple, where he had gone to give thanks for his recovery, or to see a place he had so long been excluded from, or merely because it was a place of public resort, our Lord addressed him in the emphatic words, "Sin no more, lest a worse thing come upon thee." The natural inference from these words is that his disease had been brought on by sin in early life--another instance of the lifelong misery a man may incur by almost his earliest responsible acts, of the difficulties and shame with which a lad or a boy may unwittingly fill his life, but an instance also of the willingness with which Christ delivers us even from miseries we have rashly brought upon ourselves. Further still, it is an instance of the vitality of sin. This man's lifelong punishment had not broken the power of sin within him. He knew why he was diseased and shattered. Every pain he felt, every desire which through weakness he could not gratify, every vexing thought of what he might have made of life, made him hate his sin as the cause of all his wretchedness; and yet at the end of these thirty-eight years of punishment Christ recognised in him, even in the first days of restored health, a liability to return to his sin. But every day we see the same; every day we see men keeping themselves down, and gathering all kinds of misery round them by persisting in sin. We say of this man and that, "How is it possible he can still cleave to his sin, no better, no wiser for all he has come through? One would have thought former lessons sufficient." But no amount of mere suffering purifies from sin. One has sometimes a kind of satisfaction in reaping the consequences of sin, as if that would deter from future sin; but if this will not hold us back, what will? Partly the perception that already God forgives us, and partly the belief that when Christ commands us to sin no more He can give us strength to sin no more. Who believes with a deep and abiding conviction that Christ's will can raise him from all spiritual impotence and uselessness? He, and he only, can hope to conquer sin. To rely upon Christ's word, "Sin no more," with the same confident faith with which this man acted on His word, "Rise, take up thy bed"--this alone gives victory over sin. If our own will is too weak, Christ's will is always mighty. Identify your will with Christ's, and you have His strength.

But the fear of punishment has also its place. The man is warned that a worse thing will fall upon him if he sins. Sinning after the beginning of deliverance, we not only fall back into such remorse, darkness, and misery as have already in this life followed our sin, but a worse thing will come upon us. But "worse." What can be worse than the loss of an entire life; like this man, passing in disappointment, in uselessness, in shame, the time which all naturally expect shall be filled with activity, success, and happiness; losing, and losing early, and losing by one's own fault, and losing hopelessly, everything that makes life desirable? Few men so entirely miss life as this man did, though perhaps our activities are often more hurtful than his absolute inactivity, and under an appearance of prosperity the heart may have been torn with remorse as painful as his. Yet let no man think that he knows the worst that sin can do. After the longest experience we may sink deeper still, and indeed must do so unless we listen to Christ's voice saying, "Behold, thou art made whole: sin no more, lest a worse thing come upon thee."

Footnotes:

14. Verse 4 is omitted by recent editors on the authority of the best ancient MSS.

XIII. JESUS LIFE-GIVER AND JUDGE

"The man went away, and told the Jews that it was Jesus which had made him whole. And for this cause did the Jews persecute Jesus, because He did these things on the sabbath. But Jesus answered them, My Father worketh even until now, and I work. For this cause therefore the Jews sought the more to kill Him, because He not only brake the sabbath, but also called God His own Father, making Himself equal with God. Jesus therefore answered and said unto them, Verily, verily, I say unto you, The Son can do nothing of Himself, but what He seeth the Father doing: for what things soever He doeth, these the Son also doeth in like manner. For the Father loveth the Son, and sheweth Him all things that Himself doeth: and greater works than these will He shew Him, that ye may marvel. For as the Father raiseth the dead and quickeneth them, even so the Son also quickeneth whom He will. For neither doth the Father judge any man, but He hath given all judgement unto the Son; that all may honour the Son, even as they honour the Father. He that honoureth not the Son honoureth not the Father which sent Him. Verily, verily, I say unto you, He that heareth My word, and believeth Him that sent Me, hath eternal life, and cometh not into judgement, but hath passed out of death into life. Verily, verily, I say unto you, The hour cometh, and now is, when the dead shall hear the voice of the Son of God; and they that hear shall live. For as the Father hath life in Himself, even so gave He to the Son also to have life in Himself: and He gave Him authority to execute judgement, because He is the Son of man. Marvel not at this: for the hour cometh, in which all that are in the tombs shall hear His voice, and shall come forth; they that have done good, unto the resurrection of life; and they that have done ill, unto the resurrection of judgement. I can of Myself do nothing; as I hear, I judge: and My judgement is righteous; because I seek not Mine own will, but the will of Him that sent Me. If I bear witness of Myself, My witness is not true. It is another that beareth witness of Me; and I know that the witness which He witnesseth of Me is true. Ye have sent unto John, and he hath borne witness unto the truth. But the witness which I receive is not from man: howbeit I say these things, that ye may be saved. He was the lamp that burneth and shineth: and ye were willing to rejoice for a season in his light. But the witness which I have is greater than that of John: for the works which the Father hath given Me to accomplish, the very works that I do, bear witness of Me, that the Father hath sent Me. And the Father which sent Me, He hath borne witness of Me. Ye have neither heard His voice at any time, nor seen His form. And ye have not His word abiding in you: for whom He sent, Him ye believe not. Ye search the scriptures, because ye think that in them ye have eternal life; and these are they which bear witness of Me; and ye will not come to Me, that ye may have life. I receive not glory from men. But I know you, that ye have not the love of God in yourselves. I am come in My Father's name, and ye receive Me not: if another shall come in his own name, him ye will receive. How can ye believe, which receive glory one of another, and the glory that cometh from the only God ye seek not? Think not that I will accuse you to the Father: there is one that accuseth you, even Moses, on whom ye have set your hope. For if ye believed Moses, ye would believe Me; for he wrote of Me. But if ye believe not his writings, how shall ye believe My words?"--John v. 15--47.

As soon as the impotent man discovered who it was that had given him strength, he informed the authorities, either from sheer thoughtlessness, or because he considered that they had a right to know, or because he judged that, like himself, they would rather admire the miracle than take exception to the Sabbath-breaking. If this last was his idea, he had not gauged the obtuseness and self-righteous spite of honest and pious literalism. "For this cause did the Jews persecute Jesus, because He did these things on the Sabbath." [15] In what particular form the charge of Sabbath-breaking was brought against our Lord, whether formal or conversational and tentative, John does not say. He is more concerned to give us in full the substance of His apology. For the first time our Lord now gave in public an explanation of His claims; and this five minutes' talk with the Jews contains probably the most important truth ever uttered upon earth.

The passage embodies the four following assertions: that the healing of the incurable on the Sabbath resulted from and exhibited His perfect unison with the Father; that this giving of life to an impotent man was an illustration or sign of His power to quicken whom He would, to communicate life Divine and eternal to all in whatsoever stage of spiritual or physical deadness they were; that His claim to possess this supreme power was not mere idle assertion, but was both guaranteed by this miracle, and otherwise was amply attested; and that the real root of their rejection of Him and His claims was to be found, not in their superior knowledge of God and regard for His will, but in their worldly craving for the applause of men. [16]

1. Our Lord's reply to the charge of Sabbath-breaking is, "My Father worketh hitherto, and I work." He did not make any comment on the Sabbath law. He did not defend Himself by showing that works of mercy such as He had done Were admissible. On other occasions He adopted this line of defence, but now He took higher ground. The rest of God is not inactivity. God does not on the Sabbath cease to communicate life to all things. He does not refrain from blessing men till the sun of the Sabbath is set. The tides rise and fall; the plants grow; the sun completes his circuit on the Sabbath as on other days. "Why does not God keep the Sabbath?" a caviller asked of a Jew. "Is it not lawful," was the answer, "for a man to move about in his own house on the Sabbath? The house of God is the whole realm above and the whole realm below." For God the Sabbath has no existence; it is a boon He has given to His creatures because they need it. His untiring beneficence is needful for the upholding and for the happiness of all. And it is the same superiority to the Sabbath which Jesus claims for Himself. He claims that His unceasing work is as necessary to the world as the Father's--or rather, that He and the Father are together carrying out one work, and that in this miracle the Jews find fault with He has merely acted as the Father's agent.

From this statement the Jews concluded that He made Himself equal with God. And they were justified in so concluding. It is only on this understanding of His words that the defence of Jesus was relevant. If He meant only to say that He imitated God, and that because God did not rest on the Sabbath, therefore He, a holy Jew, might work on the Sabbath, His defence was absurd. Our Lord did not mean that He was imitating the Father, but that His work was as indispensable as the Father's, was the Father's. My Father from the beginning up till now worketh, giving life to all; and I work in the same sphere, giving life as His agent and almoner to men. The work of quickening the impotent man was the Father's work. In charging Him with breaking the Sabbath they were charging the Father with breaking it.

But this gives Jesus an opportunity of more clearly describing His relation to God. He declares He is in such perfect harmony with God that it is impossible for Him to do either that miracle or any other work at His own instigation. "The Son can do nothing of Himself, but what He seeth the Father doing." "I can of myself do nothing." He had power to do it, but no will. He had life in Himself, and could give it to whom He pleased; but so perfect was His sympathy with God, that it was impossible for Him to act where God would not have Him act. So trained was He to perceive the Divine purpose, so habituated to submit Himself to it, that He could neither mistake His Father's will nor oppose it. As a conscientious man when pressed to do a wrong thing says, No, really I cannot do it; as a son who might happen to be challenged for injuring His father's business would indignantly repudiate the possibility of such a thing. "What do I live for," he would say, "but to further my father's views? My father's interests and mine are identical, our views and purposes are identical. I cannot do anything antagonistic to him." So Jesus had from the first recognised God as His Father, and had so true and deep a filial feeling that really it was the joy of His life to do His will.

This, then, was the idea the Lord sought to impress on the people on the first occasion on which He had a good opportunity of speaking in public. He cannot do anything save what is suggested to Him by consideration of God's will. Even as a boy He had begun to have this filial feeling. "Wist ye not that I must be about My Father's business?" That in Him which is most conspicuous and which He wishes to be most conspicuous is perfect sonship; filial trust and duty carried to its perfect height. It is this perfect filial unanimity with the Father which makes His life valuable, significant, different from all other lives. It is this which makes Him the perfect representative of the Father; which enables Him to be God's perfect messenger to men, doing always and only the will of God in men's sight. He is in the world not for the sake of fulfilling any private schemes of His own, but having it as His sole motive and aim to do the Father's will.

This perfect filial feeling had no doubt its root in the eternal relation of the Son to the Father. It was the continuance, upon earth and under new conditions, of the life He already had enjoyed with the Father. Having assumed human nature, He could reveal Himself only so far as that nature allowed Him. His revelation, for example, was not universal, but local, confined to one place; His human nature being necessarily confined to one place. He did not assert superiority to all human law; He paid taxes; He recognised lawful authority; He did not convince men of His Divinity by superiority to all human infirmities; He ate, slept, died as ordinary men. But through all this He maintained a perfect harmony with the Divine will. It was this which differentiated Him from ordinary men, that He maintained throughout His life an attitude of undoubting trust in the Father and devotion to Him. It was through the human will of the Lord that the Divine will of the Eternal Son uniformly worked and used the whole of His human nature.

It is in this perfect Sonship of Christ we first learn what a son should be. It is by His perfect loyalty to the Father's will, by His uniform adoption of it as the best, the only, thing He can do, that we begin to understand our connection with God, and to recognise that in His will alone is our blessedness.

Naturally we resent the rule of any will but our own; we have not by nature such love for God as would put His will first. To our reason it becomes manifest that there is nothing higher or happier for us than to sink ourselves in God; we see that there is nothing more elevating, nothing more essential to a hopeful life than that we make God's purposes in the world our own, and do that very thing which He sees to be worth doing and which He desires to do. Yet we find that the actual adoption of this filial attitude, natural, rational, and inviting as it seems, is just the most difficult of all difficulties, is indeed the battle of life. Who among us can say that we do nothing of ourselves, nothing at our own instance, that our life is entirely at God's disposal?

To this filial disposition on the part of the Son the Father responds: "The Father loveth the Son, and showeth Him all things that Himself doeth" (ver. 20). If we ask how Jesus saw the Father's works, or how, for example, He saw that the Father wished Him to heal the impotent man, the answer must be that it is by inward sympathy the Son apprehends what the Father wills. We in our measure can see what God is doing in the world, and can forward God's work. But not by mere observation of what God had done and was doing through others did Jesus see what the Father did, but rather by His own inward perception of the Father's will. By His own purity, love, and goodness He knew what the Father's goodness willed. But the Father was not passive in the matter, merely allowing the Son to discover what He could of His will. Godet illustrates this active revelation on the Father's part by the simile of the father in the carpenter's shop at Nazareth showing the son the things he made and the method of making them. This simile, however, being external, is apt to misdirect the mind. It was by a wholly inward and spiritual process the Father made known to the Son His purposes and mind.

2. This quickening of the impotent man was meant to be an object lesson, a sign of the power of Jesus to communicate life, Divine and eternal, to whom He would. "Greater works" than this of curing the paralytic "will the Father show to the Son, that ye may marvel" (ver. 20). As through His word vigour had been imparted to the impotent man, so all who listen to His word will receive everlasting life (ver. 24). As the impotent man, after thirty-eight years of deadness, found life on the moment by believing Christ's word, so every one who listens to that same voice as the word of God receives life eternal. Through that word he connects himself with the source of life. He becomes obedient to the life-giving will of God.

The question, How can the spiritually dead hear and believe? is the question. How could the impotent man rise in response to Christ's word? Psychologically inexplicable it may be, but happily it is practically possible. And here, as elsewhere, theory must wait upon fact. One thing is plain: that faith is the link between the Divine life and human weakness. Had the impotent man not believed, he would not have risen. Christ quickens "whom He will;" that is to say, there is no limit to His life-giving power; but He cannot quicken those who will not have life or who do not believe He can give it. Hence necessarily "the Father hath committed all judgement unto the Son." To the impotent man Jesus put the question, "Wilt thou be made whole?" and by that question the man was judged. By the answer he gave to it he determined whether he would remain dead or receive life. Had he not on the moment believed, he would have doomed himself to permanent and hopeless imbecility. Christ's question judged him.

Precisely so, says Jesus, are all men judged by My presence among them, and My offer of life to them. For the Father has not only given to the Son to have life in Himself, that He may thus communicate it (ver. 26), but "He hath given Him authority to execute judgement also, because He is a Son of man." For these words do not mean that Jesus will be Judge because men should be judged by one who shares their nature, [17] or because they must be judged by the holiest and most loving of men [18] --as if God Himself were not sufficiently loving--but, as the object-lesson shows us, Jesus is necessarily Judge by appearing as God's messenger, and by offering to men life everlasting. By becoming a son of man, by living in human form as the embodied love and life of God, and by making intelligible God's good-will and His invitation to life, Christ necessarily sifts men and separates them into two classes. Every one who hears the word of Jesus is judged. He either accepts quickening and passes into life, or he rejects it and abides in death. This human appearance, Jesus seems to say, which stumbles you, and makes you think that My pretensions of judging all men are absurd, is the very qualification which makes judgment one of My necessary functions.

And this explains why we find Christ uttering apparent contradictions: at one time saying, "For judgment came I into this world," and at another time saying, "I came not to judge the world." The object of His coming into the world was to give life, not to condemn men, not to cut them off finally from life and from God, but to open a way to the Father, and to be their life. But this very coming of Christ and the offers He makes to men constitute the critical test of every soul that is brought into contact with them. Judgment is the necessary accompaniment of salvation. Man's will being free, it must be so. And this judgment, determined in this life, will one day appear in final, irreversible, manifested result. "The hour is coming, in the which all that are in the graves shall hear His voice, and shall come forth; they that have done good, unto the resurrection of life; and they that have done evil, unto the resurrection of damnation."

3. But naturally the Jews would say: "These are extraordinary and apparently extravagant claims

to make. It is not easily credible that this voice which now so quietly speaks to us is one day to wake the dead. It is not easily credible that one whom we can carry before our courts is to judge all men." To which thoughts Jesus replies: "I do not expect you to take My word for these things, but there are three guarantees of My truth to which I point you. There is first of all (1) the testimony of John [19] --a man in whose prophetic gift you for a while prided yourselves, rejoicing that God had sent you so powerful and enlightening a messenger. His whole function was to testify of Me. This lamp, in the light of which you rejoiced, was lit solely for the purpose of making quite visible to you that which you now say you cannot see. But this is not the best witness I have, although those of you who cannot see for themselves might be saved if only you would believe John's testimony. But (2) I have greater witness than that of John. John said that I should come as the Father's agent. Well, if you cannot believe John's words, can you not believe the things you see? This impotent man raised to health, is this not a little hint of the Divine power that is in your midst? And are not all the works I do the Father's works, done by His power and for His purposes? Is not My whole career its own best evidence? But besides, (3) the Father Himself has borne witness to Me. He has not appeared to you. You have not heard His voice nor seen His shape, but His word, His own sufficient account of His nature and connection with you, you have. You search the Scriptures, and rightly, for they are they which testify of Me. They are the Father's word which, had you listened to, you would have known Me as sent by Him. Had you not mumbled only the husk of Scripture, counting its letters and wearing it on your foreheads, but had you, through God's law, entered into sympathy with His purpose on earth, had you, through all that Scripture tells you of Him, learned His nature, and learned to love Him, you would at once have recognised Me as His messenger. Ye have not His word abiding in you;' ye have not let it lie in your minds and colour them; ye have not chewed, and digested, and assimilated the very quintessence of it, for had you done so you would have learned to know God and seen Him in Me. [20] But whom He sent, Him ye believe not.'"

    The very Scriptures which had been given to guide them to Christ they used as a veil to blind themselves to His presence. Jesus points out where their mistake lay. "You search the Scriptures, because you suppose that in them, a mere book, you have eternal life; the truth being that life is in Me. The Scriptures do not give life, they lead to the Life-giver. The Scriptures, by your superstitiously reverent and shallow use of them, actually prevent you from finding the life they were meant to point you to. You think you have life in them, and therefore will not come to Me." So may a book, lifted out of its subordinate place, be entirely perverted from its use, and actually hinder the purpose it was given to promote. To worship the Bible as if it were Christ is to mistake a finger-post for a house of shelter. It is possible to have a great zeal for the Bible and yet quite to misapprehend its object; and to misapprehend its object is to make it both useless and dangerous. To set it on a level with Christ is to do both it, Him, and ourselves the gravest injustice. Many who seem to exalt the Scriptures degrade them; and those who give them a subordinate place truly exalt them. God speaks in Scripture, as this passage shows, but He speaks for a definite purpose, to reveal Christ; and this fact is the key to all difficulties about the Bible and inspiration.

    4. The unbelief of the Jews is traced by Jesus to a moral root. They seemed very zealous for God's law, but beneath this superficial and ostentatious championing of God there was detected a deep-seated alienation from God which unfitted them for knowing either Him or His messenger. "Glory from men I do not receive (ver. 41). But the reason of this is that ye have not the love of God in you, and cannot appreciate Divine glory or recognise it when you see it. How can you believe, when your hearts crave the glory you can give to one another, your ambition rising no higher than to be spoken of by ignorant people as the upholders of religion? You have taught yourselves to measure men by a wholly spurious standard, and cannot believe in one who is a transparency through which the glory of God shines upon you." Had some one come in his own name, seeking a glory the Jews could give him, adapting himself to their poor conceptions, him they would have received. But Jesus being sent by God had that glory which consisted in being a perfect medium of the Father's will, doing the Father's work and never seeking His own glory.

    This, then, was the reason why the Jews could not believe in Jesus. Their idea of glory was earthly, and they were unfitted to see and appreciate such glory as He showed in deeds of kindness. And those sayings of Jesus penetrate deeply into the permanent roots of unbelief.

    It was certainly a great demand on their faith which Jesus made. He asked them to believe that the most Divine of prerogatives, life-giving and judging, belonged to Him. But He gave them evidence. He only asks them to believe what they have seen exemplified. He does not as yet even ask them to draw inferences. He does not blame them for not seeing what is implied regarding His eternal relation to the Father. He adduces evidence "that they may be saved;" that they may be induced to partake of the life He dispenses; and He laments that they will not believe that He is commissioned by God to speak words of life to men, although He has given them demonstration of His commission and power to give life.

    To us also He speaks--for plainly such powers as He here claims are not such as can be capriciously given and withdrawn, rendered accessible to one age but not to another, exhibited on earth once but never more to be exercised. They are not powers that could be given to more than one messenger of God. To suppose more than one source of spiritual life or more than one seat of judgment is against reason.

Footnotes:

15. Similarly in the Synoptical Gospels the hostility of the Jews is traced to His apparent breach of the Sabbath law.

16. The following division of the former part of this Apology may help the reader to follow the sequence of thought. In vv. 19, 20, Jesus enounces the general features of His relation to the Father. In vv. 21--23 the works dictated by this relation and resulting from it are spoken of generally as "quickening" and "judging." These works are in vv. 24--27 exhibited in the spiritual sphere, and in vv. 28, 29, in the physical sphere. The first part of the defence is closed in ver. 30 with a re-affirmation of His absolute unison with the Father.

17. Westcott.

18. Stier.

19. It is very doubtful whether ver. 32 refers to John. I think it refers to the Father. Still Jesus, in vv. 33--35, refers the Jews to the testimony of John, although for His own part He depends on higher testimony.

20. The same idea is resumed in vv. 45--47. If you have not understood the writings of Moses which you have heard from Sabbath to Sabbath, and have not received the knowledge of God they were meant to give you, how shall ye believe the once heard words of Him whose coming was meant to be prepared for, and His identification made easy by all that Moses wrote and by the institutions he established.

Marcus Dods, D.D.

XIV. JESUS THE BREAD OF LIFE

John vi. 1--59.

In this chapter John follows the same method as in the last. He first relates the sign, and then gives our Lord's interpretation of it. As to the Samaritan woman, and to the inhabitants of Jerusalem, so now to the Galileans, Jesus manifests Himself as sent to communicate to man life eternal. The sign by means of which He now manifests Himself is, however, so new that many fresh aspects of His own person and work are disclosed. [21]

The occasion for the miracle arose, as usual, quite simply. Jesus had retired to the east side of the sea of Tiberias, probably to a spot near Bethsaida Julias, that He might have some rest. But the people, eager to see more miracles, followed Him round the head of the lake, and, as they went, their number was augmented by members of a Passover caravan which was forming in the neighbourhood or was already on the march. This inconsiderate pursuit of Jesus, instead of offending Him, touched Him; and as He marked them toiling up the hill in groups, or one by one, some quite spent with a long and rapid walk, mothers dragging hungry children after them, His first thought was, What can these poor tired people get to refresh them here? He turns therefore to Philip with the question, "Whence are we to buy bread that these may eat?" This he said, John tells us, "to prove" or test Philip. Apparently this disciple was a shrewd business man, quick to calculate ways and means, and rather apt to scorn the expectations of faith. Every man must rid himself of the defects of his qualities. And Jesus now gave Philip an opportunity to overcome his weakness-in-strength by at last boldly confessing his inability and the Lord's ability,--by saying, We have neither meat nor money, but we have Thee. But Philip, like many another, missed his opportunity, and, wholly oblivious of the resources of Jesus, casts His eye rapidly over the crowd and estimates that "two hundred pennyworth" [22] of bread would scarcely suffice to give each enough to stay immediate cravings. Philip's friend Andrew as little as himself divines the intention of Jesus, and naÃ¯vely suggests that the whole provision he can hear of in the crowd is a little boy's five loaves and two fishes. These helpless, meagrely furnished and meagrely conceiving disciples, meagre in food and meagre in faith, are set in contrast to the calm faith and infinite resource of Jesus.

The moral ground being thus prepared for the miracle in the confessed inability of the disciples and of the crowd, Jesus takes the matter in hand. With that air of authority and calm purpose which must have impressed the onlookers at all His miracles, He says, "Make the men sit down." And there where they happened to be, and without further preparation, on a grassy spot near the left bank of the Jordan, and just where the river flows into the lake of Galilee, with the evening sun sinking behind the hills on the western shore and the shadows lying across the darkened lake, the multitude break up into groups of hundreds and fifties, and seat themselves in perfect confidence that somehow food is to be furnished. They seat themselves as those who expect a full meal, and not a mere snack they could eat standing, though where the full meal was to come from who could tell? This expectation must have deepened into faith as the thousands listened to their Host giving thanks over the scanty provision. One would fain have heard the words in which Jesus addressed the Father, and by which He caused all to feel how near to each was infinite resource. And then, as He proceeded to distribute the ever-multiplying food, the first awe-struck silence of the multitude gave way to exclamations of surprise and to excited and delighted comments. The little lad, as he watched with widening eyes his two fishes doing the work of two thousand, would feel himself a person of consequence, and that he had a story to tell when he went back to his home on the beach. And ever and anon, as our Lord stood with a smile on His face enjoying the congenial scene, the children from the nearest groups would steal to His side, to get their supplies from His own hand.

1. Before touching upon the points in this sign emphasised by our Lord Himself, it is perhaps legitimate to indicate one or two others. And among these it may first of all be remarked that our Lord sometimes, as here, gives not medicine but food. He not only heals, but prevents disease. And however valuable the one blessing is--the blessing of being healed--the other is even greater. The weakness of starvation exposes men to every form of disease; it is a lowered vitality which gives disease its opportunity. In the spiritual life it is the same. The preservative against any definite form of sin is a strong spiritual life, a healthy condition not easily fatigued in duty, and not easily overcome by temptation. Perhaps the gospel has come to be looked upon too exclusively as a remedial scheme, and too little as the means of maintaining spiritual health. So marked is its efficacy in reclaiming the

vicious, that its efficacy as the sole condition of healthy human life is apt to be overlooked. Christ is needful to us not only as sinners; He is needful to us as men. Without Him human life lacks the element which gives reality, meaning, and zest to the whole. Even to those who have little present sense of sin He has much to offer. A sense of sin grows with the general growth of the Christian life; and that at first it should be small need not surprise us. But the present absence of a profound sorrow for sin is not to bar our approach to Christ. To the impotent man, conscious of his living death, Christ offered a life that healed and strengthened--healed by strengthening. But equally to those who now conversed with Him, and who, conscious of life, asked Him how they might work the work of God, He gave the same direction, that they must believe in Him as their life.

2. Our Lord here supplied the same plain food to all.

In the crowd were men, women, and children, old and young, hard-working peasants, shepherds from the hillside, and fishermen from the lake; as well as traders and scribes from the towns. No doubt it elicited remark that fare so simple should be acceptable to all. Had the feast been given by a banqueting Pharisee, a variety of tastes would have been provided for. Here the guests were divided into groups merely for convenience of distribution, not for distinction of tastes. There are few things which are not more the necessity of one class of men than of another, or that while devotedly pursued by one nation are not despised across the frontier, or that do not become antiquated and obsolete in this century though considered essential in the last. But among these few things is the provision Christ makes for our spiritual well-being. It is like the supply of our deep natural desires and common appetites, in which men resemble one another from age to age, and by which they recognise their common humanity. All the world round, you may find wells whose water you could not say was different from what you daily use, at any rate they quench your thirst as well. You could not tell what country you were in nor what age by the taste of the water from a living well. And so what God has provided for our spiritual life bears in it no peculiarities of time or place; it addresses itself with equal power to the European of to-day as it did to the Asiatic during our Lord's own lifetime. Men have settled down by hundreds and by fifties, they are grouped according to various natures and tastes, but to all alike is this one food presented. And this, because the want it supplies is not fictitious, but as natural and veritable a want as is indicated by hunger or thirst.

We must beware then of looking with repugnance on what Christ calls us to, as if it were a superfluity that may reasonably be postponed to more urgent and essential demands; or as if He were introducing our nature to some region for which it was not originally intended, and exciting within us spurious and fanciful desires which are really alien to us as human beings. This is a common thought. It is a common thought that religion is not an essential but a luxury. But in point of fact all that Christ calls us to, perfect reconcilement with God, devoted service of His will, purity of character,--these are the essentials for us, so that until we attain them we have not begun to live, but are merely nibbling at the very gate of life. God, in inviting us to these things, is not putting a strain on our nature it can never bear. He is proposing to impart new strength and joy to our nature. He is not summoning us to a joy that is too high for us, and that we can never rejoice in, but is recalling us to that condition in which alone we can live with comfort and health, and in which alone we can permanently delight. If we cannot now desire what Christ offers, if we have no appetite for it, if all that He speaks of seems uninviting and dreary, then this is symptomatic of a fatal loss of appetite on our part. But as Jesus would have felt a deeper compassion for any in that crowd who were too faint to eat, or as He would quickly have laid His healing hand on any diseased person who could not eat, so does He still more deeply compassionate all of us who would fain eat and drink with His people, and yet nauseate and turn from their delights as the sickly from the strong food of the healthy.

3. But what Jesus especially emphasises in the conversation arising out of the miracle is that the food He gives is Himself. He is the Bread of Life, the Living Bread. What is there in Christ which constitutes Him the Bread of Life? There is, first of all, that which He Himself constantly presses, that He is sent by the Father, that He comes out of heaven, bringing from the Father a new source of life into the world.

When our Lord pointed out to the Galileans that the work of God was to believe in Him, they demanded a further sign as evidence that He was God's Messenger: "What sign doest Thou that we may see and believe Thee? What dost Thou work? Our fathers did eat manna in the desert; they had bread from heaven, not common barley loaves such as we got from You yesterday. Have You any such sign as this to give? If You are sent from God, we may surely expect you to rival Moses." [23] To which Jesus replies: "The bread which your fathers received did not prevent them dying; it was meant to sustain physical life, and yet even in that respect it was not perfect. God has a better bread to give, a bread which will sustain you in spiritual life, not for a few years but for ever" (vv. 49, 50). "I am the living bread which came down out of heaven: if any man eat of this bread, he shall live for ever."

This they could not understand. They believed that the manna came from heaven. Not the richest field of Egypt had produced it. It seemed to come direct from God's hand. The Israelites could neither raise it nor improve upon it. But how Jesus, "whose father and mother we know," whom they could trace to a definite human origin, could say that He came from heaven they could not understand. And yet, even while they stumbled at His claim to a superhuman origin, they felt there might be something in it. Everyone with whom He came in contact felt there was in Him something unaccountable. The Pharisees feared while they hated Him. Pilate could not classify Him with any variety of offender he had met with. Why do men still continually attempt afresh to account for Him, and to give at last a perfectly satisfactory explanation, on ordinary principles, of all that He was and did? Why, but because it is seen that as yet He has not been so accounted for? Men do not thus strive to prove that Shakespeare was a mere man, or that Socrates or Epictetus was a mere man. Alas! that is only too obvious. But to Christ men turn and turn again with the feeling that here is something which human nature does not account for; something different, and something more than what results from human parentage and human environment, something which He Himself accounts for by the plain and unflinching statement that He is "from heaven."

For my part, I do not see that this can mean anything less than that Christ is Divine, that in Him we have God, and in Him touch the actual Source of all life. In Him we have the one thing within our reach which is not earth-grown, the one uncorrupted Source of life to which we can turn from the inadequacy, impurity, and emptiness of a sin-sick world. No pebble lies hid in this bread on which we can break our teeth; no sweetness in the mouth turning afterwards to bitterness, but a new, uncontaminated food, prepared independently of all defiling influences, and accessible to all. Christ is the Bread from heaven, because in Christ God gives Himself to us, that by His life we may live.

There is another sense in which Christ probably used the word "living." In contrast to the dead bread He had given them He was alive. The same law seems to hold good of our physical and of our spiritual life. We cannot sustain physical life except by using as food that which has been alive. The nutritive properties of the earth and the air must have been assimilated for us by living plants and animals before we can use them. The plant sucks sustenance out of the earth--we can live upon the plant but not on the earth. The ox finds ample nourishment in grass; we can live on the ox but not on the grass. And so with spiritual nutriment. Abstract truth we can make little of at first hand; it needs to be embodied in a living form before we can live upon it. Even God is remote and abstract, and non-Christian theism makes thin-blooded and spectral worshippers; it is when the Word becomes flesh; when the hidden reason of all things takes human form and steps out on the earth before us, that truth becomes nutritive, and God our life.

4. Still more explicitly Christ says: "The bread which I will give is My flesh, which I will give for the life of the world." For it is in this great act of dying that He becomes the Bread of Life. God sharing with us to the uttermost; God proving that His will is our righteousness; God bearing our sorrows and our sins; God coming into our human race, and becoming a part of its history--all this is seen in the cross of Christ; but it is also seen that absolute love for men, and absolute submission to God, were the moving forces of Christ's life. He was obedient even unto death. This was His life, and by the cross He made it ours. The cross subdues our hearts to Him, and gives us to feel that self-sacrifice is the true life of man.

A man in a sickly state of body has sometimes to make it matter of consideration, or even of consultation, what he shall eat. Were anyone to take the same thought about his spiritual condition, and seriously ponder what would bring health to his spirit, what would rid it of distaste for what is right, and give it strength and purity to delight in God and in all good, he would probably conclude that a clear and influential exhibition of God's goodness, and of the fatal effects of sin, a convincing exhibition, an exhibition in real life, of the unutterable hatefulness of sin, and inconceivable desirableness of God; an exhibition also which should at the same time open for us a way from sin to God--this, the inquirer would conclude, would bring life to the spirit. It is such an exhibition of God and of sin, and such a way out of sin to God, as we have in Christ's death.

5. How are we to avail ourselves of the life that is in Christ? As the Jews asked, How can this man give us His flesh to eat? Our Lord Himself uses several terms to express the act by which we make use of Him as the Bread of Life. "He that believeth on Me," "He that cometh to Me," "He that eateth My flesh and drinketh My blood, hath eternal life." Each of these expressions has its own significance. Belief must come first--belief that Christ is sent to give us life; belief that it depends upon our connection with that one Person whether we shall or shall not have life eternal. We must also "come to Him." The people He was addressing had followed Him for miles, and had found Him and were speaking to Him, but they had not come to Him. To come to Him is to approach Him in spirit and with submissive trust; it is to commit ourselves to Him as our Lord; it is to rest in Him as our all; it is to come to Him with open heart, accepting Him as all He claims to be; it is to meet the eye of a present, living Christ, who knows what is in man, and to say to Him "I am Thine, Thine most gladly, Thine for evermore."

But most emphatically of all does our Lord say that we must "eat His flesh and drink His blood" if we are to partake of His life. That is to say, the connection between Christ and us must be of the closest possible kind; so close that the assimilation of the food we eat is not too strong a figure to express it.

The food we eat becomes our blood and flesh; it becomes our life, our self. And it does so by our eating it, not by our talking of it, not by our looking at it, and admiring its nutritive properties, but only by eating it. And whatever process can make Christ entirely ours, and help us to assimilate all that is in Him, this process we are to use. The flesh of Christ was given for us; by the shedding of Christ's blood, by the pouring out of His life upon the cross, spiritual life was prepared for us. Cleansing from sin and restoration to God were provided by the offering of His life in the flesh; and we eat His flesh when we use in our own behalf the death of Christ, and take the blessings it has made possible to us; when we accept the forgiveness of sins, enter into the love of God, and adopt as our own the spirit of the cross. His flesh or human form was the manifestation of God's love for us, the visible material of His sacrifice; and we eat His flesh when we make this our own, when we accept God's love and adopt Christ's sacrifice as our guiding principle of life. We eat His flesh when we take out of His life and death the spiritual nutriment that is actually there; when we let our nature be penetrated by the spirit of the cross, and actually make Christ the Source and the Guide of our spiritual life.

This figure of eating has many lessons for us. Above all, it reminds us of the poor appetite we have for spiritual nourishment. How thoroughly by this process of eating does the healthy body extract from its food every particle of real nutriment. By this process the food is made to yield all that it contains of nourishing substance. But how far is this from representing our treatment of Christ. How much is there in Him that is fitted to yield comfort and hope, and yet to us it yields none. How much that should fill us with assurance of God's love, yet how fearfully we live. How much to make us admire self-sacrifice and fill us with earnest purpose to live for others, and yet how little of this becomes in very deed our life. God sees in Him all that can make us complete, all that can fill and gladden and suffice the soul, and yet how bare and troubled and defeated do we live. [24]

6. The mode of distribution was also significant. Christ gives life to the world not directly, but through His disciples. The life He gives is Himself, but He gives it through the instrumentality of men. The bread is His. The disciples may manipulate it as they will, but it remains five loaves only. None but He can relieve the famishing multitude. Still not with His own hands does He feed them, but through the believing service of the Twelve. And this He did not merely for the sake of teaching us that only through the Church is the world supplied with the life He furnishes, but primarily because it was the natural and fit order then, as it is the natural and fit order now, that they who themselves believe in the power of the Lord to feed the world should be the means of distributing what He gives. Each of the disciples received from the Lord no more than would satisfy himself, yet held in his hand what would through the Lord's blessing satisfy a hundred besides. And it is a grave truth we here meet, that every one of us who has received life from Christ has thereby in possession what may give life to many other human souls. We may give it or we may withhold it; we may communicate it to the famishing souls around us or we may hear unconcerned the weary heart-faint sigh; but the Lord knows to whom He has given the bread of life, and He gives it not solely for our own consumption but for distribution. It is not the privilege of the more enlightened or more fervent disciple, but of all. He who receives from the Lord what is enough for himself holds the lives of some of his fellows in his hand.

Doubtless the faith of the disciples was severely tried when they were required to advance each man to his separate hundred with his morsel of bread. There would be no struggling for the first place then. But encouraged in their faith by the simple and confident words of prayer their Master had addressed to the Father, they are emboldened to do His bidding, and if they gave sparingly and cautiously at first, their parsimony must soon have been rebuked and their hearts enlarged.

Theirs is also our trial. We know we should be more helpful to others; but in presence of the sorrowful we seem to have no word of comfort; seeing this man and that pursuing a way the end of which is death, we have yet no wise word of remonstrance, no loving entreaty; lives are trifled away at our side, and we are conscious of no ability to elevate and dignify; lives are worn out in crushing toil and misery, and we feel helpless to aid. The habit grows upon us of expecting rather to get good than to do good. We have long recognised that we are too little influenced by God's grace, and only at long intervals now are we ashamed of this; it has become our acknowledged state. We have found that we are not the kind of people who are to influence others. Looking at our slim faith, our stunted character, our slender knowledge, we say, "What is this among so many?" These feelings are inevitable. No man seems to have enough even for his own soul. But giving of what he has to others he will find his own store increased. "There is that scattereth abroad and yet increaseth," is the law of spiritual growth.

But the thought which shines through all others as we read this narrative is the genial tenderness of Christ. He is here seen to be considerate of our wants, mindful of our weaknesses, quick to calculate our prospects and to provide for us, simple, practical, earnest in His love. We see here how He withholds no good thing from us, but considers and gives what we actually need. We see how reasonable it is that He should require us to trust Him. To every fainting soul, to every one who has wandered far and whose strength is gone, and round whom the shadows and chills of night are gathering, He says through this miracle: "Wherefore do ye spend money for that which is not bread, and your labour for that which satisfieth not? Hearken diligently unto Me, and eat ye that which is good, and let your soul delight itself in fatness." [25]

Footnotes:

21. At the risk of omitting points of interest, I have thought it advisable to treat this whole representation of Christ, as far as possible, within the limits of one chapter.

22. Roughly speaking, Â£8.

23. From Psalm lxxii. 16 the Rabbis gathered that the Messiah when He came would renew the gift of manna.

24. The figure of eating reminds us that the acceptance of Christ is an act which each man must do for himself. No other man can eat for me. It also reminds us that as the food we eat is distributed, without our own will or supervision, to every part of the body, giving light to the eye and strength to the arm, making bone or skin in one place, nerve or blood-vessel in another, so, if only we make Christ our own, the life that is in Him suffices for all the requirements of human nature and human duty.

25. On verses 37, 44, and 45 see note at the end of this volume.

XV. THE CRISIS IN GALILEE

"Many therefore of His disciples, when they heard this, said, This is a hard saying; who can hear it? But Jesus knowing in Himself that His disciples murmured at this, said unto them, Doth this cause you to stumble? What then if ye should behold the Son of man ascending where He was before? It is the spirit that quickeneth; the flesh profiteth nothing: the words that I have spoken unto you are spirit, and are life. But there are some of you that believe not. For Jesus knew from the beginning who they were that believed not, and who it was that should betray Him. And He said, For this cause have I said unto you, that no man can come unto Me, except it be given unto him of the Father. Upon this many of His disciples went back, and walked no more with Him. Jesus said therefore unto the twelve, Would ye also go away? Simon Peter answered Him, Lord, to whom shall we go? thou hast the words of eternal life. And we have believed and know that Thou art the Holy One of God. Jesus answered them, Did not I choose you the twelve, and one of you is a devil? Now He spake of Judas the son of Simon Iscariot, for he it was that should betray Him, being one of the twelve."--John vi. 60--71.

The situation in which our Lord found Himself at this stage of His career is full of pathos. He began His ministry in Judæa, and His success there seemed to be all that could be desired. But it soon became apparent that the crowds who followed Him misunderstood or wilfully ignored His purpose. They resorted to Him chiefly, if not solely, for material advantages and political ends. He was in danger of being accounted the most skilful metropolitan physician; or in the greater danger of being courted by politicians as a likely popular leader, who might be used as a revolutionary flag or party cry. He, therefore, left Jerusalem at an early period in His ministry and betook Himself to Galilee; and now, after some months' preaching and mingling with the people, things have worked round in Galilee to precisely the same point as they had reached in Judæa. Great crowds are following Him to be healed and to be fed, while the politically inclined have at last made a distinct effort to make Him a king, to force Him into a collision with the authorities. His proper work is in danger of being lost sight of. He finds it necessary to sift the crowds who follow Him. And He does so by addressing them in terms which can be acceptable only to truly spiritual men--by plainly assuring them that He was among them, not to give them political privileges and the bread that perisheth, but the bread that endureth. They found Him to be what they would call an impracticable dreamer. They profess to go away because they cannot understand Him; but they understand Him well enough to see He is not the person for their purposes. They seek earth, and heaven is thrust upon them. They turn away disappointed, and many walk no more with Him. The great crowd melts away, and He is left with His original following of twelve men. His months of teaching and toil seem to have gone for nothing. It might seem doubtful if even the twelve would be faithful--if any result of His work would remain, if any would cordially and lovingly adhere to Him.

One cannot, I think, view this situation without perceiving how analogous it is in many respects to the aspect of things in our own day. In all ages of course this sifting of the followers of Christ goes on. There are experiences common to all times and places which test men's attachment to Christ. But in our own day exceptional causes are producing a considerable diminution of the numbers who follow Christ, or at least are altering considerably the grounds on which they profess to follow Him. When one views the defection of men of influence, of thought, of learning, of earnest and devout spirit, one cannot but wonder what is to be the end of this, and how far it is to extend. One cannot but look anxiously at those who seem to remain, and to say, "Will ye also go away?" No doubt such times of sifting are of eminent service in winnowing out the true from the mistaken followers, and in summoning all men to revise the reason of their attachment to Christ. When we see men of serious mind and of great attainments deliberately abandoning the Christian position, we cannot but anxiously inquire whether we are right in maintaining that position. When the question comes to us, as in Providence it does, "Will ye also go away?" we must have our answer ready.

The answer of Peter clearly shows what it was that bound the faithful few to Jesus; and in his answer three reasons for faith may be discerned.

1. Jesus satisfied their deepest spiritual wants. They had found in Him provision for their whole nature, and had learned the truth of His saying, "He that cometh to Me shall never hunger, and He that believeth on Me shall never thirst." They could now say, "Thou hast the words of eternal life." His words made water into wine, and five loaves into five thousand, but His words did what was far more to

their purpose,--they fed their spirit. His words brought them nearer to God, promised them eternal life, and began it within them. From the lips of Jesus had actually fallen words which quickened within them a new life--a life which they recognised as eternal, as lifting them up into another world. These words of His had given them new thoughts about God and about righteousness, they had stirred hopes and feelings of an altogether new kind. And this spiritual life was more to them than anything else. No doubt these men, like their neighbours, had their faults, their private ambitions, their hopes. Peter could not forget that he had left all for his Master, and often thought of his home, his plentiful table, his family, when wandering about with Jesus. They all, probably, had an expectation that their abandonment of their occupations would not be wholly without compensation in this life, and that prominent position and worldly advantage awaited them. Still, when they discovered that these were mistaken expectations, they did not grumble nor go back, for such were not their chief reasons for following Jesus. It was chiefly by His appeal to their spiritual leanings that He attracted them. It was rather for eternal life than for present advantage they attached themselves to Him. They found more of God in Him than elsewhere, and listening to Him they found themselves better men than before; and having experienced that His words were "spirit and life" (ver. 63), they could not now abandon Him though all the world did so.

So is it always. When Christ sifts His followers those remain who have spiritual tastes and wants. The spiritual man, the man who would rather be like God than be rich, whose efforts after worldly advancement are not half as earnest and sustained as His efforts after spiritual health; the man, in short, who seeks first the kingdom of God and His righteousness, and lets other things be added or not to this prime requisite, cleaves to Christ because there is that in Christ which satisfies his tastes and gives him the life he chiefly desires. There is in Christ a suitableness to the wants of men who live in view of God and eternity, and who seek to adjust themselves, not only to the world around them so as to be comfortable and successful in it, but also to the things unseen, to the permanent laws which are to govern human beings and human affairs throughout eternity. Such men find in Christ that which enables them to adjust themselves to things eternal. They find in Christ just that revelation of God, and that reconcilement to Him, and that help to abiding in Him, which they need. They cannot imagine a time, they cannot picture to themselves a state of society, in which the words and teaching of Jesus would not be the safest guide and the highest law. Life eternal, life for men as men, is taught by Him; not professional life, not the life of a religious rule that must pass away, not life for this world only, but life eternal, life such as men everywhere and always ought to live--this is apprehended by Him and explained by Him; and power and desire to live it is quickened within men by His words. Coming into His presence we recognise the assuredness of perfect knowledge, the simplicity of perfect truth. That which outrides all such critical times as the disciples were now passing through is true spirituality of mind. The man who is bent on nourishing his spirit to life everlasting simply cannot dispense with what he finds in Christ.

We need not then greatly fear for our own faith if we are sure that we covet the words of eternal life more than the path to worldly advantage. Still less need we tremble for the faith of others if we know that their tastes are spiritual, their leanings Godward. Parents are naturally anxious about their children's faith, and fear it may be endangered by the advances of science or by the old props of faith being shaken. Such anxiety is in great measure misdirected. Let parents see to it that their children grow up with a preference for purity, unselfishness, truth, unworldliness; let parents set before their children an example of real preference for things spiritual, and let them with God's aid cultivate in their children an appetite for what is heavenly, a craving to live on terms with God and with conscience; and this appetite will infallibly lead them to Christ. Does Christ supply the wants of our spirits? Can He show us the way to eternal life? Have men found in Him all needed help to godly living? Have the most spiritual and ardent of men been precisely those who have most clearly seen their need of Him, and who have found in Him everything to satisfy and feed their own spiritual ardour? Has He, that is to say, the words of eternal life? Is He the Person to whom every man must listen if he would find his way to God and a happy eternity? Then, depend upon it, men will believe in Christ in every generation, and none the less firmly because their attention is called off from non-essential and external evidences to the simple sufficiency of Christ.

2. Peter was convinced not only that Jesus had the words of eternal life, but that no one else had. "To whom shall we go?" Peter had not an exhaustive knowledge of all sources of human wisdom; but speaking from his own experience he affirmed his conviction that it was useless to seek life eternal anywhere else than in Jesus. And it seems equally hopeless still to look to any other quarter for sufficient teaching, for words that are "spirit and life." Where but in Christ do we find a God we can accept as God? Where but in Him do we find that which can not only encourage men striving after virtue, but also reclaim the vicious? To put anyone alongside of Christ as a revealer of God, as a pattern of virtue, as a Saviour of men, is absurd. There is that in Him which we recognise as not merely superior, but of another kind. So that those who reject Him, or set Him on a level with other teachers, have first of all to reject the chief part of what His contemporaries were struck with and reported, and to

fashion a Christ of their own.

And it should be observed that Christ claims this exceptional homage from His people. The "following" He requires is not a mere acceptance of His teaching alongside of other teaching, nor an acceptance of His teaching apart from Himself, as if a man should listen to Him and go home and try to practise what he has heard; but He requires men to form a connection with Himself as their King and Life, as that One who can alone give them strength to obey Him. To call Him "the Teacher," as if this were His sole or chief title, is to mislead.

The alternative, then, as Peter saw, was Christ or nothing. And every day it is becoming clearer that this is the alternative, that between Christianity and the blankest Atheism there is no middle place. Indeed we may say that between Christianity, with its supernatural facts, and materialism, which admits of no supernatural at all, and of nothing spiritual and immortal, there is no logical standing-ground. A man's choice lies between these two--either Christ with His claims in all their fulness, or a material universe working out its life under the impulse of some inscrutable force. There are of course men who are neither Christians nor materialists; but that is because they have not yet found their intellectual resting-place. As soon as they obey reason, they will travel to one or other of these extremes, for between the two is no logical standing-ground. If there is a God, then there seems nothing incredible, nothing even very surprising, in Christianity. Christianity becomes merely the flower or fruit for which the world exists, the element in the world's history which gives meaning and glory to the whole of it: without Christianity and all it involves the world lacks interest of the highest kind. If a man finds he cannot admit the possibility of such an interference in the world's monotonous way as the Incarnation implies, it is because there is in his mind an Atheistic tendency, a tendency to make the laws of the world more than the Creator; to make the world itself God, the highest thing. The Atheist's position is thoroughgoing and logical; and against the Atheist the man who professes to believe in a Personal God and yet denies miracle is helpless. And in point of fact Atheistic writers are rapidly sweeping the field of all other antagonists, and the intermediate positions between Christianity and Atheism are becoming daily more untenable.

Any one then who is offended at the supernatural in Christianity, and is disposed to turn away and walk no more with Christ, should view the alternative, and consider what it is with which he must throw in his lot. To retain what is called the spirit of Christ, and reject all that is miraculous and above our present comprehension, is to commit oneself to a path which naturally leads to disbelief in God. We must choose between Christ as He stands in the gospels, claiming to be Divine, rising from the dead and now alive; and a world in which there is no God manifest in the flesh or anywhere else, a world that has come into being no one knows how or whence, and that is running on no one knows whither, unguided by any intelligence outside of itself, wholly governed by laws which have grown out of some impersonal force of which nobody can give any good account. Difficult as it is to believe in Christ, it is surely still more difficult to believe in the only alternative, a world wholly material, in which matter rules and spirit is a mere accident of no account. If there are inexplicable things in the gospel, there are also in us and around us facts wholly inexplicable on the atheistic theory. If the Christian must be content to wait for the solution of many mysteries, so certainly must the materialist be content to leave unsolved many of the most important problems of human life. [26]

3. The third reason which Peter assigns for the unalterable loyalty of the Twelve is expressed in the words, "We have believed and know that Thou art the Holy One of God." By this he probably meant that he and the rest had come to be convinced that Jesus was the Christ, the Messiah, the consecrated One, whom God had set apart to this office. The same expression was used by the demoniac in the synagogue at Capernaum. [27] But although the idea of consecration to an office rather than the idea of personal holiness is prominent in the word, it may very well have been the personal holiness of their Master which bore in upon the minds of the disciples that He was indeed the Messiah. By His life with them from day to day He revealed God to them. They had seen Him in a great variety of circumstances. They had seen His compassion for every form of sorrow and misery, and His regardlessness of self; they had marked His behaviour when offered a crown and when threatened with the cross; they had seen Him at table in gay company, and they had seen Him fasting and in houses of mourning, in danger, in vehement discussion, in retirement; and in all circumstances and scenes they had found Him holy, so holy that to turn from Him they felt would be to turn from God.

The emphasis with which they affirm their conviction is remarkable: "We have believed and we know." It is as if they felt, We may be doubtful of much and ignorant of much, but this at least we are sure of. We see men leaving our company who are fit to instruct and guide us in most matters, but they do not know our Lord as we do. What they have said has disturbed our minds and has caused us to revise our beliefs, but we return to our old position, "We have believed and we know." It may be true that devils have been cast out by the prince of the devils; we do not know. But a stainless life is more miraculous and Divine than the casting out of devils; it is more unknown in the world, referrible to no freak of nature, accomplished by no sleight of hand or jugglery, but due only to the presence of God. Here we have not the sign or evidence of the thing but the thing itself, God not using man as an external agent for operating upon the material world, but God present in the man, living in his life, one with him.

Upon our faith nothing is more influential than the holiness of Christ. Nothing is more certainly Divine. Nothing is more characteristic of God--not His power, not His wisdom, not even His eternal Being. He who in his own person and life represents to us the holiness of God is more certainly superhuman than he who represents God's power. A power to work miracles has often been delegated to men, but holiness cannot be so delegated. It belongs to character, to the man's self; it is a thing of nature, of will, and of habit; a king may give to his ambassador ample powers, he may fill his hands with credentials, and load him with gifts which shall be acceptable to the monarch to whom he is sent, but he cannot give him a tact he does not naturally possess, a courtesy he has not acquired by dealing with other princes, nor the influence of wise and magnanimous words, if these do not inherently belong to the ambassador's self. So the holiness of Christ was even more convincing than His power or His message. It was such a holiness as caused the disciples to feel that He was not a mere messenger. His holiness revealed Himself as well as Him that sent Him; and the self that was thus revealed they felt to be more than human. When, therefore, their faith was tried by seeing the multitudes abandon their Lord, they were thrown back on their surest ground of confidence in Him; and that surest ground was not the miracles which all had seen, but the consecrated and perfect life which was known to them.

To ourselves, then, I say, by the circumstances of our time this question comes, "Will ye also go away?" Will you be like the rest, or will exceptional fidelity be found in you? Is your attachment to Christ so based on personal conviction, is it so truly the growth of your own experience, and so little a mere echo of popular opinion, that you say in your heart, "Though all men should forsake Thee, yet will not I"? It is difficult to resist the current of thought and opinion that prevails around us; difficult to dispute or even question the opinion of men who have been our teachers, and who have first awakened our mind to see the majesty of truth and the beauty of the universe; it is difficult to choose our own way, and thus tacitly condemn the choice and the way of men we know to be purer in life, and in every essential respect better than ourselves. And yet, perhaps, it is well that we are thus compelled to make up our own mind, to examine the claims of Christ for ourselves, and so follow Him with the resolution that comes of personal conviction. It is this our Lord desires. He does not compel nor hasten our decision. He does not upbraid His followers for their serious misunderstandings of His person. He allows them to be familiar with Him even while labouring under many misconceptions, because He knows that these misconceptions will most surely pass away in His society and by further acquaintance with Him. One thing He insists upon, one thing He asks from us--that we follow Him. We may only have a vague impression that He is quite different from all else we know; we may be doubtful, as yet, in what sense some of the highest titles are ascribed to Him; we may be quite mistaken about the significance of certain important parts of His life; we may disagree among ourselves regarding the nature of His kingdom and regarding the conditions of entrance into it; but, if we follow Him, if we join our fortunes to His, and wish nothing better than to be within the sound of His voice and to do His bidding; if we truly love Him, and find that He has taken a place in our life we cannot ever give to another; if we are conscious that our future lies His way, and that we must in heart abide with Him, then all our slowness to understand is patiently dealt with, all our underrating of His real dignity is forgiven us, and we are led on in His company to perfect conformity, perfect union, and perfect knowledge.

All that He desires, then, is, in the first place, not something we cannot give, not a belief in certain truths about which doubt may reasonably be entertained, not an acknowledgment of facts that are as yet beyond our vision; but, that we follow Him, that we be in this world as He was in it. Shall we, then, let Him pursue His way alone, shall we do nothing to forward His purposes, shall we show no sympathy, address no word to Him, and pretend not to hear when He speaks to us? To drag ourselves along murmuring, doubting, making difficulties, a mere dead weight on our Leader, this is not to follow as He desires to be followed. To take our own way in the main, and only appear here and there on the road He has taken; to be always trying to combine the pursuit of our own private ends with the pursuance of His ends, is not to follow. Had we seen these men asking leave of absence two or three times a month to go and look after the fishing, even though they promised to overtake their Master somewhere on the road, we should scarcely have recognised them as His followers. Had we found them, on reaching a village at night, leaving Him, and preferring to spend their leisure with His enemies, we should have been inclined to ask an explanation of conduct so inconsistent. Yet is not our own following very much of this kind? Is there not too little of the following that says, "What is enough for the Lord is enough for me; His aims are enough for me"? Is there not too little of the following that springs from a frank and genuine dealing with the Lord from day to day, and from a conscientious desire to meet His will with us, and satisfy His idea of how we should follow Him? May we each have the peace and joy of the man who, when this question, "Will ye also go away?" comes to him, quickly and from the heart responds, "I will never forsake Thee."

Footnotes:

26. "Those who turn their backs on the Eternal Son must understand, then, that they are on their way to a creed which denies an Eternal Father, and puts in His place an unconscious impersonal soul of nature, a dead central force, of which all the forces in the universe are manifestations; or an unknown, unknowable cause, remaining to be postulated after the series of physical causes has been traced as far back as science can go; and which robs mortal man of the hope that the seed sown in the churchyard shall one day be reaped in the harvest of the resurrection.... Your so-called Christianity independent of dogmas is but the evening twilight of faith, the light which lingers in the spiritual atmosphere after the sun of truth has gone down."--Dr. Bruce, Training of the Twelve, p. 154, a book to which I am greatly indebted here and elsewhere.

27. Mark i. 24.

Marcus Dods, D.D.

XVI. JESUS DISCUSSED IN JERUSALEM

"And after these things Jesus walked in Galilee: for He would not walk in Judæa, because the Jews sought to kill Him. Now the feast of the Jews, the feast of tabernacles, was at hand. His brethren therefore said unto Him, Depart hence, and go into Judæa, that Thy disciples also may behold Thy works which Thou doest. For no man doeth anything in secret, and himself seeketh to be known openly. If Thou doest these things, manifest Thyself to the world. For even His brethren did not believe on Him. Jesus therefore saith unto them, My time is not yet come; but your time is alway ready. The world cannot hate you; but Me it hateth, because I testify of it, that its works are evil. Go ye up unto the feast: I go not up yet unto this feast; because My time is not yet fulfilled. And having said these things unto them, He abode still in Galilee. But when His brethren were gone up unto the feast, then went He also up, not publicly, but as it were in secret. The Jews therefore sought Him at the feast, and said, Where is He? And there was much murmuring among the multitudes concerning Him: some said, He is a good man; others said, Not so, but He leadeth the multitude astray. Howbeit no man spoke openly of Him for fear of the Jews. But when it was now the midst of the feast Jesus went up into the temple, and taught. The Jews therefore marvelled, saying, How knoweth this man letters, having never learned? Jesus therefore answered them, and said, My teaching is not Mine but His that sent Me. If any man willeth to do His will he shall know of the teaching, whether it be of God, or whether I speak from Myself. He that speaketh from himself seeketh his own glory: but he that seeketh the glory of him that sent him, the same is true, and no unrighteousness is in him. Did not Moses give you the law, and yet none of you doeth the law? Why seek ye to kill Me? The multitude answered, Thou hast a devil: who seeketh to kill Thee? Jesus answered and said unto them, I did one work, and ye all marvel. For this cause hath Moses given you circumcision (not that it is of Moses, but of the fathers); and on the Sabbath ye circumcise a man. If a man receiveth circumcision on the Sabbath, that the law of Moses may not be broken; are ye wroth with Me, because I made a man every whit whole on the Sabbath? Judge not according to appearance, but judge righteous judgement. Some therefore of them of Jerusalem said, Is not this He whom they seek to kill? And lo, He speaketh openly, and they say nothing unto Him. Can it be that the rulers indeed know that this is the Christ? Howbeit we know this man whence He is; but when the Christ cometh, no one knoweth whence He is. Jesus therefore cried in the temple, teaching and saying, Ye both know Me, and know whence I am; and I am not come of Myself, but He that sent Me is true, whom ye know not. I know Him; because I am from Him, and He sent Me. They sought therefore to take Him: and no man laid his hand on Him, because His hour was not yet come. But of the multitude many believed on Him; and they said, When the Christ shall come, will He do more signs than those which this man hath done? The Pharisees heard the multitude murmuring these things concerning Him; and the chief priests and the Pharisees sent officers to take Him. Jesus therefore said, Yet a little while am I with you, and I go unto Him that sent Me. Ye shall seek Me, and shall not find Me: and where I am, ye cannot come. The Jews therefore said among themselves, Whither will this man go that we shall not find Him? will He go unto the Dispersion among the Greeks, and teach the Greeks? What is this word that He said, Ye shall seek Me, and shall not find Me: and where I am, ye cannot come? Now on the last day, the great day of the feast, Jesus stood and cried, saying, If any man thirst, let him come unto Me and drink. He that believeth on Me, as the Scripture hath said, out of his belly shall flow rivers of living water. But this spake He of the Spirit, which they that believed on Him were to receive: for the Spirit was not yet given: because Jesus was not yet glorified. Some of the multitude therefore, when they heard these words, said, This is of a truth the prophet. Others said, This is the Christ. But some said, What, doth the Christ come out of Galilee? Hath not the Scripture said that the Christ cometh of the seed of David, and from Bethlehem, the village where David was? So there arose a division in the multitude because of Him. And some of them would have taken Him; but no man laid hands on Him. The officers therefore came to the chief priests and Pharisees; and they said unto them, Why did ye not bring Him? The officers answered, Never man so spake. The Pharisees therefore answered them, Are ye also led astray? Hath any of the rulers believed on Him, or of the Pharisees? But this multitude which knoweth not the law are accursed. Nicodemus saith unto them (he that came to Him before, being one of them), Doth our law judge a man, except it first hear from himself and know what he doeth? They answered and said unto him, Art thou also of Galilee? Search, and see that out of Galilee ariseth no prophet."--John vii.

After describing how matters were brought to a crisis in Galilee, and pointing out that, as the result of our Lord's work there, only twelve men adhered to Him, and in even this final selection not all were to be trusted,--John passes on to describe the state of feeling towards Jesus in Jerusalem, and how the storm of unbelief gathered until it broke in violence and outrage. [28] This seventh chapter is intended to put us in the right point of view by exhibiting the various estimates that were formed of the work and person of Jesus, and the opinions which any one might hear uttered regarding Him at every table in Jerusalem.

But the motive of His going to Jerusalem at all calls for remark. His brothers, who might have been expected to understand His character best, were very slow to believe in Him. They only felt He was different from themselves, and they were nettled by His peculiarity. But they felt that the credit of the family was involved, and also that if His claims should turn out to be true, their position as brothers of the Messiah would be flattering. Accordingly they betray considerable anxiety to have His claims pronounced upon; and seeing that His work in Galilee had come to so little, they do their utmost to provoke Him to appeal at once to the central authority at Jerusalem. They did not as yet believe in Him, they could not entertain the idea that the boy they had knocked about and made to run their messages could be the long-expected King; and yet there was such trustworthy report of the extraordinary things He had done, that they felt there was something puzzling about Him, and for the sake of putting an end to their suspense they do what they can to get Him to go again to Jerusalem. The lever they use to move Him is a taunt: "If these works of yours are genuine miracles, don't hang about villages and little country towns, but go and show yourself in the capital. No one who is really confident that he has a claim on public attention wanders about in solitary places, but repairs to the most crowded haunts of men. Go up now to the feast, and your disciples will gather round you, and your claims will be settled once for all."

To this Jesus replies that the hour for such a proclamation of Himself has not yet come. That hour is to come. At the following Passover He entered Jerusalem in the manner desired by His brethren, and the result, as He foresaw, was His death. As yet such a demonstration was premature. The brothers of Jesus did not apprehend the virulence of hatred which Jesus aroused, and did not perceive how surely His death would result from His going up to the feast as the acknowledged King of the GalilÃ¦ans. He Himself sees all this plainly, and therefore declines the plan of operation proposed by His brothers; and instead of going up with them as the proclaimed Messiah, He goes up quietly by Himself a few days after. To go up as His brothers' nominee, or to go up in the way they proposed, was counter to the whole plan of His life. Their ideas and proposals were made from a point of view wholly different from His. Very often we can do at our own instance, in our own way and at our own time, what it would be a vast mistake to do at the instigation of people who look at the matter differently from ourselves, and have quite another purpose to serve. Jesus could safely do without display what He could not do ostentatiously; and He could do as His Father's servant what He could not do at the whim of His brothers.

The feast to which He thus quietly went up was the Feast of Tabernacles. This feast was a kind of national harvest home; and consequently in appointing it God commanded that it should be held "in the end of the year, when thou hast gathered in thy labours out of the field;" that is to say, in the end of the natural year, or in early autumn, when the farm operations finished one rotation and began a new series. It was a feast, therefore, full of rejoicing. [29] Every Israelite appeared in holiday attire, bearing in his hands a palm-branch, or wearing some significant emblem of earth's fruitfulness. At night the city was brilliantly illuminated, especially round the Temple, in which great lamps, used only on these occasions, were lit, and which possibly occasioned our Lord's remark at this time, as reported in the following chapter, "I am the Light of the world." There can be little doubt that when, on the last day of the feast, He stood and cried, "If any man thirst, let him come unto Me and drink," the form of his invitation was moulded by one of the customs of the feast. For one of the most striking features of the feast was the drawing of water in a golden vessel from the pool of Siloam, and carrying it in procession to the Temple, where it was poured out with such a burst of triumph from the trumpets of the Levites, aided by the Hallelujahs of the people, that it became a common Jewish saying, "He who has not seen the rejoicing at the pouring out of the water from the pool of Siloam has never seen rejoicing in his life." This pouring out of the water before God seemed to be an acknowledgment of His goodness in watering the corn-lands and pastures, and also a commemoration of the miraculous supply of water in the desert; while to some of the more enlightened it bore also a spiritual significance, and recalled the words of Isaiah, "With joy shall ye draw water out of the wells of salvation."

But this feast was not solely a celebration of the ingathering, or a thanksgiving for the harvest. The name of it reminds us that another feature was quite as prominent. In its original institution God commanded, "Ye shall dwell in booths or tabernacles seven days; all that are Israelites born shall dwell in booths," the reason being added, "that your generations may know that I made the children of Israel to dwell in booths when I brought them out of the land of Egypt." The particular significance of the Israelites dwelling in booths seems to be that it marked their deliverance from a life of bondage to a life of freedom; it reminded them how they had once no settled habitation, but yet found a booth in the desert preferable to the well-provided residences of Egypt. And every Feast of Tabernacles seemed intended to recall these thoughts. In the midst of their harvest, at the end of the year, when they were once more laying up store for winter, and when every one was reckoning whether it would be an abundant and profitable year for him or no, they were told to live for a week in booths, that they might think of that period in their fathers' experience when God was their all, when they had no provision for the morrow, and which was yet the most triumphant period of their history. All wealth, all distinctions of rank, all separation between rich and poor, was for a while forgotten, as each man dwelt in his little green hut as well sheltered as his neighbour. And to every one was suggested the thought, that let the coming winter be well provided or ill provided, let it be bleak to some and bright to others, at bottom the provision of this world is to all alike but as a green bough between them and destitution; but that all alike, reduce them if you will to a booth which has neither store nor couch in it, have still the Most High God for their deliverer, and provider, and habitation.[30]

Even before Jesus appeared at this feast He was the subject of much talk and exchange of opinions.

1. The first characteristic of the popular mind, as exhibited here by John, is its subservience to authority. Those who had a favourable opinion of Jesus uttered it with reserve and caution, "for fear of the Jews"--that is, of the Jerusalem Jews, who were known to be adverse to His claims. And the authorities, knowing the subservience of the people, considered it a sufficient reply to the favourable reports brought them by their own officers, to say, "Have any of the rulers or of the Pharisees believed on Him?" This seems a very childish mode of settling a great question, and we are ready to charge the Jews with a singular lack of independence; but we reflect that among ourselves great questions are settled very much by authority still. In politics we take our cue from one or two newspapers, conducted by men who show themselves quite fallible; and in matters of even deeper moment, how many of us can say we have thought out a creed for ourselves, and have not accepted our ideas from recognised teachers? And whether these teachers be the accredited representatives of traditional theology, or have secured an audience by their departure from ordinary views, we have in our own conscience a surer guide to the truth about Christ. For much that we may build upon the foundation we must be indebted to others; but for that which is radical, for the determination of the relation we ourselves are to hold to Christ, we must follow not authority but our own conscience.

Our equanimity need not, then, be greatly disturbed by the fact that so many of the rulers of public opinion do not believe in Christ. We need not tremble for Christianity when we see how widely extended is the opinion that miracles are the fancy of a credulous age. We need not be over-anxious or altogether downcast when we hear philosophers sublimely talk as if they had seen all round Christ, and taken His measure, and rendered satisfactory account of the pious delusions He Himself was subject to, and the groundless hallucinations which misled His followers into unheard-of virtue, and made them good men by mistake. Consider the opinions of men of insight and of power, but do not be overawed by them, for you have in yourself a surer guide to truth. Look at Christ with your own eyes, frankly open your own soul before Him, and trust the impression He makes upon you.

2. Again, John notices the perplexity of the people. They saw that, much as the authorities desired to put Him out of the way, they shrank from decisive measures. And from this they naturally gathered that the rulers had some idea that this was the Christ. Then besides, they saw the miracles Jesus did, and asked whether the Christ would do more miracles. They saw, too, that He was "a good Man," and on the whole, therefore, they were disposed to look favourably on His claims; but then there always recurred the thought, "We know this Man whence He is; but when Christ cometh, no man knoweth whence He is." They thought they could account for Christ and trace Him to His origin; and therefore they could not believe He was from God. This is the common difficulty. Men find it difficult to believe that One who was really born on earth and did not suddenly appear, nobody knew whence, can in any peculiar sense be from God. They dwell upon the truly human nature of Christ, and conceive that this precludes the possibility of His being from God in any sense in which we are not from God.

To this perplexity Jesus addresses Himself in the words (ver. 28), "Me you do in a sense know, and also whence I come, but that does not give you the full knowledge you need, for it is not of Myself I am come; your knowledge of Me cannot solve your perplexity, because I am not sent by Myself; He that sent Me is the real[31] one, and Him you do not know. I know Him because I am from Him, and He hath sent Me." That is to say: Your knowledge of Me is insufficient, because you do not, through Me, recognise God. Your knowledge of Me is insufficient so long as you construe Me into a mere earthly product. To know Me, as you know Me, is not enough; for not in Myself can you find the originating cause of what I am and what I do. You must go behind my earthly origin, and the human appearance which you know, if you are to account for My presence among you, and for My conduct and teaching. It matters little what you know of Me, if through Me you are not brought to the knowledge of God. He is the real One, He is the Supreme Truth; and Him, alas! you do not know while you profess to know Me.

3. John notes the insufficient tests used both by the people and by the authorities for ascertaining

whether Jesus was or was not their promised King. The tests they used were such as these, "Will Christ do more miracles?" "Will He come from the same part of the country?" and so forth. Among ourselves it has become customary to speak as if it were impossible to find or apply any sufficient test to the claims of Christ; impossible to ascertain whether He is, in a peculiar sense, Divine, and whether we can absolutely trust all He said, and accept the views of God He cherished and proclaimed. Certainly Christ Himself does not countenance this mode of speaking. In all His conversations with the unbelieving Jews He condemned them for their unbelief, ascribed it to moral defects, and persistently maintained that it was within the reach of any man to ascertain whether He was true or a pretender. There is a class of expressions which occur in this Gospel which clearly show what Jesus Himself considered to be the root of unbelief. To Pilate He says, "Every one that is of the truth heareth My voice." To the Jews He says, "He that is of God, heareth God's words; ye therefore hear them not, because ye are not of God." And again in this seventh chapter, "If any man is desirous to do the will of God, he will know of My doctrine whether it be of God, or whether I speak of Myself." All these statements convey the impression that Christ's person and teaching will uniformly be acceptable to those who love the truth, and who are anxious to do the will of God.

Faith in Christ is thus represented as an act rather of the spiritual nature than of the intellect, and as the result of sympathy with the truth rather than of critical examination of evidence. A painter or art-critic familiar with the productions of great artists feels himself insulted if you offer him evidence to convince him of the genuineness of a work of art over and above the evidence which it carries in itself, and which to him is the most convincing of all. If one of the lost books of Tacitus were recovered, scholars would not judge it by any account that might be given of its preservation and discovery, but would say, Let us see it and read it, and we will very soon tell you whether it is genuine or not. When the man you have seen every day for years, and whose character you have looked into under the strongest lights, is accused of dishonesty, and damaging evidence is brought against him, does it seriously disturb your confidence in him? Not at all. No evidence can countervail the knowledge gained by intercourse. You know the man, directly, and you believe in him without regard to what other persons advance in his favour or against him. Christ expects acceptance on similar grounds. Look at Him, listen to Him, pass with Him from day to day of His life, and say whether it is possible that He can be a deceiver, or that He can be deceived. He Himself is confident that those who seek the truth, and are accustomed to acknowledge and follow the truth always, will follow Him. He is confident that they will find that He so fits in with what they have already learnt, that naturally and instinctively they will accept Him.

It is at the point in which all men are interested that Christ appeals to us--at the point of life or conduct; and He says that whoever truly desires to do God's will, will find that His teaching leads him right. And if men would only acknowledge Christ in this respect, and begin, as conscience bids them, by accepting His life as exhibiting the highest rule of conduct, they would sooner or later acknowledge Him in all. A man may not at once see all that is involved in the fact that Christ exhibits, as no one else exhibits, the will of God; but if He will but acknowledge Him as the Teacher of God's will, not coming to Him with a spirit of suspicion but of earnest desire to do God's will, that man will become a convinced follower of Christ. There are, of course, persons of a sound moral disposition who get entangled intellectually in perplexing difficulties about the person of Christ and His relation to God; but if such persons are humble--and humility is a virtue of decisive consequence--they will, by virtue of their experience in moral questions, and by their practical knowledge of the value of harmony with God, prize the teaching of Christ, and recognise its superiority, and submit themselves to its influence.

It was on the last day of the feast that our Lord made the most explicit revelation of Himself to the people. For seven days the people dwelt in their booths; on the eighth day they celebrated their entrance into the promised land, forsook their booths, and, as it is said in the end of the chapter, "went every man to his own house." But on this great day of the feast no water was drawn from the pool of Siloam. On each of the preceding days the golden pitcher was in request, and the procession that followed the priest who carried it praised God who had brought water out of the rock in the desert; but on the eighth day, commemorating their entrance into "a land of springs of water," this rite of drawing the water ceased.

But the true worshippers among these Israelites had been seeing a spiritual meaning in the water, and had been conscious of an uneasy feeling of thirst still in the midst of these Temple services--an uneasy questioning whether even yet Israel had passed the thirsty desert, and had received the full gift God had meant to give. There were thinking men and thirsty souls then as there are now; and to these, who stood perhaps a little aside, and looked half in compassion, half in envy, at the merry-making of the rest, it seemed a significant fact that, in the Temple itself, with all its grandeur and skilful appliances, there was yet no living fountain to quench the thirst of men--a significant fact that to find water the priest had to go outside the gorgeous Temple to the modest "waters of Siloah that go softly." All through the feast these men wondered morning by morning when the words of Joel were to come true, when it should come to pass that "a fountain should come forth of the house of the Lord," or when that great and deep river should begin to flow which Ezekiel saw in vision issuing from the threshold of the

Marcus Dods, D.D.

Lord's house, and waxing deeper and wider as it flowed. And now once more the last day of the feast had come, the water was no longer drawn, and yet no fountain had burst up in the Temple itself, their souls were yet perplexed, unsatisfied, craving, athirst, when suddenly, as if in answer to their half-formed thoughts and longings, a clear, assured, authoritative voice passed through their ear to their inmost soul: "If any man thirst, let him come unto Me and drink. He that believeth on Me, out of his belly shall flow rivers of living water."

In these words Christ proclaims that He is the great Temple-fountain; or rather, that He is the true Temple, and that the Holy Ghost proceeding from Him, and dwelling in men, is the life-giving fountain. [32] All the cravings after a settled and eternal state, all the longings for purity and fellowship with the Highest, which the Temple services rather quickened than satisfied, Christ says He will satisfy. The Temple service had been to them as a screen on which the shadows of things spiritual were thrown; but they longed to see the realities face to face, to have God revealed, to know the very truth of things, and set foot on eternal verity. This thirst is felt by all men whose whole nature is alive, whose experience has shaken them out of easy contentment with material prosperity; they thirst for a life which does not so upbraid and mock them as their own life does; they thirst to be able to live, so that the one half of their life shall not be condemned by the other half; they thirst to be once for all in the "ampler ether" of happy and energetic existence, not looking through the bars and fumbling at the lock. This thirst and all legitimate cravings we feel Christ boldly and explicitly promises to satisfy; nay more, all illegitimate cravings, all foolish discontent, all vicious dissatisfaction with life, all morbid thirst that is rapidly becoming chronic disease in us, all weak and false views of life, He will rid us of, and give us entrance into the life that God lives and imparts--into pure, healthy, hopeful life.

Christ stands and cries still in the midst of a thirsting world: "Whosoever will let him take of the water of life freely." Has His voice become so familiar that it has lost all significance? For all who can hear and believe, His truth remains. There is life--abundant life for us. Drink of any other fountain, and you only intensify thirst, and make life more difficult, spending energy without renewing it. Live in Christ and you live in God. You have found the centre, the heart, the eternal life. As Christ stood and cried to the people He was conscious of power to impart to them a freshly welling spring of life--a life that would overflow for the strengthening and gladdening of others besides themselves. He has the same consciousness to-day; the deep, living benefits He confers are as open to all ages as the sunshine and the air; there is no necessity binding any one soul to feel that life is a failure, an empty, disappointing husk, serving no good purpose, bringing daily fresh misery and deeper hopelessness, a thing perhaps manfully to fight our way through but certainly not to rejoice in. If any one has such views of life it is because he has not honestly, believingly, and humbly responded to Christ's word and come to Him.

Footnotes:

28. It will be observed that the remaining part of the Gospel goes into very small compass as regards time. Chapters vii.--x. 21 are occupied with what was said and done at the Feast of Tabernacles, chapters xii.--xx. with the last Passover.

29. A mixture of religious thanksgiving and unrestrained social hilarity, analogous to the English celebration of Christmas.

30. Psalm xc. 1.

31. á¼   □Î»Î·Î¸Î½½á½½¹Ï,.

32. On ver. 39 see p. 48 of this volume.

XVII. THE WOMAN TAKEN IN ADULTERY

"And they went every man unto his own house: but Jesus went unto the mount of Olives. And early in the morning He came again into the temple, and all the people came unto Him; and He sat down, and taught them. And the scribes and the Pharisees bring a woman taken in adultery; and having set her in the midst, they say unto Him, Master, this woman hath been taken in adultery, in the very act. Now in the law Moses commanded us to stone such; what then sayest Thou of her? And this they said, tempting Him, that they might have whereof to accuse Him. But Jesus stooped down, and with His finger wrote on the ground. But when they continued asking Him, He lifted up Himself, and said unto them, He that is without sin among you, let him first cast a stone at her. And again He stooped down, and with His finger wrote on the ground. And they, when they heard it, went out one by one, beginning from the eldest, even unto the last: and Jesus was left alone, and the woman, where she was, in the midst. And Jesus lifted up Himself, and said unto her, Woman, where are they? did no man condemn thee? And she said, No man, Lord. And Jesus said, Neither do I condemn thee; go thy way; from henceforth sin no more."--John vii. 53--viii. 11.

This paragraph, from chap. vii. 53--viii. 11 inclusive, is omitted from modern editions of the Greek text on the authority of the best manuscripts. Internal evidence is also decidedly against its admission. The incident may very well have happened, and it bears every appearance of being accurately reported. We are glad to have so characteristic an exposure of the malignity of the Jews, and a view of our Lord which, although from a novel standpoint, is yet quite consistent with other representations of His manner and spirit. But here it is out of place. No piece of literary work is so compact and homogeneous as this Gospel. And an incident such as this, which would be quite in keeping with the matter of the synoptical Gospels, is felt rather to interrupt than to forward the purpose of John to record the most characteristic and important self-manifestations of Christ.

But as the paragraph is here, and has been here from very early times, and as it is good Gospel material, it may be well briefly to indicate its significance.

1. First, it reveals the unscrupulous malignity of the leading citizens, the educated and religious men, "the Scribes and Pharisees." They brought to Jesus the guilty woman, "tempting Him" (ver. 6); not because they were deeply grieved or even shocked at her conduct; nay, so little were they impressed with that aspect of the case, that, with a cold-blooded indelicacy which is well-nigh incredible, they actually used her guilt to further their own designs against Jesus. They conceived that by presenting her before Him for judgment, He would be transfixed on one or other horn of the following dilemma: If He said, Let the woman die in accordance with the law of Moses, they would have a fair ground on which they could frame a dangerous accusation against Him, and would inform Pilate that this new King was actually adjudging life and death. If, on the other hand, He bid them let the woman go, then He could be branded before the people as traversing the law of Moses.

Underhand scheming of this kind is of course always to be condemned. Setting traps and digging pitfalls are illegitimate methods even of slaughtering wild animals, and the sportsman disdains them. But he who introduces such methods into human affairs, and makes his business one concatenated plot, does not deserve to be a member of society at all, but should be banished to the unreclaimed wilderness. These men posed as sticklers for the Law, as the immovably orthodox, and yet had not the common indignation at crime which would have saved them from making a handle of this woman's guilt. No wonder that their unconscious and brazen depravity should have filled Jesus with wonder and embarrassment, so that for a space He could not utter a word, but could only fix His eyes on the ground.

Making all allowance for the freedom of Oriental manners from some modern refinements, one cannot but feel some surprise that such a scene should be possible on the streets of Jerusalem. It reveals a hardened and insensible condition of public opinion which one is scarcely prepared for. And yet it may well be questioned whether it was a more ominous state of public sentiment than that in the midst of which we are living, when scenes, in character if not in appearance similar to this, are constantly reproduced by our novelists and play-writers, who harp upon this one vile string, professing, like these Pharisees, that they drag such things before the public gaze for the sake of exposing vice and making it hateful, but really because they know that there is a large constituency to whom they can best appeal by what is sensational, and prurient, and immoral, though to the masculine and healthy mind disgusting. Many of our modern writers might take a hint from our German forefathers, who, in their barbarian days, held that some vices were to be punished in public, but others buried quickly in oblivion, and who, therefore, punished crime of this sort by binding it in a wicker crate, and sinking it in a pit of mud out of sight for ever. We certainly cannot congratulate ourselves on our advancement in moral perception so long as we pardon to persons of genius and rank what would be loathed in persons of no brilliant parts and in our own circles. When such things are thrust upon us, either in literature or elsewhere, we have always the resource of our Lord; we can turn away, as though we heard not; we can refuse to inquire further into such matters, and turn away our eyes from them.

Few positions could be more painful to a pure-minded man than that in which our Lord was placed. What hope could there be for a world where the religious and righteous had become even more detestable than the coarse sin they proposed to punish? No wonder our Lord was silent, silent in sheer disturbance of mind and sympathetic shame. He stooped down and wrote on the ground, as one who does not wish to answer a question will begin drawing lines on the ground with his foot or his stick. His silence was a broad hint to the accusers; but they take it for mere embarrassment, and all the more eagerly press their question. They think Him at a loss when they see Him with hanging head tracing figures on the ground; they fancy their plot is successful, and, flushed with expected victory, they close in and lay their hands on his shoulder as He stoops, and demand an answer. And so He lifts Himself up, and they have their answer: "He that is without sin among you, let him first cast a stone at her." They fall into the pit they have digged.

This answer was not a mere clever retort such as a self-possessed antagonist can always command. It was not a mere dexterous evasion. What these scribes would say of it to one another afterwards, or with what nervous anxiety they would altogether avoid the subject, we can scarcely conjecture; but probably none of them would affect to say, as has since been said, that it was a confounding of things that differ, that by demanding that every one who brought an accusation, against another should himself be open to no accusation Jesus subverted the whole administration of law. For what criminal could fear condemnation, if his doom were to be suspended until a judge whose heart is as pure as his ermine be found who may pronounce it? Might not these scribes have replied that they were quite aware that they themselves were guilty men, but no law could lay hold of any outward actions of theirs, and that they were there not to talk of their relation to God or of purity of heart, but to vindicate the outward purity of the morals of their city by bringing to judgment this offender? They did not thus bandy words with our Lord, and they could not; because they knew that it was not He who was trying to confound private morality and the administration of law but themselves. They had brought this woman to Jesus as if He were a magistrate, though often enough He had declined to interfere with civil affairs and with the ordinary administration of justice. And in His answer He still shows the same spirit of non-interference. He does not pronounce upon the woman's guilt at all. Had they taken her before their ordinary courts He would have raised no word in her favour; did her husband after this prosecute her he can have feared no interference on the part of Jesus. His answer is the answer not of one pronouncing from a judgment-seat, nor of a legal counsel, but of a moral and spiritual teacher. And in this capacity He had a perfect right to say what He did. We have no right to say to an official who in condemning culprits or in prosecuting them is simply discharging a public duty, "See that your own hands be clean, and your own heart pure, before you condemn another," but we have a perfect right to silence a private individual who is officiously and not officially exposing another's guilt, by bidding him remember that he has a beam in his own eye which he must first be rid of, a stain on his own hands he must first wash out. The public prosecutor, or judge is a mere mouthpiece and representative among us of absolute justice; in him we see not his own private character at all, but the purity and rectitude of law and order. But these scribes were acting as private individuals, and came to Jesus professing that they were so shocked with this woman's sin that they wished the long-disused punishment of stoning to be revived. And therefore Jesus had not only a perfect right, as any other man would have had, to say to them, "Thou that sayest a man should not commit adultery, dost thou commit adultery?" but also, as the searcher of hearts; as He who knew what is in man, He could risk the woman's life on the chance of there being a single man of them who was really as shocked as he pretended to be, who was prepared to say he had in his own soul no taint of the sin he was loudly professing his abhorrence of, who was prepared to say, Death is due to this sin, and then to accept such proportionate punishment as would fall to his own share.

Having given His answer His eye again falls, His former stooping attitude is resumed. He does not mean to awe them by a defiant look; He lets their own conscience do the work. But that their conscience should have produced such a result deserves our attention. The woman, when she heard His answer, may for a moment have trembled and shrunk together, expecting the crashing blow of the first stone. Could she expect that these Pharisees, some of them at least good men, were all involved somehow in her sin, tainted in heart with the pollution that had wrought such destruction in herself, or supposing they were so tainted, did they know it; or supposing they knew it, would they not be ashamed to own it in the face of the surrounding crowd; would they not sacrifice her life rather than their own character? But every man waited for some other to lift the first stone; every man thought that some one of their number would be pure enough and bold enough, if not to throw the first stone, at least to assert that he fulfilled the condition of doing so that Jesus had laid down. None was willing to put himself forward to be searched by the eyes of the crowd, and to be exposed to the still more trying judgment of Jesus, and to risk the possibility of His, in some more definite way, revealing his past life. And so they edged their way out through the crowd from before Him, each desiring to have no more to do with the business; the oldest not so old as to forget his sin, the youngest not daring to say he was not already corrupt.

This reveals two things, the amount of unascertained guilt every man carries with him, guilt that he is not distinctly conscious of, but that a little shake awakens, and that weakens him all through his life in ways that he may be unable to trace.

Further, this encounter of Jesus with the leading men gives significance to His subsequent challenge: "Which of you convinceth Me of sin?" He had shown them how easy it was to convict the guilty; but the very ease and boldness with which He had touched their conscience convinced them His own was pure. In a society honeycombed with vice He stood perfect, untouched by evil.

This searching purity, this stainless mirror, the woman felt it more difficult to face than the accusing scribes. Alone with Him who had so easily unmasked their wickedness, she feels that now she has to do with something much more awful than the accusations of men--the actual irrevocable sin. There was no voice now accusing her, no hand laid in arrest upon her. Why does she not go? Because, now that others are silent, her own conscience speaks; now that her accusers are silenced, she must listen to Him whose purity has saved her. The presence among us of a true and perfect human holiness in the person of Christ, that is the true touchstone of character; and he who does not feel that this is what actually judges all his own ways and actions, has but a dim apprehension of what human life is--of its dignity, its responsibilities, its risks, its reality. Our sin, no doubt, hems us round with a thousand disabilities, and fears, and anxieties in this world, often dreadful to bear as the shame of this woman; there gradually gathers round us a brood of mischiefs we have given birth to by overstepping God's law, a brood that throngs our steps, and makes a peaceful and happy life impossible. Other men come to recognise some of our infirmities, and we feel the depressing influence of their unfavourable judgment, and in the secresy of our own self-reflection we think meanly of ourselves; but this, overwhelming as it sometimes becomes, is not the worst of sin. Were all these evil consequences abated or removed, were we as free from accusing voices, either from the reflected judgment of the world or from our own memory, as that woman when she stood alone in the midst, yet there would then only the more clearly emerge into view the essential and inseparable evil of sin, the actual breach between us and holiness. The accusation and misery which sin brings generally either make us feel that we are expiating sin by what we suffer, or put us into a self-defensive attitude. It is when Jesus lifts His true eye to meet ours that the heart sinks humbled, and recognises that apart from all punishment and in itself sin is sin, an injury to God's love, a grievous wrong to our own humanity. In the attitude of Christ towards sin and the sinner there is an exposure of the real nature of sin which makes an ineffaceable impression.

But what will Jesus do with this woman thus left on His hands? Will He not visit her with punishment, and so assert His superiority to the accusers who had slunk away? He shows His superiority in a much more real fashion. He sees that now the woman is self-condemned, lies under that condemnation in which alone there is hope, and which alone leads to good. She could not misunderstand the significance of her acquittal. Her surprise must only have deepened her gratitude. He who had stood her friend and brought her through so critical a passage in her history could scarcely be forgotten. And yet, considering the net she had thrown around herself, could our Lord say "Sin no more" with any hope? He knew what she was going back to--a blighted home-life, a life full now of perplexity, of regret, of suspicion, probably of ill-usage, of contempt, of everything that makes men and women bitter and drives them on to sin. Yet He implies that the legitimate result of forgiveness is renunciation of sin. Others might expect her to sin; He expected her to abandon sin. If the love shown us in forgiveness is no barrier to sin, it is because we have not been in earnest as yet about our sin, and forgiveness is but a name. Do we need an external scene such as that before us as the setting which may enable us to believe that we are sinners, and that there is forgiveness for us? The entrance to life is through forgiveness. Possibly we have sought forgiveness; but if there follows us no serious estimate of sin, no fruitful remembrance of the holiness of Him who forgave us, then our severance from sin will last only until we meet the first substantial temptation.

We do not know what became of this woman, but she had an opportunity of regarding Jesus with reverence and affection, and thus of bringing a saving influence into her life. This scene, in which He was the chief figure, must always have remained the most vivid picture in her memory; and the more she thought of it the more clearly must she have seen how different He was from all besides. And unless in our hearts Christ finds a place, there is no other sufficient purifying influence. We may be convinced He is all He claims to be, we may believe He is sent to save, and that He can save; but all this belief may be without any cleansing effect upon us. What is wanted is an attachment, a real love that will prompt us always to regard His will, and to make our life a part of His. It is our likings that have led us astray, and it is by new likings implanted within us that we can be restored. So long as our knowledge of Christ is in our head only, it may profit us a little, but it will not make new creatures of us. To accomplish that, He must command our heart. He must control and move what is most influential within us; there must arise in us a real and ruling enthusiasm for Him.

Perhaps, however, the chief lesson taught by this incident is that the best way to reform society is to reform ourselves. There is of course a great deal done in our own day to reclaim the vicious, to succour the poor, and so on; and nothing is to be said against these efforts when they are the outcome of a humble and sympathising charity. But they are very often adulterated with a spirit of condemnation and a sense of superiority, which on closer inspection is found to be unjust. These scribes and Pharisees, when they dragged this woman before Jesus, felt themselves on quite another platform than that which she occupied; but a word from Christ convinced them how hollow this self-righteous spirit was. He made them feel that they too were sinners even as she, and none of them was sufficiently hardened to lift a stone against her. This is creditable to the Pharisees. There are many among us who would very quickly have lifted the stone. Even while striving to reclaim the drunkard, for example, they arraign him with an implacable ferocity that shows they are quite unconscious of being sharers in his sin. If you challenged them, they would clear themselves by vehemently protesting that they had not touched strong drink for years; but do they not consider that the almost universal intemperance of the lowest class in society has a far deeper root than individual appetite; that it is rooted in the whole miserable condition of that class, and cannot be cured till the luxuries of the rich are by some means sacrificed for the bitter need of the poor, and the rational enjoyments which save the well-to-do from coarse and open vice are put within reach of the whole population? Poverty, and the necessity it entails of being content with a wage which barely keeps in life, are not the sole roots of vice, but they are roots; and so long as we ourselves, in common with the society in which we live, are involved in the guilt of upholding a social condition which tempts to every kind of iniquity, we dare not cast the first stone at the drunkard, the thief, or even their more sunken associates. No one man, and no one class, is more guilty than another in this great blot on our Christianity. Society is guilty; but as members who happen by the accident of our birth to have enjoyed advantages saving us from much temptation which we know we could not have stood, we must learn at least to consider those who in a very real sense are sacrificed for us. Among certain savage tribes, when a chief's house is built, slaughtered slaves are laid in pits as its foundation; the structure of our vaunted civilisation has a very similar basement.

Still it is one of the most hopeful features of present-day Christianity that men are becoming sensible that they are not mere individuals, but are members of a society; and that they must bear the shame of the existing condition of things in society. Intelligent Christian men now feel that the saving of their own souls is not enough, and that they cannot with complacency rest satisfied with their own happy condition and prospects if the society to which they belong is in a state of degradation and misery. It is by the growth of this sympathetic shame that reformation on a great scale will be brought about. It is by men learning to see in all misery and vice their own share of guilt that society will gradually be leavened. To those who cannot own their connection with their fellow-men in any such sense, to those who are quite satisfied if they themselves are comfortable, I do not know what can be said. They break themselves off from the social body, and accept the fate of the amputated limb.

XVIII. CHRIST THE LIGHT OF THE WORLD

"Again therefore Jesus spake unto them, saying, I am the light of the world: he that followeth Me shall not walk in the darkness, but shall have the light of life. The Pharisees therefore said unto Him, Thou bearest witness of Thyself; Thy witness is not true. Jesus answered and said unto them, Even if I bear witness of Myself, My witness is true; for I know whence I came, and whither I go; but ye know not whence I come, or whither I go. Ye judge after the flesh; I judge no man. Yea and if I judge, My judgement is true; for I am not alone, but I and the Father that sent Me. Yea and in your law it is written, that the witness of two men is true. I am He that beareth witness of Myself, and the Father that sent Me beareth witness of Me. They said therefore unto Him Where is Thy Father? Jesus answered, Ye know neither Me, nor My Father: if ye knew Me, ye would know My Father also."--John viii. 12--19.

At the Feast of Tabernacles Jesus, who knew that He was sent to confer upon men the realities which had been symbolised and promised in all religious rites, proclaimed that He was the fountain of life (vii. 37); and thus responded to the unuttered prayer of those who looked with some weariness at the old routine of drawing water in remembrance of the provision God had made for their fathers in the desert. Another feature of the same Feast leads Him now to declare a further characteristic of His person. In commemoration of the Pillar of Fire that led their fathers in the trackless desert, the people lit large lamps round the Temple, and gave themselves up to dancing and revelry. But this, too, was no doubt felt to be for the superficial souls that can live upon rites and symbols, and do not seek to lay bare their inmost being to the very touch of eternal reality. Not merely the cynic would smile as venerable men joined in the lamp-light dance, but possibly even the grave and pious onlooker, looking back on his own mistakes in life, and conscious of the blind way in which he was still blundering on, stood wondering where the true Guide of Israel, the real Light of human life was to be found. In sympathy with all such longing after truth and clear vision Jesus cries, "I am the light of the world; he that followeth Me shall not walk in darkness, but shall have the light of life."

His words must be interpreted by their reference to the light which was then being celebrated. Of that light we read that "the Lord went before them by day in a pillar of cloud, to lead them the way, and by night in a pillar of fire, to give them light." This was a customary mode of directing the movements of large bodies of men, whether caravans or armies. In the case of an army a tall pole was erected in front of the chief's tent, and from it a basket of fire was suspended, so that the glare of it was visible by night, and its smoke by day. The head of a marching column could thus be descried from a great distance, especially in wide level tracts with little or no vegetation and few inequalities of surface to interrupt the view. The distinctive peculiarity of the Israelitish march was that Jehovah was in the fire, and that He alone controlled its movements, and thereby the movements of the camp. When the pillar of cloud left its place and advanced the tents were struck, lest they should be separated, from Jehovah and be found unfaithful to Him. During the whole course of their sojourn in the wilderness their movements were thus controlled and ordered. The beacon-fire that led them was unaffected by atmospheric influences. Dispelled by no gales, and evaporated by no fiercest heat of the Eastern sun, it hovered in the van of the host as the guiding angel of the Lord. The guidance it gave was uninterrupted and unerring; it was never mistaken for an ordinary cloud, never so altered its shape as to become unrecognisable. And each night the flame shot up, and assured the people they might rest in peace.

Two obvious characteristics of this guiding Light must be kept in view.

1. God's people were not led by a road already made and used, and which they could have studied from beginning to end on a map before starting; but they were led day by day, and step by step, by a living guide, who chose a route never before trodden. In the morning they did not know whether they were to go forward or back, or to stay where they were. They had to wait in ignorance till their guiding pillar moved, and follow in ignorance till it halted. Our passage through life is similar. It is not a chart we are promised but a guide. We cannot tell where next year or next month may be spent. We are not informed of any part of our future, and have no means of ascertaining the emergencies which may try us, the new ingredients which may suddenly be thrown into our life, and reveal in us what till now has lain hidden and dormant. We cannot tell by what kind of path we shall be led onwards to our end; and our security from day to day consists not at all in this, that we can penetrate the future, and see no dangers in it, but our security is that we shall always be guided by infallible and loving wisdom. We have learned a chief article of human wisdom if we have learned to leave to-morrow to God and

faithfully follow Him to-day. A road as it lies in the distance often looks impassably steep, but as we approach and walk it step by step, we find it almost level and fairly easy.

2. This light was to guide, not their conduct, but their movements. All men need similar guidance. All men have practical matters to determine which often greatly perplex them; they must make a choice between one or other course of action that is possible. Steps which will determine their whole subsequent life must be taken or declined; and for the determining of such alterations in the place or mode of their life there is often felt great need of a guidance which can be entirely relied upon. Sometimes, indeed, our course is determined for us, and we are not consulted in the matter; as the pillar of fire was silent, assigning no reasons, condescending to no persuasion or argument, but simply moving forwards; passing over rugged and steep mountain ridges, past inviting and sheltered glens, offering no present explanation of the route, but justified always by the result. So we often find that our course is determined apart from our own choice, wishes, judgment, or prayers. But this we commonly resent, and crave a guidance which shall approve itself to our own judgment and yet be infallible; which shall leave us our freedom of choice, and yet carry us forwards to all possibilities of good. In fact, we would rather have our freedom of choice and the responsibility of guiding our own life, with all its risks, than be carried forward without choice of our own.

This is the great distinction between the light which Christ is and the light by which the Israelites were led from day to day. They had an external means of ascertaining promptly which way they should go. Their whole life was circumscribed, and its place and mode determined for them. The guidance offered to us by Christ is of an inward kind. A God without might seem perfect as a guide, but a God within is the real perfection. God does not now lead us by a sign which we could follow, though we had no real sympathy with Divine ways and no wisdom of our own; but He leads us by communicating to us His own perceptions of right and wrong, by inwardly enlightening us, and by making us ourselves of such a disposition that we naturally choose what is good.

When matters difficult to handle and to manage come into our life, and when we are tempted to long for some external sign which would show us infallibly the right thing to do and the right way to follow, let this be our consolation, that this very exercise of judgment and bearing of responsibility in matters where right and wrong are not broadly distinguished are among the chief instruments for the formation of character; and that even though we err in the choice we make, yet by our error and by all honest effort to keep right with God in the matter, we shall certainly have made growth in ability to understand and to do what is right. No doubt it is easier to believe in a guide we can see and that moves before us like a pillar of fire; but supposing for a moment that this dispensation under which we are living is not a great deception, supposing for a moment that God is doing that one thing which He pledged Himself to do, namely, giving a Divine Spirit to men, Himself dwelling with men and in them, then we cannot fail to see that this guidance is of a much higher kind, and has much more lasting results than any external guidance could have. If, by allowing us to determine our own course and find our own way through all the hazards and perplexities of life, God is teaching us to estimate actions and their results more and more by their moral value, and if thereby He is impregnating you with His own mind and character, surely that is a much better thing than if He were keeping us in the right way merely by outward signs and irrespective of our own growth in wisdom.

Persons whose opinion is not to be lightly esteemed say that if we honestly seek God's guidance in any matter we cannot err, and have no business to reflect afterwards on our conduct as if we had made a wrong choice. I cannot think that is so. Sincere people who ask God's guidance, it seems to me, frequently make mistakes. In fact, our past mistakes are a great part of our education. Unless we are habitually in sympathy with God we are not infallible even in matters where a moral judgment is all that is required; and sometimes more is required of us than to say what is right and what is wrong. Other points have to be considered--points which call for a knowledge of life, of places, and professions, of the trustworthiness of other men, and a thousand matters in which we are liable to err. It is of course a great satisfaction to know that we wished to do right, even if we discover we have blundered; and it is also a satisfaction to know that God can use us for good in any position, even in that we have blundered into, although meanwhile we have lost some present good.

The light which Christ brought to the world was the light "of life." This additional description "of life" He commonly appended to distinguish the real and eternal good He bestowed from the figure by which it had been hinted at. He calls Himself the Bread of life, the Water of life, to point out that He is really and eternally what these material things are in the present physical world. All this present constitution of things may pass away, and the time may come when men shall no longer need to be sustained by bread, but the time shall never come when they shall not need life; and this fundamental gift Christ pledges Himself evermore to give. And when He names Himself the light of life He indicates that it is on the true, eternal life of man He sheds light.

There may, then, be many things and important things on which Christ sheds no direct light, although there is nothing of importance on which He does not shed light indirectly. He brought into the world no direct light upon scientific questions; He did not hasten the development of art by any special light thrown on its objects and methods. There was no great need for light on such matters. These are not the distressing difficulties of human existence. Indeed, men find stimulus and joy in overcoming these difficulties, and resent being told nature's secrets, and not being allowed to find them out. But the darkness that settles on the life of the individual, and upon the condition of large classes of people through what is human, personal, and practical is often overwhelming, and compels men to cry for light. The strange miscarriage of justice in the life of many individuals; the compulsion put upon them to sin and to disbelieve through the pressure of unceasing failure and privation; the triumph of cold-hearted villainy; the bitterness of separation and death; the impenetrable darkness of the future; the incomprehensible dimness, in which the most important truths are involved--all this men find no pleasure in, but rather a torment that is sometimes maddening, often destructive of all faith, and always painful. This is the kind of darkness that causes men to sink; they run upon the rocks, and go down in darkness, no living soul hearing their cry. This is the darkness which wrings from many a heart at this moment the question of despair, "What has become, of God?"

The darkness regarding conduct in which men are involved has largely a moral root. Men are blinded by their appetites and passions, so that they cannot see the best ends and enjoyments of life. It is the strong craving we have for gratifications of sense and of worldly desire that misleads us in life. As some creatures have the faculty of emitting a dark and turbid matter that discolours the water, and hides them from their pursuers, so it is a self-evolved and home-made darkness that involves us. False expectations are the atmosphere of our life; we live in an unreal world created by our own tastes and desires, which misinform us, and bid us seek the good of life where it is not to be found.

It is then this light that Christ is and brings, light upon human life, light upon all that most intimately concerns human character, human conduct, and human destiny. What each of us chiefly needs to know is, what is the best kind of human life--how can I best spend my energies, and how can I best sustain them? Are there any results of life which are satisfying and which are certain; and if so, how can I attain them? Do not all things happen alike to all; is it not with the wise man and the righteous as with the fool? Is life worth serious devotion; will it repay what is spent upon it? Is not cynical indifference, or selfish caring for present interests, the most philosophical as well as the most pleasant and easy attitude towards life to assume? These are the questions which we find answered in Christ.

The expression, "the light of life," may, however, have a somewhat different meaning. It may mean that he who follows Christ shall have that light which accompanies, and is fed by, the life which Christ gives. At the outset of the Gospel John declared that "the Life was the light of men." And this is true in the sense that they who accept Christ as their life, and truly live in Him and by Him, walk in light and not in darkness. The clouds and gloom which overhung their life are dissipated. Their horizon is widened, their prospect cleared, and all things with which they have presently to do are seen in their true dimensions and relations. They who live with the life of Christ have a clear light regarding duty. The man who has entered into the life Christ opens to us, however slow and dull in intellect he may be, may indeed make many mistakes, but he will find his way through life, and issue from it, in his measure, triumphant.

It is further to be remarked that Jesus does not content Himself with a place beside other teachers, saying, "I will give you light," but affirms that the light is inseparable from His own person. "I am the light." By this He means, as already observed, that it is by receiving Him as our life that we have light. But His words also mean that He imparts this light not by oral teaching, but by being what He is, and living as He does. Teaching by word and precept is well, when nothing better can be had; [33] but it is the Word made flesh that commands the attention of all. This is a language universally intelligible. "A life, the highest conceivable, on almost the lowest conceivable stage, and recorded in the simplest form, with indifference to all outward accompaniments attractive whether to the few or to the many, is set before us as the final and unalterable ideal of human life, amid all its continual and astonishing changes." It is by this life led here on earth He becomes our Light. It is by His faith maintained in the utmost of trial; His calmness and hopefulness amidst all that shrouds human life in darkness; His constant persuasion that God is in this world, present, loving, and working. It is by His habitual attitude towards this life, and towards the unseen, that we receive light to guide us. In His calmness we take refuge from our own dismay. In His hopefulness we refresh ourselves in every time of weariness. In His confidence our timorous anxieties are rebuked. Upon the darkest parts of our life there falls from Him some clear ray that brightens and directs. Thousands of His followers, in every age, have verified His words: "I am the light of the world: he that followeth Me shall not walk in darkness, but shall have the light of life."

And as the Teacher taught by living so must the scholar learn by living. Christ brings light by passing through all human experiences and situations, and "he that followeth" Him, not he that reads about Him, "shall have the light of life." There are very few men in the world who can think to much purpose on truths so abstruse and complicated as the Divinity of Christ and the Atonement and Miracles; but there is no man so dull as not to see the difference between Christ's life and His own. Few men may be able to explain satisfactorily the relation Christ holds to God on the one hand and to us on the other; but every man who knows Christ at all even as he knows his friend or his father, is conscious that a new light falls upon sin of all kinds, upon sins of appetite and sins of temper and sins of disposition, since Christ lived. It is in this light Christ would have us walk, and if we follow as He leads on, we shall never lack the light of life. We need not be seriously disturbed about the darkness that hangs round the horizon if light falls on our own path; we need not be disturbed by our ignorance of many Divine and human things, nor by our inability to answer many questions which may be put to us, and which indeed we naturally put to ourselves, so long only as we are sure we are living so as to please and satisfy Christ. If our life runs on the lines His life marked out, we shall certainly arrive where He now is, in the happiest and highest human condition.

Footnotes:

33. "Many had spoken wonderfully the truths concerning our state, and even concerning our hopes; they had sounded great depths in the sea of wisdom; they had drawn the line between what is solid and what is vain in life; they had caught, firmly and clearly, what was worth living for; they had measured truly the relative value of the flesh and the Spirit."--Dean Church, Gifts of Civilisation, p. 105.

XIX. JESUS REJECTED IN JERUSALEM

"He said therefore again unto them, I go away, and ye shall seek Me, and shall die in your sin: whither I go, ye cannot come. The Jews therefore said, Will He kill Himself, that He saith, Whither I go, ye cannot come? And He said unto them, Ye are from beneath; I am from above: ye are of this world; I am not of this world. I said therefore unto you, that ye shall die in your sins: for except ye believe that I am He, ye shall die in your sins. They said therefore unto Him, Who art Thou? Jesus said unto them, Even that which I have also spoken unto you from the beginning. I have many things to speak and to judge concerning you: howbeit He that sent Me is true; and the things which I heard from Him, these speak I unto the world. They perceived not that He spake to them of the Father. Jesus therefore said, When ye have lifted up the Son of man, then shall ye know that I am He, and that I do nothing of Myself, but as the Father taught Me, I speak these things. And He that sent Me is with Me; He hath not left Me alone; for I do always the things that are pleasing to Him. As He spake these things, many believed on Him. Jesus therefore said to those Jews which had believed Him, If ye abide in My word, then are ye truly My disciples; and ye shall know the truth, and the truth shall make you free. They answered unto Him, We be Abraham's seed, and have never yet been in bondage to any man: how sayest Thou, Ye shall be made free? Jesus answered them, Verily, verily, I say unto you, Every one that committeth sin is the bondservant of sin. And the bondservant abideth not in the house for ever: the son abideth for ever. If therefore the Son shall make you free, ye shall be free indeed. I know that ye are Abraham's seed; yet ye seek to kill Me, because My word hath not free course in you. I speak the things which I have seen with My Father: and ye also do the things which ye heard from your father. They answered and said unto Him, Our father is Abraham. Jesus saith unto them, If ye were Abraham's children, ye would do the works of Abraham. But now ye seek to kill Me, a man that hath told you the truth, which I heard from God: this did not Abraham. Ye do the works of your father. They said unto Him, We were not born of fornication; we have one Father, even God. Jesus said unto them, If God were your Father, ye would love Me: for I came forth and am come from God; for neither have I come of Myself, but He sent Me. Why do ye not understand My speech? Even because ye cannot hear My word. Ye are of your father the devil, and the lusts of your father it is your will to do. He was a murderer from the beginning, and stood not in the truth, because there is no truth in him. When he speaketh a lie, he speaketh of his own: for he is a liar, and the father thereof. But because I say the truth, ye believe Me not. Which of you convicteth Me of sin? If I say truth, why do ye not believe Me? He that is of God heareth the words of God: for this cause ye hear them not, because ye are not of God. The Jews answered and said unto Him, Say we not well that Thou art a Samaritan, and hast a devil? Jesus answered, I have not a devil; but I honour My Father, and ye dishonour Me. But I seek not mine own glory: there is One that seeketh and judgeth. Verily, verily, I say unto you, If a man keep My word, he shall never see death. The Jews said unto Him, Now we know that Thou hast a devil. Abraham is dead, and the prophets; and Thou sayest, If a man keep My word, he shall never taste of death. Art Thou greater than our father Abraham, which is dead? and the prophets are dead: whom makest Thou Thyself? Jesus answered, If I glorify Myself, My glory is nothing: it is My Father that glorifieth Me; of whom ye say, that He is your God; and ye have not known Him: but I know Him; and if I should say, I know Him not, I shall be like unto you, a liar: but I know Him, and keep His word. Your father Abraham rejoiced to see My day; and he saw it, and was glad. The Jews therefore said unto Him, Thou art not yet fifty years old, and hast Thou seen Abraham? Jesus said unto them, Verily, verily, I say unto you, Before Abraham was, I am. They took up stones therefore to cast at Him: but Jesus hid Himself, and went out of the temple."--John viii. 21--59.

John has now briefly detailed the self-manifestations of Jesus which He considered sufficient to induce the Jews to believe in Him; and he has shown us how, both in Galilee and in Jerusalem, the people, with few exceptions, remained unconvinced. He has also very clearly shown the reason of His rejection in Galilee. The reason was that the blessings He proposed to bestow were spiritual, while the blessings they craved were physical. Their Messianic expectation was not satisfied in Him. So long as He healed their sick, and by His mere will furnished famishing thousands with food, they thought, This is the King for us. But when He told them that these things were mere signs of higher blessings, and when He urged them to seek these spiritual gifts, they left Him in a body.

In Jerusalem opinion has followed a similar course. There also Jesus has exemplified His power to impart life. He has carefully explained the significance of that sign, and has explicitly claimed Divine prerogatives. But although individuals believe, the mass of the people are only perplexed, and the authorities are exasperated. The rulers, however, find it impossible to proceed against Him, owing to the influence He has with the people, and even with their own servants. This state of matters, however, was not destined to continue; and in the eighth chapter John traces the course of popular opinion from a somewhat hopeful perplexity to a furious hostility that, at length, for the first time, broke out in actual violence (viii. 59). Jesus did not indeed immediately retire, as if further efforts to induce faith were useless, but when the storm broke out a second time (x. 39, 40) He finally withdrew, and taught only such as sought Him out.

At this point, then, in the history we are invited to inquire what grounds of faith Jesus had presented, and what were the true reasons of His rejection.

1. But first we must ask, In what character or capacity did Jesus present Himself to men? What did He declare Himself to be? What demand did He make on the faith of those to whom He presented Himself? When He required that they should believe in Him, what exactly did He mean? Certainly He did not mean less than that they should believe He was the Messiah, and should accept Him as such. The "Messiah" was an elastic title, perhaps not conveying to any two minds in Israel precisely the same idea. It had indeed for all Israelites some contents in common. It meant that here was One upon earth and accessible, who was sent to be the Bearer of God's good-will to men, a Mediator through whom God meant to make His presence felt and His will known. But some who believed Jesus was the Christ had so poor a conception of the Christ, that He could not accept theirs as a sound faith. The minimum of acceptable faith must believe in the actual Jesus, and allow the idea of the Christ to be formed by what was seen in Jesus. Those who believed must so trust Jesus as to be willing that He should fashion the Messiahship as He saw fit. It was therefore primarily in Himself the true believer trusted. He did not, in the first instance, believe He was this or that, but he felt, "Here is the greatest and best I know; I give myself to Him." Of course this involved that whatever Christ claimed to be, He was believed to be. But it is of importance to observe that the confession, "I believe that Jesus is the Christ," was not enough in Christ's own day to guarantee the soundness of the faith of the confessor. He had further to answer the question, "What do you mean by the Christ'? For if you mean a national Messiah, coming to give you political freedom and social blessings only, this faith cannot be trusted." But if any one could say, "I believe in Jesus," and if by this he meant, "I so believe in Him that whatever He says He is, I believe He is, and whatever be the contents with which He fills the Messianic name, these contents I accept as belonging to the office," this faith was sound and acceptable.

And, according to this Gospel, Jesus at once made it plain that His idea of the Messianic office was not the popular idea. It was "eternal life" He constantly proclaimed as the gift the Father had commissioned Him to bestow; not physical life, not revived political life. So that it very shortly became impossible for any one to make the confession that Jesus was the Christ, in ignorance of what He Himself judged the Christ to be. It may be said, therefore, that when Jesus required men to believe in Him, He meant that they should trust Him as mediating efficiently between God and them, and should accept His view of all that was needful for this mediation. He meant that they should look to Him for life eternal and for perfect fellowship with God. What was doctrinally involved in this, what was implied in His claim regarding His eternal nature, might or might not at once be understood. What must be understood and believed was, that Jesus was empowered by God to act for Him, to represent Him, to impart to men all that God would impart.

II. This being so, we may now inquire, what sufficient reason Jesus, as already reported in this Gospel, has given why the people should accept Him as the Christ. In these eight chapters what do we find related which should have furnished the Jews with all the evidence which reasonable minds would require?

1. He was definitely identified as the Christ by the Baptist. It was John's function to recognise the person sent by God to fulfil all His will, and to found a kingdom of God among men. For this John lived; and if any man was in a position to say "yes" or "no" in response to the question, Is this the Christ, the Anointed and commissioned of God? John was that man. No man was in himself better qualified to judge, and no man had such material for judging, and his judgment was explicit and assured. To put aside this testimony as valueless is out of the question. It is more reasonable to ask whether it is even possible that in this matter the Baptist should be mistaken.

Jesus Himself indeed did not rest upon this testimony. For His own certification of His dignity He did not require it. He did not require the corroborative voice of one human being. It was not by what He was told regarding Himself that He became conscious of His Sonship; nor was it by an external testimony, even from such a man as John, that He was encouraged to make the claims He made. John was but a mirror reflecting what was already in Him, possibly stimulating self-consciousness, but adding nothing to His fitness for His work.

2. He expected that His claim to have come forth from God would be believed on His own word. The Samaritans believed Him on His own word. This does not mean that they believed a mere assertion;

they believed the assertion of One whom they felt to be speaking the truth. There was that in His character and bearing which compelled their faith. Through all He said there shone the self-evidencing light of truth. They might not have been able to stand a cross-examination as to the reason of the faith that was in them, they might not have been able to satisfy any other person or induce him to believe, but they were justified in following an instinct which said to them, This man is neither deceiver nor deceived. There was nothing in the claim of Jesus absolutely incredible. Nay, it rather fell in with their idea of God and with the knowledge of their own needs. They wished a revelation, and saw nothing impossible in it. This may nowadays be judged a homely rather than a philosophical view to take of God and of His relation to men. But primary and universal instincts have their place, and, if scientific knowledge does not contradict them, should be trusted. It was because the Samaritans had not tampered with their natural cravings and hopes, and had not allowed their idea of the Messiah to harden into a definite conception, that they were able to welcome Jesus with a faith which He rarely met with elsewhere.

And the main authentication of Christ's claim at all times is simply this, that He makes the claim, and that there is that in Him which testifies to His truth, while there is that in the claim itself which is congruous to our instincts and needs. There was that in the bearing of Christ which commanded belief in natures which were not numbed and blunted by prejudice. The Capernaum courtier who came to Jesus expecting to bring Him down with him to heal his boy, when he saw Him felt he could trust Him, and returned alone. Jesus was conscious that He spoke of what He knew, and spoke of it truly. "I speak that which I have seen with My Father" (ver. 38). "My record is true" (ver. 14). "If I say the truth, why do ye not believe Me?" (ver. 46.) This consciousness, both of an intention to speak the truth and of a knowledge of the truth, in a mind so pellucid and sane, justly impressed candid minds in His own day, and is irresistibly impressive still.

Again, we judge of what is probable or improbable, credible or incredible, mainly by its congruity with our previous belief. Is our idea of God such that a personal revelation seems credible and even likely? Does this supposed revelation in Christ consist with previous revelations and with the knowledge of God and His will which those revelations have fostered? Does this final revelation actually bring us the knowledge of God, and does it satisfy the longings and pure aspirations, the thirst for God and the hunger for righteousness, which assert themselves in us like natural appetites? If so, then the untutored human heart accepts this revelation. It is its own verification. Light is its own authentication. Christ brings within our ken a God whom we cannot but own as God, and who is nowhere else so clearly revealed. It is this immediacy of authentication, this self-verification, to which our Lord constantly appeals.

3. But a great part of the self-revelation of Christ could best be made in action. Such a work as the healing of the impotent man was visible to all and legible by the dullest. If His words were sometimes enigmatic, such an action as this was full of significance and easily understood. By this compassionate restoration of the vital powers He proclaimed Himself the Father's Delegate, commissioned to express the Divine compassion and to exercise the Divine power to communicate life. This was meant to be an easy lesson by which men might learn that God is full of compassion, ceaselessly working for the good of men; that He is present among us seeking to repair the mischief resulting from sin, and to apply to our needs the fulness of His own life, and that Jesus Christ is the medium through whom He makes Himself accessible to us and available for us.

These works were done by our Lord not only to convince the people that they should listen to Him, but also to convince them that God Himself was present. "If I do not the works of My Father, believe Me not. But if I do, though ye believe not Me, believe the works, that ye may know, and believe, that the Father is in Me, and I in Him." It was this He strove to impress on the people, that God was with them. It was not Himself He wished them to recognise, but the Father in Him. "I seek not Mine own glory" (ver. 50). And therefore it was the kindness of the works He pointed to: "Many good works have I showed you from My Father" (x. 32). He sought through these works to lead men to see how in His Person the Father was applying Himself to the actual needs of mankind. To accept God for one purpose is to accept Him for all. To believe in Him as present to heal naturally leads to belief in Him as our Friend and Father. Hence these signs, manifesting the presence and good-will of God, were a call upon men to trust Him and accept His messenger. They spoke of gifts still more akin to the Divine nature, of gifts not merely physical, but spiritual and eternal. Possibly in allusion to these intelligible and earthly signs our Lord said to Nicodemus, "If I have told you earthly things, and ye believe not, how shall ye believe, if I tell you of heavenly things?" If ye are blind to these earthly signs, what hope is there of your understanding things eternal in their own impalpable essence?

III. What were the true reasons of our Lord's rejection?

1. The first reason no doubt was that He so thoroughly disappointed the popular Messianic expectation. This comes out very conspicuously in His rejection in Galilee, where the people were on the point of crowning Him, but at once deserted Him as soon as it became clear that His idea of the needs of men was quite different from their's. The same reason lies at the root of His rejection by the

authorities and people of Jerusalem. This is brought out in this eighth chapter. "Many had believed on Him" (ver. 30); that is to say, they believed on Him as Nicodemus had believed; they believed He was the Christ. But as soon as He explained to them (vers. 32, 34) that the freedom He brought was a freedom attained through knowing the truth, a freedom from sin, they either were unable to understand Him or were repelled, and from believers became enemies and assailants.

It may have been with reluctance our Lord disclosed to those who had some faith in Him, that in order to be His disciples (ver. 31) they must accept His word, and find in it the freedom He proclaimed. He knew that this was not the freedom they sought. But it was compulsory that He should leave them in no dubiety regarding the blessings He promised. It was impossible that they should accept the eternal life He brought to them, unless there was quickened within them some genuine desire for it. For what prevented them from receiving Him was not a mere easily rectified blunder about the Messianic office, it was an alienation in heart from a spiritual conception of God. And accordingly in depicting the climax of unbelief John is careful in this chapter to bring out that our Lord traced His rejection by the Jews to their inveterate repugnance to spiritual life, and their consequent blinding of themselves to the knowledge of God. "He that is of God heareth God's words: ye therefore hear them not, because ye are not of God" (ver. 47). "Ye seek to kill Me, because My word hath no place in you [finds no room in you]. I speak that which I have seen with My Father; and ye do that which ye have seen with your father" (vers. 37, 38).

2. Here, as elsewhere, therefore, our Lord traces the unbelief of the Jews to the blindness induced by alienation from the Divine. They do not understand Him, because they have not that thirst for truth and righteousness which is the best interpreter of His words. "Why do ye not understand My speech? even because ye cannot bear My word." It was this word of His, the truth regarding sin and the way out of it, which sifted men. Those who eagerly welcomed salvation from sin because they knew that bondage to sin was the worst of bondages (ver. 34), accepted Christ's word, and continued in it, and so became His disciples (ver. 31). Those who rejected Him were prompted to do so by their indifference to the Kingdom of God as exhibited in the person of Christ. He was not their ideal. And He was not their ideal, because however much they boasted of being God's people God was not their ideal. "If God were your Father, ye would love Me; for I proceeded forth and came from God" (ver. 42). Jesus is conscious of adequately representing God, so that to be repelled by Him is to be repelled by God. It is really God in Him that they dislike. This is not only His own judgment of the matter. It is not a mere fancy of His own that He truly represents the Father, for "neither came I of Myself, but He sent me." He was sent into the world because He could represent the Father.

The rejection of Jesus by the Jews was therefore due to their moral condition. Their condition is such that our Lord does not scruple pungently to say, "Ye are of your father the devil." Their blindness to the truth and virulent opposition to Him proved their kinship with him who was from the beginning a liar and a murderer. They are so completely under the influence of sin that they are unable to appreciate emancipation from it. They look for satisfaction so determinedly in an anti-spiritual direction, that they are positively enraged at One who certainly has power, but who steadfastly uses it for spiritual purposes. Out of this condition they can be rescued by believing in Christ. Into the mystery which surrounds the possibility that such a belief should be cherished by any one in this condition, our Lord does not here enter. That it is possible, He implies by blaming them for not believing.

It is, then, those who are unconscious of the bondage of sin who reject Christ. One of the sayings with which He sifted His profoundly attached followers from the mass is this: "If ye continue in My word, then are ye My disciples indeed; and ye shall know the truth, and the truth shall make you free." The "word" of which Jesus here speaks is His whole revelation, all He taught by word and action, by His own habitual conduct and by His miracles. This it is which gives knowledge of the truth. That is to say, all the truth which men require for living they have in Christ. All knowledge of duty, and all that knowledge of our spiritual relations, out of which we can draw perennial motive and unfailing hope, we have in Him. The "truth" disclosed in Christ, and which emancipates from sin, must not be too carefully defined. But while leaving it in all its comprehensiveness, it must be noted that the truth which especially emancipates from sin and gives us our place as children in God's house, is the truth revealed in Christ's Sonship, the truth that God, in love and forgiveness, claims us as His children. In its own measure every truth we learn gives us a sense of liberty. The truth emancipates from superstition, from timorous waiting upon the opinion of authorities, from all that cramps mental movement and stunts mental growth; but the freedom here in view is freedom from sin, and the truth which brings that freedom is the truth about God our Father, and Jesus Christ whom He has sent.

XX. SIGHT GIVEN TO THE BLIND

"And as He passed by, He saw a man blind from his birth. And His disciples asked Him, saying, Rabbi, who did sin, this man, or his parents, that he should be born blind? Jesus answered, Neither did this man sin, nor his parents: but that the works of God should be made manifest in him. We must work the works of Him that sent Me, while it is day; the night cometh, when no man can work. When I am in the world, I am the Light of the world. When He had thus spoken, He spat on the ground, and made clay of the spittle, and anointed his eyes with the clay, and said unto him, Go, wash in the pool of Siloam (which is by interpretation, Sent). He went away, therefore, and washed, and came seeing. The neighbours therefore, and they which saw him aforetime, that he was a beggar, said, Is not this he that sat and begged? Others said, It is he: others said, No, but he is like him. He said, I am he. They said therefore unto him, How then were thine eyes opened? He answered, The man that is called Jesus made clay, and anointed mine eyes, and said unto me, Go to Siloam, and wash: so I went away and washed, and I received sight. And they said unto him, Where is He? He saith, I know not. They bring to the Pharisees him that aforetime was blind. Now it was the sabbath on the day when Jesus made the clay, and opened his eyes. Again therefore the Pharisees also asked him how he received his sight. And he said unto them, He put clay upon mine eyes, and I washed, and do see. Some therefore of the Pharisees said, This man is not from God, because He keepeth not the sabbath. But others said, How can a man that is a sinner do such signs? And there was a division among them. They say therefore unto the blind man again, What sayest thou of Him, in that He opened thine eyes? And he said, He is a prophet. The Jews therefore did not believe concerning him, that he had been blind, and had received his sight, until they called the parents of him that had received his sight, and asked them, saying, Is this your son, who ye say was born blind? how then doth he now see? His parents answered and said, We know that this is our son, and that he was born blind: but how he now seeth, we know not; or who opened his eyes, we know not: ask him; he is of age; he shall speak for himself. These things said his parents, because they feared the Jews: for the Jews had agreed already, that if any man should confess Him to be Christ, he should be put out of the synagogue. Therefore said his parents, He is of age; ask him. So they called a second time the man that was blind, and said unto him, Give glory to God: we know that this man is a sinner. He therefore answered, Whether He be a sinner, I know not: one thing I know, that, whereas I was blind, now I see. They said therefore unto him, What did He to thee? how opened He thine eyes? He answered them, I told you even now, and ye did not hear: wherefore would ye hear it again? would ye also become His disciples? And they reviled him, and said, Thou art His disciple; but we are disciples of Moses, We know that God hath spoken unto Moses: but as for this man, we know not whence He is. The man answered and said unto them, Why, herein is the marvel, that ye know not whence He is, and yet He opened mine eyes. We know that God heareth not sinners: but if any man be a worshipper of God, and do His will, him He heareth. Since the world began it was never heard that any one opened the eyes of a man born blind. If this man were not from God, He could do nothing. They answered and said unto him, Thou wast altogether born in sins, and dost thou teach us? And they cast him out. Jesus heard that they had cast him out; and finding him, He said, Dost thou believe on the Son of God? He answered and said, And who is He, Lord, that I may believe on Him? Jesus said unto him, Thou hast both seen Him, and He it is that speaketh with thee. And he said, Lord, I believe. And he worshipped Him. And Jesus said, For judgment came I into this world, that they which see not may see; and that they which see may become blind. Those of the Pharisees which were with Him heard these things, and said unto Him, Are we also blind? Jesus said unto them, If ye were blind, ye would have no sin: but now ye say, We see: your sin remaineth."--John ix.

We have already considered the striking use our Lord made of the Temple illumination to proclaim Himself the Light of the world. A still more striking physical symbol of this aspect of our Lord's person and work is found in His healing of the blind man. It is, as we have already had occasion to see, the manner of this evangelist to select for narration those miracles of Christ's which are especially "signs," outward embodiments of spiritual truth. Accordingly he now proceeds to exhibit Christ as the Light of the world in His bestowal of sight on the blind.

The disciples of Jesus had apparently been exercised by one of the outstanding problems of human life which perplex all thoughtful men: What regulates the distribution of suffering; why is it that while many of the most criminal and noxious men are prosperous and exempt from pain, many of the gentlest and best are broken and tortured by constant suffering? Why is it that inexplicable suffering seems so often to fall on the wrong people, on the innocent not on the guilty, on those who already are of refined and chastened disposition, not on those who seem urgently to need correction and the rod? Is suffering sent that character may be improved? But in Job's case it was sent because he was already irreproachable, not to make him so. Is it sent because of a man's early transgressions? But this man was born blind; his punishment preceded any possible transgression of his own. Was he then the victim of his parent's wrong-doing? But suffering is often the result of accident or of malice, or of mistake, which cannot be referred to hereditary sin. Are we then to accept the belief that this world is far from perfect as yet; that God begins at the beginning in all His works, and only slowly works towards perfection, and that in the progress, and while we are only moving towards an eternal state, there must be pains manifold and bitter? They are the shavings and sawdust and general disorder of the carpenter's workshop, which are necessarily thrown off in the making of the needful article. [34] It is to it, to the finished work, we must look, and not to the shavings, if we would understand and be reconciled to the actual state of things around us.

When Jesus said, "Neither hath this man sinned, nor his parents, but that the works of God should be made manifest in him," He of course did not mean to suggest that there is no such thing as suffering for individual or hereditary sin. By breaking the great moral laws of human life men constantly involve both themselves and their children in lifelong suffering. There is often so direct a connection between sin and suffering that the most hardened and insensible do not dream of denying that their pain and misery are self-inflicted. Sometimes the connection is obscure, and though every one else sees the source of a man's misfortunes in his own careless habits, or indolence, or bad temper, he himself may constantly blame his circumstances, his ill-luck, his partners, or his friends. It was our Lord's intention to warn the disciples against a curious and uncharitable scrutiny of any man's life to find the cause of his misfortunes. We have to do rather with the future than with the past, rather with the question how we can help the man out of his difficulties, than with the question how he got himself into them. The one question may indeed be involved in the other, but all suffering is, in the first place, a field in which the works of God may be exhibited. Wherever suffering has come from, there can be no manner of doubt that it calls out all that is best in human nature--sympathy, self-denial, gentleness, compassion, forgiveness of spirit, patient forbearance, all that is most Divine in man. To seek for the cause of suffering in order to blame and exonerate ourselves from all responsibility and claim on our pity and charity is one thing, quite another to inquire into the cause for the sake of more effectually dealing with the effect. No matter what has caused the suffering, here certainly it is always with us, and what we have to do with it is to find in it material and opportunity for a work of God. To rid the world of evil, of wretchedness, lonely sorrow, destitution, and disease is, if anything, the work of God; if God is doing anything He is carrying the world on towards perfection, and if the world is ever to be perfect it must be purged from agony and wretchedness, irrespective of where these come from. Our duty then, if we would be fellow-workers with God in what is real and abiding, is plain.

To the work of healing the blind man Jesus at once applies Himself. While the lifted stones were yet in His pursuers hands He paused to express His Father's love. He must, He says, work the works of Him who sent Him. He represented the Father not mechanically, not by getting well off by rote the task His Father had set Him, not by a studied imitation, but by being Himself of one mind with the Father, by loving that blind man just as the Father loved him, and by doing for him just what the Father would have done for him. We do the works of God when in our measure we do the same, becoming eyes to the blind, feet to the lame, help any way to the helpless. We cannot lay our hand on the diseased and heal them; we cannot give sight to the blind and make a man thus feel, this is God's power reaching to me; this is God stooping to me and caring for my infirmity; but we can cause men to feel that God is thinking of them, and has sent help through us to them. If we will only be humble enough to run the risk of failure, and of being held cheap, if we will only in sincerity take by the hand those who are ill-off and strive to better them, then these persons will think of God gratefully; or if they do not, there is no better way of making them think of God, for this was Christ's way, who had rarely need to add much explanation of His kind deeds, but letting them speak for themselves, heard the people giving God the glory. If men can be induced to believe in the love of their fellow-men, they are well on the road to belief in the love of God. And even though it should not be so, though all our endeavours to help men should fail to make them think of God as their helper, who has sent us and all help to them, yet we have helped them, and some at least of God's love for these suffering people has got itself expressed through us. God has got at least a little of His work done, has in one direction stopped the spread of evil.

Neither are we to wait until we can do things on a great scale, and attack the evils of human life with elaborate machinery. Our Lord was not a great organiser. He did not busy Himself with forming societies for this, that, and the other charitable work. He did not harangue assemblies convened to consider the relief of the poor; He did not press the abolition of slavery; He did not found orphanages or hospitals; but "as He passed by," He saw one blind man, and judged this a call sufficiently urgent. Sometimes we feel that, confronted as we are with a whole world full of deep-rooted and inveterate evils, it is useless giving assistance to an individual here and there. It is like trying to dry up the ocean with a sponge. We feel impatient with individual acts, and crave national action and radical measures. And that is very well, so long as we do not omit to use the opportunities we actually have of doing even little kindnesses, of undergirding the shattered life of individuals, and so enabling them to do what otherwise they could not do. But we shall never do our part, either to individuals or on a large scale, until we apprehend that it is only through us and others that God works, and that when we pass by a needy person we prevent God's love from reaching him, and disappoint the purpose of God. It was this feeling that imparted to Christ so intense and wakeful an energy. He felt it was God's work He was on earth to do. "I must work the works of Him that sent Me while it is day." He recognised that God was in the world looking with compassion on all human sorrow, but that this compassion could find expression only through His own instrumentality and that of all other men. We are the channels or pipes through which the inexhaustible source of God's goodness flows to the world; but it is in our power to turn off that flow, and prevent it from reaching those for whom it is intended. We do less than we ought for our fellow-men until we believe that we are the bearers of God's gifts to men; that to however few a number and in however small a way we are the media through which God finds way for His love to men, and that if we refuse to do what we can we disappoint and thwart His love and His purpose of good.

The blind man, with the quickened hearing of the blind, heard with interest the talk about himself; and a new awe fell upon his spirit as he heard that his blindness was to be the object of a work of God. He had learned to judge of men by the tones of their voice; and the firm, clear, penetrating voice which had just uttered these all-important words, "I am the Light of the world," could not, he knew, belong to a deceiver. In other ways also Jesus compensated for his lack of sight, and encouraged his faith by touching him and by laying on the closed eyes an extemporised ointment. But the miracle was not completed on the spot. The patient was required to go to the pool of Siloam and wash. John tells us that the name Siloam means Sent, and evidently connects this name with the claim Jesus constantly made to be the Sent of God.

But as the peculiarity of the miracle consisted in this, that the man was sent to the pool to be healed, we may be sure this arrangement was made to meet some element in the case. The man, with his bespattered eyes, had to grope his way to the pool, or get some kindly soul to lead him through the scoffing, doubtful crowd. And whatever this taught the man himself, it is to us a symbol of the truth that light does not come by the instantaneous touch of Christ's hand so much as by our faithfully doing His bidding. It is He who gives and is the light; but it does not stream in suddenly upon the soul, but comes upon the man who, though blindly, yet faithfully, gropes his way to the place Christ has bid him to, and uses the means prescribed by Him. "He that doeth the will of God, shall know of the doctrine whether it be of God." All the commands of Christ are justified in their performance; and clear light upon the meaning of much that we are commanded to do is only found in the doing of it.

But no doubt the special significance of the man's being sent to the pool of Siloam lay in the circumstance that it was in John's eyes a symbol of Christ Himself. He was sent by God. The people found it difficult to believe this, because He had slowly and unostentatiously grown up like any other man. "We know this Man, whence He is." "Is not this the carpenter's Son?" "How sayest Thou, I came down from heaven?" They could trace Him to His source. He did not appear fullgrown in their midst, without home, without any who had watched over His boyhood and growth. He was like the river whose sources were known, not like the stream bursting in full volume from the rock. The people felt ashamed to laud and celebrate as sent by God One who had grown up so quietly among themselves, and whose whole demeanour was so unostentatious. So had their fathers despised the waters of Siloam, "because they went softly;" because there was no mighty stream and roar, but a quiet pool and a little murmuring stream.

So might this blind man have reasoned when sent to Siloam: "Why, herein is a marvellous thing that I am to be healed by what has been within my reach since I was born, by the pool I used to dip my hand in when a boy, and wonder what like was the coolness to the sight. What hidden virtue can there be in that spring? Am I not exposing myself to the ridicule of all Jerusalem?" But, as this blind man's conduct afterwards showed, he was heedless of scorn and independent of other people's opinion, a fearless and trenchant reasoner who stands alone in the Gospel history for the firmness and sarcasm with which he resisted the bullying tone of the Pharisees, and compelled them to face, even though they would not acknowledge, the consequences of incontrovertible facts. This characteristic contempt of contempt, and scorn of scorn served him well now, for straight he went to the pool in the face of discouragements, and had his reward.

And the Pharisees might, with their gift of interpreting trifles, have deduced from this cure at the humble and noiseless Siloam some suggestion that though Jesus did seem a powerless and common Man, and though for thirty years His life had been flowing quietly on without violently changing the established order of things, yet He might, like this pool, be the Sent of God, to whom if a man came feeling his need of light and expecting in Him to find it, there was a likelihood of his blindness being taken away. This, however, as our Lord had afterwards occasion to tell them, was precisely what they could not submit to do. They could not, in the presence of a wondering and scorning crowd, admit that they needed light, nor could they condescend to seek for light from so commonplace a source. And no doubt it was a very severe trial--it was well-nigh impossible, that men in high esteem for religious knowledge, and who had been accustomed to reckon themselves the protectors of the faith, should own that they were in darkness, and should seek to be instructed by a youth from the benighted district of Galilee. Even now, when the dignity of Jesus is understood, many are prevented from giving themselves cordially to the life He insists upon by mere pride. There are men in such repute as leaders of opinion, and so accustomed to teach rather than to learn, and to receive homage rather than to give it, that scarcely any greater humiliation could be required of them, than to publicly profess themselves followers of Christ. For ourselves even, who might not seem to have much on which to pride ourselves, it is yet sometimes difficult to believe that a mere application to Christ, a mere sprinkling of this fountain, can change our inborn disposition, and make us so different from our former selves, that close observers might well doubt our identity, some saying, "This is he," others more cautiously only venturing to assert, "He is like him."

Though very pleasant to contemplate, it is impossible adequately to imagine the sensations of a man who for the first time sees the world in which he has for years been living blind. The sensation of light itself, the new sense of room and distance, the expansion of the nature, as if ushered into a new and ampler world, the glory of colour, of the skies; of the sun, of the moon walking in brightness, the first recognition of the "human face Divine," and the joy of watching the unspoken speech of its ever-changing expression, the thrill of first meeting parent, child, or friend eye to eye; the sublimity of the towers of Jerusalem, the glittering Temple, the marble palaces, by the base of which he had before dimly crept, feeling with his hand or tapping with his stick. To a man who, by the opening of one sealed sense, was thus ushered into so new a world, nothing can have seemed "too grand and good" for him to expect. He was prepared to believe in the glory and perfectness of God's world, and in Christ's power to bring him into contact with that glory. If the opening of his bodily organs of vision had given him such exquisite pleasure, and given him entrance to so new a life, what might not the opening of his inward eye accomplish? He had no patience with the difficulties raised by those who had not his experience: "How can a man that is a sinner do such miracles?" "Give God the praise; we know that this man is a sinner." To all these slow-brained, bewildered pedants, he had but the answer, "Whether He be a sinner or no, I know not; one thing I know, that, whereas I was blind, now I see." No arguments, happily, can rob me of the immense boon this Man has conferred upon me. If it gives you any satisfaction to apply your paltry tests to Him, and prove that He cannot have done this miracle, you are welcome to your conclusions; but you cannot alter the facts that I was blind, and that now I see. He who has given me so Divine a gift seems to me to carry with Him in some true form the Divine presence. I believe Him when He says, "I am the Light of the world."

This miracle was so public as to challenge scrutiny. It was not performed in the privacy of a sick-room, with none present but one or two disciples, who might be supposed ready to believe anything. It was performed on a public character and in broad day. And we nowadays may congratulate ourselves that there was a strong party in the community, whose interest it was to minimise the miracles of our Lord, and who certainly did what they could to prove them fictitious. In the case of this blind man, the authorities took steps to sift the matter; the parents were summoned, and then the man himself. They did precisely what sceptical writers in recent years have desiderated; they instituted a jealous examination of the affair. And so straightforward was the man's testimony, and so well-known was he in Jerusalem, that instead of denying the miracle, they adopted the easier course of excommunicating him for acknowledging Jesus as the Christ.

Ready witted, bold, and independent as this man was, he cannot but have felt keenly this punishment. His hope of employment was gone, and even his new joy in seeing would scarcely compensate for his being shunned by all as a tainted person. Had he been of a fainthearted and moody disposition he might have thought it had been as well had he been left in his blindness, and not become an object of abhorrence to all. But Jesus heard of his punishment, and sought him out, and declared to him more fully who He Himself was. He thus gave to the man assurance of a friendship outweighing in value what he had lost. He made him feel that though cut off from the fellowship of the visible Church, he was made a member of the true commonwealth of men--numbered among those who are united in friendship, and in work, and in destiny to Him who heads the real work of God, and promotes the abiding interests of men. And such is ever the reward of those who make sacrifices for Christ, who lose employment or friends by too boldly confessing their indebtedness to Him. They will themselves tell you that Christ makes up to them for their losses by imparting clearer knowledge of Himself, by making them conscious that they are remembered by Him, and by giving them a conscience void of offence, and a spirit superior to worldly misfortunes.

As a final reflection on the miracle and its results our Lord says: "For judgement am I come into the world, that they which see not might see, and that they which see might be made blind." A kind of sad humour betrays itself in His language, as He sees how easily felt-blindness is removed, but how absolutely blind presumed knowledge is. Humility ever wins the day. The blind man now saw because he knew he was blind, and trusted that Christ could give him sight; the Pharisees were stone-blind to the world Christ opened to them and carried in His person, because they thought that already they had all the knowledge they required. And wherever Christ comes men thus form themselves around Him in two groups, blind and seeing. "For judgment," for testing and dividing men, He is come. Nothing goes more searchingly into a man's character than Christ's offer to be to him the Light of life, to be his leader to a perfect life. This offer discloses what the man is content with, and what he really sighs for. This offer, which confronts us with the possibility of living in close fellowship and love with God, discloses whether our real bent is towards what is pure, and high, and holy, or towards what is earthly. This man who eagerly asked, "Who is the Son of God that I might believe on Him?" acknowledged his blindness and his longing for light, and he got it. The Pharisees, who claimed to see, condemned themselves by their rejection of Christ. "If," says our Lord, "ye were blind, if you were ignorant like this poor man, your ignorance would excuse you. But now ye say, We see, you boast that you can discern the Christ, you have tests of all kinds that you plume yourselves on, therefore your darkness and your sin remain." That is to say, the one sufficient test of Christ's claim is need. He presents Himself as the Light of the world, but if we are unconscious of darkness we cannot appreciate Him. But surely there are many of us who feel as if we were born blind, unable to see things spiritual as we ought; as if we had a sense too little, and could not find our way satisfactorily through this life. We hear of God with the hearing of the ear, but do not see Him; we have not the close and unmistakable discernment that comes by sight.

Footnotes:

34. See the Meditations of Marcus Aurelius.

Marcus Dods, D.D.

XXI. JESUS THE GOOD SHEPHERD

"Verily, verily, I say unto you, he that entereth not by the door into the fold of the sheep, but climbeth up some other way, the same is a thief and a robber. But he that entereth in by the door is the shepherd of the sheep. To him the porter openeth; and the sheep hear his voice: and he calleth his own sheep by name, and leadeth them out. When he hath put forth all his own, he goeth before them, and the sheep follow him: for they know his voice. And a stranger will they not follow, but will flee from him: for they know not the voice of strangers. This parable spake Jesus unto them; but they understood not what things they were which He spake unto them. Jesus therefore said unto them again, Verily, verily, I say unto you, I am the door of the sheep. All that came before me are thieves and robbers: but the sheep did not hear them. I am the door: by Me if any man enter in, he shall be saved, and shall go in and out, and shall find pasture. The thief cometh not, but that he may steal, and kill, and destroy: I came that they may have life, and may have it abundantly. I am the good shepherd: the good shepherd layeth down His life for the sheep. He that is a hireling, and not a shepherd, whose own the sheep are not, beholdeth the wolf coming, and leaveth the sheep, and fleeth, and the wolf snatcheth them, and scattereth them: he fleeth because he is a hireling, and careth not for the sheep. I am the good shepherd; and I know Mine own, and Mine own know Me, even as the Father knoweth Me, and I know the Father; and I lay down My life for the sheep. And other sheep I have, which are not of this fold: them also I must bring, and they shall hear My voice; and they shall become one flock, one shepherd. Therefore doth the Father love Me, because I lay down My life, that I may take it again. No one taketh it away from Me, but I lay it down of Myself. I have power to lay it down, and I have power to take it again. This commandment received I from My Father."--John x. 1--18.

This paragraph continues the conversation which arose out of the healing of the blind man. Jesus has pointed out to the Pharisees that they are affected with a more deplorable blindness than the born-blind beggar; He now proceeds to contrast their harsh treatment of the healed man with His own care of him, and uses this contrast as evidence of the illegitimacy of their usurpation of authority and the legitimacy of His own claim. It has been related (ix. 34) that the Jews had excommunicated the blind man because he had presumed to think for himself, and acknowledge as the Christ One regarding whom they had quietly enacted (ver. 22) that if any one acknowledged Him he should be banished from the synagogue. Very naturally the poor man would feel that this was a heavy price to pay for his eyesight. Brought up as he had been to consider the ecclesiastical authorities of Jerusalem as representing the Divine voice, he would feel that this excommunication cut him off from fellowship with all good men, and from the sources of a hopeful and godly life. Therefore, in pity for this poor sheep, and in indignation at those who thus assumed authority, Jesus explicitly declares, "I am the door." Not through the word of men who tyrannize over the flock to serve their own ends are you either admitted to or debarred from the real sources of spiritual life and fellowship with the true and good. Through Me only can you find access to permanent security and the free enjoyment of all spiritual nutriment; "By Me if any man enter in he shall be saved, and shall go in and out, and find pasture."

The primary object, then, of this allegorical passage is to impart to those who believe in Jesus the truest independence of spirit. This our Lord accomplishes by explicitly claiming for Himself the sole right of admission or rejection from the true fold of God's people. He comes into direct collision with the ecclesiastical authorities, denying that they are the true spiritual guides of the people, and presenting Himself as the supreme authority in matters spiritual. This uncompromising assertion of His own authority He makes in parabolic language; but that no one may misapprehend His meaning He Himself appends the interpretation. And in this interpretation it will be observed that, while the great ideas are explained and applied, there is no attempt to make these ideas square with the figure in every particular. In the figure, for example, the Door and the Shepherd are necessarily distinct; but our Lord does not on that account scruple to apply both figures to Himself. The rigidly logical explanation is thrown to the winds to make way for the substantial teaching.

I. First, then, Jesus here claims to be the sole means of access to security and life eternal. "I am the door: by Me if any man enter in, he shall be saved, and shall go in and out, and find pasture," Prompted by consideration for the feelings of the blind man, this expression would by him be interpreted as meaning, These arrogant Pharisees, then, can after all do me no injury; they can neither exclude nor admit; but only this Person, who has shown Himself so compassionate, so courageous, so ready to be my champion and my friend. He is the door. And this simple and memorable claim has remained through all the Christian centuries the bulwark against ecclesiastical tyranny, not indeed preventing injustice and outrage, but entirely robbing excommunication of its sting in the conscience that is right with its Lord. Outcast from the fellowship and privileges of so-called Churches of Christ many have been, who had yet the assurance in their own heart that by their attachment to Him they had entered into a more lasting fellowship and unspeakably higher privileges.

By this claim to be the Door, Jesus claims to be the Founder of the one permanent society of men. Through Him alone have men access to a position of security to association with all that is worthiest among men, to a never-failing life and a boundless freedom. He did not use His words at random, and this at least is contained in them. He gathers men round His Person, and assures us that He holds the key to life; that if He admits us, words of exclusion pronounced by others are but idle breath; that if He excludes us, the approval and applause of a world will not waft us in. No claim could possibly be greater.

II. Jesus also claims to be the Good Shepherd, and sets Himself in contrast to hirelings and robbers. This claim He proves in five particulars: He uses a legitimate mode of access to the sheep; His object is the welfare of the sheep; His Spirit is self-devoted; He knows and is known by His sheep; and all He does the Father has given Him commandment to do.

1. First, then, Jesus proves His claim to be the Good Shepherd by using the legitimate means of access to the sheep. He enters by the door. The general description of the relation between sheep and shepherd was drawn from what might be seen any morning in Palestine. At night the sheep are driven into a fold, that is, a walled enclosure, such as may be seen on our own sheep farms, only with higher walls for protection, and with a strongly-barred door in place of a hurdle or light gate. Here the sheep rest all night, guarded by a watchman or porter. In the morning the shepherds come, and at the recognised signal or knock are admitted by the porter, and each man calls his own sheep. The sheep, knowing his voice, follow him, and if any are lazy, or stubborn, or stupid, he goes in and drives them out, with a gentle, kindly compulsion, A stranger's voice they do not recognise, and do not heed. Besides, not only do they disregard a stranger's voice, but the porter also would do so, so that no robber thinks of appealing to the porter, but climbs the wall and lays hold of the sheep he wants.

Here, then, we have a picture of the legitimate and illegitimate modes of finding access to men and of gaining power over them. The legitimate leader of men comes by the door and invites: the illegitimate gets in anyhow and compels. The true shepherd is distinguished from the robber by both the action of the porter and the action of the sheep. But who is the porter who gives Christ access to the fold? Possibly, as some have suggested, the mind of Christ's contemporaries would revert to John the Baptist. The claim of Jesus to deal with men as their spiritual protector and leader had been legitimated by John, and no other pretended Messiah had been. And certainly, if any individual is indicated by the porter, it must be John the Baptist. But probably the figure includes all that introduces Jesus to men, His own life, His miracles, His loving words, providential circumstances. At all events, He makes His appeal openly, and has the requisite pass-word. There is nothing of the thief or the robber about His approach--nothing underhand and stealthy, nothing audaciously violent. On the other hand, "All that ever came before Me are thieves and robbers." The contemporary authorities in Jerusalem had come "before" Jesus, in so far as they had prepossessed the minds of the people against Him, and forcibly kept the sheep from Him. Their prior claims were the great obstacle to His being admitted. They held the fold against Him. It must have been plain to the people who heard His words that their own ecclesiastical authorities were meant. And this is not contradicted by the added clause, "but the sheep did not hear them." For these usurping leaders did not find the ear of the people, although they terrified them into obedience.

2. The Good Shepherd is identified and distinguished from the hireling by His object and His spirit of devotion--for these two characteristics may best be considered together (vv. 10--13). The hireling takes up this business of shepherding for his own sake, and just as he might take to keeping swine, or watching vineyards, or making bricks. It is not the work nor the sheep he has any interest in, but the pay. It is for himself he does what he does. His object is to make gain for himself, and his spirit is therefore a spirit of self-regard. Necessarily he flees from danger, having more regard for himself than for the sheep. The object of the good shepherd, on the contrary, is to find for the sheep a more abundant life. It is regard for them that draws him to the work. Consequently, as all love is self-devoting, so the regard of the shepherd for the sheep prompts him to devote himself, and, at the risk or expense of his own life, to save them from danger.

This differentiation of the hireling and the good shepherd was, in the first instance, exemplified in the different conduct of the authorities and Jesus towards the blind man. The authorities having fallen into the idea which commonly ensnares ecclesiastical magnates, that the people existed for them, not they for the people, persecuted him because he had followed his conscience: Jesus, by interposing in his favour, risked His own life. This collision with the Pharisees materially contributed to their determination to put Him to death.

Marcus Dods, D.D.

Probably our Lord intended that a larger meaning should be found in His words. To all His sheep He acts the part of a good shepherd by interposing, at the sacrifice of Himself, between them and all that threatens (vv. 17, 18). His death was voluntary, not necessitated either by the machinations of men or by His being human. His life was His own, to use as He saw best; and when He laid it down He did so freely. It was not that He succumbed to the wolf, to any power stronger than His own will and His own discernment of what was right. We may resign ourselves to death or choose it; but even though we did not, we could not escape it. Christ could. He "laid down" His life; and He did so, moreover, that He might "take it again." His sheep were not to be left defenceless, shepherdless: on the contrary, He died that He might free them from all danger and become to them an ever-living, omnipresent Shepherd. In these words the figure is lost in the reality.

In the words themselves, indeed, there is no direct suggestion that the penalty of sin is that which chiefly threatens Christ's sheep, but Christ could hardly use the words, and His people can hardly read them, without having this idea suggested. It was by interposing between us and sin that our Shepherd was slain. At first sight, indeed, we seem to be exposed to the very danger that slew the Shepherd: the wolf seems to be alive even after slaying Him. In spite of His death, we also die. What then is the danger from which He by His death has saved us?

The danger which threatened us was not bodily death, for from that we are not delivered. But it was something with which the death of the body is intimately connected. Bodily death is as it were the symptom, but not the disease itself. It is that which reveals the presence of the pestilence, but is not itself the real danger. It is like the plague-spot that causes the beholder to shudder, though the spot itself is only slightly painful. Now a skilful physician does not treat symptoms, does not apply his skill to allay superficial distresses, but endeavours to remove the radical disease. If the eye becomes bloodshot he does not treat the eye, but the general system. If an eruption comes out on the skin, he does not treat the skin, but alters the condition of the blood; and it is a small matter whether the symptom goes on to its natural issue, if thereby the eradication of the disease is rather helped than hindered. So it is with death: it is not our danger; no man can suppose that the mere transference from this state to another is injurious; only, death is in our case the symptom of a deep disease, of a real, fatal ailment of soul. We know death not as a mere transference from one world to another, but as our transference from probation to judgment, which sin makes us dread; and also as a transference which in form forcibly exhibits the weakness, the imperfection, the shame of our present state. Thus death connects itself with sin, which our conscience tells us is the great root of all our present misery. It is to us the symptom of the punishment of sin, but the punishment itself is not the death of the body but of the soul; the separation of the soul from all good, from all hope,--in a word, from God. This is the real danger from which Christ delivers us. If this be removed, it is immaterial whether bodily death remain or not; or rather, bodily death is used to help out our complete deliverance, as a symptom of the disease sometimes promotes the cure. Christ has tasted death for every man, and out of each man's cup has sucked the poison, so that now, as we in turn drink it, it is but a sleeping draught. There was a chemistry in His love and perfect obedience which drew the poison to His lips; and absorbing into His own system all the virulence of it, by the immortal vigour of His own constitution, He overcame its effects, and rose again triumphing over its lethargic potency.

It was not mere bodily death, then, which our Lord endured. That was not the wolf which the Good Shepherd saved us from. It was death with the sting of sin in it. It is this fact which shows us, from one point of view, the place of Christ's death in the work of atonement Death sets the seal on a man's spiritual condition. It utters the final word: He that is holy, let him be holy still; he that is filthy, let him be filthy still. The biblical view of death is that it marks the transition from a state of probation to a state of retribution. "It is appointed unto men once to die, and after death the judgment." There is no coming back again to make another preparation for judgment. We cannot have two lives, one after the flesh, and another after the spirit, but one life, one death, one judgment. Bodily death therefore thus becomes not only the evidence of spiritual death, but its seal. But this, falling upon Christ, fell harmless. Separation from God must be separation of the will, separation accomplished by the soul's self. In Christ there was no such separation. Sinners abide in death, because not only are they judicially separated, but they are in will and disposition separate. Plunge iron and wood into water: the one sinks, the other rises immediately, cannot be kept under, has a native buoyancy of its own that brings it to the surface, immerse it as often as we please. And Christ is as the wood cut by the prophet, that not only floats itself, but brings to the surface the heaviest weight.

3. It is the mutual recognition of sheep and shepherd which decisively exhibits the difference between the true shepherd and the robber. The timid animals that start and flee at the sound of a stranger's voice suffer their own shepherd to come among them and handle them. As the ownership of a dog is easily determined by his conduct towards two claimants, at one of whom he growls and round the other of whom he joyously barks and jumps; so you can tell who is the shepherd and who is the stranger by the different way in which a sheep behaves in the presence of each. If a shepherd's claim were doubtful, it might be settled either by his familiarity with its marks and ways, or by its familiarity with

him, its sufferance of his hand, its answer to his voice. Christ stakes His claim on a similar mutual recognition. If the soul does not respond to His call and follow Him, he will admit that His claim is ill-founded. He may require to enter the fold, to rouse the slumbering by a tap of His staff, to lift the sickly, to use a measure of severity with the dull and slow; but ultimately and mainly He bases His claim to be the true Leader and Lord of men simply on His power to attract them to Him. If there is not that in Him which causes us to mark Him off from all other persons, and makes us expect different things from Him, and causes us to trust ourselves with Him, then He does not expect that any other force will draw us to acknowledge Him.

The application of this to the attitude the blind man had assumed towards the Pharisees and towards Jesus was sufficiently obvious. He had disowned the Pharisees; he had acknowledged Jesus. It was plain therefore that Jesus was the Shepherd, and it was also plain that the Pharisees were not among Christ's sheep; they might be in the fold, but as they did not recognise and follow Christ they showed that they did not belong to His flock. And Christ trusts still to His own attractiveness and fitness to our needs. It is very remarkable how insufficient an account of their own conversion highly educated persons can give. Professor Clifford's favourite pupil was, like himself, an atheist; but racked by distress on account of Clifford's death, and being obliged to pass through other circumstances fitted to disclose the weakness of human nature, this pupil became an ardent Christian. One reads the record of this conversion expecting to find the reasoning power of the mathematician adding something to the demonstration of God's personality, or building a sure foundation for Christian faith. There is nothing of the kind. The experience of life gave new meaning to Christ's offer and to His revelation--that was all. So too in criticizing Renan's "Life of Christ," a French critic more profound than himself says: "The characteristic thing in this analysis of Christianity is that sin does not appear in it at all. Now if there is anything which explains the success of the Good News among men, it is that it offered deliverance from sin--salvation. It certainly would have been more appropriate to explain a religion religiously, and not to evade the very core of the subject. This Christ in white marble' is not He who made the strength of the martyrs." All this just means that if men have no sense of need they will not own Christ; and that if Christ's own presence and words do not draw them, they are not to be drawn. Of course much may be done in the way of presenting Christ to men, but beyond the simple exhibition of His person by word or in conduct not much can be done. It is a mystery, often oppressive, that men seem quite unattracted and unmoved by the Figure that so transcends all others, and gives a heart to the world. But Christ is known by His own.

This great fact of the mutual recognition of Christ and His people has an application not only to the first acceptance of Christ by the soul, but also to the Christian experience throughout. A mutual recognition and deep-lying affinity not only at first forms but for ever renews and maintains the bond between Christ and the Christian. He knows His sheep and is known by them. Often they do not know themselves;[35] but the Shepherd knows them. Many of us are frequently brought into doubt of our interest in Christ, but the foundation of God standeth sure, having this seal, "The Lord knoweth them that are His." We go astray, and get so torn with thorns, so fouled with mire, that few can tell to what fold we belong--our owner's marks are obliterated; but the Good Shepherd in telling His sheep has missed us, and come after us, and recognises and claims us even in our pitiable state. Who could tell to whom we belong when we lie absolutely content with the poisonous pasture of this world's vanities and rank gains; when the soul is stained with impurity, torn with passion, and has every mark that distinguishes Christ's people obscured? Is it surprising we should begin then ourselves to doubt whether we belong to the true fold or whether there is any true fold? Shameful are the places where Christ has found us, among prayerless days, unrestrained indulgences, with hardened heart and cynical thoughts, far from any purpose of good; and still again and again His presence has met us, His voice recalled us, His nearness awakened once more in us the consciousness that with Him we have after all a deeper sympathy than with any besides.

The whole experience of Christ as our Shepherd gives Him an increasing knowledge of us. The shepherd is the first to see the lamb at its birth, and not one day goes by but he visits it. So needful and merciful a work is it that it has no Sabbath, but as on the day of rest the shepherd feeds his own children so he cares for the lambs of his flock, sees that no harm is befalling them, remembers their dependence on him, observes their growth, removes what hinders it, hangs over the pale of the fold, watching with a pleased and fond observance their ways, their beauty, their comfort. And thus he becomes intimately acquainted with his sheep. So Christ becomes increasingly acquainted with us. We have thought much of Him; we have again and again pondered His life, His death, His words. We have endeavoured to understand what He requires of us, and day by day He has somehow been in our thoughts. Not less but far more constantly have we been in His thoughts, not a day has passed without His recurrence to this subject. He has looked upon and considered us, has marked the working of our minds, the forming of our purposes. He knows our habits by watching against them; our propensities by turning us from them. We are not left alone with our awful secret of sin: there is another who comprehends our danger, and is bent upon securing us against it.

Marcus Dods, D.D.

Slowly but surely does Christ thus win the confidence of the soul; doing for it a thousand kind offices that are not recognised, patiently waiting for the recognition and love which He knows must at last be given; quietly making Himself indispensable to the soul ere ever it discerns what it is that is bringing to it so new a buoyancy and hope. Slowly but surely grows in every Christian a reciprocal knowledge of Christ. More and more clearly does His Person stand out as the one on whom our expectation must rest. With Him we are brought into connection by every sin of ours, and by every hope. Is it not He before whom and about whom our hearts thrill and tremble time after time with a depth and awe of emotion which nothing else excites? Is it not to Him we owe it that this day we live in peace, knowing that our God is a loving Father? Is it not still His grace we must learn more deeply, His patient righteous way we must more exactly fall in with, if we are to forget our loved sin in the love of God, ourselves in the Eternal One? What is growth in grace but the laying bare of the sinner's heart to Christ, fold after fold being removed, till the very core of our being opens to Him and accepts Him, and the reciprocal laying bare of the heart of Christ toward the sinner?

For this growth in mutual understanding must advance till that perfect sympathy is attained which Christ indicates in the words: "I know My sheep and am known of Mine, as the Father knoweth Me and I know the Father." The mutual understanding between the Eternal Father and the Son is the only parallel to the mutual understanding of Christ and His people. In the loving union of husband and wife we see how intimate is the understanding, how the one is dissatisfied if any anxiety is not uttered and shared, how there can be no secret on either side. We see how a slight movement, a look, betrays intention more than many words of a stranger could reveal it; we see what confidence in one another is established, how the one is not satisfied until his thought is ratified by the other, his opinion reflected and better judged in the other, his emotion partaken of and again expressed by the other. But even this, though suggestive, is but a suggestion of the mutual intelligence subsisting between the Father and the Son, the absolute confidence in one another, the perfect harmony in purpose and feeling, the delight in knowing and being known. Into this perfect harmony of feeling and of purpose with the Supreme does Christ introduce His people. Gradually their thoughts are disengaged from what is trivial, and expand to take in the designs of the Eternal Mind. Gradually their tastes and affections are loosened from lower attachments, and are wrought to a perfect sympathy with what is holy and abiding.

Footnotes:

35. St. Augustine.

XXII. JESUS, SON OF GOD

"And it was the feast of the dedication at Jerusalem: it was winter; and Jesus was walking in the temple in Solomon's porch. The Jews therefore came round about Him, and said unto Him, How long dost Thou hold us in suspense? If Thou art the Christ, tell us plainly. Jesus answered them, I told you, and ye believe not: the works that I do in My Father's name, these bear witness of Me. But ye believe not, because ye are not of My sheep. My sheep hear My voice, and I know them, and they follow Me: and I give unto them eternal life; and they shall never perish, and no one shall snatch them out of My hand. My Father, which hath given them unto Me, is greater than all; and no one is able to snatch them out of the Father's hand. I and the Father are one. The Jews took up stones again to stone Him. Jesus answered them, Many good works have I showed you from the Father; for which of those works do ye stone Me? The Jews answered Him, For a good work we stone Thee not, but for blasphemy; and because that Thou, being a man, makest Thyself God. Jesus answered them, Is it not written in your law, I said, Ye are gods? If He called them gods, unto whom the word of God came (and the Scripture cannot be broken), say ye of Him, whom the Father sanctified and sent into the world, Thou blasphemest; because I said, I am the Son of God? If I do not the works of My Father, believe Me not. But if I do them, though ye believe not Me, believe the works: that ye may know and understand that the Father is in Me, and I in the Father. They sought again to take Him: and He went forth out of their hand. And He went away again beyond Jordan into the place where John was at the first baptizing; and there He abode. And many came unto Him; and they said, John indeed did no sign: but all things whatsoever John spake of this man were true. And many believed on Him there."--John x. 22--42.

After our Lord's visit to Jerusalem at the Feast of Tabernacles, and owing to His collision with the authorities in regard to the blind man whom He healed, He seems to have retired from the metropolis for some weeks, until the Feast of the Dedication. This Feast had been instituted by the Maccabees to celebrate the Purification of the Temple after its profanation by Antiochus Epiphanes. It began about the 20th December, and lasted eight days. As it was winter, possibly raining, and certainly cold, Jesus walked about in Solomon's Porch, where at all events He was under cover and had some shelter. Here the Jews gradually gathered, until at length He found Himself ringed round by hostile questioners, who bluntly, almost threateningly asked Him, "How long dost Thou make us to doubt? If Thou be the Christ, tell us plainly," a question which shows that, although they inferred from the assertions He had made regarding Himself that He claimed to be the Messiah, He had not directly and explicitly proclaimed Himself in terms no one could misunderstand.

At first sight their request seems fair and reasonable. In fact it is neither. The mere affirmation that He was the Christ would not have helped those whom His works and words had only prejudiced against Him. As He at once explained to them, He had made the affirmation in the only way possible, and their unbelief arose not from any want of explicitness on His part, but because they were not of His sheep (ver. 26). "My sheep hear My voice, and I know them, and they follow Me." Here, as elsewhere, He points in confirmation of His claim to the works His Father had given Him to do, and to the response His manifestation awakened in those who were hungering for truth and for God. Those who were given to Him by the Father, who were taught and led by God, acknowledged Him, and to such He imparted all those eternal and supreme blessings He was commissioned to bestow upon men.

But in describing the safety of those who believe in Him, Jesus uses an expression which gives umbrage to those who hear it--"I and the Father are one." Those who trust themselves to Christ shall not be plucked out of His hand: they are eternally secure. The guarantee of this is, that those who thus trust in Him are given to Him by the Father for this very purpose of safe-keeping: the Father Himself therefore watches over and protects them. "No man is able to pluck them out of My Father's hand. I and My Father are one." In this matter Christ acts merely as the Father's agent. The Pharisees might excommunicate the blind man and threaten him with penalties present and to come, but he is absolutely beyond their reach. Their threats are the pattering of hail on a bomb-proof shelter. The man is in Christ's keeping, and thereby is in God's keeping.

But this assertion the Jews at once construed into blasphemy, and took up stones to stone Him. With marvellous calmness Jesus arrests their murderous intention with the quiet question: "Many good works have I showed you from My Father; for which of these do you stone Me? You question whether I am the Father's Agent: does not the benignity of the works I have done prove Me such? Do not My works evince the indwelling power of the Father?" The Jews reply, and from their point of view quite reasonably: "For a good work we stone Thee not; but because Thou, being a man, makest Thyself God." How far they were justified in this charge we must inquire.

In this conversation two points are of the utmost significance.

1. The comparative equanimity with which they consider the claim of Jesus to be the Messiah is changed into fury when they imagine that He claims also equality with God. Their first appeal, "If Thou be the Christ, tell us plainly," is calm; and His answer, though it distinctly involved an affirmation that He was the Christ, was received without any violent demonstration of rage or of excitement. But their attitude towards Him changes in a moment and their calmness gives place to uncontrollable indignation as soon as it appears that He believes Himself to be one with the Father. They themselves would not have dreamed of putting such a question to Him: the idea of any man being equal with God was too abhorrent to the rigid monotheism of the Jewish mind. And when it dawned upon them that this was what Jesus claimed, they could do nothing but stop their ears and lift stones to end such blasphemy. No incident could more distinctly prove that the claim to be the Messiah was in their judgment one thing, the claim to be Divine another thing.

2. The contrast our Lord draws between Himself and those who had in Scripture been called "gods" is significant. It is the eighty-second Psalm He cites; and in it the judges of Israel are rebuked for abusing their office. It is of these unjust judges the psalm represents God as saying, "I have said, Ye are gods, and all of you are children of the Most High. But ye shall die like men, and fall like one of the princes." To these judges this word of God, "Ye are gods," had come at their consecration to their office. Having been occupied with other work they were now set apart to represent to men the authority and justice of God. But, argues our Lord, if men were called gods, to whom God's word came,--and they are so called in Scripture, which cannot be broken,--appointing them to their office, may He not rightly be called Son of God who is Himself sent to men; whose original and sole destiny it was to come into the world to represent the Father? The words are overweighted with manifold contrast. The judges were persons "to whom" the word of God came, as from without; Jesus was a person Himself "sent into the world" from God, therefore surely more akin to God than they were. The judges represented God by virtue of a commission received in the course of their career--the word of God came to them: Jesus, on the other hand, represented God because "sanctified," that is, set apart or consecrated for this purpose before He came into the world, and therefore obviously occupying a higher and more important position than they. But, especially, the judges were appointed to discharge one limited and temporary function, for the discharge of which it was sufficient that they should know the law of God; whereas it was "the Father," the God of universal relation and love, who consecrated Jesus and sent Him into the world, meaning now to reveal to men what lies deepest in His nature, His love, His fatherhood. The idea of the purpose for which Christ was sent into the world is indicated in the emphatic use of "the Father." He was sent to do the works of the Father (ver. 37); to manifest to men the benignity, tenderness, compassion of the Father; to encourage them to believe that the Father, the Source of all life, was in their midst accessible to them. If Jesus failed to reveal the Father, He had no claim to make. "If I do not the works of My Father, believe Me not." But if He did such works as declared the Father to be in their midst, then, as bearing the Father in Him and doing the Father's will, He might well be called "the Son of God." "Though ye believe not Me, believe the works; that ye may know, and believe, that the Father is in Me, and I in Him."

There can be no question, then, of the conclusiveness with which our Lord rebutted the charge of blasphemy. By a single sentence He put them in the position of presumptuously contradicting their own Scriptures. But weightier questions remain behind. Did Jesus merely seek to parry their thrust, or did He mean positively to affirm that He was God? His words do not carry a direct and explicit affirmation of His Divinity. Indeed, to a hearer His comparison of Himself with the judges would necessarily rather tend to veil the full meaning of His previous claims to pre-existence and superhuman dignity. On reflection, no doubt the hearers might see that a claim to Divinity was implied in His words; but even in the saying which first gave them offence, "I and the Father are one," it is rather what is implied than what is expressed that carries with it such a claim. For Calvin is unquestionably right in maintaining that these words were not intended to affirm identity of substance with the Father.[36] An ambassador whose actions or claims were contested might very naturally say, "I and my Sovereign are One"; not meaning thereby to claim royal dignity, but meaning to assert that what he did, his Sovereign did; that his signature carried his Sovereign's guarantee, and that his pledges would be fulfilled by the entire resources of his Sovereign. And as God's delegate, as the great Messianic Viceroy among men, it was no doubt this that our Lord wished in the first place to affirm, that He was the representative of God, doing His will, and backed by all His authority. "See the Father in Me," was His constant demand. All His self-assertion and self-revelation were meant to reveal the Father.

But although He does not directly and explicitly say, "I am God"; although He does not even use such language of Himself as John uses, when he says, "The Word was God"; yet is not His Divine nature a reasonable inference from such affirmations as that which we are here considering? Some interpreters very decidedly maintain that when Christ says, "I and the Father are one," He means one in power. They affirm that this assertion is made to prove that none of His sheep will be plucked out of His hand, and that this is secured because His Father is "greater than all," and He and His Father are one. Accordingly they hold that neither the old orthodox interpretation nor the Arian is correct: not the orthodox, because not unity of essence but unity of power is meant; not the Arian, because something more is meant than moral harmony. This, however, is difficult to maintain, and it is safer to abide by Calvin's interpretation, and believe that what Jesus means is that what He does will be confirmed by the Father. It is the Father's power He introduces as the final guarantee, not His own power.

Still, although the very terms He here uses may not even by implication affirm His Divinity, it remains to be asked whether there are not parts of Christ's work as God's commissioner on earth which could be accomplished by no one who was not Himself Divine. An ambassador may recommend his offers and guarantees by affirming that his power and that of his Sovereign are one, but in many cases he must have actual power on the spot. If a commissioner is sent to reduce a mutinous army or a large warlike tribe in rebellion, or to define a frontier in the face of an armed claimant, he must in such cases be no mere lay-figure, whose uniform tells what country he belongs to, but he must be a man of audacity and resource, able to act for himself without telegraphing for orders, and he must be backed by sufficient military force on the spot. It comes therefore to be a question whether the work on which Christ was sent was a work which could be accomplished by a man however fully equipped? Jesus though nothing more than human might have said, if commissioned by God to say so, "The promises I make, God will perform. The guarantees I give, God will respect." But is it possible that a man, however holy, however wise, however fully possessed by the Holy Spirit, could reveal the Father to men and adequately represent God? Could He influence, guide, and uplift individuals? Could He give life to men, could He assume the function of judging, could He bear the responsibility of being sole mediator between God and men? Must we not believe that for the work Christ came to do it was needful that He should be truly Divine?

While therefore it is quite true that Christ here rebuts the charge of blasphemy in His usual manner, not by directly affirming His Divine nature, but only by declaring that His office as God's representative gave Him as just a claim to the Divine name as the judges had, this circumstance cannot lead us to doubt the Divine nature of Christ, or prompt us to suppose He Himself was shy in affirming it, because the question is at once suggested whether the office He assumed is not one which only a Divine Person could undertake. It need not stumble our faith, if we find that not only in this passage but everywhere Jesus refrains from explicitly saying: "I am God." Not even among His Apostles, who were so much in need of instruction, does He definitely announce His Divinity. This is consistent with His entire method of teaching. He was not aggressive nor impatient. He sowed the seed, and knew that in time the blade would appear. He trusted more to the faith which slowly grew with the growth of the believer's mind than to the immediate acceptance of verbal assertions. He allowed men gradually to find their own way to the right conclusions, guiding them, furnishing them with sufficient evidence, but always allowing the evidence to do its work, and not breaking in upon the natural process by His authoritative utterances. But when, as in Thomas's case, it did dawn on the mind of any that this Person was God manifest in the flesh, He accepted the tribute paid. The acceptance of such a tribute proves Him Divine. No good man, whatever his function or commission on earth, could allow another to address him, as Thomas addressed Jesus, "My Lord and my God."

In the paragraph we are considering a very needful reminder is given us that the Jews of our Lord's time used the terms "God" and "Son of God" in a loose and inexact manner. Where the sense was not likely to be misunderstood, they did not scruple to apply these terms to officials and dignitaries. The angels they called sons of God; their own judges they called by the same name. The whole people considered collectively was called "God's son." And in the 2nd Psalm, speaking of the Messianic King, God says, "Thou art My Son: this day have I begotten Thee." It was therefore natural that the Jews should think of the Messiah not as properly Divine, but merely as being of such surpassing dignity as to be worthily though loosely called "Son of God." No doubt there are passages in the Old Testament which intimate with sufficient clearness that the Messiah would be truly Divine: "Thy throne, O God, is for ever and ever;" "Unto us a Child is born ... and His name shall be called the Mighty God;" "Behold the days come that I will raise unto David a righteous Branch, and this is the name whereby He shall be called, Jehovah our Righteousness." But though these passages seem decisive to us, looking on the fulfilment of them in Christ, we must consider that the Jewish Bible did not lie on every table for consultation as our Bibles do, and also that it was easy for the Jews to put a figurative sense on all such passages.

In a word, it was a Messiah the Jews looked for, not the Son of God. They looked for one with Divine powers, the delegate of God, sent to accomplish His will and to establish His kingdom, the representative among them of the Divine presence; but they did not look for a real dwelling of a Divine Person among them. It is quite certain that the Jews of the second century thought it silly of the Christians to hold that the Christ pre-existed from eternity as God, and condescended to be born as man.

"No Jew would allow," says a writer of that time, "that any prophet ever said that a Son of God would come; but what the Jews do say is that the Christ of God will come."

This circumstance, that the Jews did not expect the Messiah to be a Divine Person, throws light upon certain passages in the Gospels. When, for example, our Lord put the question, "What think ye of Christ? Whose Son is He?" The Pharisees promptly answer, "He is the Son of David." And, that they had no thought of ascribing to the Messiah a properly Divine origin, is shown by their inability to answer the further question, "How then does David call Him Lord?"--a question presenting no difficulty at all to any one who believed that the Messiah was to be Divine as well as human. [37]

So, too, if the Jews had expected the Messiah to be a Divine person, the ascription of Messianic dignity to one who was not the Messiah was blasphemy, being equivalent to ascribing Divinity to one who was not Divine. But in no case in which Jesus was acknowledged as the Messiah were those who so acknowledged Him proceeded against as blasphemous. The blind men who appealed to Him as the Son of David were told to be quiet; the crowd who hailed His entrance to Jerusalem scandalized the Pharisees but were not proceeded against. And even the blind beggar who owned Him was excommunicated by a special act passed for the emergency, which proves that the standing statute against blasphemy could not in such a case be enforced.

Again, this fact, that the Jews did not expect the Messiah to be strictly Divine, sheds light on the real ground of accusation against Jesus. So long as it was supposed that He merely claimed to be the promised Christ, and used the title "Son of God" as equivalent to a Messianic title, many of the people admitted His claim and were prepared to own Him. But when the Pharisees began to apprehend that He claimed to be the Son of God in a higher sense, they accused Him of blasphemy, and on this charge He was condemned. The account of His trial as given by Luke is most significant. He was tried in two courts, and in each upon two charges. When brought before the Sanhedrim He was first asked, "Art Thou the Christ?" a question which, as He at once pointed out, was useless; because He had taught quite openly, and there were hundreds who could testify to the claims He had put forward. He merely says that they themselves will one day own His claim. "Hereafter shall the Son of Man sit on the right hand of the power of God." This suggests to them that His claim was to something more than they ordinarily considered to be involved in the claim to Messiahship, and at once they pass to their second question, "Art Thou then the Son of God?" And on His refusing to disown this title, the High Priest rends His clothes, and Jesus is there and then convicted of blasphemy.

The different significance of the two claims is brought out more distinctly in the trial before Pilate. At first Pilate treats Him as an amiable enthusiast who fancies Himself a King and supposes He has been sent into the world to lead men to the truth. And accordingly after examining Him he presents Him to the people as an innocent person, and makes light of their charge that He claims to be King of the Jews. On this the Jews with one voice cry out, "We have a law, and by our law He ought to die, because He made Himself the Son of God." The effect of this charge upon Pilate is immediate and remarkable: "When Pilate heard that saying he was the more afraid, and went again into the judgment hall, and saith unto Jesus, Whence art Thou?" But Jesus gave him no answer.

It is plain then that it was for blasphemy Christ was condemned; and not simply because He claimed to be the Messiah. But if this is so, then how can we evade the conclusion that He was in very truth a Divine person? The Jews charged Him with making Himself equal with God; and, if He was not equal with God, they were quite right in putting Him to death. Their law was express, that no matter what signs and wonders a man performed, if he used these to draw them from the worship of the true God he was to be put to death. They crucified Jesus on the ground that He was a blasphemer, and against this sentence He made no appeal. He showed no horror at the accusation, as any good man must have shown. He accepted the doom, and on the Cross prayed, "Father, forgive them, for they know not what they do." That which they considered an act of piety was in truth the most frightful of crimes. But if He was not Divine, it was no crime at all, but a just punishment.

But no doubt that which lodges in the heart of each of us the conviction that Christ is Divine is the general aspect of His life, and the attitude He assumes towards men and towards God. We may not be able to understand in what sense there are Three Persons in the Godhead, and may be disposed with Calvin to wish that theological terms and distinctions had never become necessary. [38] We may be unable to understand how if Christ were a complete Person before the Incarnation, the humanity He assumed could also be complete and similar to our own. But notwithstanding such difficulties, which are the necessary result of our inability to comprehend the Divine nature, we are convinced, when we follow Christ through His life and listen to His own assertions, that there is in Him something unique and unapproached among men, that while He is one of us He yet looks at us also from the outside, from above. We feel that He is Master of all, that nothing in nature or in life can defeat Him; that while dwelling in time, He is also in Eternity, seeing before and after. The most stupendous claims He makes seem somehow justified; assertions which in other lips would be blasphemous are felt to be just and natural in His. It is felt that somehow, even if we cannot say how, God is in Him.

Footnotes:

36. Calvin says: "The ancients misinterpreted this passage to prove that Christ is of one substance with the Father. For Christ is not here disputing regarding unity of substance, but regarding the harmony of will (consensu) which he has with the Father, maintaining that whatever He does will be confirmed by the Father's power."

37. In this passage I borrow the convincing argument of Treffry in his too little read treatise On the Eternal Sonship. He says, p. 89: "Had the Jews regarded the Messiah as a Divine person, the claims of Jesus to that character had been in all cases equivalent to the assertion of His Deity. But there is not upon record one example in which any considerable emotion was manifested against these claims; while, on the other hand, a palpable allusion to His higher nature never failed to be instantly and most indignantly resented. The conclusion is obvious."

38. "Utinam quidem sepulta essent" (Instit., I., 13, 5).

XXIII. JESUS THE RESURRECTION AND LIFE

"Now a certain man was sick, Lazarus of Bethany, of the village of Mary and her sister Martha. And it was that Mary which anointed the Lord with ointment, and wiped His feet with her hair, whose brother Lazarus was sick. The sisters therefore sent unto Him, saying, Lord, behold, he whom Thou lovest is sick. But when Jesus heard it, He said, This sickness is not unto death, but for the glory of God, that the Son of God may be glorified thereby. Now Jesus loved Martha, and her sister, and Lazarus. When therefore He heard that he was sick, He abode at that time two days in the place where He was. Then after this He saith to the disciples, Let us go into Judæa again. The disciples say unto Him, Rabbi, the Jews were but now seeking to stone Thee; and goest Thou thither again? Jesus answered, Are there not twelve hours in the day? If a man walk in the day, he stumbleth not, because he seeth the light of this world. But if a man walk in the night, he stumbleth, because the light is not in him. These things spake He: and after this he saith unto them, Our friend Lazarus is fallen asleep; but I go, that I may awake him out of sleep. The disciples therefore said unto Him, Lord, if he is fallen asleep, he will recover. Now Jesus had spoken of his death: but they thought that He spake of taking rest in sleep. Then Jesus therefore said unto them plainly, Lazarus is dead. And I am glad for your sakes that I was not there, to the intent ye may believe; nevertheless let us go unto him. Thomas, therefore, who is called Didymus, said unto his fellow-disciples, Let us also go, that we may die with Him. So when Jesus came, He found that he had been in the tomb four days already. Now Bethany was nigh unto Jerusalem, about fifteen furlongs off; and many of the Jews had come to Martha and Mary, to console them concerning their brother. Martha, therefore, when she heard that Jesus was coming, went and met Him; but Mary still sat in the house. Martha, therefore, said unto Jesus, Lord, if Thou hadst been here, my brother had not died. And even now I know that, whatsoever Thou shalt ask of God, God will give Thee. Jesus saith unto her, Thy brother shall rise again. Martha saith unto Him, I know that he shall rise again in the resurrection at the last day. Jesus said unto her, I am the Resurrection, and the Life: he that believeth on Me, though he die, yet shall he live: and whosoever liveth and believeth on me shall never die. Believest thou this? She saith into Him, Yea, Lord: I have believed that Thou art the Christ, the Son of God, even He that cometh into the world. And when she had said this, she went away, and called Mary her sister secretly, saying, The Master is here, and calleth thee. And she, when she heard it, arose quickly, and went unto Him. (Now Jesus was not yet come into the village, but was still in the place where Martha met Him.) The Jews then which were with her in the house, and were comforting her, when they saw Mary, that she rose up quickly and went out, followed her, supposing that she was going unto the tomb to weep there. Mary therefore, when she came where Jesus was, and saw Him, fell down at His feet, saying unto Him, Lord, if Thou hadst been here, my brother had not died. When Jesus therefore saw her weeping, and the Jews also weeping which came with her, He groaned in the spirit, and was troubled, and said, Where have ye laid him? They say unto Him, Lord, come and see. Jesus wept. The Jews therefore said, Behold how He loved him! But some of them said, Could not this man, which opened the eyes of him that was blind, have caused that this man also should not die? Jesus therefore again groaning in Himself cometh to the tomb. Now it was a cave, and a stone lay against it. Jesus saith, Take ye away the stone. Martha, the sister of him that was dead, saith unto Him, Lord, by this time he stinketh: for he hath been dead four days. Jesus saith unto her, Said I not unto thee, that, if thou believedst, thou shouldest see the glory of God? So they took away the stone. And Jesus lifted up His eyes, and said, Father, I thank Thee that Thou heardest Me. And I know that Thou hearest Me always: but because of the multitude which standeth around I said it, that they may believe that Thou didst send Me. And when He had thus spoken, He cried with a loud voice, Lazarus, come forth. He that was dead came forth, bound hand and foot with grave-clothes; and his face was bound about with a napkin. Jesus saith unto them, Loose him, and let him go."--John xi. 1--44.

    In this eleventh chapter it is related how the death of Jesus was finally determined upon, on the occasion of His raising Lazarus. The ten chapters which precede have served to indicate how Jesus revealed Himself to the Jews in every aspect that was likely to win faith, and how each fresh revelation only served to embitter them against Him, and harden their unbelief into hopeless hostility. In these few pages John has given us a wonderfully compressed but vivid summary of the miracles and conversations of Jesus, which served to reveal His true character and work. Jesus has manifested Himself as the Light of the World, yet the darkness does not comprehend Him; as the Shepherd of the

Sheep, and they will not hear His voice; as the Life of men, and they will not come unto Him that they might have Life; as the impersonated love of God come to dwell among men, sharing their sorrows and their joys, and men hate Him the more, the more love He shows; as the Truth which could make men free, and they choose to serve the father of lies, and to do his work. And now, when He reveals Himself as the Resurrection and the Life, possessed of the key to what is inaccessible to all others, of the power most essential to man, they resolve upon His death. There was an appropriateness in this. His love for His friends drew Him back at the risk of His life to the neighbourhood of Jerusalem: it is as if to His eye Lazarus represented all His friends, and He feels constrained to come out from His safe retreat, and, at the risk of His own life, deliver them from the power of death.

That this was in the mind of Jesus Himself is obvious. When He expresses His resolve to go to His friends in Bethany, He uses an expression which shows that He anticipated danger, and which at once suggested to the disciples that He was running a great risk. "Let us go," not "to Bethany" but "into JudÃ¦a again." His disciples say unto Him, "Master, the Jews of late sought to stone Thee, and goest Thou thither again?" The answer of Jesus is significant: "Are there not twelve hours in the day?" That is to say: Has not every man his allotted time to work, his day of light, in which he can walk and work, and which no danger nor calamity can shorten? Can men make the sun set one hour earlier? So neither can they shorten by one hour the day of life, of light, and toil your God has appointed to you. Wicked men may grudge that God's sun shine on the fields of their enemies and prosper them, but their envy cannot darken or shorten the course of the sun: so may wicked men grudge that I work these miracles, and do these deeds of My loving Father, but I am as far above their reach as the sun in the heavens; until I have run My appointed course their envy is impotent. The real danger begins when a man tries to prolong his day, to turn night into day; the danger begins when a man through fear turns aside from duty; he then loses the only true guide and light of his life. A man's knowledge of duty, or God's will, is the only true light he has to guide him in life: that duty God has already measured, to each man his twelve hours; and only by following duty into all hazards and confusion can you live out your full term; if, on the other hand, you try to extend your term, you find that the sun of duty has set for you, and you have no power to bring light on your path. A man may preserve his life on earth for a year or two more by declining dangerous duty, but his day is done, he is henceforth only stumbling about on earth in the outer cold and darkness, and had far better have gone home to God and been quietly asleep, far better have acknowledged that his day was done and his night come, and not have striven to wake and work on. If through fear of danger, of straitened circumstances, of serious inconvenience, you refuse to go where God--i.e., where duty--calls you, you make a terrible mistake; instead of thereby preserving your life you lose it, instead of prolonging your day of usefulness and of brightness and comfort, you lose the very light of life, and stumble on henceforward through life without a guide, making innumerable false steps as the result of that first false step in which you turned in the wrong direction; not dead indeed, but living as "the very ghost of your former self" on this side of the grave--miserable, profitless, benighted.

John apparently had two reasons for recording this miracle; firstly, because it exhibited Jesus as the Resurrection and the Life; secondly, because it more distinctly separated the whole body of the Jews into believers and unbelievers. But there are two minor points which may be looked at before we turn to these main themes.

First, we read that when Jesus saw Mary weeping, and the Jews also weeping which came with her, He groaned in spirit and was troubled, and then wept. But why did He show such emotion? The Jews who saw Him weep supposed that His tears were prompted, as their own were, by sorrow for their loss and sympathy with the sisters. To see a woman like Mary casting herself at His feet, breaking into a passion of tears, and crying with intense regret, if not with a tinge of reproach, "Lord, if Thou hadst been here, my brother had not died," was enough to bring tears to the eyes of harder natures than our Lord's. But the care with which John describes the disturbance of His spirit, the emphasis he lays upon His groaning, the notice he takes of the account the Jews give of His tears,--all seem to indicate that something more than ordinary grief or sympathy was the fountain of these tears, the cause of the distress which could vent itself only in audible groans. He was in sympathy with the mourners and felt for them, but there was that in the whole scene with which He had no sympathy; there was none of that feeling He required His disciples to show at His own death, no rejoicing that one more had gone to the Father. There was a forgetfulness of the most essential facts of death, an unbelief which seemed entirely to separate this crowd of wailing people from the light and life of God's presence. "It was the darkness between God and His creatures that gave room for, and was filled with, their weeping and wailing over their dead." It was the deeper anguish into which mourners are plunged by looking upon death as extinction, and by supposing that death separates from God and from life, instead of giving closer access to God and more abundant life,--it was this which caused Jesus to groan. He could not bear this evidence that even the best of God's children do not believe in God as greater than death, and in death as ruled by God.

This gives us the key to Christ's belief in immortality, and to all sound belief in immortality. It was Christ's sense of God, His uninterrupted consciousness of God, His distinct knowledge that God the loving Father is the existence in whom all live,--it was this which made it impossible for Christ to think of death as extinction or separation from God. For one who consciously lived in God to be separated from God was impossible. For one who was bound to God by love, to drop out of that love into nothingness or desolation was inconceivable. His constant and absolute sense of God gave Him an unquestioning sense of immortality. We cannot conceive of Christ having any shadow of doubt of a life beyond death; and if we ask why it was so, we further see it was because it was impossible for Him to doubt of the existence of God--the ever-living, ever-loving God.

And this is the order or conviction in us all. It is vain to try and build up a faith in immortality by natural arguments, or even by what Scripture records. As Bushnell truly says: "The faith of immortality depends on a sense of it begotten, not on an argument for it concluded." And this sense of immortality is begotten when a man is truly born again, and instinctively feels himself an heir of things beyond this world into which his natural birth has ushered him; when he begins to live in God; when the things of God are the things among which and for which he lives; when his spirit is in daily and free communication with God; when he partakes of the Divine nature, finding his joy in self-sacrifice and love, in those purposes and dispositions which can be exercised in any world where men are, and with which death seems to have no conceivable relation. But, on the other hand, for a man to live for the world, to steep his soul in carnal pleasures and blind himself by highly esteeming what belongs only to earth,--for such a man to expect to have any intelligent sense or perception of immortality is out of the question.

2. Another question, which may, indeed, be inquisitive, but can scarcely be reprehended, is sure to be asked: What was the experience of Lazarus during these four days? To speculate on what he saw or heard or experienced, to trace the flight of his soul through the gates of death to the presence of God, may perhaps seem to some as foolish as to go with those curious Jews who flocked out to Bethany to set eyes on this marvel, a man who had passed to the unseen world and yet returned. But although no doubt good and great purposes are served by the obscurity that involves death, our endeavour to penetrate the gloom, and catch some glimpses of a life we must shortly enter, cannot be judged altogether idle. Unfortunately, it is little we can learn from Lazarus. Two English poets, the one fitted to deal with this subject by an imagination that seems capable of seeing and describing whatever man can experience, the other by an insight that instinctively apprehends spiritual things, and both by reverential faith, have taken quite opposite views of the effect of death and resurrection upon Lazarus. The one describes him as living henceforth a dazed life, as if his soul were elsewhere; as if his eye, dazzled with the glory beyond, could not adjust itself to the things of earth. He is thrown out of sympathy with the ordinary interests of men, and seems to live at cross purposes with all around him. This was a very inviting view of the matter to a poet: for here was an opportunity of putting in a concrete way an experience quite unique. It was a task worthy of the highest poetic genius to describe what would be the sensations, thoughts, and ways of a man who had passed through death and seen things invisible, and been "exalted above measure," and become certified by face to face vision of all that we can only hope and believe, and had yet been restored to earth. The opportunity of contrasting the paltriness of earth with the sublimity and reality of the unseen was too great to be resisted. The opportunity of flouting our professed faith by exhibiting the difference between it and a real assurance, by showing the utter want of sympathy between one who had seen and all others on earth who had only believed,--this opportunity was too inviting to leave room for a poet to ask whether there was a basis in fact for this contrast; whether it was likely that in point of fact Lazarus did conduct himself, when restored to earth, as one who had been plunged into the full light and thronging life of the unseen world. And, when we consider the actual requirements of the case, it seems most unlikely that Lazarus can have been recalled from a clear consciousness and full knowledge of the heavenly life--unlikely that he should be summoned to live on earth with a mind too large for the uses of earth, overcharged with knowledge he could not use, as a poor man suddenly enriched beyond his ability to spend, and thereby only confused and stupefied. Apparently the idea of the other poet is the wiser when he says:--

> "Where wert thou, brother, those four days?'
> There lives no record of reply,
> Which, telling what it is to die,
> Had surely added praise to praise.
> "From every house the neighbours met,
> The streets were fill'd with joyful sound,
> A solemn gladness even crown'd
> The purple brows of Olivet.
> "Behold a man raised up by Christ!
> The rest remaineth unrevealed;
> He told it not; or something seal'd
> The lips of that Evangelist."

The probability is, he had nothing to reveal. As Jesus said, He came "to awake him out of sleep." Had he learned anything of the spirit world, it must have oozed out. The burden of a secret which all men craved to know, and which the scribes and lawyers from Jerusalem would do all in their power to elicit from him, would have damaged his mind and oppressed his life. His rising would be as the awaking of a man from deep sleep, scarcely knowing what he was doing, tripping and stumbling in the grave-clothes and wondering at the crowd. What Mary and Martha would prize would be the unchanged love that shone in his face as he recognized them, the same familiar tones and endearments,--all that showed how little change death brings, how little rupture of affection or of any good thing, how truly he was their own brother still.

To our Lord Himself it was a grace that so shortly before His own death, and in a spot so near where He Himself was buried, He should be encouraged by seeing a man who had been three days in the grave rise at His word. The narrative of His last hours reveals that such encouragement was not useless. But for us it has a still more helpful significance. Death is a subject of universal concern. Every man must have to do with it; and in presence of it every man feels his helplessness. Nowhere do we so come to the limit and end of our power as at the door of a vault; nowhere is the weakness of man so keenly felt. There is the clay, but who shall find the spirit that dwelt in it? Jesus has no such sense of weakness. Believing in the fatherly and undying love of the Eternal God, He knows that death cannot harm, still less destroy, the children of God. And in this belief He commands back to the body the soul of Lazarus; through the ear of that dead and laid-aside body He calls to His friend, and bids him from the unseen world. Surely we also may say, with Himself, we are glad that He was not with Lazarus in his sickness, that we might have this proof that not even death carries the friend of Christ beyond His reach and power.

There is no one who can afford to look at this scene with indifference. We have all to die, to sink in utter weakness past all strength of our own, past all friendly help of those around us. It must always remain a trying thing to die. In the time of our health we may say,--

> "Since Nature's works be good, and Death doth serve
> As Nature's work, why should we fear to die?"

but no argument should make us indifferent to the question whether at death we are to be extinguished or to live on in happier, fuller life. If a man dies in thoughtlessness, with no forecasting or foreboding of what is to follow, he can give no stronger proof of thoughtlessness. If a man faces death cheerfully through natural courage, he can furnish no stronger evidence of courage; if he dies calmly and hopefully through faith, this is faith's highest expression. And if it is really true that Jesus did raise Lazarus, then a world of depression and fear and grief is lifted off the heart of man. That very assurance is given to us which we most of all need. And, so far as I can see, it is our own imbecility of mind that prevents us from accepting this assurance and living in the joy and strength it brings. If Christ raised Lazarus He has a power to which we can safely trust; and life is a thing of permanence and joy. And if a man cannot determine for himself whether this did actually happen or not, he must, I think, feel that the fault is his, and that he is defrauding himself of one of the clearest guiding lights and most powerful determining influences we have.

This miracle is itself more significant than the explanation of it. The act which embodies and gives actuality to a principle is its best exposition. But the main teaching of the miracle is enounced in the words of Jesus: "I am the Resurrection and the Life." In this statement two truths are contained: (1) that resurrection and life are not future only, but present; and (2) that they become ours by union with Christ.

(1) Resurrection and Life are not blessings laid up for us in a remote future: they are present. When Jesus said to Martha, "Thy brother shall rise again," she answered, "I know that he shall rise again in the resurrection at the last day,"--meaning to indicate that this was small consolation. There was her brother lying in the tomb dead, and there he would lie for ages dead; no more to move about in the home she loved for his sake, no more to exchange with her one word or look. What comfort did the vague and remote hope of reunion after long ages of untold change bring? What comfort is to sustain her through the interval? When parents lose the children whom they could not bear to have for a day out of their sight, whom they longed for if they were absent an hour beyond their time, it is no doubt some comfort to know that one day they will again be folded to their breast. But this is not the comfort Christ gives Martha. He comforts her, not by pointing her to a far-off event which was vague and remote, but to His own living person, whom she knew, saw, and trusted. And He assured her that in Him were resurrection and life; that all, therefore, who belonged to Him were uninjured by death, and had in Him a present and continuous life.

Christ, then, does not think of immortality as we do. The thought of immortality is with Him involved in, and absorbed by, the idea of life. Life is a present thing, and its continuance a matter of course. When life is full, and abundant, and glad, the present is enough, and past and future are unthought of. It is life, therefore, rather than immortality Christ speaks of; a present, not a future, good;

an expansion of the nature now, and which necessarily carries with it the idea of permanence. Eternal life He defines, not as a future continuance to be measured by ages, but as a present life, to be measured by its depth. It is the quality, not the length, of life He looks at. Life prolonged without being deepened by union with the living God were no boon. Life with God, and in God, must be immortal; life without God He does not call life at all.

In evidence of this present continued life Lazarus was called back, and shown to be still alive. In him the truth of Christ's words was exemplified: "He that believeth in Me, though he were dead yet shall he live; and whosoever liveth and believeth in Me shall never die." He will doubtless, like all men, undergo that change which we call death; he will become disconnected from this present earthly scene, but his life in Christ will suffer no interruption. Dissolution may pass on his body, but not on his life. His life is hid with Christ in God. It is united to the unfailing source of all existence.

(2) Such life, now abundant and evermore abiding, Christ affords to all who believe in Him. To Martha He intimates that He has power to raise the dead, and that this power is so much His own that He needs no instrument or means to apply it; that He Himself, as He stood before her, contained all that was needful for resurrection and life. He intimates all this, but He intimates much more than this. That He had the power to raise the dead it would, no doubt, revive the heart of Martha to hear, but what guarantee, what hope, was there that He would exercise that power? And so Christ does not say, I have the power, but, I am. Is any one, is Lazarus, joined to Me? has he attached himself confidingly to My Person: then whatever I am finds exercise in him. It is not only that I have this power to exercise on whom I may; but I am this power, so that if he be one with Me I cannot withhold the exercise of that power from him.

They who have learned to obey Christ's voice in life will most quickly hear it, and recognise its authority, when they sleep in death. They who have known its power to raise them out of spiritual death will not doubt its power to raise them from bodily death to a more abundant life than this world affords. They once felt as if nothing could deliver them; they were dead--deaf to Christ's commands, bound in bonds which they thought would hold them till they themselves should rot away from within them; they were buried out of sight of all that could give spiritual life, and the heavy stone of their own hardened will lay on their ruined and outcast condition. But Christ's love sought them out and called them into life. Assured that He has had power to do this, conscious in themselves that they are alive with a life given by Christ, they cannot doubt that the grave will be but a bed of rest, and that neither things present nor things to come can separate them from a love which already has shown itself capable of the utmost.

XXIV. JESUS THE SCAPEGOAT

"Many therefore of the Jews, which came to Mary and beheld that which He did, believed on Him. But some of them went away to the Pharisees, and told them the things which Jesus had done. The chief priests therefore and the Pharisees gathered a council, and said, What do we? for this man doeth many signs. If we let Him thus alone, all men will believe on Him: and the Romans will come and take away both our place and our nation. But a certain one of them, Caiaphas, being high priest that year, said unto them, Ye know nothing at all, nor do ye take account that it is expedient for you that one man should die for the people, and that the whole nation perish not. Now this he said not of himself: but being high priest that year he prophesied that Jesus should die for the nation; and not for the nation only, but that he might also gather together into one the children of God that are scattered abroad. So from that day forth they took counsel that they might put Him to death. Jesus therefore walked no more openly among the Jews, but departed thence into the country near to the wilderness, into a city called Ephraim; and there He tarried with the disciples."--John xi. 45--54.

When Jesus raised Lazarus from the dead He was quite aware that He was risking His own life. He knew that a miracle so public, so easily tested, so striking, could not be overlooked, but must decisively separate between those who yielded to what was involved in the miracle, and those who hardened themselves against it. It is remarkable that none had the hardihood to deny the fact. Those who most determinedly proceeded against Jesus did so on the very ground that His miracles were becoming too numerous and too patent. They perceived that in this respect Jesus answered so perfectly to the popular conception of what the Messiah was to be, that it was quite likely He would win the multitude to belief in Him as the long-looked-for King of the Jews. But if there were any such popular enthusiasm aroused, and loudly declared, then the Romans would interfere, and, as they said, "come and take away both our place and nation." They felt themselves in a great difficulty, and looked upon Jesus as one of those fatal people who arise to thwart the schemes of statesmen, and spoil well-laid plans, and introduce disturbing elements into peaceful periods.

Caiaphas, astute and unscrupulous, takes a more practical view of things, and laughs at their helplessness. "Why!" he says, "do you not see that this Man, with His éclat and popular following, instead of endangering us and bringing suspicion on our loyalty to Rome, is the very person we can use to exhibit our fidelity to the Empire. Sacrifice Jesus, and by His execution you will not merely clear the nation of all suspicion of a desire to revolt and found a kingdom under Him, but you will show such a watchful zeal for the integrity of the Empire as will merit applause and confidence from the jealous power of Rome." Caiaphas is the type of the bold, hard politician, who fancies he sees more clearly than all others, because he does not perplex himself by what lies below the surface, nor suffer the claims of justice to interfere with his own advantage. He looks at everything from the point of view of his own idea and plan, and makes everything bend to that. He had no idea that in making Jesus a scapegoat he was tampering with the Divine purposes.

John, however, in looking back upon this council, sees that this bold, unflinching diplomatist, who supposed he was moving Jesus and the council and the Romans as so many pieces in his own game, was himself used as God's mouthpiece to predict the event which brought to a close his own and all other priesthood. In the strange irony of events he was unconsciously using his high-priestly office to lead forward that one Sacrifice which was for ever to take away sin, and so to make all further priestly office superfluous. Caiaphas saw and said that it was expedient that one man die for the nation; but, as in all prophetic utterance, so in these words, says John, a very much deeper sense lay than was revealed by their primary application. It is, says John, quite true that Christ's death would be the saving of a countless multitude, only it was not from the Roman legions that it would long save men, but from an even more formidable visitation. Caiaphas saw that the Romans were within a very little of terminating the ceaseless troubles which arose out of this Judæan province, by transporting the inhabitants and breaking up their nationality; and he supposed that by proclaiming Jesus as an aspirant to the throne and putting Him to death, he would cleanse the nation of all complicity in His disloyalty and stay the Roman sword. And John says, that in carrying out this idea of his, he unwittingly carried out the purpose of God that Jesus should die for that nation--"and not for that nation only, but that also He should gather together in one the children of God that were scattered abroad."

Now it must be owned that it is much easier to understand what Caiaphas meant than what John meant; much easier to see how fit Jesus was to be a national scapegoat than to understand how His death removes the sin of the world. There are, however, one or two points regarding the death of Christ which become clearer in the light of Caiaphas's idea.

First, the very characteristics of Christ which made Caiaphas think of Him as a possible scapegoat for the nation, are those which make it possible that His death should serve a still larger purpose. When the brilliant idea of propitiating the Roman government by sacrificing Jesus flashed into the mind of Caiaphas, he saw that Jesus was in every respect suited to this purpose. He was in the first place a person of sufficient importance. To have seized an unknown peasant, who never had, and never could have, much influence in Jewish society, would have been no proof of zeal in extinguishing rebellion. To crucify Peter or John or Lazarus, none of whom had made the most distant claim to kingship, would not serve Caiaphas's turn. But Jesus was the head of a party. In disposing of Him they disposed of His followers. The sheep must scatter, if the Shepherd were put out of the way.

Then, again, Jesus was innocent of everything but this. He was guilty of attaching men to Himself, but innocent of everything besides. This also fitted Him for Caiaphas's purpose, for the high priest recognised that it would not do to pick a common criminal out of the prisons and make a scapegoat of him. That had been a shallow fiction, which would not for a moment stay the impending Roman sword. Had the Russians wished to conciliate our Government and avert war, this could not have been effected by their selecting for execution some political exile in Siberia, but only by recalling and degrading such an outstanding person as General Komaroff. In every case where any one is to be used as a scapegoat these two qualities must meet--he must be a really, not fictitiously, representative person, and he must be free from all other claims upon his life. It is not everyone who can become a scapegoat. The mere agreement between the parties, that such and such a person be a scapegoat, is only a hollow fiction which can deceive no one. There must be underlying qualities which constitute one person, and not another, representative and fit.

Now John does not expressly say that the deliverance Jesus was to effect for men generally was to be effected in a similar manner to that which Caiaphas had in view. He does not expressly say that Jesus was to become the scapegoat of the race: but impregnated as John's mind was with the sacrificial ideas in which he had been nurtured, the probability is that the words of Caiaphas suggested to him the idea that Jesus was to be the scapegoat of the race. And, certainly, if Jesus was the scapegoat on whom our sins were laid, and who carried them all away, He had these qualities which fitted Him for this work: He had a connection with us of an intimate kind, and He was stainlessly innocent.

This passage then compels us to ask in what sense Christ was our sacrifice.

With remarkable, because significant, unanimity the consciences of men very differently situated have prompted them to sacrifice. And the idea which all ancient nations, and especially the Hebrews, entertained regarding sacrifice is fairly well ascertained. Both the forms of their rites and their explicit statements are conclusive on this point,--that in a certain class of sacrifices they looked on the victim as a substitute bearing the guilt of the offerer and receiving the punishment due to him. This seems, after all discussion, to be the most reasonable interpretation to put upon expiatory sacrifice. Both heathens and Jews teach that without the shedding of blood there is no remission of sins; that the life of the sinner is forfeited, and that in order to the sparing of his life, another life is rendered instead; and that as the life is in the blood, the blood must be poured out in sacrifice. Heathens were as punctilious as Hebrews in their scrutiny of the victims, to ascertain what animals were fit for sacrifice by the absence of all blemish. They used forms of deprecation as exactly expressing the doctrines of substitution and of atonement by vicarious punishment. In one significant, though repulsive, particular some of the heathen went farther than the Hebrews: occasionally, the sinner who sought cleansing from defilement was actually washed in the blood of the victim slain for him. By an elaborate contrivance the sinner sat under a stage of open woodwork on which the animal was sacrificed, and through which its blood poured upon him.

The idea expressed by all sacrifices of expiation was, that the victim took the place of the sinner, and received the punishment due to him. The sacrifice was an acknowledgment on the sinner's part that by his sin he had incurred penalty; and it was a prayer on the sinner's part that he might be washed from the guilt he had contracted, and might return to life with the blessing and favour of God upon him. Of course, it was seen, and said by the heathen themselves, as well as by the Jews, that the blood of bulls and goats had in itself no relation to moral defilement. It was used in sacrifice merely as a telling way of saying that sin was acknowledged and pardon desired, but always with the idea of substitution more or less explicitly in the mind. And the ideas which were inevitably associated with sacrifice were transferred to Jesus by His immediate disciples. And this transference of the ideas connected with sacrifice to Himself and His death was sanctioned--and indeed suggested--by Jesus, when, at the Last Supper, He said, "This cup is the New Testament in My Blood, which is shed for many, for the remission of sins."

But here the question at once arises: In what sense was the Blood of Christ shed for the remission of sins? In what sense was He a substitute and victim for us? Before we try to find an answer to this question, two preliminary remarks may be made--first, that our salvation depends not on our understanding how the death of Christ takes away sin, but upon our believing that it does so. It is very possible to accept the pardon of our sin, though we do not know how that pardon has been obtained. We do not understand the methods of cure prescribed by the physician, nor could we give a rational account of the efficacy of his medicines, but this does not retard our cure if only we use them. To come into a perfect relation to God we do not require to understand how the death of Christ has made it possible for us to do so; we need only to desire to be God's children, and to believe that it is open to us to come to Him. Not by the intellect, but by the will, are we led to God. Not by what we know, but by what we desire, is our destiny determined. Not by education in theological requirements, but by thirst for the living God, is man saved.

And, second, even though we carry over to the death of Christ the ideas taught by Old Testament sacrifice, we commit no enormous or misleading blunder. Christ Himself suggested that His death might be best understood in the light of these ideas, and even though we are unable to penetrate through the letter to the spirit, through the outward and symbolic form to the real and eternal meaning of the sacrifice of Christ, we are yet on the road to truth, and hold the germ of it which will one day develop into the actual and perfect truth. Impatience is at the root of much unbelief and misconception and discontent; the inability to reconcile ourselves to the fact that in our present stage there is much we must hold provisionally, much we must be content to see through a glass darkly, much we can only know by picture and shadow. It is quite true the reality has come in the death of Christ, and symbol has passed away; but there is such a depth of Divine love, and so various a fulfilment of Divine purpose in the death of Christ, that we cannot be surprised that it baffles comprehension. It is the key to a world's history; for aught we know, to the history of other worlds than ours; and it is not likely that we should be able to gauge its significance and explain its rationale of operation. And therefore, if, without any sluggish indifference to further knowledge, or merely worldly contentment to know of spiritual things only so much as is absolutely necessary, we yet are able to use what we do know and to await with confidence further knowledge, we probably act wisely and well. We do not err if we think of Christ as our Sacrifice; nor even if we somewhat too literally think of Him as the Victim substituted for us, and ascribe to His Blood the expiatory and cleansing virtue which belonged symbolically to the blood of the ancient sacrifices.

And, indeed, there are grave difficulties in our path as soon as we strive to advance beyond the sacrificial idea, and try to grasp the very truth regarding the death of Christ. The Apostles with one voice affirm that Christ's death was a propitiation for the sins of the world: that He died for us; that He suffered not only for His contemporaries, but for all men; that He was the Lamb of God, the innocent Victim, whose blood cleansed from sin. They affirm, in short, that in Christ's death we are brought face to face, not with a symbolic sacrifice, but with that act which really takes away sin.

If we read the narrative given us in the Gospels of the death of Christ, and the circumstances that led to it, we see that the sacrificial idea is not kept in the foreground. The cause of His death, as explained in the Gospels, was His persistent claim to be the Messiah sent by God to found a spiritual kingdom. He steadily opposed the expectations and plans of those in authority until they became so exasperated that they resolved to compass His death. The real and actual cause of His death was His fidelity to the purpose for which He had been sent into the world. He might have retired and lived a quiet life in Galilee or beyond Palestine altogether; but He could not do so, because He could not abandon the work of His life, which was to proclaim the truth about God and God's kingdom. Many a man has felt equally constrained to proclaim the truth in the face of opposition; and many a man has, like Jesus, incurred death thereby. That which makes the death of Jesus exceptional in this aspect of it is, that the truth He proclaimed was what may be called the truth, the essential truth for men to know-- the truth that God is the Father, and that there is life in Him for all who will come to Him. This was the kingdom of God among men--He proclaimed a kingdom based only on love, on spiritual union between God and man; a kingdom not of this world, and that came not with observation; a kingdom within men, real, abiding, universal. It was because He proclaimed this kingdom, exploding the cherished expectations and merely national hopes of the Jews, that the authorities put Him to death.

So much is obvious on the very face of the narrative. No one can read the life of Christ without perceiving this at least--that He was put to death because He persisted in proclaiming truths essential to the happiness and salvation of men. By submitting to death for the sake of these truths He made it for ever clear that they are of vital consequence. Before Pilate He calmly said, "To this end was I born, and for this cause came I into the world, that I should bear witness unto the truth." He knew that it was this witnessing to the truth that had enraged the Jews against Him, and even in prospect of death He could not refrain from proclaiming what He felt it was vital for men to know. In this very true sense, therefore, He died for our sakes--died because He sought to put us in possession of truths without which our souls cannot be lifted into life eternal. He has given us life by giving us the knowledge of the Father. His love for us, His ceaseless and strong desire to bring us near to God, was the real cause of His death. And, recognising this, we cannot but feel that He has a claim upon us of the most commanding kind. Not for

Marcus Dods, D.D.

His contemporaries alone, not for one section of men only, did Christ die, but for all men, because the truths which He sealed by His death are of universal import. No man can live eternal life without them.

But again, Jesus Himself explained to His disciples in what sense His death would benefit them. "It is expedient for you that I go away, for if I go not away the Comforter will not come unto you." The spiritual kingdom He proclaimed could not be established while He was visibly present. His death and ascension put an end to all hopes that diverted their minds from that which constituted their real union to God and satisfaction in Him. When He disappeared from earth and sent the Holy Spirit to them, what remained to them was God's kingdom within them, His true rule over their spirits, their assimilation to Him in all things. What they now clearly saw to be still open to them was to live in Christ's spirit, to revive in their memories the truths His life had proclaimed, to submit themselves entirely to His influence, and to make known far and near the ideas He had communicated to them, and especially the God He had revealed. It was His death which set their minds free from all other expectations and fixed them exclusively on what was spiritual. And this salvation they at once proclaimed to others. What were they to say about Jesus and His death? How were they to win men to Him? They did so in the first days by proclaiming Him as raised by God to be a Prince and a Saviour, to rule from the unseen world, to bless men with a spiritual salvation, by turning them from their iniquities. And the instrumentality, the actual spiritual experience through which this salvation is arrived at is the belief that Jesus was sent by God and did reveal Him, that in Jesus God was present revealing Himself, and that His Spirit can bring us also to God and to His likeness.

Still further, and not going beyond the facts apparent in the Gospel, it is plain that Christ died for us, in the sense that all He did, His whole life on earth from first to last, was for our sake. He came into the world, not to serve a purpose of His own, and forward His own interests, but to further ours. He took upon Him our sins and their punishment in this obvious sense, that He voluntarily entered into our life, polluted as it was all through with sin and laden with misery in every part. Our condition in this world is such that no person can avoid coming in contact with sin, or can escape entirely the results of sin in the world. And in point of fact persons with any depth of sympathy and spiritual sensibility cannot help taking upon them the sins of others, and cannot help suffering their own life to be greatly marred and limited by the sins of others. In the case of our Lord this acceptance of the burden of other men's sins was voluntary. And it is the sight of a holy and loving person, enduring sorrows and opposition and death wholly undeserved, that is at all times affecting in the experience of Christ. It is the sight of this suffering, borne with meekness and borne willingly, that makes us ashamed of our sinful condition, which inevitably entails such suffering on the self-sacrificing and holy. It enables us to see, more distinctly than anything besides, the essential hatefulness and evil of sin. Here is an innocent person, filled with love and compassion for all, His life a life of self-sacrifice and devotion to human interests, carrying in His person infinite benefits to the race--this person is at all points thwarted and persecuted and finally put to death. In this most intelligible sense He very truly sacrificed Himself for us, bore the penalty of our sins, magnified the law, illustrated and rendered infinitely impressive the righteousness of God, and made it possible for God to pardon us, and in pardoning us to deepen immeasurably our regard for holiness and for Himself.

Still further, it is obvious that Christ gave Himself a perfect sacrifice to God by living solely for Him. He had in life no other purpose than to serve God. Again and again during His life God expressed His perfect satisfaction with the human life of Christ. He who searches the heart saw that into the most secret thought, down to the most hidden motive, that life was pure, that heart in perfect harmony with the Divine will. Christ lived not for Himself, He did not claim property in His own person and life, but gave Himself up freely and to the uttermost to God: more thoroughly, more spontaneously, and with an infinitely richer material did He offer Himself to God than ever burnt-offering had been offered. And God, with an infinite joy in goodness, accepted the sacrifice, and found on earth in the person of Jesus an opportunity for rejoicing in man with an infinite satisfaction.

And this sacrifice which Christ offered to God tends to reproduce itself continually among men. As Christ said, no sooner was He lifted up than He drew all men to Him. That perfect life and utter self-surrender to the highest purposes, that pure and perfect love and devotion to God and man, commands the admiration and cordial worship of serious men. It stands in the world for ever as the grand incentive to goodness, prompting men and inspiring them to sympathy and imitation. It is in the strength of that perfect sacrifice men have ceaselessly striven to sacrifice themselves. It is through Christ they strive to come themselves to God. In Him we see the beauty of holiness; in Him we see holiness perfected, and making the impression upon us which a perfect thing makes, standing as a reality, not as a theory; as a finished and victorious achievement, not as a mere attempt. In Christ we see what love to God and faith in God really are; in Him we see what a true sacrifice is and means; and in Him we are drawn to give ourselves also to God as our true life.

Looking then only at those facts which are apparent to every one who reads the life of Christ, and putting aside all that may over and above these facts have been intended in the Divine mind, we see how truly Christ is our Sacrifice; and how truly we can say of Him that He gave Himself, the just for the unjust, that He might bring us to God. We see that in the actual privations, disappointments, temptations, mental strain, opposition, and suffering of His life, and in the final conflict of death, He bore the penalty of our sins; underwent the miseries which sin has brought into human life. We see that He did so with so entire and perfect a consent to all God's will, and with so ready and unreserved a sacrifice of Himself, that God found infinite satisfaction in this human obedience and righteousness, and on the basis of this sacrifice pardons us.

Some may be able to assure themselves better of the forgiveness of God, if they look at what Christ has done as a satisfaction for or reparation of the ill that we have done. He properly satisfies for an offence who offers to the offended party that which he loves as well or better than he hates the offence. If your child has through carelessness broken or spoiled something you value, but seeing your displeasure is at pains to replace it, and does after long industry put into your hands an article of greater value than was lost to you, you are satisfied, and more than forgive your child. If a man fails in business, but after spending a lifetime to recover himself restores to you not only what you lost by him, but more than could possibly have been made by yourself with the original sum lost, you ought to be satisfied. And God is satisfied with the work of Christ because there is in it a love and an obedience to Him, and a regard to right and holiness, that outweigh all our disobedience and alienation. Often, when some satisfaction or reparation of injury or loss is made to ourselves, it is done in so good-hearted a manner, and displays so much right feeling, and sets us on terms of so much closer intimacy with the party who injured us, that we are really glad, now that all is over, that the misunderstanding or injury took place. The satisfaction has far more than atoned for it. So is it with God: our reconciliation to Him has called out so much in Christ that would otherwise have been hidden, has so stirred the deepest part, if we may say so, of the Divine nature in Christ, and has called out also so signally the whole strength and beauty of human nature, that God is more than satisfied. We cannot see how without sin there could have been that display of love and obedience that there has been in the death of Christ. Where there is no danger, nothing tragic, there can be no heroism: human nature, not to speak of Divine, has not scope for its best parts in the ordinary and innocent traffic and calm of life. It is when danger thickens, and when death draws near and bares his hideous visage, that devotion and self-sacrifice can be exercised. And so, in a world filled with sin and with danger, a world in which each individual's history has something stirring and tragic in it, God finds room for the full testing and utterance of our natures and of His own. And in the redemption of this world there occurred an emergency which called forth, as nothing else conceivably could call forth, everything that the Divine and human natures of Christ are capable of.

Another result of Christ's death is mentioned by John: "That the children of God which were scattered abroad might be gathered together in one." It was for a unity Christ died, for that which formed one whole. When Caiaphas sacrificed Christ to propitiate Rome, he knew that none but Christ's own countrymen would benefit thereby. The Romans would not recall their legions from Africa or Germany because Judæa had propitiated them. And supposing that the Jews had received some immunities and privileges from Rome as an acknowledgment of its favour, this would affect no other nation. But if any members of other nations coveted these privileges, their only course would be to become naturalized Jews, members and subjects of the favoured community. So Christ's death has the effect of gathering into one all those who seek God's favour and fatherhood, no matter in what ends of the earth they be scattered. It was not for separate individuals Christ died, but for a people, for an indivisible community; and we receive the benefits of His death no otherwise than as we are members of this people or family. It is the attractive power of Christ that draws us all to one centre, but being gathered round Him we should be in spirit and are in fact as close to one another as to Him.

Marcus Dods, D.D.

NOTE ON CHAP. VI., Vers. 37, 44, 45

Three terms are used in these verses which call for examination,--"giving," "drawing," "teaching." The two latter are used in a connection which leaves little room for doubt as to their meaning. "No man can come to Me, except the Father which hath sent Me draw him.... It is written in the prophets, And they shall be all taught of God. Every man, therefore, that hath heard and hath learned of the Father, cometh unto Me;" but, by implication, no man who has not so learned. Both verses express the thought that without special aid from God no man can come to Christ. There must be a Divine illumination of the human faculties, enabling the man to apprehend that Jesus is the Christ, and to receive Him as such. These expressions cannot refer to the outward illumination which is communicated by Scripture, by the miracles of Christ, and so forth; because the whole of the crowd addressed by our Lord had such illumination, and yet not all of them were "taught of God." The "hearing," and "learning," or "being taught of God," here spoken of must signify the opening of the inner ear by the unseen operation of God Himself. Most emphatically does Jesus affirm that without this exercise of the Divine will and Divine power upon the individual no man can receive Him. The mere manifestation of God in the flesh is not enough: an inward and special enlightenment is required to enable a man to recognise God manifest in the flesh. The words, then, of ver. 44 can only mean that in order to apprehend the significance of Christ and to yield ourselves to Him we must be aided individually and inwardly by God.

Whether the "giving" of ver. 37 is intended to signify an act prior to the teaching and drawing may reasonably be doubted. It is prior to the "coming" to Christ, as the terms of the verse prove: "All that the Father giveth Me shall come to Me: and him that cometh to Me I will in no wise cast out." Principal Reynolds says it is "the present activity of the Father's grace that is meant, not a foregone conclusion," No doubt that is in strictness true. Our Lord, in the face of general unbelief, is comforting Himself with the assurance that after all He will draw to Himself all whom the Father gives Him; and this implies that the Father's giving is the main factor in His success.

VOLUME II

I. THE ANOINTING OF JESUS.

"Jesus therefore six days before the Passover came to Bethany, where Lazarus was, whom Jesus raised from the dead. So they made Him a supper there: and Martha served; but Lazarus was one of them that sat at meat with Him. Mary therefore took a pound of ointment of spikenard, very precious, and anointed the feet of Jesus, and wiped His feet with her hair: and the house was filled with the odour of the ointment. But Judas Iscariot, one of His disciples, which should betray Him, saith, Why was not this ointment sold for three hundred pence, and given to the poor? Now this he said, not because he cared for the poor; but because he was a thief, and having the bag took away what was put therein. Jesus therefore said, Suffer her to keep it against the day of My burying. For the poor ye have always with you; but Me ye have not always. The common people therefore of the Jews learned that He was there: and they came, not for Jesus' sake only, but that they might see Lazarus also, whom He had raised from the dead. But the chief priests took counsel that they might put Lazarus also to death; because that by reason of him many of the Jews went away, and believed on Jesus."--John xii. 1-11.

This twelfth chapter is the watershed of the Gospel. The self-manifestation of Jesus to the world is now ended; and from this point onwards to the close we have to do with the results of that manifestation. He hides Himself from the unbelieving, and allows their unbelief full scope; while He makes further disclosures to the faithful few. The whole Gospel is a systematic and wonderfully artistic exhibition of the manner in which the deeds, words, and claims of Jesus produced,--on the one hand, a growing belief and enthusiasm; on the other, a steadily hardening unbelief and hostility. In this chapter the culmination of these processes is carefully illustrated by three incidents. In the first of these incidents evidence is given that there was an intimate circle of friends in whose love Jesus was embalmed, and His work and memory insured against decay; while the very deed which had riveted the faith and affection of this intimate circle is shown to have brought the antagonism of His enemies to a head. In the second incident the writer shows that on the whole popular mind Jesus had made a profound impression, and that the instincts of the Jewish people acknowledged Him as King. In the third incident the influence He was destined to have and was already to some extent exerting beyond the bounds of Judaism is illustrated by the request of the Greeks that they might see Jesus.

In this first incident, then, is disclosed a devotedness of faith which cannot be surpassed, an attachment which is absolute; but here also we see that the hostility of avowed enemies has penetrated even the inner circle of the personal followers of Jesus, and that one of the chosen Twelve has so little faith or love that he can see no beauty and find no pleasure in any tribute paid to his Master. In this hour there meet a ripeness of love which suddenly reveals the permanent place which Jesus has won for Himself in the hearts of men, and a maturity of alienation which forebodes that His end cannot be far distant. In this beautiful incident, therefore, we turn a page in the gospel and come suddenly into the presence of Christ's death. To this death He Himself freely alludes, because He sees that things are now ripe for it, that nothing short of His death will satisfy His enemies, while no further manifestation can give Him a more abiding place in the love of His friends. The chill, damp odour of the tomb first strikes upon the sense, mingling with and absorbed in the perfume of Mary's ointment. If Jesus dies, He cannot be forgotten. He is embalmed in the love of such disciples.

On His way to Jerusalem for the last time Jesus reached Bethany "six days before the Passover"-- that is to say, in all probability [1] on the Friday evening previous to His death. It was natural that He should wish to spend His last Sabbath in the congenial and strengthening society of a family whose welcome and whose affection He could rely upon. In the little town of Bethany He had become popular, and since the raising of Lazarus He was regarded with marked veneration. Accordingly they made Him a feast, which, as Mark informs us, was given in the house of Simon the leper. Any gathering of His friends in Bethany must have been incomplete without Lazarus and his sisters. Each is present, and each contributes an appropriate addition to the feast. Martha serves; Lazarus, mute as he is throughout the whole story, bears witness by his presence as a living guest to the worthiness of Jesus; while Mary makes the day memorable by a characteristic action. Coming in, apparently after the guests had reclined at table, she broke an alabaster of very costly spikenard [2] and anointed the feet of Jesus and wiped His feet with her hair.

This token of affection took the company by surprise. Lazarus and his sisters may have been in sufficiently good circumstances to admit of their making a substantial acknowledgment of their indebtedness to Jesus; and although this alabaster of ointment had cost as much as would keep a labouring man's family for a year, this could not seem an excessive return to make for service so valuable as Jesus had rendered. It was the manner of the acknowledgment which took the company by surprise. Jesus was a poor man, and His very appearance may have suggested that there were other things He needed more urgently than such a gift as this. Had the family provided a home for Him or given Him the price of this ointment, no one would have uttered a remark. But this was the kind of demonstration reserved for princes or persons of great distinction; and when paid to One so conspicuously humble in His dress and habits, there seemed to the uninstructed eye something incongruous and bordering on the grotesque. When the fragrance of the ointment disclosed its value, there was therefore an instantaneous exclamation of surprise, and at any rate in one instance of blunt disapproval. Judas, instinctively putting a money value on this display of affection, roundly and with coarse indelicacy declared it had better have been sold and given to the poor.

Jesus viewed the act with very different feelings. The rulers were determining to put Him out of the way, as not only worthless but dangerous; the very man who objected to this present expenditure was making up his mind to sell Him for a small part of the sum; the people were scrutinising His conduct, criticising Him;--in the midst of all this hatred, suspicion, treachery, coldness, and hesitation comes this woman and puts aside all this would-be wisdom and caution, and for herself pronounces that no tribute is rich enough to pay to Him. It is the rarity of such action, not the rarity of the nard, that strikes Jesus. This, He says, is a noble deed she has done, far rarer, far more difficult to produce, far more penetrating, and lasting in its fragrance than the richest perfume that man has compounded. Mary has the experience that all those have who for Christ's sake expose themselves to the misunderstanding and abuse of vulgar and unsympathetic minds; she receives from Himself more explicit assurance that her offering has given pleasure to Him and is gratefully accepted. We may sometimes find ourselves obliged to do what we perfectly well know will be misunderstood and censured; we may be compelled to adopt a line of conduct which seems to convict us of heedlessness and of the neglect of duties we owe to others; we may be driven to action which lays us open to the charge of being romantic and extravagant; but of one thing we may be perfectly sure--that however our motives are mis-read and condemned by those who first make their voices heard, He for whose sake we do these things will not disparage our action nor misunderstand our motives. The way to a fuller intimacy with Christ often lies through passages in life we must traverse alone.

But we are probably more likely to misunderstand than to be misunderstood. We are so limited in our sympathies, so scantily furnished with knowledge, and have so slack a hold upon great principles, that for the most part we can understand only those who are like ourselves. When a woman comes in with her effusiveness, we are put out and irritated; when a man whose mind is wholly uneducated utters his feelings by shouting hymns and dancing on the street, we think him a semi-lunatic; when a member of our family spends an hour or two a day in devotional exercises, we condemn it as waste of time which might be better spent on practical charities or household duties.

Most liable of all to this vice of misjudging the actions of others, and indeed of misapprehending generally wherein the real value of life consists, are those who, like Judas, measure all things by a utilitarian, if not a money, standard. Actions which have no immediate results are pronounced by such persons to be mere sentiment and waste, while in fact they redeem human nature and make life seem worth living. The charge of the Light Brigade at Balaclava served none of the immediate purposes of the battle, and was indeed a blunder and waste from that point of view; yet are not our annals enriched by it as they have been by few victories? On the Parthenon there were figures placed with their backs hard against the wall of the pediment; these backs were never seen and were not intended to be seen, but yet were carved with the same care as was spent upon the front of the figures. Was that care waste? There are thousands of persons in our own society who think it essential to teach their children arithmetic, but pernicious to instil into their minds a love of poetry or art. They judge of education by the test, Will it pay? can this attainment be turned into money? The other question, Will it enrich the nature of the child and of the man? is not asked. They proceed as if they believed that the man is made for business, not business for the man; and thus it comes to pass that everywhere among us men are found sacrificed to business, stunted in their moral development, shut off from the deeper things of life. The pursuits which such persons condemn are the very things which lift life out of the low level of commonplace buying and selling, and invite us to remember that man liveth not by bread alone, but by high thoughts, by noble sacrifice, by devoted love and all that love dictates, by the powers of the unseen, mightier by far than all that we see.

In the face, then, of so much that runs counter to such demonstrations as Mary's and condemns them as extravagance, it is important to note the principles upon which our Lord proceeds in His justification of her action.

First, He says, this is an occasional, exceptional tribute. "The poor always ye have with you, but me ye have not always." Charity to the poor you may continue from day to day all your life long: whatever you spend on me is spent once for all. You need not think the poor defrauded by this expenditure. Within a few days I shall be beyond all such tokens of regard, and the poor will still claim your sympathy. This principle solves for us some social and domestic problems. Of many expenses common in society, and especially of expenses connected with scenes such as this festive gathering at Bethany, the question always arises, Is this expenditure justifiable? When present at an entertainment costing as much and doing as little material good as the spikenard whose perfume had died before the guests separated, we cannot but ask, Is not this, after all, mere waste? had it not been better to have given the value to the poor? The hunger-bitten faces, the poverty-stricken outcasts, we have seen during the day are suggested to us by the superabundance now before us. The effort to spend most where least is needed suggests to us, as to these guests at Bethany, gaunt, pinched, sickly faces, bare rooms, cold grates, feeble, dull-eyed children--in a word, starving families who might be kept for weeks together on what is here spent in a few minutes; and the question is inevitable, Is this right? Can it be right to spend a man's ransom on a mere good smell, while at the end of the street a widow is pining with hunger? Our Lord replies that so long as one is day by day considering the poor and relieving their necessities, he need not grudge an occasional outlay to manifest his regard for his friends. The poor of Bethany would probably appeal to Mary much more hopefully than to Judas, and they would appeal all the more successfully because her heart had been allowed to utter itself thus to Jesus. There is, of course, an expenditure for display under the guise of friendship. Such expenditure finds no justification here or anywhere else. But those who in a practical way acknowledge the perpetual presence of the poor are justified in the occasional outlay demanded by friendship.

2. But our Lord's defence of Mary is of wider range. "Let her alone," He says, "against the day of my burying hath she kept this." It was not only occasional, exceptional tribute she had paid Him; it was solitary, never to be repeated. Against my burial she has kept this unguent; for me ye have not always. Would you blame Mary for spending this, were I lying in my tomb? Would you call it too costly a tribute, were it the last? Well, it is the last. [3] Such is our Lord's justification of her action. Was Mary herself conscious that this was a parting tribute? It is possible that her love and womanly instinct had revealed to her the nearness of that death of which Jesus Himself so often spoke, but which the disciples refused to think of. She may have felt that this was the last time she would have an opportunity of expressing her devotion. Drawn to Him with unutterable tenderness, with admiration, gratitude, anxiety mingling in her heart, she hastens to spend upon Him her costliest. Passing away from her world she knows He is; buried so far as she was concerned she knew Him to be if He was to keep the Passover at Jerusalem in the midst of His enemies. Had the others felt with her, none could have grudged her the last consolation of this utterance of her love, or have grudged Him the consolation of receiving it. For this made Him strong to die, this among other motives--the knowledge that His love and sacrifice were not in vain, that He had won human hearts, and that in their affection He would survive. This is His true embalming. This it is that forbids that His flesh see corruption, that His earthly manifestation die out and be forgotten. To die before He had attached to Himself friends as passionate in their devotion as Mary would have been premature. The recollection of His work might have been lost. But when He had won men like John and women like Mary, He could die assured that His name would never be lost from earth. The breaking of the alabaster box, the pouring out of Mary's soul in adoration of her Lord--this was the signal that all was ripe for His departure, this proof that His manifestation had done its work. The love of His own had come to maturity and burst thus into flower. Jesus therefore recognises in this act His true embalming.

And it is probably from this point of view that we may most readily see the appropriateness of that singular commendation and promise which our Lord, according to the other gospels, added: "Verily I say unto you, wherever this gospel shall be preached throughout the whole world, this also that she hath done shall be spoken for a memorial of her."

At first sight the encomium might seem as extravagant as the action. Was there, a Judas might ask, anything deserving of immortality in the sacrifice of a few pounds? But no such measurements are admissible here. The encomium was deserved because the act was the irrepressible utterance of all-absorbing love--of a love so full, so rich, so rare that even the ordinary disciples of Christ were at first not in perfect sympathy with it. The absolute devotedness of her love found a fit symbol in the alabaster box or vase which she had to break that the ointment might flow out. It was not a bottle out of which she might take the stopper and let a carefully measured quantity dribble out, reserving the rest for other and perhaps very different uses--fit symbol of our love to Christ; but it was a hermetically sealed casket or flask, out of which, if she let one drop fall, the whole must go. It had to be broken; it had to be devoted to one sole use. It could not be in part reserved or in part diverted to other uses. Where you have such love as this, have you not the highest thing humanity can produce? Where is it now to be had on earth, where are we to look for this all-devoting, unreserving love, which gathers up all its possessions and pours them out at Christ's feet, saying, "Take all, would it were more"?

The encomium, therefore, was deserved and appropriate. In her love the Lord would ever live: so long as she existed the remembrance of Him could not die. No death could touch her heart with his chilly hand and freeze the warmth of her devotion. Christ was immortal in her, and she was therefore immortal in Him. Her love was a bond that could not be broken, the truest spiritual union. In embalming Him, therefore, she unconsciously embalmed herself. Her love was the amber in which He was to be preserved, and she became inviolable as He. Her love was the marble on which His name and worth were engraven, on which His image was deeply sculptured, and they were to live and last together. Christ "prolongs His days" in the love of His people. In every generation there arise those who will not let His remembrance die out, and who to their own necessities call out the living energy of Christ. In so doing they unwittingly make themselves undying as He; their love of Him is the little spark of immortality in their soul. It is that which indissolubly and by the only genuine spiritual affinity links them to what is eternal. To all who thus love Him Christ cannot but say, "Because I live, ye shall live also."

Another point in our Lord's defence of Mary's conduct, though it is not explicitly asserted, plainly is, that tributes of affection paid directly to Himself are of value to Him. Judas might with some plausibility have quoted against our Lord His own teaching that an act of kindness done to the poor was kindness to Him. It might be said that, on our Lord's own showing, what He desires is, not homage paid to Himself personally, but loving and merciful conduct. And certainly any homage paid to Himself which is not accompanied by such conduct is of no value at all. But as love to Him is the spring and regulator of all right conduct, it is necessary that we should cultivate this love; and because He delights in our well-being and in ourselves, and does not look upon us merely as so much material in which He may exhibit His healing powers, He necessarily rejoices in every expression of true devotedness that is paid to Him by any of us.

And on our side wherever there is true and ardent love it must crave direct expression. "If ye love me," says our Lord, "keep my commandments"; and obedience certainly is the normal test and exhibition of love. But there is that in our nature which refuses to be satisfied with obedience, which craves fellowship with what we love, which carries us out of ourselves and compels us to express our feeling directly. And that soul is not fully developed whose pent-up gratitude, cherished admiration, and warm affection do not from time to time break away from all ordinary modes of expressing devotion and choose some such direct method as Mary chose, or some such straightforward utterance as Peter's: "Lord, Thou knowest all things, Thou knowest that I love Thee."

It may, indeed, occur to us, as we read of Mary's tribute to her Lord, that the very words in which He justified her action forbid our supposing that any so grateful tribute can be paid Him by us. "Me ye have not always" may seem to warn us against expecting that so direct and satisfying an intercourse can be maintained now, when we no longer have Him. And no doubt this is one of the standing difficulties of Christian experience. We can love those who live with us, whose eye we can meet, whose voice we know, whose expression of face we can read. We feel it easy to fix our affections on one and another of those who are alive contemporaneously with ourselves. But with Christ it is different: we miss those sensible impressions made upon us by the living bodily presence; we find it difficult to retain in the mind a settled idea of the feeling He has towards us. It is an effort to accomplish by faith what sight without any effort effectually accomplishes. We do not see that He loves us; the looks and tones that chiefly reveal human love are absent; we are not from hour to hour confronted, whether we will or no, with one evidence or other of love. Were the life of a Christian nowadays no more difficult than it was to Mary, were it brightened with Christ's presence as a household friend, were the whole sum and substance of it merely a giving way to the love He kindled by palpable favours and measurable friendship, then surely the Christian life would be a very simple, very easy, very happy course.

But the connection between ourselves and Christ is not of the body that passes, but of the spirit which endures. It is spiritual, and such a connection may be seriously perverted by the interference of sense and of bodily sensations. To measure the love of Christ by His expression of face and by His tone of voice is legitimate, but it is not the truest measurement: to be drawn to Him by the accidental kindnesses our present difficulties must provoke is to be drawn by something short of perfect spiritual affinity. And, on the whole, it is well that our spirit should be allowed to choose its eternal friendship and alliance by what is specially and exclusively its own, so that its choice cannot be mistaken, as the choice sometimes is when there is a mixture of physical and spiritual attractiveness. So much are we guided in youth and in the whole of our life by what is material, so freely do we allow our tastes to be determined and our character to be formed by our connection with what is material, that the whole man gets blunted in his spiritual perceptions and incapable of appreciating what is not seen. And the great part of our education in this life is to lift the spirit to its true place and to its appropriate company, to teach it to measure its gains apart from material prosperity, and to train it to love with ardour what cannot be seen.

Besides, it cannot be doubted that this incident itself very plainly teaches that Christ came into this world to win our love and to turn all duty into a personal acting towards Him; to make the whole of life like those parts of it which are now its bright exceptional holiday times; to make all of it a pleasure by making all of it and not merely parts of it the utterance of love. Even a little love in our life is the sunshine that quickens and warms and brightens the whole. There seems at length to be a reason and a satisfaction in life when love animates us. It is easy to act well to those whom we really love, and Christ has come for the express purpose of bringing our whole life within this charmed circle. He has come not to bring constraint and gloom into our lives, but to let us out into the full liberty and joy of the life that God Himself lives and judges to be the only life worthy of His bestowal upon us.

Footnotes:

1. It is uncertain whether the "six days" are inclusive or exclusive of the day of arrival and of the first day of the Feast. It is also uncertain on what day of the week the Crucifixion happened.

2. In The Classical Review for July 1890 Mr. Bennett suggests that the difficult word pistikes should be written pistakes, and that it refers to the Pistacia terebinthus, which grows in Cyprus and Judæa, and yields a very fragrant and very costly unguent.

3. So Stier.

Marcus Dods, D.D.

II. THE ENTRY INTO JERUSALEM

"On the morrow a great multitude that had come to the feast, when they heard that Jesus was coming to Jerusalem, took the branches of the palm trees, and went forth to meet Him, and cried out, Hosanna: Blessed is He that cometh in the name of the Lord, even the King of Israel. And Jesus, having found a young ass, sat thereon; as it is written, Fear not, daughter of Zion: behold, thy King cometh, sitting on an ass's colt. These things understood not His disciples at the first: but when Jesus was glorified, then remembered they that these things were written of Him, and that they had done these things unto Him. The multitude therefore that was with Him when He called Lazarus out of the tomb, and raised him from the dead, bare witness. For this cause also the multitude went and met Him, for that they heard that He had done this sign. The Pharisees therefore said among themselves, Behold, how ye prevail nothing: lo, the world is gone after Him."--John xii. 12-19.

If our Lord arrived in Bethany on Friday evening and spent the Sabbath with His friends there, "the next day" of ver. 12 is Sunday; and in the Church year this day is known as Palm Sunday, from the incident here related. It was also the day, four days before the Passover, on which the Jews were enjoined by the law to choose their paschal lamb. Some consciousness of this may have guided our Lord's action. Certainly He means finally to offer Himself to the people as the Messiah. Often as He had evaded them before, and often as He had forbidden His disciples to proclaim Him, He is now conscious that His hour has come, and by entering Jerusalem as King of peace He definitely proclaims Himself the promised Messiah. As plainly as the crowning of a new monarch and the flourish of trumpets and the kissing of his hand by the great officers of state proclaim him king, so unmistakably does our Lord by riding into Jerusalem on an ass and by accepting the hosannas of the people proclaim Himself the King promised to men through the Jews, as the King of peace who was to win men to His rule by love and sway them by a Divine Spirit.

The scene must have been one not easily forgotten. The Mount of Olives runs north and south parallel to the east wall of Jerusalem, and separated from it by a gully, through which flows the brook Kidron. The Mount is crossed by three paths. One of these is a steep footpath, which runs direct over the crest of the hill; the second runs round its northern shoulder; while the third crosses the southern slope. It was by this last route the pilgrim caravans were accustomed to enter the city. On the occasion of our Lord's entry the road was probably thronged with visitors making their way to the great annual feast. No fewer than three million persons are said to have been sometimes packed together in Jerusalem at the Passover; and all of them being on holiday, were ready for any kind of excitement. The idea of a festal procession was quite to their mind. And no sooner did the disciples appear with Jesus riding in their midst than the vast streams of people caught the infection of loyal enthusiasm, tore down branches of the palms and olives which were found in abundance by the roadside, and either waved them in the air or strewed them in the line of march. Others unwrapped their loose cloaks from their shoulders and spread them along the rough path to form a carpet as He approached--a custom which is still, it seems, observed in the East in royal processions, and which has indeed sometimes been imported into our own country on great occasions. Thus with every demonstration of loyalty, with ceaseless shoutings that were heard across the valley in the streets of Jerusalem itself, and waving the palm branches, they moved towards the city.

Those who have entered the city from Bethany by this road tell us that there are two striking points in it. The first is when at a turn of the broad and well-defined mountain track the southern portion of the city comes for an instant into view. This part of the city was called "the city of David," and the suggestion is not without probability that it may have been at this point the multitude burst out in words that linked Jesus with David. "Hosanna to the Son of David. Blessed is the King that cometh in the name of the Lord. Blessed is the kingdom of our father David. Hosanna, peace and glory in the highest." This became the watchword of the day, so that even the boys who had come out of the city to see the procession were heard afterwards, as they loitered in the streets, still shouting the same refrain.

After this the road again dips, and the glimpse of the city is lost behind the intervening ridge of Olivet; but shortly a rugged ascent is climbed and a ledge of bare rock is reached, and in an instant the whole city bursts into view. The prospect from this point must have been one of the grandest of its kind in the world, the fine natural position of Jerusalem not only showing to advantage, but the long line of city wall embracing, like the setting of a jewel, the marvellous structures of Herod, the polished marble and the gilded pinnacles glittering in the morning sun and dazzling the eye. It was in all probability at this point that our Lord was overcome with regret when He considered the sad fate of the beautiful city, and when in place of the smiling palaces and apparently impregnable walls His imagination filled His eye with smoke-blackened ruins, with pavements slippery with blood, with walls breached at all points and choked with rotting corpses.

Our Lord's choice of the ass was significant. The ass was commonly used for riding, and the well-cared-for ass of the rich man was a very fine animal, much larger and stronger than the little breed with which we are familiar. Its coat, too, is as glossy as a well-kept horse's--"shiny black, or satiny white, or sleek mouse colour." It was not chosen by our Lord at this time that He might show His humility, for it would have been still humbler to walk like His disciples. So far from being a token of humility, He chose a colt which apparently had never borne another rider. He rather meant by claiming the ass and by riding into Jerusalem upon it to assert His royalty; but He did not choose a horse, because that animal would have suggested royalty of quite another kind from His--royalty which was maintained by war and outward force; for the horse and the chariot had always been among the Hebrews symbolic of warlike force. The disciples themselves, strangely enough, did not see the significance of this action, although, when they had time to reflect upon it, they remembered that Zechariah had said: "Rejoice greatly, O daughter of Zion; shout, O daughter of Jerusalem: behold, thy King cometh unto thee: He is just, and having salvation; lowly, and riding upon an ass, and upon a colt the foal of an ass. And I will cut off the chariot from Ephraim, and the horse from Jerusalem, and the battle bow shall be cut off: and He shall speak peace unto the heathen."

When John says, "these things understood not His disciples at the first," he cannot mean that they did not understand that Jesus by this act claimed to be the Messiah, because even the mob perceived the significance of this entry into Jerusalem and hailed Him "Son of David." What they did not understand, probably, was why He chose this mode of identifying Himself with the Messiah. At any rate, their perplexity brings out very clearly that the conception was not suggested to Jesus. He was not induced by the disciples nor led on by the people to make a demonstration which He Himself scarcely approved or had not intended to make. On the contrary, from His first recorded act that morning He had taken command of the situation. Whatever was done was done with deliberation, at His own instance and as His own act. [4]

This then in the first place; it was His own deliberate act. He put Himself forward, knowing that He would receive the hosannas of the people, and intending that He should receive them. All His backwardness is gone; all shyness of becoming a public spectacle is gone. For this also is to be noted--that no place or occasion could have been more public than the Passover at Jerusalem. Whatever it was He meant to indicate by His action, it was to the largest possible public He meant to indicate it. No longer in the retirement of a Galilean village, nor in a fisherman's cottage, nor in dubious or ambiguous terms, but in the full blaze of the utmost publicity that could possibly be given to His proclamation, and in language that could not be forgotten or misinterpreted, He now declared Himself. He knew He must attract the attention of the authorities, and His entrance was a direct challenge to them.

What was it then that with such deliberation and such publicity He meant to proclaim? What was it that in these last critical hours of His life, when He knew He should have few more opportunities of speaking to the people, He sought to impress upon them? What was it that, when free from the solicitations of men and the pressure of circumstances, He sought to declare? It was that He was the Messiah. There might be those in the crowd who did not understand what was meant. There might be persons who did not know Him, or who were incompetent judges of character, and supposed He was a mere enthusiast carried away by dwelling too much on some one aspect of Old Testament prophecy. In every generation there are good men who become almost crazed upon some one topic, and sacrifice everything to the promotion of one favourite hope. But however He might be misjudged, there can be no question of His own idea of the significance of His action. He claims to be the Messiah.

Such a claim is the most stupendous that could be made. To be the Messiah is to be God's Viceroy and Representative on earth, able to represent God adequately to men, and to bring about that perfect condition which is named "the kingdom of God." The Messiah must be conscious of ability perfectly to accomplish the will of God with man, and to bring men into absolute harmony with God. This is claimed by Jesus. He stands in His sober senses and claims to be that universal Sovereign, that true King of men, whom the Jews had been encouraged to expect, and who when He came would reign over Gentiles as well as Jews. By this demonstration, to which His previous career had been naturally leading up, He claims to take command of earth, of this world in all its generations, not in the easier sense of laying down upon paper a political constitution fit for all races, but in the sense of being able to deliver mankind from the source of all their misery and to lift men to a true superiority. He has gone about on earth, not secluding Himself from the woes and ways of men, not delicately isolating Himself, but exposing Himself freely to the touch of the malignities, the vulgarities, the ignorance and wickedness of all; and He now claims to rule all this, and implies that earth can present no complication of distress or iniquity which he cannot by the Divine forces within Him transform into health and purity and hope.

Marcus Dods, D.D.

This then is His deliberate claim. He quietly but distinctly proclaims that He fulfils all God's promise and purpose among men; is that promised King who was to rectify all things, to unite men to Himself, and to lead them on to their true destiny; to be practically God upon earth, accessible to men and identified with all human interests. Many have tested His claim and have proved its validity. By true allegiance to Him many have found that they have gained the mastery over the world. They have entered into peace, have felt eternal verities underneath their feet, and have attained a connection with God such as must be everlasting. They are filled with a new spirit towards men and see all things with purged eyes. Not abruptly and unintelligibly, by leaps and bounds, but gradually and in harmony with the nature of things, His kingdom is extending. Already His Spirit has done much: in time His Spirit will everywhere prevail. It is by Him and on the lines which He has laid down that humanity is advancing to its goal.

This was the claim He made; and this claim was enthusiastically admitted by the popular instinct. [5] The populace was not merely humouring in holiday mood a whimsical person for their own diversion. Many of them knew Lazarus and knew Jesus, and taking the matter seriously gave the tone to the rest. The people indeed did not, any more than the disciples, understand how different the kingdom of their expectation was from the kingdom Jesus meant to found. But while they entirely misapprehended the purpose for which He was sent, they believed that He was sent by God: His credentials were absolutely satisfactory, His work incomprehensible. But as yet they still thought He must be of the same mind as themselves regarding the work of the Messiah. To His claim, therefore, the response given by the people was loud and demonstrative. It was indeed a very brief reign they accorded to their King, but their prompt acknowledgment of Him was the instinctive and irrepressible expression of what they really felt to be His due. A popular demonstration is notoriously untrustworthy, always running to extremes, necessarily uttering itself with a loudness far in excess of individual conviction, and gathering to itself the loose and floating mass of people who have no convictions of their own, and are thankful to any one who leads them and gives them a cue, and helps them to feel that they have after all a place in the community. Who has not stood by as an onlooker at a public demonstration and smiled at the noise and glare that a mass of people will produce when their feelings are ever so little stirred, and marked how even against their own individual sentiments they are carried away by the mere tide of the day's circumstances, and for the mere sake of making a demonstration? This crowd which followed our Lord with shoutings very speedily repented and changed their shouts into a far blinder shriek of rage against Him who had been the occasion of their folly. And it must indeed have been a humbling experience for our Lord to have Himself ushered into Jerusalem by a crowd through whose hosannas He already heard the mutter of their curses. Such is the homage He has to content Himself with--such is the homage a perfect life has won.

For He knew what was in man; and while His disciples might be deceived by this popular response to His claim, He Himself was fully aware how little it could be built upon. Save in His own heart, there is no premonition of death. More than ever in His life before does His sky seem bright without a cloud. He Himself is in His early prime with life before Him; His followers are hopeful, the multitude jubilant; but through all this gay enthusiasm He sees the scowling hate of the priests and scribes; the shouting of the multitude does not drown in His ear the mutterings of a Judas and of the Sanhedrim. He knew that the throne He was now hailed to was the cross, that His coronation was the reception on His own brows of all the thorns and stings and burdens that man's sin had brought into the world. He did not fancy that the redemption of the world to God was an easy matter which could be accomplished by an afternoon's enthusiasm. He kept steadily before His mind the actual condition of the men who were by His spiritual influence to become the willing and devoted subjects of God's kingdom. He measured with accuracy the forces against Him, and understood that His warfare was not with the legions of Rome, against whom this Jewish patriotism and indomitable courage and easily roused enthusiasm might tell, but with principalities and powers a thousandfold stronger, with the demons of hatred and jealousy, of lust and worldliness, of carnality and selfishness. Never for a moment did He forget His true mission and sell His spiritual throne, hard-earned as it was to be, for popular applause and the glories of the hour. Knowing that only by the utmost of human goodness and self-sacrifice, and by the utmost of trial and endurance, could any true and lasting rule of men be gained, He chose this path and the throne it led to. With the most comprehensive view of the kingdom He was to found, and with a spirit of profound seriousness strangely contrasting in its composed and self-possessed insight with the blind tumult around Him, He claimed the crown of the Messiah. His suffering was not formal and nominal, it was not a mere pageant; equally real was the claim He now made and which brought Him to that suffering.

Footnotes:

4. This is more distinctly brought out in the Synoptic Gospels than in St. John: cp. Mark xi. 1-10.
5. According to the reading of the scene by St. John, the people needed no prompting.

III. THE CORN OF WHEAT

"Now there were certain Greeks among those that went up to worship at the feast: these therefore came to Philip, which was of Bethsaida of Galilee, and asked him, saying, Sir, we would see Jesus. Philip cometh and telleth Andrew: Andrew cometh, and Philip, and they tell Jesus. And Jesus answereth them, saying, The hour is come, that the Son of man should be glorified. Verily, verily, I say unto you, Except a grain of wheat fall into the earth and die, it abideth by itself alone; but if it die, it beareth much fruit. He that loveth his life loseth it; and he that hateth his life in this world shall keep it unto life eternal."--John xii. 20-26.

St. John now introduces a third incident to show that all is ripe for the death of Jesus. Already he has shown us that in the inmost circle of His friends He has now won for Himself a permanent place, a love which ensures that His memory will be had in everlasting remembrance. Next, he has lifted into prominence the scene in which the outer circle of the Jewish people were constrained, in an hour when their honest enthusiasm and instincts carried them away, to acknowledge Him as the Messiah who had come to fulfil all God's will upon earth. He now goes on to tell us how this agitation at the centre was found rippling in ever-widening circles till it broke with a gentle whisper on the shores of the isles of the Gentiles. This is the significance which St. John sees in the request of the Greeks that they might be introduced to Jesus.

These Greeks were "of those that came up to worship at the feast." They were proselytes, Greeks by birth, Jews by religion. They suggest the importance for Christianity of the leavening process which Judaism was accomplishing throughout the world. They may not have come from any remoter country than Galilee, but from traditions and customs separate as the poles from the Jewish customs and thoughts. From their heathen surroundings they came to Jerusalem, possibly for the first time, with wondering anticipations of the blessedness of those who dwelt in God's house, and feeling their thirst for the living God burning within them as their eyes lighted on the pinnacles of the Temple, and as at last their feet stood within its precincts. But up through all these desires grew one that overshadowed them, and, through all the petitions which a year or many years of sin and difficulty had made familiar to their lips, this petition made its way: "Sir, we would see Jesus."

This petition they address to Philip, not only because he had a Greek name, and therefore presumably belonged to a family in which Greek was spoken and Greek connections cultivated, but because, as St. John reminds us, he was "of Bethsaida of Galilee," and might be expected to understand and speak Greek, if, indeed, he was not already known to these strangers in Jerusalem. And by their request they obviously did not mean that Philip should set them in a place of vantage from which they might have a good view of Jesus as He passed by, for this they could well have accomplished without Philip's friendly intervention. But they wished to question and make Him out, to see for themselves whether there were in Jesus what even in Judaism they felt to be lacking--whether He at last might not satisfy the longings of their Divinely awakened spirits. Possibly they may even have wished to ascertain His purposes regarding the outlying nations, how the Messianic reign was to affect them. Possibly they may even have thought of offering Him an asylum where He might find shelter from the hostility of His own people.

Evidently Philip considered that this request was critical. The Apostles had been charged not to enter into any Gentile city, and they might naturally suppose that Jesus would be reluctant to be interviewed by Greeks. But before dismissing the request, he lays it before Andrew his friend, who also bore a Greek name; and after deliberation the two make bold, if not to urge the request, at least to inform Jesus that it had been made. At once in this modestly urged petition He hears the whole Gentile world uttering its weary, long-disappointed sigh, "We would see." This is no mere Greek inquisitiveness; it is the craving of thoughtful men recognising their need of a Redeemer. To the eye of Jesus, therefore, this meeting opens a prospect which for the moment overcomes Him with the brightness of its glory. In this little knot of strangers He sees the firstfruits of the immeasurable harvest which was henceforth to be continuously reaped among the Gentiles. No more do we hear the heart-broken cry, "O Jerusalem, Jerusalem!" no longer the reproachful "Ye will not come to Me, that ye might have life," but the glad consummation of His utmost hope utters itself in the words, "The hour is come that the Son of man should be glorified."

But while promise was thus given of the glorification of the Messiah by His reception among all men, the path which led to this was never absent from the mind of our Lord. Second to the inspiriting thought of His recognition by the Gentile world came the thought of the painful means by which alone He could be truly glorified. He checks, therefore, the shout of exultation which He sees rising to the lips of His disciples with the sobering reflection: "Verily, verily, I say unto you, except a corn of wheat fall into the ground and die, it abideth alone: but if it die, it bringeth forth much fruit." As if He said, Do not fancy that I have nothing to do but to accept the sceptre which these men offer, to seat Myself on the world's throne. The world's throne is the Cross. These men will not know My power until I die. The manifestation of Divine presence in My life, has been distinct enough to win them to inquiry; they will be for ever won to Me by the Divine presence revealed in My death. Like the corn of wheat, I must die if I would be abundantly fruitful. It is through death My whole living power can be disengaged and can accomplish all possibilities.

Two points are here suggested: (I.) That the life, the living force that was in Christ, reached its proper value and influence through His death; and (II.) that the proper value of Christ's life is that it propagates similar lives.

I. The life of Christ acquired its proper value and received its fit development through His death. This truth He sets before us in the illuminating figure of the corn of wheat. "Except a corn of wheat fall into the ground and die, it abideth alone." There are three uses to which wheat may be put: it may be stored for sale, it may be ground and eaten, it may be sown. For our Lord's purposes these three uses may be considered as only two. Wheat may be eaten, or it may be sown. With a pickle of wheat or a grain of oats you may do one of two things: you may eat it and enjoy a momentary gratification and benefit; or you may put it in the ground, burying it out of sight and suffering it to pass through uncomely processes, and it will reappear multiplied a hundredfold, and so on in everlasting series. Year by year men sacrifice their choicest sample of grain, and are content to bury it in the earth instead of exposing it in the market, because they understand that except it die it abideth alone, but if it die it bringeth forth much fruit. The proper life of the grain is terminated when it is used for immediate gratification: it receives its fullest development and accomplishes its richest end when it is cast into the ground, buried out of sight, and apparently lost.

As with the grain, so is it with each human life. One of two things you can do with your life; both you cannot do, and no third thing is possible. You may consume your life for your own present gratification and profit, to satisfy your present cravings and tastes and to secure the largest amount of immediate enjoyment to yourself--you may eat your life; or you may be content to put aside present enjoyment and profits of a selfish kind and devote your life to the uses of God and men. In the one case you make an end of your life, you consume it as it goes; no good results, no enlarging influence, no deepening of character, no fuller life, follows from such an expenditure of life--spent on yourself and on the present, it terminates with yourself and with the present. But in the other case you find you have entered into a more abundant life; by living for others your interests are widened, your desire for life increased, the results and ends of life enriched. "He that loveth his life shall lose it; and he that hateth his life in this world shall keep it unto life eternal." It is a law we cannot evade. He that consumes his life now, spending it on himself--he who cannot bear to let his life out of his own hand, but cherishes and pampers it and gathers all good around it, and will have the fullest present enjoyment out of it,--this man is losing his life; it comes to an end as certainly as the seed that is eaten. But he who devotes his life to other uses than his own gratification, who does not so prize self that everything must minister to its comfort and advancement, but who can truly yield himself to God and put himself at God's disposal for the general good,--this man, though he may often seem to lose his life, and often does lose it so far as present advantage goes, keeps it to life everlasting.

The law of the seed is the law of human life. Use your life for present and selfish gratification and to satisfy your present cravings, and you lose it for ever. Renounce self, yield yourself to God, spend your life for the common good, irrespective of recognition or the lack of it, personal pleasure or the absence of it, and although your life may thus seem to be lost, it is finding its best and highest development and passes into life eternal. Your life is a seed now, not a developed plant, and it can become a developed plant only by your taking heart to cast it from you and sow it in the fertile soil of other men's needs. This will seem, indeed, to disintegrate it and fritter it away, and leave it a contemptible, obscure, forgotten thing; but it does, in fact, set free the vital forces that are in it, and give it its fit career and maturity.

Looking at the thing itself, apart from figure, it is apparent that "he that loveth his life shall lose it; and he that hateth his life in this world shall keep it unto life eternal." The man who most freely uses his life for others, keeping least to himself and living solely for the common interests of mankind, has the most enduring influence. He sets in motion forces which propagate fresh results eternally. And not only so. He who freely sows his life has it eternally, not only in so far as he has set in motion an endless series of beneficent influences, but inasmuch as he himself enters into life eternal. An immortality of influence is one thing and a very great thing; but an immortality of personal life is another, and this also is promised by our Lord when He says (ver. 26), "Where I am, there shall also My servant be."

This, then, being the law of human life, Christ, being man, must not only enounce but observe it. He speaks of Himself even more directly than of us when He says, "He that loveth his life shall lose it." His disciples thought they had never seen such promise in His life as at this hour: seedtime seemed to them to be past, and the harvest at hand. Their Master seemed to be fairly launched on the tide that was to carry Him to the highest pinnacle of human glory. And so He was, but not, as they thought, by simply yielding Himself to be set as King and to receive adoration from Jew and Gentile. He saw with different eyes, and that it was a different exaltation which would win for Him lasting sovereignty: "I, if I be lifted up, will draw all men unto Me." He knew the law which governed the development of human life. He knew that a total and absolute surrender of self to the uses and needs of others was the one path to permanent life, and that in His case this absolute surrender involved death.

A comparison of the good done by the life of Christ with that done by His death shows how truly He judged when He declared that it was by His death He should effectually gather all men to Him. His death, like the dissolution of the seed, seemed to terminate His work, but really was its germination. So long as He lived, it was but His single strength that was used; He abode alone. There was great virtue in His life--great power for the healing, the instruction, the elevation, of mankind. In His brief public career He suggested much to the influential men of His time, set all men who knew Him a-thinking, aided many to reform their lives, and removed a large amount of distress and disease. He communicated to the world a mass of new truth, so that those who have lived after Him have stood at quite a different level of knowledge from that of those who lived before Him. And yet how little of the proper results of Christ's influence, how little understanding of Christianity, do you find even in His nearest friends until He died. By the visible appearance and the external benefits and the false expectations His greatness created, the minds of men were detained from penetrating to the spirit and mind of Christ. It was expedient for them that He should go away, for until He went they depended on His visible power, and His spirit could not be wholly received by them. They were looking at the husk of the seed, and its life could not reach them. They were looking for help from Him instead of themselves becoming like Him.

And therefore He chose at an early age to cease from all that was marvellous and beneficent in His life among men. He might, as these Greeks suggested, have visited other lands and have continued His healing and teaching there. He might have done more in His own time than He did, and His time might have been indefinitely prolonged; but He chose to cease from all this and voluntarily gave Himself to die, judging that thereby He could do much more good than by His life. He was straitened till this was accomplished; He felt as a man imprisoned and whose powers are held in check. It was winter and not spring-time with Him. There was a change to pass upon Him which should disengage the vital forces that were in Him and cause their full power to be felt--a change which should thaw the springs of life in Him and let them flow forth to all. To use His own figure, He was as a seed unsown so long as He lived, valuable only in His own proper person; but by dying His life obtained the value of seed sown, propagating its kind in everlasting increase.

II. The second point suggested is, that the proper value of Christ's life consists in this--that it propagates similar lives. As seed produces grain of its own kind, so Christ produces men like Christ. He ceasing to do good in this world as a living man, a multitude of others by this very cessation are raised in His likeness. By His death we receive both inclination and ability to become with Him sons of God. "The love of Christ constraineth us, because we thus judge that if one died for all, then all died; and that He died for all, that they which live should not henceforth live unto themselves, but unto Him that died for them." By His death He has effected an entrance for this law of self-surrender into human life, has exhibited it in a perfect form, and has won others to live as He lived. So that, using the figure He used, we may say that the company of Christians now on earth are Christ in a new form, His body indeed. "That which thou sowest, thou sowest not that body which shall be, but bare grain: but God giveth it a body as it hath pleased Him, and to every seed his own body." Christ having been sown, lives now in His people. They are the body in which He dwells. And this will be seen. For standing and looking at a head of barley waving on its stalk, no amount of telling would persuade you that that had sprung from a seed of wheat; and looking at any life which is characterised by selfish ambition and eagerness for advancement and little regard for the wants of other men, no persuasion can make it credible that that life springs from the self-sacrificing life of Christ.

What Christ here shows us, then, is that the principle which regulates the development of seed regulates the growth, continuance, and fruitfulness of human life; that whatever is of the nature of seed gets to its full life only through death; that our Lord, knowing this law, submitted to it, or rather by His native love was attracted to the life and death which revealed this law to Him. He gave His life away for the good of men, and therefore prolongs His days and sees His seed eternally. There is not one way for Him and another for us. The same law applies to all. It is not peculiar to Christ. The work He did was peculiar to Him, as each individual has his own place and work; but the principle on which all right lives are led is one and the same universally. What Christ did He did because He was living a human life on right principles. We need not die on the cross as He did, but we must as truly yield ourselves as living sacrifices to the interests of men. If we have not done so, we have yet to go back to the very beginning of all lasting life and progress; and we are but deceiving ourselves by attainments and successes which are not only hollow, but are slowly cramping and killing all that is in us. Whoever will choose the same destiny as Christ must take the same road to it that He took. He took the one right way for men to go, and said, "If any man follow Me, where I am there will he be also." If we do not follow Him, we really walk in darkness and know not whither we go. We cannot live for selfish purposes and then enjoy the common happiness and glory of the race. Self-seeking is self-destroying.

And it is needful to remark that this self-renunciation must be real. The law of sacrifice is the law not for a year or two in order to gain some higher selfish good--which is not self-sacrifice, but deeper self-seeking; it is the law of all human life, not a short test of our fidelity to Christ, but the only law on which life can ever proceed. It is not a barter of self I make, giving it up for a little that I may have an enriched self to eternity; but it is a real foregoing and abandonment of self for ever, a change of desire and nature, so that instead of finding my joy in what concerns myself only I find my joy in what is serviceable to others.

Thus only can we enter into permanent happiness. Goodness and happiness are one--one in the long-run, if not one in every step of the way. We are not asked to live for others without any heart to do so. We are not asked to choose as our eternal life what will be a constant pain and can only be reluctantly done. The very heathen would not offer in sacrifice the animal that struggled as it was led to the altar. All sacrifice must be willingly made; it must be the sacrifice which is prompted by love. God and this world demand our best work, and only what we do with pleasure can be our best work. Sacrifice of self and labour for others are not like Christ's sacrifice and labour unless they spring from love. Forced, reluctant, constrained sacrifice or service--service which is no joy to ourselves through the love we bear to those for whom we do it--is not the service that is required of us. Service into which we can throw our whole strength, because we are convinced it will be of use to others, and because we long to see them enjoying it--this is the service required. Love, in short, is the solution of all. Find your happiness in the happiness of many rather than in the happiness of one, and life becomes simple and inspiring.

Nor are we to suppose that this is an impracticable, high-pitched counsel of perfection with which plain men need not trouble themselves. Every human life is under this law. There is no path to goodness or to happiness save this one. Nature herself teaches us as much. When a man is truly attracted by another, and when genuine affection possesses his heart, his whole being is enlarged, and he finds it his best pleasure to serve that person. The father who sees his children enjoying the fruit of his toil feels himself a far richer man than if he were spending all on himself. But this family affection, this domestic solution of the problem of happy self-sacrifice, is intended to encourage and show us the way to a wider extension of our love, and thereby of our use and happiness. The more love we have, the happier we are. Self-sacrifice looks miserable, and we shrink from it as from death and destitution, because we look at it in separation from the love it springs from. Self-sacrifice without love is death; we abandon our own life and do not find it again in any other. It is a seed ground under the heel, not a seed lightly thrown into prepared soil. It is in love that goodness and happiness have their common root. And it is this love which is required of us and promised to us. So that as often as we shudder at the dissolution of our own personal interests, the scattering of our own selfish hopes and plans, the surrender of our life to the service of others, we are to remember that this, which looks so very like death, and which often throws around our prospects the chilling atmosphere of the tomb, is not really the termination, but the beginning of the true and eternal life of the spirit. Let us keep our heart in the fellowship of the sacrifice of Christ, let us feel our way into the meanings and uses of that sacrifice, and learn its reality, its utility, its grace, and at length it will lay hold of our whole nature, and we shall find that it impels us to regard other men with interest and to find our true joy and life in serving them.

IV. THE ATTRACTIVE FORCE OF THE CROSS

"Now is my soul troubled; and what shall I say? Father, save Me from this hour. But for this cause came I unto this hour. Father, glorify Thy name. There came therefore a voice out of heaven, saying, I have both glorified it, and will glorify it again. The multitude therefore, that stood by, and heard it, said that it had thundered: others said, An angel hath spoken to Him. Jesus answered and said, This voice hath not come for My sake, but for your sakes. Now is the judgment of this world: now shall the prince of this world be cast out. And I, if I be lifted up from the earth, will draw all men unto Myself. But this He said, signifying by what manner of death He should die. The multitude therefore answered Him, We have heard out of the law that the Christ abideth for ever: and how sayest thou, The Son of man must be lifted up? who is this Son of man? Jesus therefore said unto them, Yet a little while is the light among you. Walk while ye have the light, that darkness overtake you not: and he that walketh in the darkness knoweth not whither he goeth. While ye have the light, believe on the light, that ye may become sons of light."--John xii. 27-36.

The presence of the Greeks had stirred in the soul of Jesus conflicting emotions. Glory by humiliation, life through death, the secured happiness of mankind through His own anguish and abandonment,--well might the prospect disturb Him. So masterly is His self-command, so steadfast and constant His habitual temper, that one almost inevitably underrates the severity of the conflict. The occasional withdrawal of the veil permits us reverently to observe some symptoms of the turmoil within--symptoms which it is probably best to speak of in His own words: "Now is My soul troubled; and what shall I say? Shall I say, Father, save Me from this hour'? But for this cause came I unto this hour. Father, glorify Thy name." This Evangelist does not describe the agony in the Garden of Gethsemane. It was needless after this indication of the same conflict. Here is the same shrinking from a public and shameful death conquered by His resolution to deliver men from a still darker and more shameful death. Here is the same foretaste of the bitterness of the cup as it now actually touches His lips, the same clear reckoning of all it meant to drain that cup to the dregs, together with the deliberate assent to all that the will of the Father might require Him to endure.

In response to this act of submission, expressed in the words, "Father, glorify Thy name," there came a voice from heaven, saying, "I have both glorified it, and will glorify it again." The meaning of this assurance was, that as in all the past manifestation of Christ the Father had become better known to men, so in all that was now impending, however painful and disturbed, however filled with human passions and to all appearance the mere result of them, the Father would still be glorified. Some thought the voice was thunder; others seemed almost to catch articulate sounds, and said, "An angel spake to Him." But Jesus explained that it was not "to Him" the voice was specially addressed, but rather for the sake of those who stood by. And it was indeed of immense importance that the disciples should understand that the events which were about to happen were overruled by God that He might be glorified in Christ. It is easy for us to see that nothing so glorifies the Father's name as these hours of suffering; but how hard for the onlookers to believe that this sudden transformation of the Messianic throne into the criminal's cross was no defeat of God's purpose, but its final fulfilment. He leads them, therefore, to consider that in His judgment the whole world is judged, and to perceive in His arrest and trial and condemnation not merely the misguided and wanton outrage of a few men in power, but the critical hour of the world's history.

This world has commonly presented itself to thoughtful minds as a battle-field in which the powers of good and evil wage ceaseless war. In the words He now utters the Lord declares Himself to be standing at the very crisis of the battle, and with the deepest assurance He announces that the opposing power is broken and that victory remains with Him. "Now is the prince of this world cast out; and I will draw all men unto Me." The prince of this world, that which actually rules and leads men in opposition to God, was judged, condemned, and overthrown in the death of Christ. By His meek acceptance of God's will in the face of all that could make it difficult and dreadful to accept it, He won for the race deliverance from the thraldom of sin. At length a human life had been lived without submission at any point to the prince of this world. As man and in the name of all men Jesus resisted the last and most violent assault that could be made upon His faith in God and fellowship with Him, and so perfected His obedience and overcame the prince of this world,--overcame him not in one act alone-- many had done that--but in a completed human life, in a life which had been freely exposed to the complete array of temptations that can be directed against men in this world.

In order more clearly to apprehend the promise of victory contained in our Lord's words, we may consider (I.) the object He had in view--to "draw all men" to Him; and (II.) the condition of His attaining this object--namely, His death.

I. The object of Christ was to draw all men to Him. The opposition in which He here sets Himself to the prince of this world shows us that by "drawing" He means attracting as a king attracts, to His name, His claims, His standard, His person. Our life consists in our pursuance of one object or another, and our devotion is continually competed for. When two claimants contest a kingdom, the country is divided between them, part cleaving to the one and part to the other. The individual determines to which side he shall cleave,--by his prejudices or by his justice, as it may be; by his knowledge of the comparative capacity of the claimants, or by his ignorant predilection. He is taken in by sounding titles, or he penetrates through all bombast and promises and douceurs to the real merit or demerit of the man himself. One person will judge by the personal manners of the respective claimants; another by their published manifesto, and professed object and style of rule; another by their known character and probable conduct. And while men thus range themselves on this side or on that, they really pass judgment on themselves, betraying as they do what it is that chiefly draws them, and taking their places on the side of good or evil. It is thus that we all judge ourselves by following this or that claimant to our faith, regard, and devotion, to ourself and our life. What we spend ourselves on, what we aim at and pursue, what we make our object, that judges us and that rules us and that determines our destiny.

Christ came into the world to be our King, to lead us to worthy achievements. He came that we might have a worthy object of choice and of the devotion of our life. He serves the same purpose as a king: He embodies in His own person, and thereby makes visible and attractive, the will of God and the cause of righteousness. Persons who could only with great difficulty apprehend His objects and plans can appreciate His person and trust Him. Persons to whom there would seem little attraction in a cause or in an undefined "progress of humanity" can kindle with enthusiasm towards Him personally, and unconsciously promote His cause and the cause of humanity. And therefore, while some are attracted by His person, others by the legitimacy of His claims, others by His programme of government, others by His benefactions, we must beware of denying loyalty to any of these. Expressions of love to His person may be lacking in the man who yet most intelligently enters into Christ's views for the race, and sacrifices his means and his life to forward these views. Those who gather to His standard are various in temperament, are drawn by various attractions, and must be various in their forms of showing allegiance. And this, which is the strength of His camp, can only become its weakness when men begin to think there is no way but their own; and that allegiance which is strenuous in labour but not fluent in devout expression, or loyalty which shouts and throws its cap in the air but lacks intelligence, is displeasing to the King. The King, who has great ends in view, will not inquire what it is precisely which forms the bond between Him and His subjects so long as they truly sympathise with Him and second His efforts. The one question is, Is He their actual leader?

Of the kingdom of Christ, though a full description cannot be given, one or two of the essential characteristics may be mentioned.

1. It is a kingdom, a community of men under one head. When Christ proposed to attract men to Himself, it was for the good of the race He did so. It could achieve its destiny only if He led it, only if it yielded itself to His mind and ways. And those who are attracted to Him, and see reason to believe that the hope of the world lies in the universal adoption of His mind and ways, are formed into one solid body or community. They labour for the same ends, are governed by the same laws, and whether they know one another or not they have the most real sympathy and live for one cause. Being drawn to Christ, we enter into abiding fellowship with all the good who have laboured or are labouring in the cause of humanity. We take our places in the everlasting kingdom, in the community of those who shall see and take part in the great future of mankind and the growing enlargement of its destiny. We are hereby entered among the living, and are joined to that body of mankind which is to go on and which holds the future--not to an extinct party which may have memories, but has no hopes. In sin, in selfishness, in worldliness, individualism reigns, and all profound or abiding unity is impossible. Sinners have common interests only for a time, only as a temporary guise of selfish interests. Every man out of Christ is really an isolated individual. But passing into Christ's kingdom we are no longer isolated, abandoned wretches stranded by the stream of time, but members of the undying commonwealth of men in which our life, our work, our rights, our future, our association with all good, are assured.

2. It is a universal kingdom. "I will draw all men unto Me." The one rational hope of forming men into one kingdom shines through these words. The idea of a universal monarchy has visited the great minds of our race. They have cherished their various dreams of a time when all men should live under one law and possibly speak one language, and have interests so truly in common that war should be impossible. But an effectual instrument for accomplishing this grand design has ever been wanting. Christ turns this grandest dream of humanity into a rational hope. He appeals to what is universally

present in human nature. There is that in Him which every man needs,--a door to the Father; a visible image of the unseen God; a gracious, wise, and holy Friend. He does not appeal exclusively to one generation, to educated or to uneducated, to Orientals or to Europeans alone, but to man, to that which we have in common with the lowest and the highest, the most primitive and most highly developed of the species. The attractive influence He exerts upon men is not conditioned by their historical insight, by their ability to sift evidence, by this or that which distinguishes man from man, but by their innate consciousness that some higher power than themselves exists, by their ability, if not to recognise goodness when they see it, at least to recognise love when it is spent upon them.

But while our Lord affirms that there is that in Him which all men can recognise and learn to love and serve, He does not say that His kingdom will therefore be quickly formed. He does not say that this greatest work of God will take a shorter time than the common works of God which prolong one day of our hasty methods into a thousand years of solidly growing purpose. If it has taken a million ages for the rocks to knit and form for us a standing-ground and dwelling-place, we must not expect that this kingdom, which is to be the one enduring result of this world's history, and which can be built up only of thoroughly convinced men and of generations slowly weeded of traditional prejudices and customs, can be completed in a few years. No doubt interests are at stake in human destiny and losses are made by human waste which had no place in the physical creation of the world; still, God's methods are, as we judge, slow, and we must not think that He who "works hitherto" is doing nothing because the swift processes of jugglery or the hasty methods of human workmanship find no place in the extension of Christ's kingdom. This kingdom has a firm hold of the world and must grow. If there is one thing certain about the future of the world, it is that righteousness and truth will prevail. The world is bound to come to the feet of Christ.

3. Christ's kingdom being universal, it is also and necessarily inward. What is common to all men lies deepest in each. Christ was conscious that He held the key to human nature. He knew what was in man. With the penetrating insight of absolute purity He had gone about among men, freely mixing with rich and with poor, with the sick and the healthy, with the religious and the irreligious. He was as much at home with the condemned criminal as with the blameless Pharisee; saw through Pilate and Caiaphas alike; knew all that the keenest dramatist could tell Him of the meannesses, the depravities, the cruelties, the blind passions, the obstructed goodness, of men; but knew also that He could sway all that was in man and exhibit that to men which should cause the sinner to abhor his sin and seek the face of God. This He would do by a simple moral process, without violent demonstration or disturbance or assertion of authority. He would "draw" men. It is by inward conviction, not by outward compulsion, men are to become His subjects. It is by the free and rational working of the human mind that Jesus builds up His kingdom. His hope lies in a fuller and fuller light, in a clearer and clearer recognition of facts. Attachment to Christ must be the act of the soul's self; everything, therefore, which strengthens the will or enlightens the mind or enlarges the man brings him nearer to the kingdom of Christ, and makes it more likely he will yield to His drawing.

And because Christ's rule is inward it is therefore of universal application. The inmost choice of the man being governed by Christ, and his character being thus touched at its inmost spring, all his conduct will be governed by Christ and be a carrying out of the will of Christ. It is not the frame of society Christ seeks to alter, but the spirit of it. It is not the occupations and institutions of human life which the subject of Christ finds to be incompatible with Christ's rule, so much as the aim and principles on which they are conducted. The kingdom of Christ claims all human life as its own, and the spirit of Christ finds nothing that is essentially human alien from it. If the statesman is a Christian, it will be seen in his policy; if the poet be a Christian, his song will betray it; if a thinker be a Christian, his readers soon find it out. Christianity does not mean religious services, churches, creeds, Bibles, books, equipment of any kind; it means the Spirit of Christ. It is the most portable and flexible of all religions, and therefore the most pervasive and dominant in the life of its adherent. It needs but the Spirit of God and the spirit of man, and Christ mediating between them.

II. Such being Christ's object, what is the condition of His attaining it? "I, if I be lifted up, will draw all men unto Me." The elevation requisite for becoming a visible object to men of all generations was the elevation of the Cross. His death would accomplish what His life could not accomplish. The words betray a distinct consciousness that there was in His death a more potent spell, a more certain and real influence for good among men than in His teaching or in His miracles or in His purity of life.

What is it, then, in the death of Christ which so far surpasses His life in its power of attraction? The life was equally unselfish and devoted; it was more prolonged; it was more directly useful,--why, then, would it have been comparatively ineffective without the death? It may, in the first place, be answered, Because His death presents in a dramatic and compact form that very devotedness which is diffused through every part of His life. Between the life and the death there is the same difference as between sheet lightning and forked lightning, between the diffused heat of the sun and the same heat focussed upon a point through a lens. It discloses what was actually but latently there. The life and the death of Christ are one and mutually explain each other. From the life we learn that no motive can have prompted Christ to die but the one motive which ruled Him always--the desire to do all God willed in men's behalf. We cannot interpret the death as anything else than a consistent part of a deliberate work undertaken for men's good. It was not an accident; it was not an external necessity: it was, as the whole life was, a willing acceptance of the uttermost that was required to set men on a higher level and unite them to God. But as the life throws this light upon the death of Christ, how that light is gathered up and thrown abroad in world-wide reflection from the death of Christ! For here His self-sacrifice shines completed and perfect; here it is exhibited in that tragic and supreme form which in all cases arrests attention and commands respect. Even when a man of wasted life sacrifices himself at last, and in one heroic act saves another by his death, his past life is forgotten or seems to be redeemed by his death, and at all events we own the beauty and the pathos of the deed. A martyr to the faith may have been but a poor creature, narrow, harsh and overbearing, vain and vulgar in spirit; but all the past is blotted out, and our attention is arrested on the blazing pile or the bloody scaffold. So the death of Christ, though but a part of the self-sacrificing life, yet stands by itself as the culmination and seal of that life; it catches the eye and strikes the mind, and conveys at one view the main impression made by the whole life and character of Him who gave Himself upon the cross.

But Christ is no mere hero or teacher sealing his truth with his blood; nor is it enough to say that His death renders, in a conspicuous form, the perfect self-sacrifice with which He devoted Himself to our good. It is conceivable that in a long-past age some other man should have lived and died for his fellows, and yet we at once recognise that, though the history of such a person came into our hands, we should not be so affected and drawn by it as to choose him as our king and rest upon him the hope of uniting us to one another and to God. Wherein, then, lies the difference? The difference lies in this--that Christ was the representative of God. This He Himself uniformly claimed to be. He knew He was unique, different from all others; but He advanced no claim to esteem that did not pass to the Father who sent Him. Always he explained His powers as being the proper equipment of God's representative, "The words that I speak unto you, I speak not of Myself." His whole life was the message of God to man, the Word made flesh. His death was but the last syllable of this great utterance--the utterance of God's love for man, the final evidence that nothing is grudged us by God. Greater love hath no man than this, that he lay down his life for his friends. His death draws us because there is in it more than human heroism and self-sacrifice. It draws us because in it the very heart of God is laid bare to us. It softens, it breaks us down, by the irresistible tenderness it discloses in the mighty and ever-blessed God. Every man feels it has a message for him, because in it the God and Father of us all speaks to us.

It is this which is special to the death of Christ, and which separates it from all other deaths and heroic sacrifices. It has a universal bearing--a bearing upon every man, because it is a Divine act, the act of that One who is the God and Father of all men. In the same century as our Lord many men died in a manner which strongly excites our admiration. Nothing could well be more noble, nothing more pathetic, than the fearless and loving spirit in which Roman after Roman met his death. But beyond respectful admiration these heroic deeds win from us no further sentiment. They are the deeds of men who have no connection with us. The well-worn words, "What's Hecuba to me or I to Hecuba?" rise to our lips when we try to fancy any deep connection. But the death of Christ concerns all men without exception, because it is the greatest declarative act of the God of all men. It is the manifesto all men are concerned to read. It is the act of One with whom all men are already connected in the closest way. And the result of our contemplation of it is, not that we admire, but that we are drawn, are attracted, into new relations with Him whom that death reveals. This death moves and draws us as no other can, because here we get to the very heart of that which most deeply concerns us. Here we learn what our God is and where we stand eternally. He who is nearest us of all, and in whom our life is bound up, reveals Himself; and seeing Him here full of ungrudging and most reliable love, of tenderest and utterly self-sacrificing devotedness to us, we cannot but give way to this central attraction, and with all other willing creatures be drawn into fullest intimacy and firmest relations to the God of all.

The death of Christ, then, draws men chiefly because God here shows men His sympathy, His love, His trustworthiness. What the sun is in the solar system, Christ's death is in the moral world. The sun by its physical attraction binds the several planets together and holds them within range of its light and heat. God, the central intelligence and original moral Being, draws to Himself and holds within reach of His life-giving radiance all who are susceptible of moral influences; and He does so through the death of Christ. This is His supreme revelation. Here, if we may say so with reverence, God is seen at His best--not that at any time or in any action He is different, but here He is seen to be the God of love He ever is. Nothing is better than self-sacrifice: that is the highest point a moral nature can touch. And God, by the sacrifice which is rendered visible on the cross, gives to the moral world a real, actual, immovable centre, round which moral natures will more and more gather, and which will hold them together in self-effacing unity.

To complete the idea of the attractiveness of the Cross, it must further be kept in view that this particular form of the manifestation of the Divine love was adapted to the needs of those to whom it was made. To sinners the love of God manifested itself in providing a sacrifice for sin. The death on the cross was not an irrelevant display, but was an act required for the removal of the most insuperable obstacles that lay in man's path. The sinner, believing that in the death of Christ his sins are atoned for, conceives hope in God and claims the Divine compassion in his own behalf. To the penitent the Cross is attractive as an open door to the prisoner, or the harbour-heads to the storm-tossed ship.

Let us not suppose, then, that we are not welcome to Christ. He desires to draw us to Himself and to form a connection with us. He understands our hesitations, our doubts of our own capacity for any steady and enthusiastic loyalty; but He knows also the power of truth and love, the power of His own person and of His own death to draw and fix the hesitating and wavering soul. And we shall find that as we strive to serve Christ in our daily life it is still His death that holds and draws us. It is His death which gives us compunction in our times of frivolity, or selfishness, or carnality, or rebellion, or unbelief. It is there Christ appears in His own most touching attitude and with His own most irresistible appeal. We cannot further wound One already so wounded in His desire to win us from evil. To strike One already thus nailed to the tree in helplessness and anguish, is more than the hardest heart can do. Our sin, our infidelity, our unmoved contemplation of His love, our blind indifference to His purpose-- these things wound Him more than the spear and the scourge. To rid us of these things was His purpose in dying, and to see that His work is in vain and His sufferings unregarded and unfruitful is the deepest injury of all. It is not to the mere sentiment of pity He appeals: rather He says, "Weep not for Me; weep for yourselves." It is to our power to recognise perfect goodness and to appreciate perfect love. He appeals to our power to see below the surface of things, and through the outer shell of this world's life to the Spirit of good that is at the root of all and that manifests itself in Him. Here is the true stay of the human soul: "Come unto Me, all ye that labour and are heavy laden"; "I am come a light into the world: walk in the light."

Marcus Dods, D.D.

V. RESULTS OF CHRIST'S MANIFESTATION

"But though He had done so many signs before them, yet they believed not on Him: that the word of Isaiah the prophet might be fulfilled, which he spake, Lord, who hath believed our report? and to whom hath the arm of the Lord been revealed? For this cause they could not believe, for that Isaiah said again, He hath blinded their eyes, and He hardened their heart; lest they should see with their eyes, and perceive with their heart, and should turn, and I should heal them. These things said Isaiah, because he saw His glory; and he spake of Him. Nevertheless even of the rulers many believed on Him; but because of the Pharisees they did not confess it, lest they should be put out of the synagogue: for they loved the glory of men more than the glory of God. And Jesus cried and said, He that believeth on Me, believeth not on Me, but on Him that sent Me. And he that beholdeth Me beholdeth Him that sent Me. I am come a light into the world, that whosoever believeth on Me may not abide in the darkness. And if any man hear My sayings, and keep them not, I judge him not: for I came not to judge the world, but to save the world. He that rejecteth Me, and receiveth not My sayings, hath One that judgeth him: the word that I spake, the same shall judge him in the last day. For I spake not from Myself; but the Father which sent Me, He hath given Me a commandment, what I should say, and what I should speak. And I know that His commandment is life eternal: the things therefore which I speak, even as the Father hath said unto Me, so I speak."--John xii. 37-50.

In this Gospel the death of Christ is viewed as the first step in His glorification. When He speaks of being "lifted up," there is a double reference in the expression, a local and an ethical reference. [6] He is lifted up on the cross, but lifted up on it as His true throne and as the necessary step towards His supremacy at God's right hand. It was, John tells us, with direct reference to the cross that Jesus now used the words: "I, if I be lifted up, will draw all men unto Me." The Jews, who heard the words, perceived that, whatever else was contained in them, intimation of His removal from earth was given. But, according to the current Messianic expectation, the Christ "abideth for ever," or at any rate for four hundred or a thousand years. How then could this Person, who announced His immediate departure, be the Christ? The Old Testament gave them ground for supposing that the Messianic reign would be lasting; but had they listened to our Lord's teaching they would have learned that this reign was spiritual, and not in the form of an earthly kingdom with a visible sovereign.

Accordingly, although they had recognised Jesus as the Messiah, they are again stumbled by this fresh declaration of His. They begin to fancy that perhaps after all by calling Himself "the Son of man" He has not meant exactly what they mean by the Messiah. From the form of their question it would seem that Jesus had used the designation "the Son of man" in intimating His departure; for they say, "How sayest thou, The Son of man must be lifted up?" Up to this time, therefore, they had taken it for granted that by calling Himself the Son of man He claimed to be the Christ, but now they begin to doubt whether there may not be two persons signified by those titles.

Jesus furnishes them with no direct solution of their difficulty. He never betrays any interest in these external identifications. The time for discussing the relation of the Son of man to the Messiah is past. His manifestation is closed. Enough light has been given. Conscience has been appealed to and discussion is no longer admissible. "Ye have light: walk in the light." The way to come to a settlement of all their doubts and hesitations is to follow Him. There is still time for that. "Yet a little while is the light among you." But the time is short; there is none to waste on idle questionings, none to spend on sophisticating conscience--time only for deciding as conscience bids.

By thus believing in the light they will themselves become "children of light." The "children of light" are those who live in it as their element,--as "the children of this world" are those who wholly belong to this world and find in it what is congenial; as "the son of perdition" is he who is identified with perdition. The children of light have accepted the revelation that is in Christ, and live in the "day" that the Lord has made. Christ contains the truth for them--the truth which penetrates to their inmost thought and illuminates the darkest problems of life. In Christ they have seen that which determines their relation to God; and that being determined, all else that is of prime importance finds a settlement. To know God and ourselves; to know God's nature and purpose, and our own capabilities and relation to God,--these constitute the light we need for living by; and this light Christ gives. It was in a dim, uncertain twilight, with feebly shining lanterns, the wisest and best of men sought to make out the nature of God and His purposes regarding man; but in Christ God has made noonday around us.

They, therefore, that stood, or that stand, in His presence, and yet recognise no light, must be asleep, or must turn away from an excess of light that is disagreeable or inconvenient. If we are not the fuller of life and joy the more truth we know, if we shrink from admitting the consciousness of a present and holy God, and do not feel it to be the very sunshine of life in which alone we thrive, we must be spiritually asleep or spiritually dead. And this cry of Christ is but another form of the cry that His Church has prolonged: "Awake, thou that sleepest, and arise from the dead, and Christ shall give thee light."

The "little while" of their enjoyment of the light was short indeed, for no sooner had He made an end of these sayings than He "departed, and did hide Himself from them." He probably found retirement from the feverish, inconstant, questioning crowd with His friends in Bethany. At any rate this removal of the light, while it meant darkness to those who had not received Him and who did not keep His words, could bring no darkness to His own, who had received Him and the light in Him. Perhaps the best comment on this is the memorable passage from Comus:

"Virtue could see to do what virtue would
By her own radiant light, though sun and moon
Were in the great sea sunk.
He that has light within his own clear breast
May sit i' the centre and enjoy bright day;
But he that hides a dark soul and foul thoughts
Benighted walks under the midday sun,
Himself is his own dungeon."

And now the writer of this Gospel, before entering upon the closing scenes, pauses and presents a summary of the results of all that has been hitherto related. First, he accounts for the unbelief of the Jews. It could not fail to strike his readers as remarkable that, "though He had done so many miracles before the people, yet they believed not in Him." In this John sees nothing inexplicable, however sad and significant it may be. At first sight it is an astounding fact that the very people who had been prepared to recognise and receive the Messiah should not have believed in Him. Might not this to some minds be convincing evidence that Jesus was not the Messiah? If the same God who sent Him forth had for centuries specially prepared a people to recognise and receive Him when He came, was it possible that this people should repudiate Him? Was it likely that such a result should be produced or should be allowed? But John turns the point of this argument by showing that a precisely similar phenomenon had often appeared in the history of Israel. The old prophets had the very same complaint to make: "Who hath believed our report? and to whom hath the arm of the Lord been revealed?" The people had habitually, as a people with individual exceptions, refused to listen to God's voice or to acknowledge His presence in prophet and providence.

Besides, might it not very well be that the blindness and callousness of the Jews in rejecting Jesus was the inevitable issue of a long process of hardening? If, in former periods of their history, they had proved themselves unworthy of God's training and irresponsive to it, what else could be expected than that they should reject the Messiah when He came? This hardening and blinding process was the inevitable, natural result of their past conduct. But what nature does, God does; and therefore the Evangelist says "they could not believe, because that Esaias said again, He hath blinded their eyes, and hardened their heart; that they should not see with their eyes, nor understand with their heart." The organ for perceiving spiritual truth was blinded, and their susceptibility to religious and moral impressions had become callous and hardened and impervious.

And while this was no doubt true of the people as a whole, still there were not a few individuals who eagerly responded to this last message from God. In the most unlikely quarters, and in circumstances calculated to counteract the influence of spiritual forces, some were convinced. "Even among the chief rulers many believed on Him." This belief, however, did not tell upon the mass, because, through fear of excommunication, those who were convinced dared not utter their conviction. "They loved the praise of men more than the praise of God." They allowed their relations to men to determine their relation to God. Men were more real to them than God. The praise of men came home to their hearts with a sensible relish that the praise of God could not rival. They reaped what they had sown; they had sought the esteem of men, and now they were unable to find their strength in God's approval. The glory which consisted in following the lowly and outcast Jesus, the glory of fellowship with God, was quite eclipsed by the glory of living in the eye of the people as wise and estimable persons.

In the last paragraph of the chapter John gives a summary of the claims and message of Jesus. He has told us (ver. 36) that Jesus had departed from public view and had hidden Himself, and he mentions no return to publicity. It is therefore probable that in these remaining verses, and before he turns to a somewhat different aspect of Christ's ministry, he gives in rapid and brief retrospect the sum of what

Jesus had advanced as His claim. He introduces this paragraph, indeed, with the words, "Jesus cried and said"; but as neither time nor place is mentioned, it is quite likely that no special time or place is supposed; and in point of fact each detail adduced in these verses can be paralleled from some previously recorded utterance of Jesus.

First, then, as everywhere in the Gospel, so here, He claims to be the representative of God in so close and perfect a manner that "he that believeth on Me, believeth not on Me, but on Him that sent Me. And he that seeth Me, seeth Him that sent Me." No belief terminates in Christ Himself: to believe in Him is to believe in God, because all that He is and does proceeds from God and leads to God. The whole purpose of Christ's manifestation was to reveal God. He did not wish to arrest thought upon Himself, but through Himself to guide thought to Him whom He revealed. He was sustained by the Father, and all He said and did was of the Father's inspiration. Whoever, therefore, "saw" or understood Him "saw" the Father; and whoever believed in Him believed in the Father.

Second, as regards men, He is "come a light into the world." Naturally there is in the world no sufficient light. Men feel that they are in darkness. They feel the darkness all the more appalling and depressing the more developed their own human nature is. "More light" has been the cry from the beginning. What are we? where are we? whence are we? whither are we going? what is there above and beyond this world? These questions are echoed back from an unanswering void, until Christ comes and gives the answer. Since He came men have felt that they did not any longer walk in darkness. They see where they are going, and they see why they should go.

And if it be asked, as among the Jews it certainly must have been asked, why, if Jesus is the Messiah, does He not punish men for rejecting Him? the answer is, "I came not to judge the world, but to save the world." Judgment, indeed, necessarily results from His coming. Men are divided by His coming. "The words that I have spoken, the same shall judge men in the last day." The offer of God, the offer of righteousness, is that which judges men. Why are they still dead, when life has been offered? This is the condemnation. "The commandment of the Father is life everlasting." This is the sum of the message of God to men in Christ; this is "the commandment" which the Father has given Me; this is Christ's commission: to bring God in the fulness of His grace and love and life-giving power within men's reach. It is to give life eternal to men that God has come to them in Christ. To refuse that life is their condemnation.

Footnotes:

6. See iii. 14.

VI. THE FOOT-WASHING

"Now before the feast of the Passover, Jesus knowing that His hour was come that He should depart out of this world unto the Father, having loved His own which were in the world, He loved them unto the end. And during supper, the devil having already put into the heart of Judas Iscariot, Simon's son, to betray Him, Jesus, knowing that the Father had given all things into His hands, and that He came forth from God, and goeth unto God, riseth from supper, and layeth aside His garments; and He took a towel, and girded Himself. Then He poureth water into the basin, and began to wash the disciples' feet, and to wipe them with the towel wherewith He was girded. So He cometh to Simon Peter. He saith unto Him, Lord, dost Thou wash my feet? Jesus answered and said unto him, What I do thou knowest not now; but thou shalt understand hereafter. Peter saith unto Him, Thou shalt never wash my feet. Jesus answered him, If I wash thee not, thou hast no part with Me. Simon Peter saith unto Him, Lord, not my feet only, but also my hands and my head. Jesus saith to him, He that is bathed needeth not save to wash his feet, but is clean every whit: and ye are clean, but not all. For He knew him that should betray Him; therefore said He, Ye are not all clean. So when He had washed their feet, and taken His garments, and sat down again, He said unto them, Know ye what I have done to you? Ye call Me, Master, and, Lord: and ye say well; for so I am. If I then, the Lord and the Master, have washed your feet, ye also ought to wash one another's feet. For I have given you an example, that ye also should do as I have done to you. Verily, verily, I say unto you, A servant is not greater than his lord; neither one that is sent greater than he that sent him. If ye know these things, blessed are ye if ye do them."--John xiii. 1-17.

St. John, having finished his account of the public manifestation of Jesus, proceeds now to narrate the closing scenes, in which the disclosures He made to "His own" form a chief part. That the transition may be observed, attention is drawn to it. At earlier stages of our Lord's ministry He has given as His reason for refraining from proposed lines of action that His hour was not come: now He "knew that His hour was come, that He should depart out of this world unto the Father." This indeed was the last evening of His life. Within twenty-four hours He was to be in the tomb. Yet according to this writer it was not the paschal supper which our Lord now partook of with His disciples; it was "before the feast of the Passover." Jesus being Himself the Paschal Lamb was sacrificed on the day on which the Passover was eaten, and in this and the following chapters we have an account of the preceding evening.

In order to account for what follows, the precise time is defined in the words "supper being served" [7] or "supper-time having arrived"; not, as in the Authorised Version, "supper being ended," which plainly was not the case; [8] nor, as in the Revised Version, "during supper." The difficulty about washing the feet could not have arisen after or during supper, but only as the guests entered and reclined at table. In Palestine, as in other countries of the same latitude, shoes were not universally worn, and were not worn at all within doors; and where some protection to the foot was worn, it was commonly a mere sandal, a sole tied on with a thong. The upper part of the foot was thus left exposed, and necessarily became heated and dirty with the fine and scorching dust of the roads. Much discomfort was thus produced, and the first duty of a host was to provide for its removal. A slave was ordered to remove the sandals and wash the feet. [9] And in order that this might be done, the guest either sat on the couch appointed for him at table, or reclined with his feet protruding beyond the end of it, that the slave, coming round with the pitcher and basin, [10] might pour cool water gently over them. So necessary to comfort was this attention that our Lord reproached the Pharisee who had invited Him to dinner with a breach of courtesy because he had omitted it.

On ordinary occasions it is probable that the disciples would perform this humble office by turns, where there was no slave to discharge it for all. But this evening, when they gathered for the last supper, all took their places at the table with a studied ignorance of the necessity, a feigned unconsciousness that any such attention was required. As a matter of course, the pitcher of cool water, the basin, and the towel had been set as part of the requisite furnishing of the supper chamber; but no one among the disciples betrayed the slightest consciousness that he understood that any such custom existed. Why was this? Because, as Luke tells us (xxii. 24), "there had arisen among them a contention, which of them is accounted to be the greatest." Beginning, perhaps, by discussing the prospects of their Master's kingdom, they had passed on to compare the importance of this or that faculty for forwarding the interests of the kingdom, and had ended by easily recognised personal allusions and even the direct pitting of man against man. The assumption of superiority on the part of the sons of Zebedee and others was called in question, and it suddenly appeared how this assumption had galled the rest and rankled in their minds. That such a discussion should arise may be disappointing, but it was natural. All men are jealous of their reputation, and crave that credit be given them for their natural talent, their acquired skill, their professional standing, their influence, or at any rate for their humility.

Heated, then, and angry and full of resentment these men hustle into the supper-room and seat themselves like so many sulky schoolboys. They streamed into the room and doggedly took their places; and then came a pause. For any one to wash the feet of the rest was to declare himself the servant of all; and that was precisely what each one was resolved he, for his part, would not do. No one of them had humour enough to see the absurdity of the situation. No one of them was sensitive enough to be ashamed of showing such a temper in Christ's presence. There they sat, looking at the table, looking at the ceiling, arranging their dress, each resolved upon this--that he would not be the man to own himself servant of all.

But this unhealthy heat quite unfits them to listen to what their Lord has to say to them that last evening. Occupied as they are, not with anxiety about Him nor with absorbing desire for the prosperity of His kingdom, but with selfish ambitions that separate them alike from Him and from one another, how can they receive what He has to say? But how is He to bring them into a state of mind in which they can listen wholly and devotedly to Him? How is He to quench their heated passions and stir within them humility and love? "He riseth from the supper-table, and laid aside His garments, and took a towel, and girded Himself. After that He poureth water into the basin, and began to wash the disciples' feet, and to wipe them with the towel wherewith He was girded." Each separate action is a fresh astonishment and a deeper shame to the bewildered and conscience-stricken disciples. "Who is not able to picture the scene,--the faces of John and James and Peter; the intense silence, in which each movement of Jesus was painfully audible; the furtive watching of Him, as He rose, to see what He would do; the sudden pang of self-reproach as they perceived what it meant; the bitter humiliation and the burning shame?"

But not only is the time noted, in order that we may perceive the relevancy of the foot-washing, but the Evangelist steps aside from his usual custom and describes the mood of Jesus that we may more deeply penetrate into the significance of the action. Around this scene in the supper-chamber St. John sets lights which permit us to see its various beauty and grace. And first of all he would have us notice what seems chiefly to have struck himself as from time to time he reflected on this last evening--that Jesus, even in these last hours, was wholly possessed and governed by love. Although He knew "that His hour had come, that He should depart out of this world unto the Father, yet having loved His own which were in the world He loved them unto the end." Already the deep darkness of the coming night was touching the spirit of Jesus with its shadow. Already the pain of the betrayal, the lonely desolation of desertion by His friends, the defenceless exposure to fierce, unjust, ruthless men, the untried misery of death and dissolution, the critical trial of His cause and of all the labour of His life, these and many anxieties that cannot be imagined, were pouring in upon His spirit, wave upon wave. If ever man might have been excused for absorption in His own affairs Jesus was then that man. On the edge of what He knew to be the critical passage in the world's history, what had He to do attending to the comfort and adjusting the silly differences of a few unworthy men? With the weight of a world on His arm, was He to have His hands free for such a trifling attention as this? With His whole soul pressed with the heaviest burden ever laid on man, was it to be expected He should turn aside at such a call?

But His love made it seem no turning aside at all. His love had made Him wholly theirs, and though standing on the brink of death He was disengaged to do them the slightest service. His love was love, devoted, enduring, constant. He had loved them, and He loved them still. It was their condition which had brought Him into the world, and His love for them was that which would carry Him through all that was before Him. The very fact that they showed themselves still so jealous and childish, so unfit to cope with the world, drew out His affection towards them. He was departing from the world and they were remaining in it, exposed to all its opposition and destined to bear the brunt of hostility directed against Him--how then can He but pity and strengthen them? Nothing is more touching on a death-bed than to see the sufferer hiding and making light of his own pain, and turning the attention of those around him away from him to themselves, and making arrangements, not for his own relief, but for the future comfort of others. This which has often dimmed with tears the eyes of the bystanders struck John when he saw his Master ministering to the wants of His disciples, although He knew that His own hour had come.

Another side-light which serves to bring out the full significance of this action is Jesus' consciousness of His own dignity. "Jesus, knowing that the Father had given all things into His hands, and that He came forth from God, and goeth unto God," riseth from supper, and took a towel and girded Himself. It was not in forgetfulness of His Divine origin, but in full consciousness of it, He discharged this menial function. As He had divested Himself of the "form of God" at the first, stripping Himself of the outward glory attendant on recognised Divinity, and had taken upon Him the form of a servant, so now He "laid aside His garments and girded Himself," assuming the guise of a household slave. For a fisherman to pour water over a fisherman's feet was no great condescension; but that He, in whose hands are all human affairs and whose nearest relation is the Father, should thus condescend is of unparalleled significance. It is this kind of action that is suitable to One whose consciousness is Divine. Not only does the dignity of Jesus vastly augment the beauty of the action, but it sheds new light on the Divine character.

Still another circumstance which seemed to John to accentuate the grace of the foot-washing was this--that Judas was among the guests, and that "the devil had now put into the heart of Judas Iscariot, Simon's son, to betray him." The idea had at last formed itself in Judas' mind that the best use he could make of Jesus was to sell Him to His enemies. His hopes of gain in the Messianic kingdom were finally blighted, but he might still make something out of Jesus and save himself from all implication in a movement frowned upon by the authorities. He clearly apprehended that all hopes of a temporal kingdom were gone. He had probably not strength of mind enough to say candidly that he had joined the company of disciples on a false understanding, and meant now quietly to return to his trading at Kerioth. If he could break up the whole movement, he would be justified in his dissatisfaction, and would also be held to be a useful servant of the nation. So he turns traitor. And John does not whitewash him, but plainly brands him as a traitor. Now, much may be forgiven a man; but treachery--what is to be done with it; with the man who uses the knowledge only a friend can have, to betray you to your enemies? Suppose Jesus had unmasked him to Peter and the rest, would he ever have left that room alive? Instead of unmasking him, Jesus makes no difference between him and the others, kneels by his couch, takes his feet in His hands, washes and gently dries them. However difficult it is to understand why Jesus chose Judas at the first, there can be no question that throughout His acquaintance with him He had done all that was possible to win him. The kind of treatment Judas had received throughout may be inferred from the treatment he received now. Jesus knew him to be a man of a low type and impenitent; He knew him to be at that very time out of harmony with the little company, false, plotting, meaning to save himself by bringing ruin on the rest. Yet Jesus will not denounce him to the others. His sole weapon is love. Conquests which He cannot achieve with this He will not achieve at all. In the person of Judas the utmost of malignity the world can show is present to Him, and He meets it with kindness. Well may Astié exclaim: "Jesus at the feet of the traitor--what a picture! what lessons for us!"

Shame and astonishment shut the mouths of the disciples, and not a sound broke the stillness of the room but the tinkle and plash of the water in the basin as Jesus went from couch to couch. But the silence was broken when He came to Peter. The deep reverence which the disciples had contracted for Jesus betrays itself in Peter's inability to suffer Him to touch his feet. Peter could not endure that the places of master and servant should thus be reversed. He feels that shrinking and revulsion which we feel when a delicate person or one much above us in station proceeds to do some service from which we ourselves would shrink as beneath us. That Peter should have drawn up his feet, started up on the couch, and exclaimed, "Lord, do you actually propose to wash my feet!" is to his credit, and just what we should have expected of a man who never lacked generous impulses. Our Lord therefore assures him that his scruples will be removed, and that what he could not understand would be shortly explained to him. He treats Peter's scruples very much as He treated the Baptist's when John hesitated about baptizing Him. Let Me, says Jesus, do it now, and I will explain My reason when I have finished the washing of you all. But this does not satisfy Peter. Out he comes with one of his blunt and hasty speeches: "Lord, Thou shalt never wash my feet!" He knew better than Jesus, that is to say, what should be done. Jesus was mistaken in supposing that any explanation could be given of it. Hasty, self-confident, knowing better than anybody else, Peter once again ran himself into grave fault. The first requirement in a disciple is entire self-surrender. The others had meekly allowed Jesus to wash their feet, cut to the heart with shame as they were, and scarcely able to let their feet lie in His hands; but Peter must show himself of a different mind. His first refusal was readily forgiven as a generous impulse; the second is an obstinate, proud, self-righteous utterance, and was forthwith met by the swift rebuke of Jesus: "If I wash thee not, thou hast no part with Me."

Superficially, these words might have been understood as intimating to Peter that, if he wished to partake of the feast prepared, he must allow Jesus to wash his feet. Unless he was prepared to leave the room and reckon himself an outcast from that company, he must submit to the feet-washing which his friends and fellow-guests had submitted to. There was that in the tone of our Lord which awakened Peter to see how great and painful a rupture this would be. He almost hears in the words a sentence of expulsion pronounced on himself; and as rapidly as he had withdrawn from the touch of Christ, so rapidly does he now run to the opposite extreme and offer his whole body to be washed--"not my feet only, but my hands and my head." If this washing means that we are Thy friends and partners, let me be all washed, for every bit of me is Thine. Here again Peter was swayed by blind impulse, and here again he erred. If he could only have been quiet! If he could only have held his tongue! If only he could have allowed his Lord to manage without his interference and suggestion at every point! But this was precisely what Peter had as yet not learned to do. In after-years he was to learn meekness; he was to learn to submit while others bound him and carried him whither they would; but as yet that was impossible to him. His Lord's plan is never good enough for him; Jesus is never exactly right. What He proposes must always be eked out by Peter's superior wisdom. What gusts of shame must have stormed through Peter's soul when he looked back on this scene! Yet it concerns us rather to admire than to condemn Peter's fervour. How welcome to our Lord as He passed from the cold and treacherous heart of Judas must this burst of enthusiastic devotion have been! "Lord, if washing be any symbol of my being Thine, wash hands and head as well as feet."

Jesus throws a new light upon His action in His reply: "He that is washed, needeth not save to wash his feet, but is clean every whit: and ye are clean, but not all." The words would have more readily disclosed Christ's meaning had they been literally rendered: He that has bathed needeth not save to wash his feet. The daily use of the bath rendered it needless to wash more than the feet, which were soiled with walking from the bath to the supper-chamber. But that Christ had in view as He washed the disciples' feet something more than the mere bodily cleansing and comfort is plain from His remark that they were not all clean. All had enjoyed the feet-washing, but all were not clean. The feet of Judas were as clean as the feet of John or Peter, but his heart was foul. And what Christ intended when He girt Himself with the towel and took up the pitcher was not merely to wash the soil from their feet, but to wash from their hearts the hard and proud feelings which were so uncongenial to that night of communion and so threatening to His cause. Far more needful to their happiness at the feast than the comfort of cool and clean feet was their restored affection and esteem for one another, and that humility that takes the lowest place. Jesus could very well have eaten with men who were unwashed; but He could not eat with men hating one another, glaring fiercely across the table, declining to answer or to pass what they were asked for, showing in every way malice and bitterness of spirit. He knew that at bottom they were good men; He knew that with one exception they loved Him and one another; He knew that as a whole they were clean, and that this vicious temper in which they at present entered the room was but the soil contracted for the hour. But none the less must it be washed off. And He did effectually wash it off by washing their feet. For was there a man among them who, when he saw his Lord and Master stooping at his couch-foot, would not most gladly have changed places with Him? Was there one of them who was not softened and broken down by the action of the Lord? Is it not certain that shame must have cast out pride from every heart; that the feet would be very little thought of, but that the change of feeling would be marked and obvious? From a group of angry, proud, insolent, implacable, resentful men, they were in five minutes changed into a company of humbled, meek, loving disciples of the Lord, each thinking hardly of himself and esteeming others better. They were effectually cleansed from the stain they had contracted, and could enter on the enjoyment of the Last Supper with pure conscience, with restored and increased affection for one another, and with deepened adoration for the marvellous wisdom and all-accomplishing grace of their Master.

Jesus, then, does not mistake present defilement for habitual impurity, nor partial stain for total uncleanness. He knows whom He has chosen. He understands the difference between deep-seated alienation of spirit and the passing mood which for the hour disturbs friendship. He discriminates between Judas and Peter: between the man who has not been in the bath, and the man whose feet are soiled in walking from it; between him who is at heart unmoved and unimpressed by His love, and him who has for a space fallen from the consciousness of it. He does not suppose that because we have sinned this morning we have no real root of grace in us. He knows the heart we bear Him; and if just at present unworthy feelings prevail, He does not misunderstand as men may, and straightway dismiss us from His company. He recognises that our feet need washing, that our present stain must be removed, but not on this account does He think we need to be all washed and have never been right in heart towards Him.

These present stains, then, Christ seeks to remove, that our fellowship with Him may be unembarrassed; and that our heart, restored to humility and tenderness, may be in a state to receive the blessing He would bestow. It is not enough to be once forgiven, to begin the day "clean every whit." No sooner do we take a step in the life of the day than our footfall raises a little puff of dust which does not settle without sullying us. Our temper is ruffled, and words fall from our lips that injure and exasperate. In one way or other stain attaches to our conscience, and we are moved away from cordial and open fellowship with Christ. All this happens to those who are at heart as truly Christ's friends as those first disciples. But we must have these stains washed away even as they had. Humbly we must own them, and humbly accept their forgiveness and rejoice in their removal. As these men had with shame to lay their feet in Christ's hands, so must we. As His hands had to come in contact with the soiled feet of the disciples, so has His moral nature to come in contact with the sins from which He cleanses us. His heart is purer than were His hands, and He shrinks more from contact with moral than with physical pollution; and yet without ceasing we bring Him into contact with such pollution. When we consider what those stains actually are from which we must ask Christ to wash us, we feel tempted to exclaim with Peter, "Lord, Thou shalt never wash my feet!" As these men must have shivered with shame through all their nature, so do we when we see Christ stoop before us to wash away once again the defilement we have contracted; when we lay our feet soiled with the miry and dusty ways of life in His sacred hands; when we see the uncomplaining, unreproachful grace with which He performs for us this lowly and painful office. But only thus are we prepared for communion with Him and with one another. Only by admitting that we need cleansing, and by humbly allowing Him to cleanse us, are we brought into true fellowship with Him. With the humble and contrite spirit which has thrown down all barriers of pride and freely admits His love and rejoices in His holiness does He abide. Whoso sits down at Christ's table must sit down clean; he may not have come clean, even as those first guests were not clean, but he must allow Christ to cleanse him, must honestly suffer Christ to remove from his heart, from his desire and purpose, all that He counts defiling.

But our Lord was not content to let His action speak for itself; He expressly explains (vv. 12-17) the meaning of what He had now done. He meant that they should learn to wash one another's feet, to be humble and ready to be of service to one another even when to serve seemed to compromise their dignity. [11] No disciple of Christ need go far to find feet that need washing, feet that are stained or bleeding with the hard ways that have been trodden. To recover men from the difficulties into which sin or misfortune has brought them--to wipe off some of the soil from men's lives--to make them purer, sweeter, readier to listen to Christ, even unostentatiously to do the small services which each hour calls for--is to follow Him who girt Himself with the slave's apron. As often as we thus condescend we become like Christ. By putting Himself in the servant's place, our Lord has consecrated all service. The disciple who next washed the feet of the rest would feel that he was representing Christ, and would suggest to the minds of the others the action of their Lord; and as often as we lay aside the conventional dignity in which we are clad, and gird ourselves to do what others despise, we feel that we are doing what Christ would do, and are truly representing Him.

Footnotes:

7. Compare Mark vi. 2, genomenou sabbatou; and the Latin "posita mensa."
8. See ver. 2.
9. hupoluete, παιδες,και απονιζετε.
10. The "tûsht" and "ibrîek" of modern Palestine.
11. For the formal Foot-washing by the Lord High Almoner, the Pope, or other officials, see Augustine's Letters LV.; Herzog art. Fusswaschung; Smith's Dict. of Christian Antiq. art. Maundy Thursday.

Marcus Dods, D.D.

VII. JUDAS

"I speak not of you all: I know whom I have chosen: but that the Scripture may be fulfilled, He that eateth My bread lifted up his heel against Me. From henceforth I tell you before it come to pass, that, when it is come to pass, ye may believe that I am He. Verily, verily, I say unto you, He that receiveth whomsoever I send receiveth Me; and he that receiveth Me receiveth Him that sent Me. When Jesus had thus said, He was troubled in the spirit, and testified, and said, Verily, verily, I say unto you, that one of you shall betray Me. The disciples looked one on another, doubting of whom He spake. There was at the table reclining in Jesus' bosom one of His disciples, whom Jesus loved. Simon Peter therefore beckoneth to him, and saith unto him, Tell us who it is of whom He speaketh. He leaning back, as he was, on Jesus' breast saith unto Him, Lord, who is it? Jesus therefore answereth, He it is, for whom I shall dip the sop, and give it to him. So when He had dipped the sop, He taketh and giveth it to Judas, the son of Simon Iscariot. And after the sop, then entered Satan into him. Jesus therefore saith unto him, That thou doest, do quickly. Now no man at the table knew for what intent He spake this unto him. For some thought, because Judas had the bag, that Jesus said unto him, Buy what things we have need of for the feast; or, that he should give something to the poor. He then having received the sop went out straightway: and it was night."--John xiii. 18-30.

When Jesus had washed the disciples' feet, apparently in dead silence save for the interruption of Peter, He resumed those parts of His dress He had laid aside, and reclined at the table already spread for the supper. As the meal began, and while He was explaining the meaning of His act and the lesson He desired them to draw from it, John, who lay next Him at table, saw that His face did not wear the expression of festal joy, nor even of untroubled composure, but was clouded with deep concern and grief. The reason of this was immediately apparent: already, while washing Peter's feet, He had awakened the attention and excited the consciences of the disciples by hinting that on some one of them at least, if not on more, uncleansed guilt still lay, even though all partook in the symbolic washing. And now in His explanation of the foot-washing He repeats this limitation and warning, and also points at the precise nature of the guilt, though not yet singling out the guilty person. "I speak not of you all; I know whom I have chosen; I have not been deceived: but it was necessary that this part of God's purpose be fulfilled, and that this Scripture, He that eateth bread with Me, hath lifted up his heel against Me,' receive accomplishment in Me."

It was impossible that Jesus should undisturbedly eat out of the same dish with the man whom He knew to have already sold Him to the priests; it were unfair to the other disciples and a violence to His own feelings to allow such a man any longer to remain in their company. But our Lord does not name the traitor and denounce him; he singles him out and sends him from the table on his hateful mission by a process that left every man at the table unaware on what errand he was despatched. In this process there were three steps. First of all, our Lord indicated that among the disciples there was a traitor. With dismay these true-hearted men hear the firmly pronounced statement "one of you shall betray Me" (ver. 21). All of them, as another Evangelist informs us, were exceeding sorrowful, and looked on one another in bewilderment; and unable to detect the conscious look of guilt in the face of any of their companions, or to recall any circumstance which might fix even suspicion on any of them, each, conscious of the deep, unfathomed capacity for evil in his own heart, can but frankly ask of the Master, "Lord, is it I?" It is a question that at once proves their consciousness of actual innocence and possible guilt. It was a kindness in the Lord to give these genuine men, who were so shortly to go through trial for His sake, an opportunity of discovering how much they loved Him and how closely knit their hearts had really become to Him. This question of theirs expressed the deep pain and shame that the very thought of the possibility of their being false to Him gave them. They must at all hazards be cleared of this charge. And from this shock of the very idea of being untrue their hearts recoiled towards Him with an enthusiastic tenderness that made this moment possibly as moving a passage as any that occurred that eventful night But there was one of them that did not join in the question "Lord, is it I?"--else must not our Lord have broken silence? The Twelve are still left in doubt, none noticing in the eagerness of questioning who has not asked, each only glad to know he himself is not charged.

The second step in the process is recorded in the 26th chapter of Matthew, where we read that, when the disciples asked "Lord, is it I?" Jesus answered, "He that dippeth his hand with Me in the dish, the same shall betray Me." It was a large company, and there were necessarily several dishes on the table, so that probably there were three others using the same dish as our Lord: John we know was next Him; Peter was near enough to John to make signs and whisper to him; Judas was also close to Jesus, a position which he either always occupied as treasurer and purveyor of the company, or into which he thrust himself this evening with the purpose of more effectually screening himself from suspicion. The circle of suspicion is thus narrowed to the one or two who were not only so intimate as to be eating at the same table, but as to be dipping in the same dish.

The third step in the process of discovery went on almost simultaneously with this. The impatient Peter, who had himself so often unwittingly given offence to his Master, is resolved to find out definitely who is pointed at, and yet dare not say to Christ "Who is it?" He beckons therefore to John to ask Jesus privately, as he lay next to Jesus. John leans a little back towards Jesus and puts in a whisper the definite question "Who is it?" and Jesus in the ear of the beloved disciple whispers the reply, "He it is to whom I shall give a sop when I have dipped it." And when He had dipped the sop, He gave it to Judas Iscariot. This reveals to John, but to no one else, who the traitor was, for the giving of the sop was no more at that table than the handing of a plate or the offer of any article of food is at any table. John alone knew the significance of it. But Judas had already taken alarm at the narrowing of the circle of suspicion, and had possibly for the moment ceased dipping in the same dish with Jesus, lest he should be identified with the traitor. Jesus therefore dips for him and offers him the sop which he will not himself take, and the look that accompanies the act, as well as the act itself, shows Judas that his treachery is discovered. He therefore mechanically takes up in a somewhat colder form the question of the rest, and says, "Master, is it I?" His fear subdues his voice to a whisper, heard only by John and the Lord; and the answer, "Thou hast said. That thou doest, do quickly," is equally unobserved by the rest. Judas need fear no violence at their hands; John alone knows the meaning of his abrupt rising and hurrying from the room, and John sees that Jesus wishes him to go unobserved. The rest, therefore, thought only that Judas was going out to make some final purchases that had been forgotten, or to care for the poor in this season of festivity. But John saw differently. "The traitor," he says, "went immediately out; and it was night." As his ill-omened, stealthy figure glided from the chamber, the sudden night of the Eastern twilightless sunset had fallen on the company; sadness, silence, and gloom fell upon John's spirit; the hour of darkness had at length fallen in the very midst of this quiet feast.

This sin of Judas presents us with one of the most perplexed problems of life and character that the strange circumstances of this world have ever produced. Let us first of all look at the connection of this betrayal with the life of Christ, and then consider the phase of character exhibited in Judas. In connection with the life of Christ the difficulty is to understand why the death of Christ was to be brought about in this particular way of treachery among His own followers. It may be said that it came to pass "that Scripture might be fulfilled," that this special prediction in the 41st Psalm might be fulfilled. But why was such a prediction made? It was of course the event which determined the prediction, not the prediction which determined the event. Was it, then, an accident that Jesus should be handed over to the authorities in this particular way? Or was there any significance in it, that justifies its being made so prominent in the narrative? Certainly if our Lord was to be brought into contact with the most painful form of sin, He must have experience of treachery. He had known the sorrow that death brings to the survivors; He had known the pain and disappointment of being resisted by stupid, obstinate, bad-hearted men; but if He was to know the utmost of misery which man can inflict upon man, He must be brought into contact with one who could accept His love, eat His bread, press His hand with assurance of fidelity, and then sell Him.

When we endeavour to set before our minds a clear idea of the character of Judas, and to understand how such a character could be developed, we have to acknowledge that we could desire a few more facts in order to certify us of what we can now only conjecture. Obviously we must start from the idea that with extraordinary capacity for wickedness Judas had also more than ordinary leanings to what was good. He was an Apostle, and had, we must suppose, been called to that office by Christ under the impression that he possessed gifts which would make him very serviceable to the Christian community. He was himself so impressed with Christ as to follow Him: making those pecuniary sacrifices of which Peter boastfully spoke, and which must have been specially sore to Judas. It is possible, indeed, that he may have followed Jesus as a speculation, hoping to receive wealth and honour in the new kingdom; but this motive mingled with the attachment to Christ's person which all the Apostles had, and mingles in a different form with the discipleship of all Christians. With this motive, therefore, there probably mingled in the mind of Judas a desire to be with One who could shield him from evil influences; he judged that with Jesus he would find continual aid against his weaker nature. Possibly he wished by one bold abandonment of the world to get rid for ever of his covetousness. That Judas was trusted by the other Apostles is manifest from the fact that to him they committed their common fund,--not to John, whose dreamy and abstracted nature ill fitted him for minute practical affairs; not to Peter, whose impulsive nature might often have landed the little company in difficulties; not even to Matthew, accustomed as he was to accounts; but to Judas, who had the economical habits, the aptitude for finance, the love of bargaining, which regularly go hand in hand with the love of money.

Marcus Dods, D.D.

This practical faculty for finance and for affairs generally might, if rightly guided, have become a most serviceable element in the Apostolate, and might have enabled Judas more successfully than any other of the Apostles to mediate between the Church and the world. That Judas in all other respects conducted himself circumspectly is proved by the fact that, though other Apostles incurred the displeasure of Christ and were rebuked by Him, Judas committed no glaring fault till this last week. Even to the end he was unsuspected by his fellow-Apostles; and to the end he had an active conscience. His last act, were it not so awful, would inspire us with something like respect for him: he is overwhelmed with remorse and shame; his sense of guilt is stronger even than the love of money that had hitherto been his strongest passion: he judges himself fairly, sees what he has become, and goes to his own place; recognises as not every man does recognise what is his fit habitation, and goes to it.

But this man, with his good impulses, his resolute will, his enlightened conscience, his favouring circumstances, his frequent feelings of affection towards Christ and desire to serve Him, committed a crime so unparalleled in wickedness that men practically make very little attempt to estimate it or measure it with sins of their own. Commonly we think of it as a special, exceptional wickedness--not so much the natural product of a heart like our own and what may be reproduced by ourselves, as the work of Satan using a man as his scarcely responsible tool to effect a purpose which needs never again to be effected.

If we ask what precisely it was in the crime of Judas that makes us so abhor it, manifestly its most hateful ingredient was its treachery. "It was not an enemy that reproached me; then I could have borne it; but it was thou, a man mine equal, my guide, and mine acquaintance." Cæsar defended himself till the dagger of a friend pierced him; then in indignant grief he covered his head with his mantle and accepted his fate. You can forgive the open blow of a declared enemy against whom you are on your guard; but the man that lives with you on terms of the greatest intimacy for years, so that he learns your ways and habits, the state of your affairs and your past history--the man whom you so confide in and like that you communicate to him freely much that you keep hidden from others, and who, while still professing friendship, uses the information he has gained to blacken your character and ruin your peace, to injure your family or damage your business,--this man, you know, has much to repent of. So one can forgive the Pharisees who knew not what they did, and were throughout the declared opponents of Christ; but Judas attached himself to Christ, knew that His life was one of unmixed benevolence, was conscious that Christ would have given up anything to serve him, felt moved and proud from time to time by the fact that Christ loved him, and yet at the last used all these privileges of friendship against his Friend.

And Judas did not scruple to use this power that only the love of Jesus could have given him, to betray Him to men whom he knew to be unscrupulous and resolved to destroy Him. The garden where the Lord prayed for His enemies was not sacred to Judas; the cheek that a seraph would blush to kiss, and to salute which was the beginning of joy eternal to the devout disciple, was mere common clay to this man into whom Satan had entered. The crime of Judas is invested with a horror altogether its own by the fact that this Person whom he betrayed was the Son of God and the Saviour of the world, the Best-beloved of God and every man's Friend. The greatest blessing that God had ever given to earth Judas was forward to reject: not altogether unaware of the majesty of Christ, Judas presumed to use Him in a little money-making scheme of his own.

The best use that Judas could think of putting Jesus to, the best use he could make of Him whom all angels worship, was to sell Him for £5. [12] He could get nothing more out of Christ than that. After three years' acquaintanceship and observation of the various ways in which Christ could bless people, this was all he could get from Him. And there are still such men: men for whom there is nothing in Christ; men who can find nothing in Him that they sincerely care for; men who, though calling themselves His followers, would, if truth were told, be better content and feel they had more substantial profit if they could turn Him into money.

So difficult is it to comprehend how any man who had lived as the friend of Jesus could find it in his heart to betray Him, should resist the touching expressions of love that were shown him, and brave the awful warning uttered at the supper-table--so difficult is it to suppose that any man, however infatuated, would so deliberately sell his soul for £5, that a theory has been started to explain the crime by mitigating its guilt. It has been supposed that when he delivered up his Master into the hands of the chief priests he expected that our Lord would save Himself by a miracle. He knew that Jesus meant to proclaim a kingdom; he had been waiting for three years now, eagerly expecting that this proclamation and its accompanying gains would arrive. Yet he feared the opportunity was once more passing: Jesus had been brought into the city in triumph, but seemed indisposed to make use of this popular excitement for any temporal advantage. Judas was weary of this inactivity: might he not himself bring matters to a crisis by giving Jesus into the hands of His enemies, and thus forcing Him to reveal His real power and assert by miracle His kingship? In corroboration of this theory, it is said that it is certain that Judas did not expect Jesus to be condemned; for when he saw that he was condemned he repented of his act.

This seems a shallow view to take of Judas' remorse, and a feeble ground on which to build such a theory. A crime seems one thing before, another after, its commission. The murderer expects and wishes to kill his victim, but how often is he seized with an agony of remorse as soon as the blow is struck? Before we sin, it is the gain we see; after we sin, the guilt. It is impossible to construe the act of Judas into a mistaken act of friendship or impatience; the terms in which he is spoken of in Scripture forbid this idea; and one cannot suppose that a keen-sighted man like Judas could expect that, even supposing he did force our Lord to proclaim Himself, his own share in the business would be rewarded. He could not suppose this after the terrible denunciation and explicit statement that still rang in his ears when he hanged himself: "The Son of man goeth as it is written of Him: but woe unto that man by whom the Son of man is betrayed! it had been good for that man if he had not been born."

We must then abide by the more commonplace view of this crime. The only mitigating circumstance that can be admitted is, that possibly among the many perplexed thoughts entertained by Judas he may have supposed that Jesus would be acquitted, or would at least not be punished with death. Still, this being admitted, the fact remains that he cared so little for the love of Christ, and regarded so little the good He was doing, and had so little common honour in him, that he sold his Master to His deadly enemies. And this monstrous wickedness is to be accounted for mainly by his love of money. Naturally covetous, he fed his evil disposition during those years he carried the bag for the disciples: while the rest are taken up with more spiritual matters, he gives more of his thought than is needful to the matter of collecting as much as possible; he counts it his special province to protect himself and the others against all "the probable emergencies and changes of life." This he does, regardless of the frequent admonitions he hears from the Lord addressed to others; and as he finds excuses for his own avarice in the face of these admonitions, and hardens himself against the better impulses that are stirred within him by the words and presence of Christ, his covetousness roots itself deeper and deeper in his soul. Add to this, that now he was a disappointed man: the other disciples, finding that the kingdom of Christ was to be spiritual, were pure and high-minded enough to see that their disappointment was their great gain. The love of Christ had transformed them, and to be like Him was enough for them; but Judas still clung to the idea of earthly grandeur and wealth, and finding Christ was not to give him these he was soured and embittered. He saw that now, since that scene at Bethany the week before, his covetousness and earthliness would be resisted and would also betray him. He felt that he could no longer endure this poverty-stricken life, and had some rage at himself and at Christ that he had been inveigled into it by what he might be pleased to say to himself were false pretences. His self-restraint, he felt, was breaking down; his covetousness was getting the better of him; he felt that he must break with Christ and His followers; but in doing so he would at once win what he had lost during these years of poverty, and also revenge himself on those who had kept him poor, and finally would justify his own conduct in deserting this society by exploding it and causing it to cease from among men.

The sin of Judas, then, first of all teaches us the great power and danger of the love of money. The mere thirty pieces of silver would not have been enough to tempt Judas to commit so dastardly and black a crime; but he was now an embittered and desperate man, and he had become so by allowing money to be all in all to him for these last years of his life. For the danger of this passion consists very much in this--that it infallibly eats out of the soul every generous emotion and high aim: it is the failing of a sordid nature--a little, mean, earthly nature--a failing which, like all others, may be extirpated through God's grace, but which is notoriously difficult to extirpate, and which notoriously is accompanied by or produces other features of character which are among the most repulsive one meets. The love of money is also dangerous, because it can be so easily gratified; all that we do in the world day by day is in the case of most of us connected with money, so that we have continual and not only occasional opportunity of sinning if we be inclined to the sin. Other passions are appealed to only now and again, but our employments touch this passion at all points. It leaves no long intervals, as other passions do, for repentance and amendment; but steadily, constantly, little by little, increases in force. Judas had his fingers in the bag all day; it was under his pillow and he dreamt upon it all night; and it was this that accelerated his ruin. And by this constant appeal it is sure to succeed at one time or other, if we be open to it. Judas could not suppose that his quiet self-aggrandisement by pilfering little coins from the bag could ever bring him to commit such a crime against his Lord: so may every covetous person fancy that his sin is one that is his own business, and will not damage his religious profession and ruin his soul as some wild lust or reckless infidelity would do. But Judas and those who sin with him in making continually little gains to which they have no right are wrong in supposing their sin is less dangerous; and for this reason--that covetousness is more a sin of the will than sins of the flesh or of a passionate nature; there is more choice in it; it is more the sin of the whole man unresisting; and therefore it, above all others, is called idolatry--it, above all others, proves that the man is in his heart choosing the world and not God. Therefore it is that even our Lord Himself spoke almost despairingly, certainly quite differently, of covetous men in comparison with other sinners.

Disappointment in Christ is not an unknown thing among ourselves. Men still profess to be Christians who are so only in the degree in which Judas was. They expect some good from Christ, but

Marcus Dods, D.D.

not all. They attach themselves to Christ in a loose, conventional way, expecting that, though they are Christians, they need not lose anything by their Christianity, nor make any great efforts or sacrifices. They retain command of their own life, and are prepared to go with Christ only so far as they find it agreeable or inviting. The eye of an observer may not be able to distinguish them from Christ's true followers; but the distinction is present and is radical. They are seeking to use Christ, and are not willing to be used by Him. They are not wholly and heartily His, but merely seek to derive some influences from Him. The result is that they one day find that, through all their religious profession and apparent Christian life, their characteristic sin has actually been gaining strength. And finding this, they turn upon Christ with disappointment and rage in their hearts, because they become aware that they have lost both this world and the next--have lost many pleasures and gains they might have enjoyed, and yet have gained no spiritual attainment. They find that the reward of double-mindedness is the most absolute perdition, that both Christ and the world, to be made anything of, require the whole man, and that he who tries to get the good of both gets the good of neither. And when a man awakes to see that this is the result of his Christian profession, there is no deadliness of hatred to which the bitter disappointment of his soul will not carry him. He has himself been a dupe, and he calls Christ an impostor. He know himself to be damned, and he says there is no salvation in Christ.

But to this disastrous issue any cherished sin may also in its own way lead; for the more comprehensive lesson which this sin of Judas brings with it is the rapidity of sin's growth and the enormous proportions it attains when the sinner is sinning against light, when he is in circumstances conducive to holiness and still sins. To discover the wickedest of men, to see the utmost of human guilt, we must look, not among the heathen, but among those who know God; not among the profligate, dissolute, abandoned classes of society, but among the Apostles. The good that was in Judas led him to join Christ, and kept him associated with Christ for some years; but the devil of covetousness that was cast out for a while returned and brought with him seven devils worse than himself. There was everything in his position to win him to unworldliness: the men he lived with cared not one whit for comforts or anything that money could buy; but instead of catching their spirit he took advantage of their carelessness. He was in a public position, liable to detection; but this, instead of making him honest perforce, made him only the more crafty and studiedly hypocritical. The solemn warnings of Christ, so far from intimidating him, only made him more skilful in evading all good influence, and made the road to hell easier. The position he enjoyed, and by which he might have been for ever enrolled among the foremost of mankind, one of the twelve foundations of the eternal city, he so skilfully misused that the greatest sinner feels glad that he has yet not been left to commit the sin of Judas. Had Judas not followed Christ he could never have attained the pinnacle of infamy on which he now for ever stands. In all probability he would have passed his days as a small trader with false weights in the little town of Kerioth, or, at the worst, might have developed into an extortionous publican, and have passed into oblivion with the thousands of unjust men who have died and been at last forced to let go the money that should long ago have belonged to others. Or had Judas followed Christ truly, then there lay before him the noblest of all lives, the most blessed of destinies. But he followed Christ and yet took his sin with him: and thence his ruin.

Footnotes:

12. More exactly, £3 10 8, the legal value of a slave.

VIII. JESUS ANNOUNCES HIS DEPARTURE

"When therefore he was gone out, Jesus saith, Now is the Son of man glorified, and God is glorified in Him; and God shall glorify Him in Himself, and straightway shall He glorify Him. Little children, yet a little while I am with you. Ye shall seek Me: and as I said unto the Jews, Whither I go, ye cannot come; so now I say unto you. A new commandment I give unto you, that ye love one another; even as I have loved you, that ye also love one another. By this shall all men know that ye are My disciples, if ye have love one to another. Simon Peter saith unto Him, Lord, whither goest Thou? Jesus answered, Whither I go, thou canst not follow Me now; but thou shalt follow afterwards. Peter saith unto Him, Lord, why cannot I follow Thee even now? I will lay down my life for Thee. Jesus answereth, Wilt thou lay down thy life for Me? Verily, verily, I say unto thee, The cock shall not crow, till thou hast denied Me thrice. Let not your heart be troubled: ye believe in God, believe also in Me. In My Father's house are many mansions; if it were not so, I would have told you; for I go to prepare a place for you. And if I go and prepare a place for you, I come again, and will receive you unto Myself; that where I am, there ye may be also. And whither I go, ye know the way."--John xiii. 31-xiv. 4.

When Judas glided out of the supper-room on his terrible mission, a weight seemed to be lifted from the spirit of Jesus. The words which fell from Him, however, indicated that He not only felt the relief of being rid of a disturbing element in the company, but that He recognised that a crisis in His own career had been reached and successfully passed through. "Now is the Son of man glorified, and God is glorified in Him." In sending Judas forth He had in point of fact delivered Himself to death. He had taken the step which cannot be withdrawn, and He is conscious of taking it in fulfilment of the will of the Father. The conflict in His own mind is revealed only by the decision of the victory. No man in soundness of body and of mind can voluntarily give himself to die without seeing clearly other possibilities, and without feeling it to be a hard and painful thing to relinquish life. Jesus had made up His mind. His death is the beginning of His glorification. In choosing the cross He chooses the crown. "The Son of man is glorified" in His perfect self-sacrifice that wins all men to Him; and God is glorified in Him because this sacrifice is a tribute at once to the justice and the love of God. The Cross reveals God as nothing else does.

Not only has this decision glorified the Son of man and God through Him and in Him, but as a consequence "God will glorify" the Son of man "in Himself." He will lift Him to participation in the Divine glory. It was well that the disciples should know that this would "straightway" result from all that their Master was now to pass through; that the perfect sympathy with the Father's will which He was now showing would be rewarded by permanent participation in the authority of God. It must be through such an one as their Lord, who is absolutely at one with God, that God fulfils His purpose towards men. By this life and death of perfect obedience, of absolute devotedness to God and man, Christ necessarily wins dominion over human affairs and exercises a determining influence on all that is to be. In all that Christ did upon earth God was glorified; His holiness, His fatherly love were manifested to men: in all that God now does upon earth Christ will be glorified; the uniqueness and power of His life will become more manifest, the supremacy of His Spirit be more and more apparent.

This glorification was not the far-off result of the impending sacrifice. It was to date from the present hour and to begin in the sacrifice. God will glorify Him "straightway." "Yet a little while" was He to be with His disciples. Therefore does He tenderly address them, recognising their incompetence, their inability to stand alone, as "little children"; and in view of the exhibition of bad feeling, and even of treachery, which the Twelve had at that very hour given, His commandment, "Love one another," comes with a tenfold significance. I am leaving you, He says: put away, then, all heart-burnings and jealousies; cling together; do not let quarrels and envyings divide you. This was to be their safeguard when He left them and went where they could not come. "A new commandment I give unto you, That ye love one another; as I have loved you, that ye also love one another. By this shall all men know that ye are My disciples, if ye have love one to another."

The commandment to love our neighbour as ourselves was no new commandment. But to love "as I have loved you" was so new that its practice was enough to identify a man as a disciple of Christ. The manner and the measure of the love that is possible and that is commanded could not even be understood until Christ's love was revealed. But probably what Jesus had even more directly in view was the love that was to bind His followers together [13] and make them one solid body. It was on their mutual attachment that the very existence of the Christian Church depended; and this love of men to one another springing out of the love of Christ for them, and because of their acknowledgment and love of a common Lord, was a new thing in the world. The bond to Christ proved itself stronger than all other ties, and those who cherished a common love to Him were drawn to one another more closely than even to blood relations. In fact, Christ, by His love for men, has created a new bond, and that the strongest by which men can be bound to one another. As the Christian Church is a new institution upon earth, so is the principle which forms it a new principle. The principle has, indeed, too often been hidden from sight, if not smothered, by the institution; too little has love been regarded as the one thing by which the disciple of Christ is to be recognised, the one note of the true Church. But that this form of love was a new thing upon earth is apparent. [14]

Tenderly as Jesus made the announcement of His departure, it filled the minds of the disciples with consternation. Even the buoyant and hardy Peter felt for the moment staggered by the intelligence, and still more by the announcement that he was not able to accompany his Lord. He was assured that one day he should follow Him, but at present this was impossible. This, Peter considered a reflection upon his courage and fidelity; and although his headlong self-confidence had only a few minutes before been so severely rebuked, he exclaims, "Lord, why cannot I follow Thee now? I will lay down my life for Thy sake." This was the true expression of Peter's present feeling, and he was allowed in the end to give proof that these vehement words were not mere bluster. But as yet he had not at all apprehended the separateness of his Lord and the uniqueness of His work. He did not know precisely what Jesus alluded to, but he thought a strong arm would not be out of place in any conflict that was coming. The offers which even true fidelity makes are often only additional hindrances to our Lord's purposes, and additional burdens for Him to bear. On Himself alone must He depend. No man can counsel Him, and none can aid save by first receiving from Him His own spirit.

Peter thus rebuked falls into unwonted silence, and takes no further part in the conversation. The rest, knowing that Peter has more courage than any of them, fear that if he is thus to fall it cannot be hopeful for themselves. They feel that if they are left without Jesus they have no strength to make head against the rulers, no skill in argument such as made Jesus victorious when assailed by the scribes, no popular eloquence which might enable them to win the people. Eleven more helpless men could not well be. "Sheep without a shepherd" was not too strong an expression to depict their weakness and want of influence, their incompetence to effect anything, their inability even to keep together. Christ was their bond of union and the strength of each of them. It was to be with Him that they had left all. And in forsaking all--father and mother, wife and children, home and kindred and calling--they had found in Christ that hundredfold more even in this life which He had promised. He had so won their hearts, there was about Him something so fascinating, that they felt no loss when they enjoyed His presence, and feared no danger in which He was their leader. They had perhaps not thought very definitely of their future; they felt so confident in Jesus that they were content to let Him bring in His kingdom as He pleased; they were so charmed with the novelty of their life as His disciples, with the great ideas that dropped from His lips, with the wonderful works He did, with the new light He shed upon all the personages and institutions of the world, that they were satisfied to leave their hope undefined. But all this satisfaction and secret assurance of hope depended on Christ. As yet He had not given to them anything which could enable them to make any mark upon the world. They were still very ignorant, so that any lawyer could entangle and puzzle them. They had not received from Christ any influential position in society from which they could sway men. There were no great visible institutions with which they could identify themselves and so become conspicuous.

It was with dismay, therefore, that they heard that He was going where they could not accompany Him. A cloud of gloomy foreboding gathered on their faces as they lay round the table and fixed their eyes on Him as on one whose words they would interpret differently if they could. Their anxious looks are not disregarded. "Let not your heart be troubled," He says: "believe in God, and in Me, too, believe." Do not give way to disturbing thoughts; do not suppose that only failure, disgrace, helplessness, and calamity await you. Trust God. In this, as in all matters, He is guiding and ruling and working His own good ends through all present evil. Trust Him, even when you cannot penetrate the darkness. It is His part to bring you successfully through; it is your part to follow where He leads. Do not question and debate and vex your soul, but leave all to Him. "Why art thou cast down, O my soul? and why art thou disquieted within me? Hope thou in God; for I shall yet praise Him who is the health of my countenance and my God."

"And in Me, too, trust." I would not leave you had I not a purpose to serve. It is not to secure My own safety or happiness I go. It is not to occupy the sole available room in My Father's house. There are many rooms there, and I go to prepare a place for you. Trust Me. In order that they may fully understand the reasonableness of His departure He assures them, first of all, that it has a purpose. The parent mourns over the son who in mere waywardness leaves his home and his occupation; but with very different feelings does he follow one who has come to see that the greater good of the family requires that he should go, and who has carefully ascertained where and how he can best serve those he leaves behind. To such an absence men can reconcile themselves. The parting is bitter, but the greater good to be gained by it enables them to approve its reasonableness and to submit. And what our Lord says to His disciples is virtually this: I have not wearied of earth and tired of your company, neither do I go because I must. I could escape Judas and the Jews. But I have a purpose which requires that I should go. You have not found Me impulsive, neither am I now acting without good reason. Could I be of more use to you by staying, I would stay.

This is a new kind of assertion to be made by human lips: "I am going into the other world to effect a a purpose." Often the sense of duty has been so strong in men that they have left this world without a murmur. But no one has felt so clear about what lies beyond, or has been so confident of his own power to effect any change for the better in the other world, that he has left this for a sphere of greater usefulness. This is what Christ does.

But He also explains what His purpose is: "In My Father's house are many mansions. I go to prepare a place for you." The Father's house was a new figure for heaven. The idea of God's house was, however, familiar to the Jews. But in the Temple the freedom and familiarity which we associate with home were absent. It was only when One came who felt that His real home was in God that the Temple could be called "the Father's house." Yet there is nothing that the heart of man more importunately craves than the freedom and ease which this name implies. To live unafraid of God, not shrinking from Him, but so truly at one with Him that we live as one household brightened by His presence--this is the thirst for God which is one day felt in every heart. And on His part God has many mansions in His house, proclaiming that He desires to have us at home with Him; that He wishes us to know and trust Him, not to change our countenances when we meet Him at a corner, save by an added brightness of joy. And this is what we have to look forward to--that after all our coldness and distrust have been removed and our hearts thawed by His presence, we shall live in the constant enjoyment of a Father's love, feeling ourselves more truly at home with Him than with any one else, delighting in the perfectness of His sympathy and the abundance of His provision.

Into this intimacy with God, this freedom of the universe, this sense that "all things are ours" because we are His, this entirely attractive heaven, we are to be introduced by Christ. "I go to prepare a place for you." It is He who has transformed the darkness of the grave into the bright gateway of the Father's home, where all His children are to find eternal rest and everlasting joy. As an old writer says, "Christ is the quartermaster who provides quarters for all who follow Him." He has gone on before to make ready for those whom He has summoned to come after Him.

If we ask why it was needful that Christ should go forward thus, and what precisely He had to do in the way of preparation, the question may be answered in different ways. These disciples in after-years compared Christ's passing into the Father's presence to the high priest's entrance within the veil to present the blood of sprinkling and to make intercession. But in the language of Christ there is no hint that such thoughts were in His mind. It is the Father's house that is in His mind, the eternal home of men; and He sees the Father welcoming Him as the leader of many brethren, and with gladness in His heart going from room to room, always adding some new touch for the comfort and surprise of the eagerly expected children. If God, like a grieved and indignant father whose sons have preferred other company to his, had dismantled and locked the rooms that once were ours, Christ has made our peace, and has given to the yearning heart of the Father opportunity to open these rooms once more and deck them for our home-coming. With the words of Christ there enters the spirit a conviction that when we pass out of this life we shall find ourselves as much fuller of life and deeper in joy as we are nearer to God, the source of all life and joy; and that when we come to the gates of God's dwelling it will not be as the vagabond and beggar unknown to the household and who can give no good account of himself, but as the child whose room is ready for him, whose coming is expected and prepared for, and who has indeed been sent for.

This of itself is enough to give us hopeful thoughts of the future state. Christ is busied in preparing for us what will give us satisfaction and joy. When we expect a guest we love and have written for, we take pleasure in preparing for his reception,--we hang in his room the picture he likes; if he is infirm, we wheel in the easiest chair; we gather the flowers he admires and set them on his table; we go back and back to see if nothing else will suggest itself to us, so that when he comes he may have entire satisfaction. This is enough for us to know--that Christ is similarly occupied. He knows our tastes, our capabilities, our attainments, and he has identified a place as ours and holds it for us. What the joys and the activities and occupations of the future shall be we do not know. With the body we shall lay aside many of our appetites and tastes and proclivities, and what has here seemed necessary to our comfort will at once become indifferent. We shall not be able to desire the pleasures that now allure and draw us. The need of shelter, of retirement, of food, of comfort, will disappear with the body; and what the joys and the requirements of a spiritual body will be we do not know. But we do know that at home with God the fullest life that man can live will certainly be ours.

It is a touching evidence of Christ's truthfulness and fidelity to His people that is given in the words, "If it were not so, I would have told you"--that is to say, if it had not been possible for you to follow Me into the Father's presence and find a favourable reception there, I would have told you this long ago. I would not have taught you to love Me, only to have given you the grief of separation. I would not have encouraged you to hope for what I was not sure you are to receive. He had all along seen how the minds of the disciples were working; He had seen that by being admitted to familiarity with Him they had learnt to expect God's eternal favour; and had this been a deceitful expectation He would have undeceived them. So it is with Him still. The hopes His word begets are not vain. These dreams of glory that pass before the spirit that listens to Christ and thinks of Him are to be realised. If it were not so, He would have told us. We ourselves feel that we are scarcely acting an honest part when we allow persons to entertain false hopes, even when these hopes help to comfort and support them, as in the case of persons suffering from disease. So our Lord does not beget hopes He cannot satisfy. If there were still difficulties in the way of our eternal happiness, He would have told us of these. If there were any reason to despair, He Himself would have been the first to tell us to despair. If eternity were to be a blank to us, if God were inaccessible, if the idea of a perfect state awaiting us were mere talk, He would have told us so.

Neither will the Lord leave His disciples to find their own way to the Father's home: "If I go and prepare a place for you, I will come again, and receive you unto Myself; that where I am, there ye may be also." Present separation was but the first step towards abiding union. And as each disciple was summoned to follow Christ in death, he recognised that this was the summons, not of an earthly power, but of his Lord; he recognised that to him the Lord's promise was being kept, and that he was being taken into eternal union with Jesus Christ. From many all the pain and darkness of death have been taken away by this assurance. They have accepted death as the needful transition from a state in which much hinders fellowship with Christ to a state in which that fellowship is all in all.

Footnotes:

13. "That ye love one another" is the twice-expressed commandment.

14. "Any Church that professes to be the Church of Christ cannot be that Church. The true Church refuses to be circumscribed or parted by any denominational wall. It knows that Christ is repudiated when His people are repudiated. Not even a Biblical creed can yield satisfactory evidence that a specified Church is the true Church. True Christians are those who love one another across denominational differences, and exhibit the spirit of Him who gave Himself to death upon the cross that His murderers might live."

IX. THE WAY, THE TRUTH, AND THE LIFE

"Thomas saith unto Him, Lord, we know not whither Thou goest; how know we the way? Jesus saith unto him, I am the Way, and the Truth, and the Life: no one cometh unto the Father, but by Me. If ye had known Me, ye would have known My Father also: from henceforth ye know Him, and have seen Him."--John xiv. 5-7.

It surprises us to find that words which have become familiar and most intelligible to us should have been to the Apostles obscure and puzzling. Apparently they were not yet persuaded that their Master was shortly to die; and, accordingly, when He spoke of going to His Father's house, it did not occur to them that He meant passing into the spiritual world. His assuring words, "Where I am, there ye shall be also," therefore fell short. And when He sees their bewilderment written on their faces, He tentatively, half interrogatively, adds, "And whither I go ye know, and the way ye know." [15] Unless they knew where He was going, there was less consolation even in the promise that He would come for them after He had gone and prepared a place for them. And when He thus challenges them candidly to say whether they understood where He was going, and where He would one day take them also, Thomas, always the mouthpiece for the despondency of the Twelve, at once replies, "Lord, we know not whither Thou goest; and how can we know the way?"

This interruption by Thomas gives occasion to the great declaration, "I am the Way, and the Truth, and the Life: no man cometh unto the Father, but by Me." It is, then, to the Father that Christ is the Way. And He is the Way by being the Truth and the Life. We must first, then, consider in what sense He is the Truth and the Life.

I. I am the Truth. Were these words merely equivalent to "I speak the truth," it would be much to know this of One who tells us things of so measureless a consequence to ourselves. The faith of the disciples was being strained by what He had just been saying to them. Here was a man in most respects like themselves: a man who got hungry and sleepy, a man who was to be arrested and executed by the rulers, assuring them that He was going to prepare for them everlasting habitations, and that He would return to take them to these habitations. He saw that they found it hard to believe this. Who does not find it hard to believe all our Lord tells us of our future? Think how much we trust simply to His word. If He is not true, then the whole of Christendom has framed its life on a false issue, and is met at death by blank disappointment. Christ has aroused in our minds by His promises and statements a group of ideas and expectations which nothing but His word could have persuaded us to entertain. Nothing is more remarkable about our Lord than the calmness and assurance with which He utters the most astounding statements. The ablest and most enlightened men have their hesitations, their periods of agonising doubt, their suspense of judgment, their laboured inquiries, their mental conflicts. With Jesus there is nothing of this. From first to last He sees with perfect clearness to the utmost bound of human thought, knows with absolute certainty whatever is essential for us to know. His is not the assurance of ignorance, nor is it the dogmatism of traditional teaching, nor the evasive assurance of a superficial and reckless mind. It is plainly the assurance of One who stands in the full noon of truth and speaks what He knows.

But in His endeavours to gain the confidence of men there is discernible no anger at their incredulity. Again and again He brings forward reasons why His word should be believed. He appeals to their knowledge of His candour: "If it were not so, I would have told you." It was the truth He came into the world to bear witness to. Lies enough were current already. He came to be the Light of the world, to dispel the darkness and bring men into the very truth of things. But with all His impressiveness of asseveration there is no anger, scarcely even wonder that men did not believe, because He saw as plainly as we see that to venture our eternal hope on His word is not easy. And yet He answered promptly and with authority the questions which have employed the lifetime of many and baffled them in the end. He answered them as if they were the very alphabet of knowledge. These alarmed and perturbed disciples ask Him: "Is there a life beyond? is there another side of death?" "Yes," He says, "through death I go to the Father." "Is there," they ask, "for us also a life beyond? shall such creatures as we find sufficient and suitable habitation and welcome when we pass from this warm, well-known world?" "In My Father's house," He says, "are many mansions." Confronted with the problems that most deeply exercise the human spirit, He without faltering pronounces upon them. For every question which our most anxious and trying experiences dictate He has the ready and sufficient answer. "He is the

Truth."

But more than this is contained in His words. He says not merely "I speak the truth," but "I am the Truth." In His person and work we find all truth that it is essential to know. He is the true Man, the revelation of perfect manhood, in whom we see what human life truly is. In His own history He shows us our own capacities and our own destiny. An angel or an inanimate law might tell us the truth about human life, but Christ is the Truth. He is man like ourselves. If we are extinguished at death, so is He. If for us there is no future life, neither is there for Him. He is Himself human.

Further and especially, He is the truth about God: "If ye had known Me, ye had known My Father also." Strenuous efforts are being made in our day to convince us that all our search after God is vain, because by the very nature of the case it is impossible to know God. We are assured that all our imaginations of God are but a reflection of ourselves magnified infinitely; and that what results from all our thinking is not God, but only a magnified man. We form in our thoughts an ideal of human excellence--perfect holiness and perfect love; and we add to this highest moral character we can conceive a supernatural power and wisdom, and this we call God. But this, we are assured, is but to mislead ourselves; for what we thus set before our minds as Divine is not God, but only a higher kind of man. But God is not a higher kind of man: He is a different kind of being--a Being to whom it is absurd to ascribe intelligence, or will, or personality, or anything human.

We have felt the force of what is thus urged; and feeling most deeply that for us the greatest of all questions is, What is God? we have been afraid lest, after all, we have been deluding ourselves with an image of our own creating very different from the reality. We have felt that there is a great truth lying at the heart of what is thus urged, a truth which the Bible makes as much of as philosophy does--the truth that we cannot find out God, cannot comprehend Him. We say certain things about Him, as that He is a Spirit; but which of us knows what a pure spirit is, which of us can conceive in our minds a distinct idea of what we so freely speak of as a spirit? Indeed, it is because it is impossible for us to have any sufficient idea of God as He is in Himself that He has become man and manifested Himself in flesh.

This revelation of God in man implies that there is an affinity and likeness between God and man--that man is made in God's image. Were it not so, we should see in Christ, not God at all, but only man. If God is manifest in Christ, it is because there is that in God which can find suitable expression in a human life and person. In fact, this revelation takes for granted that in a sense it is quite true that God is a magnified Man--that He is a Being in whom there is much that resembles what is in man. And it stands to reason that this must be so. It is quite true that man can only conceive what is like himself; but that is only half the truth. It is also true that God can only create what is consistent with His own mind. In His creatures we see a reflection of Himself. And as we ascend from the lowest of them to the highest, we see what He considers the highest qualities. Finding in ourselves these highest qualities--qualities which enable us to understand all lower creatures and to use them--we gather that in God Himself there must be something akin to our mind and to our inner man.

Christ, then, is "the Truth," because He is the Revealer of God. In Him we learn what God is and how to approach Him. But knowledge is not enough. It is conceivable that we should have learned much about God and yet have despaired of ever becoming like Him. It might gradually have become our conviction that we were for ever shut out from all good, although that is incompatible with a true knowledge of God; for if God is known at all, He must be known as Love, as self-communicating. But the possibility of having knowledge which we cannot use is precluded by the fact that He who is the Truth is also the Life. In Him who is the Revealer we at the same time find power to avail ourselves of the revelation. For:

II. "I am the Life." The declaration need not be restricted to the immediate occasion, Christ imparts to men power to use the knowledge of the Father He gives them. He gives men desire, will, and power to live with God and in God. But is not all life implied in this? This is life as men are destined to know it.

In every man there is a thirst for life. Everything that clogs, impedes, or retards life we hate; sickness, imprisonment, death, whatever diminishes, enfeebles, limits, or destroys life, we abhor. Happiness means abundant life, great vitality finding vent for itself in healthy ways. Great scope or opportunity of living to good purpose is useless to the invalid who has little life in himself; and, on the other hand, abundant vitality is only a pain to the man who is shut up and can spend his energy only in pacing a cell eight feet by four. Our happiness depends upon these two conditions--perfect energy and infinite scope.

But can we assure ourselves of either? Is not the one certainty of life, as we know it, that it must end? Is it not certain that, no matter what energy the most vigorous of us enjoy, we shall all one day "lie in cold obstruction"? Naturally we fear that time, as if all life were then to end for us. We shrink from that apparent termination, as if beyond it there could be but a shadowy, spectral life in which nothing is substantial, nothing lively, nothing delightsome, nothing strong. That state which we shrink from our Lord chooses as a condition of perfect life, abundant and untrammelled. And what He has chosen for Himself He means to bestow upon us.

The Expositor's Bible: The Gospel of St. John Volumes I & II

Why should we find it so hard to believe in that abundant life? There is a sufficient source of physical life which upholds the universe and is not burdened, which in continuance and exuberantly brings forth life in inconceivably various forms. The world around us indicates a source of life which seems always to grow and expand rather than to be exhausted. So there is a source of spiritual life, a force sufficient to uphold all men in righteousness and in eternal vitality of spirit, and which can give birth to ever new and varied forms of heroic, holy, godly living--a force which is ever pressing forward to find expression through all moral beings, and capable of making all human action as perfect, as beautiful, and infinitely more significant than the products of physical life which we see around us. If the flowers profusely scattered by the wayside are marvels of beauty, if the bodily frame of man and of the other animals is continually surprising us with some new revelation of exquisite arrangement of parts, if nature is so lavish and so perfect in physical life, may we not believe that there is as rich a fountain of moral and spiritual life? Nay, "the youths may faint and be weary, and the young men utterly fall," physical life may fail and in the nature of things must fail, "but they that wait upon the Lord shall renew their strength, they shall run and not be weary."

It is Jesus Christ who brings us into connection with this source of life eternal--He bears it in His own person. In Him we receive a new spirit; in Him our motive to live for righteousness is continually renewed; we are conscious that in Him we touch what is undying and never fails to renew spiritual life in us. Whatever we need to give us true and everlasting life we have in Christ. Whatever we need to enable us to come to the Father, whatever we shall need between this present stage of experience and our final stage, we have in Him.

The more, then, we use Christ, the more life we have. The more we are with Him and the more we partake of His Spirit, the fuller does our own life become. It is not by imitating successful men we become influential for good, but by living with Christ. It is not by adopting the habits and methods of saints we become strong and useful, but by accepting Christ and His Spirit. Nothing can take the place of Christ. Nothing can take His words and say to us, "I am the Life." If we wish life, if we see that we are doing little good and desire energy to overtake the good that needs to be done, it is to Him we must go. If we feel as if all our efforts were vain, and as if we could not bear up any longer against our circumstances or against our wicked nature we can receive fresh vigour and hopefulness only from Christ. We need not be surprised at our failures if we are not receiving from Christ the life that is in Him. And nothing can give us the life that is in Him but our own personal application to Him, our direct dealing with Himself. Ordinances and sacraments help to bring Him clearly before us, but they are not living and cannot give us life. It is only in so far as through and in them we reach Christ and receive Him that we partake of that highest of all forms of life--the life that is in Him, the living One, by whom all things were made, and who in the very face of death can say, "Because I live ye shall live also."

III. Being the Revealer of the Father, and giving men power to approach God and live in Him, Jesus legitimately designates Himself "the Way." Jesus never says "I am the Father"; He does not even say "I am God," for that might have produced misunderstanding. He uniformly speaks as if there were One on whom He Himself leant, and to whom He prayed, and with whom, as with another person, He had fellowship. "I am the Way," He says; and a way implies a goal beyond itself, some further object to which it leads and brings us. He is not the Being revealed, but the Revealer; not the terminal object of our worship, but the image of the invisible God, the Priest, the Sacrifice.

Christ announces Himself to Thomas as the Way, in order to remove from the mind of the disciple the uncertainty he felt about the future. He knew there were heights of glory and blessedness to which the Messiah would certainly attain, but which seemed dim and remote and even quite unattainable to sinful men. Jesus defines at once the goal and the way. All our vague yearnings after what will satisfy us He reduces to this simple expression: "the Father." This, He implies, is the goal and destiny of man; to come to the Father, who embraces in His loving care all our wants, our incapacities, our sorrows; to reach and abide in a love that is strong, wise, educative, imperishable; to reach this love and be so transformed by it as to feel more at home with this perfectly holy God than with any besides. And to bring us to this goal is the function of Christ, the Way. It is His to bring together what is highest and what is lowest. It is His to unite those who are separated by the most real obstacles: to bring us, weak and unstable and full of evil imaginings, into abiding union with the Supreme, glad to be conformed to Him and to accomplish His purposes. In proclaiming Himself "the Way," Christ pronounces Himself able to effect the most real union between parties and conditions as separate as heaven and earth, sin and holiness, the poor creature I know myself to be and the infinite and eternal God who is so high I cannot know Him.

Further, the way to which we commit ourselves when we seek to come to the Father through Christ is a Person. "I am the Way." It is not a cold, dead road we have to make the most of for ourselves, pursuing it often in darkness, in weakness, in fear. It is a living way--a way that renews our strength as we walk in it, that enlivens instead of exhausting us, that gives direction and light as we go forward. Often we seem to find our way barred; we do not know how to get farther forward; we wonder if there is no book in which we can find direction; we long for some wise guide who could show us how to proceed. At such times Christ would have us hear Him saying, "I am the Way. If you abide in Me, if you continue in My love, you are in the way and must be carried forward to all good." Often we seem to lose ourselves and cannot tell whether our faces and our steps are directed aright or not; we become doubtful whether we have been making any progress or have not rather been going back. Often we lose heart and begin to doubt whether it is possible for us men ever to reach any purer, higher life; we are going, we say, we know not whither; this life is full of blunders and failures. Many of the best and most earnest and gifted men have owned their ignorance of the purpose of life and of its end. No voice comes to us out of the unseen world to give us assurance that there is life there. How can lonely, ignorant, irresolute, weak, and helpless creatures such as we are ever attain to anything we can call blessedness? To all such gloom and doubting Christ, with the utmost confidence, says, "I am the Way. Wherever you are, at whatever point of experience, at whatever stage of sin, this way begins where you are, and you have but to take it and it leads to God, to that unknown Highest you yearn for even while you shrink from Him. From your person, as you are at this moment, there leads a way to the Father."

Footnotes:

15. Or, "And whither I go ye know the way."

X. THE FATHER SEEN IN CHRIST

"Philip saith unto Him, Lord, show us the Father, and it sufficeth us. Jesus saith unto him, Have I been so longtime with you, and dost thou not know Me, Philip? he that hath seen Me hath seen the Father; how sayest thou, Show us the Father? Believest thou not that I am in the Father, and the Father in Me? the words that I say unto you I speak not from Myself: but the Father abiding in Me doeth His works. Believe Me that I am in the Father, and the Father in Me: or else believe Me for the very works' sake. Verily, verily, I say unto you, He that believeth on Me, the works that I do shall he do also; and greater works than these shall he do; because I go unto the Father. And whatsoever ye shall ask in My name, that will I do, that the Father may be glorified in the Son. If ye shall ask Me anything in My name, that will I do. If ye love Me, ye will keep My commandments. And I will pray the Father, and He shall give you another Comforter, that He may be with you for ever, even the Spirit of truth: whom the world cannot receive; for it beholdeth Him not, neither knoweth Him: ye know Him; for He abideth with you, and shall be in you. I will not leave you desolate: I come unto you. Yet a little while, and the world beholdeth Me no more; but ye behold Me: because I live, ye shall live also. In that day ye shall know that I am in My Father, and ye in Me, and I in you. He that hath My commandments, and keepeth them, he it is that loveth me: and he that loveth Me shall be loved of My Father and I will love him, and will manifest Myself unto him."--John xiv. 8-21.

A third interruption on the part of one of the disciples gives the Lord occasion to be still more explicit. Philip is only further bewildered by the words, "from henceforth ye know the Father and have seen Him." He catches, however, at the idea that the Father can be seen, and eagerly exclaims, "Lord, show us the Father, and it sufficeth us." In this exclamation there may be a little of that vexed and almost irritated feeling that every one at times has felt in reading the words of Christ. We feel as if He might have made things plainer. We unconsciously reproach Him with making a mystery, with going about and about a subject and refusing to speak straight at it. Philip felt that if Christ could show the Father, then there was no need of any more enigmatical talk.

Ignorant as this request may be, it sprang from the thirst for God which was felt by an earnest and godly man. It arose from the craving that now and again visits every soul to get to the heart of all mystery. Here in this life we are much in the dark. We feel ourselves to be capable of better enjoyments, of a higher life. The whole creation groaneth and travaileth, as if striving towards some better and more satisfying state. There is a something not yet attained which we feel we must reach. Were this life all, we should pronounce existence a failure. And yet there is great uncertainty over our future. There is no familiar intercourse with those who have passed on and are now in the other world. We have no opportunity of informing ourselves of their state and occupations. We go on in great darkness and often with a feeling of great insecurity and trepidation; feeling lost, in darkness, not knowing whither we are going, not sure that we are in the way to life and happiness. Why, we are tempted to ask, should there be so much uncertainty? Why should we live so remote from the centre of things, and have to grope our way to life and light, clouded by doubts, beset by misleading and disturbing influences? "Show us the Father," we are tempted to say with Philip--show us the Father and it sufficeth us. Show us the Supreme. Show us the eternal One who governs all. Take us but once to the centre of things and show us the Father in whom we live. Take us for once behind the scenes and let us see the hand that moves all things; let us know all that can be known, that we may see what it is we are going to, and what is to become of us when this visible world is done. Give us assurance that behind all this dumb, immovable mask of outward things there is a living God whose love we can trust and whose power can preserve us to life everlasting.

To Philip's eager request Jesus replies: "Have I been so long time with you, and hast thou not known Me, Philip? He that hath seen Me hath seen the Father; how sayest thou, Show us the Father?" And it is thus our Lord addresses all whose unsatisfied craving finds voice in Philip's request. To all who crave some more immediate, if not more sensible manifestation of God, to all who live in doubt and feel as if more might be done to give us certitude regarding the relation we hold to God and to the future, Christ says: No further revelation is to be made, because no further revelation is needed or can be made. All has been shown that can be shown. There is no more of the Father you can see than you have seen in Me. God has taken that form which is most comprehensible to you--your own form, the form of man. You have seen the Father. I am the truth, the reality. It is no longer a symbol telling you something about a distant God, but the Father Himself is in Me, speaking and acting among you through Me.

What do we find in Christ? We find perfection of moral character, superiority to circumstances, to the elements, to disease, to death. We find in Him One who forgives sin and brings peace of conscience, who bestows the Holy Spirit and leads to perfect righteousness. We cannot imagine anything in God which is not made present to us in Christ In any part of the universe we should feel secure with Christ. In the most critical spiritual emergency we should have confidence that He could right matters. In the physical and in the spiritual world He is equally at home and equally commanding. We can believe Him when He says that he that has seen Him has seen the Father.

What precisely does this utterance mean? Does it only mean that Jesus in His holy and loving ways and in the whole of His character was God's very image? As you might say of a son who strongly resembles his father, "If you have seen the one, you have seen the other." It is true that the self-sacrifice and humility and devotedness of Jesus did give men new views of the true character of God, that His conduct was an exact transcript of God's mind and conveyed to men new thoughts of God.

But it is plain that the connection between Jesus and God was a different kind of connection from that which subsists between every man and God. Every man might in a sense say, "I am in the Father and the Father in me." But plainly the very fact that Jesus said to Philip, "Believest thou not that I am in the Father and the Father in Me?" is proof that it was not this ordinary connection He had in view. Philip could have had no difficulty in perceiving and acknowledging that God was in Jesus as He is in every man. But if that were all that Jesus meant, then it was wholly out of place to appeal to the works the Father had given Him to do in proof of this assertion.

When, therefore, Jesus said, "He that hath seen Me hath seen the Father," He did not merely mean that by His superior holiness He had revealed the Father as no other man had done (although even this would be a most surprising assertion for any mere man to make—that He was so holy that whoever had seen Him had seen the absolutely holy God), but He meant that God was present with Him in a special manner.

So important was it that the disciples should firmly grasp the truth that the Father was in Christ that Jesus proceeds to enlarge upon the proof or evidence of this. In the course of doing so He imparts to them three assurances fitted to comfort them in the prospect of His departure: first, that so far from being weakened by His going to the Father, they will do greater works than even those which had proved that the Father was present with Him; second, that He would not leave them friendless and without support, but would send them the Paraclete, the Spirit of truth, who should abide with them; and third, that although the world would not see Him, they would, and would recognise that He was the maintainer of their own life.

But all this experience would serve to convince them that the Father was in Him. He had, He says, lived among them as the representative of the Father, uttering His will, doing His works. These works might have convinced them even if they were not spiritual enough to perceive that His words were Divine utterances. But a time was coming when a satisfying conviction of the truth that God had been present with them in the presence of Jesus would be wrought in them. When, after His departure, they found themselves doing the works of God, greater works than Jesus had done, when they found that the Spirit of truth dwelt in them, imparting to them the very mind and life of Christ Himself, then they should be certified of the truth that Jesus now declared, that the Father was in Him and He in the Father. "At that day ye shall know that I am in My Father, and you in Me, and I in you." What their understanding could not at present quite grasp, the course of events and their own spiritual experience would make plain to them. When in the prosecution of Christ's instructions they strove to fulfil His commands and carry out His will upon earth, they would find themselves countenanced and supported by powers unseen, would find their life sustained by the life of Christ.

Jesus, then, speaks here of three grades of conviction regarding His claim to be God's representative: three kinds of evidence—a lower, a higher, and the highest. There is the evidence of His miracles, the evidence of His words or His own testimony, and the evidence of the new spiritual life He would maintain in His followers.

Miracles are not the highest evidence, but they are evidence. One miracle might not be convincing evidence. Many miracles of the same kind, such as a number of cures of nervous complaints, or several successful treatments of blind persons, might only indicate superior knowledge of morbid conditions and of remedies. A physician in advance of his age might accomplish wonders. Or had all the miracles of Jesus been such as the multiplication of the loaves and fishes, it might, with a shade of plausibility, have been urged that this was legerdemain. But what we see in Jesus is not power to perform an occasional wonder to make men stare or to win for Himself applause, but power as God's representative on earth to do whatever is needful for the manifestation of God's presence and for the fulfilment of God's will. It may surely at this time of day be taken for granted that Jesus was serious and true. The works are given Him by the Father to do: it is as an exhibition of God's power He performs them. They are therefore performed not in one form only, but in every needed form. He shows command over all nature, and gives evidence that spirit is superior to matter and rules it.

The miracles of Christ are also convincing because they are performed by a miraculous Person. That an ordinary man should seem to rule nature, or should exhibit wonders on no adequate occasion, must always seem unlikely, if not incredible. But that a Person notoriously exceptional, being what no other man has ever been, should do things that no other man has done, excites no incredulity. That Christ was supremely and absolutely holy no one doubts; but this itself is a miracle; and that this miraculous Person should act miraculously is not unlikely. Moreover, there was adequate occasion both for the miracle of Christ's person and the miracle of His life and separate acts. There was an end to be served so great as to justify this interruption of the course of things as managed by men. If miracles are possible, then they could never be more worthily introduced. If at any time it might seem appropriate and needful that the unseen, holy, and loving God should assert His power over all that touches us His children, so as to give us the consciousness of His presence and of His faithfulness, surely that time was precisely then when Christ came forth from the Father to reveal His holiness and His love, to show men that supreme power and supreme holiness and love reside together in God.

At present men are swinging from an excessive exaltation of miracles to an excessive depreciation of them. They sometimes speak as if no one could work a miracle, and sometimes as if any one could work a miracle. Having discovered that miracles do not convince every one, they leap to the conclusion that they convince no one; and perceiving that Christ does not place them on the highest platform of evidence, they proceed to put them out of court altogether. This is inconsiderate and unwise. The miracles of Christ are appealed to by Himself as evidence of His truth; and looking at them in connection with His person, His life, and His mission or object, considering their character as works of compassion, and their instructive revelation of the nature and purpose of Him who did them, we cannot, I think, but feel that they carry in them a very strong claim upon our most serious attention and do help us to trust in Christ.

But Christ Himself, in the words before us, expects that those who have listened to His teaching and seen His life should need no other evidence that God is in Him and He in God--should not require to go down and back to the preliminary evidence of miracles which may serve to attract strangers. And, obviously, we get closer to the very heart of any person, nearer to the very core of their being, through their ordinary and habitual demeanour and conversation than by considering their exceptional and occasional acts. And it is a great tribute to the power and beauty of Christ's personality that it actually is not His miracles which solely or chiefly convince us of His claims upon our confidence, but rather His own character as it shines through His talks with His disciples and with all men He met. This, we feel, is the Person for us. Here we have the human ideal. The characteristics here disclosed are those which ought everywhere to prevail.

But the crowning evidence of Christ's unity with the Father can be enjoyed only by those who share His life. The conclusive evidence which for ever scatters doubt and remains abidingly as the immovable ground of confidence in Christ is our individual acceptance of His Spirit. Christ's life in God, His identification with the ultimate source of life and power, is to become one of the unquestioned facts of consciousness, one of the immovable data of human existence. We shall one day be as sure of His unity with the Father, and that in Christ our life is hid in God, as we are sure that now we are alive. Faith in Christ is to become an unquestioned certainty. How then is this assurance to be attained? It is to be attained when we ourselves as Christ's agents do greater works than He Himself did, and when by the power of His spiritual presence with us we live as He lived.

Christ calls our attention to this with His usual formula when about to declare a surprising but important truth: "Verily, verily, I say unto you, He that believeth on Me shall do greater works than these." Beginning with such evidence and such trust as we can attain, we shall be encouraged by finding the practical strength which comes of union with Christ. It speedily became apparent to the disciples that our Lord meant what He said when He assured them that they would do greater works than He had done. His miracles had amazed them and had done much good. And yet, after all, they were necessarily very limited in number, in the area of their exercise, and in the permanence of their results. Many were healed; but many, many more remained diseased. And even those who were healed were not rendered permanently unassailable by disease. The eyes of the blind which were opened for a year or two must close shortly in death. The paralysed, though sent from Christ's presence healed, must yield to the debilitating influences of age and betake themselves again to the crutch or the couch. Lazarus given back for a time to his sorrowing sisters must again, and this time without recall, own the power of death. And how far did the influence of Christ penetrate into these healed persons? Did they all obey His words and sin no more? or did some worse thing than the disease He freed them from fall upon some of them? Was there none who used his restored eyesight to minister to sin, his restored energies to do more wickedness than otherwise would have been possible? In one word, the miracles of Christ, great as they were and beneficent as they were, were still confined to the body, and did not directly touch the spirit of man.

But was this the object of Christ's coming? Did He come to do a little less than several of the great medical discoverers have done? Assuredly not. These works of healing which He wrought on the bodies of men were, as John regularly calls them, "signs"; they were not acts terminating in themselves, and finding their full significance in the happiness communicated to the healed persons; they were signs pointing to a power over men's spirits, and suggesting to men analogous but everlasting benefits. Christ wrought His miracles that men, beginning with what they could see and appreciate, might be led on to believe in and trust Him for power to help them in all their matters. And now He expressly announces to His disciples that these works which He had been doing were not miracles of the highest kind; that miracles of the highest kind were works of healing and renewal wrought not on the bodies but on the souls of men, works whose effects would not be deleted by disease and death, but would be permanent, works which should not be confined to Palestine, but should be coextensive with the human race. And these greater works He would now proceed to accomplish through His disciples. By His removal from earth His work was not to be stopped, but to pass into a higher stage. He had come to earth not to make a passing display of Divine power, not to give a tantalising glimpse of what the world might be were His power acting freely and continuously in it; but He had come to lead us to apprehend the value of spiritual health and to trust Him for that. And now that He had won men's trust and taught a few to love Him and to value His Spirit, He removes Himself from their sight, and puts Himself beyond the reach of those who merely sought for earthly benefits, that He may through the Spirit come to all who understood how much greater are spiritual benefits.

This crowning evidence of Christ's being with the Father and in Him the disciples very soon enjoyed. On the day of Pentecost they found such results following from their simple word as had never followed the word of Christ. Thousands were renewed in heart and life. And from that day to this these greater works have never ceased. And why? "Because I go to the Father." And two reasons are given in these simple words. In the first place, no such results could be accomplished by Christ because not till He died was the Father's love fully known. It was the death and resurrection of Christ that convinced men of the truth of what Christ had proclaimed in His life and in His words regarding the Father. The tender compunction which was stirred by His death gave a purchase to the preacher of repentance which did not previously exist. It is Christ's death and resurrection which have been the converting influence through all the ages, and these Christ Himself could not preach. It was only when He had gone to the Father that the greater works of His kingdom could be done. Besides, it was only then that the greater works could be understood and longed for. The fact is, that the death and resurrection of Christ radically altered men's conceptions of the spiritual world, and gave them a belief in a future life of the spirit such as they previously had not and could not have. When men came experimentally into contact with One who had passed through death, and who now entered the unseen world full of plans and of vitality to execute them, a new sense of the value of spiritual benefits was born within them. The fact of being associated with a living Christ at God's right hand has refined the spiritual conceptions of men, and has given a quality to holiness which was not previously conspicuous. The spiritual world is now real and near, and men no longer think of Christ as a worker of miracles on physical nature, but as the King of the world unseen and the willing Source of all spiritual good. We sometimes wonder Christ preached so little and spoke so little as men do now in directing sinners to Him; but He knew that while He lived this was almost useless, and that events would proclaim Him more effectually than any words.

But when Christ gives as a reason for the greater works of His disciples that He Himself went to the Father, He also means that, being with the Father, He would be in the place of power, able to respond to the prayers of His people. "I go unto the Father, and whatsoever ye shall ask in My name that will I do." No man in Christ's circumstances would utter such words at random. They are uttered with a perfect knowledge of the difficulties and in absolute good faith. But praying "in Christ's name" is not so easy an achievement as we are apt to think. Praying in Christ's name means, no doubt, that we go to God, not in our own name, but in His. He has given us power to use His name, as when we send a messenger we bid him use our name. Sometimes when we send a person to a friend we are almost afraid to give him our name, knowing that our friend will be anxious for our sakes to do all he can and perhaps too much for the applicant. And in going to God in the name of Christ, as those who can plead His friendship and are identified with Him, we know we are sure of a loving and liberal reception.

But praying in Christ's name means more than this. It means that we pray for such things as will promote Christ's kingdom. When we do anything in another's name, it is for him we do it. When we take possession of a property or a legacy in the name of some society, it is not for our own private advantage but for the society we take possession. When an officer arrests any one in the Queen's name, it is not to satisfy his private malice he does so; and when he collects money in the name of government, it is not to fill his own pocket. Yet how constantly do we overlook this obvious condition of acceptable prayer! To pray in Christ's name is to seek what He seeks, to ask aid in promoting what He has at heart. To come in Christ's name and plead selfish and worldly desires is absurd. To pray in Christ's name is to pray in the spirit in which He Himself prayed and for objects He desires. When we measure our prayers by this rule, we cease to wonder that so few seem to be answered. Is God to answer prayers that positively lead men away from Him? Is He to build them up in the presumption that happiness can be found in the pursuit of selfish objects and worldly comfort? It is when a man stands, as these disciples stood, detached from worldly hopes and finding all in Christ, so clearly apprehending the sweep and benignity of Christ's will as to see that it comprehends all good to man, and that life can serve no purpose if it do not help to fulfil that will--it is then a man prays with assurance and finds his prayer answered. Christ had won the love of these men and knew that their chief desire would be to serve Him, that their prayers would always be that they might fulfil His purposes. Their fear was, not that He would summon them to live wholly for the ends for which He had lived, but that when He was gone they should find themselves unfit to contend with the world.

And therefore He gives them the final encouragement that He would still be with them, not indeed in a visible form apparent to all eyes, but in a valid and powerful spiritual manner appreciable by those who loved Christ and strove to do His will. "If ye love Me, keep My commandments. And I will pray the Father, and He shall give you another Comforter," another Advocate, one called to your aid, and who shall so effectually aid you that in His presence and help you will know Me present with you. "I will not leave you comfortless, like orphans: I will come to you." Christ Himself was still to be with them. He was not merely to leave them His memory and example, but was to be with them, sustaining and guiding and helping them even as He had done. The only difference was to be this--that whereas up to this time they had verified His presence by their senses, seeing His body, hearing His words, and so forth, they should henceforward verify His presence by a spiritual sense which the world of those who did not love Him could not make use of. "Yet a little while, and the world seeth Me no more; but ye see Me: because I live, ye shall live also." They would find that their life was bound up in His; and as that new life of theirs grew strong and proved itself victorious over the world and powerful to subdue men's hearts to Christ and win the world to Christ's kingdom, they should feel a growing persuasion, a deepening consciousness, that this life of theirs was but the manifestation of the continued life of Christ. "At that day they would know that Christ was in the Father, and they in Him, and He in them."

Consciousness, then, of Christ's present life and of His close relation to ourselves is to be won only by loving Him and living in Him and for Him. Lower grades of faith there are on which most of us stand, and by which, let us hope, we are slowly ascending to this assured and ineradicable consciousness. Drawn to Christ we are by the beauty of His life, by His evident mastery of all that concerns us, by His knowledge, by the revelation He makes; but doubts assail us, questionings arise, and we long for the full assurance of the personal love of God and of the continued personal life and energy of Christ which would give us an immovable ground to stand on. According to Christ's explanation given in this passage to His disciples, this deepest conviction, this unquestionable consciousness of His presence, is attained only by those who proceed upon the lower grades of faith, and with true love for Him seek to find their life in Him. It is a conviction which can only be won experimentally. The disciples passed from the lower to the higher faith at a bound. The sight of the risen Lord, the new world vividly present to them in His person, gave their devotedness an impulse which carried them at once and for ever to certainty. There are many still who are so drawn by spiritual affinity to Christ that unhesitatingly and unrepentingly they give themselves wholly to Him, and have the reward of a conscious life in Christ. Others have more slowly to win their way upwards, fighting against unbelief, striving to give themselves more undividedly to Christ, and encouraging themselves with the hope that from their hearts also all doubts will one day for ever vanish. Certain it is that Christ's life can only be given to those who are willing to receive it--certain it is that only those who seek to do His work seek to be sustained by His life. If we are not striving to attain those ends which He gave His life to accomplish, we cannot be surprised if we are not sensible of receiving His aid. If we aim at worldly ends, we shall need no other energy than what the world supplies; but if we throw ourselves heartily into the Christian order of things and manner of life, we shall at once be sensible of our need of help, and shall know whether we receive it or not.

Christ's promise is explicit--a promise given as the stay of His friends in their bitterest need: "He that hath My commandments, and keepeth them, he it is that loveth Me: and he that loveth Me shall be loved of My Father, and I will love Him, and will manifest Myself to him." It will still be a spiritual manifestation which can be perceived only by those whose spirits are exercised to discern such things; but it will be absolutely satisfying. We shall find one day that Christ's work has been successful, that He has brought men and God into a perfect harmony. "That day" shall arrive for us also, when we shall find that Christ has actually accomplished what He undertook, and has set our life and ourselves on an enduring foundation--has given us eternal life in God, a life of perfect joy. Things are under God's guidance progressive, and Christ is the great means He uses for the progress of all that concerns ourselves. And what Christ has done is not to be fruitless or only half effective; He will see of the travail of His soul and be satisfied--satisfied because in us the utmost of happiness and the utmost of good have been attained, because greater and richer things than man has conceived have been made ours.

These utterances are fitted to dispel a form of unbelief which seriously hinders many sincere inquirers. It arises from the difficulty of believing in Christ as now alive and able to afford spiritual assistance. Many persons who enthusiastically admit the perfectness of Christ's character and of the morality He taught, and who desire above all else to make that morality their own, are yet unable to believe that He can give them any real and present assistance in their efforts after holiness. A teacher is a very different thing from a Saviour. They are satisfied with Christ's teaching; but they need more than teaching--they need not only to see the road, but to be enabled to follow it. Unless a man can find some real connection between himself and God, unless he can rely upon receiving inward support from God, he feels that there is nothing which can truly be called salvation.

This form of unbelief assails almost every man. Very often it results from the slow-growing conviction that the Christian religion is not working in ourselves the definite results we expected. When we read the New Testament, we see the reasonableness of faith, we cannot but subscribe to the theory of Christianity; but when we endeavour to practise it we fail. We have tried it, and it does not seem to work. At first we think this is something peculiar to ourselves, and that through some personal carelessness or mistake we have failed to receive all the benefit which others receive. But as time goes on the suspicion strengthens in some minds that faith is a delusion: prayer seems to be unanswered; effort seems to be unacknowledged. The power of an almighty spirit within the human spirit cannot be traced. Perhaps this suspicion, more than all other causes put together, produces undecided, heartless Christians.

What, then, is to be said in view of such doubts? Perhaps it may help us past them if we consider that spiritual things are spiritually discerned, and that the one proof of His ascension to God's right hand which Christ Himself promised was the bestowal of His Spirit. If we find that, however slowly, we are coming into a truer harmony with God; if we find that we can more cordially approve the Spirit of Christ, and give to that Spirit a more real place in our life; if we are finding that we can be satisfied with very little in the way of selfish and worldly advancement, and that it is a greater satisfaction to us to do good than to get good; if we find ourselves in any degree more patient, more temperate, more humble,-- then Christ is manifesting in us His present life in the only way in which He promised to do so. Even if we have more knowledge, more perception of what moral greatness is, if we see through the superficial formalisms which once passed for religion with us, this is a step in the right direction, and if wisely used may be the foundation of a superstructure of intelligent service and real fellowship with God. Every discovery and abandonment of error, every unmasking of delusion, every attainment of truth, is a step nearer to permanent reality, and is a true spiritual gain; and if in times past we have had little experience of spiritual joy and confidence, if our thoughts have been sceptical and questioning and perplexed, all this may be the needful preliminary to a more independent and assured and truer faith, and may be the very best proof that Christ is guiding our mind and attending to our prayers. It is for "the world" to refuse to believe in the Spirit, because "it beholdeth Him not, neither knoweth Him."

It may also be said that to think of Christ as a good man who has passed away like other good men, leaving an influence and no more behind Him, to think of Him as lying still in His tomb outside Jerusalem, is to reverse not only the belief of those who knew Christ best, but the belief of godly men in all ages. For in all ages both before and after Christ it has been the clear conviction of devout souls that God sought them much more ardently and persistently than they sought God. The truth which shines most conspicuously in the experience of all the saved is that they were saved by God and not by themselves. If human experience is to be trusted at all, if it in any case reflects the substantial verities of the spiritual world, then we may hold it as proved in the uniform experience of men that God somehow communicated to them a living energy, and not only taught them what to do, but gave them strength to do it. If under the Christian dispensation we are left to make the best we can for ourselves of the truth taught by Christ and of the example He set us in His life and death, then the Christian dispensation, so far from being an advance on all that went before, fails to supply us with that very thing which is sought through all religions--actual access to a living source of spiritual strength. I believe that the resurrection of Christ is established by stronger evidence than exists for any other historical fact; but apart altogether from the historical evidence, the entire experience of God's people goes to show that Christ, as the mediator between God and man, as the representative of God and the channel of His influence upon us, must be now alive, and must be in a position to exert a personal care and a personal influence, and to yield a present and inward assistance. Were it otherwise, we should be left without a Saviour to struggle against the enemies of the soul in our own strength, and this would be a complete reversal of the experience of all those who in past ages have been engaged in the same strife and have been victorious.

XI. THE BEQUEST OF PEACE

"Judas (not Iscariot) saith unto Him, Lord, what is come to pass that Thou wilt manifest Thyself unto us, and not unto the world? Jesus answered and said unto him, If a man love Me, he will keep My word: and My Father will love him, and We will come unto him, and make our abode with him. He that loveth Me not keepeth not My words: and the word which ye hear is not Mine, but the Father's who sent Me. These things have I spoken unto you, while yet abiding with you. But the Comforter, even the Holy Spirit, whom the Father will send in My name, He shall teach you all things, and bring to your remembrance all that I said unto you. Peace I leave with you; My peace I give unto you: not as the world giveth, give I unto you. Let not your heart be troubled, neither let it be fearful. Ye heard how I said to you, I go away, and I come unto you. If ye loved Me, ye would have rejoiced, because I go unto the Father: for the Father is greater than I. And now I have told you before it come to pass, that, when it is come to pass, ye may believe. I will no more speak much with you, for the prince of the world cometh: and he hath nothing in Me; but that the world may know that I love the Father, and as the Father gave Me commandment, even so I do. Arise, let us go hence."--John xiv. 22-31.

The encouraging assurances of our Lord are interrupted by Judas Thaddeus. As Peter, Thomas, and Philip had availed themselves of their Master's readiness to solve their difficulties, so now Judas utters his perplexity. He perceives that the manifestation of which Jesus has spoken is not public and general, but special and private; and he says, "Lord, what has happened, that Thou art to manifest Thyself to us, and not to the world?" It would seem as if Judas had been greatly impressed by the public demonstration in favour of Jesus a day or two previously, and supposed that something must have occurred to cause Him now to wish to manifest Himself only to a select few.

Apparently Judas' construction of the future was still entangled with the ordinary Messianic expectation. He thought Jesus, although departing for a little, would return speedily in outward Messianic glory, and would triumphantly enter Jerusalem and establish Himself there. But how this could be done privately he could not understand. And if Jesus had entirely altered His plan, and did not mean immediately to claim Messianic supremacy, but only to manifest Himself to a few, was this possible?

By His reply our Lord shows for the hundredth time that outward proclamation and external acknowledgment were not in His thoughts. It is to the individual and in response to individual love He will manifest Himself. It is therefore a spiritual manifestation He has in view. Moreover, it was not to a specially privileged few, whose number was already complete, that He would manifest Himself. Judas supposed that to him and his fellow-Apostles, "us," Jesus would manifest Himself, and over against this select company he set "the world." But this mechanical line of demarcation our Lord obliterates in His reply, "If any man loveth Me, ... We will come to him." He enounces the great spiritual law that they who seek to have Christ's presence manifested to them must love and obey Him. He that longs for more satisfying knowledge of spiritual realities, he that thirsts for certainty and to see God as if face to face, must expect no sudden or magical revelation, but must be content with the true spiritual education which proceeds by loving and living. To the disciples the method might seem slow--to us also it often seems slow; but it is the method which nature requires. Our knowledge of God, our belief that in Christ we have a hold of ultimate truth and are living among eternal verities, grow with our love and service of Christ. It may take us a lifetime--it will take us a lifetime--to learn to love Him as we ought, but others have learned and we also may learn, and there is no possible experience so precious to us.

It is, then, to those who serve Him that Christ manifests Himself, and manifests Himself in an abiding, spiritual, influential manner. That those who do not serve Him do not believe in His presence and power is to be expected. But were those who have served Him asked if they had become more convinced of His spiritual and effectual presence, their voice would be that this promise had been fulfilled. And this is the very citadel of the religion of Christ. If Christ does not now abide with and energetically aid those who serve Him, then their faith is vain. If His spiritual presence with them is not manifested in spiritual results, if they have no evidence that He is personally and actively employed in and with them, their faith is vain. To believe in a Christ long since removed from earth and whose present life cannot now influence or touch mankind is not the faith which Christ Himself invites. And if His promise to abide with those who love and serve Him is not actually performed, Christendom has been produced by a mistake and has lived on a delusion.

Marcus Dods, D.D.

At this point (ver. 25) Jesus pauses; and feeling how little He had time to say of what was needful, and how much better they would understand their relation to Him after He had finally passed from their bodily sight, He says: "These things I have spoken to you, while yet I remain with you; but the Paraclete, the Holy Spirit, which the Father will send in My name, He will teach you all things, and will remind you of all that I have said to you." Jesus cannot tell them all He would wish them to know; but the same Helper whom He has already promised will especially help them by giving them understanding of what has already been told them, and by leading them into further knowledge. He is to come "in the name" of Jesus--that is to say, as His representative--and to carry on His work in the world.
16

Here, then, the Lord predicts that one day His disciples will know more than He has taught them. They were to advance in knowledge beyond the point to which He had brought them. His teaching would necessarily be the foundation of all future attainment, and whatever would not square with that they must necessarily reject; but they were to add much to the foundation He had laid. We cannot therefore expect to find in the teaching of Jesus all that His followers ought to know regarding Himself and His connection with them. All that is absolutely necessary we shall find there; but if we wish to know all that He would have us know, we must look beyond. The teaching which we receive from the Apostles is the requisite and promised complement of the teaching which Christ Himself delivered. He being the subject taught as much as the teacher, and His whole experience as living, dying, rising, and ascending, constituting the facts which Christian teaching was to explain, it was impossible that He Himself should be the final teacher. He could not at once be text and exposition. He lived among men, and by His teaching shed much light on the significance of His life; He died, and was not altogether silent regarding the meaning of His death, but it was enough that He furnished matter for His Apostles to explain, and confined Himself to sketching the mere outline of Christian truth.

Again and again throughout this last conversation Jesus tries to break off, but finds it impossible. Here (ver. 27), when He has assured them that, although He Himself leaves them in ignorance of many things, the Spirit will lead them into all truth, He proceeds to make His parting bequest. He would fain leave them what will enable them to be free from care and distress; but He has none of those worldly possessions which men usually lay up for their children and those dependent on them. House, lands, clothes, money, He had none. He could not even secure for those who were to carry on His work an exemption from persecution which He Himself had not enjoyed. He did not leave them, as some initiators have done, stable though new institutions, an empire of recent origin but already firmly established. "Not as the world giveth, give I unto you."

But He does give them that which all other bequests aim at producing: "Peace I leave with you." Men may differ as to the best means of attaining peace, or even as to the kind of peace that is desirable, but all agree in seeking an untroubled state. We seek a condition in which we shall have no unsatisfied desires gnawing at our heart and making peace impossible, no stings of conscience, dipped in the poison of past wrong-doing, torturing us hour by hour, no foreboding anxiety darkening and disturbing a present which might otherwise be peaceful. The comprehensive nature of this possession is shown by the fact that peace can be produced only by the contribution of past, present, and future. As health implies that all the laws which regulate bodily life are being observed, and as it is disturbed by the infringement of any one of these, so peace of mind implies that in the spiritual life all is as it should be. Introduce remorse or an evil conscience, and you destroy peace; introduce fear or anxiety, and peace is impossible. Introduce anything discordant, ambition alongside of indolence, a sensitive conscience alongside of strong passions, and peace takes flight. He, therefore, who promises to give peace promises to give unassailable security, inward integrity and perfectness, all which goes to make up that perfect condition in which we shall be for ever content to abide.

Jesus further defines the peace which He was leaving to the disciples as that peace which He had Himself enjoyed: "My peace I give unto you,"--as one hands over a possession he has himself tested, the shield or helmet that has served him in battle. "That which has protected Me in a thousand fights I make over to you." The peace which Christ desires His disciples to enjoy is that which characterised Himself; the same serenity in danger, the same equanimity in troublous circumstances, the same freedom from anxiety about results, the same speedy recovery of composure after anything which for a moment ruffled the calm surface of His demeanour. This is what He makes over to His people; this is what He makes possible to all who serve Him.

There is nothing which more markedly distinguishes Jesus and proves His superiority than His calm peace in all circumstances. He was poor, and might have resented the incapacitating straitness of poverty. He was driven from place to place, His purpose and motives were suspected, His action and teaching resisted, the good He strove to do continually marred; but He carried Himself through all with serenity. It is said that nothing shakes the nerve of brave men so much as fear of assassination: our Lord lived among bitterly hostile men, and was again and again on the brink of being made away with; but He was imperturbably resolute to do the work given Him to do. Take Him at an unguarded moment, tell Him the boat is sinking underneath Him, and you find the same undisturbed composure. He was never troubled at the results of His work or about His own reputation; when He was reviled, He reviled not again.

This unruffled serenity was so obvious a characteristic of the demeanour of Jesus, that as it was familiar to His friends, so it was perplexing to His judges. The Roman governor saw in His bearing an equanimity so different from the callousness of the hardened criminal and from the agitation of the self-condemned, that he could not help exclaiming in astonishment, "Dost Thou not know that I have power over Thee?" Therefore without egotism our Lord could speak of "My peace." The world had come to Him in various shapes, and He had conquered it. No allurement of pleasure, no opening to ambition had distracted Him and broken up His serene contentment; no danger had filled His spirit with anxiety and fear. On one occasion only could He say, "Now is My soul troubled." Out of all that life had presented to Him He had wrought out for Himself and for us peace.

By calling it specifically "My peace" our Lord distinguishes it from the peace which men ordinarily pursue. Some seek it by accommodating themselves to the world, by fixing for themselves a low standard and disbelieving in the possibility of living up to any high standard in this world. Some seek peace by giving the fullest possible gratification to all their desires; they seek peace in external things--comfort, ease, plenty, pleasant connections. Some stifle anxiety about worldly things by impressing on themselves that fretting does no good, and that what cannot be cured must be endured; and any anxiety that might arise about their spiritual condition they stifle by the imagination that God is too great or too good to deal strictly with their shortcomings. Such kinds of peace, our Lord implies, are delusive. It is not outward things which can give peace of mind, no more than it is a soft couch which can give rest to a fevered body. Restfulness must be produced from within.

There are, in fact, two roads to peace--we may conquer or we may be conquered. A country may always enjoy peace, if it is prepared always to submit to indignities, to accommodate itself to the demands of stronger parties, and absolutely to dismiss from its mind all ideas of honour or self-respect. This mode of obtaining peace has the advantages of easy and speedy attainment--advantages to which every man naturally attaches too high a value. For in the individual life we are daily choosing either the one peace or the other; the unrighteous desires which distract us we are either conquering or being conquered by. We are either accepting the cheap peace that lies on this side of conflict, or we are attaining or striving towards the peace that lies on the other side of conflict. But the peace we gain by submission is both short-lived and delusive. It is short-lived, for a gratified desire is like a relieved beggar, who will quickly find his way back to you with his request rather enlarged than curtailed; and it is delusive, because it is a peace which is the beginning of bondage of the worst kind. Any peace that is worth the having or worth the speaking about lies beyond, at the other side of conflict. We cannot long veil this from ourselves: we may decline the conflict and put off the evil day; but still we are conscious that we have not the peace our natures crave until we subdue the evil that is in us. We look and look for peace to distil upon us from without, to rise and shine upon us as to-morrow's sun, without effort of our own, and yet we know that such expectation is the merest delusion, and that peace must begin within, must be found in ourselves and not in our circumstances. We know that until our truest purposes are in thorough harmony with our conscientious convictions we have no right to peace. We know that we can have no deep and lasting peace until we are satisfied with our own inward state, or are at least definitely on the road to satisfaction.

Again, the peace of which Christ here speaks may be called His, as being wrought out by Him, and as being only attainable by others through His communication of it to them. We do at first inquire with surprise how it is possible that any one can bequeath to us his own moral qualities. This, in fact, is what one often wishes were possible--that the father who by long discipline, by many painful experiences, has at last become meek and wise, could transmit these qualities to his son who has life all before him. As we read the notices of those who pass away from among us, it is the loss of so much moral force we mourn; it may be, for all we know, as indispensable elsewhere, but nevertheless it is our loss, a loss for which no work done by the man, nor any works left behind him, compensate; for the man is always, or generally, greater than his works, and what he has done only shows us the power and possibilities that are in him. Each generation needs to raise its own good men, not independent, certainly, of the past, but not altogether inheriting what past generations have done; just as each new year must raise its own crops, and only gets the benefit of past toil in the shape of improved land, good seed, better implements and methods of agriculture. Still, there is a transmission from father to son of moral qualities. What the father has painfully acquired may be found in the son by inheritance. And this is analogous to the transfusion of moral qualities from Christ to His people. For it is true of all the graces of the Christian, that they are first acquired by Christ, and only from Him derived to the Christian. It is of His fulness we all receive, and grace for grace. He is the Light at whom we must all kindle, the Source from whom all flows.

How, then, does Christ communicate to us His peace or any of His own qualities--qualities in some instances acquired by personal experience and personal effort? He gives us peace, first, by reconciling us to God by removing the burden of our past guilt and giving us access to God's favour. His work sheds quite a new light upon God; reveals the fatherly love of God following us into our wandering and misery, and claiming us in our worst estate as His, acknowledging us and bidding us hope. Through Him we are brought back to the Father. He comes with this message from God, that He loves us. Am I, then, troubled about the past, about what I have done? As life goes on, do I only see more and more clearly how thoroughly I have been a wrong-doer? Does the present, as I live through it, only shed a brighter and brighter light on the evil of the past? Do I fear the future as that which can only more and more painfully evolve the consequences of my past wrong-doing? Am I gradually awaking to the full and awful import of being a sinner? After many years of a Christian profession, am I coming at last to see that above all else my life has been a life of sin, of shortcoming or evasion of duty, of deep consideration for my own pleasure or my own purpose, and utter or comparative regardlessness of God? Are the slowly evolving circumstances of my life at length effecting what no preaching has ever effected? are they making me understand that sin is the real evil, and that I am beset by it and my destiny entangled and ruled by it? To me, then, what offer could be more appropriate than the offer of peace? From all fear of God and of myself I am called to peace in Christ.

Reconcilement with God is the foundation, manifestly and of course, of all peace; and this we have as Christ's direct gift to us. But this fundamental peace, though it will eventually pervade the whole man, does in point of fact only slowly develop into a peace such as our Lord Himself possessed. The peace which our Lord spoke of to His disciples, peace amidst all the ills of life, can only be attained by a real following of Christ, and a hearty and profound acceptance of His principles and spirit. And it is not the less His gift because we have thus to work for it, to alter or be altered wholly in our own inward being. It is not therefore a deceptive bequest. When the father gives his son a good education, he cannot do so irrespective of the hard work of the son himself. When the general promises victory to his men, they do not expect to have it without fighting. And our Lord does not upset or supersede the fundamental laws of our nature and of our spiritual growth. He does not make effort of our own unnecessary; He does not give us a ready-made character irrespective of the laws by which character grows, irrespective of deep-seated thirst for holiness in ourselves and long-sustained conflict with outward obstacles and internal weaknesses and infidelities.

But He helps us to peace, not only though primarily by bringing us back to God's favour, but also by showing us in His own person and life how peace is attained and preserved, and by communicating to us His Spirit to aid us in our efforts to attain it. He found out more perfectly than any one else the secret of peace; and we are stirred by His example and success, not only as we are stirred by the example of any dead saint or sage with whom we have no present personal living fellowship, but as we are stirred by the example of a living Father who is always with us to infuse new heart into us, and to give us effectual counsel and aid. While we put forth our own efforts to win this self-conquest, and so school all within us as to enter into peace, Christ is with us securing that our efforts shall not be in vain, giving us the fixed and clear idea of peace as our eternal condition, and giving us also whatever we need to win it.

These words our Lord uttered at a time when, if ever, He was not likely to use words of course, to adopt traditional and misleading phrases. He loved the men He was speaking to, He knew He was after this to have few more opportunities of speaking with them, His love interpreted to Him the difficulties and troubles which would fall upon them, and this was the armour which He knew would bear them scathless through all. That His promise was fulfilled we know. We do not know what became of the majority of the Apostles, whether they did much or little; but if we look at the men who stood out prominently in the early history of the Church, we see how much they stood in need of this peace and how truly they received it. Look at Stephen, sinking bruised and bleeding under the stones of a cursing mob, and say what characterises him--what makes his face shine and his lips open in prayer for his murderers? Look at Paul, driven out of one city, dragged lifeless out of another, clinging to a spar on a wild sea, stripped by robbers, arraigned before magistrate after magistrate--what keeps his spirit serene, his purpose unshaken through a life such as this? What put into his lips these valued words and taught him to say to others, "Rejoice evermore, and let the peace of God which passeth understanding keep your heart and mind"? It was the fulfilment of this promise--a promise which is meant for us as for them. It will be fulfilled in us as in these men, not by a mere verbal petition, not by a craving however strong, or a prayer however sincere, but by a true and profound acceptance of Christ, by a conscientious following of Him as our real leader, as that One from whom we take our ideas of life, of what is worthy and what is unworthy.

Footnotes:

16. "In this designation of the teaching Spirit as holy, there lie lessons for two classes of people. All fanatical professions of possessing Divine illumination, which are not warranted and sealed by purity of life, are lies or self-delusion. And, on the other hand, cold-blooded intellectualism will never force the locks of the palace of Divine truth; but they that come there must have clean hands and a pure heart; and only those who have the love and the longing for goodness will be wise scholars in Christ's school."--Maclaren.

Marcus Dods, D.D.

XII. THE VINE AND THE BRANCHES

"Arise, let us go hence. I am the true Vine, and My Father is the Husbandman. Every branch in Me that beareth not fruit, He taketh it away: and every branch that beareth fruit, He cleanseth it, that it may bear more fruit. Already ye are clean because of the word which I have spoken unto you. Abide in Me, and I in you. As the branch cannot bear fruit of itself, except it abide in the vine; so neither can ye, except ye abide in Me. I am the Vine, ye are the branches: He that abideth in Me, and I in him, the same beareth much fruit: for apart from Me ye can do nothing. If a man abide not in Me, he is cast forth as a branch, and is withered; and they gather them, and cast them into the fire, and they are burned. If ye abide in Me, and My words abide in you, ask whatsoever ye will, and it shall be done unto you. Herein is My Father glorified, that ye bear much fruit; and so shall ye be My disciples. Even as the Father hath loved Me, I also have loved you; abide ye in My love. If ye keep My commandments, ye shall abide in My love; even as I have kept My Father's commandments, and abide in His love. These things have I spoken unto you, that My joy may be in you, and that your joy may be fulfilled. This is My commandment, that ye love one another, even as I have loved you."--John xiv. 31-xv. 12.

Like a friend who cannot tear himself away and has many more last words after he has bid us good-bye, Jesus continues speaking to the disciples while they are selecting and putting on their sandals and girding themselves to face the chill night air. He had to all appearance said all He meant to say. He had indeed closed the conversation with the melancholy words, "Henceforth I will not talk much with you." He had given the signal for breaking up the feast and leaving the house, rising from table Himself and summoning the rest to do the same. But as He saw their reluctance to move, and the alarmed and bewildered expression that hung upon their faces, He could not but renew His efforts to banish their forebodings and impart to them intelligent courage to face separation from Him. All He had said about His spiritual presence with them had fallen short: they could not as yet understand it. They were possessed with the dread of losing Him whose future was their future, and with the success of whose plans all their hopes were bound up. The prospect of losing Him was too dreadful; and though He had assured them He would still be with them, there was an appearance of mystery and unreality about that presence which prevented them from trusting it. They knew they could effect nothing if He left them: their work was done, their hopes blighted.

As Jesus, then, rises, and as they all fondly cluster round Him, and as He recognises once more how much He is to these men, there occurs to His mind an allegory which may help the disciples to understand better the connection they have with Him, and how it is still to be maintained. It has been supposed that this allegory was suggested to Him by some vine trailing round the doorway or by some other visible object, but such outward suggestion is needless. Recognising their fears and difficulties and dependence on Him as they hung upon Him for the last time, what more natural than that He should meet their dependence and remove their fears of real separation by saying, "I am the Vine, ye the branches"? What more natural, when He wished to set vividly before them the importance of the work He was bequeathing to them, and to stimulate them faithfully to carry on what He had begun, than to say, "I am the Vine, ye the fruit-bearing branches: abide in Me, and I in you"?

Doubtless our Lord's introduction of the word "true" or "real"--"I am the true Vine"--implies a comparison with other vines, but not necessarily with any vines then outwardly visible. Much more likely is it that as He saw the dependence of His disciples upon Him, He saw new meaning in the old and familiar idea that Israel was the vine planted by God. He saw that in Himself [17] and His disciples all that had been suggested by this figure was in reality accomplished. God's intention in creating man was fulfilled. It was secured by the life of Christ and by the attachment of men to Him that the purpose of God in creation would bear fruit. That which amply satisfied God was now in actual existence in the person and attractiveness of Christ. Seizing upon the figure of the vine as fully expressing this, Christ fixes it for ever in the mind of His disciples as the symbol of His connection with them, and with a few decisive strokes He gives prominence to the chief characteristics of this connection.

I. The first idea, then, which our Lord wished to present by means of this allegory is, that He and His disciples together form one whole, neither being complete without the other. The vine can bear no fruit if it has no branches; the branches cannot live apart from the vine. Without the branches the stem is a fruitless pole; without the stem the branches wither and die. Stem and branches together constitute one fruit-bearing tree. I, for my part, says Christ, am the Vine; ye are the branches, neither perfect without the other, the two together forming one complete tree, essential to one another as stem and branches.

The significance underlying the figure is obvious, and no more welcome or animating thought could have reached the heart of the disciples as they felt the first tremor of separation from their Lord. Christ, in His own visible person and by His own hands and words, was no longer to extend His kingdom on earth. He was to continue to fulfil God's purpose among men, no longer however in His own person, but through His disciples. They were now to be His branches, the medium through which He could express all the life that was in Him, His love for man, His purpose to lift and save the world. Not with His own lips was He any longer to tell men of holiness and of God, not with His own hand was He to dispense blessing to the needy ones of earth, but His disciples were now to be the sympathetic interpreters of His goodness and the unobstructed channels through which He might still pour out upon men all His loving purpose. As God the Father is a Spirit and needs human hands to do actual deeds of mercy for Him, as He does not Himself in His own separate personality make the bed of the sick poor, but does it only through the intervention of human charity, so can Christ speak no audible word in the ear of the sinner, nor do the actual work required for the help and advancement of men. This He leaves to His disciples, His part being to give them love and perseverance for it, to supply them with all they need as His branches.

This, then, is the last word of encouragement and of quickening our Lord leaves with these men and with us: I leave you to do all for Me; I entrust you with this gravest task of accomplishing in the world all I have prepared for by My life and death. This great end, to attain which I thought fit to leave the glory I had with the Father, and for which I have spent all--this I leave in your hands. It is in this world of men the whole results of the Incarnation are to be found, and it is on you the burden is laid of applying to this world the work I have done. You live for Me. But on the other hand I live for you. "Because I live, ye shall live also." I do not really leave you. If I say, "Abide in Me," I none the less say, "and I in you." It is in you I spend all the Divine energy you have witnessed in my life. It is through you I live. I am the Vine, the life-giving Stem, sustaining and quickening you. Ye are the branches, effecting what I intend, bearing the fruit for the sake of which I have been planted in the world by My Father, the Husbandman.

II. The second idea is that this unity of the tree is formed by unity of life. It is a unity brought about, not by mechanical juxtaposition, but by organic relationship. "As the branch cannot bear fruit of itself, but must abide in the vine, so neither can ye except ye abide in Me." A ball of twine or a bag of shot cannot be called a whole. If you cut off a yard of the twine, the part cut off has all the qualities and properties of the remainder, and is perhaps more serviceable apart from the rest than in connection with it. A handful of shot is more serviceable for many purposes than a bagful, and the quantity you take out of the bag retains all the properties it had while in the bag; because there is no common life in the twine or in the shot, making all the particles one whole. But take anything which is a true unity or whole--your body, for example. Different results follow here from separation. Your eye is useless taken from its place in the body. You can lend a friend your knife or your purse, and it may be more serviceable in his hands than in yours; but you cannot lend him your arms or your ears. Apart from yourself, the members of your body are useless, because here there is one common life forming one organic whole.

It is thus in the relation of Christ and His followers. He and they together form one whole, because one common life unites them. "As the branch cannot bear fruit of itself, so neither can ye." Why can the branch bear no fruit except it abide in the vine? Because it is a vital unity that makes the tree one. And what is a vital unity between persons? It can be nothing else than a spiritual unity--a unity not of a bodily kind, but inward and of the spirit. In other words, it is a unity of purpose and of resources for attaining that purpose. The branch is one with the tree because it draws its life from the tree and bears the fruit proper to the tree. We are one with Christ when we adopt His purpose in the world as the real governing aim of our life, and when we renew our strength for the fulfilment of that purpose by fellowship with His love for mankind and His eternal purpose to bless men.

We must be content, then, to be branches. We must be content not to stand isolated and grow from a private root of our own. We must utterly renounce selfishness. Successful selfishness is absolutely impossible. The greater the apparent success of selfishness is, the more gigantic will the failure one day appear. An arm severed from the body, a branch lopped off the tree, is the true symbol of the selfish man. He will be left behind as the true progress of mankind proceeds, with no part in the common joy, stranded and dying in cold isolation. We must learn that our true life can only be lived when we recognise that we are parts of a great whole, that we are here not to prosecute any private interest of our own and win a private good for ourselves, but to forward the good that others share in and the cause that is common.

How this unity is formed received no explanation on this occasion. The manner in which men become branches of the true Vine was not touched upon in the allegory. Already the disciples were branches, and no explanation was called for. It may, however, be legitimate to gather a hint from the allegory itself regarding the formation of the living bond between Christ and His people. However ignorant we may be of the propagation of fruit trees and the processes of grafting we can at any rate understand that no mere tying of a branch to a tree, bark to bark, would effect anything save the withering of the branch. The branch, if it is to be fruitful, must form a solid part of the tree, must be grafted so as to become of one structure and life with the stem. It must be cut through, so as to lay bare the whole interior structure of it, and so as to leave open all the vessels that carry the sap; and a similar incision must be made in the stock upon which the branch is to be grafted, so that the cut sap-vessels of the branch may be in contact with the cut sap-vessels of the stock. Such must be our grafting into Christ. It must be a laying bare of our inmost nature to His inmost nature, so that a vital connection may be formed between these two. What we expect to receive by being connected with Christ is the very Spirit which made Him what He was. We expect to receive into the source of conduct in us all that was the source of conduct in Him. We wish to be in such a connection with Him that His principles, sentiments, and aims shall become ours.

On His side Christ has laid bare His deepest feelings and spirit. In His life and in His death He submitted to that severest operation which seemed to be a maiming of Him, but which in point of fact was the necessary preparation for His receiving fruitful branches. He did not hide the true springs of His life under a hard and rough bark; but submitting Himself to the Husbandman's knife, He has suffered us through His wounds to see the real motives and vital spirit of His nature--truth, justice, holiness, fidelity, love. Whatever in this life cut our Lord to the quick, whatever tested most thoroughly the true spring of His conduct, only more clearly showed that deepest within Him and strongest within Him lay holy love. And He was not shy of telling men His love for them: in the public death He died He loudly declared it, opening His nature to the gaze of all. And to this open heart He declined to receive none; as many as the Father gave Him were welcome; He had none of that aversion we feel to admit all and sundry into close relations with us. He at once gives His heart and keeps back nothing to Himself; He invites us into the closest possible connection with Him, with the intention that we should grow to Him and for ever be loved by Him. Whatever real, lasting, and influential connection can be established between two persons, this He wishes to have with us. If it is possible for two persons so to grow together that separation in spirit is for ever impossible, it is nothing short of this Christ seeks.

But when we turn to the cutting of the branch, we see reluctance and vacillation and much to remind us that, in the graft we now speak of, the Husbandman has to deal, not with passive branches which cannot shrink from his knife, but with free and sensitive human beings. The hand of the Father is on us to sever us from the old stock and give us a place in Christ, but we feel it hard to be severed from the root we have grown from and to which we are now so firmly attached. We refuse to see that the old tree is doomed to the axe, or after we have been inserted into Christ we loosen ourselves again and again, so that morning by morning as the Father visits His tree He finds us dangling useless with signs of withering already upon us. But in the end the Vinedresser's patient skill prevails. We submit ourselves to those incisive operations of God's providence or of His gentler but effective word which finally sever us from what we once clung to. We are impelled to lay bare our heart to Christ and seek the deepest and truest and most influential union.

And even after the graft has been achieved the husbandman's care is still needed that the branch may "abide in the vine," and that it may "bring forth more fruit." There are two risks--the branch may be loosened, or it may run to wood and leaves. Care is taken when a graft is made that its permanent participation in the life of the tree be secured. The graft is not only tied to the tree, but the point of juncture is cased in clay or pitch or wax, so as to exclude air, water, or any disturbing influence. Analogous spiritual treatment is certainly requisite if the attachment of the soul to Christ is to become solid, firm, permanent. If the soul and Christ are to be really one, nothing must be allowed to tamper with the attachment. It must be sheltered from all that might rudely impinge upon it and displace the disciple from the attitude towards Christ he has assumed. When the graft and the stock have grown together into one, then the point of attachment will resist any shock; but, while the attachment is recent, care is needed that the juncture be hermetically secluded from adverse influences.

The husbandman's care is also needed that after the branch is grafted it may bring forth fruit increasingly. Stationariness is not to be tolerated. As for fruitlessness, that is out of the question. More fruit each season is looked for, and arranged for by the vigorous prunings of the husbandman. The branch is not left to nature. It is not allowed to run out in every direction, to waste its life in attaining size. Where it seems to be doing grandly and promising success, the knife of the vinedresser ruthlessly cuts down the flourish, and the fine appearance lies withering on the ground. But the vintage justifies the husbandman.

III. This brings us to the third idea of the allegory--that the result aimed at in our connection with Christ is fruit-bearing. The allegory bids us think of God as engaged in the tendance and culture of men with the watchful, fond interest with which the vinedresser tends his plants through every stage of growth and every season of the year, and even when there is nothing to be done gazes on them admiringly and finds still some little attention he can pay them; but all in the hope of fruit. All this interest collapses at once, all this care becomes a foolish waste of time and material, and reflects discredit and ridicule on the vinedresser, if there is no fruit. God has prepared for us in this life a soil than which nothing can be better for the production of the fruit He desires us to yield; He has made it possible for every man to serve a good purpose; He does His part not with reluctance, but, if we may say so, as His chief interest; but all in the expectation of fruit. We do not spend days of labour and nights of anxious thought, we do not lay out all we have at command, on that which is to effect nothing and give no satisfaction to ourselves or any one else; and neither does God. He did not make this world full of men for want of something better to do, as a mere idle pastime. He made it that the earth might yield her increase, that each of us might bring forth fruit. Fruit alone can justify the expense put upon this world. The wisdom, the patience, the love that have guided all things through the slow-moving ages will be justified in the product. And what this product is we already know: it is the attainment of moral perfection by created beings. To this all that has been made and done in the past leads up. "The whole creation groaneth and travaileth,"--for what? "For the manifestation of the sons of God." The lives and acts of good men are the adequate return for all past outlay, the satisfying fruit.

The production of this fruit became a certainty when Christ was planted in the world as a new moral stem. He was sent into the world not to make some magnificent outward display of Divine power, to carry us to some other planet, or alter the conditions of life here. God might have departed from His purpose of filling this earth with holy men, and might have used it for some easier display which for the moment might have seemed more striking. He did not do so. It was human obedience, the fruit of genuine human righteousness, of the love and goodness of men and women, that He was resolved to reap from earth. He was resolved to train men to such a pitch of goodness that in a world contrived to tempt there should be found nothing so alluring, nothing so terrifying, as to turn men from the straight path. He was to produce a race of men who, while still in the body, urged by appetites, assaulted by passions and cravings, with death threatening and life inviting, should prefer all suffering rather than flinch from duty, should prove themselves actually superior to every assault that can be made on virtue, should prove that spirit is greater than matter. And God set Christ in the world to be the living type of human perfection, to attract men by their love for Him to His kind of life, and to furnish them with all needed aid in becoming like Him--that as Christ had kept the Father's commandments, His disciples should keep His commandments, that thus a common understanding, an identity of interest and moral life, should be established between God and man.

Perhaps it is not pressing the figure too hard to remark that the fruit differs from timber in this respect--that it enters into and nourishes the life of man. No doubt in this allegory fruit-bearing primarily and chiefly indicates that God's purpose in creating man is satisfied. The tree He has planted is not barren, but fruitful. But certainly a great distinction between the selfish and the unselfish man, between the man who has private ambitions and the man who labours for the public good, lies in this-- that the selfish man seeks to erect a monument of some kind for himself, while the unselfish man spends himself in labours that are not conspicuous, but assist the life of his fellows. An oak carving or a structure of hard wood will last a thousand years and keep in memory the skill of the designer: fruit is eaten and disappears, but it passes into human life, and becomes part of the stream that flows on for ever. The ambitious man longs to execute a monumental work, and does not much regard whether it will be for the good of men or not; a great war will serve his turn, a great book, anything conspicuous. But he who is content to be a branch of the True Vine will not seek the admiration of men, but will strive to introduce a healthy spiritual life into those he can reach, even although in order to do so he must remain obscure and must see his labours absorbed without notice or recognition.

Does the teaching of this allegory, then, accord with the facts of life as we know them? Is it a truth, and a truth we must act upon, that apart from Christ we can do nothing? In what sense and to what extent is association with Christ really necessary to us?

Something may of course be made of life apart from Christ. A man may have much enjoyment and a man may do much good apart from Christ. He may be an inventor, who makes human life easier or safer or fuller of interest. He may be a literary man, who by his writings enlightens, exhilarates, and elevates mankind. He may, with entire ignorance or utter disregard of Christ, toil for his country or for his class or for his cause. But the best uses and ends of human life cannot be attained apart from Christ. Only in Him does the reunion of man with God seem attainable, and only in Him do God and God's aim and work in the world become intelligible. He is as necessary for the spiritual life of men as the sun is for this physical life. We may effect something by candle-light; we may be quite proud of electric light, and think we are getting far towards independence; but what man in his senses will be betrayed by these attainments into thinking we may dispense with the sun? Christ holds the key to all that is most permanent in human endeavour, to all that is deepest and best in human character. Only in Him can we take our place as partners with God in what He is really doing with this world. And only from Him can we draw courage, hopefulness, love to prosecute this work. In Him God does reveal Himself, and in Him the fulness of God is found by us. He is in point of fact the one moral stem apart from whom we are not bearing and cannot bear the fruit God desires.

If, then, we are not bringing forth fruit, it is because there is a flaw in our connection with Christ; if we are conscious that the results of our life and activity are not such results as He designs, and are in no sense traceable to Him, this is because there is something about our adherence to Him that is loose and needs rectification. Christ calls us to Him and makes us sharers in His work; and he who listens to this call and counts it enough to be a branch of this Vine and do His will is upheld by Christ's Spirit, is sweetened by His meekness and love, is purified by His holy and fearless rectitude, is transformed by the dominant will of this Person whom he has received deepest into his soul, and does therefore bring forth, in whatever place in life he holds, the same kind of fruit as Christ Himself would bring forth; it is indeed Christ who brings forth these fruits, Christ at a few steps removed--for every Christian learns, as well as Paul, to say, "Not I, but Christ in me." If, then, the will of Christ is not being fulfilled through us, if there is good that it belongs to us to do, but which remains undone, then the point of juncture with Christ is the point that needs looking to. It is not some unaccountable blight that makes us useless; it is not that we have got the wrong piece of the wall, a situation in which Christ Himself could bear no precious fruit. The Husbandman knew His own meaning when He trained us along that restricted line and nailed us down; He chose the place for us, knowing the quality of fruit He desires us to yield. The reason of our fruitlessness is the simple one, that we are not closely enough attached to Christ.

How, then, is it with ourselves? By examining the results of our lives, would any one be prompted to exclaim, "These are trees of righteousness, the planting of the Lord that He may be glorified"? For this examination is made, and made not by one who chances to pass, and who, being a novice in horticulture, might be deceived by a show of leaves or poor fruit, or whose examination might terminate in wonder at the slothfulness or mismanagement of the owner who allowed such trees to cumber his ground; but the examination is made by One who has come for the express purpose of gathering fruit, who knows exactly what has been spent upon us and what might have been made of our opportunities, who has in His own mind a definite idea of the fruit that should be found, and who can tell by a glance whether such fruit actually exists or no. To this infallible Judge of produce what have we to offer? From all our busy engagement in many affairs, from all our thought, what has resulted that we can offer as a satisfactory return for all that has been spent upon us? It is deeds of profitable service such as men of large and loving nature would do that God seeks from us. And He recognises without fail what is love and what only seems so. He infallibly detects the corroding spot of selfishness that rots the whole fair-seeming cluster. He stands undeceivable before us, and takes our lives precisely for what they are worth.

It concerns us to make such inquiries, for fruitless branches cannot be tolerated. The purpose of the tree is fruit. If, then, we would escape all suspicion of our own state and all reproach of fruitlessness, what we have to do is, not so much to find out new rules for conduct, as to strive to renew our hold upon Christ and intelligently to enter into His purposes. "Abide in Him." This is the secret of fruitfulness. All that the branch needs is in the Vine; it does not need to go beyond the Vine for anything. When we feel the life of Christ ebbing from our soul, when we see our leaf fading, when we feel sapless, heartless for Christian duty, reluctant to work for others, to take anything to do with the relief of misery and the repression of vice, there is a remedy for this state, and it is to renew our fellowship with Christ--to allow the mind once again to conceive clearly the worthiness of His aims, to yield the heart once again to the vitalising influence of His love, to turn from the vanities and futilities with which men strive to make life seem important to the reality and substantial worth of the life of Christ. To abide in Christ is to abide by our adoption of His view of the true purpose of human life after testing it by actual experience; it is to abide by our trust in Him as the true Lord of men, and as able to supply us with all that we need to keep His commandments. And thus abiding in Christ we are sustained by Him; for He abides in us, imparts to us, His branches now on earth, the force which is needful to accomplish His purposes.

Footnotes:

17. That the vine was a recognised symbol of the Messiah is shown by Delitzsch in the Expositor, 3rd series, vol. iii., pp. 68, 69. See also his Iris, pp. 180-190, E. Tr.

XIII. NOT SERVANTS, BUT FRIENDS

"Greater love hath no man than this, that a man lay down his life for his friends. Ye are My friends, if ye do the things which I command you. No longer do I call you servants; for the servant knoweth not what his lord doeth: but I have called you friends; for all things that I heard from My Father I have made known unto you. Ye did not choose Me, but I chose you, and appointed you, that ye should go and bear fruit, and that your fruit should abide: that whatsoever ye shall ask of the Father in My name, He may give it you. These things I command you, that ye may love one another."--John xv. 13-17.

These words of our Lord are the charter of our emancipation. They give us entrance into true freedom. They set us in the same attitude towards life and towards God as Christ Himself occupied. Without this proclamation of freedom and all it covers we are the mere drudges of this world,--doing its work, but without any great and far-reaching aim that makes it worth doing; accepting the tasks allotted to us because we must, not because we will; living on because we happen to be here, but without any part in that great future towards which all things are running on. But this is of the very essence of slavery. For our Lord here lays His finger on the sorest part of this deepest of human sores when He says, "The slave knows not what his master does." It is not that his back is torn with the lash, it is not that he is underfed and overworked, it is not that he is poor and despised; all this would be cheerfully undergone to serve a cherished purpose and accomplish ends a man had chosen for himself. But when all this must be endured to work out the purposes of another, purposes never hinted to him, and with which, were they hinted, he might have no sympathy, this is slavery, this is to be treated as a tool for accomplishing aims chosen by another, and to be robbed of all that constitutes manhood. Sailors and soldiers have sometimes mutinied when subjected to similar treatment, when no inkling has been given them of the port to which they are shipped or the nature of the expedition on which they are led. Men do not feel degraded by any amount of hardship, by going for months on short rations or lying in frost without tents; but they do feel degraded when they are used as weapons of offence, as if they had no intelligence to appreciate a worthy aim, no power of sympathising with a great design, no need of an interest in life and a worthy object on which to spend it, no share in the common cause. Yet such is the life with which, apart from Christ, we must perforce be content, doing the tasks appointed us with no sustaining consciousness that our work is part of a great whole working out the purposes of the Highest. Even such a spirit as Carlyle is driven to say: "Here on earth we are soldiers, fighting in a foreign land, that understand not the plan of campaign and have no need to understand it, seeing what is at our hand to be done,"--excellent counsel for slaves, but not descriptive of the life we are meant for, nor of the life our Lord would be content to give us.

To give us true freedom, to make this life a thing we choose with the clearest perception of its uses and with the utmost ardour, our Lord makes known to us all that He heard of the Father. What He had heard of the Father, all that the Spirit of the Father had taught Him of the need of human effort and of human righteousness, all that as He grew up to manhood He recognised of the deep-seated woes of humanity, and all that He was prompted to do for the relief of these woes, He made known to His disciples. The irresistible call to self-sacrifice and labour for the relief of men which He heard and obeyed, He made known and He makes known to all who follow Him. He did not allot clearly defined tasks to His followers; He did not treat them as slaves, appointing one to this and another to that: He showed them His own aim and His own motive, and left them as His friends to be attracted by the aim that had drawn Him, and to be ever animated with the motive that sufficed for Him. What had made His life so glorious, so full of joy, so rich in constant reward, He knew would fill their lives also; and He leaves them free to choose it for themselves, to stand before life as independent, unfettered, undriven men, and choose without compulsion what their own deepest convictions prompted them to choose. The "friend" is not compelled blindly to go through with a task whose result he does not understand or does not sympathise with; the friend is invited to share in a work in which he has a direct personal interest and to which he can give himself cordially. All life should be the forwarding of purposes we approve, the bringing about of ends we earnestly desire: all life, if we are free men, must be matter of choice, not of compulsion. And therefore Christ, having heard of the Father that which made Him feel straitened until the great aim of His life could be accomplished, which made Him press forward through life attracted and impelled by the consciousness of its infinite value as achieving endless good, imparts to us what moved and animated Him, that we may freely choose as He chose and enter into the joy of our Lord.

This, then, is the point of this great utterance: Jesus takes our lives up into partnership with His own. He sets before us the same views and hopes which animated Himself, and gives us a prospect of being useful to Him and in His work. If we engage in the work of life with a dull and heartless feeling of its weariness, or merely for the sake of gaining a livelihood, if we are not drawn to labour by the prospect of result, then we have scarcely entered into the condition our Lord opens to us. It is for the merest slaves to view their labour with indifference or repugnance. Out of this state our Lord calls us, by making known to us what the Father made known to Him, by giving us the whole means of a free, rational, and fruitful life. He gives us the fullest satisfaction moral beings can have, because He fills our life with intelligent purpose. He lifts us into a position in which we see that we are not the slaves of fate or of this world, but that all things are ours, that we, through and with Him, are masters of the position, and that so far from thinking it almost a hardship to have been born into so melancholy and hopeless a world, we have really the best reason and the highest possible object for living. He comes among us and says, "Let us all work together. Something can be made of this world. Let us with heart and hope strive to make of it something worthy. Let unity of aim and of work bind us together." This is indeed to redeem life from its vanity.

He says this, and lest any should think, "This is fantastic; how can such an one as I am forward the work of Christ? It is enough if I get from Him salvation for myself," He goes on to say, "Ye have not chosen Me, but I have chosen you, and ordained you that ye should go and bring forth fruit, and that your fruit should remain. It was," He says, "precisely in view of the eternal results of your work that I selected you and called you to follow Me." It was true then, and it is true now, that the initiative in our fellowship with Christ is with Him. So far as the first disciples were concerned Jesus might have spent His life making ploughs and cottage furniture. No one discovered Him. Neither does any one now discover Him. It is He who comes and summons us to follow and to serve Him. He does so because He sees that there is that which we can do which no one else can: relationships we hold, opportunities we possess, capacities for just this or that, which are our special property into which no other can possibly step, and which, if we do not use them, cannot otherwise be used.

Does He, then, point out to us with unmistakable exactness what we are to do, and how we are to do it? Does He lay down for us a code of rules so multifarious and significant that we cannot mistake the precise piece of work He requires from us? He does not. He has but one sole commandment, and this is no commandment, because we cannot keep it on compulsion, but only at the prompting of our own inward spirit: He bids us love one another. He comes back and back to this with significant persistence, and declines to utter one other commandment. In love alone is sufficient wisdom, sufficient motive, and sufficient reward for human life. It alone has adequate wisdom for all situations, new resource for every fresh need, adaptability to all emergencies, an inexhaustible fertility and competency; it alone can bring the capability of each to the service of all. Without love we beat the air.

That love is our true life is shown further by this--that it is its own reward. When a man's life is in any intelligible sense proceeding from love, when this is his chief motive, he is content with living, and looks for no reward. His joy is already full; he does not ask, What shall I be the better of thus sacrificing myself? what shall I gain by all this regulation of my life? what good return in the future shall I have for all I am losing now? He cannot ask these questions, if the motive of his self-sacrificing life be love; just as little as the husband could ask what reward he should have for loving his wife. A man would be astounded and would scarcely know what you meant if you asked him what he expected to get by loving his children or his parents or his friends. Get? Why he does not expect to get anything; he does not love for an object: he loves because he cannot help it; and the chief joy of his life is in these unrewarded affections. He no longer looks forward and thinks of a fulness of life that is to be; he already lives and is satisfied with the life he has. His happiness is present; his reward is that he may be allowed to express his love, to feed it, to gratify it by giving and labouring and sacrificing. In a word, he finds in love eternal life--life that is full of joy, that kindles and enlivens his whole nature, that carries him out of himself and makes him capable of all good.

This truth, then, that whatever a man does from love is its own reward, is the solution of the question whether virtue is its own reward. Virtue is its own reward when it is inspired by love. Life is its own reward when love is the principle of it. We know that we should always be happy were we always loving. We know that we should never weary of living nor turn with distaste from our work were all our work only the expression of our love, of our deep, true, and well-directed regard for the good of others. It is when we disregard our Lord's one commandment and try some other kind of virtuous living that joy departs from our life, and we begin to hope for some future reward which may compensate for the dulness of the present--as if a change of time could change the essential conditions of life and happiness. If we are not joyful now, if life is dreary and dull and pointless to us, so that we crave the excitement of a speculative business, or of boisterous social meetings, or of individual success and applause, then it should be quite plain to us that as yet we have not found life, and have not the capacity for eternal life quickened in us. If we are able to love one human being in some sort as Christ loved us--that is to say, if our affection is so fixed upon any one that we feel we could give our life for that person--let us thank God for this; for this love of ours gives us the key to human life, and will better instruct us in what is most essential to know, and lead us on to what is most essential to be and to do than any one can teach us. It is profoundly and widely true, as John says, that every one that loveth is born of God and knoweth God. If we love one human being, we at least know that a life in which love is the main element needs no reward and looks for none. We see that God looks for no reward, but is eternally blessed because simply God is eternally love. Life eternal must be a life of love, of delight in our fellows, of rejoicing in their good and seeking to increase their happiness.

Sometimes, however, we find ourselves grieving at the prosperity of the wicked: we think that they should be unhappy, and yet they seem more satisfied than ourselves. They pay no regard whatever to the law of life laid down by our Lord; they never dream of living for others; they have never once proposed to themselves to consider whether His great law, that a man must lose his life if he is to have it eternally, has any application to them; and yet they seem to enjoy life as much as anybody can. Take a man who has a good constitution, and who is in easy circumstances, and who has a good and pure nature; you will often see such a man living with no regard to the Christian rule, and yet enjoying life thoroughly to the very end. And of course it is just such a spectacle, repeated everywhere throughout society, that influences men's minds and tempts all of us to believe that such a life is best after all, and that selfishness as well as unselfishness can be happy; or at all events that we can have as much happiness as our own disposition is capable of by a self-seeking life. Now, when we are in a mood to compare our own happiness with that of other men, our own happiness must obviously be at a low ebb; but when we resent the prosperity of the wicked, we should remember that, though they may flourish like the green bay tree, their fruit does not remain: living for themselves, their fruit departs with themselves, their good is interred with their bones. But it is also to be considered that we should never allow ourselves to get the length of putting this question or of comparing our happiness with that of others. For we can only do so when we are ourselves disappointed and discontented and have missed the joy of life; and this again can be only when we have ceased to live lovingly for others.

But this one essential of Christian service and human freedom--how are we to attain it? Is it not the one thing which seems obstinately to stand beyond our grasp? For the human heart has laws of its own, and cannot love to order or admire because it ought. But Christ brings, in Himself, the fountain out of which our hearts can be supplied, the fire which kindles all who approach it. No one can receive His love without sharing it. No one can dwell upon Christ's love for him and treasure it as his true and central possession without finding his own heart enlarged and softened. Until our own heart is flooded with the great and regenerating love of Christ, we strive in vain to love our fellows. It is when we fully admit it that it overflows through our own satisfied and quickened affections to others.

And perhaps we do well not too curiously to question and finger our love, making sure only that we are keeping ourselves in Christ's fellowship and seeking to do His will. Affection, indeed, induces companionship, but also companionship produces affection, and the honest and hopeful endeavour to serve Christ loyally will have its reward in a deepening devotion. It is not the recruit but the veteran whose heart is wholly his chief's. And he who has long and faithfully served Christ will not need to ask where his heart is. We hate those whom we have injured, and we love those whom we have served; and if by long service we can win our way to an intimacy with Christ which no longer needs to question itself or test its soundness, in that service we may most joyfully engage. For what can be a happier consummation than to find ourselves finally overcome by the love of Christ, drawn with all the force of a Divine attraction, convinced that here is our rest, and that this is at once our motive and our reward?

Marcus Dods, D.D.

XIV. THE SPIRIT CHRIST'S WITNESS

"If the world hateth you, ye know that it hath hated Me before it hated you. If ye were of the world, the world would love its own: but because ye are not of the world, but I chose you out of the world, therefore the world hateth you. Remember the word that I said unto you, A servant is not greater than his lord. If they persecuted Me, they will also persecute you; if they kept My word, they will keep yours also. But all these things will they do unto you for My name's sake, because they know not Him that sent Me. If I had not come and spoken unto them, they had not had sin: but now they have no excuse for their sin. He that hateth Me hateth My Father also. If I had not done among them the works which none other did, they had not had sin: but now have they both seen and hated both Me and My Father. But this cometh to pass, that the word may be fulfilled that is written in their law, They hated Me without a cause. But when the Comforter is come, whom I will send unto you from the Father, even the Spirit of truth, which proceedeth from the Father, He shall bear witness of Me: and ye also bear witness, because ye have been with Me from the beginning. These things have I spoken unto you, that ye should not be made to stumble. They shall put you out of the synagogues: yea, the hour cometh, that whosoever killeth you shall think that he offereth service unto God. And these things will they do, because they have not known the Father, nor Me. But these things have I spoken unto you, that when their hour is come, ye may remember them, how that I told you. And these things I said not unto you from the beginning, because I was with you. But now I go unto Him that sent Me; and none of you asketh Me, Whither goest Thou? But because I have spoken these things unto you, sorrow hath filled your heart. Nevertheless I tell you the truth; It is expedient for you that I go away: for if I go not away, the Comforter will not come unto you; but if I go, I will send Him unto you. And He, when He is come, will convict the world in respect of sin, and of righteousness, and of judgment: of sin, because they believe not on Me; of righteousness, because I go to the Father, and ye behold Me no more; of judgment, because the prince of this world hath been judged. I have yet many things to say unto you, but ye cannot bear them now. Howbeit when He, the Spirit of truth, is come, He shall guide you into all the truth: for He shall not speak from Himself; but what things soever He shall hear, these shall He speak: and He shall declare unto you the things that are to come. He shall glorify Me: for He shall take of Mine, and shall declare it unto you. All things whatsoever the Father hath are Mine: therefore said I, that He taketh of Mine, and shall declare it unto you."--John xv. 18-xvi. 15.

Having shown His disciples that by them only can His purposes on earth be fulfilled, and that He will fit them for all work that may be required of them, the Lord now adds that their task will be full of hazard and hardship: "They shall put you out of the synagogues: yea, the time cometh that whosoever killeth you will think that he offereth service unto God." This was but a dreary prospect, and one to make each Apostle hesitate, and in the privacy of his own thoughts consider whether he should face a life so devoid of all that men naturally crave. To live for great ends is no doubt animating, but to be compelled in doing so to abandon all expectation of recognition, and to lay one's account for abuse, poverty, persecution, calls for some heroism in him that undertakes such a life. He forewarns them of this persecution, that when it comes they may not be taken aback and fancy that things are not falling out with them as their Lord anticipated. And He offers them two strong consolations which might uphold and animate them under all they should be called upon to suffer.

I. "If the world hateth you, ye know that it hath hated Me before it hated you. If ye were of the world, the world would love its own; but because ye are not of the world, but I chose you out of the world, therefore the world hateth you." Persecution is thus turned into a joy, because it is the testimony paid by the world to the disciples' identity with Christ. The love of the world would be a sure evidence of their unfaithfulness to Christ and of their entire lack of resemblance to Him; but its hate was the tribute it would pay to their likeness to Him and successful promotion of His cause. They might well question their loyalty to Christ, if the world which had slain Him fawned upon them. The Christian may conclude he is reckoned a helpless and harmless foe if he suffers no persecution, if in no company he is frowned upon or felt to be uncongenial, if he is treated by the world as if its aims were his aims and its spirit his spirit. No faithful follower of Christ who mixes with society can escape every form of persecution. It is the seal which the world puts on the choice of Christ. It is proof that a man's attachment to Christ and endeavour to forward His purposes have been recognised by the world. Persecution, then, should be welcome as the world's testimony to the disciple's identity with Christ.

No idea had fixed itself more deeply in the mind of John than this of the identity of Christ and His people. As he brooded upon the life of Christ and sought to penetrate to the hidden meanings of all that appeared on the surface, he came to see that the unbelief and hatred with which He was met was the necessary result of goodness presented to worldliness and selfishness. And as time went on he saw that the experience of Christ was exceptional only in degree, that His experience was and would be repeated in every one who sought to live in His Spirit and to do His will. The future of the Church accordingly presented itself to him as a history of conflict, of extreme cruelty on the part of the world and quiet conquering endurance on the part of Christ's people. And it was this which he embodied in the Book of Revelation. This book he wrote as a kind of detailed commentary on the passage before us, and in it he intended to depict the sufferings and final conquest of the Church. The one book is a reflex and supplement to the other; and as in the Gospel he had shown the unbelief and cruelty of the world against Christ, so in the Revelation he shows in a series of strongly coloured pictures how the Church of Christ would pass through the same experience, would be persecuted as Christ was persecuted, but would ultimately conquer. Both books are wrought out with extreme care and finished to the minutest detail, and both deal with the cardinal matters of human history--sin, righteousness, and the final result of their conflict. Underneath all that appears on the surface in the life of the individual and in the history of the race there are just these abiding elements--sin and righteousness. It is the moral value of things which in the long run proves of consequence, the moral element which ultimately determines all else.

II. The second consolation and encouragement the Lord gave them was that they would receive the aid of a powerful champion--the Paraclete, the one effectual, sufficient Helper. "When the Paraclete is come, whom I will send unto you from the Father, even the Spirit of truth, which proceedeth from the Father, he shall bear witness of Me: and ye also bear witness, because ye have been with Me from the beginning." Inevitably the disciples would argue that, if the words and works of Jesus Himself had not broken down the unbelief of the world, it was not likely that anything which they could say or do would have that effect. If the impressive presence of Christ Himself had not attracted and convinced all men, how was it possible that mere telling about what He had said and done and been would convince them? And He has just been reminding them how little effect His own words and works had had. "If I had not come and spoken unto them, they had not had sin: ... if I had not done among them the works which none other did, they had not had sin: but now have they both seen and hated both Me and My Father." What power, then, could break down this obstinate unbelief?

Our Lord assures them that together with their witness-bearing there will be an all-powerful witness--"the Spirit of truth"; one who could find access to the hearts and minds to which they addressed themselves and carry truth home to conviction. It was on this account that it was "expedient" that their Lord should depart, and that His visible presence should be superseded by the presence of the Spirit. It was necessary that His death, resurrection, and ascension to the right hand of the Father should take place, in order that His supremacy might be secured. And in order that He might be everywhere and inwardly present with men, it was necessary that He should be visible nowhere on earth. The inward spiritual presence depended on the bodily absence.

Before passing to the specific contents of the Spirit's testimony, as stated in vv. 8-11, it is necessary to gather up what our Lord indicates regarding the Spirit Himself and His function in the Christian dispensation. First, the Spirit here spoken of is a personal existence. Throughout all that our Lord says in this last conversation regarding the Spirit personal epithets are applied to Him, and the actions ascribed to Him are personal actions. He is to be the substitute of the most marked and influential Personality with whom the disciples had ever been brought in contact. He is to supply His vacated place. He is to be to the disciples as friendly and staunch an ally and a more constantly present and efficient teacher than Christ Himself. What as yet was not in their minds He was to impart to them; and He was to mediate and maintain communication between the absent Lord and themselves. Was it possible that the disciples should think of the Spirit otherwise than as a conscious and energetic Person when they heard Him spoken of in such words as these: "Howbeit when He, the Spirit of truth, is come, He shall guide you into all the truth: for He shall not speak from Himself; but what things soever He shall hear, these shall He speak: and He shall declare unto you the things that are to come. He shall glorify Me: for He shall take of Mine, and shall declare it unto you"? From these words it would seem as if the disciples were justified in expecting the presence and aid of One who was very closely related to their Lord, but yet distinct from Him, who could understand their state of mind and adapt Himself to them, who is not identical with the Master they are losing, and yet comes into still closer contact with them. What underlies this, and what is the very nature of the Spirit and His relation to the Father and the Son, we do not know; but our Lord chose these expressions which to our thought involve personality because this is the truest and safest form under which we can now conceive of the Spirit.

The function for the discharge of which this Spirit is necessary is the "glorification" of Christ. Without Him the manifestation of Christ will be lost. He is needed to secure that the world be brought into contact with Christ, and that men recognise and use Him. This is the most general and comprehensive aspect of the Spirit's work: "He shall glorify Me" (ver. 14). In making this announcement our Lord assumes that position of commanding importance with which this Gospel has made us familiar. The Divine Spirit is to be sent forth, and the direct object of His mission is the glorifying of Christ. The meaning of Christ's manifestation is the essential thing for men to understand. In manifesting Himself He has revealed the Father. He has in His own person shown what a Divine nature is; and therefore in order to His glorification all that is required is that light be shed upon what He has done and been, and that the eyes of men be opened to see Him and His work. The recognition of Christ and of God in Him is the blessedness of the human race; and to bring this about is the function of the Spirit. As Jesus Himself had constantly presented Himself as the revealer of the Father and as speaking His words, so, in "a rivalry of Divine humility," the Spirit glorifies the Son and speaks "what He shall hear."

To discharge this function a twofold ministry is undertaken by the Spirit: He must enlighten the Apostles, and He must convince the world.

He must enlighten the Apostles. From the nature of the case much had to be left unsaid by Christ. But this would not prevent the Apostles from understanding what Christ had done, and what applications His work had to themselves and their fellow-men. "I have yet many things to say unto you, but ye cannot bear them now. Howbeit when He, the Spirit of truth, is come, He will guide you into all the truth." A great untravelled country lay before them. Their Master had led them across its border, and set their faces in the right direction; but who was to find a way for them through all its intricacies and perplexities? The Spirit of truth, He who is Himself perfect knowledge and absolute light, "will guide you"; He will go before you and show you your way. [18] There may be no sudden impartation of truth, no lifting of the mist that hangs on the horizon, no consciousness that now you have mastered all difficulties and can see your way to the end; there may be no violation of the natural and difficult processes by which men arrive at truth; the road may be slow, and sometimes there may even be an appearance of ignominious defeat by those who use swifter but more precarious means of advance; much will depend on your own patience and wakefulness and docility; but if you admit the Spirit, He will guide you into all the truth.

This promise does not involve that the Apostles, and through them all disciples, should know everything. "All the truth" is relative to the subject taught. All that they need to know regarding Christ and His work for them they will learn. All that is needed to glorify Christ, to enable men to recognise Him as the manifestation of God, will be imparted. To the truth which the Apostles learn, therefore, nothing need be added. Nothing essential has been added. Time has now been given to test this promise, and what time has shown is this--that while libraries have been written on what the Apostles thought and taught, their teaching remains as the sufficient guide into all the truth regarding Christ. Even in non-essentials it is marvellous how little has been added. Many corrections of misapprehensions of their meaning have been required, much laborious inquiry to ascertain precisely what they meant, much elaborate inference and many buildings upon their foundations; but in their teaching there remain a freshness and a living force which survive all else that has been written upon Christ and His religion.

This instruction of the Apostles by the Spirit was to recall to their minds what Christ Himself had said, and was also to show them things to come. The changed point of view introduced by the dispensation of the Spirit and the abolition of earthly hopes would cause many of the sayings of Jesus which they had disregarded and considered unintelligible to spring into high relief and ray out significance, while the future also would shape itself quite differently in their conception. And the Teacher who should superintend and inspire this altered attitude of mind is the Spirit. [19]

Not only must the Spirit enlighten the Apostles; He must also convince the world. "He shall bear witness of Me," and by His witness-bearing the testimony of the Apostles would become efficacious. They had a natural fitness to witness about Christ, "because they had been with Him from the beginning." No more trustworthy witnesses regarding what Christ had said or done or been could be called than those men with whom He had lived on terms of intimacy. No men could more certainly testify to the identity of the risen Lord. But the significance of the facts they spoke of could best be taught by the Spirit. The very fact of the Spirit's presence was the greatest evidence that the Lord had risen and was using "all power in heaven" in behalf of men. And possibly it was to this Peter referred when he said: "We are His witnesses of these things; and so is also the Holy Ghost, whom God hath given to them that obey Him." Certainly the gifts of the Holy Ghost, the power to speak with tongues or to work miracles of healing, were accepted by the primitive Church as a seal of the Apostolic word and as the appropriate evidence of the power of the risen Christ.

But it is apparent from our Lord's description of the subject-matter of the Spirit's witness that here He has especially in view the function of the Spirit as an inward teacher and strengthener of the moral powers. He is the fellow-witness of the Apostles, mainly and permanently, by enlightening men in the significance of the facts reported by them, and by opening the heart and conscience to their influence.

The subject-matter of the Spirit's testimony is threefold: "He will convict the world in respect of sin, and of righteousness, and of judgment."

I. He should convict the world of sin. No conviction cuts so deeply and produces results of such magnitude as the conviction of sin. It is like subsoil ploughing: it turns up soil that nothing else has got down to. It alters entirely a man's attitude towards life. He cannot know himself a sinner and be satisfied with that condition. This awakening is like the waking of one who has been buried in a trance, who wakes to find himself bound round with grave-clothes, hemmed in with all the insignia of corruption, terror and revulsion distracting and overwhelming his soul. In spirit he has been far away, weaving perhaps a paradise out of his fancies, peopling it with choice and happy society, and living through scenes of gorgeous beauty and comfort in fulness of interest and life and felicity; but suddenly comes the waking, a few brief moments of painful struggle and the dream gives place to the reality, and then comes the certain accumulation of misery till the spirit breaks beneath its fear. So does the strongest heart groan and break when it wakes to the full reality of sin, when the Spirit of Christ takes the veil from a man's eyes and gives him to see what this world is and what he has been in it, when the shadows that have occupied him flee away and the naked inevitable reality confronts him.

Nothing is more overwhelming than this conviction, but nothing is more hopeful. Given a man who is alive to the evil of sin and who begins to understand his errors, and you know some good will come of that. Given a man who sees the importance of being in accord with perfect goodness and who feels the degradation of sin, and you have the germ of all good in that man. But how were the Apostles to produce this? how were they to dispel those mists which blurred the clear outline of good and evil, to bring to the self-righteous Pharisee and the indifferent and worldly Sadducee a sense of their own sin? What instrument is there which can introduce to every human heart, howsoever armoured and fenced round, this healthy revolution? Looking at men as they actually are, and considering how many forces are banded together to exclude the knowledge of sin, how worldly interest demands that no brand shall be affixed to this and that action, how the customs we are brought up in require us to take a lenient view of this and that immorality, how we deceive ourselves by sacrificing sins we do not care for in order to retain sins that are in our blood, how the resistance of certain sins makes us a prey to self-righteousness and delusion--considering what we have learnt of the placidity with which men content themselves with a life they know is not the highest, does there seem to be any instrument by which a true and humbling sense of sin can be introduced to the mind?

Christ, knowing that men were about to put Him to death because He had tried to convict them of sin, confidently predicts that His servants would by His Spirit's aid convince the world of sin and of this in particular--that they had not believed in Him. That very death which chiefly exhibits human sin has, in fact, become the chief instrument in making men understand and hate sin. There is no consideration from which the deceitfulness of sin will not escape, nor any fear which the recklessness of sin will not brave, nor any authority which self-will cannot override but only this: Christ has died for me, to save me from my sin, and I am sinning still, not regarding His blood, not meeting His purpose. It was when the greatness and the goodness of Christ were together let in to Peter's mind that he fell on his face before Him, saying, "Depart from me, O Lord, for I am a sinful man." And the experience of thousands is recorded in that more recent confession:

> "In evil long I took delight, unawed by shame or fear,
> Till a new object struck my sight and stopped my wild career:
> I saw One hanging on a tree in agonies and blood.
> Who fixed His languid eyes on me as near His cross I stood.
> Sure never till my latest breath can I forget that look;
> It seemed to charge me with His death, though not a word He spoke."

Of other convictions we may get rid; the consequences of sin we may brave, or we may disbelieve that in our case sin will produce any very disastrous fruits; but in the death of Christ we see, not what sin may possibly do in the future, but what it actually has done in the past. In presence of the death of Christ we cannot any longer make a mock of sin or think lightly of it, as if it were on our own responsibility and at our own risk we sinned.

But not only does the death of Christ exhibit the intricate connections of our sin with other persons and the grievous consequence of sin in general, but also it exhibits the enormity of this particular sin of rejecting Christ. "He will convince the world of sin, because they believe not on Me." It was this sin in point of fact which cut to the heart the crowd at Jerusalem first addressed by Peter. Peter had nothing to say of their looseness of life, of their worldliness, of their covetousness: he did not go into particulars of conduct calculated to bring a blush to their cheeks; he took up but one point, and by a few convincing remarks showed them the enormity of crucifying the Lord of glory. The lips which a few days before had cried out "Crucify Him, crucify Him!" now cried, Men and brethren, what shall we do, how escape from the crushing condemnation of mistaking God's image for a criminal? In that hour Christ's words were fulfilled; they were convinced of sin because they believed not on Him.

This is ever the damning sin--to be in presence of goodness and not to love it, to see Christ and to see Him with unmoved and unloving hearts, to hear His call without response, to recognise the beauty of holiness and yet turn away to lust and self and the world. This is the condemnation--that light is come into the world and we have loved darkness rather than the light. "If I had not come and spoken unto them, they had not had sin: but now they have no cloke for their sin. He that hateth Me, hateth My Father also." To turn away from Christ is to turn away from absolute goodness. It is to show that however much we may relish certain virtues and approve particular forms of goodness, goodness absolute and complete does not attract us.

II. The conviction of righteousness is the complement, the other half, of the conviction of sin. In the shame of guilt there is the germ of the conviction of righteousness. The sense of guilt is but the acknowledgment that we ought to be righteous. No guilt attaches to the incapable. The sting of guilt is poisoned with the knowledge that we were capable of better things. Conscience exclaims against all excuses that would lull us into the idea that sin is insuperable, and that there is nothing better for us than a moderately sinful life. When conscience ceases to condemn, hope dies. A mist rises from sin that obscures the clear outline between its own domain and that of righteousness, like the mist that rises from the sea and mingles shore and water in one undefined cloud. But let it rise off the one and the other is at once distinctly marked out; and so in the conviction of sin there is already involved the conviction of righteousness. The blush of shame that suffuses the face of the sinner as the mist-dispelling Sun of righteousness arises upon him is the morning flush and promise of an everlasting day of righteous living.

For each of us it is of the utmost importance to have a fixed and intelligent persuasion that righteousness is what we are made for. The righteous Lord loveth righteousness and made us in His image to widen the joy of rational creatures. He waits for righteousness and cannot accept sin as an equally grateful fruit of men's lives. And though in the main perhaps our faces are turned towards righteousness, and we are on the whole dissatisfied and ashamed of sin, yet the conviction of righteousness has much to struggle against in us all. Sin, we unconsciously plead, is so finely interwoven with all the ways of the world that it is impossible to live wholly free from it. As well cast a sponge into the water and command that it absorb none nor sink as put me in the world and command that I do not admit its influences or sink to its level. It presses in on me through all my instincts and appetites and hopes and fears; it washes ceaselessly at the gateways of my senses, so that one unguarded moment and the torrent bursts in on me and pours over my wasted bulwarks, resolves, high aims, and whatever else. It is surely not now and here that I am expected to do more than learn the rudiments of righteous living and make small experiments in it; endeavours will surely stand for accomplishment, and pious purposes in place of heroic action and positive righteousness. Men take sin for granted and lay their account for it. Will not God also, who remembers our frailty, consider the circumstances and count sin a matter of course? Such thoughts haunt and weaken us; but every man whose heart is touched by the Spirit of God clings to this as his hopeful prayer: "Teach me to do Thy will, for Thou art my God: Thy Spirit is good; lead me into the land of uprightness."

But, after all, it is by fact men are convinced; and were there no facts to appeal to in this matter conviction could not be attained. It does seem that we are made for righteousness, but sin is in this world so universal that there must surely be some way of accounting for it which shall also excuse it. Had righteousness been to be our life, surely some few would have attained it. There must be some necessity of sin, some impossibility of attaining perfect righteousness, and therefore we need not seek it. Here comes in the proof our Lord speaks of: "The Spirit will convince of righteousness, because I go to the Father." Righteousness has been attained. There has lived One, bone of our bone, and flesh of our flesh, tempted in all points like as we are, open to the same ambitious views of life, growing up with the same appetites and as sensitive to bodily pleasure and bodily pain, feeling as keenly the neglect and hatred of men, and from the very size of His nature and width of His sympathy tempted in a thousand ways we are safe from, and yet in no instance confounding right and wrong, in no instance falling from perfect harmony with the Divine will to self-will and self-seeking; never deferring the commandments of God to some other sphere or waiting for holier times; never forgetting and never renouncing the purpose of God in His life; but at all times, in weariness and lassitude, in personal danger and in domestic comfort, putting Himself as a perfect instrument into God's hand, ready at all cost to Himself to do the Father's will. Here was One who not only recognised that men are made to work together with God, but who actually did so work; who not only approved, as we all approve, of a life of holiness and sacrifice, but actually lived it; who did not think the trial too great, the privation and risk too dreadful, the self-effacement too humbling; but who met life with all it brings to all of us--its conflict, its interests, its opportunities, its allurements, its snares, its hazards. But while out of this material we fail to make a perfect life, He by His integrity of purpose and devotedness and love of good fashioned a perfect life. Thus He simply by living accomplished what the law with its commands and threats had not accomplished: He condemned sin in the flesh.

But it was open to those whom the Apostles addressed to deny that Jesus had thus lived; and therefore the conviction of righteousness is completed by the evidence of the resurrection and ascension of Christ. "Of righteousness, because I go to My Father, and ye see Me no more." Without holiness no man shall see God. It was this that the Apostles appealed to when first moved to address their fellow-men and proclaim Christ as the Saviour. It was to His resurrection they confidently appealed as evidence of the truth of His claim to have been sent of God. The Jews had put Him to death as a deceiver; but God proclaimed His righteousness by raising Him from the dead. "Ye denied the Holy One and the Just, and desired a murderer to be granted unto you, and killed the Prince of life whom God hath raised from the dead, whereof we are witnesses."

Probably, however, another idea underlies the words "because I go to My Father, and ye see Me no more." So long as Christ was on earth the Jews believed that Jesus and His followers were plotting a revolution: when He was removed beyond sight such a suspicion became ludicrous. But when His disciples could no longer see Him, they continued to serve Him and to strive with greater zeal than ever to promote His cause. Slowly then it dawned on men's minds that righteousness was what Christ and His Apostles alone desired and sought to establish on earth. This new spectacle of men devoting their lives to the advancement of righteousness, and confident they could establish a kingdom of righteousness and actually establishing it--this spectacle penetrated men's minds, and gave them a new sense of the value of righteousness, and quite a new conviction of the possibility of attaining it.

III. The third conviction by which the Apostles were to prevail in their preaching of Christ was the conviction "of judgment, because the prince of this world is judged." Men were to be persuaded that a distinction is made between sin and righteousness, that in no case can sin pass for righteousness and righteousness for sin. The world that has worldly ends in view and works towards them by appropriate means, disregarding moral distinctions, will be convicted of enormous error. The Spirit of truth will work in men's minds the conviction that all and every sin is mistake and productive of nothing good, and can in no instance accomplish what righteousness would have accomplished. Men will find, when truth shines in their spirit, that they have not to await a great day of judgment in the end, when the good results of sin shall be reversed and reward allotted to those who have done righteously, but that judgment is a constant and universal element in God's government and to be found everywhere throughout it, distinguishing between sin and righteousness in every present instance, and never for one moment allowing to sin the value or the results which only righteousness has. In the minds of men who have been using the world's unrighteous methods and living for the world's selfish ends, the conviction is to be wrought that no good can come of all that--that sin is sin and not valid for any good purpose. Men are to recognise that a distinction is made between human actions, and that condemnation is pronounced on all that are sinful.

And this conviction is to be wrought in the light of the fact that in Christ's victory the prince of this world is judged. The powers by which the world is actually led are seen to be productive of evil, and not the powers by which men can permanently be led or should at any time have been led. The prince of this world was judged by Christ's refusal throughout His life to be in anything guided by him. The motives by which the world is led were not Christ's motives.

But it is in the death of Christ the prince of this world was especially judged. That death was brought about by the world's opposition to unworldliness. Had the world been seeking spiritual beauty and prosperity, Christ would not have been crucified. He was crucified because the world was seeking material gain and worldly glory, and was thereby blinded to the highest form of goodness. And unquestionably the very fact that worldliness led to this treatment of Christ is its most decided condemnation. We cannot think highly of principles and dispositions which so blind men to the highest form of human goodness and lead them to actions so unreasonable and wicked. As an individual will often commit one action which illustrates his whole character, and flashes sudden light into the hidden parts of it, and discloses its capabilities and possible results, so the world has in this one act shown what worldliness essentially is and at all times is capable of. No stronger condemnation of the influences which move worldly men can be found than the crucifixion of Christ.

But, besides, the death of Christ exhibits in so touching a form the largeness and power of spiritual beauty, and brings so vividly home to the heart the charm of holiness and love, that here more than anywhere else do men learn to esteem beauty of character and holiness and love more than all the world can yield them. We feel that to be wholly out of sympathy with the qualities and ideas manifested in the Cross would be a pitiable condition. We adopt as our ideal the kind of glory there revealed, and in our hearts condemn the opposed style of conduct that the world leads to. As we open our understanding and conscience to the meaning of Christ's love and sacrifice and devotedness to God's will, the prince of this world is judged and condemned within us. We feel that to yield to the powers that move and guide the world is impossible for us, and that we must give ourselves to this Prince of holiness and spiritual glory.

In point of fact the world is judged. To adhere to worldly motives and ways and ambitions is to cling to a sinking ship, to throw ourselves away on a justly doomed cause. The world may trick itself out in what delusive splendours it may; it is judged all the same, and men who are deluded by it and still in one way or other acknowledge the prince of this world destroy themselves and lose the future.

Such was the promise of Christ to His disciples. Is it fulfilled in us? We may have witnessed in others the entrance and operation of convictions which to all appearance correspond with those here described. We may even have been instrumental in producing these convictions. But a lens of ice will act as a burning-glass, and itself unmelted will fire the tinder to which it transmits the rays. And perhaps we may be able to say with much greater confidence that we have done good than that we are good. Convinced of sin we may be, and convinced of righteousness we may be--so far at least as to feel most keenly that the distinction between sin and righteousness is real, wide, and of eternal consequence--but is the prince of this world judged? has the power that claims us as the servants of sin and mocks our strivings after righteousness been, so far as we can judge from our own experience, defeated? For this is the final test of religion, of our faith in Christ, of the truth of His words and the efficacy of His work. Does He accomplish in me what He promised?

Now, when we begin to doubt the efficacy of the Christian method on account of its apparent failure in our own case, when we see quite clearly how it ought to work and as clearly that it has not worked, when this and that turns up in our life and proves beyond controversy that we are ruled by much the same motives and desires as the world at large, two subjects of reflection present themselves. First, have we remembered the word of Christ, "The servant is not greater than his Lord"? Are we so anxious to be His servants that we would willingly sacrifice whatever stood in the way of our serving Him? Are we content to be as He was in the world? There are always many in the Christian Church who are, first, men of the world, and, secondly, varnished with Christianity; who do not seek first the kingdom of God and His righteousness; who do not yet understand that the whole of life must be consecrated to Christ and spring from His will, and who therefore without compunction do make themselves greater in every worldly respect than their professed Lord. There are also many in the Christian Church at all times who decline to make more of this world than Christ Himself did, and whose constant study it is to put all they have at His disposal. Now, we cannot too seriously inquire to which of these classes we belong. Are we making a bonâ-fide thing of our attachment to Christ? Do we feel it in every part of our life? Do we strive, not to minimise our service and His claims, but to be wholly His? Have His words, "The servant is not greater than his Lord," any meaning to us at all? Is His service truly the main thing we seek in life? I say we should seriously inquire if this is so; for not hereafter, but now, are we finally determining our relation to all things by our relation to Christ.

But, secondly, we must beware of disheartening ourselves by hastily concluding that in our case Christ's grace has failed. If we may accept the Book of Revelation as a true picture, not merely of the conflict of the Church, but also of the conflict of the individual, then only in the end can we look for quiet and achieved victory--only in the closing chapters does conflict cease and victory seem no more doubtful. If it is to be so with us, the fact of our losing some of the battles must not discourage us from continuing the campaign. Nothing is more painful and humbling than to find ourselves falling into unmistakable sin after much concernment with Christ and His grace; but the very resentment we feel and the deep and bitter humiliation must be used as incentive to further effort, and must not be allowed to sound permanent defeat and surrender to sin.

Footnotes:

18. hodegesei.

19. Godet says: "The saying xiv. 26 gives the formula of the inspiration of our Gospels; ver. 13 gives that of the inspiration of the Epistles and the Apocalypse."

XV. LAST WORDS

"A little while, and ye behold Me no more; and again a little while, and ye shall see Me. Some of His disciples therefore said one to another, What is this that He saith unto us, A little while, and ye behold Me not; and again a little while, and ye shall see Me: and, Because I go to the Father? They said therefore, What is this that He saith, A little while? We know not what He saith. Jesus perceived that they were desirous to ask Him, and He said unto them, Do ye inquire among yourselves concerning this, that I said, A little while, and ye behold Me not, and again a little while, and ye shall see Me? Verily, verily, I say unto you, that ye shall weep and lament, but the world shall rejoice: ye shall be sorrowful, but your sorrow shall be turned into joy. A woman when she is in travail hath sorrow, because her hour is come: but when she is delivered of the child, she remembereth no more the anguish, for the joy that a man is born into the world. And ye therefore now have sorrow: but I will see you again, and your heart shall rejoice, and your joy no one taketh away from you. And in that day ye shall ask Me nothing. Verily, verily, I say unto you, If ye shall ask anything of the Father, He will give it you in My name. Hitherto have ye asked nothing in My name: ask, and ye shall receive, that your joy may be fulfilled. These things have I spoken unto you in proverbs: the hour cometh, when I shall no more speak unto you in proverbs, but shall tell you plainly of the Father. In that day ye shall ask in My name: and I say not unto you, that I will pray the Father for you; for the Father Himself loveth you, because ye have loved Me, and have believed that I came forth from the Father. I came out from the Father, and am come into the world: again, I leave the world, and go unto the Father. His disciples say, Lo, now speakest Thou plainly, and speakest no proverb. Now know we that Thou knowest all things, and needest not that any man should ask Thee: by this we believe that Thou camest forth from God. Jesus answered them, Do ye now believe? Behold, the hour cometh, yea, is come, that ye shall be scattered, every man to his own, and shall leave Me alone: and yet I am not alone, because the Father is with Me. These things have I spoken unto you, that in Me ye may have peace. In the world ye have tribulation: but be of good cheer; I have overcome the world."--John xvi. 16-33.

In the intercourse of Jesus with His disciples He at all times showed one of the most delightful qualities of a friend--a quick and perfect apprehension of what was passing in their mind. They did not require to bring their mental condition before Him by laboured explanations. He knew what was in man, and He especially knew what was in them. He could forecast the precise impression which His announcements would make upon them, the doubts and the expectations they would give rise to. Sometimes they were surprised at this insight, always they profited by it. In fact, on more occasions than one this insight convinced them that Jesus had this clear knowledge of men given to Him that He might effectually deal with all men. It seemed to them, as of course it is, one of the essential equipments of One who is to be a real centre for the whole race and to bring help to each and all men. How could a person who was deficient in this universal sympathy and practical understanding of the very thoughts of each of us offer himself as our helper? There is therefore evidence in the life of Jesus that He was never non-plussed, never at a loss to understand the kind of man He had to do with. There is evidence of this, and it would seem that we all receive this evidence; for are we not conscious that our spiritual condition is understood, our thoughts traced, our difficulties sympathised with? We may feel very unlike many prominent Christians; we may have no sympathy with a great deal that passes for Christian sentiment; but Christ's sympathy is universal, and nothing human comes wrong to Him. Begin with Him as you are, without professing to be, though hoping to be, different from what you are, and by the growth of your own spirit in the sunshine of His presence and under the guidance of His intelligent sympathy your doubts will pass away, your ungodliness be renounced. He is offered for your help as the essential condition of your progress and your growth.

Seeing the perplexity which certain of His expressions had created in the minds of His disciples, He proceeds to remove it. They had great need of hopefulness and courage, and He sought to inspire them with these qualities. They were on the edge of a most bitter experience, and it was of untold consequence that they should be upheld in it. He does not hide from them the coming distress, but He reminds them that very commonly pain and anxiety accompany the birth-throes of a new life; and if they found themselves shortly in depression and grief which seemed inconsolable, they were to believe that this was the path to a new and higher phase of existence and to a joy that would be lasting. Your grief, He says, will shortly end: your joy never. Your grief will soon be taken away: your joy no one shall take away. When Christ rose again, the disciples remembered and understood these words; and a few chapters further on we find John returning upon the word and saying, "When they saw the Lord, they were glad,"--they had this joy. It was a joy to them, because love for Christ and hope in Him were their dominant feelings. They had the joy of having their Friend again, of seeing Him victorious and proved to be all and more than they had believed. They had the first glowing visions of a new world for which the preparation was the life and resurrection of the Son of God. What were they not prepared to hope for as the result of the immeasurably great things they had themselves seen and known? It was a mere question now of Christ's will: of His power they were assured.

The resurrection of Christ was, however, meant to bring lasting joy, not to these men only, but to all. These greatest of all events, the descent to earth of the Son of God with all Divine power and love, and His resurrection as the conqueror of all that bars the path of men from a life of light and joy, became solid facts in this world's history, that all men might calculate their future by such a past, and might each for himself conclude that a future of which such events are the preparation must be great and happy indeed. Death, if not in all respects the most desolating, is the most certain of all human ills. Anguish and mourning it has brought and will bring to many human hearts. Do what we will we cannot save our friends from it; by us it is unconquerable. Yet it is in this most calamitous of human ills God has shown His nearness and His love. It is to the death of Christ men look to see the full brightness of God's fatherly love. It is this darkest point of human experience that God has chosen to irradiate with His absorbing glory. Death is at once our gravest fear and the spring of our hope; it cuts short human intercourse, but in the cross of Christ it gives us a never-failing, divinely loving Friend. The death of Christ is the great compensation of all the ill that death has brought into human life; and when we see death made the medium of God's clearest manifestation, we are almost grateful to it for affording material for an exhibition of God's love which transforms all our own life and all our own hopes.

Lasting joy is the condition in which God desires us to be, and He has given us cause of joy. In Christ's victory we see all that is needed to give us hopefulness about the future. Each man finds for himself assurance of God's interest in us and in our actual condition: assurance that whatever is needful to secure for us a happy eternity has been done; assurance that in a new heavens and a new earth we shall find lasting satisfaction. This true, permanent, all-embracing joy is open to all, and is actually enjoyed by those who have something of Christ's Spirit, whose chief desire is to see holiness prevail and to keep themselves and others in harmony with God. To such the accomplishment of God's will seems a certainty, and they have learned that the accomplishment of that will means good to them and to all who love God. The holiness and harmony with God that win this joy are parts of it. To be the friends of Christ, imbued with His views of life and of God, this from first to last is a thing of joy.

That which the disciples at length believed and felt to be the culmination of their faith was that Jesus had come forth from God. He Himself more fully expresses what He desired them to believe about Him in the words: "I came forth from the Father, and am come into the world: again I leave the world, and go to the Father." No doubt there is a sense in which any man may use this language of himself. We can all truthfully say we came forth from God and came into the world; and we pass out from the world and return to God. But that the disciples did not understand the words in this sense is obvious from the difficulty they found in reaching this belief. Had Jesus merely meant that it was true of Him, as of all others, that God is the great existence out of whom we spring and to whom we return, the disciples could have found no difficulty and the Jews must all have believed in Him. In some special and exceptional sense, then, He came forth from God. What, then, was this sense?

When Nicodemus came to Jesus, he addressed Him as a teacher "come from God," because, he added, "no man can do these miracles which Thou doest except God be with Him." In Nicodemus' lips, therefore, the words "a teacher come from God" meant a teacher with a Divine mission and credentials. In this sense all the prophets were teachers "come from God." And accordingly many careful readers of the Gospels believe that nothing more than this is meant by any of those expressions our Lord uses of Himself, as "sent from God," "come forth from God," and so on. The only distinction, it is supposed, between Christ and other prophets is that He is more highly endowed, is commissioned and equipped as God's representative in a more perfect degree than Moses or Samuel or Elijah. He had their power to work miracles, their authority in teaching; but having a more important mission to accomplish, He had this power and authority more fully. Now, it is quite certain that some of the expressions which a careless reader might think conclusive in proof of Christ's divinity were not intended to express anything more than that He was God's commissioner. Indeed, it is remarkable how He Himself seems to wish men to believe this above all else--that He was sent by God. In reading the Gospel of John one is tempted to say that Jesus almost intentionally avoids affirming His divinity explicitly and directly when there seemed opportunity to do so. Certainly His main purpose was to reveal the Father, to bring men to understand that His teaching about God was true, and that He was sent by God.

There are, however, some expressions which unquestionably affirm Christ's pre-existence, and convince us that before He appeared in this world He lived with God. And among these expressions the words He uses in this passage hold a place: "I came forth from the Father, and am come into the world:

again, I leave the world, and go to the Father." These words, the disciples felt, lifted a veil from their eyes; they told Him at once that they found an explicitness in this utterance which had been a-wanting in others. And, indeed, nothing could be more explicit: the two parts of the sentence balance and interpret one another. "I leave the world, and go to the Father," interprets "I came forth from the Father, and am come into the world." To say "I leave the world" is not the same as to say "I go to the Father": this second clause describes a state of existence which is entered upon when existence in this world is done. And to say "I came forth from the Father" is not the same as to say "I came into the world"; it describes a state of existence antecedent to that which began by coming into the world.

Thus the Apostles understood the words, and felt therefore that they had gained a new platform of faith. This they felt to be plain-speaking, meant to be understood. It so precisely met their craving and gave them the knowledge they sought, that they felt more than ever Christ's insight into their state of mind and His power to satisfy their minds. At length they are able to say with assurance that He has come forth from God. They are persuaded that behind what they see there is a higher nature, and that in Christ's presence they are in the presence of One whose origin is not of this world. It was this pre-existence of Christ with God which gave the disciples assurance regarding all He taught them. He spoke of what He had seen with the Father.

This belief, however, assured though it was, did not save them from a cowardly desertion of Him whom they believed to be God's representative on earth. They would, when confronted with the world's authorities and powers, abandon their Master to His fate, and "would leave Him alone." He had always, indeed, been alone. All men who wish to carry out some novel design or accomplish some extensive reform must be prepared to stand alone, to listen unmoved to criticism, to estimate at their real and very low value the prejudiced calumnies of those whose interests are opposed to their design. They must be prepared to live without reward and without sympathy, strong in the consciousness of their own rectitude and that God will prosper the right. Jesus enjoyed the affection of a considerable circle of friends; He was not without the comfort and strength which come of being believed in; but in regard to His purpose in life He was always alone. And yet, unless He won men over to His views, unless He made some as ardent as Himself regarding them, His work was lost. This was the special hardship of Christ's solitariness. Those whom He had gathered were to desert Him in the critical hour; but the sore part of this desertion was that they were to go "each to his own"--oblivious, that is to say, of the great cause in which they had embarked with Christ.

At all times this is the problem Christ has to solve: how to prevail upon men to look at life from His point of view, to forget their own things and combine with Him, to be as enamoured of His cause as He Himself is. He looks now upon us with our honest professions of faith and growing regard, and He says: Yes, you believe; but you scatter each to his own at the slightest breath of danger or temptation. This scattering, each to his own, is that which thwarts Christ's purpose and imperils His work. The world with its enterprises and its gains, its glitter and its glory, its sufficiency for the present life, comes in and tempts us; and apart from the common good, we have each our private schemes of advantage. And yet there is nothing more certain than that our ultimate advantage is measured by the measure in which we throw in our lot with Christ--by the measure in which we practically recognise that there is an object for which all men in common can work, and that to scatter "each to his own" is to resign the one best hope of life, the one satisfying and remunerative labour.

In revealing what sustained Himself Christ reveals the true stay of every soul of man. His trial was indeed severe. Brought without a single friend to the bar of unsympathetic and unscrupulous judges: the Friend of man, loving as no other has ever loved, and craving love and sympathy as no other has craved it, yet standing without one pitying eye, without one voice raised in His favour. Alone in a world He came to convince and to win; at the end of His life, spent in winning men, left without one to say He had not lived in vain; abandoned to enemies, to ignorant, cruel, profane men. He was dragged through the streets where He had spoken words of life and healed the sick, but no rescue was attempted. So outcast from all human consideration was He, that a Barabbas found friendly voices where He found none. Hearing the suborned witnesses swear His life away, He heard at the same time His boldest disciple deny that he knew any person of the name of Jesus. But through this abandonment He knew the Father's presence was with Him. "I am not alone, because the Father is with Me."

Times which in their own degree try us with the same sense of solitariness come upon us all. All pain is solitary; you must bear it alone: kind friends may be round you, but they cannot bear one pang for you. You feel how separate and individual an existence you have when your body is racked with pain and healthy people are by your side; and you feel it also when you visit some pained or sorrowing person and sit silently in their presence, feeling that the suffering is theirs and that they must bear it. We should not brood much over any apparent want of recognition we may meet with; all such brooding is unwholesome and weak. Many of our minor sufferings we do best to keep to ourselves and say nothing about them. Let us strive to show sympathy, and we shall feel less the pain of not having it. To a large extent every one must be alone in life--forming his own views of things, working out his own idea of life, conquering his own sins, and schooling his own heart. And every one is more or less misunderstood even by his most intimate friends. He finds himself congratulated on occurrences which are no joy to him, applauded for successes he is ashamed of; the very kindnesses of his friends reveal to him how little they understand his nature. But all this will not deeply affect a healthy-minded man, who recognises that he is in the world to do good, and who is not always craving applause and recognition.

But there are occasional times in which the want of sympathy is crushingly felt. Some of the most painful and enduring sorrows of the human heart are of a kind which forbid that they be breathed to the nearest friend. Even if others know that they have fallen upon us they cannot allude to them; and very often they are not even known. And there are times even more trying, when we have not only to bear a sorrow or an anxiety all our own, but when we have to adopt a line of conduct which exposes us to misunderstanding, and to act continuously in a manner which shuts us off from the sympathy of our friends. Our friends remonstrate and advise, and we feel that their advice is erroneous: we are compelled to go our own way and bear the charge of obstinacy and even of cruelty; for sometimes, like Abraham offering Isaac, we cannot satisfy conscience without seeming to injure or actually injuring those we love.

It is in times like these that our faith is tested. We gain a firmer hold of God than ever before when we in actual life prefer His countenance and fellowship to the approbation and good-will of our friends. When in order to keep conscience clean we dare to risk the good-will of those we depend upon for affection and for support, our faith becomes a reality and rapidly matures. For a time we may seem to have rendered ourselves useless, and to have thrown ourselves out of all profitable relations to our fellow-men: we may be shunned, and our opinions and conduct may be condemned, and the object we had in view may seem to be further off than ever; but such was the experience of Christ also, till even He was forced to cry out, not only Why have ye, My friends, forsaken Me? but "My God, why hast Thou forsaken Me?" But as in His case, so in ours--this is only the natural and necessary path to the perfect justification of ourselves and of the principles our conduct has represented. If in obedience to conscience we are exposed to isolation and the various loss consequent upon it, we are not alone--God is with us. It is in the line of our conduct He is working and will carry out His purposes. And well might such an one be envied by those who have feared such isolation and shrunk from the manifold wretchedness that comes of resisting the world's ways and independently following an unworldly and Christian path.

For really in our own life, as in the life of Christ, all is summed up in the conflict between Christ and the world; and therefore the last words of this His last conversation are: "In the world ye shall have tribulation: but be of good courage. I have overcome the world." When Christ speaks of "the world" as comprising all that was opposed to Him, it is not difficult to understand His meaning. By "the world" we sometimes mean this earth; sometimes all external things, sun, moon, and stars as well as this earth; sometimes we mean the world of men, as when we say "All the world knows" such and such a thing, or as when Christ said "God so loved the world that He gave His only-begotten Son." But much more commonly Christ uses it to denote all in the present state of things which opposes God and leads man away from God. We speak of worldliness as fatal to the spirit, because worldliness means preference for what is external and present to what is inward and both present and future. Worldliness means attachment to things as they are--to the ways of society, to the excitements, the pleasures, the profits, of the present. It means surrender to what appeals to the sense--to comfort to vanity, to ambition, to love of display. Worldliness is the spirit which uses the present world without reference to the lasting and spiritual purposes for the sake of which men are in this world. It ignores what is eternal and what is spiritual; it is satisfied with present comfort, with what brings present pleasure, with what ministers to the beauty of this present life, to the material prosperity of men. And no soul whatsoever or wheresoever situated can escape the responsibility of making his choice between the world and God. To each of us the question which determines all else is, Am I to live for ends which find their accomplishment in this present life, or for ends which are eternal? Am I to live so as to secure the utmost of comfort, of ease, of money, of reputation, of domestic enjoyment, of the good things of this present world? or am I to live so as to do the most I can for the forwarding of God's purposes with men, for the forwarding of spiritual and eternal good? There is no man who is not living for one or other of these ends. Two men enter the same office and transact the same business; but the one is worldly, the other Christian: two men do the same work, use the same material, draw the same salary; but one cherishes a spiritual end, the other a worldly,--the one works, always striving to serve God and his fellows, the other has nothing in view but himself and his own interests. Two women live in the same street, have children at the same school, dress very much alike; but you cannot know them long without perceiving that the one is worldly, with her heart set on position and earthly advancement for her children, while the other is unworldly and prays that her children may learn to conquer the world and to live a stainless and self-sacrificing life though it be a poor one. This is the determining probation of life; this it is which determines what we are and shall be. We are, every one of us, living either with the world as our end or for God. The difficulty of choosing rightly and abiding by our choice is extreme: no man has ever found it easy; for every man it is a sufficient test of his reality, of his dependence on principle, of his moral clear-sightedness, of his strength of character.

Therefore Christ, as the result of all His work, announces that He has "overcome the world." And on the ground of this conquest of His He bids His followers rejoice and take heart, as if somehow His conquest of the world guaranteed theirs, and as if their conflict would be easier on account of His. And so indeed it is. Not only has every one now who proposes to live for high and unworldly ends the satisfaction of knowing that such a life is possible, and not only has he the vast encouragement of knowing that One has passed this way before and attained His end; but, moreover, it is Christ's victory which has really overcome the world in a final and public way. The world's principles of action, its pleasure-seeking, its selfishness, its childish regard for glitter and for what is present to sense, in a word, its worldliness when set over against the life of Christ, is for ever discredited. The experience of Christ in this world reflects such discredit upon merely worldly ways, and so clearly exhibits its blindness, its hatred of goodness, its imbecility when it strives to counterwork God's purposes, that no man who morally has his eyes open can fail to look with suspicion and abhorrence on the world. And the dignity, the love, the apprehension of what is real and abiding in human affairs, and the ready application of His life to a real and abiding purpose--all this, which is so visible in the life of Christ, gives certainty and attractiveness to the principles opposed to worldliness. We have in Christ's life at once an authoritative and an experimental teaching on the greatest of all human subjects--how life should be spent.

Christ has overcome the world, then, by resisting its influence upon Himself, by showing Himself actually superior to its most powerful influences; and His overcoming of the world is not merely a private victory availing for Himself alone, but it is a public good, because in His life the perfect beauty of a life devoted to eternal and spiritual ends is conspicuously shown. The man who can look upon the conflict between the world and Christ as John has shown it, and say, "I would rather be one of the Pharisees than Christ," is hopelessly blind to the real value of human life. But what says our life regarding the actual choice we have made?

Marcus Dods, D.D.

XVI. CHRIST'S INTERCESSORY PRAYER

"These things spake Jesus; and lifting up His eyes to heaven, He said, Father, the hour is come; glorify Thy Son, that the Son may glorify Thee: even as Thou gavest Him authority over all flesh, that whatsoever Thou hast given Him, to them He should give eternal life. And this is life eternal, that they should know Thee the only true God, and Him whom Thou didst send, even Jesus Christ. I glorified Thee on the earth, having accomplished the work which Thou hast given Me to do. And now, O Father, glorify Thou Me with Thine own self with the glory which I had with Thee before the world was. I manifested Thy name unto the men whom Thou gavest Me out of the world: Thine they were, and Thou gavest them to Me; and they have kept Thy word. Now they know that all things whatsoever Thou hast given Me are from Thee: for the words which Thou gavest Me I have given unto them; and they received them, and knew of a truth that I came forth from Thee, and they believed that Thou didst send Me. I pray for them: I pray not for the world, but for those whom Thou hast given Me; for they are Thine: and all things that are Mine are Thine, and Thine are Mine: and I am glorified in them. And I am no more in the world, and these are in the world, and I come to Thee. Holy Father, keep them in Thy name which Thou hast given Me, that they may be one, even as We are. While I was with them, I kept them in Thy name which Thou hast given Me: and I guarded them, and not one of them perished, but the son of perdition; that the Scripture might be fulfilled. But now I come to Thee; and these things I speak in the world, that they may have My joy fulfilled in themselves. I have given them Thy word; and the world hated them, because they are not of the world, even as I am not of the world. I pray not that Thou shouldest take them from the world, but that Thou shouldest keep them from the evil one. They are not of the world, even as I am not of the world. Sanctify them in the truth: Thy word is truth. As Thou didst send Me into the world, even so sent I them into the world. And for their sakes I sanctify Myself, that they themselves also may be sanctified in truth. Neither for these only do I pray, but for them also that believe on Me through their word; that they may all be one; even as Thou, Father, art in Me, and I in Thee, that they also may be in Us: that the world may believe that Thou didst send Me. And the glory which Thou hast given Me I have given unto them; that they may be one, even as We are one; I in them, and Thou in Me, that they may be perfected into one; that the world may know that Thou didst send Me, and lovedst them, even as Thou lovedst Me. Father, that which Thou hast given Me, I will that, where I am, they also may be with Me; that they may behold My glory, which Thou hast given Me: for Thou lovedst Me before the foundation of the world. O righteous Father, the world knew Thee not, but I knew Thee; and these knew that Thou didst send Me; and I made known unto them Thy name, and will make it known; that the love wherewith Thou lovedst me may be in them, and I in them."--John xvii.

This prayer of Christ is in some respects the most precious relic of the past. We have here the words which Christ addressed to God in the critical hour of His life--the words in which He uttered the deepest feeling and thought of His Spirit, clarified and concentrated by the prospect of death. What a revelation it would be to us had we Christ's prayers from His boyhood onwards! what a liturgy and promptuary of devotion if we knew what He had desired from His early years--what He had feared, what He had prayed against, what He had never ceased to hope for; the things that one by one dropped out of His prayers, the things that gradually grew into them; the persons He commended to the Father and the manner of this commendation; His prayers for His mother, for John, for Peter, for Lazarus, for Judas! But here we have a prayer which, if it does not so abundantly satisfy pardonable curiosity, does at least bring us into as sacred a presence. For even among the prayers of Christ this stands by itself as that in which He gathered up the retrospect of His past and surveyed the future of His Church; in which, as if already dying, He solemnly presented to the Father Himself, His work, and His people. Recognising the grandeur of the occasion, we may be disposed to agree with Melanchthon, who, when giving his last lecture shortly before His death, said: "There is no voice which has ever been heard, either in heaven or in earth, more exalted, more holy, more fruitful, more sublime, than this prayer offered up by the Son of God Himself."

The prayer was the natural conclusion to the conversation which Jesus and the disciples had been carrying on. And as the Eleven saw Him lifting His eyes to heaven, as if the Father He addressed were visible, they no doubt felt a security which had not been imparted by all His promises. And when in after-life they spoke of Christ's intercession, this instance of it must always have risen in memory and have formed all their ideas of that part of the Redeemer's work. It has always been believed that those who have loved and cared for us while on earth continue to do so when through death they have passed nearer to the Source of all love and goodness; this lively interest in us is supposed to continue because it formed so material an element in their life here below; and it was impossible that those who heard our Lord thus awfully commending them to the Father should ever forget this earnest consideration of their state or should ever come to fancy that they were forgotten.

Beginning with prayer for Himself, our Lord passes at the sixth verse into prayer for His disciples, and at the twentieth verse the prayer expands still more widely and embraces the world, all those who should believe on Him.

First, Jesus prays for Himself; and His prayer is, "Father, glorify Thy Son; glorify Thou Me with Thine own self with the glory which I had with Thee before the world was." The work for which He came into the world was done; "I have finished the work which Thou gavest Me to do." There remains no more reason why He should stay longer on earth; "the hour is come," the hour for closing His earthly career and opening to Him a new period and sphere. He does not wish and does not need a prolongation of life. He has found time enough in less than a half of three-score years and ten to do all He can do on earth. It is character, not time, we need to do our work. To make a deep and abiding impression it is not longer life we need, but intensity. Jesus did not find Himself cramped, limited, or too soon hurried out of life. He viewed death as the suitable timely step, and took it with self-command and in order to pass to something better than earthly life.

How immeasurably beneath this level is the vaunted equanimity of the thinker who says, "Death can be no evil because it is universal"! How immeasurably beneath it is the habit of most of us! Which of us can stand in that clear air on that high point which separates life from what is beyond and can say, "I have finished the work which Thou gavest Me to do"? A broken column is the fit monument of our life, unfinished, frustrated, useless. Wasted energy, ill-repaired blunders, unfulfilled purposes, fruitless years, much that is positively evil, much that was done mechanically and carelessly and for the day; plans ill conceived and worse executed; imperfect ideals of life imperfectly realised; pursuits dictated by uneducated tastes, unchastened whims, accidental circumstances,--such is the retrospect which most of us have as we look back over life. Few men even recognise the reality of life as part of an eternal order, and, of the few who do so, still fewer seriously and persistently aim at fitting in their life as a solid part of that order.

Before we know whether we have finished the work given us to do we must know what that work is. At the outset of his account of Christ's work John gives us his conception of it. "The Word was made flesh, and dwelt among us; and we beheld His glory, the glory as of the Only-begotten of the Father." This work was now accomplished, and Jesus can say, "I have glorified Thee on the earth"; "I have manifested Thy name unto the men which Thou gavest Me out of the world." We may all add our humble responsive "Amen" to this account of His finished work. John has carried us through the scenes in which Jesus manifested the glory of the Father and showed the full meaning of that name, displaying the Father's love in His self-sacrificing interest in men, the Father's holiness and supremacy in His devoted filial obedience. Never again can men separate the idea of the true God from the life of Jesus Christ; it is in that life we come to know God, and through that life His glory shines. This many a man has felt is the true Divine glory; this God yearning over His lost and wretched children, coming down and sharing in their wretchedness to win them to Himself and blessedness--this is the God for us. This alone is glory such as we bow before and own to be infinitely worthy of trust and adoration, almightiness applying itself to the necessities and fears of the weak, perfect purity winning to itself the impure and the outcast, love showing itself to be Divine by its patience, its humility, its absolute sacrifice. It is Christ who has found entrance for these conceptions of God once for all into the human mind; it is to Christ we owe it that we know a God we can entirely love and increasingly worship. With the most assured truth He could say, "I have finished the work which Thou gavest Me to do; I have glorified Thee on the earth; I have manifested Thy name unto the men which Thou gavest Me out of the world."

But Christ recognises a work which ran parallel with this, a work which continually resulted from His manifestation of the Father. By His manifesting the Father He gave eternal life to those who accepted and believed His revelation. The power to reveal the Father which Christ had received He had not on His own account, but that He might give eternal life to men. For "this is life eternal, that they might know Thee the only true God, and Jesus Christ, whom Thou hast sent." Eternal life is not merely life indefinitely prolonged. It is rather life under new conditions and fed from different sources. It can be entered upon now, but a full understanding of it is now impossible. The grub might as well try to understand the life of the butterfly, or the chick in the shell the life of the bird. To know what Christ revealed, this is the birth to life eternal. To know that love and holiness are the governing powers in conformity with which all things are carried onward to their end; to know what God is, that He is a Father who cannot leave us His children of earth behind and pass on to His own great works and purposes in the universe, but stoops to our littleness and delays that He may carry every one of us with

Him,--this is life eternal. This it is that subdues the human heart and cleanses it from pride, self-seeking, and lust, and that inclines it to bow before the holy and loving God, and to choose Him and life in Him. This it is that turns it from the brief joys and imperfect meanings of time and gives it a home in eternity--that severs it in disposition and in destiny from the changing, passing world and gives it an eternal inheritance as God's child. To as many as believed Christ, to them He gave power to become the sons of God. To believe Him and to accept the God He reveals is to become a son of God and is to enter into life eternal. To be conquered by the Divine love shown us; to feel that not in worldly ambition or any self-seeking, but only in devotion to interests that are spiritual and general, is the true life for us; to yield ourselves to the Spirit of Christ and seek to be animated and possessed by that Spirit,--this is to throw in our lot with God, to be satisfied in Him, to have eternal life.

The earthly work of Christ, then, being finished, He asks the Father to glorify Him with His own self, with the glory He had with Him before the world was. It seems to me vain to deny that this petition implies on Christ's part a consciousness of a life which He had before He appeared on earth. His mind turns from the present hour, from His earthly life, to eternity, to those regions beyond time into which no created intelligence can follow Him, and in which God alone exists, and in that Divine solitude He claims a place for Himself. If He merely meant that from eternity God had conceived of Him, the ideal man, and if the existence and glory He speaks of were merely existence in God's mind, but not actual, His words do not convey His meaning. The glory which He prayed for now was a conscious, living glory; He did not wish to become extinct or to be absorbed in the Divine being; He meant to continue and did continue in actual, personal, living existence. This was the glory He prayed for, and this therefore must also have been the glory He had before the world was. It was a glory of which it was proper to say, "I had it," and not merely God conceived it: it was enjoyed by Christ before the worlds were, and was not only in the mind of God.

What that glory was, who can tell? We know it was a glory not of position only, but of character--a glory which disposed and prepared Him to sympathize with suffering and to give Himself to the actual needs of men. From that glory He came to share with men in their humiliation, to expose Himself to their scorn and abuse, to win them to eternal life and to some true participation in His glory.

But Christ's removal from the earthly and visible life involved a great change in the condition of the disciples. Hitherto He had been present with them day by day, always exhibiting to them spiritual glory, and attracting them to it in His own person. So long as they saw God's glory in so attractive and friendly a form it was not difficult for them to resist the world's temptations. "While I was with them in the world, I kept them in Thy name"--that is, by revealing the Father to them; but "now I am no more in the world, but these are in the world, and I come to Thee. Holy Father, keep through Thine own name those whom Thou hast given Me. Sanctify them through Thy truth: Thy word is truth." Christ had been the Word Incarnate, the utterance of God to men; in Him men recognised what God is and what God wills. And this sanctified them; this marvellous revelation of God and His love for men drew men to Him: they felt how Divine and overcoming a love this was; they adored the name Father which Christ the Son made known to them; they felt themselves akin to God and claimed by Him, and spurned the world; they recognised in themselves that which could understand and be appealed to by such a love as God's. Their glory was to be God's children.

But now the visible image, the Incarnate Word, is withdrawn, and Christ commits to the Father those whom He leaves on earth. "Holy Father," Thou whose holiness moves Thee to keep men separate to Thyself from every evil contagion, "keep through Thine own name those whom Thou hast given Me." It is still by the recognition of God in Christ that we are to be kept from evil, by contemplating and penetrating this great manifestation of God to us, by listening humbly and patiently to this Incarnate Word. Knowledge of the God whose the world and all existence is, knowledge of Him in whom we live and whose holiness is silently judging and ruling all things, knowledge that He who rules all and who is above all gives Himself to us with a love that thinks no sacrifice too great--it is this knowledge of the truth that saves us from the world. It is the knowledge of those abiding realities which Christ revealed, of those great and loving purposes of God to man, and of the certainty of their fulfilment, which recalls us to holiness and to God. There is reality here; all else is empty and delusive.

But these realities are obscured and thrust aside by a thousand pretentious frivolities which claim our immediate attention and interest. We are in the world, and day by day the world insists that we shall consider it the great reality. Christ had conquered it and was leaving it. Why, then, did He not take with Him all whom He had won to Himself out of the world? He did not do so because they had a work to accomplish which could only be accomplished in the world. As He had consecrated Himself to the work of making known the Father, so must they consecrate themselves to the same work. As Christ in His own person and life had brought clear before their minds the presence of the Father, so must they by their person and life manifest in the world the existence and the grace of Christ. They must make permanent and universal the revelation He had brought, that all the world might believe that He was the true representative of God. Christ had lighted them, and with their light they were to kindle all men, till the world was full of light. A share in this work is given to each of us. We are permitted to mediate between God and men, to carry to some the knowledge which gives life eternal. It is made possible to us to be benefactors in the highest kind, to give to this man and that a God. To parents it is made possible to fill the opening and hungry mind of their child with a sense of God which will awe, restrain, encourage, gladden him all his life through. To relieve the wants of to-day, to refresh any human spirit by kindness, and to forward the interests of any struggler in life is much; but it is little compared with the joy and solid utility of disclosing to a human soul that which he at last recognises as Divine, and before which at last he bows in spontaneous adoration and absolute trust. To the man who has long questioned whether there is a God, who has doubted whether there is any morally perfect Being, any Spirit existent greater and purer than man, you have but to show Christ, and through His unconquerable love and untemptable holiness reveal to him a God.

But as it was not by telling men about God that Christ convinced men that somewhere there existed a holy God who cared for them, but by showing God's holiness and love present to them in His own person, so our words may fail to accomplish much if our life does not reveal a presence men cannot but recognise as Divine. It was by being one with the Father Christ revealed Him; it was the Father's will His life exhibited. And the extension of this to the whole world of men is the utmost of Christ's desire. All will be accomplished when all men are one, even as Christ and the Father are already one.

This text is often cited by those who seek to promote the union of churches. But we find it belongs to a very different category and much higher region. That all churches should be under similar government, should adopt the same creed, should use the same forms of worship, even if possible, is not supremely desirable; but real unity of sentiment towards Christ and of zeal to promote His will is supremely desirable. Christ's will is all-embracing; the purposes of God are wide as the universe, and can be fulfilled only by endless varieties of dispositions, functions, organisations, labours. We must expect that, as time goes on, men, so far from being contracted into a narrow and monotonous uniformity, will exhibit increasing diversities of thought and of method, and will be more and more differentiated in all outward respects. If the infinitely comprehensive purposes of God are to be fulfilled, it must be so. But also, if these purposes are to be fulfilled, all intelligent agents must be at one with God, and must be so profoundly in sympathy with God's mind as revealed in Christ that, however different one man's work or methods may be from another's, God's will shall alike be carried out by both. If this will can be more freely carried out by separate churches, then outward separation is no great calamity. Only when outward separation leads one church to despise or rival or hate another is it a calamity. But whether churches abide separate or are incorporated in outward unity, the desirable thing is that they be one in Christ, that they have the same eagerness in His service, that they be as regiments of one army fighting a common foe and supporting one another, diverse in outward appearance, in method, in function, as artillery, infantry, cavalry, engineers, or even as the army and navy of the same country, but fighting for one flag and one cause, and their very diversity more vividly exhibiting their real unity.

But why should unity be the ultimate desire of Christ, the highest point to which the Saviour's wishes for mankind can reach? Because spirit is that which rules; and if we be one with God in spirit the future is ours. This mighty universe in which we find ourselves, apparently governed by forces compared to which the most powerful of human engines are weak as the moth--forces which keep this earth, and orbs immeasurably larger, suspended in space,--this universe is controlled by spirit, is designed for spiritual ends, for ends of the highest kind and which concern conscious and moral beings.

It is as yet only by glimpses we can see the happiness of those who are one with God; it is only by inadequate comparisons and with mental effort we can attain to even a rudimentary conception of the future that awaits those who are thus eternally blessed. Of them well may Paul say, "All things are yours; for ye are Christ's, and Christ is God's." It is for Christ all things are governed by God; to be in Him is to be above the reach of catastrophe--to be, as Christ Himself expresses it, beside Himself on the throne, from which all things are ruled. Having been attracted by His character, by what He is and does, and having sought here on earth to promote His will, we shall be His agents hereafter, but in a life in which spiritual glory irradiates everything, and in which an ecstasy and strength which this frail body could not contain will be the normal and constant index of the life of God in us. To do good, to utter by word or deed the love and power that are in us, is the permanent joy of man. With what alacrity does the surgeon approach the operation he knows will be successful! with what pleasure does the painter put on canvas the idea which fills his mind and which he knows will appeal to every one who sees it! And whoever learns to do good by partaking of God's spirit of communicative goodness will find everlasting joy in imparting what he has and can. He will do so, not with the feeble and hesitating mind and hand which here make almost every good action partly painful, but with a spontaneity and sense of power which will be wholly pleasure; he will know that being one with God he can do good, can accomplish and effect some solid and needful work. Slowly, very slowly, is this arrived at; but time is of no consequence in work that is eternal, so long only as we are sure we do not idly miss present opportunities of learning, so long only as we know that our faces are turned in the right direction, and that a right spirit is in us.

Marcus Dods, D.D.

If there lingers in our minds a feeling that the end Christ proposes and utters as His last prayer for men does not draw us with irresistible force, it might be enough to say to our own heart that this is our weakness, that certainly in this prayer we do touch the very central significance of human life, and that however dimly human words may be able to convey thoughts regarding eternity we have here in Christ's words sufficient indication of the one abiding end and aim of all wisely directed human life. Whatever the future of man is to be, whatever joy life is to become, in whatever far-reaching and prolonged experiences we are to learn the fruitfulness and efficacy of God's love, whatever new sources and conditions of happiness we may in future worlds be introduced to, whatever higher energies and richer affections are to be opened in us, all this can only be by our becoming one with God, in whose will the future now lies. And it may also be said, if we think this the prayer of One who was not in the full current of actual human life, and had little understanding of men's ways, that this prayer is fulfilled in very many who are deeply involved and busily occupied in this world. They give their mind to their employment, but their heart goes to higher aims and more enduring results. To do good is to them of greater consequence than to make money. To see the number of Christ's sincere followers increasing is to them truer joy than to see their own business extending. In the midst of their greatest prosperity they recognise that there is something far better than worldly prosperity, and that is, to be kept from the evil that is in the world and to extend the knowledge of God. They feel in common with all men that it is not always easy to remember that great spiritual kingdom with its mighty but unobtrusive interests, but they are kept by the Father's name, and they do on the whole live under the influence of God and hoping in His salvation. And it would help us all to do so were we to believe that Christ's interest in us is such as this prayer reveals, and that the great subject of His intercession is, that we be kept from the evil that is in the world and be helpful in the great and enduring work of bringing into truer fellowship men's lives and God's goodness. Alongside of all our profitless labour and unworthiness of aim there runs this lofty aim of Christ for us; and while we are greedily following after pleasure, or thoughtlessly throwing ourselves into mere worldliness, our Lord is praying the Father that we be lifted into harmony with Him and be used as channels of His grace to others.

XVII. THE ARREST

"When Jesus had spoken these words, He went forth with His disciples over the brook Kidron, where was a garden, into the which He entered, Himself and His disciples. Now Judas also, which betrayed Him, knew the place: for Jesus ofttimes resorted thither with His disciples. Judas then, having received the band of soldiers, and officers from the chief priests and the Pharisees, cometh thither with lanterns and torches and weapons. Jesus therefore, knowing all the things that were coming upon Him, went forth, and saith unto them, Whom seek ye? They answered Him, Jesus of Nazareth. Jesus saith unto them, I am He. And Judas also, which betrayed Him, was standing with them. When therefore He said unto them, I am He, they went backward, and fell to the ground. Again therefore He asked them, Whom seek ye? And they said, Jesus of Nazareth. Jesus answered, I told you that I am He: if therefore ye seek Me, let these go their way: that the word might be fulfilled which He spake, Of those whom Thou hast given Me I lost not one. Simon Peter therefore having a sword drew it, and struck the high priest's servant, and cut off his right ear. Now the servant's name was Malchus. Jesus therefore said unto Peter, Put up the sword into the sheath: the cup which the Father hath given Me, shall I not drink it? So the band and the chief captain, and the officers of the Jews, seized Jesus and bound Him, and led Him to Annas first; for he was father-in-law to Caiaphas, which was high priest that year. Now Caiaphas was he which gave counsel to the Jews, that it was expedient that one man should die for the people."--John xviii. 1-14.

Jesus having commended to the Father Himself and His disciples, left the city, crossed the Kidron, and entered the Garden of Gethsemane, where He frequently went for quiet and to pass the night. The time He had spent in encouraging His disciples and praying for them Judas had spent in making preparations for His arrest. In order to impress Pilate with the dangerous nature of this Galilean he asks him for the use of the Roman cohort to effect His capture. It was possible His arrest might occasion a tumult and rouse the people to attempt a rescue. Perhaps Judas also had an alarming remembrance of the miraculous power he had seen Jesus put forth, and was afraid to attempt His apprehension with only the understrappers of the Sanhedrim or the Temple guard; so he takes the Roman cohort of five hundred men, or whatever number he would reckon would be more than a match for a miracle. And though the moon was full, he takes the precaution of furnishing the expedition with lanterns and torches, for he knew that down in that deep Kidron gully it was often dark when there was plenty of light above; and might not Jesus hide Himself in some of the shadows, in some thicket or cavern, or in some garden-shed or tower? He could not have made more elaborate preparations had he been wishing to take a thief or to surprise a dangerous chief of banditti in his stronghold.

The futility of such preparations became at once apparent. So far from trying to hide Himself or slip out by the back of the garden, Jesus no sooner sees the armed men than He steps to the front and asks, "Whom seek ye?" Jesus, in order that He might screen His disciples, wished at once to be identified by His captors themselves as the sole object of their search. By declaring that they sought Jesus of Nazareth, they virtually exempted the rest from apprehension. But when Jesus identified Himself as the person they sought, instead of rushing forward and holding Him fast, as Judas had instructed them, those in front shrank back; they felt that they had no weapons that would not break upon the calmness of that spiritual majesty; they went backward and fell to the ground. This was no idle display; it was not a needless theatrical garnishing of the scene for the sake of effect. If we could imagine the Divine nobility of Christ's appearance at that critical moment when He finally proclaimed His work done and gave Himself up to die, we should all of us sink humbled and overcome before Him. Even in the dim and flickering light of the torches there was that in His appearance which made it impossible for the bluntest and rudest soldier to lay a hand upon Him. Discipline was forgotten; the legionaries who had thrown themselves on spear-points unawed by the fiercest of foes saw in this unarmed figure something which quelled and bewildered them.

But this proof of His superiority was lost upon His disciples. They thought that armed force should be met by armed force. Recovering from their discomfiture, and being ashamed of it, the soldiers and servants of the Sanhedrim advance to bind Jesus. Peter, who had with some dim presentiment of what was coming possessed himself of a sword, aims a blow at the head of Malchus, who having his hands occupied in binding Jesus can only defend himself by bending his head to one side, and so instead of his life loses only his ear. To our Lord this interposition of Peter seemed as if he were dashing out of His hand the cup which the Father had put into it. Disengaging His hands from those who already held them He said, "Suffer ye thus far" [20] (Permit Me to do this one thing); and laying His hand on the wound He healed it, this forgiving and beneficent act being the last done by His unbound hands--significant, indeed, that such should be the style of action from which they prevented Him by binding His hands. Surely the Roman officer in command, if none of the others, must have observed the utter incongruity of the bonds, the fatuous absurdity and wickedness of tying hands because they wrought miracles of healing.

While our Lord thus calmly resigned Himself to His fate, He was not without an indignant sense of the wrong that was done Him, not only in His being apprehended, but in the manner of it. "Are ye come out as against a thief with swords and with staves? I sat daily teaching in the Temple, and ye laid no hold on Me." Many of the soldiers must have felt how ungenerous it was to treat such a Person as a common felon,--coming upon Him thus in the dead of night, as if He were one who never appeared in the daylight; coming with bludgeons and military aid, as if He were likely to create a disturbance. Commonly an arrest is considered to be best made if the culprit is seized red-handed in the very act. Why, then, had they not thus taken Him? They knew that the popular conscience was with Him, and they dared not take Him on the streets of Jerusalem. It was the last evidence of their inability to understand His kingdom, its nature and its aims. Yet surely some of the crowd must have felt ashamed of themselves, and been uneasy till they got rid of their unsuitable weapons, stealthily dropping their sticks as they walked or hurling them deep into the shade of the garden.

This, then, is the result produced by our Lord's labours of love and wisdom. His conduct had been most conciliatory--conciliatory to the point of meekness unintelligible to those who could not penetrate His motives. He had innovated certainly, but His innovations were blessings, and were so marked by wisdom and sanctioned by reason that every direct assault against them had broken down. He did not seek for power further than for the power of doing good. He knew He could lift men to a far other life than they were living, and permission to do so was His grand desire. The result was that He was marked as the object of the most rancorous hatred of which the human heart is capable. Why so? Do we need to ask? What is more exasperating to men who fancy themselves the teachers of the age than to find another teacher carrying the convictions of the people? What is more painful than to find that in advanced life we must revolutionise our opinions and admit the truth taught by our juniors? He who has new truths to declare or new methods to introduce must recognise that he will be opposed by the combined forces of ignorance, pride, self-interest, and sloth. The majority are always on the side of things as they are. And whoever suggests improvement, whoever shows the faultiness and falseness of what has been in vogue, must be prepared to pay the price and endure misunderstanding, calumny, opposition, and ill-usage. If all men speak well of us, it is only while we go with the stream. As soon as we oppose popular customs, explode received opinions, introduce reforms, we must lay our account for ill-treatment. It has always been so, and in the nature of things it must always be so. We cannot commit a crime more truly hated by society than to convince it there are better ways of living than its own and a truth beyond what it has conceived, and it has been the consolation and encouragement of many who have endeavoured to improve matters around them and have met with contempt or enmity that they share the lot of Him whose reward for seeking to bless mankind was that He was arrested as a common felon.

When thus treated, men are apt to be embittered towards their fellows. When all their efforts to do good are made the very ground of accusation against them, there is the strongest provocation to give up all such attempts and to arrange for one's own comfort and safety. This world has few more sufficient tests to apply to character than this; and it is only the few who, when misinterpreted and ill-used by ignorance and malignity, can retain any loving care for others. It struck the spectators, therefore, of this scene in the garden as a circumstance worthy of record, that when Jesus was Himself bound He should shield His disciples. "If ye seek Me, let these go their way." Some of the crowd had perhaps laid hands on the disciples or were showing a disposition to apprehend them as well as their Master. Jesus therefore interferes, reminding His captors that they had themselves said that He was the object of this midnight raid, and that the disciples must therefore be scatheless.

In relating this part of the scene John puts an interpretation on it which was not merely natural, but which has been put upon it instinctively by all Christians since. It seemed to John as if, in thus acting, our Lord was throwing into a concrete and tangible form His true substitution in the room of His people. To John these words He utters seem the motto of His work. Had any of the disciples been arrested along with Jesus and been executed by His side as act and part with Him, the view which the Christian world has taken of Christ's position and work must have been blurred if not quite altered. But the Jews had penetration enough to see where the strength of this movement lay. They believed that if the Shepherd was smitten the sheep would give them no trouble, but would necessarily scatter. Peter's flourish with the sword attracted little attention; they knew that great movements were not led by men of his type. They passed him by with a smile and did not even arrest him. It was Jesus who stood before them as alone dangerous. And Jesus on His side knew that the Jews were right, that He was the responsible person, that these Galileans would have been dreaming at their nets had He not summoned them to follow Him. If there was any offence in the matter, it belonged to Him, not to them.

But in Jesus thus stepping to the front and shielding the disciples by exposing Himself, John sees a picture of the whole sacrifice and substitution of Christ. This figure of his Master moving forward to meet the swords and staves of the party remains indelibly stamped upon his mind as the symbol of Christ's whole relation to His people. That night in Gethsemane was to them all the hour and power of darkness; and in every subsequent hour of darkness John and the rest see the same Divine figure stepping to the front, shielding them and taking upon Himself all the responsibility. It is thus Christ would have us think of Him--as our friend and protector, watchful over our interests, alive to all that threatens our persons, interposing between us and every hostile event. If by following Him according to our knowledge we are brought into difficulties, into circumstances of trouble and danger, if we are brought into collision with those in power, if we are discouraged and threatened by serious obstacles, let us be quite sure that in the critical moment He will interpose and convince us that, though He cannot save Himself, He can save others. He will not lead us into difficulties and leave us to find our own way out of them. If in striving to discharge our duty we have become entangled in many distressing and annoying circumstances, He acknowledges His responsibility in leading us into such a condition, and will see that we are not permanently the worse for it. If in seeking to know Him more thoroughly we have been led into mental perplexities, He will stand by us and see that we come to no harm. He encourages us to take this action of His in shielding His disciples as the symbol of what we all may expect He will do for ourselves. In all matters between God and us He interposes and claims to be counted as the true Head who is accountable, as that One who desires to answer all charges that can be made against the rest of us. If therefore, in view of much duty left undone, of many sinful imaginings harboured, of much vileness of conduct and character, we feel that it is ourselves the eye of God is seeking and with us He means to take account; if we know not how to answer Him regarding many things that stick in our memory and conscience,--let us accept the assurance here given us that Christ presents Himself as responsible.

It is not without surprise that we read that when Jesus was arrested all the disciples forsook Him and fled. John, indeed, and Peter speedily recovered themselves and followed to the hall of judgment; and the others may not only have felt that they were in danger so long as they remained in His company, but also that by accompanying Him they could not mend matters. Still, the kind of loyalty that stands by a falling cause, and the kind of courage that risks all to show sympathy with a friend or leader, are qualities so very common that one would have expected to find them here. And no doubt had the matter been to be decided in Peter's fashion, by the sword, they would have stood by Him. But there was a certain mysteriousness about our Lord's purpose that prevented His followers from being quite sure where they were being led to. They were perplexed and staggered by the whole transaction. They had expected things to go differently and scarcely knew what they were doing when they fled.

There are times when we feel a slackening of devotion to Christ, times when we are doubtful whether we have not been misled, times when the bond between us and Him seems to be of the slenderest possible description, times when we have as truly forsaken Him as these disciples, and are running no risks for Him, doing nothing to advance His interests, seeking only our own comfort and our own safety. These times will frequently be found to be the result of disappointed expectations. Things have not gone with us in the spiritual life as we expected. We have found things altogether more difficult than we looked for. We do not know what to make of our present state nor what to expect in the future, and so we lose an active interest in Christ and fall away from any hope that is living and influential.

Another point which John evidently desires to bring prominently before us in this narrative is Christ's willingness to surrender Himself; the voluntary character of all He afterwards suffered. It was at this point of His career, at His apprehension, this could best be brought out. Afterwards He might say He suffered willingly, but so far as appearances went He had no option. Previous to His apprehension His professions of willingness would not have been attended to. It was precisely now that it could be seen whether He would flee, hide, resist, or calmly yield Himself. And John is careful to bring out His willingness. He went to the garden as usual, "knowing all things that should come upon Him." It would have been easy to seek some safer quarters for the night, but He would not. At the last moment escape from the garden could not have been impossible. His followers could have covered His retreat. But He advances to meet the party, avows Himself to be the man they sought, will not suffer Peter to use his sword, in every way shows that His surrender is voluntary. Still, had He not shown His power to escape, onlookers might have thought this was only the prudent conduct of a brave man who wished to preserve His dignity, and therefore preferred delivering Himself up to being ignominiously dragged from a hiding-place. Therefore it was made plain that if He yielded it was not for want of power to resist. By a word He overthrew those who came to bind Him, and made them feel ashamed of their preparations. He spoke confidently of help that would have swept the cohort off the field. [21] And thus it was brought out that, if He died, He laid down His life and was not deprived of it solely by the hate and violence of men.

Marcus Dods, D.D.

The hate and violence were there; but they were not the sole factors. He yielded to these because they were ingredients in the cup His Father wished Him to drink.

The reason of this is obvious. Christ's life was to be all sacrifice, because self-sacrifice is the essence of holiness and of love. From beginning to end the moving spring of all His actions was deliberate self-devotement to the good of men or to the fulfilment of God's will; for these are equivalents. And His death as the crowning act of this career was to be conspicuously a death embodying and exhibiting the spirit of self-sacrifice. He offered Himself on the cross through the eternal Spirit. That death was not compulsory; it was not the outcome of a sudden whim or generous impulse; it was the expression of a constant uniform "eternal" Spirit, which on the cross, in the yielding of life itself, rendered up for men all that was possible. Unwillingly no sacrifice can be made. When a man is taxed to support the poor, we do not call that a sacrifice. Sacrifice must be free, loving, uncompelled; it must be the exhibition in act of love, the freest and most spontaneous of all human emotions. "It is a true Christian instinct in our language which has seized upon the word sacrifice to express the self-devotion prompted by an unselfish love for others: we speak of the sacrifices made by a loving wife or mother; and we test the sincerity of a Christian by the sacrifices he will make for the love of Christ and the brethren.... The reason why Christianity has approved itself a living principle of regeneration to the world is specially because a Divine example and a Divine spirit of self-sacrifice have wrought together in the hearts of men, and thereby an ever-increasing number have been quickened with the desire and strengthened with the will to spend and be spent for the cleansing, the restoration, and the life of the most guilty, miserable, and degraded of their fellows." It was in Christ's life and death this great principle of the life of God and man was affirmed: there self-sacrifice is perfectly exhibited.

It is to this willingness of Christ to suffer we must ever turn. It is this voluntary, uncompelled, spontaneous devotion of Himself to the good of men which is the magnetic point in this earth. Here is something we can cleave to with assurance, something we can trust and build upon. Christ in His own sovereign freedom of will and impelled by love of us has given Himself to work out our perfect deliverance from sin and evil of every kind. Let us deal sincerely with Him, let us be in earnest about these matters, let us hope truly in Him, let us give Him time to conquer by moral means all our moral foes within and without, and we shall one day enter into His joy and His triumph.

But when we thus apply John's words we are haunted with a suspicion that they were perhaps not intended to be thus used. Is John justified in finding in Christ's surrender of Himself to the authorities, on condition that the disciples should escape, fulfilment of the words that of those whom God had given Him He had lost none? The actual occurrence we see here is Jesus arrested as a false Messiah, and claiming to be the sole culprit if any culprit there be. Is this an occurrence that has any bearing upon us or any special instruction regarding the substitution of a sin-bearer in our room? Can it mean that He alone bears the punishment of our sin and that we go free? Is it any more than an illustration of His substitutionary work, one instance out of many of His habit of self-devotion in the room of others? Can I build upon this act in the Garden of Gethsemane and conclude from it that He surrenders Himself that I may escape punishment? Can I legitimately gather from it anything more than another proof of His constant readiness to stand in the breach? It is plain enough that a person who acted as Christ did here is one we could trust; but had this action any special virtue as the actual substitution of Christ in our room as sin-bearer?

It is, I think, well that we should occasionally put to ourselves such questions and train ourselves to look at the events of Christ's life as actual occurrences, and to distinguish between what is fanciful and what is real. So much has been said and written regarding His work, it has been the subject of so much sentiment, the basis of so many conflicting theories, the text of so much loose and allegorising interpretation, that the original plain and substantial fact is apt to be overlaid and lost sight of. And yet it is that plain and substantial reality which has virtue for us, while all else is delusive, howsoever finely sentimental, howsoever rich in coincidences with Old Testament sayings or in suggestions of ingenious doctrine. The subject of substitution is obscure. Inquiry into the Atonement is like the search for the North Pole: approach it from what quarter we may, there are unmistakable indications that a finality exists in that direction; but to make our way to it and take a survey all round it at once is still beyond us. We must be content if we can correct certain variations of the compass and find so much as one open waterway through which our own little vessel can be steered.

Looking, then, at this surrender of Christ in the light of John's comment, we see clearly enough that Christ sought to shelter His disciples at His own expense, and that this must have been the habit of His life. He sought no companion in misfortune. His desire was to save others from suffering. This willingness to be the responsible party was the habit of His life. It is impossible to think of Christ as in any matter sheltering Himself behind any man or taking a second place. He is always ready to bear the burden and the brunt. We recognise in this action of Christ that we have to do with One who shirks nothing, fears nothing, grudges nothing; who will substitute Himself for others wherever possible, if danger is abroad. So far as the character and habit of Christ go, there is unquestionably here manifest a good foundation for His substitution in our stead wheresoever such substitution is possible.

It is also in this scene, probably more than in any other, that we see that the work Christ had come to do was one which He must do entirely by Himself. It is scarcely exaggeration to say He could employ no assistant even in its minor details. He did indeed send forth men to proclaim His kingdom, but it was to proclaim what He alone did. In His miracles He did not use His disciples as a surgeon uses His assistants. Here in the garden He explicitly puts the disciples aside and says that this question of the Messiahship is solely His affair. This separate, solitary character of Christ's work is important: it reminds us of the exceptional dignity and greatness of it; it reminds us of the unique insight and power possessed by Him who alone conceived and carried it through.

There is no question, then, of Christ's willingness to be our substitute; the question rather is, Is it possible that He should suffer for our sin and so save us from suffering? and does this scene in the garden help us to answer that question? That this scene, in common with the whole work of Christ, had a meaning and relations deeper than those that appear on the surface none of us doubts. The soldiers who arrested Him, the judges who condemned Him, saw nothing but the humble and meek prisoner, the bar of the Sanhedrim, the stripes of the Roman scourge, the material cross and nails and blood; but all this had relations of infinite reach, meaning of infinite depth. Through all that Christ did and suffered God was accomplishing the greatest of His designs, and if we miss this Divine intention we miss the essential significance of these events. The Divine intention was to save us from sin and give us eternal life. This is accomplished by Christ's surrender of Himself to this earthly life and all the anxiety, the temptation, the mental and spiritual strain which this involved. By revealing the Father's love to us He wins us back to the Father; and the Father's love was revealed in the self-sacrificing suffering He necessarily endured in numbering Himself with sinners. Of Christ's satisfying the law by suffering the penalty under which we lay Paul has much to say. He explicitly affirms that Christ bore and so abolished the curse or penalty of sin. But in this Gospel there may indeed be hints of this same idea, but it is mainly another aspect of the work of Christ which is here presented. It is the exhibition of Christ's self-sacrificing love as a revelation of the Father which is most prominent in the mind of John.

We can certainly say that Christ suffered our penalties in so far as a perfectly holy person can suffer them. The gnawing anguish of remorse He never knew; the haunting anxieties of the wrong-doer were impossible to Him; the torment of ungratified desire, eternal severance from God, He could not suffer; but other results and penalties of sin He suffered more intensely than is possible to us. The agony of seeing men He loved destroyed by sin, all the pain which a sympathetic and pure spirit must bear in a world like this, the contradiction of sinners, the provocation and shame which daily attended Him--all this He bore because of sin and for us, that we might be saved from lasting sin and unrelieved misery. So that even if we cannot take this scene in the garden as an exact representation of the whole substitutionary work of Christ, we can say that by suffering with and for us He has saved us from sin and restored us to life and to God.

Footnotes:

20. Luke xxii. 51.
21. Matt. xxvi. 53.

Marcus Dods, D.D.

XVIII. PETER'S DENIAL AND REPENTANCE

"So the band and the chief captain, and the officers of the Jews, seized Jesus and bound Him, and led Him to Annas first; for he was father-in-law to Caiaphas, which was high priest that year. Now Caiaphas was he which gave counsel to the Jews, that it was expedient that one man should die for the people. And Simon Peter followed Jesus, and so did another disciple. Now that disciple was known unto the high priest, and entered in with Jesus into the court of the high priest; but Peter was standing at the door without. So the other disciple, which was known unto the high priest, went out and spake unto her that kept the door, and brought in Peter. The maid therefore that kept the door saith unto Peter, Art thou also one of this man's disciples? He saith, I am not. Now the servants and the officers were standing there, having made a fire of coals; for it was cold; and they were warming themselves: and Peter also was with them, standing and warming himself.... Now Simon Peter was standing and warming himself. They said therefore unto him, Art thou also one of His disciples? He denied, and said, I am not. One of the servants of the high priest, being a kinsman of him whose ear Peter cut off, saith, Did not I see thee in the garden with Him? Peter therefore denied again: and straightway the cock crew."--John xviii. 12-18, 25-27.

The examination of Jesus immediately followed His arrest. He was first led to Annas, who at once sent Him to Caiaphas, the high priest, that he might carry out his policy of making one man a scapegoat for the nation. [22] To John the most memorable incident of this midnight hour was Peter's denial of his Master. It happened on this wise. The high priest's palace was built, like other large Oriental houses, round a quadrangular court, into which entrance was gained by a passage running from the street through the front part of the house. This passage or archway is called in the Gospels the "porch," and was closed at the end next the street by a heavy folding gate with a wicket for single persons. This wicket was kept on this occasion by a maid. The interior court upon which this passage opened was paved or flagged and open to the sky, and as the night was cold the attendants had made a fire here. The rooms round the court, in one of which the examination of Jesus was proceeding, were open in front-- separated, that is to say, from the court only by one or two pillars or arches and a railing, so that our Lord could see and even hear Peter.

When Jesus was led in bound to this palace, there entered with the crowd of soldiers and servants one at least of His disciples. He was in some way acquainted with the high priest, and presuming on this acquaintanceship followed to learn the fate of Jesus. He had seen Peter following at a distance, and after a little he goes to the gate-keeper and induces her to open to his friend. The maid seeing the familiar terms on which these two men were, and knowing that one of them was a disciple of Jesus, very naturally greets Peter with the exclamation, "Art not thou also one of this man's disciples?" Peter, confused by being suddenly confronted with so many hostile faces, and remembering the blow he had struck in the garden, and that he was now in the place of all others where it was likely to be avenged, suddenly in a moment of infatuation, and doubtless to the dismay of his fellow-disciple, denies all knowledge of Jesus. Having once committed himself, the two other denials followed as matter of course.

Yet the third denial is more guilty than the first. Many persons are conscious that they have sometimes acted under what seems an infatuation. They do not plead this in excuse for the wrong they have done. They are quite aware that what has come out of them must have been in them, and that their acts, unaccountable as they seem, have definite roots in their character. Peter's first denial was the result of surprise and infatuation. But an hour seems to have elapsed between the first and the third. He had time to think, time to remember his Lord's warning, time to leave the place if he could do no better. But one of those reckless moods which overtake good-hearted children seems to have overtaken Peter, for at the end of the hour he is talking right round the whole circle at the fire, not in monosyllables and guarded voice, but in his own outspoken way, the most talkative of them all, until suddenly one whose ear was finer than the rest detected the Galilean accent, and says, "You need not deny you are one of this man's disciples, for your speech betrays you." Another, a kinsman of him whose ear Peter had cut off, strikes in and declares that he had seen him in the garden. Peter, driven to extremities, hides his Galilean accent under the strong oaths of the city, and with a volley of profane language asseverates that he has no knowledge of Jesus. At this moment the first examination of Jesus closes and He is led across the court: the first chill of dawn is felt in the air, a cock crows, and as Jesus passes He looks upon Peter;

the look and the cock-crow together bring Peter to himself, and he hurries out and weeps bitterly.

The remarkable feature of this sin of Peter's is that at first sight it seems so alien to his character. It was a lie; and he was unusually straightforward. It was a heartless and cruel lie, and he was a man full of emotion and affection. It was a cowardly lie, even more cowardly than common lies, and yet he was exceptionally bold. Peter himself was quite positive that this at least was a sin he would never commit. "Though all men should deny Thee, yet will not I." Neither was this a baseless boast. He was not a mere braggart, whose words found no correspondence in his deeds. Far from it; he was a hardy, somewhat over-venturesome man, accustomed to the risks of a fisherman's life, not afraid to fling himself into a stormy sea, or to face the overwhelming armed force that came to apprehend his Master, ready to fight for him single-handed, and quickly recovering from the panic which scattered his fellow-disciples. If any of his companions had been asked at what point of Peter's character the vulnerable spot would be found, not one of them would have said, "He will fall through cowardice." Besides, Peter had a few hours before been so emphatically warned against denying Christ that he might have been expected to stand firm this night at least.

Perhaps it was this very warning which betrayed Peter. When he struck the blow in the garden, he thought he had falsified his Lord's prediction. And when he found himself the only one who had courage to follow to the palace, his besetting self-confidence returned and led him into circumstances for which he was too weak. He was equal to the test of his courage which he was expecting, but when another kind of test was applied in circumstances and from a quarter he had not anticipated his courage failed him utterly.

Peter probably thought he might be brought bound with his Master before the high priest, and had he been so he would probably have stood faithful. But the devil who was sifting him had a much finer sieve than that to run him through. He brought him to no formal trial, where he could gird himself for a special effort, but to an unobserved, casual questioning by a slave-girl. The whole trial was over before he knew he was being tried. So do our most real trials come; in a business transaction that turns up with others in the day's work, in the few minutes' talk or the evening's intercourse with friends, it is discovered whether we are so truly Christ's friends that we cannot forget Him or disguise that we are His. A word or two with a person he never saw before and would never see again brought the great trial of Peter's life; and as unexpectedly shall we be tried. In these battles we must all encounter, we receive no formal challenge that gives us time to choose our ground and our weapons; but a sudden blow is dealt us, from which we can be saved only by habitually wearing a shirt of mail sufficient to turn it, and which we can carry into all companies.

Had Peter distrusted himself and seriously accepted his Lord's warning, he would have gone with the rest; but ever thinking of himself as able to do more than other men, faithful where others were faithless, convinced where others hesitated, daring where others shrank, he once again thrust himself forward, and so fell. For this self-confidence, which might to a careless observer seem to underprop Peter's courage, was to the eye of the Lord undermining it. And if Peter's true bravery and promptitude were to serve the Church in days when fearless steadfastness would be above all other qualities needed, his courage must be sifted and the chaff of self-confidence thoroughly separated from it. In place of a courage which was sadly tainted with vanity and impulsiveness Peter must acquire a courage based upon recognition of his own weakness and his Lord's strength. And it was this event which wrought this change in Peter's character.

Frequently we learn by a very painful experience that our best qualities are tainted, and that actual disaster has entered our life from the very quarter we least suspected. We may be conscious that the deepest mark has been made on our life by a sin apparently as alien to our character as cowardice and lying were to the too venturesome and outspoken character of Peter. Possibly we once prided ourselves on our honesty, and felt happy in our upright character, plain-dealing, and direct speech; but to our dismay we have been betrayed into double-dealing, equivocation, evasive or even fraudulent conduct. Or the time was when we were proud of our friendships; it was frequently in our mind that, however unsatisfactory in other respects our character might be, we were at any rate faithful and helpful friends. Alas! events have proved that even in this particular we have failed, and have, through absorption in our own interests, acted inconsiderately and even cruelly to our friend, not even recognising at the time how his interests were suffering. Or we are by nature of a cool temperament, and judged ourselves safe at least from the faults of impulse and passion; yet the mastering combination of circumstances came, and we spoke the word, or wrote the letter, or did the deed which broke our life past mending.

Now, it was Peter's salvation, and it will be ours, when overtaken in this unsuspected sin, to go out and weep bitterly. He did not frivolously count it an accident that could never occur again; he did not sullenly curse the circumstances that had betrayed and shamed him. He recognised that there was that in him which could render useless his best natural qualities, and that the sinfulness which could make his strongest natural defences brittle as an egg-shell must be serious indeed. He had no choice but to be humbled before the eye of the Lord. There was no need of words to explain and enforce his guilt: the eye can express what the tongue cannot utter. The finer, tenderer, deeper feelings are left to the eye to express. The clear cock-crow strikes home to his conscience, telling him that the very sin he had an hour or two ago judged impossible is now actually committed. That brief space his Lord had named as sufficient to test his fidelity is gone, and the sound that strikes the hour rings with condemnation. Nature goes on in her accustomed, inexorable, unsympathetic round; but he is a fallen man, convicted in his own conscience of empty vanity, of cowardice, of heartlessness. He who in his own eyes was so much better than the rest had fallen lower than all. In the look of Christ Peter sees the reproachful loving tenderness of a wounded spirit, and understands the dimensions of his sin. That he, the most intimate disciple, should have added to the bitterness of that hour, should not only have failed to help his Lord, but should actually at the crisis of His fate have added the bitterest drop to His cup, was humbling indeed. There was that in Christ's look that made him feel the enormity of his guilt; there was that also that softened him and saved him from sullen despair.

And it is obvious that if we are to rise clear above the sin that has betrayed us we can do so only by as lowly a penitence. We are all alike in this: that we have fallen; we cannot any more with justice think highly of ourselves; we have sinned and are disgraced in our own eyes. In this, I say, we are all alike; that which makes the difference among us is, how we deal with ourselves and our circumstances in connection with our sin. It has been very well said by a keen observer of human nature that "men and women are often more fairly judged by the way in which they bear the burden of their own deeds, the fashion in which they carry themselves in their entanglements, than by the prime act which laid the burden on their lives and made the entanglement fast knotted. The deeper part of us shows in the manner of accepting consequences." The reason of this is that, like Peter, we are often betrayed by a weakness; the part of our nature which is least able to face difficulty is assaulted by a combination of circumstances which may never again occur in our life. There was guilt, great guilt it may be, concerned in our fall, but it was not deliberate, wilful wickedness. But in our dealing with our sin and its consequences our whole nature is concerned and searched; the real bent and strength of our will is tried. We are therefore in a crisis, the crisis, of our life. Can we accept the situation? Can we humbly, frankly own that, since that evil has appeared in our life, it must have been, however unconsciously, in ourselves first? Can we with the genuine manliness and wisdom of a broken heart say to ourselves and to God, Yes, it is true I am the wretched, pitiful, bad-hearted creature that was capable of doing, and did that thing? I did not think that was my character; I did not think it was in me to sink so very low; but now I see what I am. Do we thus, like Peter, go out and weep bitterly?

Every one who has passed through a time such as this single night was to Peter knows the strain that is laid upon the soul, and how very hard it is to yield utterly. So much rises up in self-defence; so much strength is lost by the mere perplexity and confusion of the thing; so much is lost in the despondency that follows these sad revelations of our deep-seated evil. What is the use, we think, of striving, if even in the point in which I thought myself most secure I have fallen? What is the meaning of so perplexed and deceiving a warfare? Why was I exposed to so fatal an influence? So Peter, had he taken the wrong direction, might have resented the whole course of the temptation, and might have said, Why did Christ not warn me by His look before I sinned, instead of breaking me by it after? Why had I no inkling of the enormity of the sin before as I have after the sin? My reputation now is gone among the disciples; I may as well go back to my old obscure life and forget all about these perplexing scenes and strange spiritualities. But Peter, though he was cowed by a maid, was man enough and Christian enough to reject such falsities and subterfuges. It is true we did not see the enormity, never do see the enormity, of the sin until it is committed; but is it possible it can be otherwise? Is not this the way in which a blunt conscience is educated? Nothing seems so bad until it finds place in our own life and haunts us. Neither need we despond or sour because we are disgraced in our own eyes, or even in the eyes of others; for we are hereby summoned to build for ourselves a new and different reputation with God and our own consciences--a reputation founded on a basis of reality and not of seeming.

It may be worth while to note the characteristics and danger of that special form of weakness which Peter here exhibited. We commonly call it moral cowardice. It is originally a weakness rather than a positive sin, and yet it is probably as prolific of sin and even of great crime as any of the more definite and vigorous passions of our nature, such as hate, lust, avarice. It is that weakness which prompts a man to avoid difficulties, to escape everything rough and disagreeable, to yield to circumstances, and which above all makes him incapable of facing the reproach, contempt, or opposition of his fellow-men. It is often found in combination with much amiability of character. It is commonly found in persons who have some natural leanings to virtue, and who, if circumstances would only favour them, would prefer to lead, and would lead, at least an inoffensive and respectable, if not a very useful, noble, or heroic life. Finely strung natures that are very sensitive to all impressions from without, natures which thrill and vibrate in response to a touching tale or in sympathy with fine scenery or soft music, natures which are housed in bodies of delicate nervous temperament, are commonly keenly sensitive to the praise or blame of their fellows, and are therefore liable to moral cowardice, though by no means necessarily a prey to it.

The examples of its ill-effects are daily before our eyes. A man cannot bear the coolness of a friend or the contempt of a leader of opinion, and so he stifles his own independent judgment and goes with the majority. A minister of the Church finds his faith steadily diverging from that of the creed he has subscribed, but he cannot proclaim this change because he cannot make up his mind to be the subject of public astonishment and remark, of severe scrutiny on the one side and still more distasteful because ignorant and canting sympathy on the other. A man in business finds that his expenditure exceeds his income, but he is unable to face the shame of frankly lowering his position and curtailing his expenses, and so he is led into dishonest appearances; and from dishonest appearances to fraudulent methods of keeping them up the step, as we all know, is short. Or in trade a man knows that there are shameful, contemptible, and silly practices, and yet he has not moral courage to break through them. A parent cannot bear to risk the loss of his child's good-will even for an hour, and so omits the chastisement he deserves. The schoolboy, fearing his parents' look of disappointment, says he stands higher in his class than he does; or fearing to be thought soft and unmanly by his schoolfellows, sees cruelty or a cheat or some wickedness perpetrated without a word of honest anger or manly condemnation. All this is moral cowardice, the vice which brings us down to the low level which bold sinners set for us, or which at any rate sweeps the weak soul down to a thousand perils, and absolutely forbids the good there is in us from finding expression.

But of all the forms into which moral cowardice develops this of denying the Lord Jesus is the most iniquitous and disgraceful. One of the fashions of the day which is most rapidly extending and which many of us have opportunity to resist is the fashion of infidelity. Much of the strongest and best-trained intellect of the country ranges itself against Christianity--that is, against Christ. No doubt the men who have led this movement have adopted their opinions on conviction. They deny the authority of Scripture, the divinity of Christ, even the existence of a personal God, because by long years of painful thought they have been forced to such conclusions. Even the best of them cannot be acquitted of a contemptuous and bitter way of speaking of Christians, which would seem to indicate that they are not quite at ease in their belief. Still, we cannot but think that so far as any men can be quite unbiassed in their opinions, they are so; and we have no right to judge other men for their honestly formed opinions. The moral cowards of whom we speak are not these men, but their followers, persons who with no patience or capacity to understand their reasonings adopt their conclusions because they seem advanced and are peculiar. There are many persons of slender reading and no depth of earnestness who, without spending any serious effort on the formation of their religious belief, presume to disseminate unbelief and treat the Christian creed as an obsolete thing merely because part of the intellect of the day leans in that direction. Weakness and cowardice are the real spring of such persons' apparent advance and new position regarding religion. They are ashamed to be reckoned among those who are thought to be behind the age. Ask them for a reason of their unbelief, and they are either unable to give you any, or else they repeat a time-worn objection which has been answered so often that men have wearied of the interminable task and let it pass unnoticed.

Such persons we aid and abet when we do either of two things: when we either cleave to what is old as unreasoningly as they take up with what is new, refusing to look for fresh light and better ways and acting as if we were already perfect; or when we yield to the current and adopt a hesitating way of speaking about matters of faith, when we cultivate a sceptical spirit and seem to connive at if we do not applaud the cold, irreligious sneer of ungodly men. Above all, we aid the cause of infidelity when in our own life we are ashamed to live godly, to act on higher principles than the current prudential maxims, when we hold our allegiance to Christ in abeyance to our fear of our associates, when we find no way of showing that Christ is our Lord and that we delight in opportunities of confessing Him. The confessing of Christ is a duty explicitly imposed on all those who expect that He will acknowledge them as His. It is a duty to which we might suppose every manly and generous instinct in us would eagerly respond, and yet we are often more ashamed of our connection with the loftiest and holiest of beings than of our own pitiful and sin-infected selves, and as little practically stimulated and actuated by a true gratitude to Him as if His death were the commonest boon and as if we were expecting and needing no help from Him in the time that is yet to come. [23]

Footnotes:

22 There is a difficulty in tracing the movements of Jesus at this point. John tells us He was led to Annas first, and at ver. 24 he says that Annas sent Him to Caiaphas. We should naturally conclude, therefore, that the preceding examination was conducted by Annas. But Caiaphas has been expressly indicated as chief priest, and it is by the chief priest and in the chief priest's palace the examination is conducted. The name "chief priest" was not confined to the one actually in office, but was applied to all who had held the office, and might therefore be applied to Annas. Possibly the examination recorded vv. 19-23 was before him, and probably he was living with his son-in-law in the palace of the chief priest.

23. Some of the ideas in this chapter were suggested by a sermon of Bishop Temple's.

Marcus Dods, D.D.

XIX. JESUS BEFORE PILATE

"They led Jesus therefore from Caiaphas into the palace: and it was early; and they themselves entered not into the palace, that they might not be defiled, but might eat the Passover. Pilate therefore went out unto them, and saith, What accusation bring ye against this man? They answered and said unto him, If this man were not an evil-doer, we should not have delivered Him up unto thee. Pilate therefore said unto them, Take Him yourselves, and judge Him according to your law. The Jews said unto him, It is not lawful for us to put any man to death: that the word of Jesus might be fulfilled, which He spake, signifying by what manner of death He should die. Pilate therefore entered again into the palace, and called Jesus, and said unto Him, Art Thou the King of the Jews? Jesus answered, Sayest thou this of thyself, or did others tell it thee concerning Me? Pilate answered, Am I a Jew? Thine own nation and the chief priests delivered Thee unto me: what hast Thou done? Jesus answered, My kingdom is not of this world: if My kingdom were of this world, then would My servants fight, that I should not be delivered to the Jews: but now is My kingdom not from hence. Pilate therefore said unto Him, Art Thou a king then? Jesus answered, Thou sayest that I am a king. To this end have I been born, and to this end am I come into the world, that I should bear witness unto the truth. Every one that is of the truth heareth My voice. Pilate saith unto Him, What is truth? And when he had said this, he went out again unto the Jews, and saith unto them, I find no crime in Him. But ye have a custom, that I should release unto you one at the Passover: will ye therefore that I release unto you the King of the Jews? They cried out therefore again, saying, Not this man, but Barabbas. Now Barabbas was a robber. Then Pilate therefore took Jesus, and scourged Him. And the soldiers plaited a crown of thorns, and put it on His head, and arrayed Him in a purple garment; and they came unto Him, and said, Hail, King of the Jews! and they struck Him with their hands. And Pilate went out again, and saith unto them, Behold I bring Him out to you, that ye may know that I find no crime in Him. Jesus therefore came out, wearing the crown of thorns and the purple garment. And Pilate saith unto them, Behold, the man! When therefore the chief priests and the officers saw Him, they cried out, saying, Crucify Him, crucify Him. Pilate saith unto them, Take Him yourselves, and crucify Him: for I find no crime in Him. The Jews answered him, We have a law, and by that law He ought to die, because He made Himself the Son of God. When Pilate therefore heard this saying he was the more afraid; and he entered into the palace again, and saith unto Jesus, Whence art Thou? But Jesus gave him no answer. Pilate therefore saith unto Him, Speakest Thou not unto me? knowest Thou not that I have power to release Thee, and have power to crucify Thee? Jesus answered Him, Thou wouldest have no power against Me, except it were given thee from above: therefore he that delivered Me unto thee hath greater sin. Upon this Pilate sought to release Him: but the Jews cried out, saying, If thou release this man, thou art not Cæsar's friend: every one that maketh himself a king speaketh against Cæsar. When Pilate therefore heard these words, he brought Jesus out, and sat down on the judgment-seat at a place called The Pavement, but in Hebrew, Gabbatha. Now it was the preparation of the Passover: it was about the sixth hour. And he saith unto the Jews, Behold, your King! They therefore cried out, Away with Him, away with Him, crucify Him. Pilate saith unto them, Shall I crucify your King? The chief priests answered, We have no king but Cæsar. Then therefore he delivered Him unto them to be crucified."--John xviii. 28-xix. 16.

John tells us very little of the examination of Jesus by Annas and Caiaphas, but he dwells at considerable length on His trial by Pilate. The reason of this different treatment is probably to be found in the fact that the trial before the Sanhedrim was ineffective until the decision had been ratified by Pilate, as well as in the circumstance noted by John that the decision of Caiaphas was a foregone conclusion. Caiaphas was an unscrupulous politician who allowed nothing to stand between him and his objects. To the weak councillors who had expressed a fear that it might be difficult to convict a person so innocent as Jesus he said with supreme contempt: "Ye know nothing at all. Do you not see the opportunity we have of showing our zeal for the Roman Government by sacrificing this man who claims to be King of the Jews? Innocent of course He is, and all the better so, for the Romans cannot think He dies for robbery or wrong-doing. He is a Galilean of no consequence, connected with no good family who might revenge His death." This was the scheme of Caiaphas. He saw that the Romans were within a very little of terminating the incessant troubles of this Judæan province by enslaving the whole population and devastating the land; this catastrophe might be staved off a few years by such an exhibition of zeal for Rome as could be made in the public execution of Jesus.

So far as Caiaphas and his party were concerned, then, Jesus was prejudged. His trial was not an examination to discover whether He was guilty or innocent, but a cross-questioning which aimed at betraying Him into some acknowledgment which might give colour to the sentence of death already decreed. Caiaphas or Annas [24] invites Him to give some account of His disciples and of His doctrines. In some cases His disciples carried arms, and among them was one zealot, and there might be others known to the authorities as dangerous or suspected characters. And Annas might expect that in giving some account of His teaching the honesty of Jesus might betray Him into expressions which could easily be construed to His prejudice. But he is disappointed. Jesus replies that it is not for Him, arraigned and bound as a dangerous prisoner, to give evidence against Himself. Thousands had heard Him in all parts of the country. He had delivered those supposed inflammatory addresses not to midnight gatherings and secret societies, but in the most public places He could find--in the Temple, from which no Jew was excluded, and in the synagogues, where official teachers were commonly present. Annas is silenced; and mortified though he is, he has to accept the ruling of his prisoner as indicating the lines on which the trial should proceed. His mortification does not escape the notice of one of those poor creatures who are ever ready to curry favour with the great by cruelty towards the defenceless, or at the best of that large class of men who cannot distinguish between official and real dignity; and the first of those insults is given to the hitherto sacred person of Jesus, the first of that long series of blows struck by a dead, conventional religion seeking to quench the truth and the life of what threatens its slumber with awakening.

Had the Roman governor not been present in the city the high priests and their party might have ventured to carry into effect their own sentence. But Pilate had already shown during his six years of office that he was not a man to overlook anything like contempt of his supremacy. Besides, they were not quite sure of the temper of the people; and a rescue, or even an attempted rescue, of their prisoner would be disastrous. Prudence therefore bids them hand Him over to Pilate, who had both legal authority to put Him to death and means to quell any popular disturbance. Besides, the purpose of Caiaphas could better be served by bringing before the governor this claimant to the Messiahship.

Pilate was present in Jerusalem at this time in accordance with the custom of the Roman procurators of Judæa, who came up annually from their usual residence at Cæsarea to the Jewish capital for the double purpose of keeping order while the city was crowded with all kinds of persons who came up to the feast, and of trying cases reserved for his decision. And the Jews no doubt thought it would be easy to persuade a man who, as they knew to their cost, set a very low value on human blood to add one victim more to the robbers or insurgents who might be awaiting execution. Accordingly, as soon as day dawned and they dared to disturb the governor, they put Jesus in chains as a condemned criminal and led Him away, all their leading men following, to the quarters of Pilate, either in the fortress Antonia or in the magnificent palace of Herod. Into this palace, being the abode of a Gentile, they could not enter lest they should contract pollution and incapacitate themselves for eating the Passover,--the culminating instance of religious scrupulosity going hand in hand with cruel and blood-thirsty criminality. Pilate with scornful allowance for their scruples goes out to them, and with the Roman's instinctive respect for the forms of justice demands the charge brought against this prisoner, in whose appearance the quick eye so long trained to read the faces of criminals is at a loss to discover any index to His crime.

This apparent intention on Pilate's part, if not to reopen the case at least to revise their procedure, is resented by the party of Caiaphas, who exclaim, "If He were not a malefactor we would not have delivered Him up unto thee. Take our word for it; He is guilty; do not scruple to put Him to death." But if they were indignant that Pilate should propose to revise their decision, he is not less so that they should presume to make him their mere executioner. All the Roman pride of office, all the Roman contempt and irritation at this strange Jewish people, come out in his answer, "If you will make no charge against Him and refuse to allow me to judge Him, take Him yourselves and do what you can with Him," knowing well that they dared not inflict death without his sanction, and that this taunt would pierce home. The taunt they did feel, although they could not afford to show that they felt it, but contented themselves with laying the charge that He had forbidden the people to give tribute to Cæsar and claimed to be Himself a king.

As Roman law permitted the examination to be conducted within the prætorium, though the judgment must be pronounced outside in public, Pilate re-enters the palace and has Jesus brought in, so that apart from the crowd he may examine Him. At once he puts the direct question, Guilty or not guilty of this political offence with which you stand charged?--"Art Thou the King of the Jews?" But to this direct question Jesus cannot give a direct answer, because the words may have one sense in the lips of Pilate, another in His own. Before He answers He must first know in which sense Pilate uses the words. He asks therefore, "Sayest thou this thing of thyself, or did others tell it thee?" Are you inquiring because you are yourself concerned in this question? or are you merely uttering a question which others have put in your mouth? To which Pilate with some heat and contempt replies, "Am I a Jew? How can you expect me to take any personal interest in the matter? Thine own nation and the chief priests have delivered Thee unto me."

Marcus Dods, D.D.

Pilate, that is to say, scouts the idea that he should take any interest in questions about the Messiah of the Jews. And yet was it not possible that, like some of his subordinates, centurions and others, he too should perceive the spiritual grandeur of Jesus and should not be prevented by his heathen upbringing from seeking to belong to this kingdom of God? May not Pilate also be awakened to see that man's true inheritance is the world unseen? may not that expression of fixed melancholy, of hard scorn, of sad, hopeless, proud indifference, give place to the humble eagerness of the inquiring soul? may not the heart of a child come back to that bewildered and world-encrusted soul? Alas! this is too much for Roman pride. He cannot in presence of this bound Jew acknowledge how little life has satisfied him. He finds the difficulty so many find in middle life of frankly showing that they have in their nature deeper desires than the successes of life satisfy. There is many a man who seals up his deeper instincts and does violence to his better nature because, having begun his life on worldly lines, he is too proud now to change, and crushes down, to his own eternal hurt, the stirrings of a better mind within him, and turns from the gentle whisperings that would fain bring eternal hope to his heart.

It is possible that Jesus by His question meant to suggest to Pilate the actual relation in which this present trial stood to His previous trial by Caiaphas. For nothing could more distinctly mark the baseness and malignity of the Jews than their manner of shifting ground when they brought Jesus before Pilate. The Sanhedrim had condemned Him, not for claiming to be King of the Jews, for that was not a capital offence, but for assuming Divine dignity. But that which in their eyes was a crime was none in the judgment of Roman law; it was useless to bring Him before Pilate and accuse Him of blasphemy. They therefore accused Him of assuming to be King of the Jews. Here, then, were the Jews "accusing Jesus before the Roman governor of that which, in the first place, they knew that Jesus denied in the sense in which they urged it, and which, in the next place, had the charge been true, would have been so far from a crime in their eyes that it would have been popular with the whole nation."

But as Pilate might very naturally misunderstand the character of the claim made by the accused, Jesus in a few words gives him clearly to understand that the kingdom He sought to establish could not come into collision with that which Pilate represented: "My kingdom is not of this world." The most convincing proof had been given of the spiritual character of the kingdom in the fact that Jesus did not allow the sword to be used in forwarding His claims. "If My kingdom were of this world, then would My servants fight, that I should not be delivered to the Jews: but now is My kingdom not from hence." This did not quite satisfy Pilate. He thought that still some mystery of danger might lurk behind the words of Jesus. There was nothing more acutely dreaded by the early emperors than secret societies. It might be some such association Jesus intended to form. To allow such a society to gain influence in his province would be a gross oversight on Pilate's part. He therefore seizes upon the apparent admission of Jesus and pushes Him further with the question, "Thou art a king then?" But the answer of Jesus removes all fear from the mind of His judge. He claims only to be a king of the truth, attracting to Himself all who are drawn by a love of truth. This was enough for Pilate. "Aletheia" was a country beyond his jurisdiction, a Utopia which could not injure the Empire. "Tush!" he says, "what is Aletheia? Why speak to me of ideal worlds? What concern have I with provinces that can yield no tribute and offer no armed resistance?"

Pilate, convinced of the innocence of Jesus, makes several attempts to save Him. All these attempts failed, because, instead of at once and decidedly proclaiming His innocence and demanding His acquittal, he sought at the same time to propitiate His accusers. One generally expects from a Roman governor some knowledge of men and some fearlessness in his use of that knowledge. Pilate shows neither. His first step in dealing with the accusers of Jesus is a fatal mistake. Instead of at once going to his judgment-seat and pronouncing authoritatively the acquittal of his Prisoner, and clearing his court of all riotously disposed persons, he in one breath declared Jesus innocent and proposed to treat Him as guilty, offering to release Him as a boon to the Jews. A weaker proposal could scarcely have been made. There was nothing, absolutely nothing, to induce the Jews to accept it, but in making it he showed a disposition to treat with them--a disposition they did not fail to make abundant use of in the succeeding scenes of this disgraceful day. This first departure from justice lowered him to their own level and removed the only bulwark he had against their insolence and blood-thirstiness. Had he acted as any upright judge would have acted and at once put his Prisoner beyond reach of their hatred, they would have shrunk like cowed wild beasts; but his first concession put him in their power, and from this point onwards there is exhibited one of the most lamentable spectacles in history,--a man in power tossed like a ball between his convictions and his fears; a Roman not without a certain doggedness and cynical hardness that often pass for strength of character, but held up here to view as a sample of the weakness that results from the vain attempt to satisfy both what is bad and what is good in us.

His second attempt to save Jesus from death was more unjust and as futile as the first. He scourges the Prisoner whose innocence he had himself declared, possibly under the idea that if nothing was confessed by Jesus under this torture it might convince the Jews of His innocence, but more probably under the impression that they might be satisfied when they saw Jesus bleeding and fainting from the scourge. The Roman scourge was a barbarous instrument, its heavy thongs being loaded with metal and inlaid with bone, every cut of which tore away the flesh. But if Pilate fancied that when the Jews saw this lacerated form they would pity and relent, he greatly mistook the men he had to do with. He failed to take into account the common principle that when you have wrongfully injured a man you hate him all the more. Many a man becomes a murderer, not by premeditation, but having struck a first blow and seeing his victim in agony he cannot bear that that eye should live to reproach him and that tongue to upbraid him with his cruelty. So it was here. The people were infuriated by the sight of the innocent, unmurmuring Sufferer whom they had thus mangled. They cannot bear that such an object be left to remind them of their barbarity, and with one fierce yell of fury they cry, "Crucify Him, crucify Him."[25]

A third time Pilate refused to be the instrument of their inhuman and unjust rage, and flung the Prisoner on their hands: "Take Him yourselves, and crucify Him: for I find no crime in Him." But when the Jews answered that by their law He ought to die, because "He made Himself the Son of God," Pilate was again seized with dread, and withdrew his Prisoner for the fourth time into the palace. Already he had remarked in His demeanour a calm superiority which made it seem quite possible that this extraordinary claim might be true. The books he had read at school and the poems he had heard since he grew up had told stories of how the gods had sometimes come down and dwelt with men. He had long since discarded such beliefs as mere fictions. Still, there was something in the bearing of this Prisoner before him that awakened the old impression, that possibly this single planet with its visible population was not the whole universe, that there might be some other unseen region out of which Divine beings looked down upon earth with pity, and from which they might come and visit us on some errand of love. With anxiety written on his face and heard in his tone he asks, "Whence art Thou?" How near does this man always seem to be to breaking through the thin veil and entering with illumined vision into the spiritual world, the world of truth and right and God! Would not a word now from Jesus have given him entrance? Would not the repetition of the solemn affirmation of His divinity which He had given to the Sanhedrim have been the one thing wanted in Pilate's case, the one thing to turn the scale in the favour of Jesus? At first sight it might seem so; but so it seemed not to the Lord. He preserves an unbroken silence to the question on which Pilate seems to hang in an earnest suspense. And certainly this silence is by no means easy to account for. Shall we say that He was acting out His own precept, "Give not that which is holy to dogs"? Shall we say that He who knew what was in man saw that though Pilate was for the moment alarmed and in earnest, yet there was beneath that earnestness an ineradicable vacillation? It is very possible that the treatment He had received at Pilate's hand had convinced Him that Pilate would eventually yield to the Jews; and what need, then, of protracting the process? No man who has any dignity and self-respect will make declarations about his character which he sees will do no good: no man is bound to be at the beck of every one to answer accusations they may bring against him; by doing so he will often only involve himself in miserable, petty wranglings, and profit no one. Jesus therefore was not going to make revelations about Himself which He saw would only make Him once again a shuttlecock driven between the two contending parties.

Besides--and this probably is the main reason of the silence--Pilate was now forgetting altogether the relation between himself and his Prisoner. Jesus had been accused before him on a definite charge which he had found to be baseless. He ought therefore to have released Him. This new charge of the Jews was one of which Pilate could not take cognisance; and of this Jesus reminds him by His silence. Jesus might have made influence for Himself by working upon the superstition of Pilate; but this was not to be thought of.

Offended at His silence, Pilate exclaims: "Speakest Thou not unto me? Knowest Thou not that I have power to release Thee, and have power to crucify Thee?" Here was an unwonted kind of prisoner who would not curry favour with His judge. But instead of entreating Pilate to use this power in His favour Jesus replies: "Thou wouldest have no power against Me, except it were given thee from above; therefore he that delivered Me unto thee hath greater sin." Pilate's office was the ordinance of God, and therefore his judgments should express the justice and will of God; and it was this which made the sin of Caiaphas and the Jews so great: they were making use of a Divine ordinance to serve their own God-resisting purposes. Had Pilate been a mere irresponsible executioner their sin would have been sufficiently heinous; but in using an official who is God's representative of law, order, and justice to fulfil their own wicked and unjust designs they recklessly prostitute God's ordinance of justice and involve themselves in a darker criminality.

More impressed than ever by this powerful statement falling from the lips of a man weakened by the scourging, Pilate makes one more effort to save Him. But now the Jews play their last card and play it successfully. "If thou release this man, thou art not Cæsar's friend." To lay himself open to a charge of treason or neglect of the interests of Cæsar was what Pilate could not risk. At once his compassion for the Prisoner, his sense of justice, his apprehensions, his proud unwillingness to let the Jews have their way, are overcome by his fear of being reported to the most suspicious of emperors. He prepared to give his judgment, taking his place on the official seat, which stood on a tesselated pavement, called in Aramaic "Gabbatha," from its elevated position in sight of the crowds standing outside. Here, after venting his spleen in the weak sarcasm "Shall I crucify your King?" he formally hands over his Prisoner to be crucified. This decision was at last come to, as John records, about noon of the day which prepared for and terminated in the Paschal Supper.

Pilate's vacillation receives from John a long and careful treatment. Light is shed upon it, and upon the threat which forced him at last to make up his mind, from the account which Philo gives of his character and administration. "With a view," he says, "to vex the Jews, Pilate hung up some gilt shields in the palace of Herod, which they judged a profanation of the holy city, and therefore petitioned him to remove them. But when he steadfastly refused to do so, for he was a man of very inflexible disposition and very merciless as well as very obstinate, they cried out, Beware of causing a tumult, for Tiberius will not sanction this act of yours; and if you say that he will, we ourselves will go to him and supplicate your master.' This threat exasperated Pilate in the highest degree, as he feared that they might really go to the Emperor and impeach him with respect to other acts of his government--his corruption, his acts of insolence, his habit of insulting people, his cruelty, his continual murders of people untried and uncondemned, and his never-ending and gratuitous and most grievous inhumanity. Therefore, being exceedingly angry, and being at all times a man of most ferocious passions, he was in great perplexity, neither venturing to take down what he had once set up nor wishing to do anything which could be acceptable to his subjects, and yet fearing the anger of Tiberius. And those who were in power among the Jews, seeing this and perceiving that he was inclined to change his mind as to what he had done, but that he was not willing to be thought to do so, appealed to the Emperor." [26] This sheds light on the whole conduct of Pilate during this trial--his fear of the Emperor, his hatred of the Jews and desire to annoy them, his vacillation and yet obstinacy; and we see that the mode the Sanhedrim now adopted with Pilate was their usual mode of dealing with him: now, as always, they saw his vacillation, disguised as it was by fierceness of speech, and they knew he must yield to the threat of complaining to Cæsar.

The very thing that Pilate feared, and to avoid which he sacrificed the life of our Lord, came upon him six years after. Complaints against him were sent to the Emperor; he was deposed from his office, and so stripped of all that made life endurable to him, that, "wearied with misfortunes," he died by his own hand. Perhaps we are tempted to think Pilate's fate severe; we naturally sympathise with him; there are so many traits of character which show well when contrasted with the unprincipled violence of the Jews. We are apt to say he was weak rather than wicked, forgetting that moral weakness is just another name for wickedness, or rather is that which makes a man capable of any wickedness. The man we call wicked has his one or two good points at which we can be sure of him. The weak man we are never sure of. That he has good feelings is nothing, for we do not know what may be brought to overcome these feelings. That he has right convictions is nothing; we may have thought he was convinced to-day, but to-morrow his old fears have prevailed. And who is the weak man who is thus open to every kind of influence? He is the man who is not single-minded. The single-minded, worldly man makes no pretension to holiness, but sees at a glance that that interferes with his real object; the single-minded, godly man has only truth and righteousness for his aim, and does not listen to fears or hopes suggested by the world. But the man who attempts to gratify both his conscience and his evil or weak feelings, the man who fancies he can so manipulate the events of his life as to secure his own selfish ends as well as the great ends of justice and righteousness, will often be in as great a perplexity as Pilate, and will come to as ruinous if not to so appalling an end.

In this would-be equitable Roman governor, exhibiting his weakness to the people and helplessly exclaiming, "What shall I do with Jesus which is called Christ?" [27] we see the predicament of many who are suddenly confronted with Christ--disconcerted as they are to have such a prisoner thrown on their hands, and wishing that anything had turned up rather than a necessity for answering this question, What shall I do with Jesus? Probably when Jesus was led by the vacillating Pilate out and in, back and forward, examined and re-examined, acquitted, scourged, defended, and abandoned to His enemies, some pity for His judge mingled with other feelings in His mind. This was altogether too great a case for a man like Pilate, fit enough to try men like Barabbas and to keep the turbulent Galileans in order. What unhappy fate, he might afterwards think, had brought this mysterious Prisoner to his judgment-seat, and for ever linked in such unhappy relation his name to the Name that is above every name? Never with more disastrous results did the resistless stream of time bring together and clash together the earthen and the brazen pitcher. Never before had such a prisoner stood at any judge's bar. Roman governors and emperors had been called to doom or to acquit kings and potentates of all degrees and to determine every kind of question, forbidding this or that religion, extirpating old dynasties, altering old landmarks, making history in its largest dimensions; but Pilate was summoned to adjudicate in a case that seemed of no consequence at all, yet really eclipsed in its importance all other cases put together.

Nothing could save Pilate from the responsibility attaching to his connection with Jesus, and nothing can save us from the responsibility of determining what judgment we are to pronounce on this same Person. It may seem to us an unfortunate predicament we are placed in; we may resent being called upon to do anything decided in a matter where our convictions so conflict with our desires; we may inwardly protest against human life being obstructed and disturbed by choices that are so pressing and so difficult and with issues so incalculably serious. But second thoughts assure us that to be confronted with Christ is in truth far from being an unfortunate predicament, and that to be compelled to decisions which determine our whole after-course and allow fullest expression of our own will and spiritual affinities is our true glory. Christ stands patiently awaiting our decision, maintaining His inalienable majesty, but submitting Himself to every test we care to apply, claiming only to be the King of the truth by whom we are admitted into that sole eternal kingdom. It has come to be our turn, as it came to be Pilate's, to decide upon His claims and to act upon our decision--to recognise that we men have to do, not merely with pleasure and place, with earthly rewards and relations, but above all with the truth, with that which gives eternal significance to all these present things, with the truth about human life, with the truth embodied for us in Christ's person and speaking intelligibly to us through His lips, with God manifest in the flesh. Are we to take part with Him when He calls us to glory and to virtue, to the truth and to eternal life, or yielding to some present pressure the world puts upon us attempt some futile compromise and so renounce our birthright?

Could Pilate really persuade himself he made everything right with a basin of water and a theatrical transference of his responsibility to the Jews? Could he persuade himself that by merely giving up the contest he was playing the part of a judge and of a man? Could he persuade himself that the mere words, "I am innocent of the blood of this righteous man: see ye to it," altered his relation to the death of Christ? No doubt he did. There is nothing commoner than for a man to think himself forced when it is his own fear or wickedness that is his only compulsion. Would every man in Pilate's circumstances have felt himself forced to surrender Jesus to the Jews? Would even a Gallio or a Claudius Lysias have done so? But Pilate's past history made him powerless. Had he not feared exposure, he would have marched his cohort across the square and cleared it of the mob and defied the Sanhedrim. It was not because he thought the Jewish law had any true right to demand Christ's death, but merely because the Jews threatened to report him as conniving at rebellion, that he yielded Christ to them; and to seek to lay the blame on those who made it difficult to do the right thing was both unmanly and futile. The Jews were at least willing to take their share of the blame, dreadful in its results as that proved to be.

Fairly to apportion blame where there are two consenting parties to a wickedness is for us, in many cases, impossible; and what we have to do is to beware of shifting blame from ourselves to our circumstances or to other people. However galling it is to find ourselves mixed up with transactions which turn out to be shameful, or to discover that some vacillation or imbecility on our part has made us partakers in sin, it is idle and worse to wash our hands ostentatiously and try to persuade ourselves we have no guilt in the matter. The fact that we have been brought in contact with unjust, cruel, heartless, fraudulent, unscrupulous, worldly, passionate people may explain many of our sins, but it does not excuse them. Other people in our circumstances would not have done what we have done; they would have acted a stronger, manlier, more generous part. And if we have sinned, it only adds to our guilt and encourages our weakness to profess innocence now and transfer to some other party the disgrace that belongs to ourselves. Nothing short of physical compulsion can excuse wrong-doing.

The calmness and dignity with which Jesus passed through this ordeal, alone self-possessed, while all around Him were beside themselves, so impressed Pilate that he not only felt guilty in giving Him up to the Jews, but did not think it impossible that He might be the Son of God. But what is perhaps even more striking in this scene is the directness with which all these evil passions of men--fear, and self-interest, and injustice, and hate--are guided to an end fraught with blessing. Goodness finds in the most adverse circumstances material for its purposes. We are apt in such circumstances to despair and act as if there were never to be a triumph of goodness; but the little seed of good that one individual can contribute even by hopeful and patient submission is that which survives and produces good in perpetuity, while the passion and the hate and the worldliness cease. In so wild a scene what availed it, we might have said, that one Person kept His steadfastness and rose superior to the surrounding wickedness? But the event showed that it did avail. All the rest was scaffolding that fell away out of sight, and this solitary integrity remains as the enduring monument. In our measure we must pass through similar ordeals, times when it seems vain to contend, useless to hope. When all we have done seems to be lost, when our way is hid and no further step is visible, when all the waves and billows of an ungodly world seem to threaten with extinction the little good we have cherished, then must we remember this calm, majestic Prisoner, bound in the midst of a frantic and blood-thirsty mob, yet superior to it because He was living in God.

Footnotes:

24. See note to chapter xviii.

25. The cry according to the best reading was simply "Crucify, crucify," or as it might be rendered, "The cross, the cross."
26. Philo, Ad Caium, c. 38.
27. Mark xv. 12.

XX. MARY AT THE CROSS

"They took Jesus therefore: and He went out, bearing the cross for Himself, unto the place called The place of a skull, which is called in Hebrew Golgotha: where they crucified Him, and with Him two others, on either side one, and Jesus in the midst. And Pilate wrote a title also, and put it on the cross. And there was written, Jesus of Nazareth, the King of the Jews. This title therefore read many of the Jews: for the place where Jesus was crucified was nigh to the city: and it was written in Hebrew, and in Latin, and in Greek. The chief priests of the Jews therefore said to Pilate, Write not, The King of the Jews; but, that He said, I am King of the Jews. Pilate answered, What I have written I have written. The soldiers therefore, when they had crucified Jesus, took His garments, and made four parts, to every soldier a part; and also the coat: now the coat was without seam, woven from the top throughout. They said therefore one to another, Let us not rend it, but cast lots for it, whose it shall be; that the scripture might be fulfilled, which saith, They parted My garments among them, And upon My vesture did they cast lots. These things therefore the soldiers did. But there were standing by the cross of Jesus His mother, and His mother's sister, Mary the wife of Clopas, and Mary Magdalene. When Jesus therefore saw His mother, and the disciple standing by, whom He loved, He saith unto His mother, Woman, behold thy son! Then saith He to the disciple, Behold, thy mother! And from that hour the disciple took her unto his own home."--John xix. 17-27.

If we ask on what charge our Lord was condemned to die, the answer must be complex, not simple. Pilate indeed, in accordance with the usual custom, painted on a board the name and crime of the Prisoner, that all who could understand any of the three current languages might know who this was and why He was crucified. But in the case of Jesus the inscription was merely a ghastly jest on Pilate's part. It was the coarse retaliation of a proud man who found himself helpless in the hands of people he despised and hated. There was some relish to him in the crucifixion of Jesus when by his inscription he had turned it into an insult to the nation. A gleam of savage satisfaction for a moment lit up his gloomy face when he found that his taunt had told, and the chief priests came begging him to change what he had written.

Pilate from the first look he got of his Prisoner understood that he had before him quite another kind of person than the ordinary zealot, or spurious Messiah, or turbulent Galilean. Pilate knew enough of the Jews to feel sure that if Jesus had been plotting rebellion against Rome He would not have been informed against by the chief priests. Possibly he knew enough of what had been going on in his province to understand that it was precisely because Jesus would not allow Himself to be made a king in opposition to Rome that the Jews detested and accused Him. Possibly he saw enough of the relations of Jesus to the authorities to despise the abandoned malignity and baseness which could bring an innocent man to his bar and charge Him with what in their eyes was no crime at all and make the charge precisely because He was innocent of it.

Nominally, but only nominally, Jesus was crucified for sedition. If we pass, in search of the real charge, from Pilate's judgment-seat to the Sanhedrim, we get nearer to the truth. The charge on which He was in this court condemned was the charge of blasphemy. He was indeed examined as to His claims to be the Messiah, but it does not appear that they had any law on which He could have been condemned for such claims. They did not expect that the Messiah would be Divine in the proper sense. Had they done so, then any one falsely claiming to be the Messiah would thereby have falsely claimed to be Divine, and would therefore have been guilty of blasphemy. But it was not for claiming to be the Christ that Jesus was condemned; it was when He declared Himself to be the Son of God that the high priest rent His garments and declared Him guilty of blasphemy.

Now, of course it was very possible that many members of the Sanhedrim should sincerely believe that blasphemy had been uttered. The unity of God was the distinctive creed of the Jew, that which had made his nation, and for any human lips to claim equality with the one infinite God was not to be thought of. It must have fallen upon their ears like a thunder-clap; they must have fallen back on their seats or started from them in horror when so awful a claim was made by the human figure standing bound before them. There were men among them who would have advocated His claim to be the Messiah, who believed Him to be a man sent from God; but not a voice could be raised in His defence when the claim to be Son of God in a Divine sense passed His lips. His best friends must have doubted and been disappointed, must have supposed He was confused by the events of the night, and could only await the issue in sorrow and wonder.

Was the Sanhedrim, then, to blame for condemning Jesus? They sincerely believed Him to be a blasphemer, and their law attached to the crime of blasphemy the punishment of death. It was in ignorance they did it; and knowing only what they knew, they could not have acted otherwise. Yes, that is true. But they were responsible for their ignorance. Jesus had given abundant opportunity to the nation to understand Him and to consider His claims. He did not burst upon the public with an uncertified demand to be accepted as Divine. He lived among those who were instructed in such matters; and though in some respects He was very different from the Messiah they had looked for, a little openness of mind and a little careful inquiry would have convinced them He was sent from God. And had they acknowledged this, had they allowed themselves to obey their instincts and say, This is a true man, a man who has a message for us--had they not sophisticated their minds with quibbling literalities, they would have owned His superiority and been willing to learn from Him. And had they shown any disposition to learn, Jesus was too wise a teacher to hurry them and overleap needed steps in conviction and experience. He would have been slow to extort from any a confession of his divinity until they had reached the belief of it by the working of their own minds. Enough for Him that they were willing to see the truth about Him and to declare it as they saw it. The great charge He brought against His accusers was that they did violence to their own convictions. The uneasy suspicions they had about His dignity they suppressed; the attraction they at times felt to His goodness they resisted; the duty to inquire patiently into His claims they refused. And thus their darkness deepened, until in their culpable ignorance they committed the greatest of crimes.

From all this, then, two things are apparent. First, that Jesus was condemned on the charge of blasphemy--condemned because He made Himself equal with God. His own words, pronounced upon oath, administered in the most solemn manner, were understood by the Sanhedrim to be an explicit claim to be the Son of God in a sense in which no man could without blasphemy claim to be so. He made no explanation of His words when He saw how they were understood. And yet, were He not truly Divine, there was no one who could have been more shocked than Himself by such a claim. He understood, if any man did, the majesty of God; He knew better than any other the difference between the Holy One and His sinful creatures; His whole life was devoted to the purpose of revealing to men the unseen God. What could have seemed to Him more monstrous, what could more effectually have stultified the work and aim of His life, than that He, being a man, should allow Himself to be taken for God? When Pilate told Him that He was charged with claiming to be a king, He explained to Pilate in what sense He did so, and removed from Pilate's mind the erroneous supposition this claim had given birth to. Had the Sanhedrim cherished an erroneous idea of what was involved in His claim to be the Son of God, He must also have explained to them in what sense He made it, and have removed from their minds the impression that He was claiming to be properly Divine. He did not make any explanation; He allowed them to suppose He claimed to be the Son of God in a sense which would be blasphemous in a mere man. So that if any one gathers from this that Jesus was Divine in a sense in which it were blasphemy for any other man to claim to be, he gathers a legitimate, even a necessary, inference.

Another reflection which is forced upon the reader of this narrative is, that disaster waits upon stifled inquiry. The Jews honestly convicted Christ as a blasphemer because they had dishonestly denied Him to be a good man. The little spark which would have grown into a blazing light they put their heel upon. Had they at the first candidly considered Him as He went about doing good and making no claims, they would have become attached to Him as His disciples did, and, like them, would have been led on to a fuller knowledge of the meaning of His person and work. It is these beginnings of conviction we are so apt to abuse. It seems so much smaller a crime to kill an infant that has but once drawn breath than to kill a man of lusty life and busy in his prime; but the one, if fairly dealt with, will grow to be the other. And while we think very little of stifling the scarcely breathed whisperings in our own heart and mind, we should consider that it is only such whisperings that can bring us to the loudly proclaimed truth. If we do not follow up suggestions, if we do not push inquiry to discovery, if we do not value the smallest grain of truth as a seed of unknown worth and count it wicked to kill even the smallest truth in our souls, we can scarcely hope at any time to stand in the full light of reality and rejoice in it. To accept Christ as Divine may be at present beyond us; to acknowledge Him as such would simply be to perjure ourselves; but can we not acknowledge Him to be a true man, a good man, a teacher certainly sent from God? If we do know Him to be all that and more, then have we thought this out to its results? Knowing Him to be a unique figure among men, have we perceived what this involves? Admitting Him to be the best of men, do we love Him, imitate Him, ponder His words, long for His company? Let us not treat Him as if He were non-existent because He is not as yet to us all that He is to some. Let us beware of dismissing all conviction about Him because there are some convictions spoken of by other people which we do not feel. It is better to deny Christ than to deny our own convictions; for to do so is to extinguish the only light we have, and to expose ourselves to all disaster. The man who has put out his own eyes cannot plead blindness in extenuation of his not seeing the lights and running the richly laden ship on the rocks.

Guided by the perfect taste which reverence gives, John says very little about the actual crucifixion. He shows us indeed the soldiers sitting down beside the little heap of clothes they had stripped off our Lord, parcelling them out, perhaps already assuming them as their own wear. For the clothes by which our Lord had been known these soldiers would now carry into unknown haunts of drunkenness and sin, emblems of our ruthless, thoughtless desecration of our Lord's name with which we outwardly clothe ourselves and yet carry into scenes the most uncongenial. John, writing long after the event, seems to have no heart to record the poor taunts with which the crowd sought to increase the suffering of the Crucified, and force home upon His spirit a sense of the desolation and ignominy of the cross. Gradually the crowd wearies and scatters, and only here and there a little whispering group remains. The day waxes to its greatest heat; the soldiers lie or stand silent; the centurion sits motionless on his motionless, statue-like horse; the stillness of death falls upon the scene, only broken at intervals by a groan from one or other of the crosses. Suddenly through this silence there sound the words, "Woman, behold thy son: son, behold thy mother."--words which remind us that all this dreadful scene which makes the heart of the stranger bleed has been witnessed by the mother of the Crucified. As the crowd had broken up from around the crosses, the little group of women whom John had brought to the spot edged their way nearer and nearer till they were quite close to Him they loved, though their lips apparently were sealed by their helplessness to minister consolation.

These hours of suffering, as the sword was slowly driven through Mary's soul, according to Simeon's word, who shall measure? Hers was not a hysterical, noisy sorrow, but quiet and silent. There was nothing wild, nothing extravagant, in it. There was no sign of feminine weakness, no outcry, no fainting, no wild gesture of uncontrollable anguish, nothing to show that she was the exceptional mourner and that there was no sorrow like unto her sorrow. Her reverence for the Lord saved her from disturbing His last moments. She stood and saw the end. She saw His head lifted in anguish and falling on His breast in weakness, and she could not gently take it in her hands and wipe the sweat of death from His brow. She saw His pierced hands and feet become numbed and livid, and might not chafe them. She saw Him gasp with pain as cramp seized part after part of His outstretched body, and she could not change His posture nor give liberty to so much as one of His hands. And she had to suffer this in profound desolation of spirit. Her life seemed to be buried at the cross. To the mourning there often seems nothing left but to die with the dying. One heart has been the light of life, and now that light is quenched. What significance, what motive, can life have any more? [28] We valued no past where that heart was not; we had no future which was not concentrated upon it or in which it had no part. But the absorption of common love must have been far surpassed in Mary's case. None had been blessed with such a love as hers. And now none estimated as she did the spotless innocence of the Victim; none could know as she knew the depth of His goodness, the unfathomable and unconquerable love He had for all; and none could estimate as she the ingratitude of those whom He had healed and fed and taught and comforted with such unselfish devotedness. She knew that there was none like Him, and that if any could have brought blessing to this earth it was He, and there she saw Him nailed to the cross, the end actually reached. We know not if in that hour she thought of the trial of Abraham; we know not whether she allowed herself to think at all, whether she did not merely suffer as a mother losing her son; but certainly it must have been with intensest eagerness she heard herself once more addressed by Him.

Mary was commended to John as the closest friend of Jesus. These two would be in fullest sympathy, both being devoted to Him. It was perhaps an indication to those who were present, and through them to all, that nothing is so true a bond between human hearts as sympathy with Christ. We may admire nature, and yet have many points of antipathy to those who also admire nature. We may like the sea, and yet feel no drawing to some persons who also like the sea. We may be fond of mathematics, and yet find that this brings us into a very partial and limited sympathy with mathematicians. Nay, we may even admire and love the same person as others do, and yet disagree about other matters. But if Christ is chosen and loved as He ought to be, that love is a determining affection which rules all else within us, and brings us into abiding sympathy with all who are similarly governed and moulded by that love. That love indicates a certain past experience and guarantees a special type of character. It is the characteristic of the subjects of the kingdom of God.

This care for His mother in His last moments is of a piece with all the conduct of Jesus. Throughout His life there is an entire absence of anything pompous or excited. Everything is simple. The greatest acts in human history He does on the highway, in the cottage, among a group of beggars in an entry. The words which have thrilled the hearts and mended the lives of myriads were spoken casually as He walked with a few friends. Rarely did He even gather a crowd. There was no advertising, no admission by ticket, no elaborate arrangements for a set speech at a set hour. Those who know human nature will know what to think of this unstudied ease and simplicity, and will appreciate it. The same characteristic appears here. He speaks as if He were not an object of contemplation; there is an entire absence of self-consciousness, of ostentatious suggestion that He is now making atonement for the sins of the world. He speaks to His mother and cares for her as He might have done had they been in the home at Nazareth together. One despairs of ever learning such a lesson, or indeed of seeing others learn it. How like an ant-hill is the world of men! What a fever and excitement! what a fuss and fret! what an ado! what a sending of messengers, and calling of meetings, and raising of troops, and magnifying of little things! what an absence of calmness and simplicity! But this at least we may learn-- that no duties, however important, can excuse us for not caring for our relatives. They are deceived people who spend all their charity and sweetness out of doors, who have a reputation for godliness, and are to be seen in the forefront of this or that Christian work, but who are sullen or imperious or quick-tempered or indifferent at home. If while saving a world Jesus had leisure to care for His mother, there are no duties so important as to prevent a man from being considerate and dutiful at home.

Those who witnessed the hurried events of the morning when Christ was crucified might be pardoned if their minds were filled with what their eyes saw, and if little but the outward objects were discernible to them. We are in different circumstances, and may be expected to look more deeply into what was happening. To see only the mean scheming and wicked passions of men, to see nothing but the pathetic suffering of an innocent and misjudged person, to take our interpretation of these rapid and disorderly events from the casual spectators without striving to discover God's meaning in them, would indeed be a flagrant instance of what has been called "reading God in a prose translation," rendering His clearest and most touching utterance to this world in the language of callous Jews or barbarous Roman soldiers. Let us open our ear to God's own meaning in these events, and we hear Him uttering to us all His Divine love, and in the most forcible and touching tones. These are the events in which His deepest purposes and tenderest love find utterance. How He is striving to win His way to us to convince us of the reality of sin and of salvation! To be mere spectators of these things is to convict ourselves of being superficial or strangely callous. Scarcely any criminal is executed but we all have our opinion on the justice or injustice of his condemnation. We may well be expected to form our judgment in this case, and to take action upon it. If Jesus was unjustly condemned, then we as well as His contemporaries have to do with His claims. If these claims were true, we have something more to do than merely to say so.

Footnotes:

28. See Faber's Bethlehem.

XXI. THE CRUCIFIXION

"The soldiers therefore, when they had crucified Jesus, took His garments, and made four parts, to every soldier a part; and also the coat: now the coat was without seam, woven from the top throughout. They said therefore one to another, Let us not rend it, but cast lots for it, whose it shall be: that the scripture might be fulfilled, which saith, They parted My garments among them, And upon My vesture did they cast lots. These things therefore the soldiers did.... After this Jesus, knowing that all things are now finished, that the scripture might be accomplished, saith, I thirst. There was set there a vessel full of vinegar: so they put a sponge full of the vinegar upon hyssop, and brought it to His mouth. When Jesus therefore had received the vinegar, He said, It is finished: and He bowed His head, and gave up His spirit. The Jews therefore, because it was the Preparation, that the bodies should not remain on the cross upon the Sabbath (for the day of that Sabbath was a high day), asked of Pilate that their legs might be broken, and that they might be taken away. The soldiers therefore came, and brake the legs of the first, and of the other which was crucified with Him: but when they came to Jesus, and saw that He was dead already, they brake not His legs: howbeit one of the soldiers with a spear pierced His side, and straightway there came out blood and water. And he that hath seen hath borne witness, and his witness is true: and he knoweth that he saith true, that ye also may believe. For these things came to pass, that the scripture might be fulfilled, A bone of Him shall not be broken. And again another scripture saith, They shall look on Him whom they pierced."--John xix. 23, 24, 28-37.

Possibly the account which John gives of the Crucifixion is somewhat spoiled to some readers by his frequent reference to apparently insignificant coincidences with Old Testament prophecy. It is, however, to be remembered that John was himself a Jew, and was writing for a public which laid great stress on such literal fulfilments of prophecy. The wording of the narrative might lead us to suppose that John believed Jesus to be intentionally fulfilling prophecy. Where he says, "After this, Jesus knowing that all things were now accomplished, that the scripture might be fulfilled, saith, I thirst," it might be fancied that John supposed that Jesus said "I thirst" in order that Scripture might be fulfilled. This is, of course, to misconceive the Evangelist's meaning. Such a fulfilment would have been fictitious, not real. But John believes that in each smallest act and word of our Lord the will of God was finding expression, a will which had long since been uttered in the form of Old Testament prophecy. In these hours of dismay, when Jesus was arrested, tried, and crucified before the eyes of His disciples, they tried to believe that this was God's will; and long afterwards, when they had found time to think, and when they had to deal with men who felt the difficulty of believing in a crucified Saviour, they pointed to the fact that even in small particulars the sufferings of the Messiah had been anticipated and were to be expected.

The first instance of this which John cites is the manner in which the soldiers dealt with His clothes. After fixing Jesus to the cross and raising it, the four men who were detailed to this service sat down to watch. Such was the custom, lest friends should remove the crucified before death supervened. Having settled themselves for this watch, they proceeded to divide the clothes of Jesus among them. This also was customary among the Romans, as it has been everywhere usual that the executioners should have as their perquisite some of the articles worn by the condemned. The soldiers parted the garments of Jesus among them, each of the four taking what he needed or fancied--turban, shoes, girdle, or under-coat; while for the large seamless plaid that was worn over all they cast lots, being unwilling to tear it. All this fulfilled an old prediction to the letter. The reason why it had been spoken of was that it formed a weighty element in the suffering of the crucified. Few things can make a dying man feel more desolate than to overhear those who sit round his bed already disposing of his effects, counting him a dead man who can no longer use the apparatus of the living, and congratulating themselves on the profit they make by his death. How furious have old men sometimes been made by any betrayal of eagerness on the part of their heirs! Even to calculate on a man's death and make arrangements for filling his place is justly esteemed indecorous and unfeeling. To ask a sick man for anything he has been accustomed to use, and must use again if he recovers health, is an act which only an indelicate nature could be guilty of. It was a cruel addition, then, to our Lord's suffering to see these men heartlessly dividing among them all He had to leave. It forced on His mind the consciousness of their utter indifference to His feelings. His clothes were of some little value to them: He Himself of no value. Nothing could have made Him feel more separated from the world of the living--from their hopes, their ways, their life--as if already He were dead and buried.

This distribution of His clothes was also calculated to make Him intensely sensible of the reality and finality of death. Jesus knew He was to rise again; but let us not forget that Jesus was human, liable to the same natural fears, and moved by the same circumstances as ourselves. He knew He was to rise again; but how much easier had it been to believe in that future life had all the world been expecting Him to rise! But here were men showing that they very well knew He would never again need these clothes of His.

A comparison of this narrative with the other Gospels brings out that the words "I thirst" must have been uttered immediately after the fearful cry "My God, My God, why hast Thou forsaken Me?" For when the soldier was mercifully pressing the sponge steeped in vinegar to His parched lips, some of the bystanders called out, "Let be: let us see whether Elias will come to save Him," referring to the words of Jesus, which they had not rightly understood. And this expression of bodily suffering is proof that the severity of the spiritual struggle was over. So long as that deep darkness covered His spirit He was unconscious of His body; but with the agonised cry to His Father the darkness had passed away; the very uttering of His desolation had disburdened His spirit, and at once the body asserts itself. As in the wilderness at the opening of His career He had been for many days so agitated and absorbed in mind that He did not once think of food, but no sooner was the spiritual strife ended than the keen sensation of hunger was the first thing to demand His attention, so here His sense of thirst is the sign that His spirit was now at rest.

The last act of the Crucifixion, in which John sees the fulfilment of Old Testament prophecy, is the omission in the case of Jesus of the common mode of terminating the life of the crucified by breaking the legs with an iron bar. Jesus being already dead, this was considered unnecessary; but as possibly He might only have swooned, and as the bodies were immediately taken down, one of the soldiers makes sure of His death by a lance thrust. Medical men and scholars have largely discussed the causes which might produce the outflow of blood and water which John affirms followed this spear thrust, and various causes have been assigned. But it is a point which has apparently only physiological interest. John indeed follows up his statement of what he saw with an unusually strong asseveration that what he says is true. "He that saw it bare record, and his record is true: and he knoweth that he saith true, that ye might believe." But this strong asseveration is introduced, not for the sake of persuading us to believe that water as well as blood flowed from the lance wound, but for the sake of certifying the actual death of Jesus. The soldiers who had charge of the execution discharged their duty. They made sure that the Crucified was actually dead. And John's reason for insisting on this and appending to his statement so unusual a confirmation is sufficiently obvious. He was about to relate the Resurrection, and he knows that a true resurrection must be preceded by a real death. If he has no means of establishing the actual death, he has no means of establishing the Resurrection. And therefore for the first and only time in his narrative he departs from simple narration, and most solemnly asseverates that he is speaking the truth and was an eyewitness of the things he relates.

The emphatic language John uses regarding the certainty of Christ's death is, then, only an index to the importance he attached to the Resurrection. He was aware that whatever virtue lay in the life and death of Christ, this virtue became available for men through the Resurrection. Had Jesus not risen again all the hopes His friends had cherished regarding Him would have been buried in His tomb. Had He not risen His words would have been falsified and doubt thrown upon all His teaching. Had He not risen His claims would have been unintelligible and His whole appearance and life a mystery, suggesting a greatness not borne out--different from other men, yet subject to the same defeat. Had He not risen the very significance of His life would have been obscured; and if for a time a few friends cherished His memory in private, His name would have fallen back to an obscure, possibly a dishonoured, place.

It is not at once obvious what we are to make of the physical sufferings of Christ. Certainly it is very easy to make too much of them. For, in the first place, they were very brief and confined to one part of His life. He was exempt from the prolonged weakness and misery which many persons endure throughout life. Born, as we may reasonably suppose, with a healthy and vigorous constitution, carefully reared by the best of mothers, finding a livelihood in His native village and in His father's business, His lot was very different from the frightful doom of thousands who are born with diseased and distorted body, in squalid and wicked surroundings, and who never see through the misery that encompasses them to any happy or hopeful life. And even after He left the shelter and modest comforts of the Nazareth home His life was spent in healthy conditions, and often in scenes of much beauty and interest. Free to move about through the country as He pleased, passing through vineyards and olive-groves and cornfields, talking pleasantly with His little company of attached friends or addressing large audiences, He lived an open-air life of a kind in which of necessity there must have been a great deal of physical pleasure and healthful enjoyment. At times He had not where to lay His head; but this is mentioned rather as a symptom of His want of friends than as implying any serious physical suffering in a climate like that of Palestine. And the suffering at the close of His life, though extreme, was brief, and was not to be compared in its cruelty to what many of His followers have endured for His sake.

Two things, however, the physical sufferings of Christ do secure: they call attention to His devotedness, and they illustrate His willing sacrifice of self. They call attention to His devotedness and provoke a natural sympathy and tenderness of spirit in the beholder, qualities which are much needed in our consideration of Christ. Had He passed through life entirely exempt from suffering, in high position, with every want eagerly ministered to, untouched by any woe, and at last passing away by a painless decease, we should find it much harder to respond to His appeal or even to understand His work. Nothing so quickly rivets our attention and stirs our sympathy as physical pain. We feel disposed to listen to the demands of one who is suffering, and if we have a lurking suspicion that we are somehow responsible for that suffering and are benefited by it, then we are softened by a mingled pity, admiration, and shame, which is one of the fittest attitudes a human spirit can assume.

Besides, it is through the visible suffering we can read the willingness of Christ's self-surrender. It was always more difficult for Him to suffer than for us. We have no option: He might have rescued Himself at any moment. We, in suffering, have but to subdue our disposition to murmur and our sense of pain: He had to subdue what was much more obstinate--His consciousness that He might if He pleased abjure the life that involved pain. The strain upon His love for us was not once for all over when He became man. He Himself intimates, and His power of working miracles proves, that at each point of His career He might have saved Himself from suffering, but would not.

When we ask ourselves what we are to make of these sufferings of Christ, we naturally seek aid from the Evangelist and ask what he made of them. But on reading his narrative we are surprised to find so little comment or reflection interrupting the simple relation of facts. At first sight the narrative seems to flow uninterruptedly on, and to resemble the story which might be told of the closing scenes of an ordinary life terminating tragically. The references to Old Testament prophecy alone give us the clue to John's thoughts about the significance of this death. These references show us that he considered that in this public execution, conducted wholly by Roman soldiers, who could not read a word of Hebrew and did not know the name of the God of the Jews, there was being fulfilled the purpose of God towards which all previous history had been tending. That purpose of God in the history of man was accomplished when Jesus breathed His last upon the cross. The cry "It is finished" was not the mere gasp of a worn-out life; it was not the cry of satisfaction with which a career of pain and sorrow is terminated: it was the deliberate utterance of a clear consciousness on the part of God's appointed Revealer that now all had been done that could be done to make God known to men and to identify Him with men. God's purpose had ever been one and indivisible. Declared to men in various ways, a hint here, a broad light there, now by a gleam of insight in the mind of a prophet, now by a deed of heroism in king or leader, through rude symbolic contrivances and through the tenderest of human affections and the highest human thoughts God had been making men ever more and more sensible that His one purpose was to come closer and closer into fellowship with them and to draw them into a perfect harmony with Him. Forgiveness and deliverance from sin were provided for them, knowledge of God's law and will that they might learn to know and to serve Him--all these were secured when Jesus cried, "It is finished."

Why, then, does John just at this point of the life of Jesus see so many evidences of the fulfilment of all prophecy? Need we ask? Is not suffering that which is the standing problem of life? Is it not grief and trouble and sorrow which press home upon our minds most convincingly the reality of sin? Is it not death which is common to all men of every age, race, station, or experience? And must not One who identifies Himself with men identify Himself in this if in anything? It is the cross of Jesus that stands before the mind of John as the completion of that process of incarnation, of entrance into human experience, which fills his Gospel; it is here he sees the completion and finishing of that identification of God with man he has been exhibiting throughout. The union of God with man is perfected when God submits Himself to the last darkest experience of man. To some it seems impossible such a thing should be; it seems either unreal, unthought-out verbiage, or blasphemy. To John, after he had seen and pondered the words and the life of Jesus, all his ideas of the Father were altered. He learned that God is love, and that to infinite love, while there remains one thing to give, one step of nearness to the loved to be taken, love has not its perfect expression. It came upon him as a revelation that God was really in the world. Are we to refuse to God any true participation in the strife between good and evil? Is God to be kept out of all reality? Is He merely to look on, to see how His creatures will manage, how this and that man will bear himself heroically, but Himself a mere name, a lay figure crowned but otiose, doing nothing to merit His crown, doing nothing to warrant the worship of untold worlds, commanding others to peril themselves and put all to the proof, but Himself well out of range of all risk, of all conflict, of all tragedy? How can we hope to love a God we remove to a throne remote and exalted, from which He looks down on human life, and cannot look on it as we do from the inside! Is God to be only a dramatist, who arranges thrilling situations for others to pass through, and assigns to each the part he is to play, but Himself has no real interests at stake and no actual entrance into the world of feeling, of hope, of trial?

Marcus Dods, D.D.

And if a Divine Person were in the course of things to come into this human world, to enter into our actual experiences, and feel and bear the actual strain that we bear, it is obvious He must come incognito--not distinguished by such marks as would bring the world to His feet, and make an ordinary human life and ordinary human trials impossible to Him. When sovereigns wish to ascertain for themselves how their subjects live, they do not proclaim their approach and send in advance an army of protection, provision, and display; they do not demand to be met by the authorities of each town, and to be received by artificial, stereotyped addresses, and to be led from one striking sight to another and from one comfortable palace to another: but they leave their robes of state behind them, they send no messenger in advance, and they mix as one of the crowd with the crowd, exposed to whatever abuse may be going, and living for the time on the same terms as the rank and file. This has been done often in sport, sometimes as matter of policy or of interest, but never as the serious method of understanding and lifting the general habits and life of the people. Christ came among us, not as a kind of Divine adventure to break the tedium of eternal glory, nor merely to make personal observations on His own account, but as the requisite and only means available for bringing the fulness of Divine help into practical contact with mankind. But as all filth and squalor are hidden away in the slums from the senses of the king, so that if he is to penetrate into the burrows of the criminal classes and see the wretchedness of the poor, he must do it incognito, so if Christ sought to bring Divine mercy and might within reach of the vilest, He must visit their haunts and make Himself acquainted with their habits.

It is also obvious that such a Person would concern Himself not with art or literature, not with inventions and discoveries, not even with politics and government and social problems, but with that which underlies all these and for which all these exist--with human character and human conduct, with man's relation to God. It is with the very root of human life He concerns Himself.

The sufferings of Christ, then, were mainly inward, and were the necessary result of His perfect sympathy with men. That which has made the cross the most significant of earthly symbols, and which has invested it with so wonderful a power to subdue and purify the heart, is not the fact that it involved the keenest physical pain, but that it exhibits Christ's perfect and complete identification with sinful men. It is this that humbles us and brings us to a right mind towards God and towards sin, that here we see the innocent Son of God involved in suffering and undergoing a shameful death through our sin. It was His sympathy with men which brought Him into this world, and it was the same sympathy which laid Him open to suffering throughout His life. The mother suffers more in the illness of a child than in her own; the shame of wrong-doing is often more keenly felt by a parent or friend than by the perpetrator himself. If Paul's enthusiasm and devoted life for men made him truly say, "Who is weak, and I am not weak?" who shall measure the burden Christ bore from day to day in the midst of a sinning and suffering world? With a burning zeal for God, He was plunged into an arctic region where thick-ribbed ice of indifference met His warmth; consumed with devotion to God's purposes, He saw everywhere around Him ignorance, carelessness, self-seeking, total misunderstanding of what the world is for; linked to men with a love which irrepressibly urged Him to seek the highest good for all, He was on all hands thwarted; dying to see men holy and pure and godly, He everywhere found them weak, sinful, gross. It was this which made Him a man of sorrows and acquainted with grief--loving God and man with a love which was the chief element in His being, He could not get man reconciled to God. The mere sorrows of men doubtless affected Him more than they affect the most tender-hearted of men; but these sorrows--poverty, failure, sickness--would pass away and would even work for good, and so might well be borne. But when He saw men disregarding that which would save them from lasting sorrow; when He saw them giving themselves to trivialities with all their might, and doing nothing to recover their right relation to God, the spring of all good; when He saw them day by day defeating the purpose He lived to accomplish, and undoing the one only work He thought worth doing,--who can measure the burden of shame and grief He had to bear?

But it is not the suffering that does us good and brings us to God, but the love which underlies the suffering. The suffering convinces us that it is love which prompts Christ in all His life and death,--a love we may confidently trust to, since it is staggered at no difficulty or sacrifice; a love which aims at lifting and helping us; a love that embraces us, not seeking to accomplish only one thing for us, but necessarily, because it is love for us, seeking our good in all things. The power of earthly love, of the devotedness of mother, wife, or friend, we know;--we know what length such love will go: shall we then deny to God the happiness of sacrifice, the joy of love? Let it not enter our thoughts that He who is more closely related to us than any, and who will far less disclaim this relationship than any, does not love us in practical ways, and cannot fit us by His loving care for all that His holiness requires.

XXII. THE RESURRECTION

"Now on the first day of the week cometh Mary Magdalene early, while it was yet dark, unto the tomb, and seeth the stone taken away from the tomb. She runneth therefore, and cometh to Simon Peter, and to the other disciple, whom Jesus loved, and saith unto them, They have taken away the Lord out of the tomb, and we know not where they have laid Him. Peter therefore went forth, and the other disciple, and they went toward the tomb. And they ran both together: and the other disciple outran Peter, and came first to the tomb; and stooping and looking in, he seeth the linen cloths lying; yet entered he not in. Simon Peter therefore also cometh, following him, and entered into the tomb; and he beholdeth the linen cloths lying, and the napkin, that was upon His head, not lying with the linen cloths, but rolled up in a place by itself. Then entered in therefore the other disciple also, which came first to the tomb, and he saw, and believed. For as yet they knew not the scripture, that He must rise again from the dead. So the disciples went away again unto their own home. But Mary was standing without at the tomb weeping: so, as she wept, she stooped and looked into the tomb; and she beholdeth two angels in white sitting, one at the head, and one at the feet, where the body of Jesus had lain. And they say unto her, Woman, why weepest thou? She saith unto them, Because they have taken away my Lord, and I know not where they have laid Him. When she had thus said, she turned herself back, and beholdeth Jesus standing, and knew not that it was Jesus. Jesus saith unto her, Woman, why weepest thou? whom seekest thou? She, supposing Him to be the gardener, saith unto Him, Sir, if thou hast borne Him hence, tell me where thou hast laid Him, and I will take Him away, Jesus saith unto her, Mary. She turned herself, and saith unto Him in Hebrew, Rabboni; which is to say, Master. Jesus saith to her, Touch Me not; for I am not yet ascended unto the Father: but go unto My brethren, and say to them, I ascend unto My Father and your Father, and My God and your God. Mary Magdalene cometh and telleth the disciples, I have seen the Lord; and how that He had said these things unto her."--John xx. 1-18.

John gives no narrative of the Resurrection itself. He gives us what is much more valuable--a brief account of the manner in which he himself was convinced that a resurrection had taken place. His shy nature, his modest reluctance to put himself forward or use the first person in his narrative, does not prevent him from seeing that the testimony of one who, like himself, was an eyewitness of the facts is invaluable; and nothing but additional interest and reality is added to his testimony by the varied periphrases with which he veils his identity, as "the disciple whom Jesus loved," "that other disciple," and so forth.

When Mary brought the startling intelligence that the tomb was empty, Peter and John instantly made for the spot at the top of their speed. The older man was left behind by John, but natural reverence kept him from entering the rocky chamber. He looked in, however, and to his surprise saw enough to convince him that the body had not been removed for interment elsewhere or to be cast out with the bodies of criminals. For there were the linen cloths in which He had been wrapped, carefully taken off and left behind. The impression made by this circumstance was confirmed when Peter came up, and they both entered and examined the tomb and made their inferences together. For then they saw still clearer evidence of deliberation; the napkin which had been tied round the head of the dead body was there in the tomb, and it was folded and laid in a place by itself, suggesting the leisurely manner of a person changing his clothes, and convincing them that the body had not been removed to be laid elsewhere. At once John was convinced that a resurrection had taken place; his Lord's words took a new meaning in this empty tomb. Standing and gazing at the folded cloths, the truth flashed into his mind: Jesus has Himself risen and disencumbered Himself from these wrappings, and has departed. It was enough for John: he visited no other tomb; he questioned no one; he made no inquiries of his friends in the high priest's household,--he went to his own house, filled with astonishment, with a thousand thoughts chasing one another through his mind, scarcely listening to Peter's voluble tongue, but convinced that Jesus lived.

This simple narrative will be to many minds more convincing than an accumulation of elaborate arguments. The style is that of an eyewitness. Each movement and every particular is before his eye: Mary bursting, breathless, and gasping out the startling news; the hasty springing up of the two men, and their rapid racing along the streets and out through the city gates to the garden; John standing panting at the rock-hewn sepulchre, his stooping down and peering into the dark chamber; Peter toiling up behind, but not hesitating a moment, and entering and gazing at this and that till the dumb articles tell their story; and the two men leave the sepulchre together, awed and convinced. And the eyewitness who thus graphically relates what he knew of that great morning adds with the simplicity of a truthful nature, "he saw and believed"--believed then for the first time; for as yet they had not seen the significance of certain scriptures which now seemed plainly enough to point to this.

To some minds this simple narrative will, I say, carry home the conviction of the truth of the Resurrection more than any elaborate argumentation. There is an assuring matter-of-factness about it. Sceptics tell us that visions are common, and that excited people are easily deceived. But we have no word of visions here. John does not say he saw the Lord: he tells us merely of two fishermen running; of solid, commonplace articles such as grave-clothes; and of observations that could not possibly be mistaken, such as that the tomb was empty and that they two were in it. For my part I feel constrained to believe a narrative like this, when it tells me the grave was empty. No doubt their conclusion, that Jesus had Himself emptied the tomb, was not a certain but only a probable inference, and, had nothing more occurred, even John himself might not have continued so confident; but it is important to notice how John was convinced, not at all by visions or voices or embodied expectations of his own, but in the most matter-of-fact way and by the very same kind of observation that we use and rely upon in common life. And, moreover, more did occur; there followed just such results as were in keeping with so momentous an event.

One of these immediately occurred. Mary, exhausted with her rapid carrying of the news to Peter and John, was not able to keep pace with them as they ran to the tomb, and before she arrived they were gone. Probably she missed them in the streets as she came out of the city; at any rate, finding the tomb still empty and none present to explain the reason of it, she stands there desolate and pours out her distress in tears. That grave being empty, the whole earth is empty to her: the dead Christ was more to her than a living world. She could not go as Peter and John had gone, for she had no thought of resurrection. The rigid form, the unanswering lips and eye, the body passive in the hands of others, had fixed on her heart, as it commonly does, the one impression of death. She felt that all was over, and now she had not even the poor consolation of paying some slight additional attention. She can but stand and lay her head upon the stone and let her tears flow from a broken heart. And yet again in the midst of her grief she cannot believe it true that He is lost to her; she returns, as love will do, to the search, suspects her own eyesight, seeks again where she had sought before, and cannot reconcile herself to a loss so total and overwhelming. So absorbing is her grief that the vision of angels does not astonish her; her heart, filled with grief, has no room for wonder. Their kindly words cannot comfort her; it is another voice she longs for. She had but the one thought, "They have taken away my Lord,"--my Lord, as if none felt the bereavement as she. She supposes, too, that all must know about the loss and understand what she is seeking, so that when she sees the gardener she says, "Sir, if thou hast borne Him hence." What need to say who? Can any one be thinking of any other but of Him who engrosses her thought?

In all this we have the picture of a real and profound grief, and therefore of a real and profound love. We see in Mary the kind of affection which a knowledge of Jesus was fitted to kindle. And to Mary our Lord remembered His promise: "He that loveth Me shall be loved of My Father, and I will love him and will manifest Myself to him." None is so unable as He to leave any who love Him without any response to their expressions of affection. He could not coldly look on while this woman was eagerly seeking Him; and it is as impossible that He should hide Himself now from any who seek Him with as true a heart. Sometimes it would seem as if real thirst for God were not at once allayed, as if many were allowed to spend the best part of their days in seeking; but this does not invalidate the promise, "He that seeketh, findeth." For as Christ is again and again removed from the view of men, and as He is allowed to become a remote and shadowy figure, He can be restored to a living and visible influence in the world only by this man and that man becoming sensible of the great loss we sustain by His absence, and working his own way to a clear apprehension of His continued life. No experience which an honest man has in his search for the truth is worthless; it is the solid foundation of his own permanent belief and connection with the truth, and it is useful to other men.

Mary standing without at the sepulchre weeping is a concrete representation of a not uncommon state of mind. She stands wondering why she was ever so foolish, so heartless, as to leave the tomb at all--why she had allowed it to be possible to become separated from the Lord. She looks despairingly at the empty grave-clothes which so lately had held all that was dear to her in the world. She might, she thinks, had she been present, have prevented the tomb from being emptied, but now it is empty she cannot fill it again. It is thus that those who have been careless about maintaining communion with Christ reproach themselves when they find He is gone. The ordinances, the prayers, the quiet hours of contemplation, that once were filled with Him are now, like the linen clothes and the napkin, empty, cold, pale forms, remembrances of His presence that make His absence all the more painful. When we ask where we can find Him, only the hard, mocking echo of the empty tomb replies. And yet this self-reproach is itself a seeking to which He will respond. To mourn His absence is to desire and to invite His presence; and to invite His presence is to secure it. [29]

The Evangelist Mark saw more in the Lord's appearance to Mary than a response to her seeking love. He reminds his readers that this was the woman out of whom the Lord had cast seven devils, meaning apparently to suggest that those who have most need of encouragement from Him are surest to get it. He had not appeared to Peter and John, though these men were to build up His Church and be responsible for His cause. To the man whom He loved, who had stood by Him at His trial and in His death, who had received His mother and was now to be in His place to her, He made no sign, but allowed him to examine the empty tomb and retire. But to this woman He discloses Himself at once. The love which sprang from a sense of what she owed Him kept her at the tomb and threw her in His way. Her sense of dependence was the magnetic point on earth which attracted and disclosed His presence. Observe the situation. Earth lay uncertain; some manifestation is needed to guide men at this critical time; blank disappointment or pointless waiting broods everywhere. At what point shall the presence of Christ break through and quicken expectation and faith? Shall He go to the high priest's palace or to Pilate's prætorium and triumph over their dismay? Shall He go and lay busy plans with this and that group of followers? On the contrary, He appears to a poor woman who can do nothing to celebrate His triumph and might only discredit it, if she proclaimed herself His friend and herald. But thus continuous is the character of Jesus through death and resurrection. The meekness, the true perception of the actual sorrows and wants of men, the sense for spiritual need, the utter disregard of worldly powers and glory, characterise Him now as before. The sense of need is what always effectually appeals to Him. The soul that truly recognises the value and longs for the fellowship and possession of Christ's purity, devotion to God, superiority to worldly aims and interests, always wins His regard. When a man prays for these things not with his lips but with his life's effort and his heart's true craving, his prayer is answered. To seek Christ is to feel as Mary felt, to see with practical constraining clearness as she saw, that He is the most precious of all possessions, that to be like Him is the greatest of all attainments; it is to see His character with clearness, and to be persuaded that, if the world gives us opportunity of becoming like Him and actually makes us like Him, it has done for us all that is vital and permanently important.

    As Mary answered the angels she heard a step behind or saw the tomb darkened by a shadow, and on turning discerns dimly through her tears a figure which naturally enough she supposes to be the gardener--not because Jesus had assumed the clothes or lifted the tools of the gardener, but because he was the likeliest person to be going about the garden at that early hour. As the heart overburdened with grief is often unconscious of the presence of Christ and refuses to be comforted because it cannot see Him for its sorrow, so Mary through the veil of her tears can see only a human form, and turns away again, unconscious that He for whom she seeks is with her. As she turns, one word wipes the tears from her eyes and penetrates her heart with sudden joy. The utterance of her name was enough to tell her it was some one who knew her that was there; but there was a responsive thrill and an awaking of old memories and a vibration of her nature under the tone of that voice, which told her whose alone it could be. The voice seemed a second time to command a calm within her and turn her whole soul to Himself only. Once before, that voice had banished from her nature the foul spirits that had taken possession of her; she had "awaked from hell beneath the smile of Christ," and now again the same voice brought her out of darkness into light. From being the most disconsolate, Mary became at a word the happiest creature in the world.

    Mary's happiness is easily understood. No explanation is needed of the peace and bliss she experienced when she heard herself owned as the friend of the risen Lord, and called by her name in the familiar tone by Him who stood now superior to all risk, assault, and evil. This perfect joy is the reward of all in the measure of their faith. Christ rose, not that He might bring ecstasy to Mary alone, but that He might fill all things with His presence and His fulness, and that our joy also might be full. Has He not called us also by name? Has He not given us at times a consciousness that He understands our nature and what will satisfy it, that He claims an intimacy no other can claim, that His utterance of our name has a significance which no other lips can give it? Do we find it difficult to enter into true intercourse with Him; do we envy Mary her few minutes in the garden? As truly as by the audible utterance of our name does Christ now invite us to the perfect joy there is in His friendship; so truly as if He stood with us alone, as with Mary in the garden, and as if none but ourselves were present; as if our name alone filled His lips, our wants alone occupied His heart. Let us not miss true personal intercourse with Christ. Let nothing cheat us of this supreme joy and life of the soul. Let us not slothfully or shyly say, "I can never be on such terms of intimacy with Christ,--I who am so unlike Him; so full of desires He cannot gratify; so frivolous, superficial, unreal, while He is so real, so earnest; so unloving while He is so loving; so reluctant to endure hardness, with views of life and aims so opposed to His; so unable to keep a pure and elevated purpose steadfastly in my mind." Mary was once trodden under foot of evil, a wreck in whom none but Christ saw any place for hope. It is what is in Him that is powerful. He has won His supremacy by love, by refusing to enjoy His private rights without our sharing them; and He maintains His supremacy by love, teaching all to love Him, subduing to devotedness the hardest heart--not by a remote exhibition of cold, unemotional perfection, but by the persistence and depth of His warm and individual love.

Marcus Dods, D.D.

Mary had no time to reason and doubt. With one quick exclamation of ecstatic recognition and joy she sprang towards Him. The one word "my Master," [30] uttered all her heart. It is related of George Herbert that when he was inducted into the cure of Bemerton he said to a friend: "I beseech God that my humble and charitable life may so win upon others as to bring glory to my Jesus, whom I have this day taken to be my Master and my Governor, and I am so proud of His service that I will always call Him Jesus, my Master." His biographer adds: "He seems to rejoice in that word Jesus, and says that the adding these words my Master' to it and the often repetition of them seemed to perfume his mind." With Mary the title was one of indefinite respect; she found in Jesus one she could always reverence and trust. The firm, loving hand that admits no soft evasion of duty; the steadfast step that with equanimity ever goes straight forward; the strong heart that has always room for the distresses of others; the union with God which made Him a medium to earth of God's superiority and availing compassion,--these things had made the words "my Master" His proper designation in her lips. And our spirit cannot be purified and elevated but by worthy love and deserved reverence, by living in presence of that which commands our love and lifts up our nature to what is above it. It is by letting our heart and mind be filled by what is above us that we grow in abiding stature and become in our turn helpful to what is at a still lower stage than we are.

But as Mary sprang forward, and in a transport of affection made as though she would embrace the Lord, she is met by these quick words: "Touch Me not, for I am not yet ascended to My Father." Various conjectural reasons for this prohibition have been supposed,--as, that it was indecorous, an objection which Christ did not make when at a dinner-table a woman kissed his feet, scandalising the guests and provoking the suspicions of the host; or, that she wished to assure herself by touch of the reality of the appearance, an assurance which He did not object to the disciples making, but rather encouraged them to make, as He would also have encouraged Mary had she needed any such test, which she did not; or, that this vehement embrace would disturb the process of glorification which was proceeding in His body! It is idle to conjecture reasons, seeing that He Himself gives the reason, "for I am not yet ascended," implying that such "touching" would no longer be prohibited when He was ascended. Mary seems to have thought that already the "little while" of His absence was past, and that now He was to be always with them upon earth, helping them in the same familiar ways and training them by His visible presence and spoken words. This was a misconception. He must first ascend to the Father, and those who love Him on earth must learn to live without the physical appearance, the actual seeing, touching, hearing, of the well-known Master. There must be no more kissing of His feet, but homage of a sterner, deeper sort; there must be no more sitting at table with Him, and filling the mind with His words, until they sit down with Him in the Father's presence. Meanwhile His friends must walk by faith, not by sight--by their inward light and spiritual likings; they must learn the truer fidelity that serves an absent Lord; they must acquire the independent and inherent love of righteousness which can freely grow only when relieved from the over-mastering pressure of a visible presence, encouraging us by sensible expressions of favour, guaranteeing us against defeat and danger. Thus only can the human spirit freely grow, showing its native bent, its true tastes and convictions; thus only can its capacities for self-development and for choosing and fulfilling its own destiny be matured.

And if these words of Jesus seemed at first chilling and repellent, they were followed by words of unmistakable affection: "Go to my brothers, and say unto them, I ascend unto My Father and your Father, and to My God and your God." This is the message of the risen Lord to men. He has become the link between us and all that is highest and best. We know that He has overcome all evil and left it behind; we know that He is worthy of the highest place, that by His righteousness and love He merits the highest place. We know that if such an one as He cannot go boldly to the highest heaven and claim God as His God and Father, there is no such thing as moral worth, and all effort, conscience, hope, responsibility, are vain and futile. We know that Christ must ascend to the highest, and yet we know also that He will not enter where we cannot follow. We know that His love binds Him to us as strongly as His rights carry Him to God. We can as little believe that He will abandon us and leave us out of His eternal enjoyment, as we can believe that God would refuse to own Him as Son. And it is this which Christ puts in the forefront of His message as risen and ascending: "I ascend unto My Father and your Father." The joy that awaits Me with God awaits you also; the power I go to exercise is the power of your Father. This affinity for heaven which you see in Me is coupled with affinity for you. The holiness, the power, the victory, I have achieved and now enjoy are yours; I am your Brother: what I claim, I claim for you.

Footnotes:

29. See Pusey's sermon on this subject.
30. "Rabboni" had more of reverence in it than would be conveyed by "my Teacher," and it is legitimate here to use "Master" in its wider sense.

XXIII. THOMAS' TEST

"When therefore it was evening, on that day, the first day of the week, and when the doors were shut where the disciples were, for fear of the Jews, Jesus came and stood in the midst, and saith unto them, Peace be unto you. And when He had said this, He showed unto them His hands and His side. The disciples therefore were glad, when they saw the Lord. Jesus therefore said to them again, Peace be unto you: as the Father hath sent Me, even so send I you. And when He had said this, He breathed on them, and saith unto them, Receive ye the Holy Ghost: whosesoever sins ye forgive, they are forgiven unto them; whosesoever sins ye retain, they are retained. But Thomas, one of the twelve, called Didymus, was not with them when Jesus came. The other disciples therefore said unto him, We have seen the Lord. But he said unto them, Except I shall see in His hands the print of the nails, and put my finger into the print of the nails, and put my hand into His side, I will not believe. And after eight days again His disciples were within, and Thomas with them. Jesus cometh, the doors being shut, and stood in the midst, and said, Peace be unto you. Then saith He to Thomas, Reach hither thy finger, and see My hands; and reach hither thy hand, and put it into My side: and be not faithless, but believing. Thomas answered and said unto Him, My Lord and my God. Jesus saith unto him, Because thou hast seen Me, thou hast believed: blessed are they that have not seen, and yet have believed."--John xx. 19-29.

On the evening of the day whose dawning had been signalised by the Resurrection, the disciples, and, according to Luke, some others, were together. They expected that the event which had restored hope in their own hearts would certainly excite the authorities and probably lead to the arrest of some of their number. They had therefore carefully closed the doors, that some time for parley and possibly for escape might be interposed. But to their astonishment and delight, while they were sitting thus with closed doors, the well-known figure of their Lord appeared in their midst, and His familiar greeting, "Peace be with you," sounded in their ears. Further to identify Himself and remove all doubt or dread He showed them His hands and His side; and, as St. Luke tells us, even ate before them. There is here a strange mingling of identity and difference between the body He now wears and that which had been crucified. Its appearance is the same in some respects, but its properties are different. Immediate recognition did not always follow His manifestation. There was something baffling in His appearance, suggesting a well-known face, and yet not quite the same. The marks on the body, or some characteristic action or movement or utterance, were needed to complete the identification. The properties of the body also were not reducible to any known type. He could eat, speak, walk, yet He could dispense with eating and could apparently pass through physical obstacles. His body was a glorified, spiritual body, not subject to the laws which govern the physical part of man in this life. These characteristics are worth noticing, not only as giving us some inkling of the type of body which awaits ourselves, but in connection with the identification of the risen Lord. Had the appearance been the mere fancy of the disciples, how should they have required any identification?

Having saluted them and removed their consternation, He fulfils the object of His appearance by giving them their commission, their equipment, and their authority as His Apostles: "As the Father hath sent Me, even so send I you"--to fulfil still the same purpose, to complete the work begun, to stand to Him in the same intimate relation as He had occupied to the Father. To impart to them at once all that they required for the fulfilment of this commission He bestows upon them the Holy Spirit, breathing on them, to convey to them the impression that He was actually there and then communicating to them that which constituted the very breath of His own life. This is His first act as Lord of all power in heaven and on earth, and it is an act which inevitably conveys to them the assurance that His life and theirs is one life. Impulse and power to proclaim Him as risen they did not yet experience. They must be allowed time to settle to some composure of mind and to some clear thoughts after all the disturbing events of these last days. They must also have the confirmatory testimony to the Resurrection, which could only be furnished after repeated appearances of the Lord to themselves and to others. The gift of the Spirit, therefore, as a spirit of powerful witness-bearing, was reserved for six weeks.

With this perfect equipment our Lord added the words: "Whosesoever sins ye forgive, they are forgiven unto them; whosesoever sins ye retain, they are retained." These words have been the occasion of endless controversy. [31] They certainly convey the ideas that the Apostles were appointed to mediate between Christ and their fellow-men, that the chief function they should be required to discharge in this mediation was the forgiving and retention of sins, and that they were furnished with the Holy Spirit to guide them in this mediation. Apparently this must mean that the Apostles were to be the agents through whom Christ was to proclaim the terms of admission to His kingdom. They received authority to say in what cases sins were to be forgiven and in what to be retained. To infer from this that the Apostles have successors, that these successors are constituted by an external ordinance or nomination, that they have power to exclude or admit individuals seeking entrance into the kingdom of God, is to leave logic and reason a long way behind, and to erect a kind of government in the Church of Christ which will never be submitted to by those who live in the liberty wherewith His truth has made them free. The presence of the Holy Spirit, and no bare external appointment, is that which gives authority to those who guide the Church of Christ. It is because they are inwardly one with Christ, not because they happen to be able to claim a doubtful outward connection with Him, that they have that authority which Christ's people own.

But when our Lord thus appeared on the day of His resurrection to His disciples one of their number was absent. This might not have been noticed had not the absentee been of a peculiar temper, and had not this peculiarity given rise to another visit of the Lord and to a very significant restoration of belief in the mind of a sceptical disciple. The absent disciple was commonly known as Thomas or Didymus, the Twin. On various occasions he appears somewhat prominently in the gospel-story, and his conduct and conversation on those occasions show him to have been a man very liable to take a desponding view of the future, apt to see the darker side of everything, but at the same time not wanting in courage, and of a strong and affectionate loyalty to Jesus. On one occasion, when our Lord intimated to the disciples His intention of returning within the dangerous frontier of Judæa, the others expostulated, but Thomas said, "Let us also go, that we may die with Him"--an utterance in which his devoted loyalty to his Master, his dogged courage, and his despondent temperament are all apparent. And when, some time afterwards, Jesus was warning His disciples that He must shortly leave them and go to the Father, Thomas sees in the departure of his Master the extinction of all hope; life and the way to life seem to him treacherous phrases, he has eyes only for the gloom of death: "Lord, we know not whither Thou goest; and how can we know the way?"

The absence of such a man from the first meeting of the disciples was to be expected. [32] If the bare possibility of his Lord's death had plunged this loving and gloomy heart in despondency, what dark despair must have preyed upon it when that death was actually accomplished! How the figure of his dead Master had burnt itself into his soul is seen from the manner in which his mind dwells on the print of the nails, the wound in the side. It is by these only, and not by well-known features of face or peculiarities of form, he will recognise and identify his Lord. His heart was with the lifeless body on the cross, and he could not bear to see the friends of Jesus or speak with those who had shared his hopes, but buried his disappointment and desolation in solitude and silence. His absence can scarcely be branded as culpable. None of the others expected resurrection any more than himself, but his hopelessness acted on a specially sensitive and despondent nature. Thus it was that, like many melancholy persons, he missed the opportunity of seeing what would effectually have scattered his darkness.

But though he might not be to blame for absenting himself, he was to blame for refusing to accept the testimony of his friends when they assured him they had seen Jesus risen. There is a tone of doggedness that grates upon us in the words, "Except I shall see in His hands the print of the nails, and put my finger into the print of the nails, and thrust my hand into His side, I will not believe." Some deference was due to the testimony of men whom he knew to be truthful and as little liable to delusion as himself. We cannot blame him for not being convinced on the spot; a man cannot compel himself to believe anything which does not itself compel belief. But the obstinate tone sounds as if he was beginning to nurse his unbelief, than which there is no more pernicious exercise of the human spirit. He demands, too, what may never be possible--the evidence of his own senses. He claims that he shall be on the same footing as the rest. Why is he to believe on less evidence than they? It has cost him pain enough to give up his hope: is he then to give up his hopelessness as cheaply as all this? He is supremely miserable; his Lord dead and life left to him--a life which already during these few days had grown far too long, a weary, intolerable burden. Is he in a moment and on their mere word to rise from his misery? A man of Thomas' temperament hugs his wretchedness. You seem to do him an injury if you open the shutters of his heart and let in the sunshine.

Obviously, therefore, the first inference we naturally draw from this state of mind is that it is weak and wrong to lay hold of one difficulty and insist that except this be removed we will not believe. Let this difficulty about the constitution of Christ's person, or this about the impossibility of proving a miracle, or this about the inspiration of Scripture be removed, and I will accept Christianity; let God grant me this petition, and I will believe that He is the hearer of prayer; let me see this inconsistency or that explained, and I will believe He governs the course of things in this world. The understanding begins to take a pride in demanding evidence more absolute and strict than has satisfied others, and seems to display acuteness and fairness in holding to one difficulty. The test which Thomas proposed to himself seemed an accurate and legitimate one; but that he should have proposed it shows that he was neglecting the evidence already afforded him, the testimony of a number of men whose truthfulness he had for years made proof of. True, it was a miracle they required him to believe; but would his own senses be better authentication of a miracle than the unanimous and explicit declaration of a company of veracious men? He could have no doubt that they believed they had seen the Lord. If they could be deceived, ten of them, or many more, why should his senses prove more infallible? Was he to reject their testimony on the ground that their senses had deceived them, and accept the testimony of his own senses? Was the ultimate test in his own case to be that very evidence which in the case of others he maintained was insufficient?

But if this tells seriously against Thomas, we must not leave out of account what tells in his favour. It is true he was obstinate and unreasonable and a shade vain in his refusal to accept the testimony of the disciples, but it is also true that he was with the little Christian community on the second Lord's Day. This puts it beyond a doubt that he was not so unbelieving as he seemed. That he did not now avoid the society of those happy, hopeful men shows that he was far from unwilling to become, if possible, a sharer in their hope and joy. Perhaps already he was repenting having pledged himself to unbelief, as many another has repented. Certainly he was not afraid of being convinced that his Lord had arisen; on the contrary, he sought to be convinced of this and put himself in the way of conviction. He had doubted because he wished to believe, doubted because it was the full, entire, eternal confidence of his soul that he was seeking a resting-place for. He knew the tremendous importance to him of this question--knew that it was literally everything to him if Christ was risen and was now alive and to be found by His people, and therefore he was slow to believe. Therefore also he kept in the company of believers; it was on their side he wished to get out of the terrible mire and darkness in which he was involved.

It is this which distinguishes Thomas and all right-minded doubters from thorough-going and depraved unbelievers. The one wishes to believe, would give the world to be free from doubt, will go mourning all his days, will pine in body and sicken of life because he cannot believe: "he waits for light, but behold obscurity, for brightness, but he walks in darkness." The other, the culpable unbeliever, thrives on doubt; he likes it, enjoys it, sports it, lives by it; goes about telling people his difficulties, as some morbid people have a fancy for showing you their sores or detailing their symptoms, as if everything which makes them different from other men, even though it be disease, were a thing to be proud of. Convince such a man of the truth and he is angry with you; you seem to have done him a wrong, as the mendicant impostor who has been gaining his livelihood by a bad leg or a useless eye is enraged when a skilled person restores to him the use of his limb or shows him that he can use it if he will. You may know a dishonest doubter by the fluency with which he states his difficulties or by the affectation of melancholy which is sometimes assumed. You may always know him by his reluctance to be convinced, by his irritation when he is forced to surrender some pet bulwark of unbelief. When you find a man reading one side of the question, courting difficulties, eagerly seizing on new objections, and provoked instead of thankful when any doubt is removed, you may be sure that this is not a scepticism of the understanding so much as an evil heart of unbelief.

The hesitancy and backwardness, the incredulity and niggardliness of faith, of Thomas have done as much to confirm the minds of succeeding believers as the forward and impulsive confidence of Peter. Then, as now, this critical intellect, when combined with a sound heart, wrought two great boons for the Church. The doubts which such men entertain continually provoke fresh evidence, as here this second appearance of Christ to the Eleven seems due to the doubt of Thomas. So far as one can gather it was solely to remove this doubt our Lord appeared. And, besides, a second boon which attends honest and godly doubt is the attachment to the Church of men who have passed through severe mental conflict, and therefore hold the faith they have reached with an intelligence and a tenacity unknown to other men.

These two things were simply brought about in Thomas' instance. The disciples were again assembled on the following Sunday, probably in the same place, consecrated for ever in their memories as the place where their risen Lord had appeared. It is doubtful whether they were more expectant of a fresh appearance of their Lord this day than they had been any day throughout the week, but certainly every reader feels that it is not without significance that after a blank and uneventful week the first day should again be singled out to have this honour put upon it. Some sanction is felt to be given to those meetings of His followers which ever since have been assembled on the first day of the week; and the experience of thousands can testify that this day seems still the favourite with our Lord for manifesting Himself to His people, and for renewing the joy which a week's work has somewhat dimmed. Silently and suddenly as before, without warning, without opening of doors, Jesus stood in their midst. But there was no terror now--exclamations only of delight and adoration. And perhaps it was not in human nature to resist casting a look of triumphant interrogation at Thomas, a look of inquiry to see what he would make of this. Surprise, unutterable surprise, undiminished by all he had been led to expect, must have been written on Thomas' wide-gazing eyes and riveted look. But this surprise was displaced by shame, this eager gaze cast down, when he found that his Lord had heard his obstinate ultimatum and had been witness of his sullen unbelief. As Jesus repeats almost in the same words the hard, rude, bare, material test which he had proposed, and as He holds forth His hands for his inspection, shame and joy struggle for the mastery in his spirit, and give utterance to the humble but glowing confession, "My Lord and my God." His own test is superseded; he makes no movement to put it in force; he is satisfied of the identity of his Lord. It is the same penetrating knowledge of man's inmost thoughts, the same loving treatment of the erring, the same subduing presence.

And thus it frequently happens that a man who has vowed that he will not believe except this or that be made plain finds, when he does believe, that something short of his own requirements has convinced him. He finds that though he was once so express in his demands for proof, and so clear and accurate in his declarations of the precise amount of evidence required, at the last he believes and could scarcely tell you why, could not at least show his belief as the fine and clean result of a logical process. Thomas had maintained that the rest were too easily satisfied, but at the last he is himself satisfied with precisely the same proof as they. And it is somewhat striking that in so many cases unbelief gives way to belief, not by the removal of intellectual difficulties, not by such demonstration as was granted to Thomas, but by an undefinable conquest of the soul by Christ. The glory, holiness, love of His person, subdue the soul to Him.

The faith of Thomas is full of significance. First, it is helpful to our own faith to hear so decisive and so full a confession coming from the lips of such a man. John himself felt it to be so decisive that after recording it he virtually closes the Gospel which he had undertaken to write in order to persuade men that Jesus is the Son of God. After this confession of Thomas he feels that no more can be said. He stops not for want of matter; "many other signs truly did Jesus in the presence of His disciples" which are not written in this Gospel. These seemed sufficient. The man who is not moved by this will not be moved by any further proof. Proof is not what such a doubter needs. Whatever we think of the other Apostles, it is plain that Thomas at least was not credulous. If Peter's generous ardour carried him to a confession unwarranted by the facts, if John saw in Jesus the reflection of his own contemplative and loving nature, what are we to say of the faith of Thomas? He had no determination to see only what he desired, no readiness to accept baseless evidence and irresponsible testimony. He knew the critical nature of the situation, the unique importance of the matter presented to his faith. With him there was no frivolous or thoughtless underrating of difficulties. He did not absolutely deny the possibility of Christ's resurrection, but he went very near doing so, and showed that practically he considered it either impossible or unlikely in the extreme. But in the end he believes. And the ease with which he passes from doubt to faith proves his honesty and sound-heartedness. As soon as evidence which to him is convincing is produced, he proclaims his faith.

His confession, too, is fuller than that of the other disciples. The week of painful questioning had brought clearly before his mind the whole significance of the Resurrection, so that he does not hesitate to own Jesus as his God. When a man of profound spiritual feeling and of good understanding has doubts and hesitations from the very intensity and subtlety of his scrutiny of what appears to him of transcendent importance; when he sees difficulties unseen by men who are too little interested in the matter to recognise them even though they stare them in the face,--when such a man, with the care and anxiety that befit the subject, considers for himself the claims of Christ, and as the result yields himself to the Lord, he sees more in Christ than other men do, and is likely to be steadier in his allegiance than if he had slurred over apparent obstacles instead of removing them, and stifled objections in place of answering them. It was not the mere seeing of Christ risen which prompted the full confession of Thomas. But slowly during that week of suspense he had been taking in the full significance of the Resurrection, coming at the close of such a life as he knew the Lord had lived. The very idea that such a thing was believed by the rest forced his mind back upon the exceptional character of Jesus, His wonderful works, the intimations He had given of His connection with God. The sight of Him risen came as the keystone of the arch, which being wanting all had fallen to the ground, but being inserted clenched the whole, and could now bear any weight. The truths about His person which Thomas had begun to explain away return upon his mind with resistless force, and each in clear, certain verity. He saw now that his Lord had performed all His word, had proved Himself supreme over all that affected men. He saw Him after passing through unknown conflict with principalities and powers come to resume fellowship with sinful men, standing with all things under His feet, yet giving His hand to the weak disciple to make him partake in His triumph.

This was a rare and memorable hour for Thomas, one of those moments that mark a man's spirit permanently. He is carried entirely out of himself, and sees nothing but his Lord. The whole energy of his spirit goes out to Him undoubtingly, unhesitatingly, unrestrained. Everything is before him in the person of Christ; nothing causes the least diversion or distraction. For once his spirit has found perfect peace. There is nothing in the unseen world that can dismay him, nothing in the future on which he can spend a thought; his soul rests in the Person before him. He does not draw back, questioning whether the Lord will now receive him; he fears no rebuke; he does not scrutinise his spiritual condition, nor ask whether his faith is sufficiently spiritual. He cannot either go back upon his past conduct, or analyse his present feelings, or spend one thought of any kind upon himself. The scrupulous, sceptical man is all devoutness and worship; the thousand objections are swept from his mind; and all by the mere presence of Christ He is rapt in this one object; mind and soul are filled with the regained Lord; he forgets himself; the passion of joy with which he regains in a transfigured form his lost Leader absorbs him quite: "he had lost a possible king of the Jews; he finds his Lord and his God." There can be no question here about himself, his prospects, his interests. He can but utter his surprise, his joy, and his worship in the cry, "My Lord and my God."

On such a man even the Lord's benediction were useless. This is the highest, happiest, rarest state of the human soul. When a man has been carried out of himself by the clear vision of Christ's worth; when his mind and heart are filled with the supreme excellence of Christ; when in His presence he feels he can but worship, bowing in his soul before actually achieved human perfection rooted in and expressing the true Divine glory of love ineffable; when face to face, soul to soul, with the highest and most affecting known goodness, conscious that he now in this very moment stands within touch of the Supreme, that he has found and need never more lose perfect love, perfect goodness, perfect power,-- when a man is transported by such a recognition of Christ, this is the true ecstasy, this is man's ultimate blessedness.

And this blessedness is competent not only to those who saw with the bodily eye, but much more to those who have not seen and yet have believed. Why do we rob ourselves of it, and live as if it were not so--as if such certitude and the joy that accompanies it had passed from earth and were no more possible? We cannot apply Thomas' test, but we can test his test; or, like him, we can forego it, and rest on wider, deeper evidence. Was he right in so eagerly confessing his belief? And are we right to hesitate, to doubt, to despond? Should we have counted it strange if, when the Lord addressed Thomas, he had sullenly shrunk back among the rest, or merely given a verbal assent to Christ's identity, showing no sign of joy? And are we to accept the signs He gives us of His presence as if it made little difference to us and did not lift us into heaven? Have we so little sense of spiritual things that we cannot believe in the life of Him round whom the whole fortunes of our race revolve? Do we not know the power of Christ's resurrection as Thomas could not possibly know it? Do we not see as he could not see the boundless spiritual efficacy and results of that risen life? Do we not see the full bearing of that great manifestation of God's nearness more clearly? Do we not feel how impossible it was that such an one as Christ should be holden of death, that the supremacy in human affairs which He achieved by absolute love and absolute holiness should be proved inferior to a physical law, and should be interrupted in its efficacious exercise by a physical fact? If Thomas was constrained to acknowledge Christ as his Lord and his God, much more may we do so. By the nature of the case our conviction, implying as it does some apprehension of spiritual things, must be more slowly wrought. Even if at last the full conviction that human life is a joy because Christ is with us in it, leading us to eternal partnership with Himself,-- even if this conviction flash suddenly through the spirit, the material for it must have been long accumulating. Even if at last we awake to a sense of the present glory of Christ with the suddenness of Thomas, yet in any case this must be the result of purified spiritual affinities and leanings. But on this very account is the conviction more indissolubly intertwined with all that we truly are, forming an essential and necessary part of our inward growth, and leading each of us to respond with a cordial amen to the benediction of our Lord, "Blessed are they that have not seen and yet have believed."

Footnotes:

31. See Steitz' article Schlüsselgewalt in Herzog.
32. In this chapter there are reminiscences of Trench.

Marcus Dods, D.D.

XXIV. APPEARANCE AT SEA OF GALILEE

"After these things Jesus manifested Himself again to the disciples at the Sea of Tiberias; and He manifested Himself on this wise. There were together Simon Peter, and Thomas called Didymus, and Nathanael of Cana in Galilee, and the sons of Zebedee, and two other of His disciples. Simon Peter saith unto them, I go a-fishing. They say unto him, We also come with thee. They went forth, and entered into the boat; and that night they took nothing. But when day was now breaking, Jesus stood on the beach: howbeit the disciples knew not that it was Jesus. Jesus therefore saith unto them, Children, have ye aught to eat? They answered Him, No. And He said unto them, Cast the net on the right side of the boat, and ye shall find. They cast therefore, and now they were not able to draw it for the multitude of fishes. That disciple therefore whom Jesus loved saith unto Peter, It is the Lord. So when Simon Peter heard that it was the Lord, he girt his coat about him (for he was naked), and cast himself into the sea. But the other disciples came in the little boat (for they were not far from the land, but about two hundred cubits off), dragging the net full of fishes. So when they got out upon the land, they see a fire of coals there, and fish laid thereon, and bread. Jesus saith unto them, Bring of the fish which ye have now taken. Simon Peter therefore went up, and drew the net to land, full of great fishes, a hundred and fifty and three: and for all there were so many, the net was not rent. Jesus saith unto them, Come and break your fast. And none of the disciples durst inquire of Him, Who art Thou? knowing that it was the Lord. Jesus cometh, and taketh the bread, and giveth them, and the fish likewise. This is now the third time that Jesus was manifested to the disciples, after that He was risen from the dead."--John xxi. 1-14.

The removal of the doubts of Thomas restored the Eleven to unity of faith, and fitted them to be witnesses of the Lord's resurrection. And the Gospel might naturally have closed at this point, as indeed the last verses of the twentieth chapter suggest that the writer himself felt that his task was done. But as throughout his Gospel he had followed the plan of adducing such of Christ's miracles as seemed to throw a strong light on His spiritual power, he could not well close without mentioning the last miracle of all, and which seemed to have only a didactic purpose. Besides, there was another reason for John adding this chapter. He was writing at the very close of the century. So long had he survived the unparalleled events he narrates that an impression had gone abroad that he would never die. It was even rumoured that our Lord had foretold that the beloved disciple should tarry on earth till He Himself should return. John takes the opportunity of relating what the Lord had really said, as well as of recounting the all-important event out of which the misreported conversation had arisen.

When the disciples had spent the Passover week at Jerusalem, they naturally returned to their homes in Galilee. The house of the old fisherman Zebedee was probably their rendezvous. We need not listen to their talk as they relate what had passed in Jerusalem, in order to see that they are sensible of the peculiarity of their situation and are in a state of suspense.

They are back among the familiar scenes, the boats are lying on the beach, their old companions are sitting about mending their nets as they themselves had been doing a year or two before when summoned by Jesus to follow Him on the moment. But though old associations are thus laying hold of them again, there is evidence that new influences are also at work; for with the fishermen are found Nathanael and others who were there, not for the sake of old associations, but of the new and common interest they had in Christ. The seven men have kept together; they participate in an experience of which their fellow-townsmen know nothing; but they must live. Hints have been thrown out that seven strong men must not depend on other arms than their own for a livelihood. And as they stand together that evening and watch boat after boat push off, the women wishing their husbands and sons good-speed, the men cheerily responding and busily getting their tackle in trim, with a look of pity at the group of disciples, Peter can stand it no longer, but makes for his own or some unoccupied boat with the words, "I go a-fishing." The rest were only needing such an invitation. The whole charm and zest of the old life rushes back upon them, each takes his own accustomed place in the boat, each hand finds itself once more at home at the long-suspended task, and with an ease that surprises themselves they fall back into the old routine.

And as we watch their six oars flashing in the setting sun, and Peter steering them to the familiar fishing ground, we cannot but reflect in how precarious a position the whole future of the world is. That boat carries the earthly hope of the Church; and as we weigh the feelings of the men that are in it, what we see chiefly is, how easily the whole of Christianity might here have broken short off, and never have been heard of, supposing it to have depended for its propagation solely on the disciples. Here they were, not knowing what had become of Jesus, without any plan for preserving His name among men, open to any impulse or influence, unable to resist the smell of the fishing boats and the freshness of the evening breeze, and submitting themselves to be guided by such influences as these, content apparently to fall back into their old ways and obscure village life, as if the last three years were a dream, or were like a voyage to foreign parts, which they might think of afterwards, but were not to repeat. All the facts they were to use for the conversion of the world were already in their possession; the death of Christ and His resurrection were not a fortnight old; but as yet they had no inward impulse to proclaim the truth; there was no Holy Ghost powerfully impelling and possessing them; they were not endued with power from on high. One thing only they seemed to be decided and agreed about--that they must live; and therefore they go a-fishing.

But apparently they were not destined to find even this so easy as they expected. There was One watching that boat, following it through the night as they tried place after place, and He was resolved that they should not be filled with false ideas about the satisfactoriness of their old calling. All night they toiled, but caught nothing. Every old device was tried; the fancies of each particular kind of fish were humoured, but in vain. Each time the net was drawn up, every hand knew before it appeared that it was empty. Weary with the fruitless toil, and when the best part of the night was gone, they made for a secluded part of the shore, not wishing to land from their first attempt empty in presence of the other fishermen. But when about one hundred yards from the shore a voice hails them with the words, "Children"--or, as we would say, "Lads"--"have you taken any fish?" It has been supposed that our Lord asked this question in the character of a trader who had been watching for the return of the boats that he might buy, or that it was with the natural interest every one takes in the success of a person that is fishing, so that we can scarcely pass without asking what take they have had. The question was asked for the purpose of arresting the boat at a sufficient distance from the shore to make another cast of the net possible. It has this effect; the rowers turned round to see who is calling them, and at the same time tell Him they have no fish. The Stranger then says, "Cast the net on the right side of the ship, and ye shall find"; and they do so, not thinking of a miracle, but supposing that before any man would give them such express instructions he must have had some good reason for believing there were fish there. But when they found that the net was at once absolutely loaded with fish, so that they could not draw it into the boat, John looks again at the Stranger, and whispers to Peter, "It is the Lord." This was no sooner heard by Peter than he snatched up and threw over him his upper garment, and throwing himself into the water swam or waded ashore.

In every trifling act character betrays itself. It is John who is first to recognise Jesus; it is Peter who casts himself into the sea, just as he had done once before on that same lake, and as he had been first to enter the sepulchre on the morning of the Resurrection. John recognises the Lord, not because he had better eyesight than the rest, nor because he had a better position in the boat, nor because while the rest were busied with the net he was occupied with the figure on the beach, but because his spirit had a quicker and profounder apprehension of spiritual things, and because in this sudden turn of their fortune he recognised the same hand which had filled their nets once before and had fed thousands with one or two little fishes.

The reason of Peter's impetuousness on this occasion may partly have been that their fishing vessel was now as near the land as they could get it, and that he was unwilling to wait till they should get the small boat unfastened. The rest, we read, came ashore, not in the large vessel in which they had spent the night, but in the little boat they carried with them, the reason being added, "for they were not far from land"--that is to say, not far enough to use the larger vessel any longer. Peter, therefore, ran no risk of drowning. But his action reveals the eagerness of love. No sooner has he only heard from another that his Lord is near, than the fish for which he had been watching and waiting all night are forgotten, and for him, the master of the vessel, the net and all its contents might have sunk to the bottom of the lake. What this action of Peter suggested to the Lord is apparent from the question which a few minutes later He put to him: "Lovest thou Me more than these?"

Neither would Peter have sustained any serious loss even though his nets had been carried away, for when he reaches the shore he finds that the Lord was to be their host, not their guest. A fire is ready lit, fish laid on it and bread baking. He who could so fill their nets could also provide for His own wants. But there was to be no needless multiplication of miracles; the fish already on the fire was not to be multiplied in their hands when plenty were lying in the net. He directs them, therefore, to bring of the fish they had caught. They go to the net, and mechanically, in their old fashion, count the fish they had taken, one hundred and fifty and three; and John, with a fisher's memory can tell you, sixty years after, the precise number. From these miraculously provided fish they break their long fast.

The significance of this incident has perhaps been somewhat lost by looking at it too exclusively as symbolical. No doubt it was so; but it carried in the first place a most important lesson in its bare, literal facts. We have already noticed the precarious position in which the Church at this time was. And it will be useful to us in many ways to endeavour to rid our mind of all fancies about the beginning of the Christian Church, and look at the simple, unvarnished facts here presented to our view. And the plain and significant circumstance which first invites our attention is, that the nucleus of the Church, the men on whom the faith of Christ depended for its propagation, were fishermen.

This was not merely the picturesque drapery assumed by men of ability so great and character so commanding that all positions in life were alike to them. Let us recall to memory the group of men we have seen standing at a corner in a fishing village or with whom we have spent a night at sea fishing, and whose talk has been at the best old stories of their craft or legends of the water. Such men were the Apostles. They were men who were not at home in cities, who simply could not understand the current philosophies, who did not so much as know the names of the great contemporary writers of the Roman world, who took only so much interest in politics as every Jew in those troublous times was forced to take--men who were at home only on their own lake, in their fishing boat, and who could quite contentedly, even after all they had recently gone through, have returned to their old occupation for life. They were in point of fact now returning to their old life--returning to it partly because they had no impulse to publish what they knew, and partly because, even though they had, they must live, and did not know how they should be supported but by fishing.

And this is the reason of this miracle; this is the reason why our Lord so pointedly convinced them that without Him they could not make a livelihood: that they might fish all the night through and resort to every device their experience could contrive and yet could catch nothing, but that He could give them sustenance as He pleased. If any one thinks that this is a secular, shallow way of looking at the miracle, let him ask what it is that chiefly keeps men from serving God as they think they should, what it is that induces men to live so much for the world and so little for God, what it is that prevents them from following out what conscience whispers is the right course. Is it not mainly the feeling that by doing God's will we ourselves are likely to be not so well off, not so sufficiently provided for. Above all things, therefore, both we and the Apostles need to be convinced that our Lord, who asks us to follow Him, is much better able to provide for us than we ourselves are. They had the same transition to make as every man among ourselves has to make; we and they alike have to pass from the natural feeling that we depend on our own energy and skill for our support to the knowledge that we depend on God. We have to pass from the life of nature and sense to the life of faith. We have to come to know and believe that the fundamental thing is God, that it is He who can support us when nature fails, and not that we must betake ourselves to nature at many points where God fails--that we live, not by bread alone, but by every word that proceedeth out of the mouth of God, and are much safer in doing His bidding than in struggling anxiously to make a livelihood.

And if we carefully read our own experience, might we not see, as clearly as the Apostles that morning saw, the utter futility of our own schemes for bettering ourselves in the world? Is it not the simple fact that we also have toiled through every watch of the night, have borne fatigue and deprivation, have abandoned the luxuries of life and given ourselves to endure hardness, have tried contrivance after contrivance to win our cherished project, and all in vain? Our net is empty and light at the rising sun as it was at the setting. Have we not again and again found that when every boat round was being filled we drew nothing but disappointment? Have we not many times come back empty-handed to our starting-place? But no matter how much we have thus lost or missed every man will tell you it is much better so than if he had succeeded, if only his own ill-success has induced him to trust Christ, if only it has taught him really what he used with everybody else verbally to say,--that in that Person dimly discerned through the light that begins to glimmer round our disappointments there is all power in heaven and on earth--power to give us what we have been trying to win, power to give us greater happiness without it.

But this being so, it being the case that our Lord came this second time and called them away from their occupations to follow Him, and showed them how amply He could support them, they could not but remember how He had once before in very similar circumstances summoned them to leave their occupation as fishermen and to become fishers of men. They could not but interpret the present by the former miracle, and read in it a renewed summons to the work of catching men, and a renewed assurance that in that work they should not draw empty nets. Most suitably, then, does this miracle stand alone, the only one wrought after the Resurrection, and most suitably does it stand last, giving the Apostles a symbol which should continually reanimate them to their laborious work. Their work of preaching was well symbolised by sowing; they passed rapidly through the field of the world, at every step scattering broadcast the words of everlasting life, not examining minutely the hearts into which these words might fall, not knowing where they might find prepared soil and where they might find inhospitable rock, but assured that after a time whoso followed in their track should see the fruit of their words. Not less significant is the figure of the net; they let down the net of their good tidings, not seeing what persons were really enclosed in it, but trusting that He who had said, "Cast your net on the right side of the ship," knew what souls it would fall over. By this miracle He gave the Apostles to understand that not only when with them in the flesh could He give them success. Even now after His resurrection and when they did not recognise Him on the shore He blessed their labour, that they might even when they did not see Him believe in His nearness and in His power most effectually to give them success.

This is the miracle which has again and again restored the drooping faith and discouraged spirit of all Christ's followers who endeavour to bring men under His influence, or in any way to spread out this influence over a wider surface. Again and again their hope is disappointed and their labour vain; the persons they wish to influence glide out from below the net, and it is drawn empty; new opportunities are watched for, and new opportunities arrive and are used, but with the same result; the patient doggedness of the fisherman long used to turns of ill-success is reproduced in the persevering efforts of parental love or friendly anxiety for the good of others, but often the utmost patience is at last worn out, the nets are piled away, and the gloom of disappointment settles on the mind. Yet this apparently is the very hour which the Lord often chooses to give the long-sought-for success; in the dawn, when already the fish might be supposed to see the net and more vigilantly to elude it, our last and almost careless effort is made, and we achieve a substantial, countable success--a success not doubtful, but which we could accurately detail to others, which makes a mark in the memory like the hundred and fifty and three of these fishers, and which were we to relate to others they must acknowledge that the whole weary night of toil is amply repaid. And it is then a man recognises who it is that has directed his labour--it is then he for the moment forgets even the success in the more gladdening knowledge that such a success could only have been given by One, and that it is the Lord who has been watching his disappointments, and at last turning them into triumph.

The Evangelist adds, "None of the disciples durst ask Him, Who art Thou? knowing that it was the Lord"--a remark which unquestionably implies that there was some ground for the question, Who art Thou? They knew it was the Lord from the miracle He had wrought and from His manner of speaking and acting; but yet there was in His appearance something strange, something which, had it not also inspired them with awe, would have prompted the question, Who art Thou? The question was always on their lips, as they found afterwards by comparing notes with one another, but none of them durst put it. There was this time no certification of His identity further than the aid He had given, no showing of His hands and feet. It was, that is to say, by faith now they must know Him, not by bodily eyesight; if they wished to deny Him, there was room for doing so, room for questioning who He was. This was in the most delicate correspondence with the whole incident. The miracle was wrought as the foundation and encouraging symbol of their whole vocation as fishers of men during His bodily absence; it was wrought in order to encourage them to lean on One whom they could not see, whom they could at best dimly descry on another element from themselves, and whom they could not recognise as their Lord apart from the wonderful aid He gave them; and accordingly even when they come ashore there is something mysterious and strange about His appearance, something that baffles eyesight, something that would no longer have satisfied a Thomas, something therefore which is the fit preparation for a state in which they were to live altogether by faith and not at all by sight. This is the state in which we now live. He who believes will know that his Lord is near him; he who refuses to believe will be able to deny His nearness. It is faith then that we need: we need to know our Lord, to understand His purposes and His mode of fulfilling them, so that we may not need the evidence of eyesight to say where He is working and where He is not. If we are to be His followers, if we are to recognise that He has made a new life for us and all men, if we are to recognise that He has begun and is now carrying forward a great cause in this world, and if we see that, let our lives deny it as they may, there is nothing else worth living for than this cause, and if we are seeking to help it, then let us confirm our faith by this miracle and believe that our Lord, who has all power in heaven and on earth, is but beyond eyesight, has a perfectly distinct view of all we are doing and knows when to give us the success we seek.

This, then, explains why it was that our Lord appeared only to His friends after His resurrection. It might have been expected that on His rising from the dead He would have shown Himself as openly as before He suffered, and would specially have shown Himself to those who had crucified Him; but this was not the case. The Apostles themselves were struck with this circumstance, for in one of his earliest discourses Peter remarks that He showed Himself "not to all the people, but unto witnesses chosen before of God, even to us who did eat and drink with Him after He rose from the dead." And it is obvious from the incident before us and from the fact that when our Lord showed Himself to five hundred disciples at once in Galilee, probably a day or two after this, some even of them doubted--it is obvious from this that no good or permanent effect could have been produced by His appearing to all and sundry. It might have served as a momentary triumph, but even this is doubtful; for plenty would have been found to explain away the miracle or to maintain it was a deception, and that He who appeared was not the same as He who died. Or even supposing the miracle had been admitted, why was this miracle to produce any more profound spiritual effect in hearts unprepared than the former miracles had produced. It was not by any such sudden process men could become Christians and faithful witnesses of Christ's resurrection. "Men are not easily wrought upon to be faithful advocates of any cause." They advocate causes to which they are by nature attached, or else they become alive to the merit of a cause only by gradual conviction and by deeply impressed and often repeated instruction. To such a process the Apostles were submitted; and even after this long instruction their fidelity to Christ was tested by a trial which shook to the foundations their whole character, which threw out one of their number for ever, and which revealed the weaknesses of others.

In other words, they needed to be able to certify Christ's spiritual identity as well as His physical sameness. They were so to know Him and so to sympathise with His character that they might be able after the Resurrection to recognise Him by the continuity of that character and the identity of purpose He maintained. They were by daily intercourse with Him to be gradually led to dependence upon Him, and to the strongest attachment to His person; so that when they became witnesses to Him they might not only be able to say, "Jesus whom you crucified rose again," but might be able to illustrate His character by their own, to represent the beauty of His holiness by simply telling what they had seen Him do and heard Him say, and to give convincing evidence in their own persons and lives that He whom they loved on earth lives and rules now in heaven.

And what we need now and always is, not men who can witness to the fact of resurrection, but who can bear in upon our spirits the impression that there is a risen Lord and a risen life through dependence on Him.

XXV. RESTORATION OF PETER

"So when they had broken their fast, Jesus saith to Simon Peter, Simon, son of John, lovest thou Me more than these? He saith unto Him, Yea, Lord; Thou knowest that I love Thee. He saith unto him, Feed My lambs. He saith to him again a second time, Simon, son of John, lovest thou Me? He saith unto Him, Yea, Lord; Thou knowest that I love Thee. He saith unto him, Tend My sheep. He saith unto him the third time, Simon, son of John, lovest thou Me? Peter was grieved because He said unto him the third time, Lovest thou Me? And he said unto Him, Lord, Thou knowest all things; Thou knowest that I love Thee. Jesus saith unto him, Feed My sheep."--John xxi. 15-17.

To the interpretation of this dialogue between the Lord and Peter we must bring a remembrance of the immediately preceding incident. The evening before had found several of those who had followed Jesus standing among the boats that lay by the sea of Galilee. Boat after boat put out from shore; and as the familiar sights and smells and sounds awakened slumbering instincts and stirred old associations, Peter with characteristic restlessness and independence turned away to where his own old boat lay, saying, "I go a-fishing." The rest only needed the example. And as we watch each man taking his old place at the oar or getting ready the nets, we recognise how slight a hold the Apostolic call had taken of these men, and how ready they were to fall back to their old life. They lack sufficient inward impulse to go and proclaim Christ to men; they have no plans; the one inevitable thing is that they must earn a livelihood. And had they that night succeeded as of old in their fishing, the charm of the old life might have been too strong for them. But, like many other men, their failure in accomplishing their own purpose prepared them to discern and to fulfil the Divine purpose, and from catching fish worth so much a pound they became the most influential factors in this world's history. For the Lord had need of them, and again called them to labour for Him, showing them how easily He could maintain them in life and how full their nets would be when cast under His direction.

When the Lord made Himself known by His miraculous action while yet the disciples were too far off to see His features, Peter on the moment forgot the fish he had toiled for all night, and though master of the vessel left the net to sink or go to pieces for all he cared, and sprang into the water to greet his Lord. Jesus Himself was the first to see the significance of the act. This vehemence of welcome was most grateful to Him. It witnessed to an affection which was at this crisis the most valuable element in the world. And that it was shown not by solemn protestations made in public or as part of a religious service, but in so apparently secular and trivial an incident, makes it all the more valuable. Jesus hailed with the deepest satisfaction Peter's impetuous abandonment of his fishing gear and impatient springing to greet Him, because as plainly as possible it showed that after all Christ was incomparably more to him than the old life. And therefore when the first excitement had cooled down Jesus gives Peter an opportunity of putting this in words by asking him, "Simon, son of Jonas, lovest thou Me more than these?" Am I to interpret this action of yours as really meaning what it seems to mean--that I am more to you than boat, nets, old ways, old associations? Your letting go the net at the critical moment, and so risking the loss of all, seemed to say that you love Me more than your sole means of gaining a livelihood. Well, is it so? Am I to draw this conclusion? Am I to understand that with a mind made up you do love Me more than these things? If so, the way is again clear for Me to commit to your care what I love and prize upon earth--to say again, "Feed My sheep."

Thus mildly does the Lord rebuke Peter by suggesting that in his recent conduct there were appearances which must prevent these present expressions of his love from being accepted as perfectly genuine and trustworthy. Thus gracefully does He give Peter opportunity to renew the profession of attachment he had so shamefully denied by three times over swearing that he not only did not love Jesus, but knew nothing whatever about the man. And if Peter at first resented the severity of the scrutiny, he must afterwards have perceived that no greater kindness could have been done him than thus to press him to clear and resolved confession. Peter had probably sometimes compared himself to Judas, and thought that the difference between his denial and Judas' betrayal was slight. But the Lord distinguished. He saw that Peter's sin was unpremeditated, a sin of surprise, while his heart was essentially sound.

We also must distinguish between the forgetfulness of Christ, to which we are carried by the blinding and confusing throng of this world's ways and fashions and temptations, and a betrayal of Christ that has in it something deliberate. We admit that we have acted as if we had no desire to serve

Christ and to bring our whole life within His kingdom; but it is one thing to deny Christ through thoughtlessness, through inadvertence, through sudden passion or insidious, unperceived temptation--another thing consciously and habitually to betake ourselves to ways which He condemns, and to let the whole form, appearance, and meaning of our life plainly declare that our regard for Him is very slight when compared with our regard for success in our calling or anything that nearly touches our personal interests. Jesus lets Peter breakfast first, He lets him settle, before He puts His question, because it matters little what we say or do in a moment of excitement. The question is, what is our deliberate choice and preference--not what is our judgment, for of that there can be little question; but when we are self-possessed and cool, when the whole man within us is in equilibrium, not violently pulled one way or other, when we feel, as sometimes we do, that we are seeing ourselves as we actually are, do we then recognise that Christ is more to us than any gain, success, or pleasure the world can offer?

There are many who when the alternative is laid before them in cold blood choose without hesitation to abide with Christ at all costs. Were we at this moment as conscious as Peter was when this question fell from the lips of the living Person before him, whose eyes were looking for his reply, that we now must give our answer, many of us, God helping us, would say with Peter, "Thou knowest that I love Thee." We could not say that our old associations are easily broken, that it costs us nothing to hang up the nets with which so skilfully we have gathered in the world's substance to us, or to take a last look of the boat which has so faithfully and merrily carried us over many a threatening wave and made our hearts glad within us. But our hearts are not set on these things; they do not command us as Thou dost; and we can abandon whatever hinders us from following and serving Thee. Happy the man who with Peter feels that the question is an easily answered one, who can say, "I may often have blundered, I may often have shown myself greedy of gain and glory, but Thou knowest that I love Thee."

In this restoration of Peter our Lord, then, tests not the conduct, but the heart. He recognises that while the conduct is the legitimate and normal test of a man's feeling, yet there are times at which it is fair and useful to examine the heart itself apart from present manifestations of its condition; and that the solace which a poor soul gets after great sin, in refusing to attempt to show the consistency of his conduct with love to Christ, and in clinging simply to the consciousness that with all his sin there is most certainly a surviving love to Christ, is a solace sanctioned by Christ, and which He would have it enjoy. This is encouraging, because a Christian is often conscious that, if he is to be judged solely by his conduct, he must be condemned. He is conscious of blemishes in his life that seem quite to contradict the idea that he is animated by a regard for Christ. He knows that men who see his infirmities and outbreaks may be justified in supposing him a self-deceived or pretentious hypocrite, and yet in his own soul he is conscious of love to Christ. He can as little doubt this as he can doubt that he has shamefully denied this in his conduct. He would rather be judged by omniscience than by a judgment that can scrutinise only his outward conduct. He appeals in his own heart from those who know in part to Him who knows all things. He knows perfectly well that if men are to be expected to believe that he is a Christian he must prove this by his conduct; nay, he understands that love must find for itself a constant and consistent expression in conduct; but it remains an indubitable satisfaction to be conscious that, despite all his conduct has said to the contrary, he does in his soul love the Lord.

The determination of Christ to clear away all misunderstanding and all doubtfulness about the relation His professed followers hold to Him is strikingly exhibited in His subjecting Peter to a second and third interrogation. He invites Peter to search deeply into his spirit and to ascertain the very truth. It is the most momentous of all questions; and our Lord positively refuses to take a superficial, careless, matter-of-course answer. He will thus question, and thrice question, and probe to the quick all His followers. He seeks to scatter all doubt about our relation to Him, and to make our living connection with Him clear to our own consciousness, and to place our whole life on this solid basis of a clear, mutual understanding between Him and us. Our happiness depends upon our meeting His question with care and sincerity. Only the highest degree of human friendship will permit this persistent questioning, this beating of us back and back on our own feelings, deeper and deeper into the very heart of our affections, as if still it were doubtful whether we had not given an answer out of mere politeness or profession or sentiment. The highest degree of human friendship demands certainty, a basis on which it can build, a love it can entirely trust. Christ had made good His right thus to question His followers and to require a love that was sure of itself, because on His part He was conscious of such a love and had given proof that His affection was no mere sentimental, unfruitful compassion, but a commanding, consuming, irrepressible, unconquerable love--a love that left Him no choice, but compelled Him to devote Himself to men and do them all the good in His power.

Peter's self-knowledge is aided by the form the question now takes. He is no longer asked to compare the hold Christ has upon him with his interest in other things; but he is asked simply and absolutely whether love is the right name for that which connects him with his Lord. "Lovest thou Me?" Separating yourself and Me from all others, looking straight and simply at Me only, is "love" the right name for that which connects us? Is it love, and not mere impulse? Is it love, and not sentiment or fancy? Is it love, and not sense of duty or of what is becoming? Is it love, and not mere mistake? For no mistake is more disastrous than that which takes something else for love.

Now, to apprehend the significance of this question is to apprehend what Christianity is. Our Lord was on the point of leaving the world; and He left its future, the future of the sheep He loved so well and had spent His all upon, in the keeping of Peter and the rest, and the one security He demanded of them was the confession of love for Himself. He did not draw up a creed or a series of articles binding them to this and that duty, to special methods of governing the Church or to special truths they were to teach it; He did not summon them into the house of Peter or of Zebedee, and bid them affix their signatures or marks to such a document. He rested the whole future of the work He had begun at such cost on their love for Him. This security alone He took from them. This was the sufficient guarantee of their fidelity and of their wisdom. It is not great mental ability that is wanted for the furtherance of Christ's aims in the world. It is love of what is best, devotion to goodness. No question is made about their knowledge; they are not asked what views they have about the death of Christ; they are not required to analyse their feelings and say whence their love has sprung--whether from a due sense of their indebtedness to Him for delivering them from sin and its consequence, or from the grace and beauty of His character, or from His tender and patient consideration of them. There is no omission of anything vital owing to His being hurried in these morning hours. Three times over the question comes, and the third is as the first, a question solely and exclusively as to their love. Three times over the question comes, and three times over, when love is unhesitatingly confessed, comes the Apostolic commission, "Feed My sheep." Love is enough--enough not only to save the Apostles themselves, but enough to save the world.

The significance of this cannot be exaggerated. What is Christianity? It is God's way of getting hold of us, of attaching us to what is good, of making us holy, perfect men. And the method He uses is the presentation of goodness in a personal form. He makes goodness supremely attractive by exhibiting to us its reality and its beauty and its permanent and multiplying power in Jesus Christ. Absolutely simple and absolutely natural is God's method. The building up of systems of theology, the elaborate organisation of churches, the various, expensive, and complicated methods of men, how artificial do they seem when set alongside of the simplicity and naturalness of God's method! Men are to be made perfect. Show them, then, that human perfection is perfect love for them, and can they fail to love it and themselves become perfect? That is all. The mission of Christ and the salvation of men through Him are as natural and as simple as the mother's caress of her child. Christ came to earth because He loved men and could not help coming. Being on earth, He expresses what is in Him--His love, His goodness. By His loving all men and satisfying all their needs, men came to feel that this was the Perfect One, and humbly gave themselves to Him. As simply as love works in all human affairs and relationships, so simply does it work here.

And God's method is as effectual as it is simple. Men do learn to love Christ. And this love secures everything. As a bond between two persons, nothing but love is to be depended upon. Love alone carries us out of ourselves and makes other interests than our own dear to us.

But Christ requires us to love Him and invites us to consider whether we do now love Him, because this love is an index to all that is in us of a moral kind. There is so much implied in our love of Him, and so much inextricably intertwined with it, that its presence or absence speaks volumes regarding our whole inward condition. It is quite true that nothing is more difficult to understand than the causes of love. It seems to ally itself with equal readiness with pity and with admiration. It is attracted sometimes by similarity of disposition, sometimes by contrast. It is now stirred by gratitude and again by the conferring of favours. Some persons whom we feel we ought to love we do not draw to. Others who seem comparatively unattractive strongly draw us. But there are always some persons in every society who are universally beloved; and these are persons who are not only good, but whose goodness is presented in an attractive form--who have some personal charm, in appearance or manner or disposition. If some churlish person does not own the ascendency, you know that the churlishness goes deep into the character.

But this poorly illustrates the ascendency of Christ and what our denial of it implies. His goodness is perfect and it is complete. Not to love Him is not to love goodness; it is to be out of sympathy with what attracts pure and loving spirits. For whatever be the apparent or obscure causes of love, this is certain--that we love that which best fits and stimulates our whole nature. Love lies deeper than the will; we cannot love because we wish to do so, any more than we can taste honey bitter because we wish to do so. We cannot love a person because we know that their influence is needful to forward our interests. But if love lies deeper than the will, what power have we to love what at present does not draw us? We have no power to do so immediately; but we can use the means given us for altering, purifying, and elevating our nature. We can believe in Christ's power to regenerate us, we can faithfully follow and serve Him, and thus we shall learn one day to love Him.

But the presence or absence in us of the love of Christ is an index not only to our present state, but a prophecy of all that is to be. The love of Christ was that which enabled and impelled the Apostles to live great and energetic lives. It was this simple affection which made a life of aggression and reformation possible to them. This gave them the right ideas and the sufficient impulse. And it is this affection which is open to us all and which equally now as at first impels to all good. Let the love of Christ possess any soul and that soul cannot avoid being a blessing to the world around. Christ scarcely needed to say to Peter, "Feed My sheep; be helpful to those for whom I died," because in time Peter must have seen that this was his calling. Love gives us sympathy and intelligence. Our conscience is enlightened by sympathy with the person we love; through their desires, which we wish to gratify, we see higher aims than our own, aims which gradually become our own. And wherever the love of Christ exists, there sooner or later will the purposes of Christ be understood, His aims be accepted, His fervent desire and energetic endeavour for the highest spiritual condition of the race become energetic in us and carry us forward to all good. Indeed, Jesus warns Peter of the uncontrollable power of this affection he expressed. "When you were younger," He says, "you girded yourself and walked where you would; but when you are old another shall gird you, and carry you on to martyrdom." For he who is possessed by the love of Christ is as little his own master and can as little shrink from what that love carries him to as the man that is carried to execution by a Roman guard. Self-possession terminates when the soul can truly say, "Thou knowest that I love Thee." There is henceforth no choosing of ways of our own; our highest and best self is evoked in all its power, and asserts itself by complete abnegation of self and eager identification of self with Christ. This new affection commands the whole life and the whole nature. No more can the man spend himself in self-chosen activities, in girding himself for great deeds of individual glorification, or in walking in ways that promise pleasure or profit to self; he willingly stretches forth his hands, and is carried to much that flesh and blood shrink from, but which is all made inevitable, welcome, and blessed to him through the joy of that love that has appointed it.

But are we not thus pronouncing our own condemnation? This is, it is easy to see, the true and natural education of the human spirit--to love Christ, and so learn to see with His eyes and become enamoured of His aims and grow up to His likeness. But where in us is this absorbing, educating, impelling, irresistible power? To recognise the beauty and the certainty of God's method is not the difficulty; the difficulty is to use it, to find in ourselves that which carries us into the presence of Christ, saying, "Thou knowest all things; thou knowest that I love Thee." Admiration we have; reverence we have; faith we have; but there is more than these needed. None of these will impel us to life-long obedience. Love alone can carry us away from sinful and selfish ways. But this testing question, "Lovest thou Me?" was not the first but the last put to Peter by our Lord. It was only put after they had passed through many searching experiences together. And if we feel that for us to adopt as our own Peter's assured answer would only be to deceive ourselves and trifle with the most serious of matters, we are to consider that Christ seeks to win our love also, and that the ecstasy of confessing our love with assurance is reserved even for us. It is possible we may already have more love than we think. It is no uncommon thing to love a person and not know it until some unusual emergency or conjuncture of circumstances reveals us to ourselves. But if we are neither conscious of love nor can detect any marks of it in our life, if we know ourselves to be indifferent to others, deeply selfish, unable to love what is high and self-sacrificing, let us candidly admit the full significance of this, and even while plainly seeing what we are, let us not relinquish the great hope of being at length able to give our heart to what is best and of being bound by an ever-increasing love to the Lord.

XXVI. CONCLUSION

"Verily, verily, I say unto thee, When thou wast young, thou girdedst thyself, and walkedst whither thou wouldest: but when thou shalt be old, thou shalt stretch forth thy hands, and another shall gird thee, and carry thee whither thou wouldest not. Now this he spake, signifying by what manner of death he should glorify God. And when He had spoken this, He saith unto him, Follow Me. Peter, turning about, seeth the disciple whom Jesus loved following; which also leaned back on His breast at the supper, and said, Lord, who is he that betrayed Thee? Peter therefore seeing Him saith to Jesus, Lord, and what shall this man do? Jesus saith unto him, If I will that he tarry till I come, what is that to thee? follow thou Me. This saying therefore went forth among the brethren, that that disciple should not die: yet Jesus said not unto him, that he should not die; but, If I will that he tarry till I come, what is that to thee? This is the disciple which beareth witness of these things, and wrote these things: and we know that his witness is true. And there are also many other things which Jesus did, the which if they should be written every one, I suppose that even the world itself would not contain the books that should be written."--John xxi. 18-25.

Peter, springing up in the boat, and snatching his fisher's coat, and girding it round him, and dashing into the water, seemed to Jesus a picture of impetuous, inexperienced, fearless love. And as He looked upon it another picture began to shine through it from behind and gradually take its place--the picture of what was to be some years later when that impetuous spirit had been tamed and chastened, when age had damped the ardour though it had not cooled the love of youth, and when Peter should be bound and led out to crucifixion for his Lord's sake. As Peter wades and splashes eagerly to the shore the eye of Jesus rests on him with pity, as the eye of a parent who has passed through many of the world's darkest places rests on the child who is speaking of all he is to do and to enjoy in life. Fresh from His own agony, our Lord knows how different a temper is needed for prolonged endurance. But little disposed to throw cold water on genuine, however miscalculating enthusiasm, having it for His constant function to fan not to quench the smoking flax, He does not disclose to Peter all His forebodings, but merely hints, as the disciple comes dripping out of the water, that there are severer trials of love awaiting him than those which mere activity and warmth of feeling can overcome, "When thou wast young, thou girdedst thyself and walkedst whither thou wouldest: but when thou shalt be old, thou shalt stretch forth thy hands, and another shall gird thee, and carry thee whither thou wouldest not."

To a man of Peter's impulsive and independent temperament no future could seem less desirable than that in which he should be unable to choose for himself and do as he pleased. Yet this was the future to which the love he was now expressing committed him. This love, which at present was a delightful stimulus to his activities, diffusing joy through all his being, would gain such mastery over him that he would be impelled by it to a course of life full of arduous undertaking and entailing much suffering. The free, spontaneous, self-considering life to which Peter had been accustomed; the spirit of independence and right of choosing his own employments which had so clearly shown itself the evening before in his words, "I go a-fishing"; the inability to own hindrances and recognise obstacles which so distinctly betrayed itself in his leaping into the water,--this confident freedom of action was soon to be a thing of the past. This ardour was not useless; it was the genuine heat which, when plunged in the chilling disappointments of life, would make veritable steel of Peter's resolution. But such trial of Peter's love did await it; and it awaits all love. The young may be arrested by suffering, or they may be led away from the directions they had chosen for themselves; but the chances of suffering increase with years, and what is possible in youth becomes probable and almost certain in the lapse of a lifetime. So long as our Christian life utters itself in ways we choose for ourselves and in which much active energy can be spent and much influence exerted, there is so much in this that is pleasing to self that the amount of love to Christ required for such a life may seem very small. Any little disappointment or difficulty we meet with acts only as a tonic, like the chill of the waters of the lake at dawn. But when the ardent spirit is bound in the fetters of a disabled, sickly body; when a man has to lay himself quietly down and stretch forth his hands on the cross of a complete failure that nails him down from ever again doing what he would, or of a loss that makes his life seem a living death; when the irresistible course of events leads him past and away from the hopefulness and joy of life; when he sees that his life is turning out weak and ineffectual, even as the lives of others,--then he finds he has a more difficult part to play than when he had to choose his own form of activity and vigorously put forth the energy that was in him. To suffer without repining, to be laid aside from the stir and interest of the busy world, to submit when our life is taken out of our own hands and is being moulded by influences that pain and grieve us--this is found to test the spirit more than active duty.

The contrast drawn by our Lord between the youth and age of Peter is couched in language so general that it throws light on the usual course of human life and the broad characteristics of human experience. In youth attachment to Christ will naturally show itself in such gratuitous and yet most pardonable and even touching exhibitions of love as Peter here made. There is a girding of oneself to duty and to all manner of attainment. There is no hesitation, no shivering on the brink, no weighing of difficulties; but an impulsive and almost headstrong commital of oneself to duties unthought of by others, an honest surprise at the laxity of the Church, much brave speaking, and much brave acting too. Some of us, indeed, taking a hint from our own experience, may affirm that a good deal we hear about youth being warmer in Christ's service than maturity is not true, and that it had been a very poor prospect for ourselves if it had been true; and that with greater truth it may be said that youthful attachment to Christ is often delusive, selfish, foolish, and sadly in need of amendment. This may be so.

But however this may be, there can be no doubt that in youth we are free to choose. Life lies before us like the unhewn block of marble, and we may fashion it as we please. Circumstances may seem to necessitate our departing from one line of life and choosing another; but, notwithstanding, all the possibilities are before us. We may make ours a high and noble career; life is not as yet spoiled for us, or determined, while we are young. The youth is free to walk whither he will; he is not yet irrecoverably pledged to any particular calling; he is not yet doomed to carry to the grave the marks of certain habits, but may gird on himself whatever habit may fit him best and leave him freest for Christ's service.

Peter heard the words "Follow Me," and rose and went after Jesus; John did the same without any special call. There are those who need definite impulses, others who are guided in life by their own constant love. John would always absorbedly follow. Peter had yet to learn to follow, to own a leader. He had to learn to seek the guidance of his Lord's will, to wait upon that will and to interpret it--never an easy thing to do, and least of all easy to a man like Peter, fond of managing, of taking the lead, too hasty to let his thoughts settle and his spirit fixedly consider the mind of Christ.

It is obvious that when Jesus uttered the words "Follow Me," He moved away from the spot where they had all been standing together. And yet, coming as they did after so very solemn a colloquy, these words must have carried to Peter's mind a further significance than merely an intimation that the Lord wished His company then. Both in the mind of the Lord and of Peter there seems still to have been a vivid remembrance of Peter's denial; and as the Lord has given him opportunity of confessing his love, and has hinted what this love will lead him to, He appropriately reminds him that any penalties he might suffer for his love were all in the path which led straight to where Christ Himself for ever is. The superiority to earthly distresses which Christ now enjoyed would one day be his. But while he is beginning to take in these thoughts Peter turns and sees John following; and, with that promptness to interfere which characterised him, he asked Jesus what was to become of this disciple. This question betrayed a want of steadiness and seriousness in contemplating his own duty, and met therefore with rebuke: "If I will that he tarry till I come, what is that to thee? follow thou Me." Peter was prone to intermeddle with matters beyond his sphere, and to manage other people's affairs for them. Such a disposition always betrays a lack of devotion to our own calling. To brood over the easier lot of our friend, to envy him his capacity and success, to grudge him his advantages and happiness, is to betray an injurious weakness in ourselves. To be unduly anxious about the future of any part of Christ's Church, as if He had omitted to arrange for that future, to act as if we were essential to the well-being of some part of Christ's Church, is to intermeddle like Peter. To show astonishment or entire incredulity or misunderstanding if a course in life quite different from ours is found to be quite as useful to Christ's people and to the world as ours; to show that we have not yet apprehended how many men, how many minds, how many methods, it takes to make a world, is to incur the rebuke of Peter. Christ alone is broad as humanity and has sympathy for all. He alone can find a place in His Church for every variety of man.

Coming to the close of this Gospel, we cannot but most seriously ask ourselves whether in our case it has accomplished its object. We have admired its wonderful compactness and literary symmetry. It is a pleasure to study a writing so perfectly planned and wrought out with such unfailing beauty and finish. No one can read this Gospel without being the better for it, for the mind cannot pass through so many significant scenes without being instructed, nor be present at so many pathetic passages without being softened and purified. But after all the admiration we have spent upon the form and the sympathy we have felt with the substance of this most wonderful of literary productions, there remains the question: Has it accomplished its object? John has none of the artifice of the modern teacher who veils his didactic purpose from the reader. He plainly avows his object in writing: "These signs are written that ye might believe that Jesus is the Christ, the Son of God, and that believing ye might have life through His name." After half a century's experience and consideration, he selects from the abundant material afforded him in the life of Jesus those incidents and conversations which had most powerfully impressed himself and which seemed most significant to others, and these he presents as sufficient evidence of the divinity of his Lord. The mere fact that he does so is itself very strong evidence of his truth. Here is a Jew, trained to believe that no sin is so heinous as blasphemy, as the worshipping more gods than one or making any equal with God--a man to whom the most attractive of God's attributes was His truth, who felt that the highest human joy was to be in fellowship with Him in whom is no darkness at all, who knows the truth, who is the truth, who leads and enables men to walk in the light as He is in the light. What has this hater of idolatry and of lying found as the result of a holy, truth-seeking life? He has found that Jesus, with whom he lived on terms of the most intimate friendship, whose words he listened to, the working of whose feelings he had scanned, whose works he had witnessed, was the Son of God. I say the mere fact that such a man as John seeks to persuade us of the divinity of Christ goes far to prove that Christ was Divine. This was the impression His life left on the man who knew Him best, and who was, judging from his own life and Gospel, better able to judge than any man who has since lived. It is sometimes even objected to this Gospel that you cannot distinguish between the sayings of the Evangelist and the sayings of his Master. Is there any other writer who would be in the smallest danger of having his words confounded with Christ's? Is not this the strongest proof that John was in perfect sympathy with Jesus, and was thus fitted to understand Him? And it is this man, who seems alone capable of being compared with Jesus, that explicitly sets Him immeasurably above himself, and devotes his life to the promulgation of this belief.

John, however, does not expect that men will believe this most stupendous of truths on his mere word. He sets himself therefore to reproduce the life of Jesus, and to retain in the world's memory those salient features which gave it its character. He does not argue nor draw inferences. He believes that what impressed him will impress others. One by one he cites his witnesses. In the simplest language he tells us what Christ said and what He did, and lets us hear what this man and that man said of Him. He tells us how the Baptist, himself pure to asceticism, so true and holy as to command the submission of all classes in the community, assured the people that he, though greater and felt to be greater than any of their old prophets, was not of the same world as Jesus. This man who stands on the pinnacle of human heroism and attainment, reverenced by his nation, feared by princes for the sheer purity of his character, uses every contrivance of language to make the people understand that Jesus is infinitely above him, incomparable. He himself, he said, was of the earth: Jesus was from above and above all; He was from heaven, and could speak of things He had seen; He was the Son.

The Evangelist tells us how the incredulous but guileless Nathanael was convinced of the supremacy of Jesus, and how the hesitating Nicodemus was constrained to acknowledge Him a teacher sent by God. And so he cites witness after witness, never garbling their testimony, not making all bear the one uniform testimony which he himself bears; nay, showing with as exact a truthfulness how unbelief grew, as how faith rose from one degree to another, until the climax is reached in Thomas's explicit confession, "My Lord and my God!" No doubt some of the confessions which John records were not acknowledgments of the full and proper divinity of Christ. The term "Son of God" cannot, wherever used, be supposed to mean that Christ is God. We, though human, are all of us sons of God-- in one sense by our natural birth, in another by our regeneration. But there are instances in which the interpreter is compelled to see in the term a fuller significance, and to accept it as attributing divinity to Christ. When, for example, John says, "No man hath seen God at any time: the only-begotten Son, which is in the bosom of the Father, He hath declared Him," it is evident that he thinks of Christ as standing in a unique relation to God, which separates Him from the ordinary relation in which men stand to God. And that the disciples themselves passed from a more superficial use of the term to a use which had a deeper significance is apparent in the instance of Peter. When Peter in answer to the inquiry of Jesus replied, "Thou art the Christ, the Son of the living God," Jesus replied, "Flesh and blood hath not revealed this unto thee"; but this was making far too much of Peter's confession if he only meant to acknowledge Him to be the Messiah. In point of fact, flesh and blood did reveal the Messiahship of Jesus to Peter, for it was his own brother Andrew who told Peter that he had found the Messiah, and brought him to Jesus. Plainly therefore Jesus meant that Peter had now made a further step in his knowledge and in his faith, and had learned to recognise Jesus as not only Messiah, but as Son of God in the proper sense.

In this Gospel, then, we have various forms of evidence. We have the testimonies of men who had seen and heard and known Jesus, and who, though Jews, and therefore intensely prejudiced against such a conception, enthusiastically owned that Christ was in the proper sense Divine. We have John's own testimony, who writes his Gospel for the purpose of winning men to faith in Christ's Sonship, who calls Christ Lord, applying to Him the title of Jehovah, and who in so many words declares that "the Word was God"--the Word who became flesh in Jesus Christ. And what is perhaps even more to the purpose, we have affirmations of the same truth made by Jesus Himself: "Before Abraham was I am"; "I and the Father are one"; "The glory which I had with Thee before the world was"; "He that hath seen Me hath seen the Father." Who that listens to these sayings can marvel that the horrified Jews considered that He

Marcus Dods, D.D.

was making Himself equal with God and took up stones to stone Him for blasphemy? Who does not feel that when Jesus allowed this accusation to be brought against Him at the last, and when He allowed Himself to be condemned to death on the charge, He must have put the same meaning on His words that they put? Otherwise, if He did not mean to make Himself equal with the Father, would He not have been the very first to unmask and protest against so misleading a use of language? Had He not known Himself to be Divine, no member of the Sanhedrim could have been so shocked as He to listen to such language or to use it.

But in reading this Gospel one cannot but remark that John lays great stress on the miracles which Christ wrought. In fact, in announcing his object in writing it is especially to the miracles he alludes when he says, "These signs are written that ye might believe." In recent years there has been a reaction against the use of miracles as evidence of Christ's claim to be sent by God. This reaction was the necessary consequence of a defective view of the nature, meaning, and use of miracles. For a long period they were considered as merely wonders wrought in order to prove the power and authority of the Person who wrought them. This view of miracles was so exclusively dwelt upon and urged, that eventually a reaction came; and now this view is discredited. This is invariably the process by which steps in knowledge are gained. The pendulum swings first to the one extreme, and the height to which it has swung in that direction measures the momentum with which it swings to the opposite side. A one-sided view of the truth, after being urged for a while, is found out and its weakness is exposed, and forthwith it is abandoned as if it were false; whereas it is only false because it claimed to be the whole truth. Unless it be carried with us, then, the opposite extreme to which we now pass will in time be found out in the same way and its deficiencies be exposed.

In regard to miracles the two truths which must be held are: first, that they were wrought to make known the character and the purposes of God; and, secondly, that they serve as evidence that Jesus was the revealer of the Father. They not only authenticate the revelation; they themselves reveal God. They not only direct attention to the Teacher; they are themselves the lessons He teaches.

During the Irish famine agents were sent from England to the distressed districts. Some were sent to make inquiries, and had credentials explaining who they were and on what mission; they carried documents identifying and authenticating them. Other agents went with money and waggon-loads of flour, which were their own authentication. The charitable gifts told their own story; and while they accomplished the object the charitable senders of the mission had in view, they made it easy of belief that they came from the charitable in England. So the miracles of Christ were not bare credentials accomplishing nothing else than this--that they certified that Christ was sent from God; they were at the same time, and in the first place, actual expressions of God's love, revealing God to men as their Father.

Our Lord always refused to show any bare authentication. He refused to leap off a pinnacle of the Temple, which could serve no other purpose than to prove He had power to work miracles. He resolutely and uniformly declined to work mere wonders. When the people clamoured for a miracle, and cried, "How long dost Thou make us doubt?" when they pressed Him to the uttermost to perform some marvellous work solely and merely for the sake of proving His Messiahship or His mission, He regularly declined. On no occasion did He admit that such authentication of Himself was a sufficient cause for a miracle. The main object, then, of the miracles plainly was not evidential. They were not wrought chiefly, still less solely, for the purpose of convincing the onlookers that Jesus wielded super-human power.

What, then, was their object? Why did Jesus so constantly work them? He wrought them because of His sympathy with suffering men,--never for Himself, always for others; never to accomplish political designs or to aggrandise the rich, but to heal the sick, to relieve the mourning; never to excite wonder, but to accomplish some practical good. He wrought them because in His heart He bore a Divine compassion for men and felt for us in all that distresses and destroys. His heart was burdened by the great, universal griefs and weaknesses of men: "Himself took our infirmities and bare our sicknesses." But this was the very revelation He came to make. He came to reveal God's love and God's holiness, and every miracle He wrought was an impressive lesson to men in the knowledge of God. Men learn by what they see far more readily than by what they hear, and all that Christ taught by word of mouth might have gone for little had it not been sealed on men's minds by these consistent acts of love. To tell men that God loves them may or may not impress them, may or may not be believed; but when Jesus declared that He was sent by God, and preached His gospel by giving sight to the blind, legs to the lame, health to the hopeless, that was a form of preaching likely to be effectual. And when these miracles were sustained by a consistent holiness in Him who worked them; when it was felt that there was nothing ostentatious, nothing self-seeking, nothing that appealed to mere vulgar wonder in them, but that they were dictated solely by love,--when it was found that they were thus a true expression of the character of Him who worked them, and that that character was one in which human judgment at least could find no stain, is it surprising that He should have been recognised as God's true representative?

Supposing, then, that Christ came to earth to teach men the fatherhood and fatherliness of God--

could He have more effectually taught it than by these miracles of healing? Supposing He wished to lodge in the minds of men the conviction that man, body and soul, was cared for by God; that the diseased, the helpless, the wretched were valued by Him,--were not these works of healing the most effectual means of making this revelation? Have not these works of healing in point of fact proved the most efficient lessons in those great truths which form the very substance of Christianity? The miracles are themselves, then, the revelation, and carry to the minds of men more directly than any words or arguments the conception of a loving God, who does not abhor the affliction of the afflicted, but feels with His creatures and seeks their welfare.

And, as John is careful throughout his Gospel to show, they suggest even more than they directly teach. John uniformly calls them "signs," and on more than one occasion explains what they were signs of. He that loved men so keenly and so truly could not be satisfied with the bodily relief He gave to a few. The power He wielded over disease and over nature seemed to hint at a power supreme in all departments. If He gave sight to the blind, was He not also the light of the world? If He fed the hungry, was He not Himself the bread which came down from heaven?

The miracles, then, are evidences that Christ is the revealer of the Father, because they do reveal the Father. As the rays of the sun are evidences of the sun's existence and heat, so are the miracles evidences that God was in Christ. As the natural and unstudied actions of a man are the best evidences of his character; as almsgiving that is not meant to disclose a charitable spirit, but for the relief of the poor, is evidence of charity; as irrepressible wit, and not clever sayings studied for effect, is the best evidence of wit--so these miracles, though not wrought for the sake of proving Christ's union with the Father, but for the sake of men, do most effectually prove that He was one with the Father. Their evidence is all the stronger because it was not their primary object.

But for us the question remains, What has this Gospel and its careful picture of Christ's character and work done for us? Are we to close the Gospel and shut away from us this great revelation of Divine love as a thing in which we claim no personal share? This exhibition of all that is tender and pure, touching and hopeful, in human life--are we to look at it and pass on as if we had been admiring a picture and not looking into the very heart of all that is eternally real? This accessibility of God, this sympathy with our human lot, this undertaking of our burdens, this bidding us be of good cheer--is it all to pass by us as needless for us? The presence that shines from these pages, the voice that sounds so differently from all other voices--are we to turn from these? Is all that God can do to attract us to be in vain? Is the vision of God's holiness and love to be without effect? In the midst of all other history, in the tumult of this world's ambitions and contendings, through the fog of men's fancies and theories, shines this clear, guiding light: are we to go on as if we had never seen it? Here we are brought into contact with the truth, with what is real and abiding in human affairs; here we come into contact with God, and can for a little look at things as He sees them: are we, then, to write ourselves fools and blind by turning away as if we needed no such light--by saying, "We see, and need not be taught?"

www.ingramcontent.com/pod-product-compliance
Lightning Source LLC
Chambersburg PA
CBHW032040150426
43194CB00006B/361